This is the sixth and final volume of the major Commentary on Homer's *Iliad* issued under the General Editorship of Professor G. S. Kirk. It consists of introductory chapters dealing with the structure and main themes of the poem, book division, the end of the *Iliad* in relation to the *Odyssey*, and the criticism and interpretation of the Homeric poems in antiquity. The commentary follows. (The Greek text is not included.) This volume contains a consolidated index of Greek words in all six volumes. This project is the first large-scale commentary in English on the *Iliad* for nearly one hundred years, and takes special account of language, style, thematic structure and narrative technique, as well as of the cultural and social background to the work.

The Commentary is an essential reference work for all students of Greek litera-ture, and archaeologists and historians will also find that it contains matters of relevance to them.

The Iliad: a commentary

Volume VI: books 21–24

THE ILIAD:
A COMMENTARY

GENERAL EDITOR G. S. KIRK

Volume VI: books 21–24

NICHOLAS RICHARDSON

FELLOW OF MERTON COLLEGE, OXFORD

CAMBRIDGE
UNIVERSITY PRESS

Published by the Press Syndicate of the University of Cambridge
The Pitt Building, Trumpington Street, Cambridge CB2 IRP
40 West 20th Street, New York, NY 10011-4211, USA
10 Stamford Road, Oakleigh, Melbourne 3166, Australia

First published 1993
Reprinted 1996

Printed in Great Britain by Athenaeum Press Ltd, Gateshead, Tyne & Wear

*A catalogue record for this book is
available from the British Library*

Library of Congress cataloguing in publication data

Kirk, G. S. (Geoffrey Stephen)
The Iliad, a commentary
Includes bibliographical references and indexes.
Contents: v. 1. Books 1−4   v. 6 Books 21−24
Nicholas Richardson.
1. Homer. Iliad. 2. Achilles (Greek mythology) in
literature. 3. Trojan War in literature. I. Richardson,
N. J. (Nicholas James). II. Homer. Iliad. III. Title.
PA4037.K458   1985   883´.01   84-11330

ISBN 0 521 30960 3 hardback
ISBN 0 521 31209 4 paperback

This volume
is dedicated to
Jenny, Alexis, Penelope, Andrew and Catherine

and to the memory of
H. C. A. Gaunt, T. E. B. Howarth, F. W. King, J. G. Stow

CONTENTS

PREFACE

It is just over a century since Walter Leaf published the first edition of his great commentary on the *Iliad* (1886-8), in which he set out 'to offer a guide to students anxious to know more of Homer than they can learn from elementary school-books'. It is a mark of the difference between the Victorian age and ours that what a business man and banker could then accomplish in his spare time should now require the sustained energies and varied expertise of five classical scholars. One of the advantages, however, of this collaboration has been the range of different approaches adopted throughout these six volumes, for it is as true today as in Leaf's time that 'when once the strict limits of a verbal commentary are passed, it is hard to know which path to choose from the many which open into the world revealed to us by the Homeric poems'.

That this venture has indeed been a genuine work of collaboration is largely due to the careful guidance and painstaking labours of its general editor Geoffrey Kirk, to whom I wish to pay the warmest tribute of thanks, not only for his original invitation to take part, but also for his sharp-eyed diligence and determination in seeing the project through to its completion. It is a rare privilege to join a group of scholars in studying one of the Homeric poems at such a detailed level over a prolonged period of time, and in the process the Commentary itself has come to resemble an old and familiar friend, much-loved in all its singularities, even if tiresome at times, and to which one is ultimately reluctant to bid farewell. For this opportunity I am profoundly grateful.

Some particular biases and shortcomings should be mentioned here. Had I attempted a more comprehensive review of modern secondary literature, this work would have been scarcely begun, let alone finished. I tried as a rule to approach the text with a fresh mind and to analyse my own response to it, before considering the views of others. I have also attempted to keep in mind the needs of a varied audience: despite its technicalities I should like this volume to be accessible (for example) to undergraduates as well as to the increasingly select company of specialists. Professional scholars may feel that at times too subjective a note is sounded, whereas students may sometimes find the style too compressed and technical. It has not proved entirely easy to strike the right balance, and it was only as the work progressed that a more natural and leisurely style of commentary seemed to develop of its own accord.

xi

Preface

In the last volume of this series cross-references are inevitably numerous, and I hope that this will be regarded as a useful aid, rather than as a deterrent to reading. I have also paid particular attention to what struck me as the *individuality* of Homer's language, as an antidote to excessive concern for its formular quality (cf. M. W. Edwards, vol. v, pp. 53–5 and Richardson in Bremer, *HBOP* 165–84), and I hope that the frequency of references to unusual words will not irritate the reader. It must be admitted that I have relied mainly on LSJ and concordances in doing this, and have only checked a sample of words with the data base of the *Thesaurus Linguae Graecae* (including nearly all 'absolute *hapaxes*'). It would certainly be interesting to make more extensive searches, but I do not think that the overall picture would be substantially altered by doing so.

The first part of the Introduction, on structure and themes, is not intended as a dogmatic or canonical statement of received opinions (which would be impossible), but rather as an exploration of some of the possibilities. In the section on structure a good deal of space has been given to theories of ring composition, if only in order to draw attention to what seemed a rather neglected approach. The discussion of themes is inevitably somewhat impressionistic, given the allowances of space.

The roll-call of those who have contributed to the making of this volume is long, and even then I am conscious that some names must have been omitted. Love of Homer (and of Greek literature) dates from my school days at Winchester, where besides those masters named in the dedication I am grateful for the teaching of J. B. Poynton and Colin Badcock. It was fostered at Oxford by many, including my tutor Colin Hardie and supervisor Martin West, and by the encouragement of Hugh Lloyd-Jones. As a tutor myself, I owe a great deal to the work and inspiration of my colleagues, especially Jasper Griffin, Colin Macleod, Richard Rutherford and Oliver Taplin. I have also gained immeasurably from the constant contact with Homer and the stimulus of fresh responses provided by teaching pupils over 23 years at Merton. In 1962 I had the good fortune to work at Mycenae with the late Lord William Taylour, Barbara Craig, Lisa French and others. Enthusiasm for the archaeology of the Late Bronze and Early Iron Ages, encouraged also by the teaching of the late Dorothea Gray, has remained strong ever since.

Like lexicographers, all commentators are shameless plagiarists. I have found Leaf invaluable, and have gained much from Malcolm Willcock's concise but perceptive commentary. Ameis–Hentze I have not used systematically but from time to time. For book 23 Chantraine and Goube are useful, and for book 24 Colin Macleod has set a standard I could not hope to equal. I also owe much to the new series of commentaries on the *Odyssey*, edited by Alfred Heubeck and others, and to Martin West's work on Hesiod.

Work on the book itself was made possible above all by four terms of

Preface

sabbatical leave granted by my College between 1985 and 1991. At all stages I have received many detailed comments on my drafts and constant encouragement from my collaborators, and it has been a great pleasure to share the work with them all. In addition, Richard Rutherford read through and commented on the whole work. I am especially grateful to him, and also to Jasper Griffin, for discussion of the Introduction. My debt to Oliver Taplin is long-standing: he lent me his own commentary on *Iliad* 22.1–120 (including some notes by Colin Macleod), and more recently the opening chapter of his new book *Homeric Soundings*, and I have enjoyed our stimulating discussions of Homer over many years. John Boardman, Vassos Karageorghis and Mervyn Popham have all seen the commentary on book 23, and I have benefited greatly from their detailed observations on some of the archaeological issues in that Book.

Many others have helped with specific questions, by sending me their own works, and in various other ways, and it is impossible to list them all. I am aware of debts of thanks to my colleague at Merton Tom Braun, Jan Bremer, Hector Catling, Joost Crouwel, Malcolm Davies, Vincenzo di Benedetto, Garth Fowden, Oliver Gurney, Irene de Jong, James Hooker, Gregory Hutchinson, Peter Jones, Robert Lamberton, Françoise Létoublon, Edmond Lévy, Franco Montanari, Judith Mossman, Roger Moorey, Peter Parsons, Simon Pembroke, Angeliki Petropoulou, Walter Pötscher, Maurice Pope, James Porter, Simon Pulleyn, Christopher Smith, Maro Theodossiadis and Stephanie West.

My greatest practical debt is to Rachel Chapman, who (as Rachel Woodrow) produced three successive and virtually impeccable drafts of the whole work from my execrable script over a period of six years. Her immeasurable patience and astounding accuracy must be my only excuse for failing to carry out this long and tedious labour myself, and I cannot thank her adequately for all that she has done over such a long period. Like the other authors in this series, I have very much appreciated the care taken by the staff of the Press in the production of these volumes, and wish to thank Pauline Hire for her diplomatic and patient assistance throughout, and Susan Moore for her highly skilful and sensitive copy-editing.

Finally I am immensely grateful to my wife Jenny and our children for their tolerance of much scholarly eccentricity and for rescuing me from excessive absorption in the past. To them I dedicate this book, and also to the memory of four of my teachers at Winchester,

ἔνθα με το πρῶτον λιγυρῆς ἐπέβησαν ἀοιδῆς.

Merton College, Oxford
July 1991

N. J. R.

A.M.D.G.

ABBREVIATIONS

Books

Alexiou, *Ritual Lament*   M. Alexiou, *The Ritual Lament in Greek Tradition* (Cambridge 1974)

Ameis–Hentze   K. F. Ameis and C. Hentze, *Homers Ilias* (Leipzig 1913; repr. Amsterdam 1965)

Apthorp, *MS Evidence*   M. J. Apthorp, *The Manuscript Evidence for Interpolation in Homer* (Heidelberg 1980)

Arch. Hom.   *Archaeologia Homerica: Die Denkmäler und das frühgriechische Epos*, edd. F. Matz and H.-G. Buchholz (Göttingen 1967–)

Arend, *Scenen*   W. Arend, *Die typischen Scenen bei Homer* (Berlin 1933)

Beazley, *ABV*   J. D. Beazley, *Attic Black-figure Vase-painters* (Oxford 1956)

Beck, *Stellung*   G. Beck, *Die Stellung des 24 Buches der Ilias in der alten Epentradition* (diss. Tübingen 1964)

Bolling, *External Evidence*   G. M. Bolling, *The External Evidence for Interpolation in Homer* (Oxford 1925)

Bremer, *HBOP*   *Homer: Beyond Oral Poetry*, edd. J. M. Bremer, I. J. F. de Jong, and J. Kalff (Amsterdam 1987)

Buffière *Mythes d'Homère*   F. Buffière, *Les Mythes d'Homère et la pensée grecque* (Paris 1956)

Burkert, *Religion*   W. Burkert, *Greek Religion: Archaic and Classical* (Oxford 1985); Eng. trans. by John Raffan of *Griechische Religion der archaischen und klassischen Epoche* (Stuttgart 1977)

Càssola, *Inni Omerici*   F. Càssola, *Inni Omerici* (Rome 1975)

Chantraine, *Dict.*   P. Chantraine, *Dictionnaire étymologique de la langue grecque* (Paris 1968–80)

Chantraine, *GH*   P. Chantraine, *Grammaire homérique* I–II (Paris 1958–63)

Chantraine and Goube   P. Chantraine and H. Goube, *Homère, Iliade XXIII* (Paris 1972)

Chios   *Chios: a Conference at the Homereion in Chios 1986*, edd. J. Boardman and C. E. Vaphopoulou-Richardson (Oxford 1986)

Coldstream, *Geometric Greece*   J. N. Coldstream, *Geometric Greece* (London 1977)

Cook, *Troad*   J. M. Cook, *The Troad: an Archaeological and Topographical Study* (Oxford 1973)

Crouwel, *Chariots*   J. H. Crouwel, *Chariots and Other Means of Land Transport in Bronze Age Greece* (Amsterdam 1981)

Davies, *EGF*   M. Davies, *Epicorum Graecorum Fragmenta* (Göttingen 1988)

Deichgräber, *Letzte Gesang*   K. Deichgräber, 'Der letzte Gesang der Ilias', *Abhandlungen der Mainzer Akademie der Wissenschaften und Literatur, Geistes- und sozialwiss. Klasse*, 1972, No. 5

de Jong, *Narrators*   I. J. F. de Jong, *Narrators and Focalizers: the Presentation of the Story in the Iliad* (Amsterdam 1987)

Delebecque, *Cheval*   E. Delebecque, *Le Cheval dans l'Iliade* (Paris 1951)

Denniston, *Particles*   J. D. Denniston, *The Greek Particles* (2nd edn, Oxford 1951)

Edwards, *HPI*   M. W. Edwards, *Homer, Poet of the Iliad* (Baltimore and London 1987)

Elliger, *Darstellung der Landschaft*   W. Elliger, *Die Darstellung der Landschaft in der griechischen Dichtung* (Berlin 1975)

Erbse   H. Erbse, *Scholia Graeca in Homeri Iliadem* i–vii (Berlin 1969–88)

Fenik, *TBS*   B. C. Fenik, *Typical Battle Scenes in the Iliad* (*Hermes* Einzelschriften 21, Wiesbaden 1968)

Fenik, *Tradition*   B. C. Fenik, ed., *Homer: Tradition and Invention* (Leiden 1978)

Fittschen, *Sagendarstellungen*   K. Fittschen, *Untersuchungen Zum Beginn der Sagendarstellungen bei den Griechen* (Berlin 1969)

Fränkel, *Gleichnisse*   H. Fränkel, *Die homerischen Gleichnisse* (Göttingen 1921)

Friedrich, *Verwundung*   W. H. Friedrich, *Verwundung und Tod in der Ilias* (Göttingen 1956)

Frisk   H. Frisk, *Griechisches Etymologisches Wörterbuch* (Heidelberg 1954–73)

Gardiner, *Sports*   E. N. Gardiner, *Greek Athletic Sports and Festivals* (London 1910)

Gordesiani, *Kriterien der Schriftlichkeit*   R. Gordesiani, *Kriterien der Schriftlichkeit und Mündlichkeit im homerischen Epos* (Frankfurt 1986)

Griffin, *HLD*   J. Griffin, *Homer on Life and Death* (Oxford 1980)

Grube, *Greek and Roman Critics*   G. M. A. Grube, *The Greek and Roman Critics* (London 1965)

Hainsworth, *Od.*   Alfred Heubeck, Stephanie West and J. B. Hainsworth, *A Commentary on Homer's Odyssey* vol. 1 (Oxford 1988)

Hall, *Barbarian*   E. Hall, *Inventing the Barbarian* (Oxford 1989)

Hardie, *Cosmos and Imperium*   P. R. Hardie, *Virgil's Aeneid: Cosmos and Imperium* (Oxford 1986)

Harris, *Athletes*   H. A. Harris, *Greek Athletes and Athletics* (London 1964)

Helbig, *Homerische Epos*   W. Helbig, *Das homerische Epos aus den Denkmälern erläutert: archäologische Untersuchungen* (2nd edn, Leipzig 1887)

Heubeck, *Od.* Alfred Heubeck and Arie Hoekstra, *A Commentary on Homer's Odyssey* vol. II (Oxford 1989)

Higbie, *Measure and Music* C. Higbie, *Measure and Music: Enjambement and Sentence Structure in the Iliad* (Oxford 1990)

Hoekstra, *Od.* Alfred Heubeck and Arie Hoekstra, *A Commentary on Homer's Odyssey* vol. II (Oxford 1989)

HyDem, HyAp, HyHerm, HyAphr *Homeric Hymns* to Demeter, Apollo, Hermes, Aphrodite

Johansen, *Iliad in Early Greek Art* K. F. Johansen, *The Iliad in Early Greek Art* (Copenhagen 1967)

Kakridis, *Homer Revisited* J. T. Kakridis, *Homer Revisited* (Lund 1971)

Kakridis, *Researches* J. T. Kakridis, *Homeric Researches* (Lund 1949)

Kirk, *Songs* G. S. Kirk, *The Songs of Homer* (Cambridge 1962)

Krischer, *Konventionen* T. Krischer, *Formale Konventionen der homerischen Epik* (München 1971)

Kullmann, *Quellen* W. Kullmann, *Die Quellen der Ilias* (Wiesbaden 1960)

Kurtz and Boardman, *Burial Customs* D. C. Kurtz and J. Boardman, *Greek Burial Customs* (London 1971)

Lamberton, *Homer the Theologian* R. W. Lamberton, *Homer the Theologian: Neoplatonist Allegorical Reading and the Growth of the Epic Tradition* (Berkeley 1986)

Lamberton and Keaney, *Homer's Ancient Readers* R. W. Lamberton and J. Keaney, edd., *Homer's Ancient Readers: the Hermeneutics of Greek Epic's Earliest Exegetes* (Princeton 1992)

Leaf W. Leaf, *The Iliad* I–II (2nd edn, London 1900–2)

Leaf, *Troy* W. Leaf, *Troy* (London 1912)

Lefkandi I M. Popham, L. H. Sackett and P. G. Themelis, edd., *Lefkandi I. The Iron Age* (London 1980, 2 vols.)

Lehrs, *De Aristarchi studiis* K. Lehrs, *De Aristarchi studiis homericis* (3rd edn, Leipzig 1882; repr. Hildesheim 1964)

Leumann, *HW* M. Leumann, *Homerische Wörter* (Basel 1950)

LfgrE *Lexicon des frühgriechischen Epos*, edd. B. Snell and H. Erbse (Göttingen 1955–)

LIMC *Lexicon Iconographicum Mythologiae Classicae* I.1– (Zürich 1981–)

Lohmann, *Andromache-Szenen* D. Lohmann, *Die Andromache-Szenen in der Ilias* (Hildesheim 1988)

Lohmann, *Reden* D. Lohmann, *Die Komposition der Reden in der Ilias* (Berlin 1970)

Lorimer, *HM* H. L. Lorimer, *Homer and the Monuments* (London 1950)

L–P E. Lobel and D. L. Page, *Poetarum Lesbiorum Fragmenta* (Oxford 1955)

LSJ   H. Liddell, R. Scott and H. S. Jones, *A Greek–English Lexicon* (9th edn, Oxford 1940)

Macleod, *Iliad XXIV*   C. W. Macleod, *Homer, Iliad Book XXIV* (Cambridge 1982)

Martin, *Language of Heroes*   R. P. Martin, *The Language of Heroes: Speech and Performance in the Iliad* (Ithaca 1989).

Mazon   P. Mazon, *Homère, Iliade*, Tome IV, Chants xix–xxiv (Paris 1981)

Meister, *Kunstsprache*   K. Meister, *Die homerische Kunstsprache* (Leipzig 1921)

Monro, *HG*   D. B. Monro, *A Grammar of the Homeric Dialect* (2nd edn, Oxford 1891)

Moulton, *Similes*   Carroll Moulton, *Similes in the Homeric Poems* (Hypomnemata 49, Göttingen 1977)

Mueller, *Iliad*   M. Mueller, *The Iliad* (London 1984)

M–W   R. Merkelbach and M. L. West, edd., *Fragmenta Hesiodea* (Oxford 1967)

Nagler, *Spontaneity*   M. N. Nagler, *Spontaneity and Tradition: a Study in the Oral Art of Homer* (Berkeley and Los Angeles 1974)

Neumann, *Gesten und Gebärden*   G. Neumann, *Gesten und Gebärden in der griechischen Kunst* (Berlin 1965)

Nilsson, *GgrR*   M. P. Nilsson, *Geschichte der griechischen Religion* I (3rd edn, München 1967)

OCT   Oxford Classical Texts: *Homeri Opera I–V*: I–II (*Iliad*) edd. D. B. Monro and T. W. Allen (3rd edn, Oxford 1920); III–IV (*Odyssey*) ed. T. W. Allen (2nd edn, Oxford 1917–19); V (*Hymns*, etc.) ed. T. W. Allen (Oxford 1912)

Owen, *Story of the Iliad*   E. T. Owen, *The Story of the Iliad* (Toronto 1946)

Parker, *Miasma*   Robert Parker, *Miasma* (Oxford 1983)

Parry, *Language*   A. Parry, *The Language of Achilles and Other Papers* (Oxford 1989)

Parry, *MHV*   A. Parry, ed., *The Making of Homeric Verse*. The Collected Papers of Milman Parry (Oxford 1971)

Pfeiffer, *History of Classical Scholarship*   R. Pfeiffer, *History of Classical Scholarship from the Beginnings to the Hellenistic Age* (Oxford 1968)

PMG   *Poetae Melici Graeci* ed. D. L. Page (Cambridge 1962)

Reiner, *Die rituelle Totenklage*   E. Reiner, *Die rituelle Totenklage der Griechen* (Stuttgart–Berlin 1938)

Reinhardt, *IuD*   K. Reinhardt, *Die Ilias und ihr Dichter*, ed. U. Hölscher (Göttingen 1961)

Richardson, *Hymn to Demeter*   N. J. Richardson, *The Homeric Hymn to Demeter* (Oxford 1974)

Ruijgh, ΤΕ *épique*   C. J. Ruijgh, *Autour de 'ΤΕ épique': études sur la syntaxe grecque* (Amsterdam 1971)

Schadewaldt, *Aufbau*   W. Schadewaldt, *Der Aufbau der Ilias* (Frankfurt am Main 1975)

Schadewaldt, *Iliasstudien*   W. Schadewaldt, *Iliasstudien* (Leipzig 1938)

Schadewaldt, *VHWW*   W. Schadewaldt, *Von Homers Welt und Werk* (3rd edn, Stuttgart 1959)

Scheibner, *Aufbau*   G. Scheibner, *Der Aufbau des 20 und 21 Buches der Ilias* (Leipzig 1939)

Schulze, *Quaestiones Epicae*   W. Schulze, *Quaestiones Epicae* (Gütersloh 1892)

Segal, *Mutilation of the Corpse*   C. Segal, *The Theme of the Mutilation of the Corpse in the Iliad* (Leiden 1971)

Shipp, *Studies*   G. P. Shipp, *Studies in the Language of Homer* (2nd edn, Cambridge 1972)

Silk, *Iliad*   M. S. Silk, *The Iliad* (Cambridge 1987)

Stanford, *Ulysses Theme*   W. B. Stanford, *The Ulysses Theme* (Oxford 1968)

Stengel, *Opferbräuche*   P. Stengel, *Opferbräuche der Griechen* (Leipzig 1910)

Strasburger, *Kleinen Kämpfer*   G. Strasburger, *Die kleinen Kämpfer der Ilias* (diss. Frankfurt 1954)

Thornton, *Supplication*   Agathe Thornton, *Homer's Iliad: its Composition and the Motif of Supplication* (Göttingen 1984)

Usener, *Verhältnis der Odyssee zur Ilias*   K. Usener, *Beobachtungen zum Verhältnis der Odyssee zur Ilias* (Tübingen 1990)

van der Valk, *Researches*   M. H. A. L. H. van der Valk, *Researches on the Text and Scholia of the Iliad* I–II (Leiden 1963–4)

Ventris and Chadwick, *Documents*   M. Ventris and J. Chadwick, *Documents in Mycenaean Greek* (2nd edn, Cambridge 1973)

von Kamptz, *Personennamen*   Hans von Kamptz, *Homerische Personennamen* (Göttingen 1982)

von der Mühll, *Hypomnema*   P. von der Mühll, *Kritisches Hypomnema zur Ilias* (Basel 1952)

Wace and Stubbings, *Companion*   A. J. B. Wace and F. H. Stubbings, *A Companion to Homer* (London 1962)

Wackernagel, *Kleine Schriften*   J. Wackernagel, *Kleine Schriften* (Göttingen 1953–79)

Wackernagel, *Sprachliche Untersuchungen*   J. Wackernagel, *Sprachliche Untersuchungen zu Homer* (Göttingen 1916)

Wade-Gery, *Poet of Iliad*   H. T. Wade-Gery, *Poet of the Iliad* (Cambridge 1952)

Wehrli, *Allegorischen Deutung*   F. Wehrli, *Zur Geschichte der allegorischen Deutung Homers im Altertum* (Leipzig 1928)

West, *Greek Metre*   M. L. West, *Greek Metre* (Oxford 1982)

West, *Od.*   Alfred Heubeck, Stephanie West and J. B. Hainsworth, *A Commentary on Homer's Odyssey* vol. I (Oxford 1988)

West, *Ptolemaic Papyri*   S. West, *The Ptolemaic Papyri of Homer* (Köln and Opladen 1967)

West, *Theogony*   M. L. West, *Hesiod, Theogony* (Oxford 1966)

West, *Works and Days*   M. L. West, *Hesiod, Works and Days* (Oxford 1978)

Whitman, *HHT*   C. H. Whitman, *Homer and the Heroic Tradition* (Cambridge, Mass. 1958)

Wilamowitz, *IuH*   U. von Wilamowitz-Moellendorf, *Die Ilias und Homer* (Berlin 1916)

Wilamowitz, *Untersuchungen*   U. von Wilamowitz-Moellendorf, *Homerische Untersuchungen* (Berlin 1884)

Willcock   M. M. Willcock, *The Iliad of Homer* I–II (London 1978–84)

Journals

AJA	*American Journal of Archaeology*
AJP	*American Journal of Philology*
AR	*Archaeological Reports*
BICS	*Bulletin of the Institute of Classical Studies*
BSA	*Annual of the British School at Athens*
CJ	*Classical Journal*
CP	*Classical Philology*
CQ	*Classical Quarterly*
CR	*Classical Review*
G&R	*Greece and Rome*
HSCP	*Harvard Studies in Classical Philology*
JHS	*Journal of Hellenic Studies*
MDAI(A)	*Mitteilungen des Deutschen Archäologischen Instituts (Athen. Abt)*
MDAI(R)	*Mitteilungen des Deutschen Archäologischen Instituts (Röm. Abt.)*
MH	*Museum Helveticum*
PCPS	*Proceedings of the Cambridge Philological Society*
REA	*Revue des études anciennes*
TAPA	*Transactions of the American Philological Association*
YCS	*Yale Classical Studies*
ZPE	*Zeitschrift für Papyrologie and Epigraphik*

NOTE

The text used is the OCT (see Abbreviations). As in previous volumes '*Il.*' means 'the *Iliad*', '*Od.*' 'the *Odyssey*'. Early epic fragments are cited from both the OCT and Davies.

| marks the beginning or end of a verse. The abbreviation '(etc.)' after a Greek word means that the total includes all relevant terminations. Greek names are transliterated according to the rules laid down in vol. I, x. References to the scholia follow the system set out in vol. I pp. 41ff., i.e. 'Arn/A' means 'Aristonicus in MS A', etc. 'Schol. Ge' means the 'scholia in codex Genavensis 44'. Papyri of Homer are cited as in the OCT, except that 'schol. pap. XII (Erbse)' refers to the commentary (probably by Ammonius) in P.Oxy. 221, printed in Erbse vol. v, pp. 78–121, and 'pap. 249 and 271 (Mazon)' in the notes on 21.513 and 22.255 refer to the numbering in Mazon's Budé edition. 'MSS' refers to manuscripts after *c.* A.D. 600.

INTRODUCTION

1. Structure and themes

Ut pictura poesis: erit quae si propius stes
te capiat magis, et quaedam si longius abstes.

Horace, *Ars poetica* 361–2.

Das Organische ist schwer begreifbar.

Schadewaldt, *Iliasstudien* 159.

(i) Structure

That the *Iliad*, despite its size and complexity, is a poem with a coherent structure would probably not be contested by many nowadays. How that structure may be analysed, however, is still an open question. Aristotle's characterization of it as a unified plot with beginning, middle and end might seem a simple and uncontroversial starting-point, but equally his comparison of an epic or dramatic work to a living organism serves as a warning against over-simplification. In the end one may well come to the conclusion that there are several possible ways of describing the poem's construction, none of which definitely excludes the others.

Some of these have already been briefly reviewed by G. S. Kirk in his Introduction to books 1–4 (pp. 44–7), where he considers the merits and disadvantages of dividing the poem into sections of four or six books, or of a 'three-movement' structure. Before examining any such theories, however, it would be as well to emphasize that the division of the *Iliad* into twenty-four books was surely not a feature of its original conception (see pp. 21–2). These divisions do, in fact, usually come at natural breaks in the narrative, but these are not always the most significant ones, and in some cases (for example between books 20 and 21) the division cuts into what is better regarded as a single sequence of events. The *Odyssey* seems to fall quite easily into four-book sections, and one can readily conceive that this might correspond to a series of separate recitations (e.g. two a day over a period of three days), whereas a four-book structure does not seem to work so well

I

for the *Iliad*.[1] Books 1–4 can be seen as an extended prologue, if one likes, before the first main episode of the actual fighting (the *aristeia* of Diomedes), but 4.422ff. seem to mark a new start with the beginning of serious fighting, and the break at the end of book 4 is not a strong one. The end of book 8 works much better: it coincides with the end of a day's fighting, and the narrative clearly builds up to a climax here, before the Embassy to Akhilleus. It might be possible to see this as the end of the first major 'movement' of the battle, with the Greeks suffering a reversal and the plan of Zeus beginning to take real effect. Thus if one thinks in terms of three major 'movements' (corresponding perhaps roughly to Aristotle's beginning, middle and end, or to the three parts of a trilogy), 1–8 could theoretically form the first. In reality, however, book 9 continues the action of that day into the night, and the Greek leaders only go to bed after the return of the Embassy from Akhilleus. The Doloneia is clearly an interlude (whether original or not), and it seems more appropriate therefore to see the second movement of the poem as beginning with book 11, the dawn of the great day of battle which extends right through to 18.239–42.

The end of book 12 also marks a high point in the action, the moment when Hektor breaks through the Achaean Wall and the Greeks flee to the ships, and this is followed by a major retardation (books 13–14), when Poseidon rallies the Greeks and Zeus is put to sleep by Here. The end of 12 falls quite close to the poem's central point, and it shows Hektor at his most terrible and destructive (12.437–68: see on 12.457–66; also vol. IV, p. 39, on the summary at 13.345–60). On the other hand, within the great battle of books 11–18 it is off-centre, and the breach in the Wall is only the first major event in the sequence leading up to 16.122–4, where the first Greek ship is fired. The death of Patroklos at the end of book 16 could also be seen as a moment of climax, marking the end of either a four-book section or the second third of the poem, but again the action is carried over into the struggle for his body, which stretches forward as far as 18.238.

The case for a division into four sections of six books is also briefly discussed by G. S. Kirk (vol. I, p. 45). It would theoretically be possible to see book 6 as the end of an introductory block, in which the main characters are presented to us, 12 as the central climax, and 18 as marking the turning-point before Akhilleus' return to fight. But again, as Kirk shows, such an analysis is somewhat arbitrary and unsatisfactory.

In recent scholarship there has been a stronger tendency to emphasize the idea of a tripartite structure or 'three-movement' composition, one which could correspond to recitation over three days, but would not necessarily coincide with the ancient book-divisions. An early exponent of this

---

[1] A case has, however, been made by Thornton, *Supplication* 46ff. See also vol. IV, p. 39.

approach was J. T. Sheppard, whose (now unfashionable) *Pattern of the Iliad* (London 1922) saw the first movement as stretching up to the end of the Embassy to Akhilleus (1–9), the second as covering the single long day of the central books of fighting (11–18), and the last as reaching from the dawn of 19.1–2 to the end of the poem, from the reconciliation of Agamemnon and Akhilleus to the funeral of Hektor. Within these sections he attempted a more detailed structural analysis, and he pointed to some recurrent themes which helped to emphasize the poem's structure, particularly at the beginning and end (cf. especially *Pattern of the Iliad* 204–10). In this way he anticipated and helped to inspire the later and more elaborate 'ring composition' analyses of J. L. Myres and C. H. Whitman.

A similar analysis was made by H. T. Wade-Gery in his *Poet of the Iliad* (Cambridge 1952) 15–16. His three recitations covered books 1–9, 10–18.353 (when Patroklos' body is received by Akhilleus), and 18.354 to the end of 24. Schadewaldt (*Aufbau* 24) likewise divides the poem into books 1–9, 11–18 and 19–24, and he points to the fact that the action of both books 9 and 18 extends into the night, at the end of the first two movements, with these two nightfalls coming appropriately at the close of the first two days of recitation. He too goes on to give a more detailed structural analysis of the poem, into seven separate parts (39–74).[2]

The three-movement theory has most recently been advocated by O. Taplin (*Homeric Soundings*, Oxford 1992). He emphasizes the recurrence of major motifs at key points in the composition, i.e. books 1, 9–11, 18–19 and 24 (which he sees as major weight-bearing scenes, or the four dividing piers of a three-arched structure), especially the quarrel and reconciliation of Akhilleus and Agamemnon, the episodes where Thetis visits Akhilleus (in 1, 18 and 24), and the recurrent scenes of supplication or pleas for ransom, involving Khruses in 1, the Embassy in 9 and Priam in 24. He points out that references to 'tomorrow' are clustered most frequently towards the ends of the first and second movements (at 8.470–2, 8.497–565, 9.240, 9.356–61, 9.682–3, 9.707–9, and 18.134–7, 18.254–83, 18.303–4), thereby supporting Schadewaldt's observation about the nights of books 9 and 18, since these references would act as signposts for an expectant audience at the end of the day's recitation.

These views are clearly attractive, whether or not one accepts the suggestion of a three-day period for recitation. One might object that division into books 1 to 9, 11 to 18, and 19 to 24 would make the last movement noticeably shorter than the other two, but that is not necessarily a drawback. Despite the variety of views over exactly where the divisions should fall, one may still agree that analysis into three major movements can be

---

[2] Cf. also Silk, *Iliad* 37: his three parts consist of books 1–9, 10–17, 18–24.

a significant and valuable way of articulating the poem, drawing attention to some of the most important episodes in the development of the plot, and emphasizing their relationship.

A different form of structural analysis advocated by some modern scholars is ring composition. This does not necessarily conflict with other types of division. The first to argue this in detail was Myres in 1932, taking his cue from Sheppard.[3] Unfortunately Myres' attempt to see the poem as analogous to early Greek art, and especially to large-scale Geometric vase-paintings, was received sceptically by many scholars. *A priori*, however, there seems no reason why an epic poet (especially one whose own visual imagination was so highly developed) should not have thought of his work as a series of 'panels' in a large-scale visual structure, as Myres argued.

Ring composition itself is certainly a fundamental technique of Homeric epic (see vol. v Introduction, pp. 44–8), and again there seems no *a priori* reason why a poet should not use this technique (whether fully consciously or not) in the construction of his whole work as well as in composing episodes or scenes. Myres drew attention to a series of remarkable correspondences between the opening and closing sections of the *Iliad*. Of these, the ones which have most impressed recent scholars are those between books 1 and 24, whereby the themes of book 1 are echoed in reverse order in the final Book.[4] But Myres also saw detailed parallelism between books 2 and 23, 3 and 22, and so on. Somewhat unexpectedly, however, he viewed book 9 as the centre-piece of the whole structure, and this involved some awkward and unconvincing expansion and compression in other parts of his overall schema ('Last book' 280).

A similar analysis, made independently of Myres, was attempted by

---

[3] J. L. Myres, 'The last book of the *Iliad*', *JHS* 52 (1932) 264–96 (referred to here as 'Last book'). An interesting earlier attempt to compare the *Iliad*'s narrative structure with Geometric art was made by Fr. Stählin, 'Der geometrische Stil in der Ilias', *Philologus* 78 (1923) 280–301. He bases his theory to a large extent on the movements of the fighting to and fro over the plain of Troy. By coincidence Thornton uses the ebb and flow of battle as one of the main criteria in her analysis of the poem's composition (*Supplication* 46–63 and 150–63), although she does not seem to know of Stählin's analysis. For a more recent attempt to draw analogies between the *Iliad* and late Geometric art, and between the *Odyssey* and early Orientalizing art, see B. Andreae and H. Flashar, 'Strukturäquivalenzen zwischen den homerischen Epen und der frühgriechischen Vasenkunst', *Poetica* 9.2 (1977) 217–65. They argue, however, that the *Iliad* has a basically triadic structure (books 1–7, 8–18, 19–24).

[4] Parallel verses were already noted in 1876 by R. Peppmüller in his *Commentar des vierundzwanzigsten Buches der Ilias* (Berlin 1876). C. Rothe (*Die Ilias als Dichtung*, Paderborn 1910, 329) more perceptively used the parallelism in the action and time-scheme of the two books as evidence for unity of composition. Cf. also Stählin, *op. cit.* 296–301, and for other forerunners of Myres cf. Beck, *Stellung* 53 n. 1. The parallelism between books 1–3 and 22–4 is already noted by C. M. Bowra, *Tradition and Design in the Iliad* (Oxford 1930) 15–17. After Myres see especially Whitman, *HHT* 256–60, Beck, *Stellung* 53–65, Reinhardt, *IuD* 63–8, Lohmann, *Reden* 169–73, Macleod, *Iliad XXIV* 32–4, Mueller, *Iliad* 64–5, 166–76, Silk, *Iliad* 24, 38–9.

Whitman (*HHT* 249–84, and chart at end of book). His schema is more evenly distributed, since he sees books 11–15 as the main central panel, with 9 answered by 16, 8 by 17, and so on. Once again, however, Whitman's analogies with Geometric art, together with the fact that he pursued his analysis into such detail, led to his theory being given a sceptical reception.

The most recent exponent of this approach is R. Gordesiani, in *Kriterien der Schriftlichkeit und Mündlichkeit im homerischen Epos* (Frankfurt 1986) 26–67. This makes book 12 central, with 11 balanced by 13, and so on. The variations between these three scholars over the central section of the poem are notable, suggesting that such theories become progressively less satisfactory as one approaches the central episodes.

It seems nevertheless worthwhile to review this type of analysis, and above all to ask, if one accepts the comparison between books 1 and 24, how far into the poem it might be justifiable to see such ring composition as extending. Could it be carried right through, or is it most prominent at beginning and end as a narrative frame, and if so, does it gradually fade out as we approach the central part of the work? What follows is an attempt to examine this question in more detail, but it should be treated as an exploratory essay of a somewhat speculative kind.

Book 1 is clearly marked off from what follows, just as book 24 stands apart from what precedes to some extent (see on 2.1–2 and 24.1–21): they form the Prologue and Epilogue to the work. Book 1 begins with a proem referring to Akhilleus' wrath as the cause of many deaths, and to the unburied bodies which were to be the prey of dogs and birds (1–5). Book 24 ends with the most famous example of these, Hektor, receiving burial. As the poem begins with Akhilleus, so it ends with Hektor (1.1, 24.804). The first scene of book 1 has been described as a miniature version of the main plot (Schadewaldt, *Iliasstudien* 147–8; see also R. J. Rabel, *AJP* 109 (1988) 473–81): the dishonour shown by Agamemnon to Apollo's priest leads to disaster (due to divine displeasure), and this is followed by atonement and reconciliation. The theme of the old priest's supplication (here rejected) is picked up in book 9, with the Embassy to Akhilleus, and this in turn is echoed by Patroklos' supplication of him in 16, but it is mirrored and reversed most clearly in 24, when old Priam comes to Akhilleus and is received by him, and this is emphasized by several close verbal echoes (see on 24.501–2, 24.556–8, 24.560–2, 24.568–70, 24.571).

In book 1 the rejection of Khruses leads to the plague and funeral pyres of the Greeks (1.50–2). Apollo, who sets the poem's action in motion (1.8–10), is here seen as bringer of divine punishment and death. In book 24 Apollo again sets in motion the train of events (32–54), but this leads to reconciliation and the partial restoration of moral order with the funeral of Hektor. In both cases, however, Apollo shows himself to be a god concerned

5

with the moral qualities of pity and respect, for Khruses and for Hektor. Moreover, his rôle at the beginning and end is not confined to these passages. In book 1 he appears in the central and final scenes, as god of purification and healing, and of music and dance (313–17, 430–74, 601–4), and in 24 he is mentioned at the beginning (18–21) as the god who preserves Hektor's body from disfigurement, and this is echoed once more near the end in Hekabe's lament (757–9). In this last passage Apollo's 'gentle darts' bring death, but it is an honourable and beautiful one, in balanced contrast with the terrible effect of his arrows in book 1 (43–52).[5]

The plague in book 1 leads to the quarrel of Akhilleus and Agamemnon and the seizure of Briseis, and this in turn to Thetis' visit to her son. Meanwhile the journey to Khruse to return Khruseis and appease Apollo is described. Thetis then visits Zeus and begs for his help. Finally Here quarrels with Zeus, and Hephaistos makes peace. The sequence is repeated in reverse in 24: the dispute in heaven over Hektor's body, where Here again leads the opposition, is followed by Zeus's summoning of Thetis, with orders to Akhilleus to yield to entreaty, her visit to her son (see on 126–42), and finally by Priam's journey and the ransoming of Hektor (cf. Myres, 'Last book' 287–8 and fig. 8, Whitman, *HHT* 259, Macleod, *Iliad XXIV* 33). The opening theme of Agamemnon's violent conduct is divided between the scenes involving Khruseis and Briseis, who are to some extent doublets (cf. Reinhardt, *IuD* 42ff.), and this complicates the parallelism with the last Book, but nevertheless the overall correspondences seem clear enough.

To these must be added a certain degree of parallelism in the time-scheme of the two Books.[6] The plague lasts nine days, and on the tenth Akhilleus summons an assembly (1.53–4). On the twelfth day after this Thetis visits Zeus and Here quarrels with Zeus (1.493ff.). In book 24 this scheme is reversed: on the twelfth day (i.e. since Hektor's death: see on 31) the gods quarrel and debate the fate of the body. That night Priam visits Akhilleus, and at dawn next day he returns to Troy (695-7). The preparations for Hektor's pyre last nine days, and on the tenth the body is burnt (664–5, 784–7; see on 660–7, and 788–801 for further echoes of book 1).

Myres and Whitman went on to argue for a further correspondence of days between books 2–8 and 11–23, but their counts do not tally with each other. There is some confusion here, which seems due to the fact that the *three* days of books 19–23 (Akhilleus' *aristeia*, Patroklos' funeral and the Games) are to be included *within* the twelve-day period mentioned at 24.31

---

[5] Cf. also 24.602–9, where Apollo and Artemis kill the Niobids, in punishment for Niobe's boasting.

[6] Myres, 'Last book' 285–7, Whitman, *HHT* 257–8, Macleod, *Iliad XXIV* 32–3. Beck, *Stellung* 53ff., has useful criticism and discussion.

(see comment). One cannot therefore count these three days as separate and parallel to the three days following book 1, as Myres and Whitman do. It does, however, look as if the poet may be echoing the time-scheme of the opening Book at the close, at least in his emphasis on the periods of nine plus one and twelve days. On its own this is not a particularly significant point, given the tendency of Homeric epic to use these lengths of time elsewhere, but it does add another element to the overall correspondences of the two Books.

It is natural and appropriate that Homer should recapitulate motifs and scenes at the end in such a way as to reflect the opening of his poem and to give a sense of closure, especially in relation to the major themes of quarrel and reconciliation, anger and appeasement, supplication rejected and received. It is possible that the ending of the *Odyssey* (whether part of the original composition or not) is similarly designed to echo some of the leading themes of the opening episodes.[7] Moreover, the prominence of Apollo at the beginning and end of the *Iliad* may be partly paralleled by his rôle at the climax of the *Odyssey*, where the killing of the suitors occurs on the feast-day of the archer-god (20.276–8, 21.265–8). It would be tempting to see this as a sign that the poems could have been designed for recitation at one of the great festivals of Apollo, such as the Delian one described in the *Homeric Hymn to Apollo* (146–76, and cf. Wade-Gery, *Poet of Iliad* 16–17), but of course other occasions are possible (see vol. IV, Introduction, p. 38).

That book 2 is broadly paralleled by book 23 is less obvious, but seems nonetheless true. After the compressed and dramatic narrative of book 1, the pace slows almost to a halt, and the focus is broadened to encompass the armies as a whole, and especially the Greek army, its leaders and its men, their actual statistics (in the Catalogue of Ships) and their morale. As with much of the material in books 2–7, we are looking back here towards the beginning of the Trojan War, the portent at Aulis and the marshalling of the ships, and over its subsequent course. Book 23 (although different in general tone from book 2) again gives us a final panorama of the Greeks and their leaders, and as with much of the material in the later parts of the poem, it anticipates developments beyond the end of the poem, especially in some of the events of the Games (see on 262–897). A specific link between these two Books is the fact that the main action of both is sparked off by a dream scene, in book 2 the deceptive Dream sent by Zeus to Agamemnon (1–36), in 23 the dream of Akhilleus in which Patroklos' ghost tells him to bury his body as soon as possible, and speaks of Akhilleus' own imminent

---

[7] Cf. Myres, 'Last book' 267; Heubeck on *Od.* 24.413–548, 451–62, 472–88. For a survey of views on the ending of the *Odyssey* cf. S. West, 'Laertes revisited', *PCPS* 215 (1989) 113–43.

death (62–108). These are the only extended dream scenes in the *Iliad* (unless we count 24.682–9, which is not actually said to be a dream; 10.496–7 and 22.199–201 are brief references), whereas they are commoner in the *Odyssey*. Their rarity in the *Iliad* strengthens the case for seeing a parallelism between them, as a marker of the balance between these two Books.[8]

The correspondences between books 3 and 22 are much closer. The duel of Paris and Menelaos, which needs to be considered together with its immediate sequel, the breach of the truce by Pandaros in book 4, takes us back to the origins of the War, with the conflict between the two contestants for Helen, and the original guilt of the Trojans as accomplices of Paris is echoed within the poem in Pandaros' treachery (cf. especially 4.155–68, where Agamemnon predicts their ultimate punishment by Zeus). With this inconclusive affair we should contrast the duel of Akhilleus and Hektor, which seals Troy's fate. But there are more specific links which suggest that the poet may be aware of what he is doing here. Book 3 begins with Paris coming forward boldly to issue a challenge to fight, but retreating in dismay at the sight of Menelaos, like a man seeing a snake in the mountain-glens (15–37). Hektor rebukes him, and he then offers to fight a duel with Helen's former husband (38–75). In 22 Hektor waits to fight Akhilleus outside the Scaean gate, undeterred by the pleas of his parents, like a deadly mountain-snake waiting in its lair to attack a man (93–7; see comment), but when Akhilleus comes nearer he flees (131–7). Again the two similes act as signposts for the parallelism between the two duels, and the scene in 22 gains in irony by comparison with 3, where Hektor rebuked Paris for his cowardice.

At 3.121ff. Iris comes to Helen, disguised as a daughter of Priam, and finds her at home weaving a tapestry depicting the sufferings of the Trojans and Greeks on her behalf. She invites her to come and watch the duel from the walls, and Helen goes out, wearing her veil, and shedding a tear, accompanied by two maids, to the Scaean gate. There follows the Teikhoskopia, where she joins Priam and the other elders and identifies some of the Greek leaders for him (146–244). In book 22 Priam again watches from the walls (25ff., where 46–8 resemble 3.236–8). After Hektor's death he and Hekabe lament him (405–36), while Andromakhe, unaware of his death, is at home weaving a decorative tapestry (440–1

---

[8] It is natural that nearly all of the heroes, including some minor ones, who compete in the Games should be mentioned in the Catalogue of Ships; only Epeios is not. But it is possibly significant that at the end of the Achaean Catalogue the poet should pause to discuss who were the best horses and men, and in doing so should single out those of Eumelos (763–7; cf. 713–15). Both Eumelos and his horses only reappear in the chariot-race (23.288ff.). If this passage in book 2 is an anticipation of the Games it is also appropriate that in the following passage the poet should describe how Akhilleus' Myrmidons console their inactivity with athletic exercises (773–5).

echoes 3.125–6). Hearing the lamentation she rushes out, telling two of her maids to come with her, and when she reaches the wall and sees Hektor dead she faints, and her head-dress and veil fall from her head (437–74). She then recovers and utters her own lament (475–515). There is a poignant contrast here between the unhappy woman in book 3 who was the cause of the War, and who wishes she and her present husband were dead, and the innocent wife in 22 whose fate is linked so closely to that of Troy's defender.

In book 3 the Teikhoskopia is followed by the solemn ceremony of oath-taking between Agamemnon and Priam, laying down conditions for the duel, including the return of Helen and her property and further compensation by the Trojans if Menelaos wins (245–302). Priam then leaves, unable to bear to see the fight (303–13). In 22 Hektor debates whether to return Helen and the property, and offer in addition to divide all Troy's wealth between the two sides, but rejects this as useless (111–30). When he confronts Akhilleus he proposes that they make a divinely sanctioned pact that the victor will return the body of his enemy, but Akhilleus replies that no such agreements or oaths are conceivable between them (254–69), and he again rejects Hektor's final plea for burial (337–54). In books 3–4 the Trojans are morally on the wrong footing with regard to their oaths, whereas in 22 it is Akhilleus who, in rejecting the normal conventions of war and in his subsequent mistreatment of the body, will eventually arouse the gods' displeasure (cf. 22.356–60, 24.23–76, 24.107–19). The ceremonial formality of the duel in 3 (cf. also the duel between Aias and Hektor in 7) contrasts with the complete lack of such formality in 22.

At the end of the duel in book 3 Paris is rescued by Aphrodite, concealed in a cloud, and Menelaos is left vainly searching for him (380–461). There follows a debate in heaven over Troy's fate (4.1–74), involving a proposal by Zeus for a peaceful solution, countered by Here's violent protest. This leads to Athene's deception of Pandaros (75–104). These motifs of divine rescue, debate, and deceit recur a number of times elsewhere, and so it may be less significant, but it is still interesting that we find them at the end of book 21 and in 22. Here Agenor, whose duel with Akhilleus anticipates Hektor's in various ways, is rescued by Apollo, who decoys Akhilleus into vainly pursuing Apollo himself (21.595–605; 21.597–8 ∼ 3.380–2). In 22 Zeus proposes to rescue Hektor, but Athene protests strongly and he yields to her, as he had yielded to Here in book 4 (22.166–87; 22.185 ∼ 4.37, 22.186–7 = 4.73–4). Athene then deceives Hektor into facing Akhilleus (226–305). In both cases the various divine manoeuvres are designed to bring a stage closer Troy's eventual fall. It is also striking that the motif of divine rescue, which is used to *close* the duel in book 3, should occur to the poet at the end of 21, just *before* the duel with Hektor, at a point where it has much less functional significance than some of the other motifs we have

9

considered, as well as in the course of 22 itself, where rescue is proposed but rejected.

The rest of book 4 consists of preliminaries to the first clash of both armies, with Agamemnon's review of his troops and leaders, which seems to be a further stage of the process of general survey of the armies seen in book 2 and the Teikhoskopia (cf. 4.223–421 with comments). Finally battle is joined (422–544). The next major episode, however, is the *aristeia* of Diomedes in book 5. It has often been observed that Diomedes is a more straightforward and less tragic counterpart to Akhilleus (cf. Reinhardt, *IuD* 124), and his exploits here resemble in various respects those of Akhilleus in books 20–1, the corresponding section at the end of the poem.

In particular, both heroes have duels with Aineias, ending with Aineias' divine rescue (5.166–453, 20.158–339), both fight with gods, and in both cases the pro-Greek gods triumph in conflict with the pro-Trojan ones. The Aineias episodes naturally evoke other parallels, such as the references to his ancestors Tros and Ganymede, and the divine Trojan horses (5.221–3, 5.260–73. 20.221–35), and there are parallels of phrasing in the duels themselves (see on 5.167, 5.302–10, 5.311–12, 20.259–352, 20.285–7, 20.288–91, 20.319).

There are, however, even closer resemblances between the scenes in 5 and 21 where Aphrodite and Ares are wounded (5.330–430, 5.711–909, 21.385–434; cf. also 21.505–14). In 5 Aphrodite is wounded by Diomedes with Athene's aid and Athene and Here exult over her, and in 21 with Here's support she is knocked out by Athene, who triumphs over her. In 5 Aphrodite is then consoled on Mt Olumpos by her mother Dione, a motif obliquely echoed by Zeus's consolation of Artemis in 21 (505–14, where 509–10 = 5.373–4). In 5 Here and Athene prepare, with Zeus's permission, to fight Ares, and Diomedes and Athene together wound Ares, who goes to Zeus to complain. In the Theomachy the gods are fighting with Zeus's express permission (20.23–5), and Ares is knocked out by Athene in a scene which explicitly echoes the one in 5: Ares angrily recalls his earlier defeat at 21.396–9, and his treachery in helping the Trojans instead of the Greeks is mentioned in both cases (5.832–4, 21.412–14).

The ignominious treatment of these pro-Trojan deities in both episodes is contrasted with the dignity of Apollo. In 5 he warns Diomedes that mortals should not try to fight against gods, and rescues Aineias, setting him down in his temple at Pergamon and creating an image of him to be fought over (432–53). In 21 he refuses to fight Poseidon, saying that it is absurd for gods to fight over mere mortals (461–7), and at the end of the Theomachy he enters Troy to protect it, persuades Agenor to face Akhilleus, and then rescues him and enables the Trojans to escape (515–17, 538–611).

These parallels between the two *aristeiai* of Diomedes and Akhilleus can

be explained as due to the general thematic resemblances of the two episodes, and one can view the Theomachy in 20–1 as echoing the earlier
conflicts of the gods in 5. A further thematic link (suggested by Myres,
'Last book' 281–2) is less obvious, but worth considering: the tailpiece to
Diomedes' *aristeia* is his meeting with Glaukos in book 6, ending with
the exchange of arms, where Diomedes gains gold armour for bronze
(6.234–6). This motif of the hero's acquisition of new golden armour, which
here comes at the *end* of his most successful exploits, in the case of Akhilleus
precedes and heralds his entry to battle, with the creation of the new divine
armour by Hephaistos in book 18. The episode in 6 is relatively minor
and has puzzled scholars (see on 6.234–6), whereas the theme is greatly
expanded in 18, but it may be that the thematic links between Diomedes
and Akhilleus have helped to suggest its introduction in book 6. In terms of
ring composition the appearance of this motif after Diomedes' *aristeia* and
before that of Akhilleus would fit the overall schema well.[9]

After the battle scenes of books 5–6 come Hektor's visit to Troy and his
meetings with his mother Hekabe, Helen and Paris, and Andromakhe. In
structural terms these quieter, domestic episodes may be counterbalanced
by the scenes in books 18–19 in the Greek camp, of Thetis' second visit
to Akhilleus (leading to her visit to Hephaistos), the reconciliation of
Agamemnon and Akhilleus, and the accompanying laments for Patroklos.
In both cases we are made acutely aware that the leading heroes themselves, Hektor and Akhilleus, are soon to die (cf. 6.367–8, 6.407–93, 18.94–
126, 19.408–24), and both accept this fact in similar words (cf. especially
6.486–9, 18.115–21). We see both heroes reacting to the emotional pres-
sures of those most dear to them. Akhilleus has no wife or children with him
at Troy, but in lamenting Patroklos he also thinks of his father and son, back
at home (19.321–37). Hektor's preoccupation with his pressing duty as a
soldier is such that he refuses his mother's offer of wine and Helen's of a
seat (6.258–68, 6.354–62), as Akhilleus, because of his grief for Patroklos,
refuses to eat until he has fought, although here this motif assumes far
greater significance (19.199–214, 19.303–8).

After book 6 the case for structural correspondences of this kind becomes
less strong. Book 7 contains the formal duel of Hektor and Aias, followed by
a truce for burial of the dead of both sides and the building of the Achaean
Wall. The first day of fighting ends (undramatically) at 7.380, and the truce
occupies two more days (see on 7.433). Book 8 covers one more whole day
of fighting. It begins with the momentous decree of Zeus forbidding the

[9] Other possible links are the parallel glorification by Athene of Diomedes at 5.1–8 and
Akhilleus at 18.202–31, and the echo at 21.462–6 of the simile comparing men to leaves at
6.146–9.

gods to intervene, which is lifted in book 20. Battle is joined and fortunes fluctuate, but after Here and Athene have been prevented from helping the Greeks the Trojans are dominant and the plan of Zeus is clearly taking effect (cf. especially Zeus's prophecy at 470–83). The scene is set for the Embassy to Akhilleus in book 9.

As Kirk observes (vol. II, pp. 230–1, 293), by contrast with what precedes books 7 and 8 seem less clearly motivated within the poem's design, although the building of the Wall is an important preliminary to the great central battle, and book 8 does move the plot an important stage further forward. In terms of overall ring composition one might well be inclined to see Akhilleus' rejection of the Embassy in book 9 as answered (to some extent) by 16, where he allows Patroklos to fight (Whitman, *HHT* 279–83). The opening scene of 9, where Agamemnon weeps like a dark spring (13–15), is echoed in the simile describing Patroklos' tears (16.2–4), a marker which could be regarded as similar to the two dreams in 2 and 23, or the similes at the beginning of 3 and 22. Akhilleus' renewal of his complaint about Agamemnon (16.49–63: see comments) clearly echoes book 9 (especially 644–55), and when the first ship is fired he allows Patroklos to fight, again mindful of his promise to Aias in 9 (16.122–9).

At the same time, Akhilleus' rejection of Agamemnon's offer in 9 is not finally reversed until their meeting in 19, and equally the fighting in 16, especially the major duels of Patroklos with Sarpedon and Hektor, if they do have a structural counterpart in the earlier books, could possibly find this in the duel of Aias and Hektor in 7.[10] We are then left with the narratives of more general fighting in 8 and 17, both of which broadly show the Greeks under increasingly severe pressure, and both have a similar function. As 8 prepares for the plea to Akhilleus in 9, so 17 sets the scene for Akhilleus' final entry into battle, whose prologue occurs in 18 (cf. 165–238). The scene with which 8 ends, however, the Trojan assembly on the plain by night, in which Hektor confidently predicts the defeat of the Greeks, is only answered or balanced at 18.243–314 (see comments), the corresponding assembly at nightfall where he refuses to take Pouludamas' advice to withdraw into Troy (18.303–4 = 8.530–1; cf. Whitman, *HHT* 277–8).

Thus in these parts of the poem it would still be theoretically possible to discover certain major corresponding episodes, but the sequence would become less regular. We have now reviewed the first nine and last nine books, leaving only the interlude of the Doloneia and books 11–15. In 11–12 the Greeks suffer a series of major reverses, with the wounding of several leaders, Hektor's *aristeia*, and the battle for the Wall. In 13–14 they enjoy a respite and some major successes, aided by Poseidon and Here's

---

[10] Cf. for example Gordesiani, *Kriterien der Schriftlichkeit* 32–3, 44–6.

deception of Zeus, until Hektor is eventually knocked out by Telamonian Aias and the Trojans flee. This process is again reversed in 15 after Zeus has awoken, when a further prophetic speech by Zeus (49–77) looks forward as far as the capture of Troy. This is echoed by another programmatic passage at 592–614, and it marks the beginning of a major forward movement in the plot, which then advances without any more large-scale retardations until the end of the poem. Meanwhile the other main strand of the plot has been spun between books 11 and 15, with Patroklos' mission to Nestor and consequent delay to help Eurupulos (11.596–848), resumed at 15.390–405 when he sets off to return to Akhilleus' hut. Book 15 builds up to a great climax (rather as 12 does, but still more intensely), with the *aristeia* of Telamonian Aias, as the Greeks are forced back step by step to the defence of the ships, culminating in repeated calls by the leaders of both sides to fight harder (especially 484ff., 560ff., 661ff., 773ff.), and a great series of similes (592–636). There is no strong break at the end of this Book and the battle for the ships continues directly at 16.102ff., after the dialogue of Patroklos and Akhilleus.[11]

This surely illustrates the important fact that any structural correspondences such as have been suggested here between the earlier and later parts of the poem must be seen as in counterpoint with the main forward movement of the narrative, which works in a series of increasing waves, with peaks and corresponding troughs between them. The difference depends on whether one considers the poem from a static, visual point of view (as in Myres' and Whitman's theories), or from a dynamic and aural one. An audience unfamiliar with the work can only do the latter, but a composer who has developed and expanded his work gradually over a long period of time can do both. In fact, it is probably best to view any ring-composition theory of this kind from the standpoint of the poet who is operating on the level both of detailed composition and also of large-scale planning. In doing the latter he will naturally take most care over the opening and closing parts of his work, where consequently we find the clearest correspondences, providing the narrative 'frame' (cf. Whitman, *HHT* 258–9, Mueller, *Iliad* 175, Silk, *Iliad* 39).

Thus we begin with the intensely compressed action of book 1, followed by the broader, panoramic view of 2. The focus then narrows to the duel and its aftermath in 3–4, and this is followed by the major battle sequence in 5 in which the first *aristeia* is described and Greek natural supremacy is emphasized. Then come the quieter but emotionally charged episodes in Troy which arise from this, and so on. The poet is working with large-scale

---

[11] For the structure of books 11–15 see also on 11.426–7 (11–13 seem to form 'some kind of internal unit') and on 14.1–152, 15.262–404.

blocks of scenes of contrasting character, just as he constantly maintains variety of pace and tone at a more detailed level. The overall pattern of the poem seems to fall broadly into three main sections or 'panels', the opening one with Akhilleus' withdrawal, leading up to book 9, the central Books of the great battle, whether we see this as running from 11 to Patroklos' intervention in 16 or (perhaps more convincingly) from 11 to 18, and the closing section involving Akhilleus' return to fight. In terms of the poem's larger theme of the War as a whole, the first part is to some extent retrospective and the last is prospective, and the balance and contrasts are clearest between the opening and closing sections.

The visual analogies suggested by the ring-composition theory are, as had been said, only one type of approach. Given the fundamentally formular character of Homeric composition, certain leading themes will tend to recur several times throughout a large-scale composition, and here comparison with musical motifs (or *leitmotifs*) also can be relevant.[12] It has been the special merit of Schadewaldt and Reinhardt and their followers that they have concentrated attention on the significance of such recurrent themes, the interrelationships between different episodes which they suggest, and the effects of foreshadowing and anticipation which they involve (vol. v, pp. 7–10). Typical motifs and themes have already been considered in vol. II (pp. 15–27), and composition by theme is discussed in vol. v (pp. 11–23).[13] Something more, however, needs to be said briefly in conclusion about the poem's major themes and their development.

(ii) Themes

Any attempt to categorize such themes is bound to be somewhat arbitrary and impressionistic, even more so than in the case of analyses of structure. Nevertheless, such analysis can be illuminating, whether it is purely internal, considering only the poem itself, or comparative, identifying narrative motifs and patterns shared with other literary works.

The primary theme of the *Iliad* is stated in the opening lines: it is the wrath of Akhilleus and its fatal results (1.6–7). The *Iliad* is concerned with passion (πάθος, both emotion and suffering), whereas the *Odyssey*'s subject is said to be ἄνδρα ... πολύτροπον, a man, his character (ἦθος) and his experiences, although these too involve suffering. The *Iliad* takes its

[12] This suggests one of the dangers inherent in any approach which tries to carry ring composition too far, if this involves singling out particular episodes as significantly balanced at the expense of others of a similar type: for example, the duels in 7 and 16, as opposed to those of 16 and 22 which also have close links with each other.

[13] Cf. also Edwards, *HPI* 7–12 and 61–70, and '*Topos* and transformation in Homer', in Bremer, *HBOP* 47–60.

beginning from the quarrel of Agamemnon and Akhilleus (1.6–7), tracing the immediate cause of this and following its consequences. Passion leads to strife, in this case a form of στάσις within the Greek army, due to a dispute over a woman. This theme mirrors the cause of the Trojan War itself, the passion of Paris for Helen, which led to the strife between Greeks and Trojans. Similar processes are at work both internally (within one society) and externally (between different peoples). Attempts to mend the quarrel of the Greek leaders are as fruitless as efforts to resolve the War peacefully, and whole nations suffer from the passions of their rulers (as Horace says in his summary of the *Iliad*'s significance in *Epist.* 1.2.6–16). The leading theme of the poem is thus linked closely to the broader theme which makes it an *Iliad*, the Trojan War as a whole. In both cases, the outcome of strife is the death of many on both sides (1.3–5). Passion, war, and death are the basic ingredients which go to make up much of this work.

The opening lines, however, also introduce another essential element: the poet begins by asking a goddess to sing of the wrath, and concludes the proem with 'and the plan of Zeus was fulfilled' (1.5). The narrative of the quarrel starts by asking, not what *human* action sparked it off, but 'which of the gods' (1.8). Behind the sufferings of mortals lies the will of the gods, and only divine inspiration can enable the singer to know what are the hidden springs of human action. The relationship of gods and men is as much a theme of the poem as the ones we have already identified. Moreover, it is closely linked to these, since death and immortality are opposite sides of a single concept, and this is what divides men and gods most fundamentally. This boundary is more clearly marked in the *Iliad* than in other early Greek epics.

Divine will governs the order of the world, and this order is defined in terms of such concepts as μοῖρα, a word most often used in the *Iliad* in the context of a man's life and death, but one which can also be applied more generally to aspects of human society and its ordering. Thus from the specific theme of gods and men we move on naturally to the broader issues of social order and heroic ethics, such themes as honour (τιμή), respect (αἰδώς) and pity (ἔλεος), and the conventions governing behaviour between different classes of people, men and women, rulers and ruled, Greeks and non-Greeks, old and young, one's family, ξεῖνοι, suppliants, and so on. These ethical issues take us beyond the specific terms of the *Iliad*'s story (in contrast to others), but they help to define the limits within which it operates. The working-out of the consequences of passion, war and strife is seen very much in ethical terms. How far particular forms of conduct, such as those of Agamemnon and Akhilleus, Hektor and Paris, Patroklos and others, are justified, the nature of human responsibility for error, the operation of what Homeric poetry describes as ἄτη, and the processes of restitution, reconciliation and atonement: all of these are ethical issues fundamental to the poem, and help to give it its *moral* character. Ultimately, it is surely to a large extent these aspects, together with the poet's insight into human character, which lead us to regard this as one of the greatest works of European literature still today.

Although the *Iliad* encompasses the Trojan War as a whole together with many earlier events, and although the poet's geographical terms of reference are wide, the essential plot is highly concentrated. In this respect it is very different from the *Odyssey*. It covers the events of a limited number of days, and its main scenery is the plain of Troy, which (like the battlefields of northern France in the First World War) has few features or landmarks. The starkness of the setting is impressive: the destructive forces of War have obliterated nearly all creative aspects of nature and landscape. It has been observed too that there is hardly any 'weather' in the poem's action, beyond the monotonous recurrence of sunrise, noon and sunset, the welcome respite of nightfall and the ominous return of dawn, and the supernatural phenomena of thunder and lightning, eerie mists blotting out the battlefield, or bloody rain, all signs of divine involvement in the conflict.

The range of *dramatis personae* of the action itself is also limited almost entirely to the distant world of gods and heroes, warriors whose life seems to be devoted mainly to fighting. It is very noticeable in this respect how relatively slight and debatable are the differentiating marks which might distinguish the Greeks from their eastern enemies, the Trojans and their allies.[14] The main distinction on the human level is not between Greeks and foreigners, but between different levels of society, rulers and ruled (βασιλῆες and δῆμος). We see very little of the latter in the *Iliad*. The only really 'unheroic' characters are Thersites and Dolon, and even they may perhaps belong rather to the 'upper' than the 'lower' classes (see comment on 2.212). Both names suggest that they represent types. The scenes involving them offer interludes of comic relief. They are close in tone and content to the *Odyssey*, and it is significant that Odysseus is prominent in both of them. The episode with Thersites resembles the boxing-match in which he beats up the beggar Iros (*Od.* 18.1–107; see also on 23.784), and the Doloneia displays his special Odyssean skills in deception. In the Games for Patroklos we meet a similar comic character from a lower order of society, Epeios (the carpenter of the Wooden Horse) in the boxing and weight-throwing events (see on 653–99, 665, 840). In general, however, in the poem's action on the human level we do not find the range of characters which appears in the *Odyssey*, such as slaves, farmers, craftsmen and merchants, and which makes that poem seem so much closer to the life of the poet's own day. Even priests or

---

[14] Cf. the scepticism of Hall, *Barbarian*, especially 19–55; but for some possible differences between the two sides see on 21.130–2, 24.495–7, 24.719–22 (para. 4).

seers often appear in the *Iliad* only to be killed, and may themselves be aristocratic.

This bleak concentration of theme and focus is to some extent relieved by the similes, with their vivid and refreshing *vignettes* of the world of the poet and his audience, the peaceful, everyday world of Ionia in the eighth century B.C., filled with such a wealth of details of landscape, weather, country and domestic life, and so on. The Shield of Akhilleus also gives us a microcosm of the contemporary world, in its main aspects of war and peace, countryside and town. The poignant domestic scenes of life in Troy and of Hektor's family add great depth, but essentially they heighten the pathos of the War, with all its human loss. Hektor's impending death hangs heavy over his meetings with his family in book 6. On the Greek side we have the shadowy figures of the captive women, among whom only Briseis is briefly but movingly characterized (1.348, 19.282–302), and the many moving references to the families who have been left at home. These reach their culmination in the meeting between Priam and Akhilleus in book 24, where the theme of fathers and sons, important throughout, is most powerfully represented by Priam's appeal (see on 24.486–506, and vol. V, p. 10).

As a foil to the bleakness of the human tragedy there is the 'divine comedy' of Olympian society, with its scenes of family quarrels and feuds. Without such contrasts the endless tale of killing would seem unbearable. Yet even the gods, for all their apparent freedom from care, are in fact inextricably and passionately involved in human affairs, and are themselves deeply affected by the sufferings of those whom they love (cf. especially Griffin, *HLD* 179–204).

We have briefly reviewed the broader thematic outlines of the poem: passion and its moral effects (πάθος and ἦθος), war and peace, gods and men, Achaeans and their enemies. Within this framework we might ask whether it is possible to define certain leading motifs (or 'narrative patterns') which recur significantly throughout the work and help to give the poem its shape. This may well be an even more subjective venture than our speculations so far, but nevertheless worth the attempt.

The Trojan War itself begins with the abduction of a woman, and this motif is repeated in the quarrels of Khruseis and Briseis, involving the anger of (successively) Apollo, Agamemnon and Akhilleus. This pattern occurs also in the story of Demeter and the rape of Persephone. Both Demeter and Akhilleus withdraw in anger, causing devastation. Attempts are made to appease them with offers of recompense, but these fail. Eventually they do return, and there is a reconciliation with the offending parties.[15] This narrative pattern governs the plot of the *Iliad* up to book 19. Interwoven

---

[15] Cf. M. L. Lord, 'Withdrawal and return: an epic story pattern in the Homeric Hymn to Demeter and in the Homeric Poems', *CJ* 62 (1967) 241–8; Edwards, *HPI* 62.

with it is another major theme, that of the death of the hero's closest friend, his grief and subsequent vengeance: this strand of the story effectively begins with book 11 and takes us up to book 22 or 23 (Edwards, *HPI* 8–9, 63). It is this above all which gives the plot its most tragic quality. The story could well have ended there, with Hektor's death or Patroklos' burial, but the typical theme of the fate of a dead warrior's body is here developed into a remarkable conclusion, with Priam's visit to Akhilleus to recover his son's corpse (Edwards, *HPI* 9–10, 79–81).

These three themes are, however, themselves closely linked by repeated patterns. All three involve grief or anger at the loss of a loved one (Helen, Khruseis, Briseis; Patroklos, Hektor), the infringement of honour which this implies, and the need to recover what has been lost (although in the case of Patroklos and Hektor this can only be the body). In the case of the women and Patroklos anger and grief lead to vengeance and the desire for compensation.

A motif which recurs significantly throughout is that of *supplication*, and this has been seen by some as one of the key themes of the poem (cf. especially Thornton, *Supplication* 113–42). In book 1 the rejected supplication of Agamemnon by Khruses leads to his prayer to Apollo for vengeance, and Akhilleus' request to Thetis leads to her successful supplication of Zeus. In 9 the Embassy, although not originally seen as supplication, is viewed in these terms by Phoinix and Diomedes (9.501, 9.502–12, 9.698): this again fails. In 16, however, Akhilleus yields to Patroklos' plea to pity the Greeks, to the extent that he allows him to fight instead. Finally, having refused Hektor's repeated requests for burial in book 22 (the culmination of all the 'suppliant scenes' which occur in the actual fighting), he gives way at last to Priam.

Agathe Thornton argues that this motif is closely linked to the theme of ἄτη. Agamemnon is a victim of this because of his treatment of Khruses and Akhilleus, and Akhilleus because of his own refusal to give way to the Embassy. This leads to the involvement of Patroklos (cf. especially 11.602–4). Patroklos too fails to heed Akhilleus' warning not to attack Troy, and is implicated in the process as a largely innocent victim, and equally Hektor is doomed because he refuses the advice of Pouludamas in book 18. These examples take us beyond the suppliancy theme itself. But the close association between Prayers (Λιταί) and Ate is clearly expressed in Phoinix' speech to Akhilleus (9.496–514), where he describes how Prayers are the daughters of Zeus himself, who come after Ate to heal the harm; if one hears them they help one, but if one rejects them they ask Zeus to send Ate as retribution. This clear warning is not heeded by Akhilleus, who loses Patroklos as a result. But in the end, after his reconciliation with Agamemnon and Hektor's death, he accepts the orders of Zeus (himself the guardian of suppliants) to hear the prayers of Priam (cf. Thornton, *Supplication* 135–6, 140–1). This theme of suppliancy thus does much to articulate and shape the main movement of the plot, as well as carrying great weight in terms of the poem's moral significance.

Finally, Akhilleus' rejection and later acceptance of the claims upon him of his fellow-men highlight another essential aspect of the poem, that of the isolation of this hero from society, which is linked to his foreknowledge of impending death. This theme was to have powerful repercussions in later Greek literature, especially in the tragedies of Sophocles, several of whose heroes seem to have inherited from Akhilleus their own rugged and solitary grandeur.

To isolate, as we have done, certain themes in this way from the complexity of such a vast work is clearly a highly selective process, and it would be possible to argue that the poem's significance depends as much on other factors as it does on these. One might object that more weight should be given to the themes of *honour* (τιμή) and *fame* (κλέος), which are fundamental to heroic narrative, and which govern the behaviour of all the leading characters in the poem. Alternatively, in stressing the emotional and moral aspects, have we failed to give due value to the rôle of the poem as a *historical* document in antiquity, and one with great patriotic appeal? One can point in this respect to certain crucial themes, such as the extraordinary concept of a single, united expedition of Greek peoples against their eastern neighbours in the heroic age, the strains and stresses involved in holding this together, the lack of clarity over the expedition's overall command, and the resulting clash of leaders with different claims to pre-eminence. The picture which the *Iliad* presents is in this respect curiously similar to that of the *Odyssey*, where settled government is disrupted by the absence of the titular ruler of Ithaca and the issue of succession to the kingship is unclear. It is hard to believe that such situations have no historical basis, and this suspicion is confirmed by Hesiod, whose *Works and Days* is remarkably outspoken against the local rulers, who are portrayed as corrupt and greedy (cf. for example his δωροφάγους βασιλῆας of *Erga* 38–9 with the accusation that Agamemnon is a δημοβόρος βασιλεύς at *Il.* 1.231). By contrast, Hesiod's picture of the honest peasant farmer and his lazy, dishonest brother has its close counterpart in the loyal and disloyal retainers of Odysseus.

Such historical or semi-historical issues are, however, rather shared between the *Iliad* and *Odyssey* than peculiar to one poem. Further discussion of them would be beyond the scope of this Introduction, but see J. B. Hainsworth, vol. III (pp. 32–53).

2. Two special problems

(i) Book division

There is no positive evidence that the division of the *Iliad* or *Odyssey* into twenty-four books, numbered with the letters of the Ionic alphabet, was made before the Alexandrian period. In the fifth and fourth centuries B.C. several authors refer to episodes or sections of both poems by titles, such as Διομήδεος ἀριστείη (Hdt. 2.116, quoting 6.289–92), Σκήπτρου παράδοσις, Νεῶν κατάλογος (Thuc. 1.9.4, 1.10.4), Λιταί, Τειχομαχία (Pl. *Crat.* 428c, *Ion* 539B), Ἀλκίνου ἀπόλογος (Pl. *Rep.* 614B, Arist. *Poet.* 1455a2, *Rhet.* 1417a13), Νίπτρα (Arist. *Poet.* 1454b30). It is significant that Herodotus quotes part of book 6 as from Diomedes' *aristeia* (which is the title of book 5 in our MSS), and that the reference in the *Poetics* to the 'story told to Alkinoos' is not to part of *Odyssey* 9–12, but to *Od.* 8.521ff. This indicates that in the classical period such titles did not correspond with our book-divisions, and taken by itself this tends to suggest either that the division was not yet made, or that if it was, it was not so widely used as to affect the older division by episodes.[16]

The evidence of the Ptolemaic papyri is hard to assess.[17] There is nothing to mark the end or beginning of a book of Homer in surviving papyri of the third or second century B.C., but few contain the junction between two books, and the left-hand margin is complete in only one case. In two papyri of the *Odyssey*, thought to belong to the second half of the third century B.C., the beginning of a roll or column apparently corresponded with *Od.* 9.1 and 21.1, and the second of these may possibly have contained only book 21. A few (3 or 4?) similar cases are thought to occur in the later Ptolemaic period, but not all of these are certain. On the other hand, from the first century A.D. onward the end of a book is regularly marked by a coronis and title. Moreover, the first attestation of book-numbering in Alexandrian scholarship is in the late second century B.C., the *Commentary on* Ξ (book 14) of Apollodorus of Athens (cf. Erbse III 557).

The only ancient authors who attribute the division of the poems into 24 books to particular scholars are Ps.-Plutarch (*Vita Hom.* 2.4) and Eustathius (5.29ff.). The first makes it the work of τῶν γραμματικῶν τῶν περὶ Ἀρίσταρχον, the second (whose whole account is confused) 'Aristarchus and after him Zenodotus'. Against Ps.-Plutarch's attribution to Aristarchus

---

[16] A long catalogue of such titles for episodes is given by Aelian (*VH* 13.14).
[17] Cf. West, *Ptolemaic Papyri* 20–5.

(or Aristophanes) it has been argued that they would surely have made *Od.* 23.296 the end of a book, since they regarded this as the 'end of the *Odyssey*'. But this would have resulted in a book of only 296 verses, which could well have been regarded as too short. Lachmann and Wilamowitz argued that the division was made by Zenodotus, who is also thought to have composed an essay on the number of days in the *Iliad*.[18] Alternatively, it has been suggested that the innovation made by the Alexandrian scholars was not the division into books, but simply the use of letters of the alphabet for them, the division itself being older.[19]

Those who prefer an earlier date for the book-division tend to associate it with rhapsodic practice, and the use of the term ῥαψῳδία for a book might support this.[20] But this clashes with the evidence that titles of episodes ran over book-divisions before the Hellenistic period. To some extent, however, the divisions presumably did correspond with rhapsodic breaks, in so far as they came at significant breaks in the narrative. It has also been argued that the division works better for the *Iliad* than for the *Odyssey*, where it results in some rather short books, and that the Alexandrians would have been more rational.[21] But once the division was made for one poem, it is not surprising that the same system should have been imposed on the other.

It must be admitted that the evidence is not sufficient to allow us to give a precise date for book-division. Even the early Ptolemaic papyri which seem to have begun a roll or column at (for example) *Od.* 9.1 or 21.1 may well have done so simply because these marked the beginning of significant sections of the poem (Odysseus' account of his Wanderings, and the Trial of the Bow). But such evidence as there is does seem to point to the Alexandrian period as the time when this innovation was made, rather than to an earlier date.[22]

(ii) The end of the *Iliad* in relation to the *Odyssey*

It has often been claimed that book 24 is closer in language and themes to the *Odyssey* than the rest of the *Iliad* is, but very varying conclusions have been drawn from this claim.[23]

---

[18] Cf. Pfeiffer, *History of Classical Scholarship* 116–17, Wilamowitz, *Untersuchungen* 369, and Nickau, *RE* xA (1972) s.v. Zenodotos (3), 36–7.

[19] Cf. P. Mazon, *Introduction à l'Iliade* (Paris 1912) 138ff.

[20] Cf. Mazon, *loc. cit.*, J. A. Notopoulos, *HSCP* 68 (1964) 11–12, West, *Ptolemaic Papyri* 20 and West, *Od.* 39–40, G. P. Goold, *Illinois Classical Studies* 2 (1977) 26–30.

[21] West, *Ptolemaic Papyri* 19 and West, *Od.* 40 n. 19.

[22] See also vol. IV, p. 31 n. 47 'after Apollonius Rhodius'. O. Taplin, *Homeric Soundings* (Oxford 1992) 285–93, has a detailed examination of the actual book-divisions of the *Iliad* in relation to the poem's narrative structure.

[23] Peppmüller listed Odyssean features and argued that book 24 was later than most of the *Odyssey* (*Commentar des vierundzwanzigsten Buches der Ilias*, Berlin 1876, xxxi–xl). Some later analysts followed him, others (e.g. Cauer and Wilamowitz) thought that 24 and the *Odyssey*

First we must ask whether in fact 24 really does differ from the rest of the *Iliad* in this respect. My own impression is that it does. To begin with, one can see this simply from a survey of the density of comments which look specifically to the *Odyssey* for parallels rather than the *Iliad*, i.e. about one in 5 or 6 verses of book 24, a frequency much greater than in other parts of this Commentary.[24] This survey covers a wide range of features – linguistic, stylistic and thematic – and on its own tells one little. It is also open to the objection that a commentator already aware of earlier attempts to connect book 24 to the *Odyssey* is more likely to notice such parallels here than elsewhere. However, the resemblances are particularly impressive when one considers the structure of scenes in 24.

It is surely significant that the narrative of the *Odyssey* opens in a way which is very close to the opening part of 24 (see on 22–76, 33, 33–4, 38, 77–119). The gods take pity on Odysseus as they do on Hektor, despite the hostility of Poseidon to Odysseus and the pro-Greek gods to Hektor. Athene's protests to Zeus in both *Odyssey* 1 and 5 resemble those of Apollo in *Iliad* 24. In each case Zeus agrees, and a double plan is put into action, which involves sending Athene and Hermes to Telemakhos and Kalupso, just as Zeus sends Iris to Thetis and then to Priam in the *Iliad*. Hermes is also involved in the case of Hektor: unable to steal the body, he later comes instead to escort Priam on his journey. Moreover, the beginning of Apollo's protest at the hard-heartedness of the gods is echoed by Kalupso when she is visited by Hermes (24.33, *Od.* 5.118), although here the motif is used in a different way; the journey of Iris to Thetis resembles that of Hermes to Kalupso, both being described by a simile about fishing

---

were the work of the same poet or circle of poets. Leaf (II 536) held that this Book 'resembles I, K, and Ψ, in its kinship to the *Odyssey*, but to a greater degree than any of them', concluding that 'if in the Μῆνις we have the Aischylos, in this last book we have at once the Sophokles and Euripides of the Epos'. But F. M. Stawell, in *Homer and the Iliad* (London 1909) 93ff. and 238ff., argued, with detailed evidence, that book 24 was no more Odyssean in style and language than books 1 or 22.1–404. Cf. from the same 'old unitarian' camp J. A. Scott, *The Unity of Homer* (Berkeley 1921) 73–105.

Later Reinhardt (*IuD* 469–505) took up arms against the analysts and reviewed some of the main parallels, arguing in favour of the strong influence of book 24 on the *Odyssey*. He was followed by Beck, who noted more cases of possible influence (*Stellung* 102–9, and *Philologus* 109 (1965) 1–29). Deichgräber, however (*Letzte Gesang* 114–17), observed that the similarities could be due to the use of common traditional material.

A brief attempt to identify some Odyssean features in the *Iliad* is made by E. K. Borthwick, *Odyssean Elements in the Iliad* (Inaugural Lecture given at Edinburgh University on 2 May 1983). The relationship of the *Odyssey* to the *Iliad* is reviewed more generally by R. B. Rutherford, in 'From the *Iliad* to the *Odyssey*', *BICS* 38 (1991–2). Cf. also Usener, *Verhältnis der Odyssee zur Ilias*.

[24] The frequency naturally varies widely, e.g. 1 in 45 verses of book 5, 1 in 10 of book 22, 1 in 13 of book 23. A short episode such as the sea-journey to Khruse (1.430–87) may be exceptional (about 1 in 6.5), and the subject-matter accounts for this (see on 1.432–9, 434); but I do not believe that the density is so high over any other whole Book.

(24.80–2, *Od.* 5.51–4); and Hermes' journey at 24.331–48 is echoed closely at *Od.* 5.29–49.

The preparations for Priam's journey involve a number of motifs which recur in the *Odyssey*, especially the details of the gifts and the waggon, Hekabe's reactions, and the libation, prayer and omen before departure (see on 150, 190, 191–2, 200–16, 228, 229–37, 259–61, 263, 264, 277–8, 281–321, 292–8, 308–13). The journey itself, and the return to Troy next day, naturally have parallels in Odyssean overland journeys. But it is the major episode where Hermes and Priam meet and talk which bears the closest resemblance to Odyssean scenes, especially those of Hermes' visit to Kalupso, his meeting with Odysseus in book 10, and other meetings between Athene and Odysseus or Telemakhos (see on 333–48, 347–8, 348, 349–442, 360–3, 375–7, 397–8). There is also a significant parallel here between the piety of Priam and that of Laertes at the end of the *Odyssey* (see on 425–8), which is one aspect of a larger issue, that of the parallelism between the endings of the two epics, both of which involve a sympathetic study of the aged father of one of the leading heroes, as well as the description of a funeral, and a 'moral ending'.

The portrayal of Akhilleus' quarters, and of Priam's visit and supplication, again have their closest parallels in the *Odyssey* (see especially on 469–691, and on 448–56, 450–1, 452–3, 472–6, 475–6, 482–4, 553–5, 558, 587–90, 633–76). Akhilleus' great speech of consolation to Priam (518–51) has many Odyssean features of expression (see on 518, 524, 525–6, 527–33, 529–30, 538–40, 543–6), and its moral themes (the importance of endurance, the uselessness of grief, the need to accept the will of the gods, etc.) find their clearest echoes in the *Odyssey*. Moreover, given the close relationship which we have seen between this Book and the opening of the *Odyssey*, it seems only natural to believe that Zeus's words at *Od.* 1.32–43, about how men blame the gods unfairly for all their troubles, take up and comment on Akhilleus' words about the Jars of Zeus at 24.527–33 (as bT on 527–8 already surmised; see on 527–33).

Among many other parallels one deserves to be singled out here: Hekabe's and Helen's laments, with their restrained pathos, seem to be echoed together in the touching speech of Odysseus' mother's ghost to him in the Nekuia, when she describes how she died of longing for him and for his gentleness (*Od.* 11.197–203; see on 757–9, 768–72).

Finally, as Macleod rightly says (*Iliad XXIV* 15), at the end of the *Iliad* the gods 'appear as what they are throughout the *Odyssey*, the guarantors of justice and kindness among mortals'. The moral tone of book 24, on both the divine and human levels, anticipates that of the *Odyssey*, just as much as its language, themes and scenic construction.

What conclusion are we to draw from these observations? Clearly there is a range of possible explanations, as always in such cases of epic parallels. Few nowadays would agree with the old analytical view that book 24 is later than and influenced by the *Odyssey*. More would side with Reinhardt, seeing the *Odyssey* as the work of a poet particularly heavily influenced by this part of the *Iliad*. Some, however, will prefer Deichgräber's view, that the resemblances are due to common use of traditional elements. This last view may seem to some extent satisfactory, but on its own it is surely not enough to explain what appear to be such major differences between this Book and the rest of the *Iliad*. It is surely more likely that the composer of the *Odyssey* had the end of the *Iliad* especially in mind, whether or not both poems are by the same author. It is, however, tempting to go a step further, and to see the similarities as due to the fact that when Homer gave the end of the *Iliad* the form it has, the *Odyssey* was already taking shape in his mind: i.e. not only is a single poet the composer of both, but their composition actually overlapped to some extent. Thus we find that not only does the *Iliad* itself form a great and complex ring-structure, whose end echoes and resolves the themes of its beginning, but it is also inseparably linked or dovetailed thematically with the *Odyssey*, as if the two works could really almost be regarded as one great epic *continuum*, stretching from the Wrath of Akhilleus to the safe homecoming and triumph of the last of the heroes, Odysseus.

3. Homer and his ancient critics

(i) From Homer to Aristotle[25]

The Homeric poems, and especially the *Odyssey*, have much to say about singers and audiences, and it is possible to construct from them a kind of *ars poetica*.[26] The singer's status, his ethical, didactic and commemorative rôles, the emotional impact of song, the questions of originality, of poetic technique and inspiration, of credibility, truth and fiction: these are all themes which are reflected in what the poet himself says, and they anticipate much that will be important in later criticism. The *Odyssey* even contains the first example of explicit criticism of epic song, together with an answer to this. When Phemios sings of the painful return of the Achaeans from Troy, Penelope weeps, and then asks him to change the subject, because it is so distressing for her personally. Telemakhos replies:

My mother, why do you begrudge the faithful bard the right to give pleasure in whatever way his mind prompts him? It is not bards who are to blame; no, surely Zeus is to blame, who allots to mortal men whatever he wishes for each. And this man should not be criticized if he sings of the Danaans' fate: for men always give more renown to that song which is the latest to circulate among its hearers. (1.346–52)

It can also be argued that the *Odyssey* itself, in its implied ideals of survival at all costs, homecoming and domestic harmony, forms the first commentary on – and criticism of – the *Iliad*.[27] What is clear, at any rate, is that the composer of the *Odyssey* has learnt a great deal from the extraordinary

---

[25] A version of much of this section appears as 'Aristotle's reading of Homer and its background' in Lamberton and Keaney, *Homer's Ancient Readers*.

[26] Cf. especially W. Marg, *Homer über die Dichtung* (2nd edn, Münster 1971), H. Fränkel, *Early Greek Poetry and Philosophy* (Oxford 1975) 6–25, J. Svenbro, *La Parole et le marbre* (Lund 1976) 11–45, Macleod, *Iliad XXIV* 1–8 and *Collected Essays* (Oxford 1983) 1–15, G. B. Walsh, *The Varieties of Enchantment* (Chapel Hill 1984), C. Segal, 'Bard and audience in Homer', in Lamberton and Keaney, *Homer's Ancient Readers*, S. Goldhill, *The Poet's Voice* (Cambridge 1991) 56–68.

[27] Cf. J. Griffin, in Bremer, *HBOP* 101: 'The poet of the *Odyssey* is aware of the *Iliad* and, in important respects, composing in response to it; his response makes him the first of literary critics'; and *ibid*. 102: 'A marvellous creation ... fit for the greatest of all heroes; yet grim and terrifying, immoderate, never to be repeated. That, perhaps, was the final judgment of the *Odyssey* on the *Iliad*.' Cf. also R. B. Rutherford, 'From the *Iliad* to the *Odyssey*', *BICS* 38 (1991–2).

achievement of the earlier poem, and his work may well be seen as a poetic reflection on the *Iliad*, as well as a complement to it.

One of the most fundamental issues which the narrative of the *Odyssey* seems to reflect, whereas there is no hint of this in the *Iliad*, is the question of the fictional character of epic. By making Odysseus himself the supreme master of false tales, by telling the incredible tales of his wanderings in his own mouth, and then by stressing on two occasions his resemblance to a skilful singer whose words carry conviction, however strange they may be (*Od.* 11.363–9, 17.513–21), the poet indirectly draws attention to this issue. It is surely significant that the verse which describes the disguised Odysseus' skill in deceiving his own wife by his narrative, ἴσκε ψεύδεα πολλὰ λέγων ἐτύμοισιν ὁμοῖα (19.203), is so close to that of Hesiod's Muses in their famous address to him (*Th.* 27–8): ἴδμεν ψεύδεα πολλὰ λέγειν ἐτύμοισιν ὁμοῖα, | ἴδμεν δ' εὖτ' ἐθέλωμεν ἀληθέα γηρύσασθαι. Here for the first time the Muses pose the problem explicitly: if they can sing both truth and credible fiction, how is one to distinguish between them?

During the archaic period this will be a growing preoccupation. Solon's dismissive πολλὰ ψεύδονται ἀοιδοί (fr. 29 West) anticipates the more detailed criticisms of the sixth-century B.C. philosophers Xenophanes, Heraclitus and probably also Pythagoras, and Stesichorus' explicit rejection of the Homeric and Hesiodic accounts of Helen and the Trojan War. Xenophanes is concerned to combat the epic portrayal of the gods as anthropomorphic and fallible, and the popular acceptance of Homer as a religious teacher (D–K 21 B 10–12, 14–16). Heraclitus attacks the philosophical authority of both Homer and Hesiod (22 A 22, B 40, 42, 56, 57, 106). Hesiod's breadth of learning (πολυμαθίη) should not be mistaken for wisdom (B 40), and Homer, although wiser than all other Greeks, was unable to solve a children's riddle, the riddle of the lice (B 56). Homer and Archilochus deserve to be expelled from poetic contests and flogged, presumably on moral grounds, and for misleading people (B 42). According to later legend, Pythagoras was said to have seen Homer and Hesiod being punished in the Underworld, because of their lies about the gods (Hieronymus of Rhodes, fr. 42 Wehrli). Meanwhile Stesichorus produced his own version of the story of Helen, in which she never went to Troy, but stayed in Egypt throughout the War, whilst a phantom of her appeared at Troy (*PMG* 192–3). The phantom Helen was destined later to have philosophical repercussions, as a symbol of human illusion for Euripides, Plato, and the Neoplatonists.[28]

---

[28] Revising Homer's version of the Trojan War remained a popular game throughout antiquity: cf. especially Hdt. 2.112–20, Dio Chrys. *Or.* 11, Philostratus, *Heroicus*, and the accounts ascribed to Dictys and Dares.

Such attacks, however, did not prevent people from appealing to Homer as a historical source for political reasons, as Athens is said to have done early in the sixth century in her dispute with Megara over Salamis (Arist. *Rhet.* 1375b30). The Athenian claim to Sigeum in the Troad was based at least partly on their participation in the Trojan War, as portrayed in the *Iliad* (Hdt. 5.94.2). We hear more of such appeals later, during the Persian Wars (Hdt. 7.161.3, 7.169, 7.171, 9.27.4). The authority of Homer in sixth-century Athens is shown most clearly by the regulation that the Homeric poems alone should be recited at the Panathenaia (Lycurgus, *In Leocratem* 102, Isocrates, *Paneg.* 159, Pl. *Hipparchus* 228B).[29] Although we are never explicitly told that 'Homer' means exclusively the *Iliad* and *Odyssey*, that is probably what is meant by the fourth-century B.C. authors who first mention this rule, and it seems quite possible that these two poems were already being distinguished from the other early epics loosely associated by tradition with Homer's name.

Towards the end of the sixth century, we begin to hear of an attempt to meet the attacks of the philosophers on their own ground through allegory, in the work of Theagenes of Rhegium, who is said to have been the first to use this method. The context in which this is mentioned is that of allegorical interpretations of the Theomachy in *Iliad* 20 and 21, in terms of the conflict both of physical elements and also of moral or psychological forces (D–K 8.2). This episode makes a natural starting-point for such interpretations, although exactly what Theagenes' own theory was is unclear. However, it looks as if he discussed the Homeric text in some detail, since a variant reading is ascribed to him in the Scholia (D–K 8.3), and he is said to have been the first person to write on Homer's poetry, life and date, as well as on the Greek language in general (8.1, 1A). Thus we find linguistic study already closely linked to allegorical interpretation at this early stage of scholarship.

These various responses to Homer or epic in general continue through the literature of the fifth century. Pindar is clearly sensitive to philosophical criticism of the kind expressed by Xenophanes, and he is also concerned with problems of truth, credibility, and the fictional character of poetry. The classic case is his rationalization of the myth of Pelops in *Olympian* 1, where he comments on the deceptive charm of poetic tales (μῦθοι), their power of lulling us into accepting the marvellous and fabulous as credible (*O.* 1.25ff.). More specifically, in *Nemean* 7, he speaks of Homer's exaggeration of the truth about Odysseus, and the way in which he persuades us to suspend our disbelief: 'I think that the story of Odysseus was exaggerated beyond what he experienced, because of the sweet words of Homer: for

---

[29] Cf. vol. IV, pp. 30–1.

there is an impressive dignity about his fictions and winged craft, and poetic skill deceives, leading astray with fables: the generality of men has a blind heart' (*N.* 7.20ff.). At the same time, however, the shame of the suicide of Ajax was counterbalanced by the honour paid to him by Homer, 'who set all his valour upright again, telling of it in accordance with his wand of wondrous verses, as a theme for later singers to play on' (*I.* 4.41ff.). And just before his criticism of Homer in *Nemean* 7 he refers to the idea of commemorative poetry as a 'mirror for noble deeds' (*N.* 7.14–16). Here already we see the tension between the ideas of epic song as commemoration, reflecting a true image, and poetic fiction as a distorting medium.[30]

Like Pindar, the historians Herodotus and Thucydides attempt a rationalizing approach. Herodotus argues that Homer's story of Helen at Troy cannot be true, for if she had been there the Trojans would surely have given her back, and he accepts the alternative version which left her in Egypt. Homer, he says, knew the truth, but rejected it as less appropriate (εὐπρεπής) for his poetry (2.112–20). He also observes here that the epic *Cypria* cannot be Homer's work, as it disagrees with the *Iliad* over Paris' journey to Troy (2.117). Elsewhere (4.32) Herodotus doubts whether the *Epigonoi* is Homeric. Thucydides draws detailed deductions about the historical nature of the Trojan War and early Greek society from Homer and other epic poetry, whilst stressing the tendency of poets to exaggeration (1.1–22). Thucydides' respect for Homer as a source is striking, although there is a strong note of disparagement in Perikles' funeral speech, where he says that Athens does not need a Homer to sing her praises, nor any poet whose verses will give a momentary pleasure, only to be contradicted by the truth of history (2.41.4).

So far we have to some extent been considering attitudes to epic as a whole, rather than more detailed discussion of Homer or anything approaching literary criticism in a modern sense. Close analysis and discussion of problems there must always have been, and this is already attested for Theagenes, but it is with the sophists that such discussion begins to emerge into the foreground.[31] This was encouraged by their special interest in language and also in the use of poetic texts to underpin their own theories. Echoes can be detected in chapter 25 of Aristotle's *Poetics* and in the surviving fragments of his *Homeric Problems* (see below). Debate about the detailed interpretation of a text (such as Simonides' poem on virtue in Plato's *Protagoras*) led naturally to the search for the *underlying* sense, the ὑπόνοια. For men like Protagoras, the early poets were really sophists in disguise,

---

[30] On these passages of Pindar see also Richardson, 'Pindar and later literary criticism in antiquity', *Papers of the Liverpool Latin Seminar* 5 (1985) 384–9, F. J. Nisetich, *Pindar and Homer* (Baltimore 1989), and G. Nagy, *Pindar's Homer* (Baltimore 1990) especially 414–37.

[31] Cf. Richardson, *PCPS* 201 (1975), 65–81.

clothing their philosophical wisdom in a popular dress (Pl. *Prot.* 316D–E, *Theaet.* 180C–E). From this could develop more elaborate and extraordinary allegorical constructions, such as that of Metrodorus of Lampsacus, interpreting the whole of the *Iliad* in terms of Anaxagoras' cosmology (D–K 61 A 3–4).[32] Philodemus describes such theories as the work of maniacs, and they were liable to give the whole practice of allegory a bad name.

Anaxagoras himself seems to have been far more cautious: he is said to have been 'the first to show that Homer's poetry concerned valour and justice' (D–K 59 A 1 §11). This sounds not so very different from the popular view reflected in Aristophanes' *Frogs*, that Homer teaches 'marshalling of armies, forms of valour, arming of men for war' (1034ff.). This kind of ethical or educational approach is echoed by Niceratus in Xenophon's *Symposium*, when he says that his father Nicias made him learn the whole of Homer's poetry by heart, as part of the education of a gentleman (3.5). Later on he claims him as a source of information on all kinds of ethical and practical subjects (4.6–7), as does the rhapsode Ion in Plato's dialogue (537Aff.). It is, incidentally, in these contexts that we hear the names of the various supposedly leading interpreters of the Homeric poems. Apart from Metrodorus, these include Stesimbrotus of Thasos, Anaximander and Glaucon. It is surely significant that we know so little about most of them: their views and theories about the poems were overtaken by those of later critics. But Stesimbrotus was the teacher of the first person definitely known to have 'edited' the text of Homer, the epic poet Antimachus of Colophon: here we seem to glimpse the beginnings of scholarship in its later Hellenistic and modern sense.[33]

Many of the major sophists, on the other hand, are known to have used Homeric themes and characters as vehicles for the expression of their own ethical or rhetorical ideas. We see this clearly in the debate between Socrates and Hippias over the relative merits of Akhilleus' and Odysseus' characters (Pl. *Hippias Minor*), in Gorgias' *Helen* and *Palamedes*, or in the *Aias* and *Odysseus* of Antisthenes. The long list of essays on Homeric subjects ascribed to Antisthenes includes many which probably set out to draw moral lessons from the poems (*PCPS* 201 (1975) 77–81). Socrates himself seems to have been fond of using Homer to illustrate a point, if we can judge from Xenophon and Plato, and sometimes this takes the form of moral allegory: for example the Sirens' charms strike at those ambitious for fame, and it was gluttony that turned Odysseus' men into swine, and self-restraint that saved Odysseus himself (Xen. *Mem.* 2.6.10–12, 1.3.7). In Plato's

---

[32] For details see *PCPS* 201 (1975) 68–70.
[33] Cf. Pfeiffer, *History of Classical Scholarship* 35–6. But Antimachus' edition may have been rather a critical work, discussing a series of emendations: cf. N. G. Wilson, *CR* 19 (1969) 369.

Apology (28c) Socrates defends himself from the charge of deliberately courting death by appeal to the precedent of Akhilleus.

This moralizing view of Homer may well have found its culmination as far as the classical period is concerned in the early fourth-century *Mouseion* of Alcidamas. In this he seems to have collected traditional stories about the early poets, including the old tales of the contest of Homer and Hesiod and their respective deaths, in order to illustrate the moral value of their works. It is likely that this is one of the works which Plato has in mind when he attacks such an approach in book 10 of the *Republic*, and questions whether Homer ever was of any practical or civic use to anyone.[34] Alcidamas seems to have admired Homer's poems especially for their ethical realism, and he called the *Odyssey* a 'fine mirror of human life' (Arist. *Rhet.* 1406b12). He also spoke of the honours paid to Homer and other poets, a theme which Plato again treats with sarcastic scepticism.

By contrast with this type of viewpoint the sophist Protagoras (D–K 80 A 30) gives us what seems to be the first example of interpretative criticism of a more structural type, embedded by chance in a papyrus commentary on *Iliad* 21 (see on 205–327). He apparently observed that the battle of Akhilleus with the river-god Skamandros was designed to form a transition from Akhilleus' previous exploits to the battle of the gods ('and perhaps also to increase Akhilleus' importance', adds the scholiast). Thus, in addition to showing a linguistic interest in Homer, exemplified by his criticism of the poet for addressing the Muse in the imperative (D–K 80 A 29), Protagoras may have taken a broader interest in the poet's compositional techniques. But such instances are rare and hard to detect at this period.

The attitude of Plato to Homer is deeply divided: on the one hand a deep and abiding love of the poet, whose influence on him (as Longinus observed: 13.3–4) can be detected at every turn (he quotes him some 150 times[35]); on the other, strong misgivings about the rôle of poetry in the philosophical life. His own work may be viewed as a philosophical alternative to traditional literary forms, especially epic and drama, and his own myths as designed to replace those of Homer and Hesiod. At the end of the *Republic* (614B2–3) the story of Er is said to be 'not a tale told to Alkinoos, but rather that of a courageous man ...' (οὐ ... Ἀλκίνου γε ἀπόλογον ... ἀλλ' ἀλκίμου μὲν ἀνδρός ...). Homeric fiction gives way to a tale which conveys philosophical truth in mythical form.

Allegory for Plato, although he plays with this method from time to time, is no answer to the problem of poetry. There is no way of discovering

---

[34] Cf. Richardson, *CQ* 31 (1981) 1–10.
[35] Cf. G. E. Howes, 'Homeric quotations in Plato and Aristotle', *HSCP* 6 (1895) 153–210, J. Labarbe, *L'Homère de Platon* (Liège 1949).

whether or not a particular interpretation of the text is correct. You cannot prove this philosophically, and even if you could ask the poet, he could not tell you. Poets are mouthpieces of divine inspiration, hence essentially irrational, unable to give an account (λόγος) of what they mean. Poetry is of no use as a direct source of knowledge.[36]

On the other hand, the emotional power of epic and dramatic poetry is immeasurable. The intense sensations of pity and fear, already noted by Gorgias in his *Defence of Helen* (D–K 82 B 11.9), are experienced by Ion the rhapsode and his audience at the high points of his recitation of Homer (*Ion* 535B–C). In the *Republic* the potentially damaging effect of such emotional scenes in Homer and tragedy on our own characters is one of the main themes in Plato's attack on poetry, combined with the more direct onslaught on the falsehood of poetic portrayals of gods and heroes. The stories, untrue and immoral as they are, influence our own behaviour in turn, and the insidious pleasure which they arouse must be resisted. Finally, in book 10, comes the deeper attack on artistic μίμησις in general, as an illusory portrayal of what is itself only a world of appearances. Here the old idea of narrative or dramatic poetry as a mirror of life, and hence as morally valuable, is explicitly rejected.

Despite the attack on Homer as the 'first of the tragedians' in the *Republic*, Plato clearly has a deeper admiration for him than for the tragedians themselves: in the *Laws*, for example, he dismisses tragedy as suitable for women, teenagers, and the general crowd, whereas epic is for older and wiser men (658D–E). The end of the *Republic* throws down the challenge which will lead to Aristotle's defence of both Homer and tragedy, when Socrates invites poetry to produce a justification of her value, 'as we are conscious of the fascination which she holds for us', especially when she is approached through the medium of Homer (607B–8B).

Plato's philosophical views hardly constitute an interpretation, although he often quotes the poet to illustrate a point, thereby sometimes suggesting a particular interpretation of individual passages. Aristotle, on the other hand, is said to have 'discussed Homer in detail in many dialogues, admiring and praising him' (Dio Chrys. *Or.* 53.1). There was a strong ancient tradition that Aristotle gave his pupil Alexander the Great a special text of the *Iliad*. Alexander's own passion for Homer must derive in part from Aristotle's influence, and the work *On Kingship* which he wrote for Alexander can hardly have failed to make use of Homer for this purpose.[37] In his surviving works Aristotle quotes Homer some 114 times, with a strong

---

[36] For Plato's views on allegory cf. J. Tate, *CQ* 23 (1929) 142–54, 24 (1930) 1–10, S. Weinstock, *Philologus* 82 (1926) 121–53.

[37] Cf. Pfeiffer, *History of Classical Scholarship* 71–2, Aristotle, *Fragments*, ed. Rose, 408–9.

bias towards the *Iliad* (as in the case of Plato), and these quotations show his fondness for the poet, whom like Plato he often uses for illustration.[38] For example in the *Nicomachean Ethics* the observation that people do not like to be reminded of benefits conferred on them is backed up by a reference to the scene of Thetis' supplication of Zeus in *Iliad* 1, where she tactfully omits to mention the service she had done for him in the past in rescuing him from an Olympian conspiracy, although Akhilleus had reminded her of it (*EN* 1124b12–17). This surely shows a close and sensitive psychological reading of the text, whether or not the observation is originally due to Aristotle himself.

The Aristotelian work entitled *Homeric Problems* (frr. 142–79 Rose) must reflect the whole tradition of detailed discussion of the text down to Aristotle's time as well as his own observations, and chapter 25 of the *Poetics* is a summary of the same subject, with an attempt for the first time to systematize the methods which can be used to solve difficulties.[39] Here he states the fundamental principle, so often ignored by both earlier and later critics, that poetry is not subject to the same criteria as other arts and sciences (1460b13–15). If a scene achieves the kind of effects which are described in the *Poetics* as desirable, then minor faults of accuracy, coherence, and so on, are irrelevant. With this simple observation most of the trivial objections of earlier pedants such as Zoilus are swept away. Thus, the pursuit of Hektor by Akhilleus is impossible in practice, but the dramatic effect is overwhelming (1460b23–6). Moral criticisms (such as those raised by Plato and others) can be answered by appealing to historical context or the conventions of the poet's day: for instance in the *Problems* Aristotle compares Akhilleus' brutal treatment of Hektor's body with a later Thessalian practice, to show that it was not unique to this scene in Homer (fr. 166). Religious beliefs may simply reflect those of Greek society at that stage of development, and so it is misguided to attack them from a modern viewpoint. Careful examination of the poetic context is also important in dealing with moral issues. For instance, Agamemnon lets Ekhepolos off military service, on payment of a horse, and this sounds like bribery (*Iliad* 23.295ff.): but he was right, said Aristotle in the *Problems*, to prefer a good horse to a useless man (fr. 165)! Alternatively, if something is untrue or historically impossible, it may be justified as idealization. Finally, many

---

[38] Cf. A. Römer, 'Die Homercitate und die homerische Frage des Aristoteles', *Sitzb. Bayer. Akad.* (1884), 264–314, and G. E. Howes, *HSCP* 6 (1895) 210–37.

[39] Cf. vol. IV, p. 23; Pfeiffer, *History of Classical Scholarship* 69ff., Römer, *op. cit.*, R. Wachsmuth, *De Aristotelis studiis Homericis capita selecta* (Berlin 1863), M. Carroll, 'Aristotle's *Poetics* Ch. XXV in the light of the Homeric Scholia' (diss. Baltimore 1895), A. Gudeman, *RE* XIII 251 1ff., H. Hintenlang, 'Untersuchungen zu den Homer-Aporien des Aristoteles' (diss. Heidelberg 1961), A. R. Sodano, *Rendiconti dell' Accademia di Archeologia, Lettere e Belle Arti di Napoli* 40 (1960) 227–78, G. L. Huxley, *Proceedings of the Royal Irish Academy* C 79 (1979) 73–81.

minor problems of interpretation and consistency can be solved by adopting a more flexible approach to the text and considering alternative ways of taking it, instead of assuming that the first or most obvious interpretation must be correct. To us these principles may seem largely obvious, but it is surprising how easily they can be forgotten by modern as well as ancient critics.[40]

The *Homeric Problems* constituted a preliminary ground-clearing exercise of a practical kind in preparation for the more theoretical approach of the *Poetics* as a whole. In the main body of this work Aristotle is primarily interested in tragedy, and sees Homer very much in dramatic terms. But despite his eventual conclusion in chapter 26 that tragedy is superior to epic because of its greater dramatic immediacy and concentration (reversing Plato's preference for epic), his intense admiration for Homer shines through again and again. Here for the first time the fundamental differences between the *Iliad* and *Odyssey* and other epic poems are clearly stated. Homer is outstanding for his dramatic qualities and his portrayal of character through speeches (1448b34–6, 60a5–11). His plots, even if necessarily less strictly unified than those of tragedy, are far more so than those of other epic poets, whose works are essentially episodic and often centred on a single character or concerned with a sequence of unrelated actions, rather than aiming at unity of action (51a16–30, 59a30–b7, 62b3–11). He was the first to use all the forms and parts of epic (as defined in Aristotle's chapters on tragedy), and to do so successfully, and he surpasses all others in style and thought (59b12–16). Moreover he has taught other poets the art of making fictions plausible (60a18ff.), and in his more marvellous episodes his brilliance conceals the improbability in a way which a lesser poet could not have achieved (60a34–b2). Given Aristotle's generally evolutionary approach it is really very remarkable that he should see the Homeric poems as so highly developed artistically, although they stand relatively early in his conspectus of literary development.

Aristotle provides the answers to Plato's main attacks on epic and tragedy in his discussion of the nature of poetic imitation, and his account of the κάθαρσις achieved by tragedy. The first reinstates poetry in general as a philosophically serious pursuit, and the second gives to tragedy a special value on the emotional plane. Aristotle never *explicitly* ascribes to epic a similar cathartic function, but the close analogies he draws between epic and tragedy do surely imply that epic *can* act in a similar way. More specifically the fact that epic in his view should have reversals, recognitions and sufferings (παθήματα), and should produce similarly powerful effects

---

[40] Cf. W. B. Stanford's lively book *Enemies of Poetry* (London 1980) for a demonstration of this fact.

of ἔκπληξις, must point this way. The implication of Aristotle's final comparison of epic and tragedy is most probably that the kind of pleasure which both should arouse is similar and should be associated with an emotional κάθαρσις, but that tragedy does this more powerfully and effectively than epic. At the same time, the *Iliad* is evidently much closer to tragedy than the *Odyssey*, for it is concerned above all with suffering and emotion (πάθος), whereas the *Odyssey* is primarily concerned with ἦθος (59b14–15), and its happy ending is more like that of a comedy (53a30–9). Where the *Odyssey* seems to come closest to tragedy in Aristotle's view is in its recurrent use of the device of recognition (59b15). This is a theme to which Aristotle devotes considerable attention, and it surely deserves more than it has received in modern criticism both of Homer and the *Poetics*.[41]

Aristotle's admiration for Homer is focused especially on the extraordinary skill with which he creates a single, unified story out of a vast and highly diversified body of material, incorporating many subsidiary episodes without allowing us to lose sight of the main theme. When he comes to discuss the differences between epic and tragedy (in chapter 24), he shows that epic has certain significant advantages because of its much greater scale. This gives it grandeur (and the heroic metre adds to this, by its more stately character), and also allows for more variety, which is linked to its more episodic nature. The chief technique for creating this variety is the description of different sequences of events which are happening at the same time, i.e. the epic poet's ability to freeze one sequence and shift the scene, returning later to the point where he left off. This superiority of epic is connected with its narrative mode, because events do not have to be enacted visually. This also gives it greater scope for 'the marvellous' (τὸ θαυμαστόν), as in the pursuit of Hektor, which would be impossible on the stage. Here Aristotle picks up the criticisms of earlier readers such as Pindar and Thucydides of the tendency of epic poetry to exaggeration, but makes a special poetic virtue out of this, rather than a fault. He goes on to link it with Homer's exceptional skill in creating plausible fictions, which is based on the building-up of enough realistic circumstantial detail to make his fantasies credible. This again is presumably particularly a feature of the more leisurely descriptive and narrative mode of epic as opposed to tragedy, and it leaves us with the paradox that Homer's mastery of fiction is especially to his credit, whereas in the past it was as the master of truth that he was most admired.

Although much of what Aristotle says here apparently applies to epic in

---

[41] Terence Cave's *Recognitions* (Oxford 1988), however, redresses the balance; cf. also Sheila Murnaghan, *Disguise and Recognition in the Odyssey* (Princeton 1987), Richardson, 'Recognition scenes in the Odyssey and ancient literary criticism', *Papers of the Liverpool Latin Seminar* 4 (1983) 219–35, S. Goldhill, *The Poet's Voice* (Cambridge 1991) 1–24.

general, it is clear that it is really Homer whom he has in the forefront of his mind throughout. This does not mean that he would have recommended taking him as the model for a new epic poem, which he explicitly says should be much shorter, in fact as it turns out about the length of Apollonius' *Argonautica* (1459b17–22). There is conflict here between his intense admiration for the Homeric poems, which prevents him from criticizing them as too long and complex or too episodic, and his preference for a more compressed and unified structure. But he did not set out to write a treatise on epic in the *Poetics*, and so we must not press him too hard for consistency on this subject. Doubtless he could have replied that in works on the scale of the Homeric poems one must take a broad view of the overall effect, and not subject them to the kind of detailed scrutiny which might be appropriate to works on a smaller scale.

Aristotle's whole approach to poetry is conditioned by his status as Plato's successor, and this affects his view of Homer too. He shares Plato's intense love and admiration for the poet, and wishes to rescue him from the attacks of Plato and earlier philosophers and critics. To do so, however, he shifts the focus right away from the preoccupation with the gap between Homer's portrayal of divine or heroic ethics and later moral beliefs, and also between the aesthetic criteria suitable for an early epic poem and those governing the literature of the classical period. The essential criterion is no longer that of literal truth but of dramatic effectiveness and credibility, and in aesthetic terms Aristotle's approach, although technical, is extremely flexible. Homer's status as the ancestor of tragedy allows him the credit for having anticipated in so many respects the most powerful form of poetry ever conceived, and at the same time his use of the epic narrative mode gave him a wider scope, which enabled him to become the supreme 'master of fiction' at a remarkably early stage in its development.

(ii) The Hellenistic period

The work of the three major Alexandrian scholars has been discussed by R. Janko in his Introduction to vol. IV.[42] As he says, Zenodotus' criteria for establishing a genuine text seem to show no awareness of Aristotle's work on Homeric problems, and although Aristophanes was more conservative he was also over-inclined to object to passages on grounds of impropriety. Aristarchus, however, set out to distinguish what was truly Homeric in this tradition from what he regarded as 'Cyclic' interpolations, in a way which could be considered as following broadly in Aristotle's footsteps, and his

---

[42] See also J. Porter, 'Hermeneutic lines and circles: Aristarchus and Crates on Homeric exegesis', in Lamberton and Keaney, *Homer's Ancient Readers*.

approach is a good deal more enlightened than that of his predecessors.[43] Many of his critical observations remain immensely valuable today. Nevertheless, he can still employ the same kind of ethical and aesthetic criteria as earlier scholars in a way which Aristotle would have considered narrowminded. Whether he actually knew the *Poetics* itself directly is doubtful, since an ancient tradition held that the esoteric works of Aristotle disappeared from circulation for a century or so, in the early second century B.C.[44] The *Homeric Questions*, however, and *On Poets* of Aristotle will have been available to him, and would have given a reasonable idea of his views.

The early Stoic philosophers took a lively interest in the interpretation of poetry, for which they favoured a broadly allegorical approach. It remains, however, very questionable whether any of them actually went in for extensive allegorical readings of the Homeric poems, as opposed to selecting particular passages or myths in order to support their own philosophical theories.[45] Their chief purpose seems to have been to identify the gods of Homer and Hesiod with cosmic elements and forces, using etymology to support these identifications, an approach which is recognizably similar to the allegorical methods of earlier philosophers. It is true that according to Dio Chrysostom (*Or.* 53.4) Zeno followed the lead of Antisthenes in arguing that 'the poet has written some things according to opinion and others according to truth, in order to save Homer from apparent self-contradiction where inconsistencies are supposed to exist in his narrative'. Dio adds that whereas Antisthenes stated the principle without elaboration Zeno demonstrated it in detail (ὁ δὲ καθ' ἕκαστον τῶν ἐπὶ μέρους ἐδήλωσεν). If, however, he had wanted to allegorize the poems in a thorough-going way, he would presumably have tried to show that even the most objectionable passages were true if correctly understood, as the later allegorist Heraclitus did.[46] There is no trace of allegorical interpretation of specific Homeric episodes in what little we know of Zeno's *Homeric Problems*, and in his essay *On How to Listen to Poetry* he may have suggested ways of reconciling mythology with modern religion and ethics, as Plutarch does in his work with this title, but without necessarily using physical allegory.[47]

---

[43] For some specific parallels between Aristarchus and Aristotle see Porter, 'Hermeneutic lines and circles', section I, H. Erbse, *Beiträge zum Verständnis der Odyssee* (Berlin 1972) 166–77; cf. also R. Meijering, *Literary and Rhetorical Theories in Greek Scholia* (Groningen 1987).

[44] Strabo 608–9, Plut. *Sulla* 26.

[45] Cf. Wehrli, *Allegorischen Deutung*, Ph. de Lacy, 'Stoic views on poetry', *AJP* 69 (1948) 241ff., Buffière, *Mythes d'Homère*, and A. A. Long, 'The Stoics as readers of Homer', in Lamberton and Keaney, *Homer's Ancient Readers*.

[46] Cf. Wehrli, *Allegorischen Deutung* 65.

[47] For specific interpretations by Zeno cf. *SVF* I frr. 100, 103, 153–70. Plutarch's essay (*Mor.* 14E–37B) gives an excellent survey of traditional moralizing approaches to Homer, and of how the poet's educational value could be preserved against criticism. Cf. D. Babut, *Plutarque et le Stoicisme* (Paris 1969) 87ff., L. J. R. Heirman, 'Plutarch *de audiendis poetis*' (diss. Leiden 1972), and the commentary on this essay by E. Valgiglio (Turin 1973).

Cleanthes' interests seem also to have been mainly etymological (*SVF* I 535, 539–42, 546–7) and this is even more the case with Chrysippus (*SVF* II 1021, 1061-1100). The *Concise Hellenic Theology* of Cornutus in the first century A.D. is a dry handbook which shows the heaviest debt to these early Stoic methods, and it is significant that it betrays no real interest in poetry for its own sake. We perhaps come a little closer to such an interest in the work of Zeno's pupil Ariston of Chios, if it is the case that he attached importance to euphony, and held that the trained ear, rather than reason, should be the judge of this.[48]

The two main surviving works of Homeric allegory are the *Homeric Problems* of Heraclitus (usually thought to be *c.* first century A.D.) and the essay *On the Life and Poetry of Homer* attributed to Plutarch. Heraclitus' book belongs to the general class of works which set out to defend Homer against the attacks of Plato – works which proliferated in the first and second centuries A.D.[49] He owes a certain amount to the early Stoics, but much also to other earlier and later allegorists, although the question of his sources is still a matter of debate.[50] The other work (which seems to be later than Heraclitus) is a diverse compilation which aims to show Homer as master of all arts, including (besides poetry and rhetoric) physics, ethics and theology.[51] It uses allegory as one of its techniques of interpretation, drawing on the Stoics but also showing a marked Neopythagorean tendency. It sets out to make Homer the ancestor of *all* philosophical schools, an idea satirized by Seneca (*Ep.* 88.5): as he says, if Homer is master of many conflicting doctrines then he must be really master of none.[52] Stoic allegories also find a place from time to time in the Homeric Scholia and Eustathius, but again mediated by and combined with later sources.[53]

Apart from the Alexandrian scholars the most important and original figure in Homeric scholarship of the Hellenistic period is Crates of Mallos, a contemporary of Aristarchus, who criticized many of his theories.[54] Crates in turn expressed his own estimate of his superiority over Alexandrian

---

[48] Ariston's views have to be reconstructed from the criticisms of Philodemus, and so remain rather uncertain: cf. C. Jensen, *Philodemus über die Gedichte* (Berlin 1923) 128ff.

[49] Cf. S. Weinstock, *Philologus* 82 (1926) 145ff.

[50] Cf. Buffière's introduction to the Budé edition of Heraclitus (Paris 1962).

[51] On its character, date, and relationship to Plutarch's works cf. Wehrli, *Allegorischen Deutung* 3ff., Bernadakis, *Plutarch* VII (Leipzig 1896) ixff., Buffière, *Mythes d'Homère* 72ff., Babut, *Plutarque et le Stoicisme* 161ff.

[52] Cf. also Philodemus' criticism (*Rh.* II 111 Sudhaus).

[53] Cf. K. Reinhardt, *De Graecorum theologia capita duo* (Berlin 1910) 77ff., van der Valk, *Researches* I 479ff.

[54] Cf. J. Helck, 'De Cratetis Mallotae studiis criticis quae ad Iliadem spectant' (diss. Leipzig 1905) and *De Cratetis studiis ... quae ad Odysseam spectant* (Progr. Dresden 1914), Wehrli, *Allegorischen Deutung* 40ff., H. J. Mette, *Sphairopoiia* (Munich 1936) and *Parateresis* (Halle 1952), Pfeiffer, *History of Classical Scholarship* 238–45, Porter in Lamberton and Keaney, *Homer's Ancient Readers.*

scholarship by his proud claim to be a κριτικός, rather than a mere γραμματικός, and he defined the critic's task as πάσης λογικῆς ἐπιστήμης ἔμπειρον εἶναι, in contrast to the narrow philological interest of the γραμματικός (fr. 17 ed. Mette, *Sphairopoiia*). As with the earlier Stoics, by whom he was influenced, it is doubtful whether Crates went in for extensive and detailed allegory of the poems as a whole. A reasonable interpretation of a reference to him by Philodemus is that he was much less extreme in his approach than Metrodorus (see p. 29 above). His allegorical views were also combined with a good deal of more routine philological work on the text. Moreover where he does allegorize this is in connexion with his specific interest in Homer as a potential source of cosmology and scientific knowledge.

An example of this is his interpretation of Agamemnon's shield (*Il.* 11.32–40) as a 'representation of the *cosmos*' (Mette, *Sphairopoiia* fr. 23a–c), which seems to have been worked out in considerable detail, if we can judge from Eustathius (828.39ff.).[55] The shield's complex workmanship (it is called πολυδαίδαλον) mirrors that of the *cosmos*, and it is 'man-encircling' because the human race forms part of this. Its ten concentric bronze circles represent the 'brazen heaven' (*Il.* 17.425), corresponding to the five parallel circles, i.e. the two 'colures' which link the solstitial and equinoctial points, the galaxy, zodiac and horizon. The stars are represented by its twenty bosses of white tin (and so the central boss of black κύανος is presumably the earth). It resembles the *aegis* of Athene (*Il.* 5.738ff.), Zeus's daughter, and Agamemnon himself is compared to Zeus (2.478, 10.5ff.), again suggesting the shield's significance.

The Shield of Akhilleus is the subject of even more extensive allegories of a similar kind, in both Heraclitus' *Homeric Problems* (43–51) and Eustathius (1154.42ff.). These differ from each other, and that of Heraclitus looks as if it might well derive ultimately from Crates, as he takes great trouble to establish Homer's knowledge of a spherical earth (44–7; cf. *On the Life and Poetry of Homer* 104–6, 109–10). This in turn was one of the main aims of Crates.[56] By contrast, Eustathius names his source as Demo, a learned lady mentioned as an allegorist by him and the Scholia elsewhere.[57]

Crates' scientific interest led him to discuss details of Homeric astronomy and geography both in the Shield of Akhilleus and elsewhere. Thus he

[55] For details of this, the various ancient allegories of the Shield of Akhilleus, and their possible relevance to Virgil's Shield of Aeneas see also Hardie, *Cosmos and Imperium* 340–6, and '*Imago mundi*: cosmological and ideological aspects of the Shield of Achilles', *JHS* 105 (1985) 11–31.

[56] Cf. Mette, *Sphairopoiia* 43ff., Wehrli, *Allegorischen Deutung* 28ff. Heraclitus differs from Crates, however, in his explanation of the Homeric phrase θοὴ νύξ (Heracl. 45, Crates fr. 28a Mette), and his direct source may be Posidonius (cf. D.L. 7.144).

[57] On Demo see Reinhardt, *De Graecorum theologia* 48ff., Kroll, *RE* Suppl. III 331ff.

interpreted the doves (πέλειαι) which bring ambrosia to Zeus in *Od.* 12.62ff. as the Pleiades (frr. 26a and 27) and he may well be the source of an allegory of Nestor's cup (*Il.* 11.632–5) given by Asclepiades of Myrlea, in which the doves on the cup are the Pleiades, its golden studs are stars, and the cup itself is again a 'representation of the *cosmos*' (Ath. 489Dff.).

It had been traditional to locate the voyages of Odysseus in the western Mediterranean, although such speculation was dismissed by Eratosthenes with the famous remark that 'you will find the places visited by Odysseus when you have discovered the name of the cobbler who sewed up the bag of the winds' (Strabo 1.2.15)! Aristarchus also believed that such speculation was misplaced, and he disagreed with Crates, who wished to locate the wanderings in the Atlantic or 'Outer Sea'.[58] Crates ingeniously suggested that the Laestrygonians lived in the distant north, because Homer says that a herdsman there can earn a double wage, and that 'the paths of day and night are close together' (*Od.* 10.81ff.), which he took to imply the short summer nights of the far north. Likewise the Cimmerians, living at the edge of Ocean, under perpetual cloud and darkness (*Od.* 11.13ff.), must be near one of the Poles, and he preferred to read 'Cerberians' here (frr. 37–8). In his spherical earth Hades was at the Antipodes, and Ocean ran both along the equator and from north to south, dividing the earth into four equal sections (frr. 34–5). His cosmology was equally symmetrical, and even the allegorist Heraclitus finds somewhat far-fetched Crates' interpretation of Hephaistos' fall to earth (*Il.* 1.590–4), where his arrival on Lemnos at sunset is explained as meaning that Zeus wished to measure the universe, and so threw two firebrands at equal speed, from heaven to earth and from east to west, one being Hephaistos, the other the Sun (Heraclitus 27).

This concentration on the harmony and balance of the *cosmos* is surely echoed by Crates' view of the aesthetic aspect of Homer's poetry. Like Ariston he seems to have emphasized the importance of euphony and good composition as the sources of the pleasure of poetry. Behind this there must lie the atomist tradition (cf. Democritus, D–K 68 B 21?) which saw close analogies between στοιχεῖα as elements of the *cosmos* and as the letters from which words and so discourse in general are composed, a tradition taken seriously also by Lucretius (1.196–8, 2.686–94).[59]

Suetonius (*De grammaticis et rhetoribus* 2) treats as a landmark in the development of scholarship at Rome the visit of Crates in 168 B.C. He came

---

[58] Cf. Lehrs, *De Aristarchi studiis* 241ff., Mette, *Sphairopoiia* fr. 31. An echo of the controversy appears in P. Oxy. 2888 col. iii.1ff.

[59] Cf. Jensen, *Philodemus über die Gedichte* 146ff., Wehrli, *Allegorischen Deutung* 49ff., Mette, *Parateresis* 59ff., J. Porter, *Cronache Ercolanesi* 19 (1989) 149–78 (especially 171–4); also P. Friedländer, 'Patterns of sound and atomistic theory in Lucretius', in *Probleme der Lukrezforschung* ed. C. J. Classen (Hildesheim 1986) 291–307.

on a mission from the King of Pergamon, broke his leg in a drain, and spent his convalescence giving lectures there. It was these lectures which first stimulated the Romans to pursue the more detailed study of poetry. But it was not only Roman scholarship which benefited, for it seems highly likely that Crates was one of the influences which led later Roman poets to take both cosmology and allegory in general so seriously.[60]

(iii) Rome (to the Augustan period)[61]

Study of Homer at Rome must really date at least from the time of Livius Andronicus' translation of the *Odyssey* into Saturnian verse in the late third century B.C. Livius seems to have used some form of Homeric glossary for this, if not a more detailed commentary.[62] The choice of the *Odyssey* rather than the *Iliad* is interesting, as the Romans, like the Greeks, quoted the *Iliad* far more, although both were used as school texts. The legends linking Odysseus with southern Italy and Sicily must have made him popular, and Livius himself probably came from Tarentum.[63]

But it was Ennius who claimed to have inherited the soul of Homer, in a vision in which Homer is clearly portrayed as a source of philosophical knowledge of the *cosmos*.[64] Ennius' introduction of hexameter verse also marks the beginning of a more truly Hellenized literature at Rome. This is the time when we begin to hear of quotations of Homer by leading Romans such as Cato the Elder, Aemilius Paullus, and his son, the younger Scipio. Lucilius, Scipio's friend, reflects Hellenistic literary theory when he says that Homer's critics do not find fault with his work as a whole but only with individual parts of it (401–10 Warmington).[65] Among such common subjects of criticism he mentions Homer's marvels, his *ficta monstra* such as Polyphemus and his giant walking-stick (520–3).[66] About this time or soon afterwards the *Iliad* was also translated into Latin hexameters by both Cn. Matius and Ninnius Crassus (*Fragmenta Poetarum Latinorum*, ed. Morel, pp. 48–9, 51). Later, Cicero's versions of passages from Homer are more interesting, and his frequent quotations in letters are a good index of the semi-proverbial character of much of Homer for the cultured Romans of the

---

[60] Cf. Hardie, *Cosmos and Imperium* 27–9 (etc.).
[61] See especially J. Tolkiehn, 'De Homeri auctoritate in cotidiana Romanorum vita', *Jahrb. für class. Phil.* Suppl. 23 (1896–7) 221–89, and *Homer und die römische Poesie* (Leipzig 1900), A. Ronconi, *Interpreti Latini di Omero* (Turin 1973).
[62] Cf. Ronconi, *op. cit.* 13ff., H. Fränkel, 'Griechische Bildung in altrömischen Epen', *Hermes* 67 (1932) 306ff.
[63] On Odysseus in Italy cf. E. D. Phillips, *JHS* 73 (1953) 53ff.
[64] On Ennius' vision cf. Hardie, *Cosmos and Imperium* 76–83.
[65] Cf. C. O. Brink, *Horace on Poetry* I (Cambridge 1963) 6off., and II (Cambridge 1971) 359ff.
[66] Cf. Quint. 8.3.34, 4.24, [Longinus] 9.14.

late Republic.[67] Most curious of all is the *Ilias Latina*, an epitome of the *Iliad* in 1,070 verses which is influenced by Virgil and Ovid, and which devotes over half its lines to the first five books.[68] Together with the later prose accounts of the Trojan War attributed to 'Dictys' and 'Dares' this poem became an important source for the western Middle Ages, when knowledge of Greek was lost.

The admiration of Lucretius for Homer is clear (cf. especially Lucr. 1.124–6, 3.1037–8), but for both explicit criticism and implicit interpretation we must turn rather to Horace and Virgil. The first part of Horace's second epistle (*Ep.* 1.2.1–31) reads almost like a summary of the whole earlier tradition of moralizing interpretation of Homer, especially of the *Odyssey*.[69] Horace declares Homer to be a better guide to ethics than the philosophers Chrysippus and Crantor. The *Iliad* shows clearly the effects of passion as a disruptive force in human society; the *Odyssey* by contrast gives us in Ulysses a valuable model of virtue and wisdom, portraying his broad experience of the world, his endurance, resilience, and resistance to temptations, which preserved him from the fate of his companions. They in their turn, like the worthless suitors of Penelope or the idle youth of Alkinoos' court, may be regarded as models of ourselves: unless, that is, we can rouse ourselves from our lethargy and get down to some useful work! Otherwise we too shall suffer the evil effects of our passions.

In his *Ars poetica* Horace's concern is as much aesthetic as moral, and in his approach to Homer he treads closely in the footsteps of Aristotle. Thus the brief, allusive proem to the *Odyssey* is contrasted with the typically inflated 'cyclic' prelude, and he praises Homer's rapidity in moving directly *in medias res*, his avoidance of a tediously chronological structure, his unity of plot, and the credibility of his fictions (136–52). But, as Lucilius had observed, in works on such a scale some faults are inevitable, and yet they do not spoil the effect of the whole (347–60).

Like Horace, Virgil shows in his *Aeneid* that he has learnt from Aristotle and later Hellenistic critics how to follow in Homer's track, to imitate his virtues and also as far as possible to avoid his faults.[70] Like Horace too, he clearly views Homer through the moral and cosmological spectacles of earlier Greek critics and philosophers.[71] Aeneas' adventures represent his

[67] Cf. *Fragmenta Poetarum Latinorum*, ed. Morel, pp. 73–7, Tolkiehn, *De Hom. auctoritate* 259ff., Ronconi, *op. cit.* 41ff., V. Clavel, *De M. T. Cicerone Graecorum interprete* (Paris 1968).

[68] Cf. *Poetae Latini minores* III 3, ed. Vollmer, and Tolkiehn, *op. cit.* 96ff.

[69] Cf. E. Kaiser, *MH* 21 (1964) 109ff., 197ff., J. Moles, *Papers of the Liverpool Latin Seminar* 5 (1985) 34–9, together with S. Eidinow, *CQ* 40 (1990) 566–8.

[70] Cf. especially R. Heinze, *Virgils epische Technik* (3rd edn, Leipzig and Berlin 1915), G. Knauer, *Die Aeneis und Homer* (Göttingen 1964), R. R. Schlunk, *The Homeric Scholia and the Aeneid* (Ann Arbor 1974).

[71] For Homeric allegory and the Aeneid see especially Hardie, *Cosmos and Imperium*.

progress towards the divinely ordained goal of Rome's foundation, taking us a stage further along the road towards the spiritual epics of Dante or Milton, but this notion of a moral or spiritual *Odyssey* is already present in ancient readings of the *Odyssey* itself. Aeneas is to a certain extent a hero with Stoic characteristics, in his submission to fate, his control of his emotions, and his triumph over fortune through endurance, although Virgil wisely never allows this aspect to obliterate his human fallibility.

Virgil's gods too are on the whole more remote and august than those of Homer, above all in the *Iliad*. Direct intervention in human affairs, especially to do harm, is usually through intermediary figures (Aeolus, Somnus, Allecto, etc.), avoiding some of the problems which Homer had posed for Plato, and there are clear signs of physical or cosmological allegory here: Jupiter's will is identical to Fate, Juno represents the elemental forces of disorder, Venus those of harmony; and just as Here was equated with air, so Juno is mistress of the powers of the air or winds (1.78ff., etc.), Diana is the moon (9.403ff.), Apollo the sun (11.912ff.), and Iris the rainbow (4.700ff., etc.).[72] Virgil seems to allude to earlier interpretations of divine epithets, such as those which linked Pallas with πάλλειν or Tritonia with τρεῖν (1.39ff., 2.169ff., 2.226ff.).[73] Moreover, where Homer has divine comedy, such as the scandalous tale of Ares and Aphrodite (*Od.* 8.266–366), in his parallel scene Virgil substitutes a cosmology sung by Atlas' pupil Iopas (*Aen* 1.740ff.). The song of Demodokos had already been interpreted as a cosmic allegory (cf. Heraclitus, *Homeric Problems* 69, Ps.-Plut. *On the Life and Poetry of Homer* 99–101), and Cleanthes had made Atlas a representation of Stoic Providence.[74]

One of the most acute problems of Homeric criticism was the credibility of Homer's *speciosa miracula*, as Horace called them. Virgil on the whole avoids the more fantastic aspects of the scenes he imitates, and where he does introduce the bizarre or supernatural it is usually for a specific purpose linked to his main narrative aims, as for example in his omens, visions and prophecies. And as Odysseus' travels were described in the words of the hero himself, a device by which the poet could distance himself from his fictions, so too Virgil's account of the visit to the Underworld ends with Aeneas and the Sibyl leaving by the gate of false dreams (16.893–9). This episode resembles the myths of Plato, designed as fictional images of philosophical truth, and the Neoplatonist character of the vision of Rome's future and the doctrine of reincarnation supports this form of interpretation.[75]

[72] Cf. Heinze, *op. cit.* 293ff., Knauer, *op. cit.* 289–90.
[73] Schlunk, *op. cit.* 17ff. In general cf. G. J. M. Bartelink, *Etymologiserung bij Vergilius* (Amsterdam 1965).
[74] Knauer, *op. cit.* 168 n. 2, Buffière, *Mythes d'Homère* 150, 168ff., Hardie, *Cosmos and Imperium* 52–60.
[75] Cf. also Hardie, *Cosmos and Imperium* 66–83, D. A. West, 'The bough and the gate', in *Oxford Readings in Vergil's Aeneid*, ed. S. J. Harrison (Oxford 1990) 224–38.

These are just a few of the ways in which Virgil shows himself sensitive to the earlier history of Homeric interpretation and criticism, so that the *Aeneid* in turn becomes a 'reading' of the Homeric poems, just as the *Odyssey* could be viewed as a commentary on the *Iliad*.

(iv) Later Greek criticism

Much of the significant literary criticism of later antiquity bears a heavy debt to Aristotle's pioneering work, and this is especially true of the treatise *On Style* attributed to Demetrius, whose date is uncertain, but must be somewhere between the third and first century B.C.[76] In his discussion of what he defines as the four main styles, plain, grand, elegant and forceful, Demetrius quotes many examples from Homer, especially to illustrate the grand style. It is clear that many of his quotations are standard, as they occur either in Aristotle himself, or in later sources such as Quintilian, Dionysius of Halicarnassus and Ps.-Plutarch's *Life and Poetry of Homer*, or else are singled out for praise by the Homeric Scholia.

Demetrius shows a special interest in euphony, sound effects and rhythm, an interest which he shares with Dionysius and the exegetical Scholia.[77] In his discussion of language and figures of speech he builds on Aristotelian foundations, and many of his detailed observations are interesting and memorable. For example, he preserves for us the dictum of Theophrastus, that

not everything should be given lengthy treatment with full details, but some things should be left for the hearer to grasp and work out for himself: for if he infers what is omitted by you he becomes no longer just your hearer but your witness, and one who is also more favourable, since he thinks himself intelligent, and that you have given him the opportunity to exercise his mind. To tell your hearer everything as if he were a fool suggests that you are underrating him (222).

This is related to the Homeric narrative principle formulated by Aristarchus of τὸ σιωπώμενον, whereby the poet takes many things for granted, or alludes to them in passing.[78]

Dionysius' treatise *On the Arrangement of Words* (composed in the Augustan period) is the work of a versatile essayist and historian.[79] His originality for us lies primarily in the fact that he is the first surviving critic who attempts a close critical analysis of extended passages of literature. Dionysius himself claims to be breaking new ground here (4), and it is clear that he finds his task a difficult one. He is concerned above all with the effects of word-order,

---

[76] Cf. Grube, *Greek and Roman Critics* 110–21, D. C. Innes in D. A. Russell and M. Winterbottom, *Ancient Literary Criticism: the Principal Texts in New Translations* (Oxford 1972) 171–215.

[77] Cf. Richardson, *CQ* 30 (1980) 283–7.   [78] Cf. Richardson, *CQ* 30 (1980) 271.

[79] Cf. the Loeb edition of Dionysius by S. Usher, vol. II (1985) 3–243.

sound and rhythm, and he sees Homer as a master-craftsman in all these respects (cf. 16 ὁ δὴ πολυφωνότατος ἁπάντων ποιητῶν Ὅμηρος, etc.). A good instance of Dionysius' technique at work is his elaborate analysis of *Od.* 11.593–8, the famous description of Sisuphos in Hades (20).[80] Dionysius' account of how the words and rhythms mirror the sense is obscure in some details, but he is undoubtedly right to draw attention to these aspects of the poet's technique. As Pope put it:

> See Dionysius Homer's thoughts refine,
> And call new beauties forth from ev'ry line!

(*Essay on Criticism* 665–6)

It is probably to the late Hellenistic and early Roman periods that much of the critical and interpretative material preserved in the bT Scholia belongs, and they are an invaluable source for us, filling out the more sketchy and theoretical picture given by the critics. A detailed discussion of what they have to offer is given in *CQ* 30 (1980) 265–87.[81] Likewise, we can gauge the extent of ancient discussion of Homeric speeches from the many works of rhetorical theory which quote and analyse them.[82] Perhaps the best summary, however, of the value of the Homeric poems as a whole for the ancient orator is given by Quintilian (10.1.46–51). As Okeanos is the origin of all waters, so Homer *omnibus eloquentiae partibus exemplum et ortum dedit*, a claim which Quintilian goes on to illustrate with admirable concision.

The most unexpected and original work of ancient literary criticism is the treatise *On the Sublime* attributed to Longinus, which must belong to the first century A.D. or later.[83] More than any other ancient writer, the author of this work succeeds in expressing for us his sense of Homer's genius and superiority to all man-made rules of art, although at the same time he believes that natural genius does need to be controlled and guided by certain methods and precepts (2.1–2).

The origins of his enthusiasm for Homer must lie in the earlier admiration (reflected as we have seen in Plato and Aristotle) for his more dramatic and emotionally charged episodes and for his ability to evoke wonder and surprise (τὸ θαυμαστόν, ἔκπληξις: cf. [Longinus] 1.4). It is in the famous ninth chapter, one of the finest passages of ancient criticism, that he has most to say about the poet as a model of greatness of thought (the first of Longinus'

[80] Cf. Demetrius 72 for a briefer allusion.
[81] See also R. Meijering, *Literary and Rhetorical Theories in the Greek Scholia* (Groningen 1987), and K. Snipes, 'Literary interpretation in the Homeric Scholia: the similes of the *Iliad*', *AJP* 109 (1988) 196–222.
[82] Cf. the Index to Spengel, *Rhet. gr.* III 518–22, Ps.-Plut. *On the Life and Poetry of Homer* 15–90, 161–74, Dionysius of Halicarnassus, *Opuscula* (ed. Usener and Radermacher) II 310ff., etc.
[83] Cf. D. A. Russell's edition (Oxford 1964), Grube, *Greek and Roman Critics* 340–53.

five sources of sublimity).[84] Here it is especially his descriptions of the supernatural that are singled out for praise, such as the cosmic leap of Here's horses (*Il.* 5.770–2), the introduction to the Theomachy (*Il.* 21.388 + 20.61–5), and Poseidon's journey across the sea (*Il.* 13.18ff. + 20.60). To these are added two heroic examples, the awful silence of Telamonian Aias in the Underworld (*Od.* 11.563) and Aias' prayer to Zeus for light (*Il.* 17.645–7). It is during this discussion that he makes the celebrated remark that 'Homer has done his best to make the men of the Trojan War gods and the gods men',[85] commenting that such episodes as the Theomachy are 'blasphemous and improper unless interpreted allegorically' (9.7).

These examples (combined most remarkably with quotation from the account of Creation in Genesis 1) lead on to the memorable passage contrasting the *Iliad* with the *Odyssey* as works of πάθος and ἦθος respectively.[86] The *Odyssey* is a work of old age, essentially an epilogue to the *Iliad*. It is all story-telling, in which the fabulous and incredible have replaced the dramatic intensity of the earlier poem. Odysseus' wanderings are like the 'dreams of Zeus',[87] although they are still the work of genius, and in the descriptions of Odysseus' household realism has replaced emotional power, making them a kind of 'moral comedy'. In this comparison there are many points which recall earlier criticism, but nowhere else are the differences between the two poems so well expressed.

Another celebrated passage is the discussion of literary imitation (13.2–14), where a list of those authors traditionally seen as most inspired by Homer is given – Herodotus, Stesichorus, Archilochus, and above all Plato – and the nature of this form of inspiration is discussed. Here Plato's greatness of style is seen as the direct result of his aspiration to reach Homer's height. This paradoxical view of Plato as the inheritor of Homer's genius rather than his enemy is common among the Neoplatonists, one of whose aims was to put an end to the ancient quarrel between poetry and philosophy.[88]

Finally this work gives us the classic statement of the superiority of fallible greatness over mediocre perfection (32.8–36.4): it is better to be

[84] Cf. Gibbon's comment (quoted by Russell in his edition of Longinus, 89): 'The ninth chapter is one of the finest monuments of antiquity ... I almost doubt which is most sublime, Homer's Battle of the Gods or Longinus' apostrophe to Terentianus upon it.'

[85] Cf. Cic. *Tusc.* 1.65 *fingebat haec Homerus et humana ad deos transferebat; divina mallem ad nos*; Philostr. *Her.* 2.19.

[86] Cf. C. Gill, '*The ethos/pathos* distinction in rhetorical and literary criticism', *CQ* 34 (1984) 149–66.

[87] Cf. Hor. *AP* 359, Quint. 6.2.29, 10.1.46, Plut. *Mor.* 709B, Dio Chrys. *Or.* 11.129.

[88] Cf. S. Weinstock, *Philologus* 82 (1926) 121–53, Buffière, *Mythes d'Homère* 19ff., Russell on [Longinus] 13.3 (pp. 116ff.).

like Homer or Plato, who aim high and sometimes fail, than to play safe and never leave the ground. Sublimity raises man to the divine level and it is this which guarantees immortality to literature. And yet, he adds, ideally nature's greatness should be aided by art, if *true* perfection is to be achieved (36.4).

After the technicalities of Hellenistic scholarship, the elaborate systems of rhetoric and the complex ingenuities of the allegorists, to read 'Longinus' on Homer is like emerging from the cloud enveloping a great mountain's lower slopes, and suddenly seeing around one the towering Alpine peaks. These peaks were there, but as we struggled painfully upwards through the mists of learning and speculation we could not see them clearly. The view may be selective, neglecting the quieter beauties of the valleys, but no other ancient work did so much in the immediately pre-Romantic period in Europe to encourage admiration for the genius of Homer, who was in so many ways far removed from the politer standards of that age.

(v) Neoplatonists and Christians

Glimpses of a Neoplatonic or Neopythagorean view of Homer have already been detected in Ennius' vision of the poet and in Aeneas' visit to the Underworld. But explicit Neoplatonist allegorization of Homer begins to appear in the first centuries A.D., from Plutarch onwards, and continues down to its final flowering in the work of Proclus, in the fifth century.[89] The first figures of real significance are Numenius and Cronius, in the later second century A.D., but their ideas are preserved only by later authors, especially the third-century author Porphyry in his essay on the Cave of the Nymphs in the *Odyssey* (13.102–12).[90]

Porphyry himself also wrote a *Homeric Questions*, some of which survives intact, and parts of which are quoted in the Homeric Scholia.[91] This marks the culmination in antiquity of scholarly work on Homeric problems, drawing on Aristotle and his predecessors and on later scholarship. To this work we owe the famous principle that Homer is his own best interpreter:

---

[89] Cf. especially Buffière, *Mythes d'Homère* 393–582, A. D. R. Sheppard, *Studies on the 5th and 6th Essays of Proclus' Commentary on the Republic* (Hypomnemata 61, Göttingen 1980), Lamberton, *Homer the Theologian*, and his 'The Neoplatonists and the spiritualization of Homer', in Lamberton and Keaney, *Homer's Ancient Readers*.

[90] For Porphyry's *De Antro Nympharum* cf. his *Opuscula Selecta*, ed. A. Nauck (Teubner 1886), and the translations by Buffière, *Mythes d'Homère* 595–616, and R. Lamberton (Barrytown, N.Y.: Station Hill 1983).

[91] *Quaestionum Homericarum ad Iliadem/Odysseam Reliquiae*, ed. H. Schrader (2 vols., Teubner 1880–90), and *Quaestionum Homericarum liber I*, ed. A. R. Sodano (Naples 1970). Schrader's reconstruction of the lost work is, however, very speculative: cf. H. Erbse, *Beiträge zur Überlieferung der Iliasscholien* (Zetemata 24, Munich 1960) 17–77.

ὡς αὐτὸς μὲν ἑαυτὸν τὰ πολλὰ "Ομηρος ἐξηγεῖται (*Quaest. hom.*, ed. Sodano, p. 1.12–14), a principle which corresponds with the actual practice of Aristarchus, whether or not he actually stated it in these terms.[92]

Porphyry's combination of this traditional type of exegesis (which itself sometimes uses allegory as *one* of its techniques) with the systematic allegory of his *Cave of the Nymphs* is not really so unusual as has been thought, for the evidence suggests that earlier allegorists from Theagenes onwards, and especially Crates, could go in for a similar combination of interests, and allegory itself developed from a close study of the language of texts.[93] His *De antro* itself, however, has been described as 'the earliest surviving interpretive critical essay in the European tradition'.[94] It is certainly the most remarkable and imaginative reading of Homer which survives from antiquity.

The passage in *Odyssey* 13 describes a cave in the bay of Phorkus, the old man of the sea, in Ithaca, where Odysseus is landed on his return home. At the bay's head is an olive tree, and nearby is the lovely, shadowy cave, which is sacred to the Naiads. In it there are bowls and amphorae of stone, where bees make their honey, and great stone looms, where the nymphs weave robes of sea-purple. It has two springs of ever-flowing water, and two entrances to north and south, the first for mortals, the second for gods. Later, Athene and Odysseus store his treasures in the cave and sit beneath the sacred olive tree to plan the suitors' destruction (366ff.).

Porphyry dismisses the suggestion that this is simply a real cave and nothing more, and equally that it is just poetic fantasy. The poet wishes us to ask what he really means by this detailed and mysterious description. The answer is that the cave is the material world, as in Plato's *Republic*, and the Naiads are souls, whose sea-purple robes on stone looms represent flesh and blood covering the bones of material bodies, by which the souls become incarnate. The honey bees are the souls of the just, bees being holy and honey symbolic of purity and freedom from corruption. The souls enter and leave the cave by the two doorways, entering as mortals and leaving as divine (and the symbolism of north and south is elaborately explained). The olive tree is sacred to Athene, goddess of wisdom, and it is at the head of the harbour because wisdom governs the world, Athene herself being born from Zeus's head. The olive's leaves are dark and light, symbolizing the hope of suppliants, who hold an olive branch, of passing from darkness to light, and the evergreen olive's fruit is a reward for labour as in the prizes of olive oil at the Panathenaia, just as the eternal Wisdom gives us prizes for running life's race.

[92] Cf. Pfeiffer, *History of Classical Scholarship* 226–7.
[93] Cf. Richardson, *PCPS* 201 (1975) 67ff., Lamberton, *Homer the Theologian* 109–10.
[94] Lamberton, *Homer the Theologian* 120.

Odysseus lays aside his material possessions and sits down beneath the olive tree with Athene, who transforms him into a beggar. So we must humble ourselves, give up our material concerns, and deliberate with Athene how to overcome the treacherous passions which are our enemies. Odysseus himself is the man who endures all the stages of reincarnation, until he is finally freed from the world of matter, when he 'arrives at a place where men do not know the sea', according to Teiresias' prophecy (*Od.* 11.121ff.).

This extraordinary allegory could hardly be further removed from the limpid simplicity of Homeric narrative style, but it is a remarkable testimony to the regenerative power of Homeric poetry, which could still evoke such interpretations after nearly a thousand years of tradition. Porphyry's allegory (based on the works of Numenius and Cronius) fits into the wider context of Neoplatonist views on the poems in general, for which one needs to look especially to Proclus.[95] In these the Trojan War itself becomes an image of life on earth, Helen being the beauty of the world of the senses over which souls struggle. The Trojan Helen herself is only an εἴδωλον, as in Stesichorus and Euripides, this world being only an image of reality. Troy or Ilion represents matter (ὕλη, ἰλύς), and the Greeks are souls which eventually escape and return to their true, spiritual home. The ten-year War symbolizes the ten periods of 1,000 years of successive reincarnations. As we have seen, Odysseus' wanderings again represent the soul's exile, the sea is the material world, and his trials are the soul's conflict with passions and temptations, leading to her final victory.

These wider allegories are explicitly prompted by the aim of defending Homer against the criticisms of Plato, and of reconciling poet and philosopher, and this aim is linked to an elaborate theory of poetry which restores the status it had originally enjoyed, as capable of expressing the highest forms of truth about the world[96]. From the work of Porphyry or Proclus it is a very easy step to that of the early Christian apologists (especially Justin, Clement and Origen), who set out to defend Christianity against the pagan tradition, using allegory either to reinterpret Biblical myths or else to show how Greek myths really foreshadowed the truths of Christianity.[97] In this complex process Homer played an important rôle, and on the whole he continued to enjoy a relatively privileged status as the conveyor of divinely

---

[95] Cf. Sheppard, *op. cit.*, Lamberton, *Homer the Theologian* 197–232.

[96] Cf. Lamberton, *Homer the Theologian* 162–97.

[97] Cf. especially H. Rahner, *Griechische Mythen in christliche Deutung* (Zurich 1957), G. Glockmann, *Homer in der frühchristlichen Literatur bis Justinus* (Berlin 1968), N. Zeegers-Van der Vorst, *Les Citations des poètes grecs chez les apologistes chrétiens du IIe siècle* (Louvain 1972), J. Daniélou, *A History of Christian Doctrine* II. *Gospel Message and Hellenistic Culture* (London 1973), J. Pépin, *Mythe et allégorie* (2nd edn, Paris 1976), Lamberton, *Homer the Theologian*, especially 78–82, 233ff.

inspired truth, despite the general hostility of the apologists towards pagan religion and myths. Through this channel the allegorical tradition passed to Byzantium, to the Latin Middle Ages, and ultimately into the Renaissance.[98]

Viewed from a modern perspective, ancient criticism and interpretation of Homer may well seem curiously unbalanced, especially because of its emphasis on morality and its allegorical tendencies. But we should bear in mind first of all the unique status of the Homeric poems in antiquity, and secondly the fact that all forms of literary interpretation are in a certain sense a form of allegory, since they seek to draw out of a text more than is directly expressed by the words themselves. This applies as much to modern criticism of Homer as to ancient, and from this viewpoint it is not unreasonable to see this present series of commentaries on the *Iliad* as the continuation of a tradition which stretches back through Byzantium to Alexandria, and beyond this to the first tentative efforts to expound the poem of which we are aware, in the fifth and sixth centuries B.C.

[98] This is not the place to pursue the story further. For Byzantium and the Renaissance cf. R. Browning and A. Grafton in Lamberton and Keaney, *Homer's Ancient Readers*, P. Cesaretti, *Allegoristi di Omero a Bisanzio* (Milan 1991). For general surveys of later interpretation of Homer cf. G. Finsler, *Homer in der Neuzeit* (Leipzig 1912), J. L. Myres and D. Gray, *Homer and his Critics* (London 1958), H. Clarke, *Homer's Readers* (Newark 1981). Stanford, *Ulysses Theme*, follows the fortunes of Odysseus through the centuries, as do B. Rubens and O. Taplin in *An Odyssey round Odysseus* (London 1989), and K. C. King does the same for the hero of the *Iliad* in *Achilles: Paradigms of the War Hero from Homer to the Middle Ages* (Berkeley 1987). For Homer in English, French and German literature and criticism see also G. de F. Lord, *Homeric Renaissance: the Odyssey of George Chapman* (London 1956), D. Knight, *Pope and the Heroic Tradition* (Yale 1951), D. M. Foerster, *Homer in English Criticism* (Yale 1969), H. A. Mason, *To Homer through Pope* (London 1972), K. Simonsuuri, *Homer's Original Genius* (Cambridge 1979), N. Hepp, 'Homère en France au xviᵉ siècle', *Atti della Accademia delle Scienze di Torino. Classe di scienze morali, storiche et filologiche* 96 (1962) 383–508, and *Homère en France au xviiᵉ siècle* (Paris 1968), T. Bleicher, *Homer in der deutschen Literatur 1450–1740* (Stuttgart 1972).

COMMENTARY

BOOK TWENTY-ONE

This Book cannot be considered separately from book 20. The framework of both consists in the scenes describing the Battle of the Gods. At the opening of book 20 Zeus urged the gods to intervene directly in the conflict (a reversal of the situation at the beginning of book 8), on the grounds that otherwise Akhilleus might sack Troy before the due time; and a grandiose passage described the cosmic effects of their entry into battle (47–66). After this prelude to the Theomachy the theme of direct conflict between the gods was left suspended, while Akhilleus clashed with Aineias, skirmished with Hektor, and killed other Trojans. It is resumed at 21.328–514, where a series of actions between opposing deities takes place (cf. 14.402–522n., for a similarly suspended sequence).

The earlier part of book 21 leads up to this through a succession of climactic scenes, centred on the theme of the battle in and with the river Skamandros. The Book opens with a brief but vivid description of half of the Trojans trapped and slaughtered in the river (1–33), followed by two major scenes in which Lukaon (34–138) and Asteropaios (139–201) are killed and their bodies disposed of in the stream. These actions arouse Skamandros' anger. He appeals to Akhilleus to desist, and then begins to attack him directly and protect the Trojans. In danger of being overwhelmed Akhilleus prays to Zeus, and is encouraged by Poseidon and Athene. Skamandros in turn calls to Simoeis for support, and begins to overpower his opponent (205–327).

This conflict between Akhilleus and the river-god, itself an intensely dramatic episode, leads into what is really the first major scene of the Theomachy, the clash of Skamandros and Hephaistos, water and fire (328–82), already foreshadowed in the list of divine combatants at 20.33–40 (and 67–74). Once again the tone of this scene is intense and powerful.

By contrast, the battles or squabbles of the major Olympian deities, Athene and Here against Ares, Aphrodite and Artemis, together with Hermes' light-hearted avoidance of conflict with Leto, may at first seem trivial, although Apollo's refusal to fight his uncle Poseidon strikes a deeper note (383–513). The tone is similar to that of the scenes in book 5, where

51

Athene helps Diomedes to defeat Aphrodite and Ares, and there are echoes of these scenes which should probably be seen as part of a larger pattern of correspondences between the 'Diomedeia' and books 20–1 (see Introduction, 'Structure and themes'). But the divine battles in book 21 do have their functions within the poet's design. Not only do they give a cosmic dimension to Akhilleus' own *aristeia*, forming a series of stages leading up to the final confrontation between him and Hektor (cf. the interesting early comment on this technique by the sophist Protagoras, cited on 205–327), but throughout the Books in which Akhilleus is in action there also run the themes of the imminent threat of Troy's destruction and of its constant postponement. Skamandros' defeat by Hephaistos eliminates one divine protector, the city's chief river-god (cf. 21.372–6, where he swears not to defend Troy on the day of its sack); and the rout of three other pro-Trojan deities symbolizes their powerlessness against the forces of Here and Athene (cf. especially Athene's vaunt at 428–33). The lack of dignity with which this is accomplished has moral implications, suggesting the false position of the gods who are supporting a city doomed for Paris' treachery: his actions were instigated by Aphrodite, leading to the hateful war of which Ares is the embodiment (compare 5.832–4 and 21.412–14, where Athene accuses Ares himself of treachery in deserting the Greeks for the Trojans). On the Theomachy see also 383–513n.

The one god who preserves an awe-inspiring dignity on the Trojan side is Apollo, and it is appropriate that after the other deities have withdrawn he should enter Troy, in order to protect it from destruction. The Book closes with a rapid sequence of scenes which form a prelude to book 22 and anticipate some of its themes (see on 514–611).

The analysis by Scheibner (*Aufbau*) makes many excellent points on this part of the poem. See also Whitman, *HHT* 272–3 on the structure of books 20–1, and Bremer's discussion of the rôle of the gods in terms of narrative technique in *HBOP* 31–46.

1–33 Prelude: many of the Trojans take refuge in the river Skamandros, and are slaughtered by Akhilleus

In this opening scene the similes of slaughter and panic (13–16, 22–6 and 29) are a continuation of those (of forest fire and threshing) at the end of book 20 (490–9). For other sequences of similes running over book-divisions, see on 9.4–8, 16.823–6.

1–16 The sound-patterns of this passage are analysed by A. B. Lord in Wace and Stubbings, *Companion* 200–1, and cf. Elliger, *Darstellung der Landschaft* 72–3. The references to the river in 1–2 and 15–16 frame the description, and it is mentioned in the centre of the passage (8). Descriptions of river-battles of this kind seem to be rare in earlier Near Eastern literature, but cf. the Egyptian accounts of the battle of Kadesh (A. Gardiner, *The Kadesh Inscriptions of Ramesses II*, Oxford 1960, 10, 30, 39–41), where the Hittites are said to be driven into the Orontes and massacred, and a Hittite story of someone (Tudhalijas?) being driven into and pursued across a river, published by K. K. Riemschneider, *Journal of Cuneiform Studies* 16 (1962) 110–21.

1–11 This long periodic sentence, with quite heavy enjambment, acts as an excellent introduction to the scene of carnage.

1–2 = 14.433–4, 24.692–3. The ford is mentioned as a landmark in all these passages, rather than as a crossing-place. The scholia are in doubt whether πόρος means 'ford' or 'stream', but it is usually taken as the former. It has not featured as part of an actual battle scene until now, since at 14.433–9 it is a resting-place for Hektor on the way back to the city.

The phrases which the poet uses to refer to the river Skamandros in this Book and elsewhere form an extensive formular system.

Nominative

143, 212, 228 ποταμὸς βαθυδίνης |
329, 20.73 μέγας ποταμὸς βαθυδίνης |
130 ποταμός περ ἐΰρροος ἀργυροδίνης |
304 | εὐρὺ ῥέων ποταμός
16 | πλῆτο ῥόος κελάδων

Cf. 12.21 δῖός τε Σκάμανδρος |

Accusative

8 ἐς ποταμὸν εἰλεῦντο βαθύρροον ἀργυροδίνην
206 πὰρ ποταμὸν πεφοβῆατο διήεντα |
603 πὰρ ποταμὸν βαθυδινήεντα Σκάμανδρον |
25 ποταμοῖο κατὰ δεινοῖο ῥέεθρα |
332 | Ξάνθον διήεντα
352 τὰ περὶ καλὰ ῥέεθρα ἅλις ποταμοῖο πεφύκει

Cf. 7.329 ἐΰρροον ἀμφὶ Σκάμανδρον |

Genitive

1–2 = 14.433–4, 24.692–3:
ἀλλ' ὅτε δὴ πόρον ἷξον ἐϋρρεῖος ποταμοῖο
Ξάνθου διήεντος ὃν ἀθάνατος τέκετο Ζεύς

15 Ξάνθου βαθυδινήεντος |
148 Σκαμάνδρου διήεντος |
268 μέγα κῦμα διιπετέος ποταμοῖο |
326 πορφύρεον δ' ἄρα κῦμα διιπετέος ποταμοῖο
(διιπετέος ποταμοῖο 16.174, 17.263, 3× *Od.*)

Cf. also (*above*) 21.25 ποταμοῖο κατὰ δεινοῖο ῥέεθρα |
11.499 | ὄχθας πὰρ ποταμοῖο Σκαμάνδρου

Dative
Cf. 5.36 ἐπ' ἠϊόεντι Σκαμάνδρῳ |

Note also the use of:
21.9 αἰπὰ ῥέεθρα | ~ 8.369 Στυγὸς ὕδατος αἰπὰ ῥέεθρα |
238, 244, 361, 382 καλὰ ῥέεθρα | (*see on 238*)
352 (above) τὰ περὶ καλὰ ῥέεθρα ἅλις ποταμοῖο πεφύκει
354 | οἳ κατὰ καλὰ ῥέεθρα
365 | ὣς τοῦ καλὰ ῥέεθρα
218 ἐρατεινὰ ῥέεθρα | (*see comment*)

See also Elliger, *Darstellung der Landschaft* 54.

3–11 bT comment on Akhilleus' feat of dividing the enemy into two groups, and pursuing some towards the city and others into the river. Cf. 16.394–8, where Patroklos drives the Trojans towards the ships and cuts off their retreat, and 10.363–4.

4–5 There may be a hint of retribution in this reference to the previous day's troubles for the Greeks. For 4 cf. 6.41 πρὸς πόλιν, ᾗ περ οἱ ἄλλοι ἀτυζόμενοι φοβέοντο, and 21.554 φεύγω, τῇ περ οἱ ἄλλοι ἀτυζόμενοι κλονέονται.

6 πεφυζότες: only here, 528, 532, and 22.1, always of the Trojans, whereas we have πεφεύγοι at 609, πεφευγότες *Od.* 1.12. The original formation was probably *πεφυγϝότες, which became πεφυζότες on the analogy of φύζα, after the loss of the digamma (Chantraine, *Dict.* s.v. φεύγω 1). The poet may use it in preference to πεφευγότες because he wants to suggest the noun φύζα ('rout'), a stronger expression than φυγή.

ἠέρα δ' Ἥρη: this was later used to support the allegorical identification of Here with air (cf. Buffière, *Mythes d'Homère* 106ff.). Herē's intervention seems perfunctory, but such brief interventions are a feature of this Book. The mist stops the Trojans from escaping to the city, but the poet says no more about the fate of this group.

8 βαθύρροον: elsewhere of Okeanos (2× *Il.*, 2× *Od.*). Cf. 130 ποταμός περ ἐΰρροος ἀργυροδίνης. ἀργυροδίνης is used likewise of Peneios at 2.753.

9–10 The noise and confusion are emphasized by the onomatopoeic words πατάγῳ, βράχε, ἴαχον, ἀλαλητῷ (so T). βραχεῖν is most often used of the clash of armour, but it occurs again at 387 in a similar verse, σὺν δ' ἔπεσον μεγάλῳ πατάγῳ, βράχε δ' εὐρεῖα χθών. For αἰπὰ ῥέεθρα see on 8.369.

12–16 This vivid simile catches in only three verses the effect of the Trojan panic. ἀκρίς (only here in Homer) can mean 'locust', 'grasshopper' or 'cricket', but as it is presumably destructive here, 'locust' seems the best equivalent; cf. M. Davies and J. Kathirithamby, *Greek Insects* (London 1986) 135–44, and Gow on Theocr. *Id.* 5.108 and *CR* 6 (1956) 92. The scholia say that this method of driving locusts out of the crops was practised in Cyprus, but it would presumably have been familiar to the poet's audience also. There is a parallel to this simile in the Flood story as told in the Mesopotamian epic *Atraḥasis*. Cf. S. Dalley, *Myths from Mesopotamia* (Oxford 1989) 32–3: 'Nintu was wailing . . . | Would a true father (?) have given birth to the [rolling?] sea | (so that) they could clog the river like dragonflies?'

The contrast of fire and water foreshadows the conflict of Hephaistos and Skamandros, as does the association of Akhilleus with fire, which is frequent in books 18–22: see on 22.317–21.

12 The scholia note how the tone of the simile is raised by the language, especially ῥιπῆς and ἠερέθονται ('take wing').

16 κελάδων: 'sounding'; cf. 18.576 πὰρ ποταμὸν κελάδοντα. ἐπιμὶξ ἵππων τε καὶ ἀνδρῶν resembles 11.525 ἐπιμὶξ ἵπποι τε καὶ αὐτοί and 23.242 καίοντ' ἐπιμὶξ ἵπποι τε καὶ ἄνδρες.

17 ὁ διογενής: διογενής is used of various heroes, 7× *Il.*, but only here with a definite article. Cf. ὁ γέρων 1.33 with comment.

Akhilleus leaves his spear on the bank, but at 67–70 he is using it again. As Aristarchus observed (Arn/A), this is a typical example of the poet's economy in taking unimportant details for granted (κατὰ τὸ σιωπώμενον). Cf. bT 1.449 etc., and *CQ* 30 (1980) 271.

18 κεκλιμένον μυρίκῃσιν is a suitable topographical detail. See on 350–1, and cf. 6.39, 10.466–7. δαίμονι ἶσος (9× *Il.*) is usually applied to a sudden destructive attack.

19 Cf. 23.176 χαλκῷ δηϊόων· κακὰ δὲ φρεσὶ μήδετο ἔργα.

20–1 Cf. 10.483–4 (with κτεῖνε . . . γαῖα instead of τύπτε . . . ὕδωρ). The substitution of αἵματι ὕδωρ for the more usual αἵματι γαῖα (3× *Il.*) creates a rare type of hiatus.

22–6 This simile makes a good companion to the previous one. There the movement was from land to water: here pursuer and pursued are both in the water (cf. bT).

22 μεγακήτης is used elsewhere of a ship (3× *Il.*) or the sea (*Od.* 3.158). It is usually translated 'with mighty hollow', 'capacious' (cf. Leaf, LSJ). But the influence of κῆτος is surely felt, and the poet perhaps intended 'monstrous'. Cf. *Od.* 12.96–7 δελφῖνάς τε . . . καὶ εἴ ποθι μεῖζον ἕλῃσι | κῆτος . . . , the only other instance of dolphins in Homer.

23 λιμένος εὐόρμου: the epithet occurs only here in *Il.*; cf. *Od.* 4.358, 9.136 λιμὴν εὔορμος.

24 Cf. 3.25 μάλα γάρ τε κατεσθίει, in the same position in the verse, in a simile about a lion.

26 πτῶσσον ὑπὸ κρημνούς: the river has steep banks (cf. 171–5, etc.). πτῶσσον ('cowered') is effective, as at 14.

26–32 Akhilleus takes twelve prisoners, to be offered as a blood-price for the killing of Patroklos. He had vowed to do this when Patroklos' body was first brought back to him (18.336–7), and he fulfils his promise at 23.175–6. Within the action of the *Iliad* itself prisoners are not taken elsewhere: see on 11.111, 130ff.

28 This is suitably solemn: a four-word verse with heavy spondaic rhythm at the beginning.

29 τεθηπότας ἠΰτε νεβρούς: cf. 4.243 with comment. τεθηπώς recurs at 64 of Lukaon. This is the third simile from the animal world in this section, each one belonging to a different element (air, water, land).

30–1 There is pathos, emphasized by αὐτοί, in the use of the captives' own clothing to tie them up: so bT. The thongs are usually taken as belts. For ἐϋτμήτοισιν ἱμᾶσιν | cf. 10.567(n.), and for ἐπὶ στρεπτοῖσι χιτῶσι cf. 5.113 διὰ στρεπτοῖο χιτῶνος with comment. The best sense for στρεπτός is probably 'strongly-woven'.

34–138 Akhilleus meets Priam's son Lukaon, whom he had previously captured and sold. Ransomed by Eetion of Imbros, Lukaon had eventually returned to Troy. He supplicates Akhilleus, who kills him, throws him into the river, and makes a contemptuous speech over him which angers the river-god

This famous scene has been described as 'the climax of the set of supplications in battle' (Griffin, *HLD* 56 n. 12), although one should really reserve this description for Hektor's plea at 22.337–60. It is also the climax of all the contests involving lesser warriors (Strasburger, *Kleinen Kämpfer* 85). Akhilleus has already refused to spare Tros, a significant anticipation of this scene (20.463–72). At 11.101–12 Agamemnon killed Priam's sons Isos and Antiphos, whom Akhilleus had previously captured and ransomed. A similar motif occurs in the combat between Aineias and Akhilleus in book 20, where we hear of how Aineias had been attacked and pursued by Akhilleus on a previous occasion, but escaped (89–96, 187–94). This was when Akhilleus sacked Lurnessos and Pedasos, and Pedasos was the home of Lukaon's mother (21.84–7). There is another thematic link in that on this occasion Apollo is disguised as Lukaon when he urges Aineias to fight Akhilleus (20.81). We had already heard of Lukaon at 3.333, where Paris put on his breastplate before his duel with Menelaos (cf. Schadewaldt, *Iliasstudien* 49, Fenik, *TBS* 82–3). Cf. also Akhilleus' killing of Poludoros (20.407–18): both are sons of Priam and Laothoe, and are linked at 21.84–91, 22.46–53.

bT (34) comment on this scene as an example of περιπέτεια, and add that the details make the story vividly realistic. The basic structure is typical, consisting of (*a*) the meeting of the two warriors, (*b*) speeches, and (*c*) conflict, but in other respects it is highly individual.

34–48 These verses form one long periodic structure, explaining Lukaon's situation.

36–7 This is similar to the surprise attack on Aineias when he was cattle-herding, and on Isos and Antiphos when tending sheep, although here Akhilleus comes at night. Akhilleus refers to his many sleepless nights of campaigning at 9.325–7. ἀλωή here means 'orchard'.

37–8 ἐρινεὸν ... ὄρπηκας: a 'whole and part' construction. Cf. 24.58, *Od.* 18.396. ὄρπηξ occurs only here in Homer; cf. Hes. *Erga* 468, etc.

The verses are reminiscent of 4.485–6 (simile), where a chariot-maker cuts down a poplar to make a felloe for a chariot: τὴν μέν θ' ἁρματοπηγὸς ἀνὴρ αἴθωνι σιδήρῳ | ἐξέταμ', ὄφρα ἴτυν κάμψη περικαλλέϊ δίφρῳ. On the ἄντυγες ('chariot-rails') see Lorimer, *HM* 326; J. Wiesner, *Arch. Hom.* F 15–16. The scholia and Eustathius object to the use of wild fig branches for a rail, as being easily broken, but according to Theophrastus (*HP* 5.6.2) wild fig being tough is easily bent, and so was used to make hoops for garlands and other things. In Theocr. *Id.* 25.247ff. it is heated in order to be bent into a chariot-felloe.

39 ἀνώϊστον: 'unforeseen' (cf. οἴομαι); only here in Homer (ἀνωϊστί *Od.* 4.92), emphasizing the irony and pathos of Lukaon's fate after he had already escaped death once at Akhilleus' hands. After the enjambment of 34–8 the end-stopped verse is powerful.

40–8 These verses summarize Lukaon's past life and adventures, about which we hear again at 54–9, 74–96.

40–1 Euneos, son of Iason and Hupsipule, supplies wine to the Greek army from Lemnos at 7.467–75. At 23.740–9 we learn what the price of Lukaon was (ὦνον ἔδωκε ...'Ιησονίδης Εὔνηος 746–7): a very valuable silver mixing-bowl of Sidonian workmanship, given by Euneos to Patroklos; from 21.79 it appears that this was worth a hundred oxen! By this precious object the poet links the fates of Lukaon and Patroklos. See 23.740–9n., and cf. Griffin *HLD* 17–19 on other cups with symbolic significance.

ἐπέρασσε: 'exported for sale'; aorist of πέρνημι (related to περάω). This aorist form occurs several times in book 21 (58, 78, 102, 454), and 4 times in *Od.* 14–15.

42–4 Lukaon was ransomed by a family friend, Eetion of Imbros, who has the same name as Andromakhe's father and the father of the Trojan Podes (17.575). He sent him to Arisbe on the Hellespont (cf. 2.836), perhaps for safe-keeping there. ὑπεκπροφυγών (cf. 20.147) implies that Lukaon had to slip away unnoticed in order to get home.

45–8 There is strong pathos in the contrast between Lukaon's brief spell

57

of happiness among his family and friends and his impending death. For the twelfth day as a significant one cf. 1.425, 1.493, 24.31, 24.413 etc. Verses 46–7 are echoed at 80–4, 92–3.

47–8 There is grim irony in the addition of καὶ οὐκ ἐθέλοντα νέεσθαι, especially as νέομαι is normally used of returning home (cf. νόστος). Lukaon's several journeys and homecoming are only the prelude to his final journey to the house of Hades. Cf. 23.51 νεκρὸν ... νέεσθαι ὑπὸ ζόφον ἠερόεντα. For καὶ οὐκ ἐθέλοντα cf. 36.

49–53 Lukaon's helplessness is emphasized by this complex sentence, in anticipation of his desperate plea for salvation. His lack of armour enables Akhilleus to recognize him at once (cf. bT). γυμνόν is emphatic at the beginning of the verse: cf. e.g. 17.122, 17.693, 18.21, 22.510. For οὐδ' ἔχεν ἔγχος cf. 22.293 οὐδ' ἄλλ' ἔχε μείλινον ἔγχος (Hektor).

53–63 Akhilleus' speech of amazement is full of mocking irony. He speaks of Lukaon almost as if he had already been killed at their previous encounter, and there is word-play in 56–7, which would normally refer to death, but can be taken also of Lukaon's westward voyage into slavery.

53–4 = 20.343–4 (54 = 13.99, 15.286 followed by οἶον δή ...).

57 οἶον δή often occurs after an exclamation or similar sentence, e.g. 13.633, 15.287, 17.587, *Od.* 1.32, 5.183, 11.429.

57–63 Akhilleus contrasts Lukaon's escape from the sea with his coming journey under the earth (59 ~ 63).

58 Λῆμνον ἐς ἠγαθέην: cf. 2.722 (dative). The island was sacred to Hephaistos. The perfect form πεπερημένος occurs only here. The later perfect passive of πέρνημι is πέπρημαι, πέπραμαι.

59 There is striking alliteration, assonance and echo here: πόντος ἁλὸς πολιῆς, ὁ πολέας ἀέκοντας ἐρύκει. πόντος ἁλὸς πολιῆς occurs only here. D. H. F. Gray ('Homeric epithets for things', *CQ* 41 (1947) 112) observes that πόντος is most often used of the deep sea, ἅλς of the sea round the coast, and this expression 'is unique in implying that the difference has been wholly forgotten'. πόντος is related to Latin *pons*, Eng. 'path', etc.: cf. Chantraine *Dict.* s.v.

60–1 Cf. 20.257–8 ἀλλ' ἄγε θᾶσσον | γευσόμεθ' ἀλλήλων χαλκήρεσιν ἐγχείῃσιν (cf. *Od.* 20.181, 21.98).

61 ὄφρα ἴδωμαι ἐνὶ φρεσὶν ἠδὲ δαείω is a unique expression. Cf. ὄφρα ἴδωμαι -μεν (3× *Il.*, 1× *Od.*), ὄφρα δαείω (2× *Il.*, 1× *Od.*). The expanded expression is presumably designed to increase the irony.

62 κεῖθεν is euphemistic for Hades.

63 γῆ φυσίζοος is an adaptation of φυσίζοος αἶα (3.243, *Od.* 11.301, in both cases of the Dioskouroi: see on 3.243–4). There is a variant reading φυσίζωος here, which occurs in late Greek (and cf. schol. pap. xii (Erbse) col. ii 2, 4). Leaf would like to read γαῖα φῦσίζωος, ἥτε κρατερόν περ ἐρύκει, for no good reason. As at 3.243, *Od.* 11.301, there is surely an effect of contrast in the idea of the life-giving, or grain-bearing, earth keeping a dead hero. Actually it will be the sea which finally receives him: 125–7! The repetition of the verb at the end of 62 and 63 (cf. 59) is emphatic.

64–72 Akhilleus' attack coincides dramatically with Lukaon's assumption of a suppliant position, as he slips in under the thrust of the spear and seizes his opponent's knees with one hand, and the spear with the other to prevent another throw. bT observe that the scene is described in a very graphic way. The significance of gestures is maintained later in this episode, when Lukaon lets go of the spear and sits down with hands outspread in despair (Reinhardt, *IuD* 436–9). For scenes of supplication in Homer and later literature cf. J. Gould, 'Hiketeia', *JHS* 93 (1973) 74–103 (esp. 80–1 on Lukaon and other rejected suppliants in Homer). See also 1.512–13n., 20.463–72n., and Thornton, *Supplication* 111–42.

64 For τεθηπώς see on 29.

65–6 Schol. pap. XII (Erbse) col. II 5–11 refer to Stesichorus (*PMG* 273) in a discussion of these verses, possibly in order to give a parallel for a long speech by someone about to die, who wishes to gain time.

67–70 T assumes that Akhilleus does not throw his spear, but thrusts with it, following Aristarchus' rule that οὐτάζω is only used of thrusting (cf. Lehrs, *De Aristarchi studiis* 51ff.). Verses 67–9 resemble in construction 20.468–9, where Tros seizes Akhilleus' knees as Akhilleus strikes him.

69–70 ἐγχείη … ἱεμένη = 20.279–80 (without χροὸς … ἀνδρομέοιο). In 70 ἔστη is effective. For the rest of the verse cf. 15.317, 21.168, again of spears sticking in the ground (λιλαιόμενα -ομένη χροὸς ἆσαι). Aristotle commented on these personifications of inanimate objects in epic as examples of vivid metaphorical expression (*Rhet.* 1411b31–12a10). See also 4.126n. ἄμεναι is from ἄω ('take one's fill'). ἀνδρομέοιο ('human') is usually an epithet of skin, flesh or blood (cf. 17.571, 20.100, 4× *Od.*).

72 This additional gesture of supplication shows Lukaon's terror.

73 Aristarchus (Did/A) did not read this verse in his text. The majority of MSS read λισσόμενος instead of φωνήσας, and Didymus reports a variant καί ῥ' ὀλοφυρόμενος. A speech of supplication is introduced simply by ἐλίσσετο γούνων at 6.45, by γουναζέσθην at 11.130 and by λίσσετο … γουνούμενος at 15.660. Cf. also *Od.* 10.264–6, where most MSS and two papyri omit 265. The verse occurs after λίσσετο at *Od.* 8.344–6, and after γούνων ἐλλιτάνευσα at *Od.* 10.481–2 (although here too some MSS omit it). Van der Valk defends it, reading λισσόμενος (*Researches* II 490ff.), but it could well be an addition, as Apthorp argues (*MS Evidence* 147–52, 195–7).

74–96 Lukaon's speech is both a plea for mercy and a lament for his death, which he foresees as virtually inescapable. He begins by appealing to his claim on Akhilleus as one who has received hospitality from him as a captive, a fact which creates a religious bond between them (cf. Gould, *op. cit.* 79). The rest of the speech emphasizes his misfortune in meeting Akhilleus again after his escape, the pathos of his mother's loss of both her sons, and finally the fact that, although he is Priam's son, he does not have the same mother as Hektor, the chief target of Akhilleus' hatred.

74 *Cf. Od.* 22.312 = 344 (Leodes and Phemios), γουνοῦμαί σ', 'Οδυσσεῦ· σὺ δέ μ' αἴδεο καί μ' ἐλέησον. Akhilleus has, however, lost his sense of αἰδώς and ἔλεος: cf. especially 24.44–5, and see on 22.82. The relationship of this scene to those in *Od.* 22 (where Leodes is killed but Phemios spared) is discussed by Usener, *Verhältnis der Odyssee zur Ilias* 131–40.

75–6 These verses mean that Lukaon already has a suppliant claim on Akhilleus (cf. bT): he is 'as good as a suppliant'. For ἀντί here cf. 8.163, *Od.* 8.546. Verse 76 puzzled the early critics of Homer, and Stesimbrotus of Thasos explained it on the grounds that non-Greeks such as Lukaon only ate bread made of barley (cf. *PCPS* 201 (1975) 73–4)! Presumably it means that when captured Akhilleus was the first Greek with whom Lukaon shared bread (cf. *Od.* 6.175, 7.301, 8.462, schol. A and Porphyry). 'It would be incongruous to offer food, the source of life, to someone, and then take away his life. And he mentions Demeter to evoke religious scruples ... One should admire the poet's inventiveness: in putting a speech in an enemy's mouth he still finds a plausible argument for his salvation' (bT).

79 Lukaon implies that Akhilleus has profited greatly by his earlier capture. ἀλφάνω occurs only here in *Il.*; cf. *Od.* 15.452, 17.250, 20.383, always of profits from the sale of people.

80–5 Lukaon's agitation produces a run of enjambed verses with sentence-breaks in mid-verse, or 'skewed' sentences as defined by Higbie, *Measure and Music* 77, 112–20; cf. 24.469–76 with comment.

80 It looks as if Lukaon had to pay back to Eetion the price of his freedom. We also learn that Euneos made a profit of two hundred per cent on his buying and selling of this slave. The scholia oddly took λύμην as an optative referring to Lukaon's hope of being rescued again (cf. 99), which is impossible. It must be aorist passive indicative.

80–4 These verses recall 46–7 (θεός ~ μοῖρα), and 80–1 are echoed by 155–6.

83 For this kind of assumption of divine hostility cf. 2.116 etc. and Parker, *Miasma* 201.

84–5 μινυνθάδιον δέ με μήτηρ γείνατο ...: cf. 1.352 μῆτερ, ἐπεί μ' ἔτεκές γε μινυνθάδιόν περ ἐόντα (Akhilleus); 15.612 (Hektor). All three are doomed: cf. 106ff. Lukaon's use of this phrase suggests a bond with Akhilleus. The emphasis on Laothoe leads up to his final plea (95–6).

85–7 Laothoe and her father Altes, ruler of Pedasos, are mentioned again by Priam at 22.48–51 in connexion with Lukaon and Poludoros. The

Leleges (cf. 10.429, 20.96) were one of the peoples of the Troad, and Pedasos and the river Satnioeis must lie in the southern Troad (see on 6.21–2).

85-6 Ἄλταο ... Ἄλτεω: for the epanalepsis cf. 157–8, 2.671–3, etc. The variant Ἄλτα(ο) could be the original reading in 86 (cf. Leaf). Akhilleus has sacked Pedasos (20.92), and this may have given rise to the variant reading ἄνασσε in 86 (some city texts, one papyrus and several MSS). Aristarchus read the present, probably rightly: the city seems to be still inhabited at 6.34–5: ναῖε δὲ Σατνιόεντος ἐϋρρείταο παρ' ὄχθας | Πήδασον αἰπεινήν.

87 αἰπήεις occurs only here as an alternative for αἰπεινός, and then in Hellenistic poetry. Our MSS read ὑπό instead of ἐπί, but Strabo (605) argues for ἐπί, since Satnioeis is a river, not a mountain (cf. T).

88 On Priam's polygamy see 24.495–7n.

89-91 Cf. 20.407–18 for Poludoros' death. For δειροτομήσεις cf. 555, 23.174, and ἀποδειροτομήσω -ειν 18.336, 23.22 (all of Akhilleus); *Od.* 22.349 (in a suppliant speech again). This shocking word evokes greater pity for Lukaon. For πρυλέεσσι ('armed warriors') see on 5.744. Poludoros' rash courage was emphasized at 20.411–12.

92 ἔσσεται: the variant ἔσσεαι would be more vivid, and is possibly right.

93 ἐπεί ῥ' ἐπέλασσέ γε δαίμων: the formula recurs at 15.418, and for the divine agency cf. 47, 82–4.

94-6 Verse 94 = 1.297 etc. (7× *Il.*, 6× *Od.*); 96 ~ 17.204 (τοῦ δή ...). The repetitions give no grounds for believing the verses to be an addition (as Leaf argues). All that Lukaon has said leads up to this final, desperate plea.

95 ὁμογάστριος: the word recurs at 24.47, and thereafter rarely, in late Greek. Zenodotus read ἰογάστριος, comparing 24.496 ἰῆς ἐκ νηδύος, but no other compounds of ἴα occur in Homer (cf. Arn/A).

96 ἐνηέα: 'with this epithet of Akhilleus' friend he thinks he may soften him, by teaching him to emulate his friend's kindness' (bT). Ironically, the reference to Patroklos' death only sparks off Akhilleus' bitter reply. The verse echoes 17.204, in the speech by Zeus prophesying Hektor's death, when he puts on Akhilleus' armour after killing Patroklos, and the epithet is nearly always applied to Patroklos in the poem (see on 23.252).

97-8 Cf. 11.136–7, where Agamemnon refuses to spare the two sons of Antimakhos, especially 137 μειλιχίοις ἐπέεσσιν, ἀμείλικτον δ' ὄπ' ἄκουσαν (see comment).

99-113 Akhilleus' speech sums up the difference between the 'normal' conditions of war, before Patroklos' death, and the brutality of the present situation. He accepts Lukaon's allusion to their earlier bond of ξενία, calling him φίλος (106), and thereby suggesting a sense of sympathy which is developed in the reference to his own impending death, although at the same time there is a note of bitter irony in his use of the word 'friend'. The contrast with the ferocity of Agamemnon (6.46ff., 11.131ff.) is striking. Cf. Griffin (*HLD* 55): 'Agamemnon is ruthless and unreflective; Achilles kills in a passionate revenge, but not in blind ferocity. He sees his action in the perspective of human life and death as a whole, the perspective which puts slayer and slain on a level, so that it is more than a mere colloquialism that he calls Lycaon "friend" as he kills him.' Cf. also W. Marg, *Die Antike* 18 (1942) 175–6; Schadewaldt, *VHWW* 26off. Nevertheless, we must not exaggerate Akhilleus' sympathy here: the contemptuous tone of 122–35 shows us his other side.

The structure of the speech is effective. It begins with a single-verse sentence, rejecting Lukaon's plea. The main reason is then given in two balanced, contrasting sentences, 100–2 πρὶν μέν ... and 103–5 νῦν δ' ... (note also 102 Τρώων ..., 105 καὶ πάντων Τρώων ...). The 'consolatory' section which follows (106ff.) consists of a series of short, staccato sentences with no enjambment, often with a break at the caesura. The questions (106, 108) add to the tone of familiarity. Finally a solemn three-verse sentence announcing Akhilleus' own death expands the point of 110, leaving behind a strong sense of the inevitability of the whole process of mutual slaughter.

99 νήπιε: the opening word of Akhilleus' speech at once obliterates any hopes of mercy (cf. bT). For νήπιε at the beginning of a verse in a speech cf. 16.833 (Hektor to the dying Patroklos), 18.295 (Hektor to Pouludamas), 22.333 (Akhilleus to the dying Hektor). See also on 2.38, and vol. v, Introduction, p. 43.

100–2 Leaf notes the rarity of πρίν as a conjunction in this position, i.e. preceding the main clause (cf. *Od.* 14.229), and the unique combination of πρίν ... τόφρα ... Thus πρίν carries an unusually heavy emphasis here. ἐπισπεῖν αἴσιμον ἦμαρ is also a unique expression, instead of the normal πότμον ἐπισπεῖν, although αἴσιμον ἦμαρ alone is formular. For τι cf. 9.645.

103–5 Cf. 47–8, 82–4, 92–3. Akhilleus confirms Lukaon's fear and generalizes his experience. Ἰλίου may represent Ἰλίοο (cf. 2.518n.). In 105 καί emphasizes πάντων. περὶ δ' αὖ ... παίδων incidentally answers Lukaon's plea that although Priam's son he is not Hektor's full brother.

106–7 In 106 the juxtaposition of friendship and death makes a bitter contrast, and κάτθανε καὶ Πάτροκλος echoes ἀλλὰ ... θάνε καὶ σύ. For a similar sentiment cf. 15.139–40, where Athene consoles Ares for the loss of his son. Callisthenes, Aristotle's nephew, is said to have quoted 107 to Alexander at the time when Alexander had begun to turn against him (Plutarch, *Alex.* 54). For ὅ περ σέο πολλὸν ἀμείνων cf. 7.114, 16.709.

In later Greek literature the reflection that all men must die is a standard motif in speeches of consolation for the death of a loved one (e.g. Menander Rhetor ed. Russell and Wilson p. 162, with comments), and Akhilleus himself has already referred to the fact that not even Herakles, dearest of men to Zeus, escaped death, in relation to his own impending fate (18.115–21). Here however this theme seems to serve primarily to justify Akhilleus' desire for revenge. See also on 18.117–19.

109 πατρὸς ... ἀγαθοῖο, θεὰ ... μήτηρ: chiastic contrast of noble father and divine mother.

110 ἔπι stands for ἔπεστι (cf. *Od.* 11.367). This was Aristarchus' interpretation, and it seems likely to be correct.

111–13 Cf. the solemn prophecies of Troy's fall at 4.164–8, 6.448–9 ἔσσεται ἦμαρ ὅτ' ἄν ποτ' ὀλώλη Ἴλιος ἱρή ..., and see on 4.163–5. In 111 the careful enumeration of the three parts of the day, unique in Homer, adds to the solemnity of Akhilleus' prediction. δείλη occurs only here in Homer, but is common later. Cf. δείελος at 232, *Od.* 17.606 δείελον ἦμαρ (*Od.* 17.599 δειελιήσας). In 112 Ἄρη probably means 'in battle'.

113 'He is confident that no one will kill him in close combat' (bT and schol. pap. xii (Erbse)). Akhilleus appears uncertain whether he will die from a spear-cast or arrow-shot, although at 277–8 he says that his mother prophesied his death from 'Apollo's swift shafts', which suggests an arrow. More details about his death are given at 18.96, 19.416–17. 22.359–60: all of these together fit the story in the *Aithiopis* and later literature in which Akhilleus was shot by the arrow of Paris, with Apollo's aid (Homer, OCT vol. v, p. 106.7–9 = Davies, *EGF* p. 47.20–3, Apollodorus, *Epit.* 5.3, Virgil, *Aen* 6.56–8, Ov. *Met.* 12.597ff.). For the increasing prominence of the theme of Akhilleus' death in *Iliad* 18–24 see on 18.95–6.

114–19 The strong enjambment in this description of Lukaon's killing binds the whole sequence of actions closely together. Verses 117–18 are particularly vivid, with the monosyllabic δῦ standing at the beginning of the verse. Cf. the analysis by Friedrich, *Verwundung* 100–2.

114 Cf. 425. The other parallels for λῦτο γούνατα καὶ φίλον ἦτορ are all Odyssean (8×). Cf. γούνατ' ἔλυσεν | 8× *Il.*; φίλον ἦτορ | 14× *Il.*

115–17 Cf. 14.495–7, and for χεῖρε πετάσσας also 4.523, 13.549. In these passages, however, the victim spreads out his hands *after* he has been struck or as he is dying. Here Lukaon lets go of Akhilleus' spear and knees *before* he is struck, which Gould suggests may symbolize the fact that he is 'no longer a suppliant in the full ritual sense when he is killed' (*op. cit.* 81). But Lukaon's gesture really indicates his despair. Cf. the paralysis of Deukalion at the prospect of his impending death, at 20.480–2.

117–19 For 117–18 cf. 16.339–40 ὁ δ' ὑπ' οὔατος αὐχένα θεῖνε | Πηνέλεως, πᾶν δ' εἴσω ἔδυ ξίφος, and for ξίφος ἄμφηκες cf. *Od.* 16.80, 21.341, *Il.*

63

10.256 φάσγανον ἄμφηκες. The rare phrase perhaps draws attention to the effectiveness of this prolonged stab wound (Friedrich, *Verwundung* 102). Verse 119 = 13.655.

120–38 Akhilleus' unnecessary and contemptuous action and his insulting speech anger the river-god, who begins to think of direct intervention. For this type of thematic anticipation cf. vol. v, Introduction. p. 21.

122–3 The scholia report a variant ἦσο, which comes from *Od.* 18.105, 20.262, and cannot be right here. σ' ὠτειλὴν | αἷμ' gives us three accusatives together, unless σ' is σ(οι) as in 1.170. Aristarchus firmly supported ὠτειλήν against ὠτειλῆς (the reading of most of our MSS), which looks like an attempt to correct the text. Normally a corpse was washed before burial: here the fish will lick it clean. ἀπολιχμᾶν occurs only here in Homer; cf. λιχμᾶν Hes. *Th.* 826, λιχμάζειν *Aspis* 235, etc. ἀκηδέες means 'uncaring' (cf. 24.526). But the κῆδος which they will not provide is above all that of proper burial and mourning, and the point is stressed by οὐδέ σε μήτηρ ... γοήσεται.

123–5 Akhilleus picks up Lukaon's references to his mother (84ff.). Lukaon's funeral procession and burial will be replaced by his journey down the river to the sea. ἁλὸς εὐρέα κόλπον is a unique variation of the formula θαλάσσης εὐρέα κόλπον (18.140, *Od.* 4.435). As the maternal earth receives the dead normally, so here the sea will do so, in its 'ample bosom'. For οὐδέ σε μήτηρ | ἐνθεμένη λεχέεσσι γοήσεται cf. 22.352–3, 22.86–7 (both to Hektor, the first by Akhilleus). For other references to the grief of parents or family in vaunting speeches cf. 14.501ff., 17.27–8.

126–7 Usually an unburied body suffers mutilation from dogs and birds (1.4–5 etc.). This is a grim variation on the theme, in which the effect is made more eerie by the vivid picture of the fish darting through the dark waves, just under the rippling surface of the sea, as the pallid corpse floats among them. Soon we shall hear how Asteropaios' flesh actually is devoured by eels and fish (203–4). Cf. Segal, *Mutilation of the Corpse* 30–2.

μέλαιναν φρῖχ' ὑπαΐξει means 'will dart up to [*or* under] the dark ripple'. For φρίξ cf. 7.63–4, 23.692, *Od.* 4.402 (always in association with μέλας). ἀΐσσω always has a long α elsewhere in Homer, but usually a short one in later poetry. The variant ὑπαλύξει was actually preferred by Philetas and Callistratus, because they took φρίξ as meaning 'chill' and thought that the fish avoided the cold by diving to the bottom! ὅς κε φάγῃσι ('who shall eat') implies intention. The phrase ἀργέτα δημόν only occurs elsewhere at 11.818, in a similar context: ἄσειν ἐν Τροίῃ ταχέας κύνας ἀργέτι δημῷ. The colour contrast with μέλαιναν φρῖκα is vivid.

128 The opening spondaic word φθείρεσθ' is emphatic and contemptuous.

130–5 These verses were athetized by Aristophanes, who thought that they had been added to give a reason for the river's anger. He also objected to the use of δηθά (131), perhaps because he took it here as meaning 'often' (as Arn/A do). Probably the underlying reason was that Aristophanes found the verses shocking (cf. Pl. *Rep.* 391B). Didymus suggests that as Aristarchus did not defend them he may have agreed with Aristophanes.

130–2 For ποταμός ... ἐΰρροος ἀργυροδίνης cf. 8. δηθά means 'over a long period' ('depuis longtemps'). The verbal echo δὴ δηθά perhaps underlines the ironic tone.

A bull is sacrificed to Alpheios at 11.728, and river-gods could themselves be portrayed as bulls or as bull-headed in later art and literature. At 237 the river will actually be described as bellowing like a bull. Skamandros has a priest (5.77–8), as Sperkheios has a sanctuary and altar at his springs, where sheep are offered (23.147–8). On the cult and iconography of river-gods see Nilsson, *GgrR* 236–40, Burkert, *Religion* 174–5.

Sacrifices to river-gods were commonly lowered into the water itself. Horses were thrown into the sea by the Argives at a place where a freshwater spring rises (Pausanias 8.7.2; cf. Fraser's note), and the Rhodians were said to throw a chariot and four horses into the sea as an offering to the sun each year (Festus p. 190 ed. Lindsay). But the custom of sacrificing horses to rivers is not typically Greek. The Magi in Xerxes' army sacrificed white horses to the river Strymon (Hdt. 7.113), and horse-sacrifices were common among the Scythians (Hdt. 4.61), Massagetai (Hdt. 1.216) and Parthians (Tac. *Ann.* 6.37). It is possible that the custom mentioned by Akhilleus is intended to be specifically Trojan rather than Greek, *pace* Hall (*Barbarian* 43–4).

136–8 For Skamandros' growing anger see on 120–38

137 The variant φόνοιο for πόνοιο recurs at 249 in a similar phrase, and it was the reading of Aristophanes there, whereas Aristarchus (Arn/A) read πόνοιο. But πόνος is used elsewhere in the context of fighting (11.601, 16.568, etc.).

139–204 Akhilleus fights Asteropaios, kills him, and leaves his body in the river

The form of the fight is as follows:

139–47   Akhilleus attacks Asteropaios, whose genealogy is given. Asteropaios stands his ground.

148–60   Akhilleus asks his name and origin and Asteropaios tells him.

161–8   Asteropaios throws both spears at once, hits Akhilleus' shield with one, and grazes his arm with the other.

169–72   Akhilleus throws and misses, and the spear sticks in the riverbank.

173–82 Akhilleus attacks with his sword, as Asteropaios tries unsuccessfully to pull the spear out or break it, and Akhilleus kills him with a blow in the stomach.
182–99 He strips his armour and boasts over the body.
200–4 He then pulls out the spear, and leaves the body to be eaten by the eels and fish.

Although much of the structure is typical (see especially on 16.335–41, and Fenik, *TBS* 145–6), the poet uses the river-setting for significant details and also Asteropaios' own character. He was mentioned at 12.102, 17.217, 17.351–5, but not in the Catalogue at 2.848. He is the son of Pelegon, and grandson of the great river Axios, the modern Vardar, which flows down through Macedonia into the sea near Salonika (see on 2.848–50). Special prominence is given to his parentage here (and apart from Axios his parents and grandparents are only mentioned here in the *Iliad*). Akhilleus explicitly stresses that the river Skamandros has been of no more help to him than his own ancestry (184–99). The poet has chosen this particular victim carefully: there is a cruel irony in the manner of his death (203–4), and his descent from Axios is an added reason for Skamandros' support (145–6), and for his anger at his death (cf. bT 145–6, 192). Is he Homer's own creation?

Asteropaios is a formidable opponent, who does remarkably well. He stands up to Akhilleus and is the only hero who actually succeeds in wounding him slightly. He does not give up after his initial failure, but tries bravely to pull Akhilleus' spear from the bank. His ambidexterity is an added advantage (162–3). All this is in marked contrast with the preceding scene, where Lukaon was utterly helpless from the start.

141 Πηλεγόνος: Pelegon is presumably the eponymous ancestor of the Pelagones, who lived in the region of the Axios (Pelagonia). Cf. Strabo 331 (fr. 38 and 39, Eust. 1228.12). The Pelagones were sometimes identified with the Giants (Call. *Hy.* 1.3; cf. also Philodemus, *De pietate* 248v, p. 25 Gomperz, quoted by Erbse on Schol. 21.141), and the name Periboia appears again as that of the daughter of Eurumedon, king of the Giants and wife of Poseidon, at *Od.* 7.56–9 (where 57 ~ 142 here). Asteropaios aroused considerable interest later: a monograph on him was written by Ptolemy Pindarion (Wilamowitz, *Kleine Schriften* IV 143), and schol. pap. XII (Erbse, on 21.163) cites a fragment of lyric poetry about him (*PMG* 501).

For Ἄξιος εὐρυρέεθρος cf. 2.849 etc. Ἀξίου εὐρὺ ῥέοντος. εὐρυρέεθρος recurs only in Nonnus and Quintus of Smyrna.

145 ἔχων δύο δοῦρε: a warrior often carries or brandishes two spears, but here both will be used together (162–8).

146 δαϊκταμένων ('slain in battle') only recurs at 301; cf. ἀρηΐφατος, ἀρηϊκτάμενος. It is echoed by ἐδάϊζε (147).

148–51 Verses 148–9 = 6.121–2, in the meeting of Glaukos and Diomedes, which this episode resembles (see below). In 150 τίς πόθεν εἰς ἀνδρῶν occurs nowhere else in *Il.*, but 7× *Od.* (1.170 etc.). Cf. 6.123 τίς δὲ σύ ἐσσι, φέριστε, καταθνητῶν ἀνθρώπων; and similar enquiries at 15.247 and 24.387. Verse 151 = 6.127. This grim statement implies that 150 also asks about Asteropaios' parentage.

152–60 Asteropaios' reply is brief and to the point, being largely composed of conventional motifs. The last sentence suggests that he does not want to waste time exchanging the courtesies of heroic war. His opening question was more effective as an introduction to Glaukos' famous comparison of men to leaves (6.145). Like Glaukos, Asteropaios too gives his parentage but not his name, which would be unnecessary. Cf. 24.397, *Od.* 6.196, 15.267.

155 δολιχεγχής is an absolute *hapax*. For other descriptions of the Paeonians see on 16.287–8.

155–6 ἥδε ... εἰλήλουθα is very similar to 80–1. The motif of the latecomer to the war occurs at 10.434, 13.361, 13.792–4, 16.811, and here it adds to the poignancy of the hero's death. Asteropaios could theoretically have been mentioned in the Catalogue, since less than ten days have elapsed since the events of book 2. Hence a verse was inserted in some texts into the Paeonian entry after 2.848, in order to introduce him (cf. T on 21.140, schol. pap. XII (Erbse) 21.155).

158 This verse is omitted by several MSS. It is a variant of 2.850, which a few MSS read here. It might be thought to weaken the brevity of this speech, but it is natural for Asteropaios to dwell on his ancestry, and cf. the repetition at 85–6.

162 Πηλιάδα μελίην: Eustathius (1229.39) notices the variety of expressions for Akhilleus' spear in this episode: 169 μελίην ἰθυπτίωνα, 172 μείλινον ἔγχος, 178 δόρυ μείλινον Αἰακίδαο, 200 χάλκεον ἔγχος.

ἁμαρτῇ ... ἀμφίς: Asteropaios throws both spears at once (*sc.* βάλεν).

163 περιδέξιος occurs only here in Homer (cf. Aristophanes etc.); it must mean 'ambidextrous' in this context. ἀμφιδέξιος would not fit the metre.

165 = 20.268. On its own (i.e. apart from 20.269–72) this line most naturally implies that the gold layer is on top (see on 20.268–72).

166–8 ἐπιγράβδην ('with a graze') occurs only here in Homer; cf. Orph. *Lithica* 365. χειρός means 'arm' here, and ἡ δέ in 167 is the spear. Verse 168 resembles 15.317 (and see 21.69–70n.).

169–70 ἰθυπτίωνα occurs only here, and means 'straight-flying'; cf. 20.99 τοῦ δ' ἰθὺ βέλος πέτετ'. Zenodotus' reading ἰθυκτίωνα, supposed to mean 'straight-grained', is ingenious but less relevant. Verse 170 is very similar to 140.

171–2 'It is dramatically effective for Akhilleus to be wounded and to miss his opponent' (T). μεσσοπαγές occurs only here in early Greek literature (cf. Nonn. *D.* 1.233), and means 'driven into the ground up to the middle'. This anticipates Asteropaios' hopeless struggle to pull the spear out. Aristarchus preferred μεσσοπαλές (Did/A), which is read by some manuscripts, and was presumably intended to mean 'quivering up to [*or* in] the middle'.

174–9 Asteropaios' desperate efforts to pull out the spear and then to break it are vividly described. For τρίς ... βίης (176–7) cf. *Od.* 21.125–6. μεθίημι with the genitive is a normal construction. Most manuscripts read βίη or βίῃ, neither of which is probable. The pattern 'three times ... but on the fourth ...' is a common one: see on 22.165, and for τρὶς ... τρὶς ... τὸ δὲ τέτρατον ... see also on 16.702–6. In 178 ἄξαι ('to break') is from ἄγνυμι.

180–1 παρ' ὀμφαλόν ... κάλυψεν = 4.525–6 (see comment). χολάδες only occurs in these two passages in Homer; cf. *HyHerm* 123, etc.

182 ἐνὶ στήθεσσιν ὀρούσας: this brutal action goes beyond that of Hektor at 16.862–3.

183 = 13.619, 17.537. At 23.560–2 and 807–8 Akhilleus will offer Asteropaios' breastplate and sword as prizes in the funeral games for Patroklos.

184–99 The main theme of Akhilleus' speech of triumph, the genealogical comparison, is standard in heroic confrontations: cf. especially Aineias at 20.200–58 (with comments). But he displays an arrogance which goes still further than his speech over Lukaon's body (the opening of which is echoed at 184). The contemptuous and constant references to rivers (185, 186, 190, 191, 192, 196) rise to a magnificent, cosmic climax in the dismissal of even Okeanos, the source of all the waters of the world, as no match for the thunderbolt of Zeus. It is a superb piece of rhetoric, but seriously miscalculated, for Akhilleus himself will soon prove to be no match for Skamandros, whom he dismisses so boldly at 192–3.

184–5 Κρονίωνος | παισίν refers to Akhilleus' ultimate descent from Zeus (188–9). ἐκγεγαῶτι (read by Aristarchus, Arn/A, and most MSS) is preferable to the accusative here, as it stands in a clause which is independent of the infinitive ἐριζέμεναι and so follows the construction of τοι.

186–7 φῆσθα refers to 157. γένος, meaning 'offspring' (cf. 6.180, 9.538) or 'by birth', balances γενεήν. Notice the parallel structure of these verses, as in 20.206–9, 1.280–1, etc.

190–1 τῷ ('therefore') seems slightly incongruous here (rather in the manner of children arguing who say 'so there!'). μὲν ... αὖτε are virtually equivalent to 'just as ... so'.

For ἁλιμυρηέντων cf. *Od.* 5.460, where it refers specifically to the river's mouth, where it meets the sea. This stately compound was later thought to suggest the actual sound of the river running into the sea: cf. Eust. 1230.42 οἱ ἐν τῇ ἁλὶ μυρόμενοι, τουτέστι μετὰ ἤχου ῥέοντες ... καὶ ὡς ἂν συνηθέστερόν τις εἴποι, μορμύροντες; Leaf 'where it murmurs against the brine'. The basic sense of μύρομαι is not certain (cf. Chantraine, *Dict.*; Frisk).

αὖτε is Aristarchus' reading for δ' αὖτε (cf. 4.238). ποτάμοιο is elliptical, meaning 'than the offspring of a river'.

192–3 Akhilleus means Skamandros, rather than Axios. For 193 cf. 8.210 οὐκ ἂν ἔγωγ' ἐθέλοιμι Διὶ Κρονίωνι μάχεσθαι.

194 Akheloos, the great river of north-west Greece, and the longest one in Greece, was always regarded as specially important, and in later literature the name was sometimes used as a metonym for 'water' in general (cf. Erbse on schol. 194). It is mentioned only here in Homer, although another river of this name in Lydia occurs at 24.616.

For οὐδέ in 194 Aristarchus wanted to read οὔτε. οὔτε ... οὐδέ is perfectly possible (Denniston, *Particles* 193), and may be what he intended (rather than οὔτε ... οὔτε). For οὐδὲ ... οὐδὲ ... ('not even ... nor') cf. Kühner–Gerth II 294.

195 Megacleides and Zenodotus wanted to omit this verse, in order to make Akheloos the origin of all rivers, and Pausanias' text does not seem to have read it (8.38.10). Aristarchus and virtually all our MSS keep it. Modern scholars have tended to side with Zenodotus, but the line is surely genuine. How could Akheloos be the origin of the whole sea? Verse 195 accords with 14.201, 14.246 (see comments); cf. also Hes. *Th.* 337–70, where Okeanos is the father of rivers and springs, and A. Lesky, *Thalatta* (Vienna 1947) 81–2.

For βαθυρρείταο ...'Ωκεανοῖο cf. Hes. *Th.* 265 'Ωκεανοῖο βαθυρρείταο, and 18.607 ποταμοῖο μέγα σθένος 'Ωκεανοῖο. Leaf rightly calls this 'one of the most majestic lines ever written'. The polysyllabic phrase at each end of the verse frames the simpler μέγα σθένος in the centre, with a balanced structure of epithets and nouns. The splendid compound epithet βαθυρρείτης occurs only here in Homer (cf. Hes. *Th.* 265), and the repeated πάντες ... πᾶσα ... πᾶσαι ... and alliteration of 196–7 add to the effect. Cf. the grandeur of 7.422 ἐξ ἀκαλαρρείταο βαθυρρόου 'Ωκεάνοιο, and 14.246, 18.399.

197 φρείατα: only here in Homer; cf. *HyDem* 99, etc.

199 σμαραγήσῃ: a vivid word for the crack and rumble of thunder and a memorable ending to this speech. Elsewhere in Homer it occurs only at 2.210, of the sea breaking on the shore, and 2.463, of the Asian meadow, crowded with clamorous birds (see on 2.462–3). Cf. Hes. *Th.* 679, 693 (Titanomachy).

200 The poet here carefully notes Akhilleus' recovery of his only spear, which Asteropaios was unable to draw from the river-bank.

201–4 These verses echo the theme of 120–7. ἀμφεπένοντο (203), 'tended', is ironic, as at 23.184. It is used of care for a wounded man at 4.220 and 16.28. As in the cruel parody of Lukaon's funeral, the care of Asteropaios' body falls to the eels and fish, who attack the place where his flesh is most tender. ἔγχελυς only recurs at 353 in Homer; cf. Archilochus 189 West, etc.

204 The four-word verse with its repeated participles ('cropping ... shearing') dwells dispassionately and clinically on this unpleasant scene, before our attention is diverted elsewhere. The fact that ἐρέπτεσθαι is usually applied to animals peacefully cropping grass, grain etc. adds to the macabre incongruity, and the precise word ἐπινεφρίδιος ('around the kidneys') appears to be an absolute *hapax*. See also Richardson in Bremer, *HBOP* 170.

205–327 Skamandros intervenes. Akhilleus' slaughter of the Paeonians arouses the river, who asks him to desist. When Akhilleus fails to comply he complains to Apollo and then pursues Akhilleus over the plain. Akhilleus appeals to Zeus, and Poseidon and Athene come to his aid. Akhilleus attacks the river, who asks Simoeis for help and begins to overpower him

This is an intensely dramatic episode, in which we sense something of Akhilleus' own elemental power. In one or two places, however, the course of events has seemed to some readers slightly disjointed. Akhilleus apparently agrees to the river's request to drive the Trojans out of his waters and not to choke his streams (221), but Skamandros at once complains to Apollo, and Akhilleus then leaps into the water (227–34). Is this a sign that the poet originally had a version without the episode of Akhilleus' actual fight with the river (cf. Leaf)? That seems most unlikely, as there would be little point in introducing Skamandros at all. Akhilleus in fact only agrees to drive the Trojans out of the river, but refuses to stop slaughtering them, and his defiant words at 224–6 cause the river-god to make his appeal to Apollo. A further apparent difficulty is that at 291–2 Poseidon promises Akhilleus that the river will soon desist, but this only happens after Hephaistos' intervention at Here's request (328–82). It looks as if the poet is duplicating the motif of divine aid in order to show us the weight of support behind Akhilleus, and also as a preparation for the actual conflict between the gods at 385–514. The fight with the river is itself a stage in this process of climax, as was acutely observed by the sophist Protagoras (schol. pap. XII (Erbse) on 240).

205 Παίονας ἱπποκορυστάς: see 16.287–8 with comment.

207–8 Cf. 16.451–2 ἐνὶ κρατερῇ ὑσμίνῃ | χέρσ' ὑπὸ Πατρόκλοιο ... δαμῆναι.

209–12 Cf. 5.677–80, where Odysseus kills several Lycians, especially 679–80 καί νύ κ' ἔτι πλέονας Λυκίων κτάνε δῖος 'Οδυσσεύς, | εἰ μὴ ἄρ' ὀξὺ νόησε μέγας κορυθαίολος Ἕκτωρ ...; and for this sequence in general (catalogue of victims followed by hostile intervention, often divine) see on 16.415–18.

Mudon is perhaps related to the Paeonian place-name Amudon (2.849, 16.288). It is also the name of a Paphlagonian (5.580). Cf. von Kamptz, *Personennamen* 309. Ophelestes is possibly an Illyrian name (von Kamptz 148–9, 256). It is applied to a Trojan at 8.274.

213 A few MSS omit this verse, perhaps because of *homoeoteleuton* with 212. It could, however, have been added because it was thought that the river-god could not address Akhilleus unless he took human form, and if it were not there we should not really regret its absence. Aristarchus (Did/A) found support for both εἰσάμενος and εἰδόμενος, and both forms occur elsewhere (see on 16.710–11). ἐκ φθέγξατο (or ἐκφθέγξατο) is the reading of a few MSS for ἐφθέγξατο, and is much better with the genitive construction. Aristarchus' omission of δέ (Did/A) produces an awkward asyndeton.

214–21 Skamandros' request is courteous, considering Akhilleus' behaviour so far.

214–15 περί ... ἀνδρῶν means 'beyond all men'. For αἴσυλα ῥέζεις see on 5.403–4. The emphatic runover word ἀνδρῶν and θεοὶ αὐτοί frame 215.

216–17 The Geneva scholia say that Skamandros' real intention is to lure Akhilleus into the water to drive out the Trojans, so that he can then be destroyed. This is supported by Scheibner (*Aufbau* 36), but seems over-ingenious.

218 ἐρατεινὰ ῥέεθρα: a unique phrase, particularly effective by contrast with the river's pollution (cf. bT), a contrast implied also by 219–20 (especially ἅλα δῖαν); Arn/A misses the point. See also on 238, and Richardson in Bremer, *HBOP* 171.

220 The verse is made ugly by the repeated sigmatism, and the echo of στειν- ... κτειν- ..., suggesting the horror of the scene. For ἀϊδήλως ('destructively'), cf. ἀΐδηλος 2.455, etc.

221 ἄγη μ' ἔχει: ἄγη occurs only here in *Il.*, twice in *Od.*, both times in the same phrase as here (3.227, 16.243).

223–7 Akhilleus' assent is at best very perfunctory, referring presumably to Skamandros' request at 217, and the main weight of his reply is on his desire for more slaughter. In 225–6 Ἕκτορι ... ἀντιβίην go together. ἤ κεν ... ἤ κεν ... ('whether ... or . ...') seems better than placing a colon after ἀντιβίην and making this a separate 'either ... or ...' sentence (ἤ ... ἤ ...).

71

229–32 Apollo was last seen rescuing Hektor from Akhilleus at 20.443–54, and he is not mentioned again until 435. For the time being nothing comes of this appeal to him, but the poet wants to concentrate on Skamandros himself at this point, and the appeal stresses the river-god's desperation. In fact, Apollo does fulfil Zeus's instructions at 515–611, where 516–17 recall 20.30.

Zeus's actual instructions were that the gods should give aid to both sides, lest Akhilleus should sack Troy (20.23–30). What Skamandros says is perfectly in accord with this. True, Zeus had said nothing about a time-limit, but the point presumably is that the gods should continue to give support throughout the day's fighting.

231–2 Τρωσὶ ... ἀμύνειν resembles 15.255 (of Apollo). For the limit indicated by 231–2 cf. 11.193–4, 17.454–5. The phrase δείελος ὀψὲ δύων suggests that originally δείελος referred to the setting sun, but the etymology is not certain. σκιάζειν occurs only here in Homer; cf. Hes. *Th.* 716 (κατὰ δ᾽ ἐσκίασαν), etc.

233–50 Virtually all this passage concentrates on the river's actions. The style and structure reflect this: notice the very high frequency of enjambment, especially periodic and progressive. In 18 verses these two types occur 12 times, i.e. 66%, more than twice as often as the average frequency noted by Parry (*MHV* 254: 24.8% in 600 verses of *Iliad* 1–6). This is naturally accompanied by a high frequency of internal pauses. The effect is of a great piling-up of sentences, as the river deploys all its forces to defeat Akhilleus. Verses 241–8 are discussed by Higbie, *Measure and Music* 118–19. She also notes the low density of formulae in this passage.

234 The compound ἀπαΐσσειν occurs only here in Homer, later in fifth-century literature. For οἴδματι θύων cf. 23.230, the only other occurrence of the phrase in Homer, Hes. *Th.* 109, 131, and see Richardson on *HyDem* 14. One should perhaps read θυίων (Chantraine, *GH* 1 372).

235 πάντα δ᾽ ὄρινε ῥέεθρα κυκώμενος: the triple trochaic break in each of the first three feet has a restless effect which suits the theme of confusion; see on 406–11.

236 = 344. For ἅλις ἔσαν a minority of MSS read ἔσαν ἅλις, which Leaf prefers on the grounds that the ϝ of ἅλις is usually observed, although cf. 17.54 ὅθ᾽ ἅλις in the same position, again with -λῖς before a vowel. But in any case ἅλις hardly ever occurs before the bucolic diaeresis (*Od.* 15.77, 15.94 only), whereas it is common after the main caesura.

237 μεμυκὼς ἠΰτε ταῦρος: perhaps because (as later) rivers were seen as sometimes taking the form of a bull. Schol. B refers here to Archilochus' portrayal of Akheloos as a bull, in his fight with Herakles (fr. 287 West). Cf. S. *Tr.* 10–14, with P. E. Easterling's comments; also *Atrahasis* (S. Dalley, *Myths from Mesopotamia*, Oxford 1989, 31): 'The Flood roared like a bull.'

238 σάω: cf. 16.363 (3rd person sing. impf. as if from σάωμι). καλὰ ῥέεθρα recurs 6× in book 21, but nowhere else in *Il.* (cf. *Od.* 11.240). So it need not be merely 'formular'. See on 218.

239 T and Eustathius (1233.64) acutely observe that the repeated -ῃσι endings suggest the broad and calm expanse of the river, as saviour of the Trojans. This effect is increased by the slow pace of the spondaic opening and the way in which the words grow in length.

240 Schol. pap. xii (Erbse) compares *Od.* 11.243–4 (Turo and Poseidon): πορφύρεον δ' ἄρα κῦμα περιστάθη οὔρεϊ ἶσον, | κυρτωθέν, κρύψεν δὲ θεὸν θνητήν τε γυναῖκα.

241–2 The Shield was Hephaistos' work, and so its mention here is particularly suitable (so T). For εἶχε in 242 a minority of MSS read εἶα, which is possible.

243–6 'ἐκ ῥιζῶν is relevant, as this tree has deep roots: hence it carries all the bank with it' (bT). διωθεῖν occurs only here in Homer, later in Herodotus etc. γεφύρωσεν means 'dammed'. See on 5.87–8, 15.356–7. The fallen tree enables Akhilleus to escape from the water.

246–7 The variant λίμνης for δίνης is less suitable in this context, where the river is in motion. In 247 the variant πεδίονδε (A, schol. pap. xii) may have been designed to avoid the genitive πεδίοιο for 'over the plain', a common construction (2.785 etc.). Zoilus criticized Homer here because Akhilleus does not use his chariot and immortal horses (schol. Ge 21.256), and schol. pap. xii (Erbse, on 246–7) answers this pedantic charge.

249–50 ἀκροκελαινιόων means 'with darkening crest', a vivid Homeric *hapax* (cf. Nonnus, *D.* 18.156) which fills the first hemistich. Cf. 13.799 κυρτὰ φαληριόωντα. For ἵνα... ἀλάλκοι cf. 137–8, and for μιν... Ἀχιλλῆα (e.g.) *Od.* 6.48.

251–64 The river's pursuit of Akhilleus is expressed in two contrasting similes, a short and rapid one describing Akhilleus' flight, and a more leisurely and detailed one for the pursuit.

251–6 This description is similar to that of 22.138–44: 138 Πηλεΐδης ἐπόρουσε ...; 139–42 simile of hawk, ἐλαφρότατος πετεηνῶν, ... οἴμησε ... ἡ δέ θ' ὕπαιθα φοβεῖται ...; 141–4 flight and pursuit.

251 ὅσον τ' ἐπὶ δουρὸς ἐρωή: for this and similar estimates of distance see on 15.358–9.

252–3 Eagle-similes occur elsewhere at 15.690 (Hektor), 17.674 (Menelaos), 22.308 (Hektor), *Od.* 24.538 (Odysseus). In all these passages it is the eagle's swoop which is described, except in book 17 where it is primarily its sharp sight. Philetas read ὄμματ' for οἴματ' in 252, and some scholars read μελανόσσου ('black-eyed'), but cf. οἴμησε(ν) 22.140, 22.308 = *Od.* 24.538, and 16.752 οἶμα λέοντος ἔχων. An extraordinary conjecture, attributed to Aristotle, was μελανόστου ('black-boned'), apparently relying on Democritus' view that eagles have black bones (68 в 22 D–K)! Aristarchus wanted to read τοῦ as enclitic for τινός, although the Homeric form is τευ. The problem here was the use of the article with θηρητῆρος, but this can be explained as identifying the type of eagle concerned, 'a dark one, the hunter'. It may be the one described at 24.316 as μορφνὸν θηρητῆρ', ὃν καὶ περκνὸν καλέουσιν, although they are possibly distinguished in Arist. *HA* 9.32. Cf. A. *Ag.* 115, Fraenkel *ad loc.*, W. G. Arnott, *CQ* 29 (1979) 7–8. Ingeniously, Ahrens conjectured μελανόρσου for μέλανος τοῦ, because the eagle in Archilochus 178 (West) is black-tailed.

253 κάρτιστος: this is echoed in Arist. *HA* 9.32, 618b26, where the black eagle is said to be κράτιστος. For ὅς τε ... ὤκιστος πετεηνῶν cf. 15.238 (Apollo compared to a hawk).

254 ἐπὶ στήθεσσι ... κονάβιζε: cf. 13.497–8, with comment.

257–64 This is one of Homer's most attractive and lively similes. Part of its effect comes from the contrast between the violent scene of the river-god's pursuit and the peaceful picture of the gardener. Cf. the simile likening the destruction of the Greek wall by Apollo to a child destroying a sand-castle at 15.361–4. The scholia notice the change of style here: 'he moves from the powerful style to the plain and florid' (bT; cf. schol. Ge). Douris of Samos failed to see this, and censured the simile as inappropriate to the scene described (*FGH* 76.89). Demetrius however singles it out as a model of vividness (ἐνάργεια) arising from precise, detailed description (*On Style* 209). Virgil's admiration is shown by his imitation at *G.* 1.104–10. There is another agricultural simile at 346–7, where the wind dries a newly watered plot of land, a good contrast with this one.

The remarkably high frequency of *hapax legomena* adds greatly to the precision of the simile (ὀχετηγός, μάκελλα, ἀμάρη, ψηφίς, ὀχλεῖν, προαλής): cf. Richardson in Bremer, *HBOP* 172–3. ὀχετηγός is rare later, but ὀχετός, ὀχετεύειν are commoner. For ἀπὸ κρήνης μελανύδρου cf. 16.160 (with comments on 16.156–63). In 258 ὕδατι is preferable to the variant ὕδατος. μάκελλα ('mattock') recurs in the fifth century, but cf. Hes. *Erga* 470 (etc.) μακέλη. ἀμάρη ('trench') is doubtful in Sappho fr. 174 L–P and is found in Hellenistic poetry. It survived in Thessalian and crops up now and then in late prose. ἔχματα (4× *Il.*) means 'impediments' here. ψηφίς ('pebble') recurs in Hipponax (128.3 West) etc.; ψῆφος occurs nowhere in archaic literature.

In 261 there is assonance of χ, κ and λ, and κελαρύζειν is onomatopoeic (cf. 11.813, *Od.* 5.323). ὀχλεῖν recurs in fifth-century literature, but cf. 12.448, *Od.* 9.242 for ὀχλίζειν. προαλής ('sloping') reappears in Hellenistic poetry, and survived in Cypriote, Arcadian and Laconian. For φθάνει with ᾱ cf. 9.506, 10.346.

264 θεοὶ ... ἀνδρῶν: this gnomic hemistich, which only occurs here, neatly rounds off the comparison. Such aphorisms are more usually expressed by characters in the poem than by the narrator (cf. vol. v, Introduction, p. 6).

265–98 Akhilleus' inability to resist leads him to complain to Zeus, and Poseidon and Athene encourage him.

265–71 For ὁσσάκι δ' ὁρμήσειε ... τοσσάκι μιν ... cf. 22.194–7. In 266–7 Akhilleus has the impression that *all* the gods are against him. For διιπετέος ποταμοῖο see on 16.174. In 269 πλάζε means 'struck', apparently the basic sense of the verb (Chantraine, *Dict.* s.v.); cf. 12.285, *Od.* 5.389, and see on 17.750–1. In all four passages the verb is used in connexion with water. In 268–71 the river seems at one moment to be pounding Akhilleus' shoulders, whilst at another its current undermines his legs. ὑπέρεπτε ('eat away from below', 'undercut') is a vivid compound found only here and in Quintus of Smyrna (9.377).

272–83 Akhilleus' complaint to Zeus is not untypical of the disappointed Homeric hero: cf. 3.365 (Menelaos), 8.236 (Agamemnon), 12.164 (Asios), 13.631 (Menelaos), all beginning Ζεῦ πάτερ ... But Akhilleus' protest also reveals his greatness: it is not death he fears, but an ignoble death. Cf. the famous prayer of Aias at 17.645–7, that the Greeks may perish at least in the daylight (bT *ad loc.*, [Longinus] 9.10, and bT 21.273, 21.276, 21.279).

273–4 ὡς ... σαῶσαι means 'to think that not one of the gods has undertaken to rescue me, pitiful as I am'. The complex word-order may be due to the tendency of pronouns to come early in the sentence (see on 347). ἔπειτα ... πάθοιμι implies 'if I escape I should not mind dying later'.

276–8 Akhilleus' disappointment suggests that Thetis' prophecy of a heroic death had consoled him (see on 113). In *Il.* θέλγειν and related words are only used of the gods (12.255, 14.215, 15.322, 15.594, 21.604, 24.343). Verse 278 is a powerful four-word one, framed by λαιψηροῖς ... βελέεσσιν, to describe his death.

279–80 'Not just death in battle, but at the hands of the best of the enemy, is his wish' (bT). For ὅς ... ἄριστος cf. 23.348. The vulgate reading τέτραφ' (for γ' ἔτραφ') is found only here and as a variant at 23.348, whereas ἔτραφον as intransitive is regular in Homer. Verses 277–80 are echoed by Sophocles (*Ph.* 334–6):

NE. τέθνηκεν, ἀνδρὸς οὐδένος, θεοῦ δ' ὕπο,
 τοξευτός, ὡς λέγουσιν, ἐκ Φοίβου δαμείς.

ΦΙ. ἀλλ' εὐγενὴς μὲν ὁ κτανών τε χὡ θανών.

281–3 Verse 281 = *Od.* 5.312, at the end of a speech in which Odysseus fears an unheroic death at sea and wishes he had died at Troy, where he would have won fame and received proper burial (cf. A. B. Lord, *The Singer of Tales*, Cambridge, Mass. 1960, 196–7, and Usener, *Verhältnis der Odyssee* *zur Ilias* 141–7 for comparison of these two scenes). Virgil's Aeneas echoes them both (*Aen.* 1.94–101). In 282 ἐρχθέντα means 'trapped'. ὡς παῖδα συφορβόν stresses the pathetic and dishonourable nature of this fate. συφορβός only occurs here in *Il.*, 7× *Od.* For ἔναυλος ('torrent-bed') see on 16.70–1, and for ἀποέρσῃ of water sweeping someone away cf. 329, 6.348.

284–6 It is unusual for gods to appear together to encourage a hero. Their failure to do much more than give encouragement was explained by Aristotle as due to the fact that it was Hephaistos who was Skamandros' opponent (schol. pap. xii (Erbse) on 286; cf. bT on 288–91). However, Athene does in fact give Akhilleus the strength to resist the river-god (299–304).

285 It is also unusual in the *Iliad* for the human form taken by a deity to be so unspecific. Cf. 13.357, where Poseidon particularly wants to remain anonymous. At 213 the river wishes Akhilleus to know who he is, and presumably the same applies here.

286 χειρὶ δὲ χεῖρα λαβόντες: this phrase occurs only here for the usual formula with a singular verb, ἐν δ' ἄρα οἱ φῦ χειρί. Cf. 6.233 χεῖράς τ' ἀλλήλων λαβέτην καὶ πιστώσαντο.

287 τοῖσι: unless this is a careless use of a formula, it presumably means 'among them' (cf. *Od.* 5.202, 7.47). But the verse could be a later addition (see on 290–2, 298).

288 Gods and other visionary personages commonly say 'be not afraid'. Cf. 24.153–4, 24.171–4 with comments, and for μήτε τι τάρβει also *Od.* 7.50–1.

289 ἐπιταρρόθω: cf. 5.808 τοίη οἱ ἐγὼν ἐπιτάρροθος ἦα (~ 828), etc., and 4.390 τοίη οἱ ἐπίρροθος ἦεν Ἀθήνη, etc. The derivation of ἐπιτάρροθος is unknown; see on 4.389–90.

290–2 Aristarchus athetized 290 because Poseidon does not give his own name, although he had taken the form of a man, and so Akhilleus could not know his identity (Arn/A). It is certainly true that when a god reveals himself as such he normally does give his name (see Richardson on *HyDem* 268). Schol. pap. xii (Erbse) adds that on his departure Poseidon does not encourage Akhilleus by any clear sign, and Skamandros' violence does not abate (305–6). Seleucus defended the verse in a work Κατὰ τῶν Ἀριστάρχου σημείων, pointing out that Poseidon and Athene had already indicated their divinity by their pledge of greeting and by verse 289; and he also answered a criticism of Ζηνὸς ἐπαινήσαντος on the grounds that Zeus had not sent them, by saying that this could be taken for granted (κατὰ τὸ σιωπώμενον). It comes as a surprise, therefore, to learn that in another work (Διορθωτικά) Seleucus athetized 290–2! These verses were not in the Cretan edition (schol. pap. xii (Erbse)).

Ζηνὸς ἐπαινήσαντος may simply refer to Zeus's permission to the gods to intervene in the battle. But 292 is a weak verse: λωφᾶν on its own (without genitive or participle) is odd, and the verb otherwise only occurs in Homer at *Od.* 9.460 (λωφήσειε κακῶν); and σὺ δὲ εἴσεαι αὐτός is rather pointless. All three verses may be a later addition. In this case, 287 might also have been added. Cf. Bolling, *External Evidence* 189–90. Apthorp however defends the verses (*MS Evidence* 77–8).

293 αἴ κε πίθηαι: cf. 1.207 with comment (Athene to Akhilleus), *Od.* 1.279 (Athene in disguise to Telemakhos) σοὶ δ᾽ αὐτῷ πυκινῶς ὑποθήσομαι, αἴ κε πίθηαι.

295–7 Ἰλιόφι: the 'only example of -φι from a proper name and equivalent to pure gen. without local reference' (Shipp, *Studies* 307). On these forms cf. Chantraine, *GH* I 238–9. The poet could have used Ἰλίου (or Ἰλίοο?) as at 104. ὅς κε φύγῃσι means 'whoever of the army escapes'. For δίδομεν δέ τοι εὖχος ἀρέσθαι cf. the variant at 2.15 δίδομεν δέ οἱ εὖχος ἀρέσθαι.

298 Only Poseidon has spoken, unless we omit 287 and 290, but in itself this is not a serious objection. Cf. 10.349, where Didymus quoted 298 in support.

299–304 The gods' intervention enables Akhilleus to hold his own against Skamandros for the time being. There follows a brief, vivid picture of the flooded plain, with weapons and corpses floating everywhere, and Akhilleus in the midst.

301–2 Cf. A. *Ag.* 659–60 ὁρῶμεν ἀνθοῦν πέλαγος Αἰγαῖον νεκροῖς | ἀνδρῶν Ἀχαιῶν ναυτικοῖς τ᾽ ἐρειπίοις, and Virgil, *Aen.* 1.100–1 *ubi tot Simois correpta sub undis | scuta virum galeasque et fortia corpora volvit.* For δαϊκταμένων αἰζηῶν cf. 146.

302–4 For τοῦ δ᾽ ... ἐπήδα cf. 269 ὁ δ᾽ ὑψόσε ποσσὶν ἐπήδα, with γούνατ᾽ ἐδάμνα at the end of 270. πρὸς ῥόον ... ἀν᾽ ἰθύν means 'as he rushed straight on against the current'. This need not mean that Akhilleus is going 'upstream', but rather that he holds his footing against the current. For ἀν᾽ ἰθύν cf. *Od.* 8.377, where the sense is 'straight upwards' (cf. Hainsworth). ἴσχεν ('checked') is read by Aristarchus and a few of our MSS, against the vulgate ἔσχεν, and is clearly the more precise word here. The second hemistich of 304 picks up 299, rounding off this passage about Akhilleus' response.

305–27 Skamandros appeals again, this time to Simoeis. Once more nothing comes of this (cf. Eust. 1237.47, and see on 229–32); but it gives the opportunity for a magnificent speech, which characterizes the river-god. As at 233–50 enjambment is frequent, with emphatic runover words. At 312–15 there is a series of vivid verses with a sense-pause at the caesura, as Skamandros gives a list of urgent instructions to his brother (see also detailed comments on 311–15). At 316–23 he threatens Akhilleus with a new form of burial, in a picturesque description which echoes the ironic theme of Akhilleus' own treatment of Lukaon and Asteropaios (122–35, 200–4), and is similar to the type of mocking speech made by a successful warrior over his opponent (cf. Scheibner, *Aufbau* 99 n. 2).

305–7 For 305 cf. 248 οὐδέ τ' ἔληγε θεὸς μέγας, and for λήγειν μένος see on 13.424. κόρυσσε δέ κῦμα means 'reared up his crested wave'; cf. 4.424 πόντῳ μέν τε πρῶτα κορύσσεται (with comment), etc. The use of the active here may be a secondary development; cf. 2.273 πόλεμόν τε κορύσσων, Leumann, *HW* 210. For the river Simoeis see on 5.773–4, where the confluence of the two rivers is mentioned.

310 For κατὰ μόθον in this position cf. 18.159, 18.537.

311–12 The rhythm of ἀλλ' ἐπάμυνε τάχιστα marks the urgency. ὀροθύνειν is normally used of rousing persons in the *Iliad*; cf. *Od.* 5.292 πάσας δ' ὀρόθυνεν ἀέλλας.

313–15 ἵστη is imperative singular, like δαίνυ (9.70). The opening spondaic word, the lengthening of δέ and the simplicity of μέγα κῦμα all contribute to the impression of a single, towering wave. The onomatopoeia and assonance of ὀρυμαγδὸν ὄρινε are effective, as also the parallelism of ὀρόθυνον ... ὀρυμαγδὸν ... The heavy, spondaic phrase φιτρῶν καὶ λαῶν recurs at 12.29, where Poseidon destroys the Greek wall. The indefinite expression ἄγριον ἄνδρα is probably derogatory as at 8.96 (see on 22.38). For ὅς δὴ νῦν κρατέει cf. 5.175, 16.424 | ὅστις ὅδε κρατέει ..., and for μέμονεν δ' ὅ γε ἶσα θεοῖσι cf. 5.440–1 μηδὲ θεοῖσιν | ἶσ' ἔθελε φρονέειν.

316–17 'He has excellently listed all the attributes on which Akhilleus especially prided himself, his courage, appearance, and armour' (bT). Cf. 3.54–5 οὐκ ἄν τοι χραίσμη κίθαρις τά τε δῶρ' Ἀφροδίτης, | ἥ τε κόμη τό τε εἶδος, ὅτ' ἐν κονίῃσι μιγείης. τὰ τεύχεα καλά means 'those arms of his, fine as they are'. νειόθι occurs only here in Homer; cf. Hes. *Th.* 567 etc., and *Il.* 10.10 νειόθεν.

317–18 The arms lying in the mud of the river bed make a memorable picture, which contrasts with the flotsam of armour at 300–1. Cf. Clarence's dream of drowning in *Richard III* (Act I Sc. IV 24–33):

> Methought I saw a thousand fearful wracks;
> A thousand men that fishes gnaw'd upon;
> Wedges of gold, great anchors, heaps of pearl,
> Inestimable stones, unvalu'd jewels,
> All scatter'd in the bottom of the sea.
> Some lay in dead men's skulls; and in those holes
> Where eyes did once inhabit, there were crept,
> As 'twere in scorn of eyes, reflecting gems,
> That woo'd the slimy bottom of the deep,
> And mock'd the dead bones that lay scatter'd by.

318–19 The sound-patterns are noticed by T (319): strong repetition of κ in 318, and of σ and χ in 319 (silt and shingle silently sweeping over the bones). ἰλύς ('mud', 'slime') is a Homeric *hapax* (cf. Hdt. 2.7, etc.).

319 εἰλύσω ψαμάθοισιν: instead of the usual winding-sheet his body will be wrapped in sand. Cf. *Od.* 14.135–6 ἤ τόν γ' ἐν πόντῳ φάγον ἰχθύες, ὀστέα δ' αὐτοῦ | κεῖται ἐπ' ἠπείρου ψαμάθῳ εἰλυμένα πολλῇ.

This is the only example in Homer of εἰλύω in the active (cf. Aratus 432). It is probably a secondary formation from the perfect passive εἴλυμαι (Chantraine, *GH* 1 131, 442). The variant ἰλύσω ('I will slime him down with sand', Leaf) does not occur in surviving literature. The assonance of ἰλύος . . . εἰλύσω is effective.

χέραδος is another Homeric *hapax*; cf. Sappho 145, Alcaeus 344 L–P etc. It means either 'shingle' or else all the rubbish and silt collected in the river-bed. The variant σχέραδος was supported by πολυσχέραδος in Euphorion fr. 25 Powell (schol. Ge), but χέραδος (neuter) is the regular form. It is probably related to χέρμας ('stone') and perhaps also χαράδρα ('ravine'); cf. Chantraine, *Dict.* s.v.

320–1 Cf. the collecting of the bones after Patroklos' and Hektor's funerals at 23.252–3, 24.792–4; ἄλλεγον is used in this context at 23.253. ἄσις is another rare word for silt, only here in Homer. Cf. Nicander, *Th.* 176, Charito 2.2, and ἀσώδης A. *Supp.* 31. This great heap of silt will be Akhilleus' burial-mound!

323 τυμβοχόης: this (genitive of τυμβοχόη) is the reading of Crates, whereas Aristarchus (Arn/A) read τυμβοχοῆσ(αι), the aorist of τυμβοχοεῖν, which occurs at Hdt. 7.117 and elsewhere. For χρεώ μιν ἔσται with genitive cf. 9.75 etc. The aorist infinitive is not elided elsewhere, and τυμβοχοῆσαί μιν would be a very awkward expression (cf. Leaf). τυμβοχόη occurs nowhere else, but cf. A. *Th.* 1022 τυμβοχόος, S. *Ant.* 848 τυμβόχωστος.

324–7 This is really the climax of the episode so far, as the river-god raises himself aloft in a single towering wave, 'seething with foam and blood and corpses'. The incongruity is like that in James Elroy Flecker's poem *The Old Ships*:

> Who knows how oft with squat and noisy gun . . .
> The pirate Genoese
> Hell-raked them till they rolled
> Blood, water, fruit and corpses up the hold.

κυκώμενος . . . θύων . . . μορμύρων ἀφρῷ . . . πορφύρεον all contribute to the idea of a seething, boiling wave. μορμύρειν is onomatopoeic, and always used elsewhere in the formula ἀφρῷ μορμύρων -οντα (18.403, 5.599). πορφύρεον can be translated here 'heaving', or 'surging': cf. 1.482, *Od.* 2.428, 11.243, and πορφύρειν, with Chantraine, *Dict.* s.v. For πορφύρεον

... ἀειρόμενον cf. *Od.* 11.243–4 (quoted in comment on 240). κατὰ δ' ἦρεε Πηλεΐωνα means 'and he began to overpower the son of Peleus'.

328–82 Herē asks Hephaistos to burn up the plain and the river, and he does so, until Skamandros asks him to stop, and promises Herē not to help the Trojans any more. She agrees, and Hephaistos desists

Hephaistos' attack on Skamandros was anticipated at 20.36 and 40, and 73–4 (if those verses are original), and it leads in turn to the battle between the other gods (21.383–514). For later interpreters this opposition of fire and water gave a starting-point for cosmic interpretations of the Theomachy (cf. Buffière, *Mythes d' Homère* 100ff.). Hephaistos has a Trojan priest at 5.9–10, but is named among pro-Greek gods at 15.214. Herē is closely associated with her son here, as (for example) in 1.571–600.

329 For μέγας ποταμὸς βαθυδίνης see on 1–2.

331 κυλλοπόδιον: 'little club-foot'; see on 18.369–71. Aristarchus (Arn/A) considered the epithet inappropriate here, but it is possible that he did not actually athetize the verse (cf. Erbse *ad loc.*). Plutarch (*Mor.* 35c) points out that in Homer such an address is not a reproach: evidently the epithet was defended by some as a sign of familiarity.

331–2 ἄντα ... εἶναι: 'for it was against you, as we supposed, that swirling Xanthos was matched in battle'. This refers back to the pairing of these two gods at 20.73–4 (cf. ἄντα ... at 73).

333 ἀλλ' ἐπάμυνε τάχιστα: the repetition of this from 311 stresses the opposition of water and fire, and the fact that Here's appeal answers that of Skamandros to his brother.

πιφαύσκεο δὲ φλόγα πολλήν: note the strong plosive alliteration. For πιφαύσκεσθαι ('manifest') cf. 12.280, of snow sent by Zeus. It is an unusual word to apply to the elements, suggesting their divine or portentous nature.

334–5 Violent winds or storms in Homer are often seen as the result of more than one wind blowing at once: 2.145, 9.5, 11.306–7, 16.765, 23.194–230, *Od.* 5.295–6, 5.331–2. ἀργεστᾶο Νότοιο refers to a south wind which clears the sky of clouds; cf. 11.306. εἴσομαι ('I shall hasten'), is from ἵεμαι; cf. Chantraine, *GH* I 293, 412. Zenodotus took it as 'I shall know', reading ὄρσασα, and ἤ in 336. ἐξ ἀλόθεν occurs nowhere else.

336–7 ἀπό ... κήαι is a tmesis and κήαι optative. φλέγμα occurs only here in early Greek literature. Later it is nearly always used in a medical sense (Hdt. 4.187, Hippocrates, etc.).

338 ἐν δ' αὐτὸν ἵει πυρί means 'set him on fire'; cf. 10.88–9 τὸν ... Ζεὺς ἐνέηκε πόνοισι. For μηδέ ... ἀρειῇ cf. 20.108–9, and on ἀρειῇ ('threat') see 17.429–31n.

341–2 ἀκάματον πῦρ ... θεσπιδαὲς πῦρ: note the elegant variation of formulae. They serve different functions, after a consonant or a vowel, and σχεῖν̲ θεσπιδαές would be unattractive.

343–56 The theme of 'burning' is emphasized by the constant repetitions throughout this passage: 343 ... πῦρ δαίετο, καῖε δὲ νεκροὺς ..., 345 πᾶν δ' ἐξηράνθη πεδίον ..., 347 ... ἀγξηράνη ..., 348 ὡς ἐξηράνθη πεδίον πᾶν, κὰδ δ' ἄρα νεκροὺς, 349 κῆεν ... φλόγα παμφανόωσαν, 350 καίοντο ..., 351 καίετο δὲ ..., 356 καίετο δ' ... Cf. also 353 τείροντ' ..., 355 τειρόμενοι ... There is a good deal of assonance and alliteration throughout. The two passages describing the burning of the plain and the river are balanced (343–9 and 350–6, with transitional sentence at 349; see also on 350–6). The whole episode brilliantly describes the gradual, inexorable spread of the blaze, until it finally attacks the river-god himself.

343–4 πρῶτα μέν is not answered until 349. The scholia here (and at 365) raise the question why Akhilleus was not affected by the fire, and compare the way in which Skamandros kept the Trojans in his waters without their coming to harm (238–9).

344 = 236. αὐτόν is masculine, and at 236 refers to the river, whereas here it ought to refer to the neuter πεδίον. The verse could be an example of careless repetition by the poet, or a later expansion.

345–9 For the simile, again drawn from the peaceful and orderly life of the farmer, see on 257–64. Again there is a high proportion of unusual words: both ξηραίνειν and ἀγξηραίνειν, though common later, occur only here in Homer, νεοαρδής nowhere else; ἐθείρειν is virtually unique (ἐθείρεται Orph. *Arg.* 932). Hesychius explains ἐθείρῃ with ἐπιμελείας ἀξιώσῃ, but the derivation is unknown. If it is related to ἔθειρα the sense 'comb', 'rake' would be reasonable. ἀλωή can be used of any piece of cultivated land or of a threshing-floor, and it is not clear exactly what the agricultural process involved here is supposed to be.

346 For ὡς δ' ὅτ' ὀπωρινὸς Βορέης cf. *Od.* 5.328, in a simile of chaff being blown about. νεοαρδέα means 'freshly watered'.

347 χαίρει δέ μιν ὅς τις ἐθείρῃ: as often in the similes we have the reaction of the human participant or observer introduced. Cf. 8.559 γέγηθε δέ τε φρένα ποίμην, *Od.* 6.106 γέγηθε δέ τε φρένα Λητώ, *Il.* 4.275–9, 4.455, etc. Here Fränkel (*Gleichnisse* 46) says that the reaction of the man in the simile suggests the Greeks' sense of relief at Hephaistos' rescue of Akhilleus. But (as at 257–64) there is surely also a contrast between the scorching destruction caused by Hephaistos and the beneficial results of the drying wind.

It is interesting to find μιν outside the relative clause, when ὅς τις μιν would have been possible. Enclitic pronouns tend to come in second place in the sentence, or as near the opening as possible: cf. Wackernagel, *Kleine Schriften* I 1–103, especially 3–4.

350–6 Hephaistos' effect on the river is expressed in two balanced sentences of three verses each (350–2, 353–5), with a third single-verse sentence describing the burning of the river itself. Note the emphatic position of καίοντο … καίετο … τείροντ' … καίετο (cf. κῆεν 349), and the careful parallelism of 350 with 351, and of 352 with 354 (which incidentally helps to explain the use of τά as a heavy syllable at the beginning of 352).

350–1 The trees are elm, willow, tamarisk; the plants celandine (?), reeds, galingale (for λωτός see on 14.347–8). On the realism of this description of the banks of Skamandros see Leaf, *Troy* 10: 'Today the river-channel through the plain is marked by the line of low willows and elm bushes … and the tamarisks spread from the banks in thick copses, making with their young shoots at the end of April conspicuous patches of dull crimson.'

350 πτελέαι τε καὶ ἰτέαι: Leaf reads simply καί (for τε καί), with one MS, because the digamma of ἰτέαι is observed at *Od.* 10.510. But one should not expect consistency over this point in Homer.

351 Cf. *Od.* 4.603 ᾧ ἐνὶ μὲν λωτὸς πολύς, ἐν δὲ κύπειρον. Θρύον occurs as the name of a place by the Alpheios at 2.592, *HyAp* 423 (cf. *Il.* 11.711 Θρυόεσσα). It is not certain which plant is referred to here as λωτός, celandine, trefoil, and clover all being suggested (see on 14.348).

352 τὰ περὶ …: see on 3.355–60, and Chantraine, *GH* 1 103.

353 τείροντ': 'were troubled', 'were distressed'; it is always a strong word in Homer and later. For ἐγχέλυές τε καὶ ἰχθύες cf. 203. Athenaeus (299D) says that the eels show how deep down the fire has reached, as they live in the slime of the river-bed. οἳ κατὰ δίνας is like 11.535, 20.500 αἳ περὶ δίφρον.

354 κυβίστων: 'one could not find a more expressive word' (bT). The alliteration of *kappa* in this verse underscores the verb.

355 πολυμήτιος Ἡφαίστοιο: this is the only place in Homer where πολύμητις is used not of Odysseus, and in the nominative (18× *Il.*, 68× *Od.*). Cf. 367 Ἡφαίστοιο βίηφι πολύφρονος, *Od.* 8.297, 8.327 πολύφρονος Ἡφαίστοιο; *Il.* 1.571 Ἥφαιστος κλυτοτέχνης, 1.608 etc. Ἥφαιστος … ἰδυίῃσι πραπίδεσσι. The four-word verse effectively closes this part of the description. For its structure cf. 363.

356 καίετο δ' ἲς ποταμοῖο: this is not exactly a periphrastic use of ἲς, as the river's strength is really being burned away. Cf. 23.720 κρατερὴ δ' ἔχεν ἲς Ὀδυσῆος, and ἲς ἀνέμου -οιο 2× *Il.*, 3× *Od.* The digamma of ἲς is usually observed (at least 2× *Il.*, 8× *Od.*), but cf. 17.739 for another neglect (Chantraine, *GH* 1 143).

357 The verb ἀντιφερίζειν recurs at 488. At 411 ἰσοφαρίζεις/ἀντιφερίζεις are variants (and at 357 ἰσοφερίζειν occurs in some MSS). Cf. ἀντιφέρεσθαι 1.589, 21.482, *Od.* 16.238.

358 σοί γ' … φλεγέθοντι: 'against you, blazing thus with fire'.

359–60 Skamandros seems to say 'as long as you stop, then for all I care, he can drive the Trojans out straight away, and put an end to Troy'. For the river-god's indifference to Troy's fate cf. 373–6. The possibility that the Trojans may desert the city is envisaged at 22.381–4. τί μοι ... ἀρωγῆς; means 'What (share) do I have in combat and aid?'

361 φῆ occurs only here in Homer for 'he spoke', instead of ἦ. ἀνὰ δ' ἔφλυε ('bubbled up') is a vivid expression which anticipates the simile. The compound occurs only here and in a papyrus fragment of prose, the simple verb first in Aeschylus.

362–5 Another simile from daily life, and again one of Homer's more unusual comparisons. It describes lard being melted in a cooking pot. Cf. *Od.* 12.237–8 (Kharubdis compared to a boiling cauldron); 20.25–30 (Odysseus tossing like a roasting paunch full of fat and blood). For the unusual language and sound-effects see on 363–4.

362 ὡς δὲ λέβης ... πυρὶ πολλῷ: cf. *Od.* 12.237 λέβης ὡς ἐν πυρὶ πολλῷ. ζεῖ could originally have been ζέει; cf. 11.554 τρεῖ.

363 μέλδειν does not occur again until Hellenistic poetry, and ἀπαλοτρεφής only in a second-century A.D. verse inscription. μέλδειν (cf. 'melt'; ἀμαλδύνω?) was ousted in common Greek by τήκειν. There was a protracted debate in antiquity about the reading of the first two words of this verse, and κνίσην μελδόμενος represents the view of Aristarchus (Arn/A) and others. μελδόμενος is then middle, agreeing with λέβης. Among several alternatives κνίση μελδομένου (Crates and others) is possible. It was suggested in antiquity that the original reading might have been ΜΕΛΔΟΜΕΝΟ, i.e. μελδομένου, and that the transcribers to the Ionic script altered this to μελδόμενος. For this theory cf. Chantraine, *GH* I 5ff. and R. Janko in vol. IV, Introduction, pp. 34–7.

This is an impressive four-word verse, with opening spondaic word followed by three polysyllabic words, in which the repeated nasals, liquids and sibilants may suggest the sizzling of fat in the cauldron. If so, Aristarchus' reading has a further advantage thereby. The stately character of the verse contrasts piquantly with its homely subject.

364 ἀμβολάδην ('bubbling up') again occurs only here and at *HyHerm* 426 in early epic. Once more, note the effect of the liquid and nasals, in contrast to the dry, crackling consonants of ὑπὸ δὲ ξύλα κάγκανα κεῖται. κάγκανος occurs only here in *Il.*; cf. ξύλα κάγκανα *Od.* 18.308, κάγκανα κᾶλα *HyHerm* 112.

365 πυρὶ φλέγετο, ζέε δ' ὕδωρ: an awkward, uneven rhythm for the verse-ending, describing the water's turmoil. ζέε picks up ζεῖ (362), as often in the similes, and the whole verse recapitulates 361, rounding off the passage.

366–7 οὐδ' ἔθελε προρέειν means 'he had no mind to flow on' (Leaf). For τεῖρε ... πολύφρονος cf. 355. In 367 Leaf takes βίηφι as a genitive (cf. 295), but one could take ἀϋτμή on its own, and Ἡφαίστοιο βίηφι as 'through the might of Hephaistos'.

368–76 The river's appeal to Hephaistos has no effect, and he makes an even more urgent protest to Here.

368 Cf. *Od.* 22.311 etc. καί μιν λισσόμενος ἔπεα πτερόεντα προσηύδα.

369 ἐμὸν ῥόον ἔχραε κήδειν probably means 'has attacked my stream, so as to vex it'. Cf. *Od.* 21.68–9 οἳ τόδε δῶμα | ἔχραετ' ἐσθιέμεν καὶ πινέμεν.

370 ἐξ ἄλλων: i.e. me above all other allies of Troy. For οὐ ... αἴτιός εἰμι cf. 19.86 ἐγὼ δ' οὐκ αἴτιός εἰμι ...

372 ἐγὼν ἀποπαύσομαι: pap. 12 (3rd cent. B.C.) reads ἐγὼ λήξω (or λήγω) μένος, thus avoiding repetition with 373, but such repetition with variation is a common device of emphasis.

373–6 Here, as elsewhere in the poem, Homer looks forward beyond the bounds of his work, to Troy's destruction. Skamandros' defeat has eliminated a major defender of the city (cf. Whitman, *HHT* 272). This kind of bargaining reminds us of the dreadful pact struck between Zeus and Here at 4.25–67, and the scene between Zeus and Poseidon at 7.443–64 (cf. 12.10–35).

374–6 These verses repeat 20.315–17 (see comment). There, however, the oath was sworn by the gods who were Troy's worst enemies. The majority of MSS have δαιομένη, δαίωσι at 20.317 (actually read by Leaf there, but unlikely to be right), whereas this occurs in a minority at 21.376. δάηται | καιομένη, καίωσι δ' is again emphatic repetition.

377–82 This echoes 328–42 at the beginning of the episode (330 = 378, 331 ~ 379, 342 ~ 381), thus rounding it off effectively. Here had anticipated this moment already (340–1).

377–8 At 377 pap. 12 gives as variants θεὰ λευκώλενος Ἥρη and βοῶπις πότνια Ἥρη, and at 378 it offers two alternative verses: αὐτίκα μειλιχίοισι προσηύδα φαίδιμον υἱόν (cf. 6.214; 6.144, 21.97), and αὐτίκ' ἄρ'] Ἥφαιστον προσεφώνει σπ[ερχομένη περ.

379 τέκνον ἀγακλεές: 'the epithet is appropriate to Hephaistos' victory' (bT). Cf. 17.716 ἀγακλεὲς ὦ Μενέλαε, and ἀγακλῆος of heroes at 16.738, 23.529 (16.571 Ἀγακλῆος).

379–80 οὐ γὰρ ἔοικεν ... στυφελίζειν: cf. Skamandros' impatient question at 360. This view is repeated with greater eloquence by Apollo at 462–7, and the same theme has occurred at 1.573–6 and 8.427–31. Hephaistos' intervention was necessary, but it is nevertheless undignified for him 'to jostle (στυφελίζειν) an immortal god in this way for the sake of mortals'. ἀθάνατον θεὸν ... βροτῶν are in contrast as often.

382 'And backward rolled the wave along the lovely streams': a quiet close to this violent scene. κατασεύεσθαι recurs only in late epic (Quintus of

Smyrna 4.270, Nonnus, *D.* 5.353). Pap. 12 apparently read κατέσχετο, and
this recurs in a few MSS; κατέσσυτο may have been found obscure. After
382 it adds the verse κὰρ ῥόον, ᾗ τὸ πάροιθεν ἵει καλλίρροον ὕδωρ.

*383–513 The other gods fight. Ares attacks Athene, who knocks him out with a stone.
Aphrodite rescues him, but Athene, encouraged by Here, knocks her flat as well.
Poseidon invites Apollo to fight, reminding him of Laomedon's treachery to them, but
Apollo declines. Artemis reproaches him, and Here abuses her and boxes her ears.
Hermes refuses to fight Leto. Artemis goes to Zeus and complains about Here's treatment
of her*

This episode picks up and at the same time rounds off those passages at
20.33–40 and 67–74 where the gods are paired against each other, thereby
providing a frame to the intervening scenes. Here Aphrodite, mentioned at
20.40, is introduced as an extra victim of Athene, together with Ares.
That association reminds us of book 5, where Diomedes wounds both with
Athene's help (311–430, 793–909). Artemis' complaint to Zeus also resembles 5.370–415, where Aphrodite goes to her mother Dione for consolation,
and 5.868–87, where Ares complains to Zeus.

The opening section of the Theomachy (20.1–74) suggested a conflict on
the cosmic scale, affecting all levels of the universe (especially 56–66): it
won the praise of Longinus for its sublimity (9.6). The episode in book 21
has seemed to many a terrible anticlimax after this grandiose prologue, and
all the more so after the battle with the River. 'The Theomachy is one of
the very few passages in the *Iliad* which can be pronounced poetically bad',
declared Leaf categorically (Introduction to book 21).

From one point of view the episode is the culmination of the process
earlier in the Book whereby the gods were drawn progressively further into
the conflict. In a more significant way, however, it provides an essential
respite, between the intense scenes preceding it and the real climax of
Akhilleus' combat with Hektor (to which 520–611 are simply the prelude).
One can, if one wishes, speak here of 'comic relief', as with the divine scenes
in books 5 and 14, and certainly the contrast between the frivolity of the
gods' squabbles here and the deadly earnest of the mortal conflicts could
hardly be more acute. But more important functions of this episode can be
defined: it emphasizes the vast gulf between mortal and immortal concerns, and throws into even greater relief the tragedy of events on earth
(cf. Griffin, *HLD*, esp. 179–204; Reinhardt, *IuD* 446–50). It is surely also
a significant point that this episode symbolizes the almost total collapse of
the pro-Trojan forces in heaven, and so foreshadows Troy's fall (cf. 428–
33, 516–17, 522–5, 583–9). Only Apollo remains free to act, in order to
postpone the time of doom for the city.

The structure of the episode is worth attention:

383–90   Herē checks Hephaistos. Zeus laughs at the sight of the other gods fighting
391–415   Ares defeated by Athene   ⎱ *(comic)*
416–34   Aphrodite knocked out by Athene ⎰
435–69   Apollo refuses to fight Poseidon *(serious)*
470–96   Artemis beaten by Here   ⎱ *(comic)*
497–504   Hermes refuses to fight Leto ⎰
505–15   Artemis complains to Zeus about Here, and he laughs at the sight of her.

The laughter of Zeus on Olumpos frames the whole episode. In 391–434 the Ares and Aphrodite scenes are clearly parallel. The Aphrodite scene is also echoed by the Artemis one, but this is contrasted with the important exchange between Apollo and Poseidon, which forms the central panel of the episode (see on 435–69), and this in turn makes a good contrast with the lighter scene in which Hermes declines to fight with Leto. Thus all the episodes in the conflict are linked in a series of interlocking pairs.

383–4 These transitional verses seem to add little to what has already been said.

385 ἔρις ... βεβριθυῖα: 'momentous conflict'. Cf. the metaphorical use of βρίθειν to mean 'be preponderant', 'be mighty', at 12.346 etc.

386 δίχα ... ἄητο ('blew in different directions' like contrary winds): an appropriate expression for θυμός, if this originally refers to a 'breath-spirit'. This may well be an echo of 20.32, where the gods go to war, δίχα θυμὸν ἔχοντες.

387–8 A 'tricolon crescendo' to describe the cosmic sound effects. Note the staccato rhythm of the four opening dactyls in 387, and the heavy spondaic ending with final monosyllable. Verse 387 resembles 9, and here too in μεγάλῳ πατάγῳ βράχε δ' εὐρεῖα χθών sound echoes sense. Cf. the grandiose sound effects in the prologue to the Theomachy, at 20.47–53 and 20.56–66. For πατάγῳ most MSS have the commoner but less vivid word ὁμάδῳ, but two papyri support πατάγῳ.

388 ἀμφὶ δὲ σάλπιγξεν μέγας οὐρανός: the scholia (A and schol. Ge) note the reference to a trumpet here, whose use the poet knows but does not attribute to heroic times (cf. 18.219n.). The verb does not recur before Xenophon. The 'trumpeting heaven' announces the start of battle (so bT). Cf. 17.424–5 σιδήρειος δ' ὀρυμαγδὸς | χάλκεον οὐρανὸν ἷκε ... This is a variation on the typical theme of the sound effects which signal the opening of a major combat: cf. especially 11.45–6 (thunder by Here and Athene for Agamemnon), and 2.465–6, 2.781–5, etc. (Scheibner, *Aufbau* 70).

This verse was famous and often quoted in antiquity. Critics were divided between those who admired the metaphor and those who found it out of place. Cf. Demetrius, *On Style* 83 (disapproving: it produces μικροπρέπεια); Pliny, *Ep.* 9.26.6 (we must consider carefully whether such expressions are *incredibilia* ... *et inania*, or *magnifica caelestia*); [Longinus] 9.6 (quoting 388 with 20.61–5); schol. bT (general approval of appropriateness, novelty and striking effect); Aristides Quintilianus 2.9 (84) pp. 52.3 J. (at first sight inappropriate, but made effective by the way it is used); Philostr. *Her.* 2.19 p. 162.32 K. (along with the rest of the Theomachy praised for its dramatic effect but criticized theologically); Hermog. *Id.* 2.4 (318) p. 334.25 R. (as an example of poetic licence, with *Il.* 5.749, 13.29); Eust. 1242.27 (mixed criticism and approval). Cf. W. Bühler, *Beiträge zur Erklärung der Schrift vom Erhabenen* (Göttingen 1964) 26ff., Russell on [Longinus] 9.6.

388–90 For the scansion ἅιε see on 10.532. ἅϊε δὲ Ζεὺς ... ξυνίοντας: these verses recall 20.22–3, where Zeus announces that he will remain seated on Olumpos, taking pleasure in the spectacle of the battle. Zeus's delight in the gods' quarrels shocked later critics. Aristotle (quoted by schol. Ge on 21.390) discussed the apparent contradiction between this and 5.890–1, where Zeus hates Ares because of his perpetual love of strife. Chamaeleon (fr. 18 Wehrli) found Zeus's apparent malevolence inexplicable. Other commentators compared *Od.* 8.78, where Agamemnon rejoices at the quarrel of Odysseus and Akhilleus, and Menander (fr. 784 K.), where someone says that conflict between members of his household helps to keep the family together! Cf. also Phld. *Hom.* col. 10.13, p. 39 ed. Olivieri.

One defence offered was that Zeus was pleased because the gods were contending περὶ ἀρετῆς and yet without risk (T 21.389, schol. Ge 21.390). But there is not much sign of ἀρετή in what follows (cf. Griffin, *HLD* 183). It is the lack of risk which is perhaps the point: 'Zeus appears to have a just appreciation of the whole combat as a parody of serious fighting. It is only here and in 508 that Homer's Zeus ever goes beyond a smile, like the Zeus of the hymn to Hermes (389), who "laughs aloud" at the tricks of his naughty son' (Leaf on 390).

391–2 The god of war begins the battle (cf. 20.38 where he leads the pro-Trojan gods), and attacks the leading warrior-goddess. Cf. 20.133–55, where Poseidon advises Here to keep out of the battle, unless Ares or Apollo intervenes (138), and the gods then 'stand off'.

392 ῥινοτόρος: 'hide-piercing', i.e. 'shield-piercing', an unusual epithet, only here in Homer. Cf. Hes. *Th.* 934 (of Ares) and Nonnus. Here Ares does strike Athene's aegis (400–1).

394–9 Ares reveals his coarse character by his rudeness, and his vindictiveness by referring to his earlier defeat, which he is not ashamed to mention (cf. bT 396).

394–5 Cf. Ares' complaint about Athene at 5.875–6, and for the wording cf. 7.24–5 (Apollo to Athene).

394 κυνάμυια: only here and at 421 in Homer; cf. Ath. 126A, 157A. The variant κυνόμυια is found in later Greek (*LXX*, *AP* etc.), but κυνάμυια is probably original, replacing *κυα-μυια: cf. Chantraine, *Dict.* s.v.

'Dog-fly' is splendidly abusive, suggesting both the proverbial shamelessness of the dog and the recklessness (θάρσος) of the fly. If it actually refers to a tick, then it also suggests a love of blood (αἱμοπότις ὅ ἐστι κρότων, T). At 17.570–3 Athene inspires μυίης θάρσος in Menelaos.

395 ἄητον: only here in Homer, but connected in antiquity with ἀΐητον at 18.410 (πέλωρ). Aeschylus seems to have used the word to mean 'great' (fr. 3 N.), but numerous other explanations were offered. Modern philology has not progressed much further. Risch, in *LfgrE* s.v., supports a connection with ἄημι, which was one ancient view. See also on 18.410.

396 ἦ οὐ μέμνῃ ὅτε . . . : so also 15.18 (Zeus to Here), 20.188. The episode occurred at 5.855–8, and this reference marks the link between these two episodes, which seem to offset each other in the poem's structure (cf. Introduction, 'Structure').

395–6 ἀνῆκεν . . . ἀνῆκας: this kind of repetition does not seem to have troubled the epic poets. Two papyri give separate variants in both verses: 395 ἀνώγει, 396 Τυδείδη Διομήδει ἄνωγας.

397 πανόψιον ἔγχος: the epithet occurs only here and in Nonnus (*D.* 14.169). Apparently it means 'fully visible', in contrast to Athene who was invisible at 5.844–5. On παν- compounds see 22.490n. Antimachus and pap. 12 read ὑπονόσφιον, which should mean 'surreptitious' (cf. νοσφίδιος), although the scholia were puzzled as to the sense (T 397, Eust. 1243.40). It is presumably a conjecture, to avoid the difficulty of Athene's invisibility: cf. West, *Ptolemaic Papyri* 157.

398 Cf. 5.858 διὰ δὲ χρόα καλὸν ἔδαψεν, which this echoes.

399 ὅσσα ἔοργας: this is the reading of a late papyrus and one MS, omitting μ' (which ignores the digamma). Cf. however 22.347 οἷα μ' ἔοργας, 3.351, *Od.* 22.318.

440–1 αἰγίδα: this is read by some MSS, whereas pap. 12 and the majority have ἀσπίδα, but θυσσανόεσσαν is only used as an epithet with αἰγίδα (4× *Il.*). For the aegis see on 2.446–51, 15.18–31, 308–11. It is wielded by Zeus himself at 4.167, 17.593, but more often by Athene (2.447, 5.738, 18.204, *Od.* 22.297). For σμερδαλέην, ἥν etc., cf. 2.309, 20.65.

402 Pap. 12 omits this verse, which is similar to 5.844 and 15.745. It is dispensable, but probably genuine.

403–4 These verses closely resemble 7.264–5 (Hektor versus Aias) ἀλλ' ἀναχασσάμενος . . . μέγαν τε. For the formular phrase χειρὶ παχείῃ there was a variant Πάλλας Ἀθήνη, clearly because the epithet was felt to be unsuitable to the goddess, as the Geneva scholiast (on 424) indicates. Cf. similarly *Od.* 21.6 χειρὶ παχείη, applied to Penelope, where there was a variant χερσὶ φίλησιν.

405 Cf. 12.421–4 (a boundary-dispute in simile), and for a mark set up by ἄνδρες πρότεροι cf. 23.332.

406–11 These six verses form an unusual succession whose first five feet are all dactyls, and the initial three trochaic word-breaks in 407 produce a markedly bumpy rhythm, as at 235, 23.116, 23.263, *Od.* 11.598, etc.: cf. Kirk, *YCS* 20 (1966) 95ff.

407–9 ἑπτὰ δ' ἐπέσχε πέλεθρα πεσών resembles *Od.* 11.577, where Tituos ἐπ' ἐννέα κεῖτο πέλεθρα. A π(έ)λεθρον was either 100 feet long or 10,000 square feet (cf. 23.164n.). At 5.859–61 the wounded Ares shouts as loud as nine or ten thousand warriors, a similar motif. The compound ἀμφαραβεῖν occurs only here; cf. Hes. *Aspis* 64 ἀμφαράβιζον. Verse 409 = 16.829 (ἐπευχόμενος).

410 νηπύτι': for this word, which occurs 8× in books 20–1, see comment on 13.292, the only other instance in the poem. It does not occur in the *Odyssey*. The vocative is used again at 441, 474 and 585. πώ περ occurs only here in Homer, and is replaced in pap. 12 by the commoner πώ ποτ'.

411 ἰσοφαρίζεις: ἀντιφερίζεις, read by the papyrus and most MSS and mentioned as a variant by A, would be possible here. Cf. 487–8 ὄφρ' ἐῢ εἰδῇς | ὅσσον φερτέρη εἴμ', ὅτι μοι μένος ἀντιφερίζεις. See also on 357. Again the poet has shown an unusual fondness for one or both of these words in this Book (and cf. 482 μένος ἀντιφέρεσθαι).

412–14 Cf. 5.832–4 (with comment), where Athene says that Ares has broken his promise to her and Here that he would help the Greeks against the Trojans, another example of cross-reference. For τῆς μητρὸς ἐρινύας ἐξαποτίνοις cf. *Od.* 11.279–80, where Oidipous' μητρὸς ἐρινύες cause him many troubles after her death, and *Il.* 9.566–72, *Od.* 2.135 for a mother's invocation of an ἐρινύς or ἐρινύες. For the article τῆς cf. Chantraine, *GH* II 164. The compound ἐξαποτίνειν occurs only here and in the Sibylline Oracles. 'You would pay back in full your mother's Erinyes' resembles Hes. *Th.* 472 τείσαιτο δ' ἐρινῦς πατρὸς ἑοῖο.

Pap. 12 offers καὶ μητρὸς ... ἂψ ἀποτίνοις, but also what looks like ἑῆς above καί. This may be a corruption of ἧς, which had already been conjectured by Brugmann and could possibly be original: cf. West, *Ptolemaic Papyri* 159–60, Chantraine, *GH* I 273–4.

415 πάλιν τρέπεν ὄσσε φαεινώ: probably a gesture of aversion (see comment on 3.427).

416 Cf. 5.353 where Iris leads the wounded Aphrodite away from the battle. The Separatists took this as evidence that the *Iliad* and the *Odyssey* were by different poets, because in *Odyssey* 8 Aphrodite is married to

Hephaistos, whereas here they assumed that Aphrodite was openly living with Ares. The answer given to this was that the times referred to in each case were different (Arn/A). They are of course also brother and sister, and Ares lends Aphrodite his chariot after her wounding at 5.355–63. The variant reading φιλομμείδης Ἀφροδίτη is a formular doublet (see on 3.424). φιλομμείδης would have been too cheerful in this context.

417 μόγις δ' ἐσαγείρετο θυμόν: Aristarchus and some MSS prefer the imperfect here and at 15.240 (νεὸν δ' ἐσαγείρετο θυμόν), whereas the vulgate reading is ἐσαγείρατο in both cases. At 15.240 the aorist is better (see comment), but here there is some advantage in the imperfect, with its conative force.

418–34 Behind this scene of enmity between Here, Athene and Aphrodite, as with 5.418–25, Reinhardt sees the story of the Judgement of Paris (*Tradition und Geist*, Göttingen 1960, 27–8). See on 24.23–30.

418–20 Verse 418 ~ 5.711, 419–20 = 5.713–14, again in the context of conflict with Ares, when Here is urging Athene to intervene.

420–2 Here's speech is brief and impatient. Cf. especially the peremptory two final words of 422. καὶ δὴ αὖθ' means 'there she goes again . . .' (as in book 5). This is rather like the common use of δηὖτε in archaic Greek lyric poetry (cf. B. Snell, *The Discovery of the Mind*, Berkeley 1953, 57–8). For ἡ κυνάμυια cf. 394. The article is derogatory here (cf. Chantraine, *GH* II 163–4), and the echo of 394 suggests that Here is returning Ares' insult.

424–5 For ἐπιεισαμένη cf. 11.367, 20.454 ἐπιείσομαι, and on 21.335. The variant ἐπερεισαμένη (Demetrius Ixion) would be possible. The runover word ἤλασε is heavily emphatic.

426 κεῖντο ἐπὶ χθονί: the variant ποτὶ χθονί in some MSS would avoid the hiatus, but ἐπί is better. The variants κεῖτο ἐπί (some MSS) and θεῖνε ποτί (pap. 12) indicate considerable uncertainty about the reading here. It is possible that the original form was κείατ' ἐπί, as κεῖντο is unusual in Homer (only *Od.* 6.19). Cf. Chantraine, *GH* I 476; West, *Ptolemaic Papyri* 160. The idea of Ares and Aphrodite laid out together is highly comic.

427–33 Athene's speech resembles those of human warriors boasting over their enemies. For 427 cf. 121, whereas for the variant προσηύδα cf. 409 (with οἱ). The moralizing 428–9 resemble *Od.* 1.47 ὡς ἀπόλοιτο καὶ ἄλλος ὅτις τοιαῦτά γε ῥέζοι (Athene speaking). For πάντες ὅσοι Τρώεσσιν ἀρωγοί cf. 371. The phrase Ἀργείοισι . . . θωρηκτῇσιν occurs only here. Cf. 12.317, 15.689 etc. Λυκίων/Τρώων (πύκα) θωρηκτάων. Pap. 12 reads κυδα[λίμοισιν, a commoner expression and one which also eliminates the spondaic ending: cf. West, *Ptolemaic Papyri* 46–7, 160.

430–1 Verse 430 is similar to 589 ὧδ' ἔκπαγλος ἐὼν καὶ θαρσαλέος πολεμιστής. τλήμονες means 'bold', 'reckless'. For 431 ἐμῷ μένει ἀντιόωσα cf. 151 = 6.127.

433 This verse resembles 2.133, 4.33, etc.

434 = 1.595 (cf. 14.222). This is omitted by some MSS, and may be a later addition. The variant reading ὡς ἔφαθ', ἡ δ' ἐγέλασσε occurs nowhere else.

435–69 Poseidon's invitation to Apollo to fight has been thought to contradict his attitude at 20.138–43, where he advises Here that they should not intervene unless Ares or Apollo also interferes (cf. Leaf). But 436–7 actually seem to echo this passage (ἀρξάντων ἑτέρων ~ 20.138 εἰ δέ κ' Ἄρης ἄρχωσι μάχης ἢ Φοῖβος Ἀπόλλων), and Ares *has* in fact been involved in the fighting. Poseidon's suggestion that Apollo should attack first (439 ἄρχε...) also looks like an echo of his previous reluctance to start things off.

Although Poseidon's speech is provocative, this exchange with Apollo makes an effective contrast with the coarser scenes before and after. Poseidon treats the need to fight primarily as a matter of honour, in the manner of heroic duels. Apollo's reply deflates this notion: to fight in this way over mortals is beneath the dignity of gods. This is the central scene of the Theomachy, and it makes a deeply serious point (cf. Scheibner, *Aufbau* 102ff.).

437 ἀμαχητί: only here in Homer; cf. Hdt. 1.174, etc.

439–40 Cf. 13.355, 15.166 (Zeus older than Poseidon), and for similar expressions 14.112, 19.219, 23.587–8.

441–57 The service of Poseidon and Apollo to Laomedon was alluded to briefly at 7.452–3, where Poseidon says that they *both* built the Trojan wall (hardly a serious contradiction, although see on 7.443–64 for other doubts about that passage). The poet gives no reason for this period of service by the two gods: the scholia suggest either that it was a punishment for rebellion against Zeus (comparing 1.400, with Zenodotus' substitution of Apollo for Athene in that verse), or else that they wanted to test Laomedon (cf. *Od.* 17.485–7). The second reason was given by Hellanicus (*FGH* 4.26a; cf. also Apollodorus, *Bibl.* 2.5.9 and Frazer's note). The story, as told later, continued with the gods' revenge: Apollo sent a plague, and Poseidon the sea-monster referred to at 20.145–8 (cf. also 5.638–51). As usual, the poet alludes to such past events in piecemeal fashion, as and when it is convenient for him to do so.

Apollodorus pointed out the appropriateness of the two divine tasks, Poseidon being worshipped as ἀσφάλιος καὶ θεμελιοῦχος, and Apollo as νόμιος (*FGH* 244.96). A similar story was that of Apollo's service as Admetos' herdsman (see on 2.766). Laomedon's behaviour also reminds one of the imprisonment of Ares by Otos and Ephialtes (5.385–91). On these stories of the binding or imprisonment of gods see K. Meuli, *Gesammelte Schriften* (Basel 1975) II 1035–81, 'Die gefesselten Götter'.

444–5 πὰρ Διὸς ἐλθόντες suggests that they were ordered by Zeus to do this service, for whatever reason. θητεύσαμεν occurs only here in *Il.*; for the verb and related noun θής cf. *Od.* 4.644, 11.489, 18.357–8, and West on Hes. *Erga* 602. ῥητός is also found only here in Homer; cf. Hes. *Erga* 4 ('spoken of'), and in the sense 'specified' (as here) Hdt. 1.77 etc. For the phrase cf. *HyDem* 173 ἐπ' ἀπείρονι μισθῷ.

446–7 Aridices read ἤτοι μὲν γὰρ ἐγὼ πόλεως, and Aristophanes πόλει for πόλιν. For ἄρρηκτος cf. 14.56, 14.68 (of the wall round the Greek camp).

448 The formula εἰλίποδας ἕλικας βοῦς was used at 9.466 (= 23.166), and occurs 3× *Od.* For βουκολέεσκες cf. 5.313 etc.

449 Cf. 2.821, 11.105 Ἴδης ἐν κνημοῖσι, 22.171 Ἴδης ἐν κορυφῇσι πολυπτύχου; more often πολυπίδακος Ἴδης (5× *Il.*); cf. also 11.183 Ἴδης ἐν κορυφῇσι ... πιδηέσσης.

450–2 μισθοῖο τέλος means 'the due time of payment'. The epithet πολυγηθέες does not occur elsewhere in Homer (cf. Hesiod etc.). The phrase πολυγηθέες ὧραι may have a general significance (cf. Leaf), but in this context it surely suggests relief at the end of the year's labour. νῶϊ βιήσατο μισθὸν ἅπαντα means 'robbed us of all our wage', and the verb is used only here with a double accusative; cf. Hor. *C.* 3.3.21–2 *destituit deos | mercede pacta Laomedon* (as one of the reasons for the hostility of Juno and Minerva to Troy). For ἔκπαγλος cf. 589 ὥδ' ἔκπαγλος ἐών ..., and see on 1.145–6, 3.415. The structure and sound effects of this line suggest a strong, autocratic ruler: Λαομέδων | ἔκπαγλος | ἀπειλήσας δ' | ἀπέπεμπε.

453–5 Such threats are commoner in the *Odyssey*: 18.84–7, 18.115–16, 20.382–3, 21.307–9. Here 453–7 expand the theme of 450–2. In 453 the variant σοί for σύν can hardly be right, as there seems to be no reason why Apollo's punishment should be different from Poseidon's.

454 περάαν νήσων ἐπὶ τηλεδαπάων: cf. 22.45 περνὰς νήσων ἐπὶ τηλεδαπάων. In both verses there was a variant θηλυτεράων in antiquity (in the 'city' texts at 454), taken by some scholars to mean 'fertile' (T 22.45; cf. Call. fr. 548).

455 ἀπολέψεμεν was Aristarchus' reading, and it is found in a few of our MSS, the rest having ἀποκόψεμεν, ἀποκόψειν or ἀποκόπτειν. It means 'peel off' (cf. 1.236 περὶ γάρ ῥά ἑ χαλκὸς ἔλεψε), a vivid and crude metaphor. ἀπολέπειν occurs nowhere else in early epic, and is later used in comedy: cf. Epich. 158, Ar. *Av.* 673, E. *Cyc.* 237 (conjectured by Ruhnken). In *Cyclops* (if this is the right reading) the word also comes in a passage threatening various dire forms of punishment.

456 The phase κεκοτηότι θυμῷ occurs only here in *Il.*; cf. *Od.* 9.501 ἄψορρον προσέφην κεκοτηότι θυμῷ, and 19.71, 22.477.

458–60 μεθ' ἡμέων: μετά with genitive is rare in Homer and early poetry (cf. Chantraine, *GH* II 119–20: probably only 3× *Il.*, 2× *Od.*). πειρᾷ is also unusual (from *πειράεαι?), recurring at 24.390, 24.433; cf. Chantraine, *GH* I 57, and see on 14.198–9. For Τρῶες ὑπερφίαλοι cf. 13.621. πρόχνυ here and at *Od.* 14.69 (with ὀλέσθαι) must mean 'utterly'. Cf. also *Il.* 9.570 where it is used with καθεζομένη: there it is thought to have the original sense of 'on one's knees' (Chantraine, *Dict.* s.v. γόνυ). For σὺν παισὶ καὶ αἰδοίης ἀλόχοισι cf. *HyAp* 148 αὐτοῖς σὺν παίδεσσι καὶ αἰδοίης ἀλόχοισιν, *Il.* 6.250 αἰδοίης ἀλόχοισιν.

461 = 15.253. ἄναξ ἑκάεργος Ἀπόλλων (2× *Il.*, 1× *Od.*) is a slightly less common formula than the metrically equivalent ἄναξ Διὸς υἱὸς Ἀπόλλων (4× *Il.*, 1× *Od.*), but was regarded by Parry as 'undoubtedly the older' (*MHV* 178). It gains in popularity in the Hymns (6× *HyAp*, *HyHerm*) over its rival (4× *HyAp*, *HyHerm*). Διὸς υἱός is actually a variant reading both here and at 15.253; see on that verse.

462 σαόφρονα: only here in *Il.*; cf. *Od.* 4.158, and σαοφροσύνη, *Od.* 23.13, 23.30. Apollo *par excellence* displays this quality of σωφροσύνη. There are good remarks on this by W. F. Otto, *The Homeric Gods* (London 1954) 66, *à propos* of this scene.

464–6 Cf. 6.142 εἰ δέ τίς ἐσσι βροτῶν οἳ ἀρούρης καρπὸν ἔδουσιν ... and 146–9 οἵη περ φύλλων γενεή, τοίη δὲ καὶ ἀνδρῶν, etc. This coincidence shows that the two passages must be related, and they are quoted together by Plutarch (*Mor.* 104E–F). Leaf called the lines in book 21 'an obvious reminiscence of the famous simile' in book 6. He also thought the phrase ἀρούρης καρπὸν ἔδοντες 'totally incongruous', and φύλλοισιν ἐοικότες ... ζαφλεγέες a 'ludicrous confusion of metaphor'; and concluded that 'it is hard to believe that any poet could have written such a medley except in deliberate parody'. This is a totally unfair verdict. ζαφλεγέες is a strong and effective word to describe men in the fullness of their prime, contrasting with φθινύθουσιν which suggests a 'waning' light, as well as any kind of decaying life. This set of images overlaps with the brief comparison to leaves in an unusual but not inappropriate way. ἀρούρης καρπὸν ἔδοντες is also a singular phrase, only paralleled in Homer in the related passage at 6.142. Cf. ἐπὶ χθονὶ σῖτον ἔδοντες (3× *Od.*). It emphasizes the earthbound, temporal character of men, as compared with the gods (οὐ γὰρ σῖτον ἔδουσ᾽ ... 5.341).

The context here is also related to that in book 6. There Diomedes says that if Glaukos is a god he would not fight him, but if mortal he will, and Glaukos replies, comparing men's γενεή to that of leaves. In book 21 one god refuses to fight another for the sake of mortals.

For ζαφλεγέες τελέθουσιν cf. 12.347 = 360 ζαχρηεῖς τελέθουσιν. ζαφλεγής occurs only here in Homer, and nowhere later except *HyHom* 8.8 (probably by Proclus: cf. M. L. West, *CQ* 20 (1970) 300–4), an oracle quoted by Eusebius (*PE* 3.15), and Nonnus (*D.* 2.26). In 466 ἀκήριοι means 'spirit-less', 'lifeless' (cf. 5.812, 7.100 etc.). In 467 αὐτοί is 'on their own'.

468–9 The reason given by the poet for Apollo's withdrawal ironically suggests that Apollo's speech was a discreet way of avoiding an unequal contest. In 469 the long word πατροκασιγνήτοιο, filling the first hemistich, suggests the dignity of Poseidon as Apollo's uncle. Cf. the very similar context of *Od.* 6.329–30 (Athene) αἴδετο γάρ ῥα | πατροκασίγνητον, echoed at 13.341–2 ἀλλά τοι οὐκ ἐθέλησα Ποσειδάωνι μάχεσθαι | πατροκασιγνήτῳ, and *HyDem* 31 (with Richardson's comments). μιγήμεναι ἐν παλάμῃσι is a rather unusual phrase. Cf. 13.286 μιγήμεναι ἐν δαῒ λυγρῇ, and ἐν παλάμῃσι(ν) (10× *Il.*).

470–513 With Artemis' intervention we return to a more petty level.

470 πότνια θηρῶν: this title of Artemis, so often used by modern scholars, only occurs here in Homer. It may appear later at *Supplementum Hellenisticum* (edd. Lloyd-Jones and Parsons) 953.14. The scholia compare Anacreon, *PMG* 348.3 δέσποιν' Ἄρτεμι θηρῶν.

471 Aristarchus athetized this verse as unnecessary (Arn/A). There is nothing objectionable about it, but equally nothing to prove that it is not an addition. Elsewhere in Homer the epithet ἀγρότερος is used as a synonym for ἄγριος, of wild animals (e.g. 486). But it is quite a common title of Artemis in later literature and cult (cf. *RE* s.v. Agrotera).

473–4 μέλεον ... εὖχος means 'an empty vaunt', i.e. one which cost him no effort. But the idea of futility is picked up by ἀνεμώλιον αὔτως in 474. For ἀνεμώλιον cf. 5.216 ἀνεμώλια, of a bow and arrows.

475–7 These verses were athetized on the grounds that they conflict with Apollo's attitude at 468–9, and because Apollo is not a god of war (Arn/A). These reasons do not seem strong enough for rejecting the verses, which are probably an *'ad hoc* invention' (cf. Willcock, *HSCP* 81 (1977) 49–50). For 475–6 cf. 1.396–7 πολλάκι γάρ σεο πατρὸς ἐνὶ μεγάροισιν ἄκουσα | εὐχομένης ..., and 20.83–5, where Aineias boasts in his cups that he will fight (ἐναντίβιον πολεμίξειν) Akhilleus. Verse 477 is an effective four-word one.

480 Cf. 2.277 νεικείειν βασιλῆας ὀνειδείοις ἐπέεσσιν. This verse is omitted by two papyri and most MSS, and was not in Aristarchus' texts, since the scholia and Eustathius understand προσέφη with 479. It may well be an addition. For the construction ἀπὸ κοινοῦ cf. 11.56 etc. and Lehrs, *De Aristarchi studiis* 338–9.

481 κύον ἀδεές is used of Athene at 8.423; see on 1.225, 3.180, 22.345.

482–4 χαλεπή ... ἀντιφέρεσθαι presumably means 'I am dangerous to oppose in (respect of) might'; cf. 1.589, 21.411, 21.488, etc. τοξοφόρος occurs nowhere else in *Il.* or *Od.*; cf. *HyAp* 13, 126, etc. ἐπεὶ ... ἐθέλησθα explains τοξοφόρῳ περ ἐούσῃ, and γυναιξί is ironic, i.e. she only kills women, not men. For Artemis in this rôle cf. 6.205, 6.428, etc. It is particularly appropriate that the goddess who is herself πότνια θηρῶν and ἀγροτέρη should be described as a beast of prey. The point is picked up with heavy irony by 485–6.

485 θῆρας ἐναίρειν: the scholia point out that strictly speaking ἐναίρειν means 'despoil' (cf. ἔναρα).

487–8 The apodosis is left to be understood, as at 6.150–1. Here 489–92 explain clearly enough what is implied. For the genitive πολέμοιο with δαήμεναι cf. 16.211.

489–513 Herē treats Artemis like a naughty child, and she responds accordingly, as Demetrius observed (schol. Ge 491). The lack of seriousness is emphasized by 491 (μειδιόωσα) and 508 (ἡδὺ γελάσσας).

490–1 τόξα here presumably means 'bow and quiver' (cf. 502–3). In 491 αὐτοῖσιν is emphatic, 'with her own weapons'. μειδιόωσα stresses the comic character of the scene, but Here's smile is one of triumph, as at 434, 14.222–3.

492 ἐντροπαλιζομένην: 'turning (her head) away'. There are several variants: ἐντροπαλιζομένη (several MSS), ἐντροπαλιζομένης (Ptolemy of Ascalon), πολλὰ λισσομένης (Chian and Cypriote texts).

493–6 A brief but effective simile. Cf. the simile of the hawk and pigeon at 22.139–44: 21.493–4 ὕπαιθα … φύγεν ὥς τε πέλεια … ἣ ῥά θ' ὑπ' ἴρηκος … resemble 22.139–41 ἠΰτε κίρκος … μετὰ τρήρωνα πέλειαν | ἣ δέ θ' ὕπαιθα φοβεῖται … In 493 the light, dactylic rhythm suits Artemis' bird-like flight. Neither the compound εἰσπέτομαι (Hdt. 9.100, etc.) nor χηραμός recurs in Homer. χηραμός is used of a cleft where a bird nests at Arist. *HA* 614b35 and in Heliodorus. Here Homer has already explained the word's meaning in κοίλην πέτρην. For the rest of 495 cf. 15.271–6n. (274).

496 This verse elegantly repeats the most important words of 493.

497–501 Hermes light-heartedly declines to fight with Leto, and with ironic courtesy offers her the privilege of claiming a moral victory. Hermes the trickster is also shown as witty and carefree in the story of Ares and Aphrodite (*Od.* 8.338–43).

497 διάκτορος Ἀργειφόντης: see comment on 2.103. The nominative formula occurs first here, 5 times in book 24 and 6× *Od.*

498–500 These verses implicitly allude to Here's treatment of Artemis. πληκτίζεσθαι ('exchange blows') only occurs here in Homer (cf. Ar. *Ec.* 964 etc.). For πρόφρασσα in 500 cf. 10.290n. (3× *Od.*).

502–3 συναίνυτο is an absolute *hapax legomenon*. καμπύλα τόξα is a good instance of a formular phrase which does not precisely suit its context, as it must refer to bow and arrows together. The form πεπτεῶτα recurs at *Od.* 22.384; cf. Chantraine, *GH* I 428, 430. For μετὰ στροφάλιγγι κονίης cf. 16.775 ἐν ... κονίης, of Kebriones' corpse, in a more serious passage.

504 θυγατέρος ἧς: if this goes with τόξα it is unusually distant from the noun on which it depends. The alternative is to take it as genitive with κίε, 'went after her daughter', which seems more likely; cf. Chantraine, *GH* II 52–4. The verse resembles 18.138, where however πάλιν means 'back from'.

505 Διὸς ποτὶ χαλκοβατὲς δῶ: see on 1.425–7.

506–10 Cf. 5.370–4, where Aphrodite falls on her mother's knees, and is embraced by her and comforted. Verses 509–10 = 5.373–4 (see comment). Verse 510 is omitted by most MSS and could be an addition to the original text.

In 506 Artemis behaves like a child. Cf. Call. *Hy.* 3.4–5; ἀρχμενοι ὡς ὅτε πατρὸς ἐφεζομένη γονάτεσσι | παῖς ἔτι κουρίζουσα τάδε προσέειπε γονῆα, where 28–31, with Zeus's laughter and his reference to Here's jealousy, seem to recall 508 and 512–13 here. Her trembling robe in 507 delicately suggests her distress, as does the third repetition of δακρυόεσσα at 506 (cf. 493 and 496).

511 ἐϋστέφανος κελαδεινή: ἐϋστέφανος is used of Artemis only here in Homer, elsewhere of Aphrodite (*Od.* 8.267 etc.). For κελαδεινή see on 16.183.

512–13 This takes us back to what sparked off the whole episode, by a form of ring composition. But it sounds as if Artemis is blaming Here more generally for all the divine strife occasioned by the Trojan War. Cf. 4.1–74, where Here refuses to accept Zeus's proposal for an end to the War. The tone is again that of a spoilt child: 'It's all *her* fault!' For στυφέλιξε in 512 see on 380. In 513 Aristarchus seems to have read νείκε' ἐτύχθη (cf. AT), as at 11.670, *Od.* 21.303. The usual phrase is νεῖκος ὄρωρε (etc.), 10× *Il.*, 3× *Od.* νεῖκε(α) is read by one papyrus and two later MSS.

514–611 Apollo enters Troy to protect it from Akhilleus, whilst the other gods return to Olumpos. Priam urges the Trojans to keep the gates open until the army is safe inside. Apollo prompts Agenor to withstand Akhilleus, and after a soliloquy he does so. They fight briefly, but Agenor is rescued from death by Apollo, who takes his place. While Akhilleus is pursuing him, the Trojan army pours into the city

Apollo's concern for the Trojans brings us back to the human conflict, and as the other gods fade from view the focus narrows to the scene which was left suspended earlier in this Book, of Akhilleus' pursuit of the enemy. This episode forms a prelude to book 22: cf. Priam watching from the wall, and his concern for his people's safety (22.25–91), the rôle of Apollo, and above all Agenor's soliloquy, which foreshadows Hektor's (22.98–130). The deception of Akhilleus by Apollo also contrasts with the scene where Athene deceives Hektor after Apollo has left him (226–47), although the consequences of this are far more serious. Finally the combat between Akhilleus and Agenor resembles in one respect that of Akhilleus and Hektor (cf. 21.591–4n.). Cf. Fenik, *TBS* 213–14; M. Edwards in Bremer, *HBOP* 50–2, and vol. v, Introduction, p. 19.

515 Φοῖβος: schol. pap. xɪɪ (Erbse) on 229–32 reads οἶος, which is possible but may be a conjecture.

516–17 The danger that Troy will fall before its due time is averted by divine intervention, as elsewhere in the poem. Cf. 544–6, 16.698–711, 20.20–30; Fenik, *TBS* 154, 175–6, Reinhardt, *IuD* 107ff., Scheibner, *Aufbau* 49ff. For ὑπέρμορον cf. 20.30 δείδω μὴ καὶ τεῖχος ὑπέρμορον ἐξαλαπάξῃ; 2.155 ὑπέρμορα with comment, etc.

520 παρὰ πατρί is the reading of most MSS, in preference to the variant πὰρ Ζηνί, which would give an unattractively spondaic hemistich.

522–5 The simile resembles the more developed one at 18.207–14, where the fire which blazes from Akhilleus' head is like the smoke and flames rising from beacons in a besieged city. Here however it is the city itself which is on fire, and the point of comparison is between the sufferings of its people and those of the beleaguered Trojans. Although brief, impressionistic, and somewhat repetitive in its language (523–5), it emphasizes powerfully the sense of impending doom hanging over Troy as the result of Akhilleus' onslaught. The brief simile at 22.408–11, comparing the lamentation of the Trojans after Hektor's death to the emotional effect of Troy's actual fall, is the culmination of this sequence of comparisons (see also on 17.736–41). The allusion to divine wrath at 523 is relevant too, since Troy will fall as a result of divine anger. Cf. the storm sent by Zeus as a punishment for injustice in the simile at 16.384–93 (with comment), and in general see Moulton, *Similes* 35–7, 106–7, 110–11.

522–3 Cf. 18.207 ὡς δ᾽ ὅτε καπνὸς ἰὼν ἐξ ἄστεος αἰθέρ᾽ ἵκηται. Here ἵκηται is a variant in A for the vulgate ἱκάνει, which should perhaps be kept, as ἵκηται could be from 18.207. Presumably the city is burning as a result of enemy assault, although the poet does not say so. θεῶν δέ ἐ μῆνις ἀνῆκε is best taken as a parenthesis. For the expression cf. 5.178 χαλεπὴ δὲ θεοῦ ἔπι μῆνις, 22.358 and *Od.* 11.73 θεῶν μήνιμα, *Od.* 2.66 θεῶν δ᾽ ὑποδείσατε μῆνιν.

523–5 ἀνῆκε, | πᾶσι δ᾽ ἔθηκε πόνον ... κήδε᾽ ἐφῆκεν, ... πόνον καὶ κήδε᾽ ἔθηκεν: the repetition is unusual, and may be intended to emphasize the comparison. There are several variants here: 524 ἐφῆπται (cf. 2.15 etc.), 525 φόνον ... ἐφῆκεν/ἐνῆκεν/ἔτευξεν/πολύστονα κήδεα θῆκεν (cf. 1.445); cf. also 22.488 πόνος καὶ κήδε᾽ ὀπίσσω.

526–36 The high frequency of periodic and integral enjambment here suggests the urgency of the crisis.

526–9 Priam watches from the wall as at 3.146–244, where again

Agamemnon is described by him as πελώριον (166). Here too the epithet suggests Priam's view of Akhilleus, as at 22.92 (see comment). In 526 the wall is divine because it was built by Poseidon; cf. 8.519 θεοδμήτων ἐπὶ πύργων. For πεφυζότες see on 6.

530 ὀτρύνων is preferred by Aristarchus (Did/A) to the future ὀτρυνέων, rightly as it introduces Priam's speech. πυλαωρός occurs first here, again at 24.681, and perhaps 22.69.

531–6 For Priam's instructions to hold the gates open until all are inside cf. 12.120–3 οὐδὲ πύλῃσιν | εὗρ' ἐπικεκλιμένας σανίδας καὶ μακρὸν ὀχῆα | ἀλλ' ἀναπεπταμένας ἔχον ἀνέρες (etc.).

533 The variant κλονέει for κλονέων would be possible, but the participle is a less obvious construction and preferable: 'here he is, driving them on'. For νῦν ... ἔσεσθαι cf. 23.310 τῷ τ' οἴω λοίγι' ἔσεσθαι.

534 ἀλέντες: this verb is regularly used of the Trojans taking refuge in the city (16.714, 18.286, 21.607, 22.12, 22.47).

535 ἐπανθέμεναι was Aristarchus' reading (Did/A). The compound does not recur until the fifth century. Some of the city texts read ἐπ' ἂψ θεμέναι, and this has prevailed in our MSS. Aristarchus may have disliked the sound of this: he also wanted to read ἂψ ἐπὶ νῆας ἴμεν for νῆας ἐπ' ἂψ ἰέναι at 18.14. If ἐπιτιθέναι can mean 'close' (5.751 etc.), presumably ἐπανατιθέναι can mean 'close again'. Wackernagel (*Kleine Schriften* I 147) was unhappy about this, but one would like to think Aristarchus was right here. For σανίδας ... ἀραρυίας cf. 18.275, with comment.

536 ἄληται: aorist subjunctive from ἄλλομαι. Herodian read ἄληται: cf. 534 (ἐς τεῖχος ... ἀλέντες), and 16.714 ἐς τεῖχος ... ἀλῆναι. But cf. 12.438, 16.558 ἐσήλατο τεῖχος (and see on 12.438).

537 For city gates and their bars see on 11.120–1, 455–6.

538–9 Zenodotus athetized these two verses. It is hard to believe the reason given by Arn/A, that he understood φάος as 'light' rather than 'salvation', and thought it absurd for the open gates to be needed to bring this. Probably Zenodotus objected that the verses had been added merely to explain how Apollo comes to be outside the city in the following scene. But they prepare us for the god's subsequent intervention.

The variant ἀμῦναι for ἀλάλκοι in 539 could be defended on the ground that this verb more often takes a genitive than ἀλαλκεῖν. But for the genitive with ἀλαλκεῖν cf. 22.348, *Od.* 10.288, and for λοιγὸν ἀλαλκεῖν 21.138, 21.250.

540–3 The scene is closed by two sentences with heavy integral enjambment. The suspension of the verb until the beginning of 542 gives prominence to 541, a chiastic verse vividly describing the wretched state of the fleeing Trojans. καρχαλέοι ('parched') occurs only here in early epic, and then in Hellenistic poetry and later epic. The variant καρφαλέοι ('dry') would be possible, but is surely due to the replacement of a difficult word by an easier one.

In 542 ὁ δὲ is Akhilleus. For σφεδανὸν ἔφεπ' in 542 cf. ἕπετο σφεδανόν 11.165, 16.372. Aristarchus and several MSS read σφεδανῶν, the participle of σφεδανάω, which does not occur elsewhere but would be possible.

544–6 Cf. 16.698–700: ἔνθα κεν ὑψίπυλον Τροίην ἕλον υἶες Ἀχαιῶν ... εἰ μὴ Ἀπόλλων Φοῖβος ... For this type of scene see on 516–17. Agenor has already played a part in the action several times, and especially in books 11–16 (see on 4.467–9, 11.59–60). For φῶτ' Ἀντήνορος υἱὸν ἀμύμονα cf. 4.194 φῶτ' Ἀσκληπιοῦ υἱὸν ἀμύμονος, *Od.* 21.26, 4.247–8 φῶθ' Ἡρακλῆα, φωτὶ ... δέκτῃ, and similarly *Il.* 11.92 ἄνδρα Βιήνορα etc.

548 κῆρας: this is read by only one MS and also quoted by Eustathius for the vulgate χεῖρας, which is defended by Leaf and read by Allen's *editio maior*. Elsewhere we have κῆρες θανάτοιο (5× *Il.*, 1× *Od.*). Death is personified at 14.231, 16.454, 16.682, and Leaf quotes the reading of our MSS and Zenodotus at 1.97 λοιμοῖο βαρείας χεῖρας ἀφέξει, although he had himself previously argued against this. θανάτοιο χεῖρας is a very unusual expression, but there is little support for the alternative reading, and it is an effective phrase in itself. See also on 15.693–5.

549 φηγῷ κεκλιμένος: this topographical detail may hint at the motif of divine detachment and ease. Cf. 7.22 where Apollo and Athene meet παρὰ φηγῷ, and then at 58–61 they sit down as spectators of the battle φηγῷ ἐφ' ὑψηλῇ πατρὸς Διὸς αἰγιόχοιο. At 6.237 and 9.354 a φηγός is closely associated with the Scaean gate. For κεκάλυπτο δ' ἄρ' ἠέρι πολλῇ cf. 16.790 (Apollo) ἠέρι γὰρ πολλῇ κεκαλυμμένος ἀντεβόλησε, and similar expressions at 3.381, 11.751, 20.444, 21.597.

550–70 Agenor debates whether to fight Akhilleus or not. For this type of monologue cf. 11.403–10, 17.90–105, 22.98–130. In all four cases the hero is the subject of a simile just after or before the monologue. The closest parallel is with Hektor's monologue at 22.98–130, where again direct flight is considered and rejected (εἰ μέν κε(ν) ...); an alternative scheme is dismissed (εἰ δ' ἂν ... 21.556, εἰ δέ κεν ... 22.111), the objection to this having been stated (21.562 = 22.122, μή ... 21.563 ∼ 22.123); and finally the decision is made to fight (21.566–70 ∼ 22.129–30). Agenor's soliloquy follows directly after the reference to Apollo inspiring him with courage (547). As elsewhere in Homer, divine influence does not prevent a hero from having to make his own decision, and here we have a clear insight into the process by which he does so. For these monologues see on 11.403, 17.90–105, and Schadewaldt, *VHWW* 300–3, Fenik, *TBS* 96–100, 163–4, Fenik, *Tradition* 68–90, G. Petersmann, *Grazer Beiträge* 2 (1974) 147–69. This type of speech is handled by the poet with considerable variation to suit context and character. Odysseus rejects the idea of flight as dishonourable

(11.408–10), Menelaos decides on retreat as the wisest course (17.98–105), whereas Agenor realizes that flight would be disastrous. Hektor's reasoning is more complex: see on 22.98–130.

550 Ἀχιλλῆα πτολίπορθον: this epithet is used of Akhilleus at 8.372, 15.77 and 24.108, of Odysseus at 2.278, 10.363, and also of Oileus (2.728), Enuo (5.333), Ares (20.152) and Otrunteus (20.384). In the *Odyssey* it is always used of Odysseus (6×; cf. πτολιπόρθιος 2×). See on 2.278–9.

Aristarchus apparently discussed the epithet in his reply to the Separatists, but it is not clear what line was taken by either side on this question. He athetized 8.371–2 and 15.56–77, and Arn/A on 15.56 says that according to Aristarchus the epithet was *never* used of Akhilleus (so also Cic. *Ad. fam.* 10.13.2). At 21.550 however Arn/A says that it occurs *only here*, and at 24.108 there is no comment in the scholia. Evidently Aristarchus' view has become garbled in the later tradition (cf. Erbse on 21.550). Did he reject 24.108–9, and possibly also 21.550–1? He can hardly have accepted the wretched variant Ἀχιλλέα Πηλείωνα at 21.550 (τινες AT). He probably thought the epithet inappropriate because Akhilleus died before the sack of Troy, but it is fully justified by his claim to have sacked many other cities (9.328–9 etc.). At the same time, however, it may suggest Akhilleus' rôle as the *potential* destroyer of Troy itself (cf. 544 etc.), and hint at the way Agenor views him as he approaches (cf. 22.92n.).

551 Cf. *Od.* 4.427, 4.572, 10.309 ἦϊα, πολλὰ δέ μοι κραδίη πόρφυρε κιόντι. The only other occurrence of πορφύρειν in the *Iliad* neatly illustrates the relationship between metaphor and simile (14.16–20); ὡς δ' ὅτε πορφύρῃ πέλαγος μέγα κύματι κωφῷ ... | ὡς ὁ γέρων ὥρμαινε δαϊζόμενος κατὰ θυμὸν ...

552 = 11.403 etc. (7× *Il.*, 4× *Od.*). The verse recurs in all four of the monologues mentioned above (550–70n.).

553–5 ὤ μοι ἐγών, εἰ μέν κεν ... also opens the other monologues. For 554 cf. 6.41 πρὸς πόλιν, ᾗπερ οἱ ἄλλοι ἀτυζόμενοι φοβέοντο, and 21.4 πρὸς πόλιν, ᾗπερ Ἀχαιοὶ ἀτυζόμενοι φοβέοντο. φοβέονται, the reading of most MSS here, is presumably due to the influence of these parallel verses. For δειροτομήσει see on 89. The same brutality of expression here emphasizes the indignity of this cowardly end.

556–61 εἰ δ' ἂν ἐγώ ... means 'suppose I leave', with no apodosis. Cf. 567, 22.111, and comment on 1.581. Chantraine, *GH* II 362–4, has a good discussion of the periodic structure of 556–65 and 22.111–25. The compound ὑποκλονέεσθαι occurs only here in Homer, later in Quintus of Smyrna (14.572). Ἰλήϊον recurs nowhere else, and was explained as 'of Ilios' (Did/A) or 'of Ilos' (T), the hero whose tomb is mentioned at 10.415 etc. Crates read Ἰδήϊον, as an alternative form of Ἰδαῖον, but it seems awkward to describe the plain as belonging to the mountain. For Ἴδης

τε κνημούς (559) cf. Ἴδης ἐν κνημοῖσι (3× *Il.*), and 23.117 κνημούς ...
πολυπίδακος Ἴδης. The 'thickets' (ῥωπήϊα) of Mt Ida recur at 23.122.

560–1 ἑσπέριος comes only here in *Il.*, 7× *Od.* in this sense. The detail
of washing away the sweat in the river is a vivid touch, suggesting relief at
escape from death. For ἱδρῶ ἀποψυχθείς cf. 11.621, 22.2 ἱδρῶ ἀπεψύχοντο,
and 10.572–6.

562 = 11.407, 17.97, 22.122 (monologues), and also 22.385.

563–4 μή ... νοήσῃ expresses a fear that this may happen (cf. 22.123
etc.). ἀπαειρόμενον (only here in Homer) means 'as I take myself off': a
metaphor from setting sail according to T and Porphyry (*Quaest. hom.* 1
256.4, ed. Sodano); cf. ἀπαίρειν, 'sail away', in Attic. The alliteration of
π (πόλιος, πεδίονδε) and μ (με μετάιξας μάρψῃ) may be accidental. Cf.
22.455–6 δείδω μή ... μοῦνον ἀποτμήξας πόλιος πεδίονδε δίηται, in the
context of Andromakhe's fear that Hektor may be cut off by Akhilleus.

567 Most MSS have πόλιος, and this should be read here as at 2.811.
κατεναντίον occurs only here in Homer; cf. Hes. *Aspis* 73 etc.

568–70 There is never any allusion in Homer to the later legend of
Akhilleus' invulnerability. τρωτός ('vulnerable') is another Homeric *hapax*;
cf. Euripides (*Hel.* 810), etc. For ἐν δὲ ἴα cf. 9.319 ἐν δὲ ἰῇ ..., with unusual
hiatus. The sense is 'he only has *one* life'.

570 Cf. 8.141 νῦν μὲν γὰρ τούτῳ Κρονίδης Ζεὺς κῦδος ὀπάζει. Aristarchus
athetized this verse (Arn/A), regarding it as a common type of addition made
to supply a verb which can be understood with θνητὸν ... ἄνθρωποι, and
pointing out that it weakens the impression of Agenor's resolution to fight.
Hektor's monologue ends with a reference to Zeus's decisive power (22.130),
but that is not a very close parallel, and Aristarchus could be right.

571 ἀλείς: cf. 22.308 of Hektor's attack on Akhilleus. It means 'gathering
himself together' or perhaps 'crouching'.

573–82 Agenor is compared to a leopard which attacks a hunter and is
not deterred either by hounds baying or by being wounded. Cf. 11.414–20,
where Odysseus after his soliloquy is compared to a wild boar attacked by
dogs and hunters, and 11.415 ὁ δέ τ' εἶσι βαθείης ἐκ ξυλόχοιο ... is like 573.
For the animal's fearlessness (574–5) cf. 12.45–6, in a comparison of Hektor
to a boar or lion confronting dogs and hunters: τοῦ δ' οὔ ποτε κυδάλιμον
κῆρ | ταρβεῖ οὐδὲ φοβεῖται ...

573 πάρδαλις: on the variant πόρδαλις see 13.103n. bT say that the
leopard is the most aggressive of all the wild beasts, quoting Aristotle's view
that the female of this species is more deadly than the male (*HA* 9.1,
608a33–5). Leopards occur in the similes at 13.103, 17.20.

575 ὑλαγμός occurs only here in early epic, and later in Xenophon (*Cyn.*
4.5), etc. Zenodotus and others read κυνυλαγμόν, and Stesichorus (*PMG*
255) was quoted in support of this, but this word occurs nowhere else.

576 μιν ἧ: Leaf observes that ἧ is rarely shortened (10.451, 16.515, 21.113, 23.724), and that μιν is not in its normal place (i.e. after the opening, εἴ περ γάρ). He thinks that μιν should be omitted, and that the variant τις (in the city texts) suggests that both may be mere stop-gaps. But the object seems desirable here and these arguments inconclusive against it.

577-8 The phrase περὶ δουρὶ πεπαρμένη occurs only here. Support for the realism of these verses came from the scholar Heracleon, who said that he had seen this happen at Rome (bT 577).

580 This verse picks up 574-5 οὐδέ τι ... φοβεῖται (i.e. 'flees') and 578 πρίν γ' ... The conjunction πρίν alone with optative only occurs here in Homer, elsewhere with infinitive or occasionally subjunctive. Cf. Chantraine, *GH* II 264-5.

582-9 Agenor makes the usual provocative speech before a single combat. His words resemble Hektor's mocking speech of triumph over the fallen Patroklos (cf. 16.830-6).

584-5 Verse 584 is similar to 16.708. For νηπύτι' see on 410. For τετεύξεται there is a variant τετεύξεαι (most MSS), but this would have to be middle, whereas elsewhere this tense is passive (12.345 etc.). ἐπ' αὐτῇ means 'on her account' (cf. LSJ s.v. ἐπί ΙΙΙ 1).

586 For πολέες τε καὶ ἄλκιμοι cf. 11.483 Τρῶες ἕπον πολλοί τε καὶ ἄλκιμοι. The variant ἄνδρες ἔνειμεν was considered possible by Did/A, but after ἐν this is unnecessary.

587 οἳ καί was Aristarchus' reading (Did/A), whereas all but one of our MSS have οἳ κε. In spite of Leaf's objection to the latter, κε ... εἰρυόμεσθα (future) would be exactly like 1.175, 9.155, 9.297, *Od.* 5.36 (cf. Chantraine *GH* II 226). However, Aristarchus clearly regarded καί as having the support of the better MSS. It has the advantage of adding emphasis to Agenor's confident assertion, and therefore seems preferable. For τοκέων see on 15.660 and cf. Chantraine, *GH* II 224 on this form.

588 πότμον ἐφέψεις is paralleled by *Od.* 24.471 πότμον ἐφέψειν, and the more common πότμον ἐπισπεῖν etc. (6× *Il.*, 7× *Od.*). For ἔκπαγλος see on 452, and for θαρσαλέος πολεμιστής cf. 430 ὧδέ τε θαρσαλέοι ..., and 5.602 (etc.) θαρσαλέον πολεμιστήν (3× *Il.*).

590-8 The fight is briefly described, since it is really only a delaying tactic on Apollo's part, and it soon ends in Agenor's rescue by the god. This may explain its unusual features. Verse 590 is an untypical one, and elsewhere greaves are never actually hit in battle as in 591. Akhilleus' divine greaves are in any case special, but the fact that otherwise greaves belong only to the formular structure of arming-scenes has been thought to support the view that ἐϋκνήμιδες Ἀχαιοί derives from reminiscence of Late Bronze Age warfare, when the Greeks were distinguished from other peoples by their special greaves. As yet no examples of metal greaves have been found between *c.* 1100 and 700 B.C. in the Greek world (for a possible LHIIIC example cf. P. A. Mountjoy, *Opuscula Atheniensia* 15 (1984) 135–7). But non-metallic greaves, which would not normally survive to be discovered by the archaeologist, probably continued to be used during this period. See also on 3.330–1.

590 For ὀξὺν ἄκοντα cf. 10.335 (end of verse), *Od.* 14.531, 21.340 (in same position as here). For βαρείης χειρὸς ἀφῆκε cf. 13.410; βαρεῖαι -ας χεῖρες -ας 4× *Il.*, βαρείη χειρί 2× *Il.* The variant παχείης χειρός occurs nowhere else, and derives from the formula χειρὶ παχείῃ. This verse is a unique variation on the usual ἦ ῥα καὶ ἀμπεπαλὼν προΐει δολιχόσκιον ἔγχος (7× *Il.*).

591–4 A blow on the shin occurs elsewhere only at 4.518–19, with no mention of a greave. This episode anticipates 22.289–91, where Hektor's spear hits Akhilleus' shield and rebounds. Cf. also 13.586–92, where an arrow rebounds off a breastplate.

592 Leaf and Allen follow La Roche in reading the variant οἱ for the vulgate μιν. But ἀμφὶ δέ οἱ should mean 'around (*or* upon) him', and ἀμφὶ δέ μιν 'around it' (κνήμην) seems possible here (cf. 16.414 etc.).

For κνημὶς νεοτεύκτου κασσιτέροιο cf. 613 κνημῖδας ἑανοῦ κασσιτέροιο. νεότευκτος recurs only in one verse epigram; cf. 5.194 νεοτευχής. Pure tin would be useless as a protective metal. It looks as if there was already debate in antiquity over this point, for Aristotle (*Poet.* 1461a27–30) cites κνημὶς νεοτεύκτου κασσιτέροιο as an example of an extension of meaning similar to calling a mixture of wine and water 'wine' or iron-workers 'bronze-smiths', etc. This suggests that 'tin' was interpreted as meaning an alloy of tin and another metal (cf. the commentaries of Bywater, Lucas *ad loc.*). As D. Gray said (*JHS* 74 (1954) 9), 'the poet apologizes for the impossibility in Φ 594, θεοῦ δ᾽ ἠρύκακε δῶρα'; cf. Arn/A (594): Hephaistos' armour is invulnerable.

593 For σμερδάλεον κονάβησε see on 2.334.

595–6 Πηλεΐδης ... | δεύτερος is again a slightly unusual way of describing a counter-attack.

596–8 For this type of divine rescue cf. Fenik, *TBS* 12. Verse 597 resembles 3.380–1 τὸν δ᾽ ἐξήρπαξ᾽ Ἀφροδίτη ... ἐκάλυψε δ᾽ ἄρ᾽ ἠέρι πολλῇ, 20.442–3 τὸν δ᾽ ἐξήρπαξεν Ἀπόλλων ... ἐκάλυψε δ᾽ ἄρ᾽ ἠέρι πολλῇ; also 11.751–2, where Poseidon rescues the Aktorione, καλύψας ἠέρι πολλῇ. ἡσύχιος occurs only here in Homer; cf. ἡσυχίη *Od.* 18.22, ἡσυχίως *HyHerm* 438, ἥσυχος Hesiod etc. For ἔκπεμπε νέεσθαι cf. 18.240 πέμψεν ... νέεσθαι, *Od.* 4.8, 13.206 (ἔ)πεμπε νέεσθαι (etc.).

599–601 Apollo's substitution of himself for Agenor is a variant of the trick which he plays at 5.449–53, where he replaces Aineias with an εἴδωλον over which the Greeks and Trojans fight. But it is also related to the common motif of a god assuming a human disguise on the battlefield.

ἀποεργάθειν comes only here in *Il.*; cf. *Od.* 21.221. There may be word-play with ἑκάεργος in 600, as this was connected in antiquity with ἑκάς and εἴργειν (cf. Chantraine, *Dict.* s.v.). Verse 600 resembles 5.450 αὐτῷ τ' Αἰνείᾳ ἴκελον (of the εἴδωλον). In 601 the repetition ποδῶν ... ποσσί cannot be significant. For πρόσθε ποδῶν cf. 16.742, *Od.* 22.4.

602–11 This episode closes with an effective contrast between the point-less pursuit by Akhilleus of the false Agenor on the empty battlefield, and the crowded scene of panic as the Trojans pour into the city, without stopping to rescue their own comrades. The Book ends as it began with a Trojan rout. Cf. the description of the Greek retreat at the end of book 12, when Hektor breaks through the gates of the Achaean wall.

602–7 ἧος is answered by τόφρα (606), with δόλῳ ... οἷσι in parenthesis. On the form ἧος for ἕως in the MSS see Chantraine, *GH* i 11. For πὰρ ποταμὸν βαθυδινήεντα Σκάμανδρον see on 1–2, and for τυτθὸν ὑπεκπρο-θέοντα cf. 9.502 | πολλὸν ὑπεκπροθέει; 21.44 | ἔνθεν ὑπεκπροφυγών. For ἔθελγεν Ἀπόλλων see on 276.

606–7 These verses seem to echo the warning of Pouludamas (18.270–1, especially 270 ἀσπασίως). Cf. also 19.71–3 (72 ἀσπασίως). In 607 Anti-machus and Rhianus read πύλαι δ' ἔμπληντο, which would suggest an even more congested scene (also avoiding repetition of πόλις in 607–8); but cf. 22.12, 22.47 εἰς ἄστυ ἄλεν, ἀλέντων.

610–11 ἐσσυμένως, which A and some other MSS read, seems better than the vulgate ἀσπασίως, after ἀσπάσιοι in 607. σαῶσαι, 3rd person sing. aorist optative, is read by Aristarchus, for our vulgate σάωσαν (Did/A). The singular verb would go with γοῦνα, and the optative would resemble πεφεύγοι in 609. As so often, Aristarchus prefers a less obvious reading.

BOOK TWENTY-TWO

The event towards which the action of the poem has been tending, the final conflict of Akhilleus and Hektor, forms the theme of this Book. Its unity is remarkable and its structure relatively simple. After the brief opening scene in which we see Hektor alone before the walls of Troy and Apollo revealing himself to Akhilleus, there follow three speeches. In the first two Priam and Hekabe appeal to Hektor not to face Akhilleus (25–89), and in the third Hektor debates whether to do so or not (90–130). This opening triad of speeches is balanced at the end of the Book by the laments of Priam and Hekabe (405–36) and the longer scene which concludes with the lament of Andromakhe (437–515).

These speeches frame the action, which is in two main parts, the pursuit of Hektor and the duel itself. The narrative of the pursuit is 'frozen' at 166, when the gods debate the outcome (167–87), leading to Athene's intervention, and at 208–15, with extraordinary rapidity, the decisive moment is described when Zeus weighs the fates of the two heroes, Apollo leaves Hektor and Athene arrives at Akhilleus' side. The pursuit ends with brief exchanges between Athene and the two opponents, encouraging Akhilleus and deceiving Hektor into facing his enemy (216–47).

The duel itself is also framed by two exchanges between the contestants, which centre on the fate of the loser's body (248–72, 330–66). The fight is remarkably brief, and the chief impression is of the continuing divine deceit of Hektor followed by his realization of the truth (296–305), and his helplessness in the face of the combined forces of Akhilleus and Athene. Its brevity contrasts with the slowness of the build-up, in which the poet explores in depth the psychological and moral reactions of those concerned on both human and divine levels.

The theme of the mutilation of Hektor's body now dominates, as the Greek army insult the corpse and Akhilleus drags it behind his chariot. Again speeches portray the triumph of the victors, contrasted with extreme manifestations of grief at Troy, distilled above all in the laments of Hektor's family.

The narrative is intensely dramatic almost throughout the Book, rising to high emotional levels especially at the beginning and end. There are fleeting glimpses of a different world, the orderly one of normal life, as in Hektor's vision of the conversation of a pair of lovers (126–8), the reference to the women of Troy washing their clothes outside the walls in peacetime

(153–6), and (most poignant of all) the quiet domestic scene in Hektor's home of Andromakhe weaving and ordering the maids to heat the bath water for his return (440–6), and the memories of their wedding-day evoked by her veil (470–2). All of these intensify the contrast with the grimness of what is now taking place. Poignant too is the juxtaposition of the life-and-death struggle of Hektor's pursuit with the studied formality of the debate in heaven over his fate, so easily and quickly resolved by Zeus's yielding to Athene's protest (157–85).

1–24 The Trojans who have taken refuge in the city recover from their flight, but Hektor remains outside the walls. Apollo discloses his identity to Akhilleus, who is angry with him for having deceived him. Akhilleus approaches the walls

With the abrupt reference to Hektor's doom at 5–6 we are suddenly back in the mainstream of the narrative, aware that the final conflict is soon to happen.

1 πεφυζότες ἠΰτε νεβροί: for πεφυζότες see on 21.6. Cf. 4.243, 21.29 τεθηπότες -ας ἠΰτε νεβροί -ούς. This simile anticipates the longer one comparing Akhilleus and Hektor to a dog pursuing a fawn at 188–93. Cf. Moulton, *Similes* 78–80, and on the similes in this Book in general *ibid.* 76–87.

2 ἀπεψύχοντο: Aristarchus seems to have preferred ἀνεψύχοντο (Did/ AbT). Elsewhere we have ἱδρῷ ἀπεψύχοντο 11.620, ἱδρῶ ἀποψυχθείς 21.561, but ἕλκος ἀναψύχοντα 5.795, ἀνέψυχθεν φίλον ἦτορ (after washing) 10.575, ἀνέψυχον φίλον ἦτορ 13.84. These parallels suggest that ἀπε- is right here. For the metaphorical use of ἀκεῖσθαι cf. 13.115, *Od.* 10.69, 14.383.

3 κεκλιμένοι καλῇσιν ἐπάλξεσιν: this surely means leaning against the battlements rather than spaced along them (which Willcock favours). The Trojans are exhausted.

4 σάκε' ὤμοισι κλίναντες: see on 11.593. There and at 13.488 this occurs in the context of defence rather than attack, and has been taken as referring to a large (body?) shield planted on the ground, against which one could lean (e.g. Leaf *ad loc.*, Lorimer, *HM* 188). This is implausible, and here it is not possible as the Greeks are on the move. It might indicate a shield held out almost horizontally, with the top end resting on the shoulder, to guard against missiles from the walls. This seems to be the view of T (on 11.593), and cf. Heyne: *arcte iunctis ordinibus, ita ut clipeos ante se ferendo humero admotos haberent.* For a similar manoeuvre cf. 12.137–8 (with comment), *Arch. Hom.* E 49 (Borchhardt).

5–6 We last saw Hektor at 20.443–4, when he was rescued from Akhilleus by Apollo. Here the poet reintroduces him with dramatic suddenness, briefly accounting for his remaining outside Troy and at the same time announcing that his doom is impending. ὀλοιή μοῖρα only occurs here, instead of μοῖρ' ὀλοή (2× *Il*., 5× *Od*.). For μοῖρ' ἐπέδησεν cf. 4.517(n.), *Od*. 11.292, *Il*. 19.91–4 (Ἄτη), and later expressions denoting the 'binding' power of ἀνάγκη (see Richardson on *HyDem* 216–17). Ἰλίου may stand for Ἰλίοο (see on 21.104).

For the Scaean gate see on 3.145, 9.354. It was here that Hektor had met Andromakhe (6.392ff.), and here Akhilleus must eventually be killed (22.360). Cf. Schadewaldt, *VHWW* 294, Elliger, *Darstellung der Landschaft* 59–62.

7–13 Apollo's speech of self-revelation is lightly mocking (cf. 9 οὐδέ νύ πώ με, 11 ἦ νύ τοι ... etc.). He does not say which god he is, but Akhilleus realizes (15).

9–10 αὐτὸς θνητὸς ἐὼν θεὸν ἄμβροτον are contrasted as often (cf. 21.380n.). For σὺ δ' ἀσπερχὲς μενεαίνεις cf. 4.32. Here 4.33 has been added by one papyrus, presumably to supply an infinitive with μενεαίνεις.

11–12 Τρώων πόνος ('labour concerning the Trojans') is an objective genitive (cf. 2.356n.). ἐφόβησας means 'you have put to flight'. For εἰς ἄστυ ἄλεν cf. 47 εἰς ἄστυ ἀλέντων, and see on 21.534, 21.607. λιάσθης here means 'you have turned aside' (cf. Leumann, *HW* 208–9, Chantraine, *Dict*. s.v. λιάζομαι).

13 μέν is 'however' (cf. 283, and Denniston, *Particles* 362), and μόρσιμος 'fated to die'. This personal sense recurs at *Od*. 16.392 = 21.162.

14 πόδας ὠκὺς Ἀχιλλεύς: it is here that this fixed characteristic of Akhilleus is most clearly embodied in action; cf. 24 etc., and W. Whallon, *Formula, Character and Context* (Center for Hellenic Studies, Washington, D.C. 1969) 14–17.

15–20 Akhilleus' angry and defiant reply was censured by Plato, who in the *Republic* (391A) quotes verses 15 and 20 among the passages which he regards as morally reprehensible. bT (20) reply that Akhilleus shows not arrogance but μεγαλοφροσύνη (cf. 21 μέγα φρονέων). It is typical of this hero that even when confronting Apollo he should be so concerned with honour (18) and revenge (20). His readiness to defy Apollo contrasts with the helplessness of both Diomedes and Patroklos in the face of this god (5.443–4, 16.710–11).

15 ἔβλαψάς μ': 'you have fooled me'. In Homer βλάπτειν in the sense of harming one's wits is usually applied to divine powers: cf. 9.507, 9.512, 15.724, 19.94, *Od*. 14.178, 21.294 (οἶνος), 23.14. Cf. the later prose word θεοβλάβεια, which is the equivalent of ἄτη.

θεῶν ὀλοώτατε πάντων: for similar complaints about the gods cf. 3.365 with comment, *Od*. 20.201.

16–20 ἦ ... ἦ: the repeated assertions stress Akhilleus' frustration.

17 γαῖαν ὀδὰξ εἷλον: cf. 2.418 ὀδὰξ λαζοίατο γαῖαν, and similar expressions at 11.749, 19.61, *Od.* 22.269.

18–19 Verse 18 echoes 21.596. For 19 cf. 3.381 ῥεῖα μάλ' ὥς τε θεός, 16.688–90 (with comment) etc.; 1.515 ἐπεὶ οὔ τοι ἔπι δέος. ὀπίσσω means 'in future' (6.450, 24.111). On this divine ease and irresponsibility see Griffin, *HLD* 188–9.

20 Cf. *Od.* 2.62 ἦ τ' ἂν ἀμυνοίμην, εἴ μοι δύναμίς γε παρείη.

22–4 A brief simile, comparing Akhilleus to a prize-winning racehorse. As with the comparison in verse 1 this is picked up later at 162–6 by the simile comparing Hektor and Akhilleus to racehorses. Cf. also 6.506–11, where Paris is compared to a horse running over the plain, and the repetition of this at 15.263–8 where it is applied to Hektor; 15.269 is similar to 22.24.

22–3 For ἵππος ἀεθλοφόρος cf. 162 ἀεθλοφόροι ... ἵπποι. Elsewhere ἀεθλοφόρος is used (3× *Il.*). For σὺν ὄχεσφιν ... τιταινόμενος πεδίοιο cf. 23.518 πεδίοιο τιταινόμενος σὺν ὄχεσφι, 6.507 θείη πεδίοιο, 2.390, 12.58 ἅρμα τιταίνων. Verse 23 means 'who effortlessly races at full stretch over the plain'.

24 Cf. 15.269 ὡς Ἕκτωρ λαιψηρὰ πόδας καὶ γούνατ' ἐνώμα, with comment.

25–89 Priam sees Akhilleus approaching the city and entreats Hektor not to face him, describing the evils in store for the Trojans if the city is taken, but his appeal fails. Hekabe also vainly begs him not to stand against Akhilleus

We have already seen Priam watching anxiously from the wall at 21.526–36. We recall also book 3, where he and the other Trojan elders watched with Helen, and Priam took part in the preparations for the single combat between his son Paris and Menelaos. There, however, he went back to Troy because he could not bear to watch the fight (305–7), whereas here he is present throughout the whole conflict. This is one aspect of the structural balance and contrast between these two Books (cf. Introduction, 'Structure'). See also J. T. Kakridis, *Homer Revisited* (Lund 1971) 68ff., on the connexions of these appeals with Andromakhe's plea to Hektor in book 6; on the links between the speeches in 6 and 22 in general see Beck, *Stellung* 71–92.

25–32 Priam sees Akhilleus shining in his armour like the Dog-Star, whose destructive character is described. The simile suggests the way in which Priam himself reacts to the sight of Akhilleus (cf. de Jong, *Narrators* 126). At 5.4–7 a briefer version of this simile is applied to Diomedes, and at 11.61–6 Hektor in his shining armour, darting to and fro in the ranks, is compared to an οὔλιος ἀστήρ now shining and then hidden in the clouds. At 13.242–5 Idomeneus' armour is like Zeus's lightning. The present comparison is echoed at 317–20, where the glint of Akhilleus' spear-point is like the evening star at dusk. See Moulton, *Similes* 26–7, 80–1, and *Hermes* 102 (1974) 392–4.

26–7 παμφαίνονθ' ὥς τ' ἀστέρ' ... ὅς ῥά τ' ὀπώρης εἶσιν: cf. 5.5–6 ἀστέρ' ὀπωρινῷ ἐναλίγκιον, ὅς τε μάλιστα | λαμπρὸν παμφαίνῃσι ..., with comment. The star is Sirius, the brightest of the fixed stars, and the chief star of the constellation Canis Maior. The words 'which goes forth at harvest-time' refer to its heliacal rising at dawn in mid-July. The following period, until mid-September, is one of intense heat in Greece and Asia Minor, and it was thought that Sirius was responsible for fevers at this time (cf. West on Hes. *Erga* 417).

27–8 For ἀρίζηλοι δέ οἱ αὐγαί cf. the simile at 13.244, where 245 = 22.32. The obscure and impressive phrase νυκτὸς ἀμολγῷ recurs in 317 of the evening star, and cf. 11.173, 15.324, *Od.* 4.841. All four examples in the *Iliad* are in similes. Because of 317, and also the reference to Sirius' rising at dawn (27), it has been taken as referring to the twilight of evening or dawn in these two passages (Eust. 1255.5, bT 317). But Sirius would not be so bright at such a time, and this does not seem to suit the other Homeric passages where it occurs, in which the sense 'at dead of night' seems more appropriate (see on 11.173, and West on *Od.* 4.841).

29 κύν' 'Ωρίωνος: originally κύν' 'Ωαρίωνος; cf. Chantraine, *GH* 1 16. Akhilleus is later compared to a dog hunting a fawn (188–93). ἐπίκλησιν καλέουσιν recurs at 506 and 18.487 = *Od.* 5.273. ἐπίκλησις sometimes means 'second name' or 'nickname', and perhaps this is the sense here (with Sirius as the first name); see on 6.402–3.

30–2 The two hemistichs of 30 are contrasted. For κακὸν δέ τε σῆμα τέτυκται cf. 13.244 δεικνὺς σῆμα βροτοῖσιν, 6.178 σῆμα κακόν, *Od.* 23.188 σῆμα τέτυκται. The word πυρετός occurs only here in Homer. Later it meant 'fever', and Arn/A held that this, rather than 'heat', was the meaning here too. Verse 32 = 13.245.

33–4 κεφαλὴν ... χερσὶν | ὑψόσ' ἀνασχόμενος: striking the head with one's hands and raising one's hands above one's head were both traditional expressions of strong grief, found also in Greek mourning ritual: cf. Reiner, *Die rituelle Totenklage* 42–3; Neumann, *Gesten und Gebärden* 86; Alexiou, *Ritual Lament* 6. This is echoed at the end of Priam's speech, when he tears his hair in grief. With ἀνασχόμενος one should understand χεῖρας: cf. 3.362, 23.660, 23.686, *Od.* 18.95. ᾤμωξεν ... μέγα δ' οἰμώξας is an unusual repetition. Priam's appeal is desperate.

35–6 ὁ δὲ προπάροιθε πυλάων | ἑστήκει: cf. the two Lapiths at 12.131–2 τὼ μὲν ἄρα προπάροιθε πυλάων ὑψηλάων | ἕστασαν ...

36 At this stage we know nothing of the inner turmoil which Hektor is about to go through (98–130). For ἄμοτον μεμαὼς ... μάχεσθαι cf. 13.80 ἄμοτον μεμαῶτι μάχεσθαι |.

37 For χεῖρας ὀρεγνύς, a gesture of entreaty, cf. 1.351 with comment.

38–76 Priam begins his speech by begging Hektor not to risk virtually certain death by facing Akhilleus. He goes on to speak of the other sons he has lost, expresses his fears that Lukaon and Poludoros may also have been killed (cf. 20.407–18, 21.34–135), and says that Hektor is the one hope for Troy's salvation. The second half of the speech (59–76) is an appeal to Hektor to pity his father, followed by a vivid description of the horrors that await the Trojans if the city is taken, and a terrible vision of how his own dogs will eat his body after he is killed.

38–9 The oblique reference of ἀνέρα τοῦτον could be occasioned by the lack of a traditional formula for Akhilleus in the accusative, with initial vowel, and in this part of the verse. But it is effective in this context. Cf. in Hekabe's speech 84 ἄμυνε δὲ δήϊον ἄνδρα; 379, 418 (ἀνέρα τοῦτον); and similar indirect expressions at 8.96, 13.746, 14.250, 18.257, 21.314, 24.204, 24.207, 24.212. For οἶος ἄνευθ' ἄλλων see on 416.

41–3 The asyndeton in these verses indicates urgency. Cf. 295, 16.126–9, 24.354–5, with comments. This kind of effect is discussed by [Longinus] (19–20) and prose examples are collected in J. D. Denniston, *Greek Prose Style* (Oxford 1952) 99ff.

41 σχέτλιος: since the previous and following clauses have Akhilleus as their subject this presumably refers to him, rather than being addressed to Hektor. At 86 however it may well refer to Hektor (see comment).

41–2 αἴθε ... ἐμοί is an example of an unusual figure of speech, φίλος here implying its opposite by a kind of grim irony (cf. Arn/A). For κύνες καὶ γῦπες ἔδοιεν cf. 18.271 κύνες καὶ γῦπες ἔδονται, and 4.237, 16.836 γῦπες ἔδονται. This is a persistent theme throughout book 22, leading up to the issue of Hektor's burial. Cf. 66–76, 89, 335–6, 339, 348, 354, 508–10, and Segal, *Mutilation of the Corpse* 33–47. ἔδοιεν is Aristarchus' reading here (Did/A), whereas all our manuscripts read ἔδονται, probably owing to the influence of the parallel passages. The future with κεν is possible, but the optative is better in the context of 41–3.

43 ἀπὸ πραπίδων ἄχος ἔλθοι: cf. 24.514 ἀπὸ πραπίδων ἦλθ' ἵμερος.

44–5 εὖνις occurs only here and at *Od.* 9.524 in Homer, later in Empedocles (57.2) and Aeschylus (*Pers.* 289 etc.). The loss of so many of Priam's sons is an important theme, especially in the later books of the poem: cf. 423–6, 24.255–60, 24.493–501, Griffin, *HLD* 123ff. For 45 see on 21.454.

46–55 As elsewhere, the poet here binds his narrative together by linking the deaths of Poludoros and Lukaon in books 20–1 with the possibility of Hektor's death. For Laothoe and Altes see on 21.84–7.

46–8 δύο παῖδε ... οὐ δύναμαι ἰδέειν ... τούς μοι Λαοθόη τέκετο ...: cf. 3.236–8 (Helen to Priam on the walls of Troy): δοιὼ δ' οὐ δύναμαι ἰδέειν κοσμήτορε λαῶν ... αὐτοκασιγνήτω, τώ μοι μία γείνατο μήτηρ. The context is similar in both cases: Helen searches vainly for her brothers who are dead, as Priam here fails to find his sons.

48 κρείουσα γυναικῶν: κρείουσα (the feminine of κρείων) only occurs here in Homer. Cf. the proper name Kreousa, and Hes. fr. 26.7–8 τ[ά]ς ποτε [Λ]αο[θό]η κρείουσ' Ὑπερηὶς ἀ[μύ]μων | [γεί]νατο ...; 26.31a Ἀντιόχη κρείουσα; Theocr. *Id.* 17.132 οὓς τέκετο κρείουσα Ῥέα. It looks as if it belonged primarily to genealogical poetry.

49 'Their father's ignorance is very pitiable' (bT). Helen's ignorance of her brothers' deaths in book 3 evokes a similar pathos.

49–50 ἤ τ' ἄν ... ἀπολύσομεθ': ἄν can be used with the 'modal' future indicative, but ἀπολυσόμεθα is probably aorist subjunctive here; cf. Chantraine, *GH* II 225–6. The variant ἀπολύσομεν (A) is inappropriate here, as the middle is used of the person who offers a ransom. This allusion foreshadows Priam's ransoming of Hektor in book 24.

49–51 There are similar passages referring to ransoming at 6.46–50, 10.378–81 (especially 378–9 ἔστι γὰρ ἔνδον | χαλκός τε χρυσός τε), 11.131–5 and 22.340–1. Gifts provided by the bride's father or family on her marriage are mentioned or implied several times elsewhere in Homer: cf. 6.191–5, 9.147–56, *Od.* 4.735–6, 7.311–14, 20.341–2, 23.227–8, and perhaps *Od.* 1.277–8, 2.132–3. It seems most probable (despite A. M. Snodgrass, *JHS* 94 (1974) 116–17) that the conventions of marriage reflected in the poems involved an exchange of gifts between both sides, rather than simply 'purchase' of the bride. Cf. M. I. Finley, *Revue Internationale des Droits de l'Antiquité* (3ᵉ ser.) 2 (1955) 167–94 = *Economy and Society in Ancient Greece*, edd. B. D. Shaw and R. P. Salter (London 1983) 233–45; W. K. Lacey, *JHS* 86 (1966) 55–68; I. Morris, *Classical Antiquity* 5 (1986) 81–138; I. N. Perysinakis, *CQ* 41 (1991) 297–302. See also on 88.

ὀνομάκλυτος (51) is found only here in Homer, although cf. ὄνομα κλυτόν at *Od.* 9.364, 19.183; for the compound epithet cf. *HyHerm* 59, etc.

52–3 One should surely punctuate with a comma at the end of 52, rather than after τεθνᾶσι (both are discussed by Nicanor). The former is supported by the parallel verses at *Od.* 4.834 etc. ἢ ἤδη τέθνηκε (-ᾶσι) καὶ εἰν Ἀΐδαο δόμοισι.

54–8 This brings Priam's argument back to his main point, the appeal to Hektor not to risk his life too, since Troy depends on him. In 55 ἢν μὴ καὶ σὺ θάνης means 'as long as you are not killed as well'.

56–8 Priam here puts forward several arguments together, appealing to Hektor (*a*) to save the Trojans, (*b*) to avoid giving glory to Akhilleus, and (*c*) to save his own life. Finally (59–76) he launches into his passionate plea to save Priam himself from a terrible fate.

59 φρονέοντ': 'while I still have my senses', or perhaps rather 'while I still live': so bT, and LSJ s.v. φρονέω IV.

60 δύσμορος occurs only here and at 481 in *Il.*, 6× *Od*. It is confined to speeches, always at the beginning of the verse (cf. Griffin, *JHS* 106 (1986) 41–2, for such emotional language in speeches). ἐπὶ γήραος οὐδῷ recurs at 24.487 and 3× *Od*. Since Priam is already an old man γήραος is most probably a defining genitive, 'the threshold consisting of old age', implying that old age is itself seen as a transitional stage between life and death. Cf. J. T. Kakridis, *Gymnasium* 78 (1971) 512–13.

61–5 'He anticipates the fall of Troy' (A). bT comment on the grim economy of this catalogue of a sacked city's troubles, observing how the poet refrains from equipping any of the nouns with the usual epithets, and comparing 9.591–4 for a similar description; see also on 12.457–66. The repeated participial phrases produce a relentless, monotonous effect. For the mention of the θάλαμοι of Priam's extended family cf. 6.242–50. In a sack the most private family rooms are desecrated.

62–4 ἑλκηθείσας τε θύγατρας ... καὶ νήπια τέκνα | βαλλόμενα προτὶ γαίῃ: T thinks of the fate of Kassandra, raped by Locrian Aias, and of Astuanax, who was thrown from the wall of Troy in later versions of the sack (*Iliupersis*, OCT vol. v, p. 108.2–3 = Davies, *EGF* p. 62.23–4, *Ilias Parva* fr. 19 Allen = Davies, *EGF* fr. 20; see on 24.734–9). ἕλκειν is used of rape at *Od*. 11.580; cf. *Il*. 6.465 ἑλκηθμοῖο. As Schadewaldt observed (*Hellas und Hesperien*, Zürich 1960, 37), in such allusions to the sack of Troy the poet 'makes what in the tradition is simple fact into a medium for the expression of psychological themes'.

65 This verse has been suspected as repetitious after 62. Certainly without it we should have an effective climax at 63–4, but given the style of this passage the repetition could be original. Most MSS of Plutarch (*Mor.* 114A) omit the verse, but they also omit 69–73.

66–76 The common motif of a body being eaten by dogs is here developed in a unique way, since these dogs are Priam's own. Leaf calls this 'an exaggeration of horror unlike the true Epic style'. Moreover, 71–6 correspond closely with Tyrtaeus fr. 10.21–30 West:

> αἰσχρὸν γὰρ δὴ τοῦτο, μετὰ προμάχοισι πεσόντα
> κεῖσθαι πρόσθε νέων ἄνδρα παλαιότερον,
> ἤδη λευκὸν ἔχοντα κάρη πολιόν τε γένειον,
> θυμὸν ἀποπνείοντ' ἄλκιμον ἐν κονίῃ,
> αἱματόεντ' αἰδοῖα φίλαις ἐν χερσὶν ἔχοντα –
> αἰσχρὰ τά γ' ὀφθαλμοῖς καὶ νεμεσητὸν ἰδεῖν,
> καὶ χρόα γυμνωθέντα· νέοισι δὲ πάντ' ἐπέοικεν,
> ὄφρ' ἐρατῆς ἥβης ἀγλαὸν ἄνθος ἔχῃ,
> ἀνδράσι μὲν θηητὸς ἰδεῖν, ἐρατὸς δὲ γυναιξὶ
> ζωὸς ἐών, καλὸς δ' ἐν προμάχοισι πεσών.

Tyrtaeus is exhorting the young men not to neglect the defence of their elders in battle, and many modern scholars have argued that these verses suit the context there much better than the corresponding ones in the *Iliad*, where Priam is urging his son *not* to face Akhilleus, and so 71–3 are out of place. Cf. already bT 71–3: 'this appears to be an exhortation to die, rather than a discouragement' (etc.).

This has led to rejection of 69–76 as a later addition: cf. Leaf on 69, Schadewaldt, *VHWW* 300 n. 1, Von der Mühll, *Hypomnema* 332–3 (with other references), Lohmann, *Reden* 168. It is more probable, however, that both Homer and Tyrtaeus are making use of a protreptic passage belonging to the epic tradition, and that Homer has adapted it to a different context. Priam's point is that death and subsequent mutilation of one's body are disgraceful for an *old* man, and that therefore Hektor should think of the safety of his father and his people, rather than any personal honour gained by not running away. Verses 71–3 belong strictly within this context here.

As for Priam's dogs, cf. Segal, *Mutilation of the Corpse* 33: 'The threatened mutilation of Priam by his own dogs in his own house (cf. 22.69) also illustrates one of the broader implications of the corpse theme: that is, the destruction of civilized values, of civilization itself, by the savagery which war and its passions release.' It is a gruesome vision, but no more horrific than, for example, Akhilleus' wish that he might eat Hektor's raw flesh (346–7), or Hekabe's that she might eat Akhilleus' liver (24.212–13); cf. also 4.34–6. For general discussion of such passages see Segal, *Mutilation of the Corpse* 38–41, Griffin, *HLD* 20–1, 117.

In the *Ilias Parva* Priam is killed by Neoptolemus 'at the doors of his house' (fr. 16 Allen = Davies, *EGF* fr. 17): cf. here 66 πρώτῃσι θύρῃσι. In the *Iliupersis*, however, he dies at the altar of Zeus ἕρκειος (OCT vol. v, p. 107.30–1 = Davies, *EGF* p. 62.19–20), and this is the usual version later. In art his death is often associated with that of Astuanax, and sometimes also with the rape of Kassandra. Cf. Austin on Virgil, *Aen.* 2.506–58, and see on 62–4, 24.734–9.

66–7 αὐτὸν δ' ἂν ... | ὠμησταὶ ἐρύουσιν: for ἂν with the future see on 49–50. The phrase ὠμησταὶ ἐρύουσι is applied to birds devouring a corpse at 11.454.

68 For ῥέθεα, meaning 'limbs' here, see on 16.855–8.

69–71 Leaf punctuates with a colon after 68, making οὕς refer forward, and οἵ in 70 demonstrative. That is possible, but it seems preferable with the OCT to take οὕς as picking up κύνες in 66, with ἐπεί κε τις ... ἕληται as a parenthesis. For τραπεζῆας cf. 23.173, *Od.* 17.309 τραπεζῆες κύνες. θυραωρούς was Aristarchus' reading (Did/A) and that of a papyrus and a few MSS, πυλαωρούς being the vulgate text. θυραωρός occurs nowhere else in Homer (cf. later θυρωρός), πυλαωρός at 21.530, 24.681. The objection to πυλαωρός was that πύλη refers to the gate of a city, not a house, although πύλη or πύλαι are sometimes used of a house-door in Attic tragedy (cf. LSJ). It is possible that πυλαωρούς is original, and θυραωρούς an ancient conjecture: so van der Valk, *Researches* II 140.

70–1 ἀλύσσοντες means 'restless', 'maddened'. This form of the verb occurs only here in epic, and nowhere else later in the present tense, but cf. 5.352 etc. ἀλύειν. In περὶ θυμῷ, περί is probably adverbial, as in περὶ κῆρι etc. ἐν προθύροισι echoes the end of 66, rounding off this passage. For the second hemistich of 71 cf. Tyrt. fr. 10.27 νέοισι δὲ πάντ᾽ ἐπέοικεν.

72 ἀρηϊκταμένῳ: only here, but cf. ἀρηΐφατος, δαϊκτάμενος. If one were to write this as two words (Ἄρηϊ κταμένῳ) the parallelism and chiasmus with the following hemistich would be more clearly brought out. The series of dative endings, repetition of the same idea, and heavy spondaic opening all combine to give this line a dirge-like effect. δεδαϊγμένος -ον ὀξέϊ χαλκῷ occurs 4× and δεδαϊγμένος -οι 2× in books 18–19, especially of Patroklos.

73 κεῖσθαι is added somewhat awkwardly (contrast Tyrt. fr. 10.22), and the rest of the verse repeats the idea of 71–2 in a rather weak way. ὅττι φανήη was taken as meaning 'whatever befalls him' by Leaf, but the sense 'whatever is visible' (i.e. of his body) is surely better (cf. Willcock).

74–6 These verses appear to have been omitted by the Hellenistic papyrus (pap. 12): cf. West, *Ptolemaic Papyri* 161.

74 πολιόν τε κάρη πολιόν τε γένειον: cf. 24.516 for this emphatic repetition (Akhilleus pities Priam). Tyrtaeus has λευκὸν ... κάρη πολιόν τε γένειον (fr. 10.23).

75 αἰδῶ suggests αἰδοῖα. Tyrtaeus (fr. 10.25) is brutally explicit, whereas the abstract noun here implies that this form of disfigurement is a particular affront to someone's αἰδώς in general. Homeric decorum generally avoids references to αἰδοῖα: see on 2.262 (the only other Homeric use of αἰδώς in this sense), and in general Wackernagel, *Sprachliche Untersuchungen* 224–9. As with 71, κύνες picks up the beginning of this section of the speech at the end (cf. 66).

76 τοῦτο δὴ οἴκτιστον: cf. *Od.* 12.258 οἴκτιστον δὴ κεῖνο ἐμοῖς ἴδον ὀφθαλμοῖσι. οἴκτιστος occurs only here in *Il.*, but 6× *Od.*, always in speeches except once (22.472 οἴκτιστα).

77–8 Tearing one's hair is again a common feature of mourning ritual, which recurs at 405–6, 18.27, 24.710–11 and *Od.* 10.567; see also on 33–4.

79–81 Hekabe is more emotional. She weeps and laments, exposing her breast. There are parallels to this gesture of exposure by women in a conflict in Tacitus' account of the Germans and also in Irish literature: cf. Tac. *Germania* 8.1, and Griffin, *HLD* 25 n. 66. κολπὸν ἀνιεμένη means 'drawing open the fold of her dress'.

82–9 Hekabe's speech is much shorter than Priam's, but it is a more personal appeal for pity. It is a traditional feature of entreaties that she should remind Hektor of what she has given him in the past (εἴ ποτε ... τῶν μνῆσαι ...). She goes on to envisage Hektor's unburied body as a prey for the dogs, deprived of burial rites. Her thoughts turn to the funeral lament which it would be the duty of his mother and wife to make if he dies: cf. 352–4, 426–8, 508–14, and for the laments themselves 24.719–59. Notice also the rush of imperatives in 82–5, and the repeated vocatives of endearment: τέκνον ἐμὸν ... φίλε τέκνον ... φίλον θάλος. The speech is echoed in Stesichorus' *Geryoneis* by Geruon's mother, *Supplementum Lyricis Graecis* ed. Page, S 13.2–5.

82 αἴδεο καί μ' ἐλέησον: so also at 21.74. αἰδώς and ἔλεος are crucial concepts in these closing books of the poem, recurring at 123–4, 419, 24.44, 24.207–8 and 24.503.

83–4 εἴ ποτέ τοι ... τῶν μνῆσαι: cf. 1.39 εἴ ποτέ τοι etc. (in a prayer), 394–407 εἴ ποτε ... τῶν νῦν μιν μνήσασα ... (Thetis' entreaty to Zeus), etc. λαθικηδέα is an effective epithet, only here in epic; cf. Alc. 346.3 L–P οἶνον ... λαθικάδεον, etc. For δήϊον ἄνδρα see on 38.

85 ἐών is the reading of Aristarchus (Did/A) and some of our MSS for the vulgate ἰών. Leaf also prefers ἐών, but either seems possible. There are similar variants at 4.277.

86–9 Cf. especially 352–4 οὐδ' ὥς σέ γε πότνια μήτηρ | ἐνθεμένη λεχέεσσι γοήσεται, ὃν τέκεν αὐτή, | ἀλλὰ κύνες τε καὶ οἰωνοὶ κατὰ πάντα δάσονται.

86 σχέτλιος is repeated from 41. Here however it may well refer to Hektor, and this is how the OCT takes it. It means 'persistent', 'obstinate': cf. σχεθεῖν, and the etymology of Hektor's own name implied at 24.730. It is used by Diomedes to Nestor when he is woken up by him at 10.164, by Akhilleus of Patroklos at 18.13, and to Odysseus by Athene at *Od.* 13.293 and 20.45: so it does not need to be hostile.

87 φίλον θάλος: the metaphorical θάλος is more effective as a term of endearment than the variant τέκος. θάλος occurs in *Il.* only here, but it is used (metaphorically) at *Od.* 6.157, *HyDem* 66 and 187.

88 ἄλοχος πολύδωρος: as at 6.394 (Andromakhe meeting Hektor), *Od.* 24.294 (Penelope). πολύδωρος was interpreted as meaning that she had received many marriage gifts from her parents (A 6.394, Arn/A on 22.88; cf. Arn/A on 2nd hemistich of 9.147); see on 49–51. Hektor's own gifts are mentioned at 472.

ἄνευθε ... μέγα νῶϊν means 'very far away from us'. This use of μέγα with an adverb seems to be unique, but for μέγα of distance cf. 14.363 μέγα προθορών. The interlaced word-order is unusual, and these simple words have great intensity.

91–130 Hektor ignores his parents' entreaties, and waits for Akhilleus' attack. But he then begins to debate whether or not to remain after all. Eventually he resolves to stand firm

90–2 With these transitional verses the focus moves to Hektor himself. The repetition of the phrase οὐδ' Ἕκτορι θυμὸν ἔπειθε -ον (78, 91) stresses his obduracy, preparing for the simile which follows. Hektor's refusal to listen reminds us of his earlier obduracy towards Pouludamas and others, which he himself will soon recall (99–103).

92 Ἀχιλῆα πελώριον: as at 21.537. In both cases the epithet emphasizes Akhilleus' menacing and awe-inspiring approach, as seen through the eyes of Priam or Hektor. Cf. de Jong, *Narrators* 129–30 (also on the following simile).

93–7 Hektor is compared to an angry and venomous snake waiting at the entrance to its hole to attack a man. At 3.33–7 Paris retreats before Menelaos like a man confronted by a snake; and at 12.200–7 an eagle is counter-attacked by the snake which it is carrying. These passages imply the same view of snakes as vicious and courageous creatures (cf. Fränkel, *Gleichnisse* 69). The snake in its lair also suggests the idea of Hektor just outside the gate of Troy.

Notice the reversal of the simile in book 3, implying the contrast between Paris and Hektor: there the snake is Menelaos and Paris retreats, whereas here the snake is Hektor who stands and waits. But in book 3 Paris eventually does stand and fight a duel, although only after Hektor's reproaches, whereas here Hektor's resolution breaks down and he flees. It is ironic that the hero who had always urged on the other Trojans should here lose his own nerve at the supreme moment of crisis. Cf. Introduction, 'Structure', and Schadewaldt, *VHWW* 304–5; see also Fenik, *Tradition* 83–4, on the relationship of this simile to Hektor's monologue.

93 ἐπὶ χείῃ: this word for the snake's hole is repeated at 95, and occurs only here in epic. Cf. Pindar, *I.* 8.77 etc. For ὀρέστερος ἄνδρα μένῃσι some city texts read ὀρέστερον ἄνδρα δοκεύῃ. ὀρέστερος also occurs only here in *Il.*; cf. *Od.* 10.212.

94 βεβρωκὼς κακὰ φάρμακ': imitated by Virgil in a simile at *Aen.* 2.471: *coluber mala gramina pastus*. Evidently snakes were believed to get their poison from the food which they ate; this is stated by Aelian (*NA* 6.4), but it is clear that he is basing himself on Homer, whom he cites. Pliny (*HN* 8.139) says that snakes have no venom when hibernating, which seems to imply the same belief. For ἔδυ δέ τέ μιν χόλος αἰνός cf. 9.553, 19.16 ἔδυ χόλος.

95 The phrase σμερδαλέον δὲ δέδορκεν only occurs here in Homer, but cf. 3.342 δεινὸν δερκόμενοι, etc. The word δράκων itself is related to δέρκομαι, so there is probably deliberate etymological word-play here, as the D-scholiast suggests. ἑλισσόμενος περὶ χείῃ belongs to a group of formular phrases: 1.317 ἑλισσομένη περὶ καπνῷ, 18.372 -ον περὶ φύσας, 21.11 -οι περὶ δίνας.

97 The verse presents a vivid detail. The shield resting on a projecting tower, and likewise Akhilleus leaning on his spear at 225, remind T appropriately of sculpture. There are similar details at 112 and 21.17–18, 21.549(n.).

98–130 Hektor's soliloquy is the longest and most complex of its type: see on Agenor's speech (21.550–70), which it most closely resembles. After the poet's insistence on Hektor's determination this speech is at first sight a surprise. But we must judge it in its context. In the eyes of those who look on, Hektor initially displays a stubborn determination to stand firm. But the poet reveals to us that internally he is in a turmoil of uncertainty (cf. the reference to Agenor's courage at 21.547, followed by his soliloquy). Hektor's reasoning culminates in the conclusion that the only practical course is to fight, but as soon as Akhilleus is really close fear gets the upper hand, and he flees (131–7). Then, deceived into thinking he has support from Deiphobos, he again makes a stand and shows defiance (226ff.), until he realizes the truth; then he despairs, but nevertheless displays a final, desperate courage (296ff.). This oscillation, extended here over a series of episodes, might be seen as the forerunner of those more concentrated scenes in tragedy (especially in Euripides) where internal debate and conflict are shown. On these cf. W. Schadewaldt, *Monolog und Selbstgespräch* (Berlin 1926), especially 189ff.; and on Hektor's monologue the works referred to at 21.550–70n.

98–9 Verse 98 = 21.552 (see note), etc., and for ὤ μοι ἐγών, εἰ μέν κε ... see on 21.553. After 99 pap. 12 has an extra verse: λωβητός κεν πᾶσι μετὰ Τ[ρώεσσι (e.g. γενοίμην).

100–10 The debate in which Pouludamas urged retreat into Troy and Hektor rejected this advice took place at 18.243–313. Hektor actually boasted then that he would not run away from Akhilleus (306–8), and the poet commented that Athene robbed the Trojans of their wits when they agreed with him (311–13); so here (104) Hektor refers to his disastrous error. Because of this he is now afraid of the shame and disgrace of failure, and feels that it is better to face his enemy. At least he may die honourably (105–10).

We see how preoccupied Hektor still is with honour and shame, rather than with the sort of consideration for his people's future safety which had dictated Pouludamas' advice, and which Priam has also been urging. There is a significant parallel with his refusal to listen to Andromakhe's advice in book 6 (405–65). There too Hektor was concerned above all with honour and shame (6.442 = 22.105; note also the reference to Andromakhe at

22.88, picking up 6.394). Cf. J. M. Redfield, *Nature and Culture in the Iliad: the Tragedy of Hector* (Chicago 1975) 157–8: 'the same inner force that sent him into battle—his *aidōs* before the men and women of Troy—prevents him from returning home'. bT's comment is also worth quoting: 'the poet shows how disastrous is the love of honour (φιλοτιμία): for because he does not wish to be called a coward (κακός) by a baser man (κακωτέρου) ... he perishes. His reasoning displays a noble spirit, but also folly: for he wanted to cure one evil by another.'

100 For ἐλεγχείην ἀναθήσει cf. 23.408 ἐλεγχείην καταχεύῃ |. This compound verb occurs only here in Homer; cf. Hes. *Erga* 658, etc.

102 νύχθ᾽ ὕπὸ τήνδ᾽ ὀλοήν: 'in the course of this (last) cursed night'. Pap. 12 replaces this by the colourless νύκτα ποτὶ δνοφερήν, probably because this use of ὕπό in a temporal sense is so rare (cf. 16.202n.). For ὀλοή applied to νύξ see on 16.567–8.

103 = 5.201. Here and at 108 there was a variant κάλλιον (cf. 15.195–9n.).

104–5 For 104 cf. 4.409 κεῖνοι δὲ σφετέρῃσιν ἀτασθαλίῃσιν ὄλοντο (of the Seven against Thebes), with comment. ἀτάσθαλος and related words occur 5× *Il.*, but 26× *Od.* Verse 105 = 6.442. See on 100–10 above.

106 For μή ποτέ τις εἴπῃσι cf. 23.575. κακώτερος ἄλλος ἐμεῖο implies that it is more dishonourable to be criticized by a 'baser' man. Hektor is constantly concerned about what people will say: see on 6.459–62, 7.87–91 and 7.300–2, also 6.479–81, 16.838–42, and Martin, *Language of Heroes* 136–8.

108–10 τότε means 'in that case', i.e. 'because I fear disgrace'. In 109–10 κατακτείναντα ... αὐτῷ ... is the vulgate text, but Aristarchus (Did/A) knew κατακτείναντι as an alternative, and our MSS have the variants κατακτείναντι and αὐτόν. Leaf comments judiciously that κατακτείναντα 'has yielded as usual to the influence of the infin. with which it is closely connected (*to slay and return*), and is undoubtedly more Homeric', whereas 'the dative αὐτῷ seems necessary to keep up the connexion with ἐμοί: the acc. would be ambiguous, as it might refer to Achilles'.

110 κεν 'seems to serve here as a reinforcement of the ἄν above' (Leaf). Pap. 12 reads ἢ [αὐ]τῷ π[ρὸ πόλ]ηος ἐϋκλειῶς ἀπ[ολέσθαι, which would be a perfectly reasonable verse, and one which avoids the correption and awkward trochaic rhythm of αὐτῷ and ὀλέσθαι; but it may have arisen owing to objection to κεν, such as is expressed by Arn/A. Cf. van der Valk, *Researches* ii 566–7, Chantraine, *GH* ii 311. πρὸ πόληος means 'in defence of the city'.

111–30 Hektor now considers offering Akhilleus the return of Helen and the property which Paris stole, together with the further offer to divide all the wealth of Troy between Greeks and Trojans: this measure was mentioned as an alternative to the sack of a city at 18.509–12. He breaks off, however, reflecting that Akhilleus would not respect him but simply kill him, unarmed as he is. Finally he resolves to fight.

111 εἰ δέ κεν ...: see on 21.556. Here the suspension of the conditional clause is sustained over eleven whole verses, producing an effect of climax as Hektor's offer grows progressively more extraordinary in value, until it reaches the point where he himself realizes that this is all just day-dreaming. At this point (122) he breaks off, without reaching an apodosis.

112–13 For δόρυ δὲ πρὸς τεῖχος ἐρείσας see on 97. αὐτός means 'on my own', or perhaps 'unarmed', and ἀντίος perhaps 'as a suppliant' (so T).

114–18 In book 3 the duel was fought ἀμφ' Ἑλένη καὶ κτήμασι πᾶσι (70), and Agamemnon added the idea of further compensation (286–7). At 7.345–64 Paris refused to give up Helen, but was willing to return the property and to add more from his own house. Cf. 114 and 117 with 7.350–1 Ἑλένην καὶ κτήμαθ' ἅμ' αὐτῇ | δώομεν Ἀτρεΐδησιν ἄγειν.

115–16 Cf. 7.389–90 κτήματα μὲν ὅσ' Ἀλέξανδρος κοίλης ἐνὶ νηυσὶν | ἠγάγετο Τροίηνδ' ... For ἥ τ' ἔπλετο νείκεος ἀρχή cf. 11.604 (with comment) κακοῦ δ' ἄρα οἱ πέλεν ἀρχή; *Od.* 8.81 (of the Trojan War) πήματος ἀρχή. ἥ refers to the whole of what precedes, i.e. the rape of Helen, and is attracted to the case of ἀρχή.

117–18 ἀμφίς means apart from what has already been mentioned. ἀποδάσσεσθαι (future) is Aristarchus' reading (Did/A) for our vulgate ἀποδάσσασθαι.

119 Τρωσὶν ... γερούσιον ὅρκον: i.e. an oath taken by the elders in the name of the people of Troy. See on 4.259 γερούσιον αἴθοπα οἶνον.

120–1 Cf. 18.511–12 ἄνδιχα πάντα δάσασθαι | κτῆσιν ὅσην πτολίεθρον ἐπήρατον ἐντὸς ἔεργεν. Here the future δάσεσθαι seems to have been read in antiquity (cf. T), and is preferable, as in 118. Verse 121 is omitted by a papyrus and several MSS, including A. It is not really needed after 118, and is probably an addition.

122 For this 'break-off formula' see on 21.562.

123–5 We have seen what Hektor envisages actually happen in the case of Lukaon (21.34–135). For the construction μή ... ἵκωμαι ... ὁ δέ μ' οὐκ ἐλεήσει ... cf. the train of thought in Agenor's soliloquy at 21.563–5 μή μ' ... νοήσῃ ... οὐκέτ' ἔπειτ' ἔσται ... Here ἵκωμαι means 'approach as a suppliant (ἱκέτης)', as is shown by the use of the verb αἰδέσεται (so Arn/A, bT). γυμνόν must mean 'unarmed', as at 21.50 (Lukaon) etc. αὔτως ('just as I am') is often used with an implication of helplessness, e.g. 6.400 νήπιον αὔτως.

126–8 Whatever the poet may have intended by the phrase ἀπὸ δρυὸς οὐδ' ἀπὸ πέτρης (which occurs only here in *Il.*), the general point is presumably that any attempt at exchanging words of friendship with Akhilleus is a waste of time. Ancient and modern interpretations are listed and discussed by West on Hes. *Th.* 35, who concludes that 'the truth is lost in antiquity'. Cf. also *Od.* 19.163 οὐ γὰρ ἀπὸ δρυός ἐσσι παλαιφάτου οὐδ' ἀπὸ πέτρης. It may be relevant that the Hesiodic context has some resemblance to ours. Hesiod has just told of his meeting with the Muses, and breaks off with the question ἀλλὰ τίη μοι ταῦτα περὶ δρῦν ἢ περὶ πέτρην; He then urges himself to get on with the job of praising the Muses (36). The first half of *Th.* 35 is the same as that of 122, where again Hektor breaks off his speculations and brings himself down to earth. In both cases something which is either irrelevant or unrealistic is dismissed. In Hektor's case his earlier thoughts of a treaty with his enemy now suggest to his mind the conversation of two lovers 'from oak or from rock': this too may be irrelevant, trivial, fanciful, or perhaps simply long and rambling.

Whatever the original sense, to a modern reader the phrase conjures up a pastoral scene of a lover's meeting in the countryside, which (despite Leaf's odd view that this is 'neither Epic nor Greek') does form a suitable context. Hektor has just referred to being killed 'like a woman', and this is perhaps what gives rise to the idea of the two lovers conversing (cf. 13.290–1n.). The effect is extraordinarily moving: 'Hektor's mind reverts to peacetime' (Willcock), and there could be no greater contrast with the grimness of the real situation. The effect of the reference to peacetime at 153–6 is similar. The idea of φιλία between Akhilleus and Hektor is echoed at 261–7 in the elaborate simile by which Akhilleus expresses the impossibility of any such agreement.

After 126 an extra verse is added by pap. 12, whose point is unclear. It ends πολέ]μοιο μεμαότα δακρυόεντος.

127 ὀαριζέμεναι: cf. 6.516 ὅθι ἣ ὀάριζε γυναικί (Hektor and Andromakhe). ὀαριστύς is used again at 14.216 of love; and at 13.291, 17.228 of war, probably ironically as here (see on 13.290–1). The root noun ὄαρ (in the sense 'wife') occurs at 5.486, 9.327; cf. ὀαριστής of Minos as the close friend of Zeus at *Od.* 19.179. The fact that the verb is used only here and in the scene where Hektor converses with his own wife is surely significant, and the echo of the earlier scene helps to remind us of what Hektor himself stands to lose.

ἅ τε παρθένος ἠΐθεός τε: cf. 18.567 παρθενικαὶ δὲ καὶ ἠΐθεοι ἀταλὰ φρονέοντες, 593 ἠΐθεοι καὶ παρθένοι ἀλφεσίβοιαι. Both these verses occur in the Shield of Akhilleus, again in peaceful scenes set into the context of war.

127–8 Epanalepsis of this type, where the second hemistich is repeated at the beginning of the next verse, occurs only at 20.371–2 (Hektor speaking about Akhilleus) and 23.641–2; cf. *CQ* 30 (1980) 282. Here the verb, also, is repeated in 128. bT consider that the repetition reflects the talkativeness of the two lovers. Modern scholars describe the effect as 'pathetic' or 'wistful' (Willcock, Segal, *Mutilation of the Corpse* 35, Owen, *Story of the Iliad*

222). One might compare it to a momentary 'still' in the middle of a film: our minds rest, with Hektor's, on this scene of the lovers. Verse 128 is a stately one, composed of four main words, with a spondaic ending. 'We may also note how Homer, as is his custom, fills the lines [127–8] with vowels and avoids all ugly consonantal clashes, to express the implicit pleasure of the scene' (W. B. Stanford, *The Sound of Greek*, Berkeley 1967, 88). Notice also the general chiastic effect: ὀαριζέμεναι ... παρθένος (etc.) ... παρθένος ... ὀαρίζετον, with ἀλλήλοιιν at the end to draw the two parties together and round off the sentence.

129–30 The two closing verses of this speech, in contrast, are rapid and matter-of-fact, with a quick run of dactyls in both. ξυνελαυνέμεν is intransitive only here. For ὅττι τάχιστα the variant ὄφρα τάχιστα (A and one papyrus) would go with the following verse; cf. 13.326–7 ὄφρα τάχιστα | εἴδομεν ἠέ τῳ εὖχος ὀρέξομεν, ἦέ τις ἡμῖν. But it is more effective to take the two verses separately with asyndeton. In 130 pap. 12 reads ὁπποτέρῳ Κρονίδης Ζεὺς κῦδος ὀρέξῃ. Cf. for this alternative 5.33, 8.141, 21.570 (at the end of Agenor's soliloquy). Here, however, the vulgate reading with κεν is better.

131–87 When Akhilleus finally bears down upon Hektor he flees. Akhilleus pursues him around the walls of Troy three times, whilst the gods look on. Zeus asks whether they should rescue him from death, but Athene protests that his doom has been fixed long ago. Zeus gives way, and Athene leaves Olumpos

In this and the following episode (188–213) the poet maintains and increases the suspense by a series of different techniques, in a way which resembles other climactic parts of the earlier battle-scenes: for this see especially on 15.592–746, and Fenik, *TBS* 178.

131–5 This description of Akhilleus picks up 25–32. It is as if hardly any time had really elapsed, and bT comment that Akhilleus' approach, Priam's and Hekabe's supplications, and Hektor's soliloquy are all really simultaneous. As Owen says of this Book, 'everything is rushing to a climax, and yet it all stands still—as when we watched Achilles coming swiftly across the plain, the time seemed endless' (*Story of the Iliad* 227).

132 This is another four-word verse, comparing Akhilleus to Ares. Elsewhere only Meriones is compared to Enualios, in a formular verse (2.651 etc.), but cf. (θοῷ) ἀτάλαντος (etc.) Ἄρηϊ (11× *Il.*) and βροτολοιγῷ ἶσος (etc.) Ἄρηϊ (4× *Il.*), and see on 13.298–303. κορυθάϊκι means 'with quivering helmet'. The word occurs only here and perhaps in Hes. fr. 185.15 M–W κορυθά]ϊκος πολεμιστέω; cf. κορυθαίολος (2.816 etc.).

133–4 As at 26–32 and 92 Akhilleus' approach inspires terror, here especially because of the deadly spear which he brandishes. The runover word δεινήν is powerful; for a similar use cf. especially 16.788–89, where Apollo encounters Patroklos and causes his death, and see Higbie, *Measure and Music* 207–8.

134–5 In addition to the simile at 26–32 cf. 11.595 (etc.) δέμας πυρὸς αἰθομένοιο |, 18.609 θώρηκα φαεινότερον πυρὸς αὐγῆς |, 18.136 ἠελίῳ ἀνιόντι | (cf. 8.538). The threefold hiatus and sequence of vowel sounds in 135 were noticed by T, who described the verse as 'rather liquid' (ὑγρότερος); see also on 152. Such effects are discussed by Demetrius (*On Style* 68–74), who says that ἠέλιος is more euphonious than ἥλιος. For other examples in the scholia cf. *CQ* 30 (1980) 286. Here one might think that the concurrence of long vowels added to the impression of 'grandeur' (as suggested by Demetrius 72–3). This shows how difficult it is to describe such effects, although that need not debar one from trying.

136–8 Two verses containing four short, sharp sentences, which describe Hektor's terror and flight, contrast with the fluid five verses about Akhilleus' pursuit which follow at 138–42. Note the elegant variation of the colometry in 136–7, with οὐδέ ... μένειν, a more flowing clause in enjambment, enclosed within the more staccato ones:

Ἕκτορα δ᾽, ὡς ἐνόησεν, ἕλε τρόμος· οὐδ᾽ ἄρ᾽ ἔτ᾽ ἔτλη
αὖθι μένειν, ὀπίσω δὲ πύλας λίπε, βῆ δὲ φοβηθείς·

For the second hemistich of 136 cf. 19.14 ἕλε τρόμος, οὐδέ τις ἔτλη | and 20.421 οὐδ᾽ ἄρ᾽ ἔτ᾽ ἔτλη |, and for 138 cf. 6.505 ποσὶ κραιπνοῖσι πεποιθώς |. Pap. 12 reads ποσὶν ταχέεσσι, which is commoner (4× *Il.*).

139–44 Akhilleus pursuing Hektor is compared to a hawk in close pursuit of a dove. κίρκος only occurs in one other simile in the *Iliad* (17.755–9), but ἴρηξ is commoner (6×), and ἴρηξ and πέλεια appear together in the simile at 21.493–6: see comments.

139 Cf. *Od.* 13.86–7 οὐδέ κεν ἴρηξ | κίρκος ὁμαρτήσειεν, ἐλαφρότατος πετεηνῶν, and the similar expressions at *Il.* 15.237–8 and 21.253.

140 οἴμησε: the verb recurs at 308 (= *Od.* 24.538) and 311, again in a simile. Cf. the use of the noun οἶμα in comparisons at 16.352, 21.252. On τρήρωνα πέλειαν see 5.778n.

141–2 ὕπαιθα φοβεῖται in this context resembles 21.493 ὕπαιθα θεὰ φύγεν ὥς τε πέλεια. The phrase ὀξὺ λεληκώς occurs only here. At Hes. *Erga* 207 the hawk asks the nightingale τί λέληκας; The verb is used of the black eagle at Arist. *HA* 618b31. ταρφέ᾽ ἐπαΐσσει means 'makes frequent swoops'.

143 πέτετο, τρέσε δ᾽ Ἕκτωρ: the lengthened vowel before τρέσε and break in the middle of the fifth foot make an abrupt closing rhythm. τρέσε is 'fled in terror' (Arn/A, T); cf. 5.256 etc.

144 λαιψηρὰ δὲ γούνατ᾽ ἐνώμα recurs at 10.358, and is related to 15.269 = 22.24 λαιψηρὰ πόδας καὶ γούνατ᾽ ἐνώμα.

145-57 The poet gives us precise topographical details, which add to the credibility and vividness of the narrative. He may also be following his custom elsewhere of filling a space in the story, as for example where a journey is taking place. This is suggested by bT (147–56): for other examples in the scholia see *CQ* 30 (1980) 266–7. There is a much clearer example of this technique at 166–87 below, the debate in heaven before the climax of the chase.

145 παρὰ σκοπιὴν καὶ ἐρινεὸν ἠνεμόεντα: this look-out place can hardly be the one where Polites is posted at 2.793. A fig-tree is mentioned as a landmark at 6.433, 11.167: in the first case it seems to be near the wall of Troy, which fits this passage, and it may be significant that in that passage as well as in book 22 it is mentioned in close association with the fate of Hektor (cf. Elliger, *Darstellung der Landschaft* 58).

146 They follow a waggon-track which skirts the town, a short distance outside the wall. ἁμαξιτός occurs in Homer only here; cf. *HyDem* 177, etc.

147-56 'In spite of the loving detail with which the *Iliad* . . . describes the double fountain under the walls of Troy, it is no longer possible to use it as evidence: no such combination of hot and cold springs now exists in the plain' (Leaf, *Troy* 48). But 'what he gives us is in fact very characteristic of the Troad at large, though not of the immediate surroundings of Troy. The hot springs of the Troad are as marked a feature as the cold which break out all over many-fountained Ida' (*ibid.* 49–50). Already in antiquity, by the time of Demetrius of Scepsis (Strabo 13.1.43, 602), there were no hot springs by the walls of Troy, whereas such were known to exist on Mt Ida (so T on 149). Two large springs, in particular, form one of the sources of the Skamandros on Mt Ida, and some nineteenth-century travellers asserted that one was hotter than the other (Leaf, *ibid.* 50–2). The suggestion was made by R. L. K. Virchow (*Beiträge zur Landeskunde der Troas*, Berlin 1880, 33–43) that the poet transferred these in his imagination to Troy, where some springs do still exist near the walls (Leaf, *ibid.* 165–6). But Cook (*Troad* 293) has doubts about this.

Whatever the truth may be, presumably the poet had heard of two springs which were regarded as a local wonder by the people of the Troad. Why does he introduce them at this crucial point in his narrative? Partly for the reasons mentioned already in the comment on 145–57, but also because it is precisely at this point, when Akhilleus and Hektor reach these springs for the fourth time, that Hektor's doom is sealed (208–13). This is a variation of the technique which the poet uses elsewhere in order to draw our attention to the importance of what is to occur, whether he does so by describing a particular object or scene in unusual detail, or by other means such as a build-up of similes, or an invocation of the Muses. Here, however, there is in addition a dramatic contrast between the life-and-death struggle which is taking place and the recollection of a peaceful scene of women washing safely in the countryside near the city walls. Cf. S. E. Bassett, *TAPA* 61 (1930) 138–9, Schadewaldt, *VHWW* 308, Elliger, *Darstellung der Landschaft* 58–9, Griffin, *HLD* 21–2, 112.

147–8 Ancient scholars solved the problem of identification here by suggesting that the springs were either fed by Skamandros underground, or else were simply near the river (Arn/A 148, Porph. 1.256.24, Demetrius of Scepsis in Strabo *loc. cit.*). For Σκαμάνδρου δινήεντος see on 21.1–2.

149–52 The poet dwells on the contrast between the two springs, from one of which hot steam rises, whereas the other even in summer is as cold as hail, snow or ice. The two couplets are balanced, but in the second there is a climax in χαλάζη | ἢ χιόνι ψυχρῇ, ἢ ἐξ ὕδατος κρυστάλλῳ. ὕδατι λιαρῷ recurs at 11.830 and 846. For 151–2 cf. 10.6–7 ἠὲ χάλαζαν | ἢ νιφετόν, ὅτε πέρ τε χιὼν ἐπάλυνεν ἀρούρας; 15.170–1 νιφὰς ἠὲ χάλαζα | ψυχρή ...; and *Od.* 14.476–7 πηγυλίς· αὐτὰρ ὕπερθε χιὼν γένετ' ἠΰτε πάχνη, | ψυχρή, καὶ σακέεσσι περιτρέφετο κρύσταλλος (the only other use of κρύσταλλος in Homer).

T says of 152 'he has made the verse fluid by the use of the juxtaposed vowels', and this verse is quoted by Aulus Gellius (*NA* 6.20.4) as a model example of the deliberate effect of *suavitas*, produced by the elegant use of hiatus. See on 135, which this verse resembles in structure, and with which it is contrasted in subject (fire and the sun, snow and ice). The spondaic ending adds to the beauty of the verse, which must surely be the coldest in Greek poetry.

153–6 In *Odyssey* 6 Nausikaa and her maids wash εἵματα σιγαλόεντα (26) at the πλύνοι (40, 86) by the river's mouth: the phrase εἵματα σιγαλόεντα and the word πλύνοι only occur in these passages in Homer. σιγαλόεντα, however, is used of Andromakhe's head-dress at 468; cf. ἡνία σιγαλόεντα 5.226 etc., ῥήγεα σιγαλόεντα *Od.* 6.38 etc. The form λάϊνεοι occurs only here in Homer (cf. λάϊνος 3× *Il.*, 5× *Od.*), and the verb πλύνω only here in *Il.*, 5× *Od.*, 2× in book 6 (31, 59).

156 = 9.403, where Akhilleus is speaking of Troy's wealth in the past. Here, however, it carries much greater significance.

157–8 φεύγων, ὁ δ' ὄπισθε διώκων means '(one) fleeing, the other pursuing'. For this idiom cf. 7.420, 24.527. Verse 158 elaborates 157, with an elegant chiasmus.

159–66 The idea of pursuit naturally suggests a foot-race, and this in turn generates the simile of the horse-race. But the prize here is no ordinary one: it is Hektor's own life (159–61).

159 ἱερήϊον is a sacrificial animal (4× *Od.*). Oxen are used as prizes in the funeral games at 23.260. βοείην is either an ox-hide or possibly a shield (cf. 7.238 βῶν, etc.). bT say that hides were given as prizes in the four-yearly festival of Herakles celebrated by the people of Oita. Shields were also sometimes given as prizes in games in the classical period, as in the Heraia at Argos (schol. Pindar, *O.* 7.152c). Here, however, with ἱερήϊον an ox-hide is more likely.

160 ἀρνύσθην means 'they were trying to win'. For ἅ τε ποσσὶν ἀέθλια γίγνεται ἀνδρῶν cf. 9.124 etc. ἀέθλια ποσσὶν ἄροντο |.

161 περὶ ψυχῆς: cf. *Od.* 9.423 περὶ ψυχῆς, *Od.* 22.245 περί τε ψυχέων ἐμάχοντο.

162-6 This simile expands the brief one at 22-4. It has several points of contact with the narrative: the importance of the prize (161 ~ 163), the speed of the horses (163 ~ 159, 166), and by implication the repeated 'laps' of the racecourse (162 περὶ τέρματα ~ 165). It also suggests the idea of spectators: hence the gods as onlookers (166). So it not only arises out of the preceding context, but also acts as a transitional passage to the following scene in heaven.

For 162 cf. 22 ὥς θ' ἵππος ἀεθλοφόρος; 23.309 περὶ τέρματα. τρωχᾶν is used of mules at *Od.* 6.318 and later in Apollonius (3.874 τρώχων εὐρεῖαν κατ' ἀμαξιτόν).

164 ἢ τρίπος ἠὲ γυνή: at 23.262-5 the first prize in the chariot-race is a woman and a tripod together. ἀνδρὸς κατατεθνηῶτος means that it is in honour of a man who has died. For the ancient tradition that the athletic festivals all originated as funeral games see on 23.262-897.

164-5 Here two successive verses have spondaic endings. In 165 τρίς is a signal that when the fourth time comes the outcome will be decided (208-13). The same motif occurs at 5.436-9 (see comment), 16.702-6, 16.784-7, 20.445-8 and 21.176-9. Here, however, the action is suspended at this momentous point: the picture is frozen, while the gods calmly discuss Hektor's fate. The most famous example of this technique is the account of how Odysseus got his scar, at the climax of the recognition scene with Eurukleia (*Od.* 19.392-468).

πόλιν πέρι δινηθήτην: bT comment that it is 'as if they were turning on a (compass-drawn) circle, suggesting both speed and running along a single line'.

166 θεοὶ δ' ἐς πάντες ὁρῶντο: δ' ἐς is better here, for the gods looking on, than the more commonplace variant δέ τε.

166-87 The gods are like the spectators at a sporting event. They discuss the outcome, and they are also involved in what is going on, as in the quarrel between the spectators of the horse-race at 23.448-98. See Griffin, *HLD* 179-204 and *CQ* 28 (1978) 1-22.

This debate resembles that over Sarpedon's fate (16.431-61: see comment for these and other scenes of this type). Zeus pities both, Sarpedon more than Hektor because he is his own son, but Hektor also because of his piety. He asks whether both should be rescued or not. Herē protests that Sarpedon's doom has long been fixed, and Athene uses the same words of Hektor (16.441– = 22.179–81). At this point the scenes diverge. Herē has more to say about Sarpedon's fate, not all of it negative, whereas in Hektor's case Zeus simply yields to Athene, and allows her to bring about his death.

It is clear that Zeus is not bound by the fact that a person's doom has long ago been fixed: but the fear of disapproval from the other gods is enough to deter him from altering this.

168 φίλον ἄνδρα: 'a man I love'. It is curious that this very simple phrase occurs only here in Homer. In its very plainness it carries a great deal of emotional weight in this context.

169–70 For ἐμὸν δ' ὀλοφύρεται ἦτορ | Ἕκτορος cf. 16.450 τεὸν δ' ὀλοφύρεται ἦτορ, from Here's speech to Zeus in the debate about Sarpedon's fate.

170–2 Zeus's words imply that punctiliousness in sacrificing to the gods creates an obligation on their part to respond favourably. Apollo makes this point more vehemently on behalf of Hektor after his death (24.33–8), and Zeus agrees (66–70). So also Zeus loves Troy more than any other city on account of the Trojans' piety (4.44–9), and cf. 20.297–9 (Poseidon and Aineias). The same motif recurs in Athene's plea for Odysseus at *Od.* 1.60–2, and in prayers at *Il.* 1.39–41, 8.238–42, *Od.* 4.762–6, 17.240–3.

For 170 cf. 8.240 βοῶν δημὸν καὶ μηρί' ἔκηα |, 24.33–4 οὔ νύ ποθ' ὑμῖν | Ἕκτωρ μηρί' ἔκηε βοῶν αἰγῶν τε τελείων; For | Ἴδης ἐν κορυφῆσι cf. 11.183, 14.332, and 21.449 Ἴδης ... πολυπτύχου. Zeus has a precinct and altar on Gargaros, one of the peaks of Mt Ida, at 8.47–8 (cf. Cook, *Troad* 257–8). For sacrifices on the citadel cf. 6.257 (prayer to Zeus).

172–3 These verses pick up 168, and 173 is also echoed at 230.

174–81 This passage is closely parallel to 16.435–43 in the related scene discussed above. In 176 ἐσθλὸν ἐόντα means 'noble though he is'.

178 ὦ πάτερ ἀργικέραυνε, κελαινεφές: cf. 19.121 Ζεῦ πάτερ ἀργικέραυνε; for κελαινεφές (vocative, of Zeus) cf. 2.412 (see note), 15.46.

180 ἐξαναλύειν is used only here and at 16.442, and very rarely in later literature.

182–5 Zeus's reply resembles his words to Athene at 8.38–40 (8.38 ~ 182, 39–40 = 183–4). To us it seems as if Zeus gives way all too easily, and οὔ νύ τι θυμῷ | πρόφρονι μυθέομαι sounds very casual. It is as if he knew all along that nothing could be done to save Hektor. But this debate, and Zeus's consent, serve the dramatic function of re-enacting for us the process of divine decision which seals Hektor's doom, just as the weighing of the fates (208–13) gives this a final, visual expression.

185–7 ἔρξον ὅπη δή τοι νόος ἔπλετο is similar to the way in which Zeus gave way to Here at 4.37, ἔρξον ὅπως ἐθέλεις. Verses 186–7 = 4.73–4, again echoing the same scene (see comments).

The formular character of several parts of this scene in heaven gives it a rather detached and stilted quality, in contrast to the intensity of the surrounding narrative. The gods preserve an elaborate courtesy towards each other, as if excessive involvement with the struggle on earth would be undignified.

188–213 Akhilleus continues to pursue Hektor, preventing him from reaching the shelter of the walls. Hektor is given a last burst of strength by Apollo: but when they reach the springs for the fourth time Zeus weighs the fates of the two men, Hektor's doom sinks down, and Apollo leaves him

188 Ἕκτορα ... ὠκὺς Ἀχιλλεύς: the two opposing names frame the verse. The formula ὠκὺς Ἀχιλλεύς (36× *Il.*) has point here. For κλονέων ἔφεπ' cf. 11.496 ἔφεπε κλονέων.

189–201 As a fawn, started from its lair by a hound, is pursued through mountain glens, and if it hides in a thicket the dog tracks it down, so Hektor could not escape Akhilleus. Every time he tried to reach the sheltering walls, Akhilleus would cut him off, and drive him towards the plain. It was just like a dream, where neither pursuer can catch pursued, nor pursued escape.

One simile follows closely after the other, the first concentrating on Akhilleus' relentless pursuit, the second on the frustration of both parties. There are comparisons with frightened fawns at 4.243–6, 21.29, 22.1. Cf. also the simile at 10.360–4, where Diomedes and Odysseus pursue Dolon and cut him off, like two dogs chasing a young deer or a hare through a wood, and 17.673–8, where Menelaos is like an eagle which spies a hare hiding in a thicket. At 18.318–22 Akhilleus is like a lion hunting for a man who has taken its cubs, suggesting his future hunt for Hektor as the killer of Patroklos, now reaching its climax.

The dream simile is far more unusual. 'Comparisons which refer to psychological states are rare in the *Iliad*' (Moulton, *Similes* 84). At 15.80–3 Here's journey is as quick as a man's thought, and the Phaeacian ships are 'as fast as wing or thought' at *Od.* 7.36. Similes describing a state of unresolved or balanced conflict occur at 12.417–24 (417 οὔτε ... Λύκιοι ... ἐδύναντο ..., 419 οὔτε ... Δαναοὶ ... ἐδύναντο ...), 12.432–6 (432 οὐδ' ὥς ἐδύναντο ...), 15.405–13 (405–6 Ἀχαιοὶ ... οὐδ' ἐδύναντο ..., 408 οὐδέ ποτε Τρῶες ... ἐδύναντο ...). These are reviewed by Fränkel, *Gleichnisse* 58–9. The Homeric dream simile inspired Virgil's at *Aen.* 12.908–14, just before Turnus' death. There it is Turnus' sense of helplessness which is the main point of comparison.

189 The word-order is complex. For the expression cf. 8.248 νεβρὸν ... τέκος ἐλάφοιο ταχείης |, and 22.139 | ἠΰτε κίρκος ὄρεσφιν.

191 Cf. 17.676–7 οὐκ ἔλαθε πτώξ | θάμνῳ ὑπ᾽ ἀμφικόμῳ κατακείμενος. For καταπτήξας cf. 8.136 καταπτήτην, *Od.* 8.190 κατὰ δ᾽ ἔπτηξαν. The noun πτώξ is directly related to πτήσσω (Chantraine, *Dict.* s.v.).

192 ἀνιχνεύων: this is the only example of ἰχνεύειν and its compounds in Homer; for ἀνιχνεύειν cf. Arist. *HA* 624a28 etc.; ἰχνεύειν Sophocles etc.

θέει ἔμπεδον, ὄφρα κεν εὕρῃ: cf. 13.141 θέει ἔμπεδον ἧος ἵκηται, 12.281 χέει ἔμπεδον, ὄφρα καλύψῃ, both in similes.

193 οὐ λῆθε picks up εἴπερ τε λάθῃσι in 191. ποδώκεα Πηλείωνα (10× *Il.*) is here relevant to the context: see on 14 and 188.

194–8 These verses form a long and complex sentence describing Akhilleus' manoeuvres, as he constantly cuts off Hektor's line of retreat. He must be keeping on the inside of Hektor, which strictly speaking is hard to reconcile with their both being on the waggon-track (146): but we should not stop to reflect on such details here.

For ὁσσάκι δ᾽ ὁρμήσειε ... ἀΐξασθαι ... τοσσάκι μιν ... ἀποστρέψασκε cf. 21.265–9 ὁσσάκι δ᾽ ὁρμήσειε ... | στῆναι ... | τοσσάκι μιν μέγα κῦμα ... | πλάζε ...

For πυλάων Δαρδανιάων see on 3.145. In 195 Leaf favours the future ἀΐξεσθαι, but after ὁρμᾶν the aorist infinitive would be normal. In 196 οἱ is dative, with ἀλάλκοιεν. προπάροιθεν in 197 could have either a local or a temporal sense, but the latter seems better (so Arn/A, bT). For ἀποστρέψασκε T records the variant παρατρέψασκε, and some MSS read ἀποτρέψασκε. ποτὶ πτόλιος is 'on the city side'.

199–201 Aristarchus (Arn/A) athetized these verses, as 'worthless (εὐτελεῖς) in style and thought', and he objected that they contradict the simile at 162–6. This shows his limitations. Leaf defends them in his note, but reluctantly rejects them along with 202–4 in an appendix.

The repetitions are surely deliberate, suggesting constant, frustrated effort. For οὐ δύναται (etc.) cf. the parallels quoted on 189–201, and also 15.416–18 οὐδὲ δύναντο | οὔθ᾽ ὁ τὸν ἐξελάσαι ... | οὔθ᾽ ὁ τὸν ἂψ ὤσασθαι ...

199 ὡς δ᾽ ἐν ὀνείρῳ οὐ ...: as so often in similes the phrasing is untypical. ὄνειρος (etc.) elsewhere occurs at the end of the verse (4× *Il.*, 10× *Od.*), or before the third-foot caesura (2× *Il.*, 5× *Od.*); and the hiatus after the second foot is rare (cf. 4.412, 5.215). In φεύγοντα διώκειν the absence of any specified subject suits the generalizing tone and increases the compression of the sentence.

202–4 Leaf and others have made heavy weather of these verses, whose obvious sense is 'how could Hektor have escaped impending death, had not Apollo given him extra strength for the last time?' It is true that they do not add much to the story at this point, and could have been inserted as a way of explaining how Hektor was not overtaken by Akhilleus, a problem discussed by the scholia (bT 165, D 201). But the poet may have chosen to raise and answer this question himself, and the mention of Apollo has point, reminding us again of his involvement just before the moment when he will desert Hektor (213). There may be a parallel in the rhetorical question at *Od.* 22.12–14. At the moment when Odysseus hits Antinoos in the throat the poet breaks off to ask who could have expected such an event. Both questions draw attention to the impossibility of the situation, at a structurally similar point in the narrative.

202 ὑπεξέφυγεν: there was a variant ὑπεξέφερεν, which Aristarchus (Did/A) seems to have favoured, and which was perhaps taken as meaning 'kept ahead of', 'outran' (cf. Hdt. 4.125). But cf. 5.22, 16.687 ὑπέκφυγε κῆρα, etc.

203 πύματόν τε καὶ ὕστατον: this emphatic expression does not recur in *Il.*, and occurs once in *Od.* (20.116). It carries considerable weight here.

ἤντετ' Ἀπόλλων: at 16.788 (ἤντετο γάρ τοι Φοῖβος) Apollo 'meets' Patroklos, but in a hostile sense.

205–7 Aristotle alludes to this passage in the *Poetics* (1460a11–17, 60b22–6), when he says that such a scene would be impossible on the stage, but is dramatically effective in epic. He may be responding to Megacleides, who criticized the whole episode of the pursuit and duel as implausible (b 22.36, bT 205–7).

πικρὰ βέλεμνα only occurs here: cf. πικρὸς -όν ὀϊστός -όν 10× *Il.*, 1× *Od.*, and βέλεμνα | 3× *Il.* For 207 cf. 10.367–8 ἵνα μή τις ... | φθαίη ἐπευξάμενος βαλέειν, ὁ δὲ δεύτερος ἔλθοι.

208–13 At 8.68–74 Zeus weighs the fates of the Achaeans and Trojans, again at a decisive point in the action, the beginning of the long process of reversal for the Greeks in fulfilment of Zeus's pledge to Thetis (8.69–70 = 209–210, 72 ~ 212), and the scales of Zeus are mentioned at 16.658 and 19.223–4. Here Hektor's fate is already decided in advance, and this is a visual or symbolic representation of the crucial moment at which the decision becomes irrevocable.

Arn/A tells us that this scene inspired Aeschylus' play *Psychostasia*, in which it was not the fates but the souls of Akhilleus and Memnon which were weighed by Zeus: cf. *TGF* pp. 88–9 N.² = pp. 374–7 Radt. But the scene in the *Iliad* may possibly echo an earlier epic version of the fight between Akhilleus and Memnon: cf. vol. v, Introduction, p. 18, and see on 16.658.

The structure of these verses is highly dramatic: 208–10 are three whole-verse clauses (208–9 being balanced. ἀλλ' ὅτε δή ... καὶ τότε δή ...), followed by the balancing parts of 211, naming the two opposing fates. After this leisurely build-up comes the decisive moment: 212–13 contain four sentences of extraordinary brevity, which describe Zeus lifting the scales, Hektor's fate sinking, the descent to Hades, and desertion by Apollo. The four verbs in these verses all stand first in their clauses, emphatic and parallel. Cf. Griffin, *HLD* 154–5.

208 ἀλλ' ὅτε δὴ τὸ τέταρτον: as at 5.438 etc.; see also on 165.

210 τανηλεγέος θανάτοιο: this epithet occurs only in this verse (= 8.70) in *Il.*, 6× *Od.* (2× with κήρ), and is rare in later poetry. The sense is uncertain (see on 8.70), but it creates a leisurely and impressive phrase. For the nature of the κῆρε see on 9.411, 12.326–7.

212 μεσσά: Chrysippus wanted to read ῥῦμα, which was supposed to refer to the centre of the scales.

213 ᾤχετο δ' εἰς Ἀΐδαο: probably the subject is still αἴσιμον ἦμαρ. But as his fate sinks, so Hektor in effect begins his journey to the afterlife.

λίπεν δέ ἑ Φοῖβος Ἀπόλλων: Apollo's departure is instantaneous after the weighing. His desertion of Hektor both contributes to Hektor's death and is the result of its imminence, since the gods avoid contact with death where possible, as Artemis leaves Hippolutos (E. *Hipp.* 1437–41). Cf. Parker, *Miasma* 33, 67. The awful brevity of this hemistich is rather like that of 1.47 ὁ δ' ἤϊε νυκτὶ ἐοικώς, of Apollo coming down as the god of the plague. Notice too the vivid juxtaposition with Athene's arrival at Akhilleus' side in 214.

214–47 Athene comes to Akhilleus and tells him to stand and draw breath. She then goes to Hektor, disguised as Deiphobos, and encourages him to face Akhilleus.

Here begins the first stage in the process of Hektor's fatal deception by Athene. Cf. her deceit of Pandaros (4.86–104), and her rôle in the second half of the *Odyssey* (especially 13.296–9 and 20.345–72). The deception of Hektor has always disturbed Homer's readers; bT comment that 'it is inappropriate (ἄτοπον) that a goddess should deceive Hektor'. But the Homeric gods regularly use deception to bring doom, as in cases of ἄτη.

214–23 Athene appears to Akhilleus in her own person, and he evidently recognizes her at once, as at 1.197–200.

216 Διῒ φίλε φαίδιμ' Ἀχιλλεῦ: cf. 1.74 | ὦ Ἀχιλλεῦ ... Διῒ φίλε; φαίδιμ' Ἀχιλλεῦ | 4× *Il.*, 1× *Od.* θεοῖς ἐπιείκελ' Ἀχιλλεῦ | (5× *Il.*, 1× *Od.*) is metrically equivalent. But Διῒ φίλε has point here, since Akhilleus' success must depend ultimately on Zeus's favour, and perhaps the poet also felt θεοῖς ἐπιείκελε to be inappropriate in Athene's mouth.

217 Ἀχαιοῖσι: either 'for the Achaeans' (which the parallel of 391–4 might support), or 'in the Achaeans' eyes', as at 4.95, 9.303.

218 ἄατον: 'insatiate'. See West on Hes. *Th.* 714 for this form, and comment on 5.388.

219 πεφυγμένον ἄμμε γενέσθαι: for the use of a direct object in this expression cf. 6.488, *Od.* 9.455.

220–1 This is remarkably contemptuous towards Apollo, especially προπροκυλινδόμενος. Akhilleus' hostility at 15–20 is similar. προπροκυλινδόμενος means 'grovelling in front of', as a suppliant, like Priam when supplicating the Trojans, κυλινδόμενος κατὰ κόπρον, at 414; cf. Gould, *JHS* 93 (1973) 94–5. This vivid compound recurs at *Od.* 17.525, and nowhere else in later literature.

222 ἄμπνυε is from the aorist (ἄμπνυον) of ἀναπνέω.

225 χαλκογλώχινος ('bronze-barbed') occurs only here; cf. τανυ-/τριγλώχις 5.393 etc., γλωχίς 24.274.

227 Deiphobos, Hektor's brother, first appeared at 12.94 (see comment), and then frequently in book 13, where he was wounded by Meriones (527ff.). Book 13 is probably in the poet's mind during the following episode. For the expression cf. 13.45 εἰσάμενος Κάλχαντι δέμας καὶ ἀτειρέα φωνήν and 17.555 (Athene) εἰσαμένη Φοίνικι δέμας καὶ ἀτειρέα φωνήν.

228–46 The courtesy and affection of this exchange make Hektor's deception all the more poignant. Note the parallelism of the openings of the three speeches (229, 233, 239), all stressing the speakers' earnestness and sincerity.

229–31 For ἠθεῖ᾽, ἦ μάλα δή σε cf. 6.518 (Paris to Hektor), and for ἠθεῖος ('trusty friend') cf. also 239, 10.37, 23.94, *Od.* 14.147. It seems to be used especially when referring to a brother (see on 6.518–19). Verse 230 echoes 173, and 231 = 11.348.

234 γνωτῶν means 'relatives', but is used especially of brothers; cf. 17.35, A.R. 1.53 (so bT, Eust.).

239–41 This theme of supplication by one's family and companions echoes 37–91, and recurs at 9.464–5, 9.581–94.

242 ἐτείρετο πένθεϊ λυγρῷ: cf. 5.153 τείρετο γήραϊ λυγρῷ.

244 φειδωλή: only here in epic and rare later (Solon, Phanias). Cf. 7.409 οὐ γάρ τις φειδὼ νεκύων, and for another abstract expression of this kind 8.181 μνημοσύνη τις ἔπειτα πυρὸς δηΐοιο γενέσθω.

244–6 Cf. 8.532–4 εἴσομαι εἴ κέ μ᾽ ... ἀπώσεται, ἦ κεν ἐγὼ τὸν | χαλκῷ δηώσας ἔναρα βροτόεντα φέρωμαι. Similar expressions occur at the end of a speech at 130, 13.326–7, etc., especially in exhortations to a comrade (see 13.326–7n.).

245–6 φέρηται ... δαμήῃ: δαμείη, the reading of most MSS, is supported by the same variation of mood in such contexts elsewhere, e.g. 16.648–51, 18.308 etc. (but not 13.486); see on 18.308. bT observe the tactful way in which Athene 'makes the danger common to them both (νῶϊ), but gives the victory to Hektor alone (σῷ δουρί)'.

247 κερδοσύνη occurs only here in *Il.*; cf. *Od.* 4.251, 14.31 (of Odysseus), and 13.296–7 (Odysseus and Athene excel in κέρδεα). The abstract noun is very rare later. There is an unusually strong assonance of *ēta* in this verse, and the καί is rather hard to explain.

248–366 Hektor tells Akhilleus that he is ready to fight, and asks him to agree that the winner should return the corpse of the loser. Akhilleus refuses to accept this proposal. He throws and misses, but Athene returns the spear. Hektor hits Akhilleus' shield but the spear rebounds. He calls to Deiphobos for a second spear, but Deiphobos has vanished. He realizes his doom is sealed, and attacks with his sword. Akhilleus closes, drives his spear through his neck, and exults over him. Hektor entreats him to return his body, but he again refuses. Hektor warns Akhilleus of his own impending death, and dies. Akhilleus contemptuously dismisses the warning

Although many motifs of the duel are typical (cf. the detailed comments which follow), what strikes one at once as unusual is, first of all, the extent to which the combat is punctuated throughout by speeches right up to the moment of Hektor's death, and second, the rôle of Athene, whose support of Akhilleus and deception of Hektor is decisive. Neither speeches nor divine intervention and deception are without parallels, but together they raise the whole scene to a different plane from that of the other duels. Throughout it we are constantly aware of the reactions and emotions of the two contestants, of the issues behind the action, in terms of the future fate of Hektor's body and the fate of Troy itself, and also of the divine hand at work directing the course of events to their inevitable outcome. On these aspects see also Schadewaldt, *VHWW* 311–23.

248–72 The exchange of speeches before a duel is in itself a typical motif: e.g. 5.630–54, 6.120–236, 20.176–258.

248–9 Verse 248 = 3.15 etc. (12× *Il.*). For τὸν πρότερος προσέειπε cf. 5.276 etc. (10× *Il.*).

251 Cf. 165. δίον must mean 'I fled' here (cf. 250 φοβήσομαι), although elsewhere δίε means 'he was afraid' (5.566 etc.). It is usually thought that the verb has been affected by the influence of δίεσθαι meaning 'pursue'. The variant reading δίες (in 'the better texts' according to Did/A, and possibly pap. 12) would mean 'you pursued me' (cf. 18.584 ἐνδίεσαν), and may well be right; cf. Chantraine, *GH* I 293, 388, and Schulze, *Quaestiones Epicae* 355. δίεσθαι ('pursue') is probably related to διώκειν, δίε ('he was afraid') to δείδω: cf. Chantraine, *Dict.* s.v. δίεμαι, δείδω.

251–2 Cf. 1.534–5 οὐδέ τις ἔτλη | μεῖναι ἐπερχόμενον.

252–3 For ἀνῆκε pap. 12 reads ἀνώγει (cf. 21.396). For στήμεναι ἀντία σεῖο cf. 17.166–7 οὐκ ἐτάλασσας | στήμεναι ἄντα; 21.266 στῆναι ἐναντίβιον. ἕλοιμί κεν, ἤ κεν ἁλοίην are potential optatives ('I may slay or be slain', i.e. whether one or the other).

254 θεοὺς ἐπιδώμεθα: aorist subjunctive of ἐπιδίδοσθαι, 'let us give each other our gods', i.e. offer them as witnesses of an oath (254–5). This phrase only occurs here; cf. perhaps 23.485 περιδώμεθον ('let us wager').

255 This verse is probably omitted by one papyrus (pap. 271 in Mazon's Budé). For μάρτυροι cf. 2.302(n.). On the gods as overseers of human affairs, especially oaths, cf. Griffin, *HLD* 181–2. ἐπίσκοπος is used of an overseer or guardian at 24.729 (of Hektor) and *Od.* 8.163; otherwise of a spy at *Il.* 10.38, 10.342. ἁρμονίαι in the sense of 'agreements' occurs only here in Homer; cf. *Od.* 5.248, 5.361, where it means 'joints'. It is interesting to find it in a moral sense already in the *Iliad*.

256 ἔκπαγλον: see on 1.145–6, 3.415.

257 δώῃ καμμονίην: this phrase recurs at 23.661. καμμονίη ('endurance') occurs nowhere else in early Greek literature, and very rarely in later poetry. According to Plutarch (*Mor.* 22c) the word is Aeolic.

259 After this verse pap. 12 reads 342–3.

260–72 Akhilleus' reply is brutal. He absolutely rejects the possibility of any compact between them. The normal conventions of human society no longer apply, as far as he and Hektor are concerned. He is confident of success, and above all consumed by desire for vengeance.

260 = 1.148, 22.344, 24.559. See on 1.148.

261 ἄλαστε: elsewhere ἄλαστος is an epithet of ἄχος or πένθος (24.105, 3× *Od.*; cf. *Od.* 14.174 ἄλαστον ὀδύρομαι). Here, however, it seems to mean 'accursed', as at S. *OC* 1482, 1672 (and sometimes also ἀλάστωρ has this sense). The etymology is disputed: Chantraine, *Dict.* (s.v. ἀλάστωρ) favours a connexion with the verb λαθεῖν. See also 12.163n. (ἀλαστήσας), *LfgrE* s.v. ἄλαστος, Fraenkel on A. *Ag.* 1501.

συνημοσύνας: only here in early epic, picking up ἁρμονιάων, although the verb is found at 13.381 (συνώμεθα). συνημοσύναι recurs at A.R. 1.300, 3.1105.

262–7 'Achilles *utters* more similes than any character in the poem' (Moulton, *Similes* 100; cf. 16.7–10n.). This is of course not a usual type of simile, for it expresses a proverbial truth about relationships in the world of animals and men, and then transfers this in an unusual way to the present situation. Cf. Hes. *Erga* 276–80, where the lack of δίκη in the animal kingdom is contrasted with men's possession of it as a gift of Zeus.

The verses have an elaborately balanced structure, with a three-verse simile answered by a three-verse sentence referring to Hektor and Akhilleus:

ὡς οὐκ ἔστι λέουσι καὶ ἀνδράσιν ὅρκια πιστά,
οὐδὲ λύκοι τε καὶ ἄρνες ὁμόφρονα θυμὸν ἔχουσιν,
ἀλλὰ κακὰ φρονέουσι διαμπερὲς ἀλλήλοισιν,
ὡς οὐκ ἔστ' ἐμὲ καὶ σὲ φιλήμεναι, οὐδέ τι νῶϊν
ὅρκια ἔσσονται, πρίν γ' ἢ ἕτερόν γε πεσόντα
αἵματος ἆσαι Ἄρηα, ταλαύρινον πολεμιστήν.

133

The order of 262–4 and 265–7 is chiastic, the clauses about oaths framing those about friendship. For wolves and lambs in similes see on 16.352–5.

263 ὁμόφρονα θυμὸν ἔχουσιν: cf. *HyDem* 434, *HyHerm* 391 ὁμόφρονα θυμὸν ἔχουσαι -οντας. ὁμοφρονέειν and ὁμοφροσύνη occur in the *Odyssey* (2× each), ὁμόφρων only here in Homer.

265–7 For 265 see on 126–8. πρίν γ' ... πολεμιστήν are repeated from 5.288–9 (see comment); 267 also occurs at 20.78.

268–9 For παντοίης ἀρετῆς cf. 15.642 παντοίας ἀρετάς. It means 'all the valour that you can display' here. Verse 269 = 5.602. πολεμιστήν is repeated very soon after 267.

270 ὑπάλυξις occurs nowhere else in *Il.*; cf. *Od.* 23.287, and A.R. 4.1261.

271–2 For νῦν δ' ἀθρόα πάντ' ἀποτείσεις cf. *Od.* 1.43 νῦν δ' ἀθρόα πάντ' ἀπέτισε. He does not name Patroklos, but makes the reference in 272 general. For ἔγχεϊ θύων cf. 11.180, 16.699 ἔγχεϊ θῦεν.

273–360 For the pattern of the duel cf. 11.232–40, 13.604–18, Fenik, *TBS* 87–8, 145–6. In each case A misses B, B hits A but fails to wound, and A kills B.

273 = 3.355 etc. (7× *Il.*).

274–6 Cf. 13.184 etc. ἀλλ' ὁ μὲν ... χάλκεον ἔγχος (6× *Il.*); and especially 13.404–8 (404 = 22.274; 405–8 Idomeneus crouches under his shield; 408 τὸ δ' ὑπέρπτατο χάλκεον ἔγχος ~ 22.275); 13.503–5 (503 = 22.274; 504–5 the spear sticks in the ground). Similar passages are 16.610–13 and 17.526–9. In 275 ἕζετο means 'he crouched down'. For χάλκεον there was a variant μείλινον (Did/A, pap. 107 Allen). For ἐν γαίῃ δ' ἐπάγη cf. also 10.374, where a spear passes over Dolon's shoulder and ἐν γαίῃ ἐπάγη.

276–7 Hektor's escape from being hit has momentarily raised the tension, as if this were really an open fight and he had a chance (so bT 274). But immediately Athene intervenes to return Akhilleus' spear, unseen by Hektor (for this motif cf. 20.324–5, 20.438–41, and see also 16.130–54n.). This has seemed to many modern readers very unfair, robbing Hektor of his only chance of survival. It is 'the most extreme case of divine assistance to a warrior in the *Iliad*', as Willcock says. The nearest parallel comes not in battle but in the games, when Athene returns Diomedes' whip in the chariot race, in retaliation for Apollo's interference (23.382–90).

Here Athene's intervention has the effect of underscoring still more strongly the fact that Hektor is doomed, whatever he may do. But he is still ignorant of the truth, and this makes his confident speech (278–88) all the more ironic.

279–88 In Hektor's speech it is the short, staccato phrases at the beginning and end of the verses which convey his contempt and hostility most strongly: 279 ἤμβροτες ..., 280 ἦ τοι ἔφης γε ..., 286 εἴ τοι ἔδωκε θεός ...,

288 σὺ γάρ σφισι πῆμα μέγιστον. These are contrasted effectively with the longer whole-verse clauses, especially in 281–4.

280–2 ἤ τοι ἔφης γε means 'yet you *thought* you did'. Given Akhilleus' hatred of deceitful speech (9.309–13), the taunt in 281–2 is particularly wounding. ἀρτιεπής occurs only here in Homer and twice later, at Pindar, *O.* 6.61, *I.* 5.46; cf. Homeric ἀρτίφρων, ἀρτίπος, ἄρτια βάζειν, etc.; ἀρτιέπειαι of the Muses, Hes. *Th.* 29. It is odd to find it here in a bad sense, meaning 'glib'. ἐπίκλοπος is also only here in *Il.*; cf. *Od.* 21.397 ἐπίκλοπος ἔπλεο τόξων, and for ἐπίκλοπος alone *Od.* 11.364, 13.291. μένεος ἀλκῆς τε λάθωμαι occurred at 6.265.

283–4 For 283 cf. 8.95 μή τίς τοι φεύγοντι μεταφρένῳ ἐν δόρυ πήξῃ, etc., and for 284 cf. τὸν δ' ἰθὺς μεμαῶτα 2× *Il.*, διὰ δὲ στήθεσφιν ἔλασσε(ν) 4× *Il.*

286 ὡς ... κομίσαιο: 'would that you might catch it fully in your flesh'. Cf. 14.456 ἀλλά τις Ἀργείων κόμισε χροΐ, and 14.463. The sense of κομίζειν is not easy to assess exactly here, but it may be faintly colloquial. See however on 14.456 for another translation. For σῷ ἐν χροΐ the variant ἐνί is metrically preferable.

289–91 Verse 289 = 273 etc. For 290 cf. 13.160 καὶ βάλεν, οὐδ' ἀφάμαρτε, κατ' ἀσπίδα πάντοσ' ἐΐσην etc.; μέσον σάκος 5× *Il.* For 290–1 cf. the similar incident at 21.591–4(n.), and also 13.586–92, where Helenos' arrow rebounds from Menelaos' breastplate, especially 592 πολλὸν ἀποπλαγχθεὶς ἑκὰς ἔπτατο πικρὸς ὀϊστός.

291–2 χώσατο ... χειρός is repeated from 14.406–7. χώσατο means 'he was distressed', 'he was frustrated': see on 23.385.

293 κατηφήσας: 'downcast'. Cf. *Od.* 16.342 κατήφησαν; κατηφείη 3× *Il.*; 24.253 κατηφόνες. The etymology is unknown.

οὐδ' ἀλλ' ... ἔγχος: cf. 21.50 (Lukaon) οὐδ' ἔχεν ἔγχος. As bT observe, Hektor normally carries two spears, e.g. 5.495, 6.104, 11.212, 12.464–5. So why not here? 'Perhaps he threw one down when running, κατὰ τὸ σιωπώμενον [i.e. the poet takes this for granted]', bT suggest. But in the formal duels in books 3 and 7 the contestants only have a single spear each (cf. 3.338, 3.340ff., 7.244ff.), and Akhilleus above all has a single spear (cf. also Kirk, *Songs* 190–2, and comments on 3.330–8). Surely, however, this is not a question which should arise. The whole dramatic effect depends on both sides having only one spear.

294 λευκάσπις occurs only here in Homer. It is a very interesting case of a unique epithet applied to a hero. Deiphobos is θεοειδής (12.94), and in the genitive ὑπερηνορέοντος (13.258). If one looks at Parry's list of Homeric epithets used of two or more heroes (*MHV* 89–91), one can see that the only existing ones to fit here are μεγαλήτορα (1× *Il.*, 3× *Od.*) and θεοειδέα (1× *Od.*; otherwise θεοειδέα with synizesis at end of line, 3× *Il.*). Consequently it is possible that lack of choice was a contributing factor here. It may also be relevant that Deiphobos' shield is prominent in book 13, where he advances under cover of it, and Meriones breaks his spear on it and then goes to get another spear (156–68, 246–58). There are similarities with the passage in book 22, and later Deiphobos himself also retreats in search of a supporter (13.455–9). For other points of contact with book 13 see on 274–6, 288–91. But in any case Deiphobos' white shield leaves a significant mark on our minds. It is as if Hektor were looking all around the battlefield for this conspicuous sign of his brother's presence (cf. μακρὸν ἀΰσας, i.e. as if he were far away), only to find emptiness and silence. For other uses of white as a marker see 23.329, 453–5. Later this epithet is applied especially to the army of the Seven against Thebes (A. *Th.* 89, S. *Ant.* 106, E. *Phoen.* 1099). Cf. also W. K. Pritchett, *The Greek State at War*, pt III (Berkeley 1979) 261–2 n. 90.

295 ἤτεέ μιν δόρυ μακρόν: 'the poet effectively uses asyndeton here, and the repetition also evokes great pity' (T). Technically the asyndeton is due to the fact that ἤτεε (etc.) explains κάλει. But it must surely be the most dramatic use of this device in the poem.

295–305 As in Greek tragedy, delusion and error are followed by the moment of discovery or recognition. Hektor knows automatically which god is responsible (299), as for example Akhilleus knows that Apollo has rescued Hektor at 20.450. He knows too that the protection afforded him by Zeus and Apollo has gone for ever. But he resolves to die heroically. Notice the prominence of divine agents in Hektor's view of events (the gods, Athene, Zeus and Apollo, μοῖρα). At the same time, the fame which he will win by his death depends on his own human efforts (304–5).

The speech opens slowly and with great solemnity, with three end-stopped verses, and there are only two cases of integral enjambment in what follows (301–3). This suits the gravity of Hektor's tone. Contrast, for example, the style of 250–9 and 261–72, where enjambment is much more frequent.

296 Cf. 1.333 αὐτὰρ ὁ ἔγνω ᾗσιν ἐνὶ φρεσὶ φώνησέν τε.

297 ὢ πόποι, ἦ μάλα δή: for this exclamation cf. 373, 16.745 etc. For the whole verse cf. 16.693 Πατρόκλεις, ὅτε δή σε θεοὶ θάνατόνδε κάλεσσαν.

300–1 For 300 cf. 16.853 (Patroklos to Hektor) = 24.132 (Thetis to Akhilleus) ἄγχι παρέστηκεν θάνατος καὶ μοῖρα κραταιή. ἀλέη ('escape') occurs only here in Homer. Cf. Hes. *Erga* 545, and Hippocrates, *Aër.* 19; ἀλεωρή 3× *Il.*

301–2 ἦ γάρ ῥα ... ἑκηβόλῳ: i.e. 'so, after all, that was what they *really* wanted'.

302–3 οἵ με ... εἰρύατο: Zeus supported Hektor during Akhilleus' withdrawal, and Apollo did so until the last possible moment. Cf. Apollo's rescue of him at 20.443–4. For μοῖρα κιχάνει cf. 17.478 etc. (4× *Il.*).

304-5 In Hektor's final act of resolution the repeated *alpha* privative (cf. 386n.) and assonance of 304 add emphasis. Effective too is the powerful simplicity of μέγα ῥέξας τι. For μὴ μὰν ἀσπουδί γε cf. 8.512, 15.476 (with comment on this verse). ἀκλειῶς occurs only here in *Il.*; cf. *Od.* 1.241 = 14.371, again of death. However, the adjective is used 2× *Il.*, 1× *Od.* καὶ ἐσσομένοισι πυθέσθαι recurs at 2.119 and 4× *Od.* Hektor's characteristic concern with future κλέος emerges here again (see on 106).

306-21 The last phase of the duel begins with the two heroes coming to close combat, Hektor with his sword, Akhilleus with his spear: the inequality of the contest is clear. Each is given a simile: Hektor is like an eagle swooping down to catch a lamb or hare, Akhilleus' spear-point shines like the evening star. But the description of Akhilleus is elaborated, by reference to the rest of his divine armour, shield, helmet and golden helmet-crest (313–16), as if again to emphasize his superiority.

306-7 For 306 cf. 1.190 φάσγανον ὀξὺ ἐρυσσάμενος; 22.311 τινάσσων φάσγανον ὀξύ. Verse 307 is an untypical description for a sword, and λαπάρη occurs elsewhere only in the context of wounds (5× *Il.*). Cf. 3.372 of a chin-strap, ὅς οἱ ὑπ' ἀνθερεῶνος ὀχεὺς τέτατο τρυφαλείης. μέγα τε στιβαρόν τε is elsewhere used of a shield (σάκος), 5× *Il.* For the scansion | τό οἱ see on 16.228–30.

308-11 For eagle similes see on 17.674–8, 21.252–3, and Moulton, *Similes* 81–2. Verse 308 (= *Od.* 24.538) is a powerful one: 'gathering himself together he swooped like a high-soaring eagle'. The form ὑψιπετήεις recurs only in a Homeric parody by Matro (*Conv.* 78), but cf. | αἰετὸς ὑψιπετής 3× *Il.*, 1× *Od.* For διὰ νεφέων ἐρεβεννῶν cf. 5.864 ἐκ νεφέων ἐρεβεννή ... ἀήρ. The dark clouds are effective: the eagle suddenly appears through them, swift and menacing. There may be a contrast between the eagle in the dark clouds and the radiance of the evening star against the darkening sky in the simile which follows at 317–21, symbolizing Akhilleus' victory and Hektor's doom; cf. Schadewaldt, *VHWW* 320.

310 For ἁρπάξων the majority of our MSS read ἁρπάζων, but the future is preferable. ἁμαλός ('soft', 'tender') occurs only here in *Il.*; cf. *Od.* 20.14 (σκυλάκεσσι). It is rare in later literature, but survived in Thessalian, and is related to ἀμαλδύνω etc.: cf. Chantraine, *Dict.* s.v.

ἢ πτῶκα λαγωόν: πτώξ was originally an epithet ('cowering'), which became the name of an animal, like τρήρων, etc. Cf. 17.676–7 (in an eagle simile) πτῶξ | θάμνῳ ὑπ' ἀμφικόμῳ κατακείμενος.

313 ἀγρίου may originally have been ἀγρίοο; cf. 21.104n., etc.

313-20 These verses recall 19.379–83, when Akhilleus puts on his armour, and 315–16 περισσείοντο ... θαμειάς repeat 19.382–3 (see on 19.380–3). Cf. also 20.162–3 (Aineias) νευστάζων κόρυθι βριαρῇ· ἀτὰρ ἀσπίδα θοῦριν | πρόσθεν ἔχε στέρνοιο, τίνασσε δὲ χάλκεον ἔγχος, and Hektor's nodding plume at 6.469–70.

315 τετραφάλῳ: this recurs at 12.384, and probably means 'with four bosses'; see on 3.362. For καλαί the majority of MSS read δειναί (Did/A, T). Both are possible, but the emphasis on beauty would suit what follows, especially 318 κάλλιστος.

316 A few MSS omit this verse, which repeats 19.383. Pap. 12 adds 133–5 after 316.

317–21 For this simile see on 25–32, and Moulton, *Similes* 85–6, together with *Hermes* 102 (1974) 393–4, where he says: 'Perhaps the net effect ... is the extraordinary distancing from the action ... At the climax of the poem, our attention is directed to the majestic movement of the beautiful evening star through the heavens.'

The ostensible point of comparison is the brilliance of Akhilleus' spearpoint and that of the evening star. But the peculiar beauty of this star and its quiet appearance in the sky contrast with the deadliness of the attack. At the same time the evening star evokes the idea of closing day and night drawing on, which fits the theme of Hektor's coming death.

This passage is the climax of the series in which Akhilleus or his armour are depicted in terms of fire or light: 18.205–14, 19.16–17, 19.365–6, 19.373–83, 19.398, 20.371–2, 20.490–4, 21.12–16, 21.522–5, 22.25–32, 22.134–5. Cf. already Eust. 1255.31–40, and Schadewaldt, *VHWW* 320 (with n. 3), Whitman, *HHT* 132–45.

317–18 For οἶος δ' ἀστὴρ εἶσι cf. 11.62 οἶος δ' ἐκ νεφέων ἀναφαίνεται οὔλιος ἀστήρ, and for μετ' ἀστράσι νυκτὸς ἀμολγῷ see on 28. ἕσπερος is used only here in Homer of the evening star. At *Od.* 1.423 etc. it means 'evening'. For ὃς κάλλιστος cf. 2.673, and for comparable expressions of supremacy in similes 17.674–5, 21.253, 22.30, 22.139 etc.

319 ἀπέλαμπ' ('it shone') is an uncommon impersonal use; cf. perhaps 324 φαίνετο. εὐήκης recurs only in Hellenistic poetry (A.R. 2.101, etc.).

321 ὅπη εἴξειε μάλιστα means 'where it might best yield (an opening)'.

322–3 τόσον μέν is 'to a certain extent', 'so far', as at 18.378, 23.454. Verse 323 = 17.187, where Hektor actually puts on the armour of Akhilleus, taken from Patroklos' body (and see on 18.84 for τεύχεα ... | καλά). It is significant that the poet echoes 17.187 just when Akhilleus is about to strike the fatal blow. Cf. Virgil, *Aen.* 12.940–52, where Aineias is driven to kill Turnus by the sight of the belt which he had taken from the body of Pallas.

324–6 Cf. 8.325–7 παρ' ὦμον, ὅθι κληῒς ἀποέργει | αὐχένα τε στῆθός τε, μάλιστα δὲ καίριόν ἐστι, | τῇ ῥ' ἐπὶ οἷ μεμαῶτα βάλεν λίθῳ ὀκριόεντι.

φαίνετο means 'it showed', i.e. either with χρώς understood, or impersonal. Aristarchus knew of a variant φαῖνεν or φαῖνον (Did/A, T). For λαυκανίην ('gullet') cf. 24.642. The word occurs nowhere else in early epic, and otherwise only in later epic and elegiac verse (A.R. 2.192, etc.), usually in the form λευκανίη. The accusative is probably due to attraction to the case of αὐχένα, as one might have expected the nominative here after φαίνετο. Most of our MSS read λαυκανίης, which would be a partitive genitive, and might well be the right reading. Cf. Chantraine, *GH* II 51, Wackernagel, *Kleine Schriften* II 1120–1.

327 = 17.49. There is strong assonance of initial *alphas* here.

328–9 ἀσφάραγος meaning 'wind-pipe' recurs only in the medical writers, and in Hellenistic and later verse (Nicander, Nonnus, Quintus of Smyrna). For χαλκοβάρεια cf. 11.96 στεφάνη ... χαλκοβάρεια |, 15.465 ἰὸς χαλκοβαρής. Aristarchus (Arn/A) athetized 329 as ridiculous. In defence it was said that the poet treats accidental events as if they were designed (Arn/A, bT). T quotes *Od.* 9.154–5 ὦρσαν δὲ Νύμφαι ... αἶγας ὀρεσκῴους, ἵνα δειπνήσειαν ἑταῖροι, and 12.427–8 ἦλθε δ' ἐπὶ Νότος ὦκα ... ὄφρ' ἔτι τὴν ὀλοὴν ἀναμετρήσαιμι Χάρυβδιν. The death-arias of operatic heroes may be as unrealistic, but are equally essential in dramatic terms.

330–67 This death-scene, with its exchange of speeches, is closely parallel to that of Patroklos at 16.827–63 (see on 830–63, and cf. Fenik, *TBS* 217–18, Schadewaldt, *VHWW* 262, 323):

16.829–42	~	22.330–6: boasting speech by victor
16.829 ἐπευχόμενος	~	22.330 ἐπεύξατο
830 Πάτροκλ', ἦ που ἔφησθα ...	~	22.331 Ἕκτορ', ἀτάρ που ἔφης ...
833 νήπιε· τάων δὲ πρόσθ' ...	~	22.333 νήπιε· τοῖο δ' ἄνευθεν
(i.e. you did not reckon with me!)		ἀοσσητήρ ...
836 σὲ δέ τ' ἐνθάδε γῦπες ἔδονται	~	22.335–6 σὲ μὲν κύνες ἠδ' οἰωνοὶ | ἑλκήσουσ' ἀϊκῶς
16.843	~	22.337: the dying man replies
		22.338–54: Hektor asks for burial and Akhilleus refuses (expanding 335–6, which is echoed by 354)
16.844–54: Patroklos' final speech	~	22.335–60: Hektor's final speech
The gods gave you victory. It was Apollo and Euphorbos, not you, who caused my death.		I knew I could not persuade you.
But your own death is imminent, at Akhilleus' hands.		But beware of divine anger, when you die at the hands of Paris and Apollo.
16.885–7: Patroklos dies	=	22.361–3: Hektor dies.
16.858	~	22.364: the victor addresses him after his death

16.859–61 Why prophesy my
death? Perhaps I may kill
Akhilleus.

16.862–3

22.365–6: I will accept my fate,
when the gods fulfil it.

~ 22.367: the victor withdraws his
spear from the body.

The exchange between Hektor and Akhilleus about burial (338–54) is a crucial addition to the scheme in book 16, foreshadowing book 24.

In the two prophetic speeches (16.844–54, 22.355–60) reference to Apollo's agency in causing Patroklos' death is echoed in Hektor's prophecy that Apollo will cause Akhilleus' death. In both cases divine and human agency are mentioned together.

The final replies of Hektor and Akhilleus are significantly different: Hektor does not accept that Patroklos' prophecy will necessarily come true, whereas Akhilleus knows that he must die soon and is willing to accept his fate, although he wastes few words in saying so. Hektor's prophecy is the climax of a series of references to Akhilleus' impending death (see on 21.113, etc.).

330 For ἤριπε δ' ἐν κονίης cf. 5.75, 11.743 ἤριπε δ' ἐν κονίη -ῃσιν, and for ὁ δ' ἐπεύξατο δῖος Ἀχιλλεύς 20.388.

332 ὀπίζεο: cf. 18.216 ὠπίζετο, and 2× *Od.*

333 For νήπιε in emphatic initial position see on 21.99, and for ἀοσσητήρ see on 15.254–7. ἀμείνων surely means 'better than Patroklos', in spite of bT's view that it refers to Hektor, because 'he would not have compared himself with Patroklos'.

335–6 Cf. 11.453–5 in a boasting speech: ἀλλ' οἰωνοὶ | ὠμησταὶ ἐρύουσι ... | αὐτὰρ ἔμ', εἴ κε θάνω, κτεριοῦσί γε δῖοι Ἀχαιοί; 11.452–5 also resemble 22.352–4.

335 κύνες ἠδ' οἰωνοί: cf. 1.4–5 ἑλώρια τεῦχε κύνεσσιν | οἰωνοῖσί τε πᾶσι ('Hector's death is the most tragic of those rendings by dogs and birds foretold in the proem', Segal, *Mutilation of the Corpse* 37); 22.354 κύνες τε καὶ οἰωνοὶ κατὰ πάντα δάσονται; 24.411 οὔπω τόν γε κύνες φάγον, οὐδ' οἰωνοί; see on 42.

336 ἑλκήσουσ' ἀϊκῶς: cf. 17.558 κύνες ἑλκήσουσιν (of Patroklos' body). ἀϊκῶς occurs only here in epic, but cf. ἀεικής, and Attic αἰκής, αἰκῶς. Antimachus wanted to substitute the easier reading ἑλκήσουσι κακῶς (Did/A, T). We should perhaps read αἰκῶς here (Wackernagel, *Kleine Schriften* 1 222). Shipp (*Studies* 24) argues that αἰκῶς is Attic, whereas Chantraine (*GH* 1 38) prefers to read ἀεικῶς with synizesis, which seems unlikely.

337 = 15.246; cf. 16.843 τὸν δ' ὀλιγοδρανέων προσέφης, Πατρόκλεες ἱππεῦ. For the rare word ὀλιγοδρανέειν see on 15.245–6.

338 With the utmost urgency Hektor supplicates Akhilleus, by his life, his knees, and his parents: to us a curious triad. Cf. Gould, *JHS* 93 (1973) 75ff., for examples of supplication by the knees. Here Hektor cannot touch Akhilleus' knees, and so this comes under Gould's class of 'rejected "figurative" supplications' (*op. cit.* 80–1, 81 n. 42). For supplication by parents cf. 15.659–66 (parents, children, wives), 24.466–7 (parents and son), 485–92 (father), *Od.* 11.66–8 (wife, father and son); similar lists occur in S. *Ph.* 468–70, *OC* 250–1. This speech is the final one in a series of pleas by Trojans for their lives, all vain (see on 20.463–72).

339 κύνας καταδάψαι: a striking alliterative phrase. καταδάπτειν occurs only here in *Il.* Cf. 23.182–3 Ἕκτορα δ' οὔ τι | δώσω Πριαμίδην πυρὶ δαπτέμεν, ἀλλὰ κύνεσσιν; *Od.* 3.259 κύνες ... κατέδαψαν.

340–1 Here the theme of Hektor's ransoming is first introduced. Elsewhere in the poem the defeated plead for their lives, offering ransom (cf. 49–51n.), but only in this case do we hear of ransom for a dead body, for Akhilleus has already refused Hektor's plea that he should return his body for burial (258–72).

342–3 = 7.79–80, spoken also by Hektor, before his duel with Aias. There bT comment that Hektor's concern for burial is an effective anticipation of his future fate.

344–54 Akhilleus' speech is even more brutal and passionate than his earlier refusal of Hektor's request for burial. But his violent words at 346–7 must be read in their context: the wish 'is meant, while conveying hatred enough, to express that which is inconceivable' (Leaf). For this idiom, 'by which a certainty is expressed, by contrasting it with an impossibility in the form of a wish', see on 18.464–6. The desire to eat Akhilleus' liver is expressed in equally violent language by Hekabe at 24.212–14, and Zeus ascribes to Here a similar desire that she might 'eat the Trojans raw' at 4.34–6.

The structure and style of the speech are typical of Akhilleus' more passionate outbursts. He begins with a single-verse sentence, which immediately rejects Hektor's request. The remaining nine verses should probably be treated as two sentences, with a stop at the end of 348 (so Leaf). After the impossible wish and assertion of 346–8 Akhilleus repeats his rejection even more vehemently, with two οὐδ' εἴ κεν ... clauses (349–50, 351–2), and the apodosis οὐδ' ὥς ... (352–3), rounded off by the repetition in 354 of the theme of 335–6. Cf. 9.379–87 οὐδ' εἴ μοι δεκάκις τε καὶ εἰκοσάκις τόσα δοίη ... (οὐδ' ὅσ' ... οὐδ' ὅσα ...) οὐδ' εἴ μοι τόσα δοίη ὅσα ... οὐδέ κεν ὥς ..., in Akhilleus' rejection of Agamemnon's offer. The prominence of gutturals in 345, 348, 349, 354 may also not be accidental. On such sound effects and repetition in Akhilleus' rhetoric cf. Martin, *Language of Heroes* 220–2. The speech rises to a climax of passionate certainty. Yet, as with his earlier refusal to save the Greeks, Akhilleus will in the end give way. The passages in both books 9 and 22 are echoed at the climax of the *Odyssey*, in Odysseus' refusal of Eurumakhos' offer of recompense (22.61–4).

345 κύον: Hektor is called a dog by Akhilleus at 20.449 (= 11.362, addressed to him again by Diomedes), and is referred to by Teukros as such at 8.299. When used by heroes of each other in the *Iliad* this term of abuse is almost always put into the mouth of a Greek speaker (e.g. Akhilleus to Agamemnon at 1.159, 225n., 9.373). Here it comes in a speech which is concerned with the rôle of real dogs as eaters of corpses. Cf. M. Faust, 'Die künstlerische Verwendung von κύων, "Hund", in den homerischen Epen', *Glotta* 48 (1970) 8–31, especially 29–30.

γούνων γουνάζεο: emphatic repetition. γουνάζομαι or γουνοῦμαι is used of figurative supplication also at 9.583, 11.130, *Od.* 6.149.

347 'The placing of the long participle between adjective and noun, both short words, gives a striking effect' (Segal, *Mutilation of the Corpse* 40).

348 ἀπαλάλκοι: this compound recurs at *Od.* 4.766.

349–50 εἰκοσινήριτος occurs only here, and is probably from εἰκοσινήριτα (cf. ἀριθμός), 'twentyfold'. Cf. Hes. *Th.* 240 μεγήριτα, with West's comment, and Leumann, *HW* 246–7. στήσωσ' means 'weigh out', as at 19.247, 24.232. For ὑπόσχωνται δὲ καὶ ἄλλα cf. 114–18 ὑπόσχωμαι ... ἅμα δ' ... ἀλλ' ἀποδάσσεσθαι. This echo of Hektor's earlier speculations here brings home to us how pointless they were.

351–2 οὐδ' ... Πρίαμος: 'not even if Priam, Dardanos' offspring, were to bid me weigh your own body against gold', i.e. to pay your weight in gold. This hyperbole was said to have inspired Aeschylus to a literal portrayal of the scene in his Φρύγες ἢ Ἕκτορος λύτρα (p. 84 N.² = p. 365 Radt). For αὐτός of the body cf. 1.4(n.), 9.547, 23.65. For χρυσῷ ἐρύσασθαι cf. Theognis 77–8 πιστὸς ἀνὴρ χρυσοῦ τε καὶ ἀργύρου ἀντερύσασθαι | ἄξιος. The verb seems to mean 'weigh' here, from ἐρύειν = 'draw'. Leaf compares ἕλκειν = 'weigh' (212 etc.), but that refers to holding up the scales.

352–4 Cf. 21.123–4 οὐδέ σε μήτηρ | ἐνθεμένη λεχέεσσι γοήσεται, and 22.86–9 οὔ σ' ἔτ' ἔγωγε | κλαύσομαι ἐν λεχέεσσι ... ὃν τέκον αὐτή, | ... κύνες ταχέες κατέδονται. 'This statement not only negates the appeal to the sanctity of parents which runs throughout the scene (338, 341, 345); it also confirms Hecuba's near-hysterical forebodings' (Segal, *Mutilation of the Corpse* 40).

354 Cf. also 335–6 etc., and for κατὰ πάντα δάσονται cf. *Od.* 18.87 (~ 22.476) μήδεα τ' ... δώῃ κυσὶν ὠμὰ δάσασθαι. bT note the aptness of the tmesis κατὰ ... δάσονται in the context of tearing the body apart. For other examples cf. *CQ* 30 (1980) 286, and AbT 15.1 with Erbse's commentary.

The effect of this verse (gutturals and dentals, tmesis) is increased by the way in which οἰωνοί bridges the central caesura, after a weak caesura in the second foot:

1   2   3   4   5   6

ἀλλὰ κύνες τε | καὶ οἰωνοὶ | κατὰ πάντα δάσονται

On the tendency towards avoidance of a break after the trochee in the second foot see vol. I, p. 19. What we have seems to be an unusual type of 'rising threefolder', in which the first two cola might appear to be equal in weight: $-\cup\cup-\cup$ and $\cup---$; but the second actually sounds heavier owing to the three long syllables.

355–60 Hektor prophesies Akhilleus' death, as Patroklos foresaw Hektor's.

355 καταθνῄσκων: cf. 337 ὀλιγοδρανέων. 'The poet marks the different times very effectively' (bT).

356–7 Elsewhere προτιόσσομαι means 'look at' (*Od.* 7.31, 23.365) or 'forebode' (*Od.* 5.389, 14.219); cf. ὄσσομαι, 'imagine', 'forebode'. The second sense is better here: 'truly knowing you well I forebode (my fate)'. For ἦ γάρ ... θυμός cf. 24.205, 521 σιδήρειόν νύ τοι ἦτορ (of Priam).

358 μή τοί τι θεῶν μήνιμα γένωμαι: so also at *Od.* 11.73 (Elpenor), the only other instance of μήνιμα in Homer. In both cases the anger of the gods would be aroused by failure to give due burial (cf. Parker, *Miasma* 70). Precisely what its result would be is left vague, as often in prophecies, but it looks as if Akhilleus' death may be seen as retribution for his behaviour towards Hektor's corpse. Cf. the ominous warning of Apollo himself at 24.50–4.

359–60 See on 21.113, and cf. especially 19.416–17 ἀλλὰ σοὶ αὐτῷ | μόρσιμόν ἐστι θεῷ τε καὶ ἀνέρι Ἶφι δαμῆναι. For ἐνὶ Σκαιῇσι πύλῃσι see on 3.145 and 22.6, and cf. 23.80–1 (Akhilleus will die 'below the walls of Troy'). In the *Aithiopis* (OCT vol. v, ed. Allen, p. 106.7–9 = Davies, *EGF* p. 47.20–1) 'Akhilleus having routed the Trojans and broken into the city is killed by Paris and Apollo'. The Scaean gates are depicted in this context on the *Tabulae Iliacae* of the early Imperial period: *LIMC* I.1 p. 183 no. 854 (and on other portrayals in art and literature see *ibid.* 181–5).

361–3 = 16.855–7; 364 echoes 16.858. See on these verses.

364 καὶ τεθνηῶτα: 'to address him even when dead shows the extremity of his anger' (bT).

365–6 For τέθναθι cf. 15.496 | τεθνάτω, 15.497 etc. | τεθνάμεν. The imperative, standing alone at the beginning of the verse, is brutally abrupt and dismissive; see on 21.128 φθείρεσθ'. κῆρα ... ἄλλοι = 18.115–16, when

Akhilleus is replying to Thetis, after she has announced that he will die 'immediately after Hektor' (96). See on those verses.

367–404 Akhilleus strips off Hektor's armour, and the other Greeks stab his corpse. Akhilleus suggests that they attack Troy, but then remembers that Patroklos is unburied. He tells them to return to the ships with Hektor's body, singing a victory-song. He then fastens the body to his chariot by thongs passed through the ankles, and sets off, dragging it behind him

On this scene see especially Segal, *Mutilation of the Corpse* 41–2, Griffin, *HLD* 47, 84–5, 138.

367 Cf. 21.200 (ἐκ κρημνοῖο). The motif of withdrawing the spear occurred after the killing of Sarpedon by Patroklos (16.503–4), and Patroklos by Hektor (16.862–3). Cf. also 5.620–1, 6.64–5.

368–9 For ὁ δ' ἀπ' ὤμων τεύχε' ἐσύλα cf. 15.524, etc. περιτρέχειν occurs only here in early epic, but is common later (cf. Herodotus etc.).

370–1 Wonder at Hektor's beauty is combined with callous indifference, or perhaps hatred, as the Achaeans stab his body. For the wonder of the troops Leaf compares Hdt. 9.25.1, after Masistios has been killed at Plataia: ὁ δὲ νεκρὸς ἦν θέης ἄξιος μεγάθεος εἵνεκα καὶ κάλλεος· τῶν δὲ εἵνεκα καὶ ταῦτα ἐποίευν· ἐκλιπόντες τὰς τάξις ἐφοίτων θησόμενοι Μασίστιον.

The stabbing of the corpse may derive ultimately from the wish to ensure that the dead man is really and truly dead and that his ghost cannot harm his enemies after death. 'But Homer will not bring such horrors to the surface, and the scene as we have it draws a great part of its pathos and effectiveness from the heroic contrast of the impassive corpse of Hector and the small malevolence of those who ran from him in life and can face him only when he is safely dead. "The emotion (of triumph) is that of a low mob, and it magnifies the greatness of the dead man", is the correct comment of the scholiast' (Griffin, *HLD* 47). Wilamowitz made a similar point (*IuH* 103): 'Der Dichter hebt die Grösse Hektors durch die Niedrigkeit der feindlichen Menge.'

Much of the effect comes from the contrast between beauty and defilement, and this recurs still more explicitly at the end of this scene (401–4).

For φυὴν καὶ εἶδος ἀγητόν cf. *Od.* 6.16 φυὴν καὶ εἶδος (*sic*); εἶδος ἀγητοί -ός | 3× *Il.* ἀνουτητί ('without wounding him') occurs only here and in Quintus of Smyrna (3.445); cf. ἀνούτατος (4.540), ἄουτος (18.536), 'unwounded'. This stabbing is mentioned again at 24.421.

372–4 Leaf compares this grimly mocking speech with a passage in *Burnt Njal*: 'All men said that it was better to be near Skarphedinn dead than they weened, for no man was afraid of him' (cf. *Njal's Saga*, translated by M. Magnusson and H. Pálsson, Penguin 1960, p. 276). Verse 372 = 2.271 (n.)

etc. For 373 cf. 16.745 ὧ πόποι, ἦ μάλ' ἐλαφρὸς ἀνήρ· ὡς ῥεῖα κυβιστᾷ, in a mocking speech of triumph over a fallen enemy. The verb ἀμφαφάω occurs only here in *Il.*, but 6× *Od.* The predominance of *m*, *l* and *p* sounds in this line is very noticeable, and emphasized by the two long final words, and the echo μάλα ... μαλακώτερος. In 374 the variant ἐνέπρηθεν (imperfect) is preferred by Leaf, who calls it 'obviously superior' to ἐνέπρησεν.

375 That is, 'as they spoke they stabbed him' (Arn/A, bT).

376–94 Akhilleus' first suggestion, which appears to be that they should attack the city immediately, could reflect the sequence of events after the killing of Memnon, when he does attack Troy and is killed (cf. the *Aithiopis*, OCT vol. v, ed. Allen, p. 106.5–9 = Davies, *EGF* p. 47.18–21). But the risk of such an attack is constantly present in the later books (cf. 16.91–4, 16.698–9, 18.265, 20.26–30, and Poseidon's advice to Akhilleus at 21.296–7), and Hektor's death points forward to Troy's actual fall (410–11). The poet is once again leading us to expect a sequence of events which is then postponed.

378 = 2.79 etc. (8× *Il.*). The verse is used several times in an address to the Greeks in general. Zenodotus' alternative line Ἀτρείδη τε καὶ ἄλλοι ἀριστῆες Παναχαιῶν (= 7.327, 23.236) is out of place here, as Agamemnon is in his hut. There is another variant ὧ φίλοι ἥρωες Δαναοὶ θεράποντες Ἄρηος (= 2.110 etc.) in a few medieval MSS.

379 ἐπεὶ δή: cf. 23.2 for this scansion of ἐπεί (and 4× *Od.*); Chantraine, *GH* I 103. τόνδ' ἄνδρα is another oblique reference, as at 38 etc. Akhilleus does not name him yet. In θεοὶ ... ἔδωκαν he duly acknowledges the gods' rôle in his victory.

380 ὃς κακὰ πολλ' ἔρρεξεν: cf. 9.540 ὃς κακὰ πολλ' ἔρδεσκεν, where Ammonius read ἔ(ρ)ρεξεν. Here the vulgate reading is in fact ἔρδεσκεν, which is less suitable in this case.

381–3 Akhilleus does not speak in terms of a full-scale attack, but presumably what he has in mind is the capture of Troy. For expressions like εἰ δ' ἄγετε in an apodosis cf. 24.407, *Od.* 4.832. For σὺν τεύχεσι πειρηθέωμεν cf. 11.386 σὺν τεύχεσι πειρηθείης |; *Od.* 8.100 πειρηθέωμεν |. On this form see Chantraine, *GH* I 459.

383 The first alternative, desertion of the city (or strictly speaking the citadel), is very extreme: but Akhilleus is in the first flush of his victory over Hektor. Cf. however 24.383–5, where the same idea is envisaged.

385 This verse = 21.562 (see comment). This is the only case where the verse does not occur in a soliloquy, but it does not seem out of place here: in all the instances a particular train of thought is interrupted by the realization of a factor which invalidates it.

386 ἄκλαυτος ἄθαπτος recur together at *Od.* 11.54 and 11.72, and neither is used elsewhere in the *Iliad*; cf. S. *Ant.* 876 ἄκλαυτος ἄφιλος ἀνυμέναιος.

For other examples of such co-ordinated epithets with negative prefix see Richardson on *HyDem* 200.

387–8 ὄφρα . . . ὀρώρῃ: cf. 23.47 ὄφρα ζωοῖσι μετείω, and 9.610 = 10.90 καί μοι φίλα γούνατ' ὀρώρῃ. The variant verse ζωὸς ἐν ᾽Αργείοισι φιλοπτολέμοισι μετείω is quite well attested (A, Eust. and several of our MSS).

389–90 The best sense here is 'and if in Hades men forget the dead, yet even there I shall remember my dear comrade', i.e. after I too am dead. This gives a good contrast to 387–8. T mentions *Od.* 11.467–8, where Akhilleus and Patroklos appear together in the Underworld, as they do also at *Od.* 24.15–16. The compound καταλήθεσθαι occurs nowhere else in surviving literature.

391–4 These verses echo 217–18, in Athene's promise to Akhilleus. For 391 cf. 1.473 καλὸν ἀείδοντες παιήονα κοῦροι ᾽Αχαιῶν, and comments there. There the paean was sung in Apollo's honour, after the prayer and sacrifice to propitiate him for the insult to Khruses. Essentially a paean was regarded in antiquity as a song of thanksgiving for relief from trouble, or sometimes a song for the aversion of trouble (cf. AbT 1.473, T 22.391c): hence it could be sung, as here, after a victory in war. There is no compelling reason to suppose that it was addressed to Apollo here: in view of his enmity to Akhilleus and the Greeks this seems unlikely (although von Blumenthal, *RE* XVIII s.v. Paian 2341–2, thinks that it was so). For the paean as a war-song later cf. von Blumenthal, *op. cit.* 2346–8, W. K. Pritchett, *Ancient Greek Military Practices* pt i (Berkeley 1971) 105–8.

392 Before 393 pap. 12 adds [καὶ τ]εθνηότα περ· τόσα γὰρ κακ' ἐμήσατ' ᾽Αχαιούς.

393–4 Aristarchus (Arn/A) athetized these verses, ὅτι παρὰ τὴν ἀξίαν ᾽Αχίλλεως οἱ λόγοι, and he referred to 16.242–4, where Akhilleus implied that Patroklos on his own was a match for Hektor. Aristarchus' point seems to have been that 393–4 overrate Hektor by comparison with this earlier view (cf. also Eust. 1275.21ff.). bT defend the verses, saying that 'Akhilleus makes the victory a collective one, and encouraging his supporters he says that the Trojans' hopes are ended after Hektor's death'. This seems nearer the mark, and the further suggestion, that the verses represent the actual song which the Greeks are to sing, or perhaps rather the refrain, is attractive (Eust. 1275.17ff.). The asyndeton after 392 is in favour of this idea, as is the asyndetic simplicity, brevity and balance of the two separate hemistichs of 393, each composed of a 1st person plural aorist indicative verb plus a noun–epithet object. Verse 394 is more expansive, giving the reason why the glory is so great in a single-verse clause. Verse 393 is entirely dactylic (Eust. 1275.18), a suitably cheerful rhythm. For θεῷ ὣς εὐχετόωντο in 394 cf. *Od.* 8.467 = 15.181 θεῷ ὣς εὐχετοώμην. The same idea recurs at 434–5.

395–404 This ten-verse passage describing the dragging of Hektor's body is all the more shocking after the exalted tone of the previous verses. Cf. Griffin, *HLD* 84–5 on verse 395: 'The immediate juxtaposition of "god-like Hector" and "acts of humiliation" enables the poet to bring out, without sentimentality, the pathos of the greatest possible fall for a man, from god-like stature to humiliation and helplessness.'

Verses 395–400 are in the poet's most matter-of-fact style, with painfully precise description of how Akhilleus makes holes in the dead man's ankles, threads them with thongs, and fastens these to the chariot. Verses 399–400, apart from the reference to the armour, could have come in any typical scene of a departure. Verses 401–4 are also objective and detached, and yet at the same time the verses could not express more clearly the terrible contrast between Hektor's beauty and greatness and his present degradation (cf. Schadewaldt, *VHWW* 325–6, Griffin, *HLD* 138). For an anticipation of this passage in the fight over Patroklos' corpse see on 17.288–303.

395 This verse is repeated at 23.24. In ἀεικέα μήδετο ἔργα does ἀεικέα imply moral condemnation by the poet, or simply shame for Hektor's body? The two alternatives are already suggested by the scholia (b 395). That we cannot necessarily infer moral condemnation is indicated above all by Akhilleus' own words at 335–6, σὲ μὲν ... ἑλκήσουσ' ἀϊκῶς: he cannot be condemning *himself* there (cf. S. E. Bassett, *TAPA* 64 (1933) 44–6). Moreover 395 is echoed at the end of this passage by 403–4, where Zeus himself is said to allow the disfigurement (ἀεικίσσασθαι) of Hektor's head. At 24.33–54, however, Apollo protests, accusing the gods of being δηλήμονες because they allow this mutilation to continue (54 ἀεικίζει). Apollo says that this is neither κάλλιον nor ἄμεινον (52) for Akhilleus, and may incur divine anger (53 νεμεσσηθέωμεν). Despite the opposition of Here, Zeus accepts Apollo's plea (64–76). So in the end the gods uphold the principle that Hektor's body should not have been so treated. As we have seen, this may also be the implication of Hektor's warning to Akhilleus at 358–60. But this will not become clear until book 24 (although it is foreshadowed at 23.184–91), and at 22.395 there has not as yet been any *explicit* condemnation of Akhilleus' acts, however much they are portrayed as brutal and degrading. See also de Jong, *Narrators* 138.

396–7 τετραίνειν occurs only here in *Il.*; cf. *Od.* 5.247, 23.198. The term 'Achilles' tendon' derives from the use of the word τένοντε in this passage (cf. Leaf *ad loc.*). πτέρνη is only here in early epic, but common later. For βοέους ... ἱμάντας cf. 23.324 βοέοισιν ἱμᾶσιν.

399–400 For ἐς δίφρον δ' ἀναβάς cf. 16.657. Verse 400 = 5.366 etc. (3× *Il.*, 3× *Od.*).

401–4 These verses significantly echo the description of the defilement

of Patroklos' helmet, itself linked there with Hektor's impending doom
(16.793–800). Cf. 16.795–800:

> μιάνθησαν δὲ ἔθειραι
> αἵματι καὶ κονίῃσι· πάρος γε μὲν οὐ θέμις ἦεν
> ἱππόκομον πήληκα μιαίνεσθαι κονίῃσιν,
> ἀλλ' ἀνδρὸς θείοιο κάρη χαρίεν τε μέτωπον
> ῥύετ' Ἀχιλλῆος· τότε δὲ Ζεὺς Ἕκτορι δῶκεν
> ᾗ κεφαλῇ φορέειν, σχεδόθεν δέ οἱ ἦεν ὄλεθρος.

Cf. also the defilement of Sarpedon's body by blood and dust (16.638–40),
and similar descriptions at 15.537–8, 17.51–2, 439–40; see on 16.794–800,
and Fenik, *TBS* 163, Segal, *Mutilation of the Corpse* 41–2, Griffin, *HLD*
134–8. Segal comments: 'Homer has reserved the more moving and solemn
effect for Hector. He has thinned out the details ..., used three parallel
clauses with effective enjambements, and heightened this rhythmic movement by a strong alliteration of *k* and *p* sounds. The language describing
the mutilation here is distinctive and nontraditional.'

In later antiquity the dragging of Hektor was defended in two ways: (*a*)
on the grounds that Hektor himself wanted to mutilate Patroklos' corpse,
by cutting off his head and fixing it on stakes (18.176–7), and that in fact
Patroklos' body was dragged to and fro by Hektor and the Trojans in the
fight for its possession (17.125–6, 17.288–302, 17.389–95; cf. also 18.175–
6); cf. Schol. AB 22.397, Porph. 1.267.1; one could add that Hektor wanted
to throw the body to the dogs (17.127); (*b*) Aristotle (fr. 166 R.[3]) simply
observed that Akhilleus was following an existing custom, and he supported
this with evidence that the practice continued in Thessaly (cf. Call. fr. 588).
It was said that Alexander the Great imitated Akhilleus' action, by inflict-
ing the same fate on Batis, governor of Gaza (Hegesias, *FGH* 142 F 5,
Quintus Curtius 4.6.29).

401 ἀμφὶ δὲ χαῖται | recurs at 6.509 = 15.266, in the simile about the
stall-fed horse, which in the second passage refers to Hektor's success after
he has been encouraged by Apollo.

402 κυάνεαι: Poseidon is κυανοχαίτης (13.563 etc.), and the brows of
Zeus and Here are of this colour (1.528, 15.102 etc.; see on 1.528), but it
is very unusual for the epithet to be usea of a hero's hair. At *Od.* 16.176
the hair of Odysseus' beard is called κυάνεαι, when he is transformed by
Athene, and there Telemakhos actually thinks that he *is* a god (183). By
such means, with characteristic economy, the poet draws our attention to
the contrast between Hektor's 'god-like' appearance and his defilement.

πίτναντο is the reading of a minority of MSS and T, but it is clearly
preferable to the vulgate πίλναντο, or the other alternative reading
πί(μ)πλαντο.

403–4 τότε δὲ ... γαίη: after the three shorter enjambed clauses of 401–3 this longer sentence closes the description with a characteristic allusion to the divine will. Cf. 16.799–800, quoted in comment on 401–4.

404 ἑῇ ἐν πατρίδι γαίη: a similar phrase is used elsewhere in the context of dying in one's own land: cf. 3.244 φίλῃ ἐν πατρίδι γαίῃ (Dioskouroi); 8.359 φθίμενος ἐν πατρίδι γαίῃ (Hektor). 'The motif of "beauty brought low" is combined with that of "suffering in one's own country". The bitterness of the ill-treatment of Hector's head, "which before was comely", is increased by his enemy having power to inflict it in his own fatherland, before the eyes of his own people' (Griffin, *HLD* 138; cf. 112). This melancholy phrase closes the narrative of Hektor's death and prepares the way for the scenes which are about to follow. The whole of the remainder of this Book describes the immediate reactions in Troy to Hektor's death: the extreme grief and violent, unrestrained emotion of all the Trojans, and above all of his own parents and his wife.

405–36 Hektor's parents and the people of Troy lament his death. Priam begs them to let him go and entreat Akhilleus for the return of Hektor's body, and Hekabe leads the women of Troy in lamentation

This section balances the speeches by Priam and Hekabe at the beginning of the Book (25–89): see Introduction to book 22. The reference to the deaths of Priam's other sons and his grief for them, but above all for Hektor (422–6), echoes 44–55. Hekabe tears her hair (405–6) as Priam did then (77–8), and in both cases her shorter speech complements Priam's.

Priam's speech also anticipates his actual supplication of Akhilleus in book 24: there too he reminds him of his father Peleus (420–1 ~ 24.486–92), and again speaks of his lost sons (423–8 ~ 24.493–502). There is a reversal here, as what was prevented in book 22 becomes real in book 24 (cf. Macleod, *Iliad XXIV* 21–2, and Reinhardt, *IuD* 468–9). Moreover, Priam's self-abasement (414) is again referred to at 24.163–5 and 24.640. A further structural parallel can be seen between the triad of speeches by Priam, Hekabe and Andromakhe at the end of book 22 and the laments of Andromakhe, Hekabe and Helen near the close of book 24 (723–76). On these links see also Beck, *Stellung* 71–92.

405–6 ὡς ... ἅπαν: this echoes 402 κάρη ... κονίῃσι, as a transition to the following scene. For τίλλε κόμην see on 77–8.

406–7 ἀπὸ δὲ ... τηλόσε: so too Andromakhe's head-dress is thrown from her head, in the more elaborate passage at 468–72. Demeter tears her head-dress in grief at *HyDem* 40–1, in a passage perhaps influenced by these scenes (see Richardson on *HyDem* 38ff. and 41). For λιπαρὴν ... καλύπτρην cf. 18.382 λιπαροκρήδεμνος and *Od.* 1.334 etc. λιπαρὰ κρήδεμνα. Woven materials actually have oil dripping from them at 18.595–6, *Od.* 7.107. For the καλύπτρη (perhaps really a head-scarf rather than a veil) see on 14.184, and Lorimer, *HM* 386. The word itself occurs only here in *Il.*, 2× *Od.*

407–9 κώκυσεν … ὤμωξεν … κωκυτῷ … οἰμωγῇ: κωκύειν is always used of women in epic and tragedy (so bT 408 and LSJ). The repetition of the nouns in 409, after the verbs in 407–8, and the spondaic first hemistich, add to the mournful effect. κωκυτός recurs at 447, otherwise in Homer only as the name of the river in the Underworld at *Od.* 10.514.

410–11 These solemn and terrible verses are made all the more memorable by the untypical language of 411. ὀφρυόεσσα ('beetling') occurs only here in Homer, although cf. 20.151 ἐπ' ὀφρύσι Καλλικολώνης. Hes. fr. 204.48 M–W, and an oracle at Hdt. 5.92β both have ὀφρυόεντα Κόρινθον; cf. Call. fr. 186.20 ὀφρυόειν Ἴλιον. C. M. Bowra (*JHS* 80 (1960) 18 = *On Greek Margins*, Oxford 1970, 4) comments that the epithet 'not only conveys a vivid impression of Troy on its ridge overlooking the plain but helps by contrast to strengthen the note of menace in its coming doom. It is a general comment on the forbidding aspect which the city presented, especially to any possible attackers.'

σμύχοιτο ('were smouldering') is paralleled in Homer only at 9.653, where it refers to the burning of the Achaean ships by Hektor, and recurs in Hellenistic poetry and late prose. It is a particularly ugly and gloomy word.

For the Trojans Hektor's death means the end of Troy, and as in Priam's earlier speech (60–76), so here we have a vision of what is to come.

412–13 So too at 18.33–4 Antilokhos holds Akhilleus' hands, to restrain him in case he tries to kill himself in his grief at the news of Patroklos' death.

414 κυλινδόμενος κατὰ κόπρον: this is repeated at 24.640 of Priam, and the same action described more fully at 24.163–5. Akhilleus' self-abasement at 18.23–7 is similar (and compare Laertes at *Od.* 24.315–17). As in book 18 we have here the first extreme reaction of grief. That such reactions persisted in later antiquity is suggested by the criticism of Lucian, *De luctu* 12: 'dust is sprinkled on the head, and the living are more pitiful than the dead man; for they often roll on the ground and beat their heads against the earth'. Such rituals of mourning were sometimes described by the term 'self-pollution', (κατα)μιαίνεσθαι (Parker, *Miasma* 40–1). In general cf. also K. Meuli, *Gesammelte Schriften*, Basel 1975, I 333ff.

415 ἐξ ὀνομακλήδην ὀνομάζων: cf. *Od.* 4.278 ἐκ δ' ὀνομακλήδην … ὀνόμαζες. At *Od.* 12.250 ἐξονομακλήδην must be a single word, and so perhaps here also. The insistence on Priam's naming of each person individually stresses the desperation of his appeal.

416–28 Priam's speech contains a high frequency of single runover words or short phrases at the opening of a verse (420, 421, 422, 425, 426,

428), another way of emphasizing the urgency of his entreaty. Cf. vol. v, pp. 42–4.

416 οἷον: so too Hektor faced Akhilleus alone, although his parents begged him not to do so (cf. 38–9). In book 24 Priam will ignore the pleas of Hekabe, and go virtually alone to face Akhilleus (148, 177, 203, 519).

κηδόμενοί περ was preferred by Aristarchus (Did/A) to the variant κηδόμενόν περ. It presumably means 'concerned though you are for *me*'.

418 λίσσωμ' ('let me supplicate') is virtually a final clause; cf. Chantraine, *GH* II 207. For ἀνέρα τοῦτον see on 38. ἀτάσθαλον ὀβριμοεργόν means 'reckless', 'violent'; cf. Hes. *Th.* 996 ἀτάσθαλος ὀβριμοεργός |, of Pelias, ὀβριμοεργός alone of Herakles at *Il.* 5.403. 'He abuses the man whom he wishes to supplicate' (bT).

419–26 Not only is the train of thought similar to that of Priam's actual speech of supplication of Akhilleus (24.486–506: see on 405–36), with the mention of Peleus leading on to Priam's own grief for his sons, and thus to Hektor, but there are verbal parallels too. Cf. 419 with 24.503 αἰδεῖο ... αὐτόν τ' ἐλέησον; 420 ∼ 24.486–7; and the climactic positioning of Ἕκτορος (426) with 24.501 Ἕκτορα.

419 ἦν: pap. 12 reads εἰ, which was conjectured by Heyne and may be right; cf. Chantraine, *GH* II 281–2. Leaf wanted to take ἡλικίην as 'his (i.e. Akhilleus') contemporaries' (cf. 16.808). But it must surely mean 'my age'.

421–2 Cf. 6.282–3 μέγα γάρ μιν (Paris) Ὀλύμπιος ἔτρεφε πῆμα | Τρωσί τε καὶ Πριάμῳ ...

423–4 Pap. 12 reads τοίους for τόσσους, perhaps to avoid repetition with τόσσον in 424, and τῶν πολλῶν in 424. τηλεθάοντας ('flourishing') is usually of plants; see on 87 φίλον θάλος. For this theme of Priam's loss of so many sons see on 44.

425 Leaf compares Jacob's 'then shall ye bring down my gray hairs with sorrow to the grave' (Genesis 42.38). For ἄχος ὀξύ cf. 19.125, *Od.* 11.208. καταφέρειν (κατοίσεται) is only here in Homer, but common later.

426–8 Cf. 86–8 etc., and see on 82–9. Here Priam wishes that his son had died in his own arms. For 427 cf. *Od.* 20.59 κλαίουσα κορέσσατο, etc., and for 428 cf. 485, 24.727 ὃν τέκομεν σύ τ' ἐγώ τε δυσάμμοροι.

429 The Trojans take up the lament, as the women do after Andromakhe's speech at 515. The same type of refrain occurs after all the laments in book 24 (746, 760, 776), but the verse is varied at 437 to introduce the scene of Andromakhe at home. On such refrains cf. Alexiou, *Ritual Lament* 12–13, 131ff. Did/A and T quote a variant γέροντες for πολῖται, making the verse a repetition of 19.338. This is supported by T, on the grounds that Priam's speech is 'suitable to fathers'.

430–6 Hekabe's lament is more simple than Priam's, and also more resigned (430–1). It is mainly concerned with Hektor's past greatness, in contrast to his present state, a familiar feature of funerary laments in general (cf. Thetis at 18.55–7, and Alexiou, *Ritual Lament* 165–71). Her initial words 'why should I live?' are also a typical way of opening a lament with a question or a series of questions: cf. Alexiou, *op. cit.* 161–77. The speech has an alternation of progressive and integral enjambment throughout, which gives it a fluid quality.

430 This verse is very similar to 24.747. For this formal introduction to a lament see on 18.316–17.

431 τέκνον, ἐγὼ δειλή: cf. the opening of Andromakhe's lament (477). βείομαι is probably a short-vowel subjunctive, 'why should I live?'; cf. 15.194 βέομαι etc. For αἰνὰ παθοῦσα Aristarchus (Did/A) read αἰνὰ τεκοῦσα, as at 1.414 (Thetis to Akhilleus). Cf. also 18.54 (Thetis) ὤ μοι ἐγὼ δειλή, ὤ μοι δυσαριστοτόκεια.

433 εὐχωλή probably means 'something to boast about', as at 2.160, 4.173. ὄνειαρ is applied to Hektor again at 486. In the singular the word seems elsewhere in early epic to be used often to describe gods or their gifts: cf. *Od.* 4.444 (Eidothee's aid to Odysseus), Hes. *Th.* 871 (winds), *Erga* 822 (days), *HyDem* 269 (Demeter), with Richardson's comment.

434–5 οἵ σε θεὸν ὣς | δειδέχατ': 'who used to welcome you as a god'. The original form may have been δηδέχατ' (see on 4.4). Cf. 394 etc., and *Od.* 7.71–2: καὶ λαῶν, οἵ μίν ῥα θεὸν ὣς εἰσορόωντες | δειδέχαται μύθοισιν, ὅτε στείχησ' ἀνὰ ἄστυ.

437–515 Meanwhile, Andromakhe sits weaving at home knowing nothing of Hektor's death. She has just told her maids to prepare the water for his bath, when she hears the laments of Hekabe and the Trojans. Fearful for Hektor she rushes to the wall, and when she sees him she faints. Recovering, she laments his death, her own loss, and the helpless plight of their son Astuanax

This great scene is the last in the narrative of Hektor's death. It takes us back to the other scene in book 6, where the poet showed us Hektor, Andromakhe and Astuanax together (370–502). There Hektor found his wife watching anxiously on the wall, to which she had gone μαινομένη ἐϊκυῖα (389 ~ 22.460 μαινάδι ἴση), and where she stood lamenting (372–3). We heard of her father Eetion and her home Thebe, and what happened to them and her family at Akhilleus' hands (395–8, 414–28): here we are reminded again of her home and marriage (22.470–2, 22.479–81). Andromakhe had warned Hektor there of what could happen to him, and of the fate awaiting his wife and son (6.407–13, 6.429–32). Now that Hektor is dead, she foresees this fate in vivid detail (22.482–507). We were told there why their son was called Astuanax, and we are reminded of this again here, although now the name has lost its meaning (402–3 ~ 22.506–7). There

Hektor foresaw the fall of Troy, and wished that he might die rather than see Andromakhe a captive (6.447–65): his wish has now come true, and Troy's fall is near.

The picture of the timid child clinging to his nurse, afraid of his father's nodding helmet-plume, and the touching naturalness of this family scene (6.466–84) seem to find an echo too in the realistic way in which Andromakhe contrasts his gentle nursing with the rudeness that he will encounter as an orphan, causing him to run in tears to his widowed mother (22.490–504).

The scene in book 6 closed with Hektor telling his wife to go back to her loom and domestic tasks, and to bid her maids go about their work, while he returned to the war. She obeyed, and we last saw her among her maids, who were lamenting Hektor as if he were already killed (6.490–502). Now we find her again at her loom (22.440–1), giving orders to her maids for their domestic tasks (442–4). This Book too closes with her lament, echoed by the women. Her last words describe the clothes which they have woven for Hektor, which will now be useless to him, and which she will burn (510–14). Thus the scene in book 22 itself is framed by these references to the clothes made by the women (cf. 440–1).

The two episodes of books 6 and 22 also form the same pattern in reverse order. Andromakhe on the wall, her return home, and the premature laments for Hektor in book 6, are reversed with the scenes in book 22 of her at home, waiting for his return when he is already dead, then rushing to the wall, and lamenting him.

Book 6 showed us the city which Hektor was defending, the members of his own family for whom he was fighting, and above all the quiet, orderly happiness of family life which he stood to lose. Here, after the intense dramatic action of the battlefield, and the wild grief of the Trojans, we are again transported to the orderly peace of Hektor's house: the person who is dearest to him is the last to know the truth, although when she hears the laments we see that her heart was full of foreboding, and she at once guesses what has happened. The shock of seeing him dead causes her to faint: but she recovers, and her speech is remarkably controlled, in contrast to that of Priam. There is a practical side to her character, which appeared already in book 6, when she actually gave Hektor a piece of tactical advice about where to face the Greeks (433–9). It was also she who was responsible for the care of Hektor's war-horses (8.185–90), and who would receive his armour when he came home from fighting (17.207–8). Here her thoughts turn almost at once to their son, her chief surviving responsibility: it is his fate, not her own, that concerns her above all. He is also, in one sense, the image of his father, as his name suggests and as Hektor prayed that he would be (6.476–81).

Andromakhe's lament is echoed in her final speech in book 24 (725–45). This is shorter, but again she speaks mainly of what awaits their son (22.482–5 ~ 24.725–7). The two speeches complement each other, for in the first she imagined what would happen if he escaped death or captivity, whereas in the second she is more realistic and faces the truth, which is that Troy will fall and he will be enslaved or killed. This foresight parallels that of Hektor himself in book 6, when he predicted Andromakhe's enslavement (454–65).

The admiration of ancient readers for this episode is clearly shown in the detailed comments of the scholia (cf. 442–5, 448, 452, 464–5, 468–72, 474, 487, 500, 512–13). The effect of contrast between Hektor's death and the scene at his home was imitated by Juvenal in the pathetic description of a street accident in Rome, where the dead man's slaves are preparing their master's bath and dinner, while he is already waiting to cross the Styx (*S.* 3.257–67). In a later age Thackeray too may have echoed the scene, in *Vanity Fair* (chapter 32), when he describes Amelia praying for her husband to return from the battlefield of Waterloo, while he 'was lying on his face, dead, with a bullet through his heart' (cf. Griffin, *HLD* 110).

The scholia regard the motif of Andromakhe's ignorance of the truth as characteristic of the poet's skill in evoking sympathy. In a comment on 17.401–2, bT compare this with Akhilleus' ignorance of Patroklos' death and hopes of his safe return from battle, and also Dolon's expectation that those who are approaching him (at 10.349–56) are his own companions, coming to tell him to return to Troy.

For a detailed discussion of 437–76 cf. C. Segal, 'Andromache's *anagnorisis*: formulaic artistry in *Iliad* 22.437–76', *HSCP* 75 (1971) 33–57. On the relationship with book 6 cf. Wilamowitz, *IuH* 321; U. Hölscher, *Gnomon* 27 (1955) 388–9; W. Schadewaldt, *Hellas und Hesperien* (Zürich 1960) 36–8; Beck, *Stellung* 71–92; Lohmann, *Reden* 99–100, and especially his *Andromache-Szenen* 63–9.

438 Ἕκτορος is best taken with ἄλοχος. Leaf notes *Od.* 8.12 ὄφρα ξείνοιο πύθησθε, but here (as he says) one would expect a participle (θανόντος) if the noun were taken with πέπυστο. For οὐ γάρ οἵ τις ἐτήτυμος ἄγγελος ἐλθών cf. *HyDem* 46 οὔτ' οἰωνῶν τις τῇ ἐτήτυμος ἄγγελος ἦλθεν.

440–1 Cf. Helen at 3.125–8 ἥ δὲ μέγαν ἱστὸν ὕφαινε, | δίπλακα πορφυρέην, πολέας δ' ἐνέπασσεν ἀέθλους (etc.), and see comments on 3.125–7, 3.128. There are other parallels between these two scenes: both women leave their weaving in order to go to the wall, accompanied by two maids, and wearing their veils (3.141–5, 22.460–3, 22.468–72). See Introduction, 'Structure', and cf. Arend, *Scenen* 52–3, and Lohmann, *Andromache-Szenen* 59–62.

441 ἐν δὲ θρόνα ποικίλ' ἔπασσε refers to weaving, not embroidery (cf.

3.125–7n.). θρόνα is revived in literature by the Hellenistic poets, and survived in Cypriote, Thessalian and Aetolian. From this evidence it seems to mean either 'flowers' or 'figured patterns' in general (schol. Theocr. 2.59–62b). πάσσειν also survived in Cypriote, where it is said to have the same sense as ποικίλλειν (AT 441).

Helen was weaving scenes from the Trojan War itself, suffered for her sake, but Andromakhe is cut off from events outside, and the contrast of her peaceful weaving of decorative motifs with what has actually happened is all the more poignant. 'For Andromache ... the battle scenes are not reducible to art. They are too much part of a terrible present ... Her embroidery ... contains the symbols of the life and hope which the gods deny' (Segal, *HSCP* 1971, 41).

442–6 bT comment that 'he increases the pathos. For so far is she from being aware of what has occurred that she even prepares bath water, as though virtually seeing Hektor: and so the poet has added in sympathy the exclamation νηπίη, οὐδ' ἐνόησεν, as if pitying her ignorance.'

442–4 Cf. 18.343–5, 23.39–41, especially 18.344 (~ 23.40) ἀμφὶ πυρὶ στῆσαι τρίποδα μέγαν, ὄφρα τάχιστα. This passage in book 18 concerns the washing of Patroklos' corpse, making this an ominous echo. Moreover, the phrase μάχης ἐκ νοστήσαντι -ε (444) is always used of warriors who are fated *not* to survive. Cf. 17.207, where Zeus says that Hektor will *not* return from battle to Andromakhe; 24.705 (Hektor again after death), and 5.157 (two warriors who will *not* return home). For θερμὰ λόετρα see on 14.3–7.

445 For νηπίη, οὐδ' ἐνόησεν cf. 20.264 | νήπιος, οὐδ' ἐνόησε; | νηπίη 16.8; and see on 2.38. μάλα τῆλε λοετρῶν is a new and touching variation on the common motif of dying far from home and all its domestic comforts (cf. Griffin, *HLD* 109–10). Hektor is also, ironically, deprived of the washing which was part of the ritual of preparation of a body for burial.

447–9 Verse 447 echoes 409. In 448 ἐλελίχθη is a violent word, indicating a very strong reaction, emphasized by χαμαὶ δέ οἱ ἔκπεσε κερκίς. κερκίς (shuttle) occurs only here in *Il.*, once in *Od.* (5.62); see on 23.759–63. In 449 Andromakhe reacts at once, despite her agitation.

450 The structure of the verse (the opening command, followed by two clauses of increasing length, with asyndeton) expresses her urgency. For ὅτιν' the reading ὅτι (two papyri and some MSS) might be right (cf. Leaf).

451 ἑκυρή recurs at 24.770; cf. ἑκυρός 3.172, 24.770 (all in Helen's speeches).

451–3 These verses are an unusually vivid physical description of her state, with heavy enjambment. Cf. 461, and 10.93–4 κραδίη δέ μοι ἔξω | στηθέων ἐκθρῴσκει, τρομέει δ' ὑπὸ φαίδιμα γυῖα; also 15.280. On 452–3 bT compare Call. *Hy.* 5.83–4 ἐκόλασαν γὰρ ἀνίαι | γώνατα.

453 ἐγγὺς ... τέκεσσιν: she begins with the general plural, as if afraid to name Hektor.

454 αἳ γάρ ... ἔπος: cf. 18.272 αἳ γὰρ δή μοι ἀπ᾽ οὔατος ὧδε γένοιτο.

455–6 θρασὺν Ἕκτορα occurs 5× *Il.*, always in this position. Here the epithet is relevant, as also at 12.60, 12.210, and 13.725. The point is made explicitly at 457–9, and bT compare 6.407 (Andromakhe to Hektor): δαιμόνιε, φθίσει σε τὸ σὸν μένος. For 456 cf. 21.563 μή μ᾽ ἀπαειρόμενον πόλιος πεδίονδε νοήσῃ, and 21.3 ἔνθα διατμήξας τοὺς μὲν πεδίονδε δίωκε.

457–9 Cf. also 12.46, where Hektor is like a boar or lion who is fearless in face of his attackers, ἀγηνορίη δέ μιν ἔκτα; 16.753 ἥ τέ μιν ὤλεσεν ἀλκή (in a simile of Patroklos). For 458–9 cf. *Od.* 11.514–15 οὔ ποτ᾽ ἐνὶ πληθυῖ μένεν ἀνδρῶν οὐδ᾽ ἐν ὁμίλῳ, | ἀλλὰ πολὺ προθέεσκε, τὸ ὃν μένος οὐδενὶ εἴκων. Even at this moment of her supreme anxiety for Hektor's life Andromakhe's admiration for his courage comes out. But notice also how she speaks of him already in the past tense (so Willcock).

460 μεγάροιο διέσσυτο μαινάδι ἴση: cf. 6.389–90, where Andromakhe has gone to the wall to look for Hektor μαινομένῃ ἐϊκυῖα, and Hektor ἀπέσσυτο δώματος to look for *her*. μαινάδι ἴση is similar to the formular δαίμονι ἶσος (6× *Il.*). Homer knows about maenads (6.132–3), so that could be what he means here. Perhaps, however, we are wrong to attempt to draw a distinction between 'mad woman' and 'maenad'. The word μαινάς itself occurs only here in Homer; cf. *HyDem* 386, etc.

461 Cf. 452, and *HyDem* 293 δείματι παλλόμεναι.

462 Pap. 12 reads [αὐτὰρ ἐπεὶ Σκαιάς] τε πύλ[ας καὶ] πύργον ἵκανεν (cf. 6.237, where πυργόν is the reading of most MSS).

463 ἔστη παπτήνασ᾽ ἐπὶ τείχεϊ: 'it is well observed that she does not ask the truth of others: it is the mark of an agitated spirit to want to be an eyewitness' (bT).

464–5 ἑλκόμενον ... ἕλκον: the repetition emphasizes the horror of the sight. For ἕλκον ἀκηδέστως cf. 24.417 ἕλκει ἀκηδέστως, again of Akhilleus dragging Hektor; 21.123 ἀκηδέες with comment. Here too as with Lukaon the body is suffering from the denial of funeral rites.

466 = 5.659, 13.580 (τὸν δὲ ...), where it refers to death in battle.

467 ἀπὸ δὲ ψυχὴν ἐκάπυσσε: 'she breathed out her soul', i.e. fainted. The verb, which recurs only in Quintus of Smyrna (6.523), is probably related to καπνός. Cf. 5.698 (with comment on 696), *Od.* 5.468 (κακῶς) κεκαφηότα θυμόν, of fainting.

468–72 As she faints, she throws off her head-dress: perhaps the result of the violence of her fall, rather than a deliberate act, whereas Hekabe threw off her veil deliberately when she tore her hair (405–7). Here the description is far more detailed, for this is a more emotional moment and Andromakhe is a more significant figure. Not only is her head-dress extremely elaborate, but the description culminates in the history of her κρήδεμνον: it was a gift of Aphrodite on the occasion of her wedding with Hektor. Cf. bT 468–70: 'he reminds us of her former happiness, so that by stressing her change of fortune he may increase the effect of pity'. There could be no more vivid symbol of her tragedy.

468 βάλε was Aristarchus' reading (Did/A) for the vulgate χέε. The latter would be better suited to an involuntary movement, but does not go well with τῆλε; see on 468–72. For δέσματα σιγαλόεντα cf. 154 εἵματα σιγαλόεντα. 'In both cases Homer calls up these tangible reminders of a past happiness in a context which assures its destruction' (Segal, *HSCP* 1971, 49).

469–70 ἄμπυκα ... κρήδεμνόν θ': most probably the ἄμπυξ is a head-band, the κεκρύφαλος a cap (or sometimes later a net) to keep the hair in order, and the πλεκτὴ ἀναδέσμη some kind of woven or plaited binding for the hair. Over all of these was her shawl or head-scarf, κρήδεμνον (see on 14.184). Cf. Lorimer, *HM* 386–9 and *Arch. Hom.* B 21–2 (Marinatos). The three items in 469 are found only here in Homer, although χρυσάμπυκας ἵππους (4× *Il.*) implies the noun ἄμπυξ. Unless the conjecture ἀναδεσμᾶν is correct at E. *Med.* 978, ἀναδεσμή reappears only in very late literature (Nonnus, Agathias, Damascius, Photius).

470 ὅ ῥά οἱ δῶκε ... Ἀφροδίτη: Aphrodite's gifts can be figurative (e.g. 3.64–5), just as Pandaros' bow may be a gift of Apollo, although Pandaros made it himself (2.827, 4.105–11). It may, however, be wrong here to make a distinction between 'literal' and 'figurative' gifts.

The κρήδεμνον is in itself a symbol of marriage, since the Greek bride would wear this for the wedding ceremony. The poet has characteristically taken this motif from a typical scene (a woman normally covers her head when going out of the house: cf. Helen at 3.141 etc.), and used it here for a very special effect.

471–2 The event was described at 6.394–8, and the expression is similar to 16.190 ἠγάγετο πρὸς δώματ' ἐπεὶ πόρε μύρια ἕδνα.

473 γαλόῳ τε καὶ εἰνατέρες: her husband's sisters and his brother's wives. Once again we have an echo of book 6 (378, 383). The nouns recur together at 24.769. γάλως survived in Attic, and ἐνάτηρ occurs in late inscriptions from Asia Minor. These kinship terms tend to cluster around Helen and Andromakhe (see on 3.180 and 24.762–75).

474 ἀτυζομένην ἀπολέσθαι means 'distraught to the point of death'. At 412–13 and here we have two parallel tableaux, of the people gathered about Priam to prevent him from rushing out of the city, and the women clustering around Andromakhe to give her support (so bT 474).

475 Cf. *Od.* 5.458 ἀλλ' ὅτε δή ῥ' ἔμπνυτο καὶ ἐς φρένα θυμὸς ἀγέρθη and 24.349 αὐτὰρ ἐπεί ῥ' ἔμπνυτο καὶ ἐς φρένα θυμὸς ἀγέρθη. ἔμπνυτο is

Aristarchus' reading (Did/A) for the vulgate ἄμπνυτο; see on 5.697, where Kirk prefers ἀμπνύνθη. For καὶ ... ἀγέρθη cf. also 4.152 ἄψορρόν οἱ θυμὸς ἐνὶ στήθεσσιν ἀγέρθη, and see on 15.252–3, 16.481.

476 ἀμβλήδην occurs only here in Homer, and is rare later (ἀναβλήδην Arat. 1070, Maximus 287). 'With deep sobs' seems a better sense than 'lifting up her voice'. Cf. 21.364 ἀμβολάδην, and perhaps 19.314 ἀδινῶς ἀνενείκατο ('heaved deep sighs').

477–514 Andromakhe begins by lamenting the joint fate of Hektor and herself, in a series of balanced clauses (477–84), and she returns to Hektor and to her own inability to give him due burial rites at the end (508–14; cf. 482–3 νῦν δὲ σὺ μὲν ... αὐτὰρ ἐμὲ ... with 508–12 νῦν δὲ σὲ μὲν ... ἀτάρ τοι εἵματ' ... καταφλέξω ...). The central part of the speech concerns Astuanax (484–507). Consideration of his fate leads to a generalizing section about an orphan's life (490–8), with a transition at 499–500 back to Astuanax himself, leading her to reflect on the contrast with his past comfort and happiness (500–4). Verse 507 is also a transitional one, leading her back to Hektor.

There is a certain freedom in the way her thoughts develop, which seems psychologically natural. So too is the way in which she dwells on the homely details of a child's daily life, both of the orphan and the prince, and her preoccupation with something that might seem almost trivial, and which yet means so much to her, the lovely clothing made for Hektor which he will never use, even in death.

This wonderful speech has (alas!) not escaped the probing scalpel of sharp-eyed critics, from Aristarchus onwards. The Alexandrian scholar, accustomed to the manners of a Hellenistic court, could not understand why Andromakhe should speak of an orphan's lot in terms which he saw as quite inappropriate for the princeling of Priam's lineage. Such general reflections were out of place here, and 487–99 were therefore doomed to *athetesis*. Modern critics have been divided over the issue, some going still further and condemning 500–5 or 500–7. Certainly, 500–4 have no point apart from what precedes. Yet among the analysts Wilamowitz defended the lines condemned by Aristarchus (*IuH* 105–7), and so did Von der Mühll (*Hypomnema* 346–7).

An additional objection was made by Leaf (on 487), that 'the passage contains ἅπαξ λεγόμενα of a sort quite unfamiliar in Epic poetry; ἀπουρήσουσιν, παναφήλικα, ὑπεμνήμυκε, ὑπερῴην, ἀμφιθαλής'. This draws attention to the significant point that, as in the similes, Homer can use a quite distinctive vocabulary when he is speaking of more everyday matters. Leaf's view of epic propriety, like that of Aristarchus, was too narrow. For a defence of the passage see also Richardson in Bremer, *HBOP* 180–3.

477–84 Andromakhe sees her fate as linked to Hektor's. She has lost her home, as he foresaw the end of his city, and for each the other was all-important (6.411–30, 6.447–65). There is careful and elaborate rhetorical parallelism and contrast here (cf. Lohmann, *Reden* 99):

478   σὺ μὲν ἐν Τροίῃ Πριάμου κατὰ δῶμα,
     αὐτὰρ ἐγὼ Θήβῃσιν …
     ἐν δόμῳ Ἠετίωνος …

482   νῦν δὲ σὺ μὲν Ἀΐδαο δόμους ὑπὸ κεύθεσι γαίης
     ἔρχεαι, αὐτὰρ ἐμὲ στυγερῷ ἐνὶ πένθεϊ λείπεις
     χήρην ἐν μεγάροισι …

By this means Andromakhe suggests that their fates run parallel now, as they did in the past. Cf. Hor. *C.* 2.17, especially 20–30, where Horace links his destiny with that of Maecenas. On the linking of Thebe's fate with Troy's see O. Taplin in *Chios* 18–19.

477 For Ἕκτορ, ἐγὼ δύστηνος cf. 431 τέκνον, ἐγὼ δειλή at the opening of Hekabe's lament. γιγνόμεθ' is the reading of Monro and Allen, but we should probably follow the MS reading γείνομεθ', as elsewhere, with Leaf, and Allen's *editio maior* (1931).

479–80 Cf. 6.396–7 Ἠετίων, ὃς ἔναιεν ὑπὸ Πλάκῳ ὑληέσσῃ, | Θήβῃ Ὑποπλακίῃ … For ὅ μ' … ἐοῦσαν cf. 8.283 ὅ σ' ἔτρεφε τυτθὸν ἐόντα.

481 In δύσμορος αἰνόμορον the variation and repetition are pathetic. δύσμορος is used of himself by Priam at 60 (cf. 59 ἐμὲ τὸν δύστηνον), αἰνόμορος only here in *Il.*, and 2× *Od.* For ὡς μὴ … τεκέσθαι cf. 17.686, 18.19 ἢ μὴ ὤφελλε γενέσθαι, and for such a wish in a lament cf. Helen at 24.764, and Alexiou, *Ritual Lament* 178 (with n. 46).

482 Ἀΐδαο δόμους ὑπὸ κεύθεσι γαίης: cf. *Od.* 24.204 εἰν Ἀΐδαο δόμοις, ὑπὸ κεύθεσι γαίης.

484–6 Cf. 24.725–8 κὰδ δέ με χήρην | λείπεις ἐν μεγάροισι· πάϊς δ' ἔτι νήπιος αὔτως, | ὃν τέκομεν σύ τ' ἐγώ τε δυσάμμοροι, οὐδέ μιν οἴω | ἥβην ἵξεσθαι … For the complaint of desertion by the dead man cf. (for example) Alexiou, *Ritual Lament* 176, 182–4.

484 χήρη recurs at 6.408, 6.432, 22.499, 24.725. In the singular this word is used by no one else but Andromakhe in Homer, and on four occasions in association with the mention of their son. The only other occurrence is at 2.289 (χῆραι). νήπιος αὔτως means 'a mere baby'; see on 125.

485–6 οὔτε σὺ τούτῳ … οὔτε σοι οὗτος: this transposition of pronouns (T 485–6 ἀντιμεταβολή) is emphasized by the parallelism of position at the end of the verses. 'He has mingled the pathos wonderfully, arousing pity in the case of each of them, the child who is deprived of his father's valour and the father who cannot enjoy his son' (bT).

487–99 For Aristarchus' rejection of these verses (Arn/A) see on 477–514. In reality Andromakhe's vision becomes general here, because she and her son are archetypes of all widows and orphans.

487 πόλεμον ... πολύδακρυν Ἀχαιῶν: cf. 3.165 (Priam to Helen) πόλεμον πολύδακρυν Ἀχαιῶν | (another echo of book 3).

489 It is not really so surprising that Andromakhe should fear the loss of her son's royal property after Hektor's death. There were other members of the family who might step in after Priam was no longer there to defend him, for example those brothers of Hektor whom Priam regards as idle and useless (24.248–64). There is also the hostility between Priam's family and that of Aineias (13.459–61, 20.178–83), and the prophecy that Aineias and his descendants will rule the Trojans in the future (20.302–8).

ἀπουρίσσουσιν: this verb occurs only here in surviving literature. In antiquity it was connected with οὖρος ('boundary'), like the later ἀφορίζεσθαι ('to appropriate for oneself'): so Arn/A, Eust. 1282.16. An alternative modern view (Leaf, Chantraine, *GH* 1 446, *LfgrE* s.v.) connects it, or the variant ἀπουρήσουσιν, with ἀπηύρα, ἀπούρας, translating 'will take away'. The fact that the active rather than middle is used is not a valid objection to the first view, which seems preferable. Notice the strong assonance of initial *alphas* in this verse.

490–9 In this passage the verses are virtually all end-stopped, and several have a proverbial ring to them (e.g. 490, 499).

490 παναφήλικα: 'entirely cut off from his contemporaries', a good example of the expressive quality of Greek compounds; cf. 24.255, 24.493 πανάποτμος, 24.540 παναώριον. παναφῆλιξ occurs nowhere else in Greek literature. M. Pope (*CQ* 35 (1985) 5) notices that out of fifteen παν-compounds in the *Iliad* six occur only in the last four books, 'and this is most easily understood as the result of a temporary inclination of the poet's mind – especially as it is precisely in these examples that the force of the παν- is intensive (e.g. πανάποτμος "all-unhappy") instead of quantitative (e.g. πανημέριος "all-day")'. Cf. also 24.5 πανδαμάτωρ, 21.397 πανόψιον, 23.532 and 547 πανύστατος.

491 πάντα δ᾽ ὑπεμνήμυκε: another unique expression. Aristarchus (A) took the verb as meaning 'he bows his head, is downcast' (κατανένευκεν), πάντα meaning 'in everything'. This would be the perfect of ὑπημύω, ὑπἐμήμῡκἒ, with the *nu* added *metri gratia*: so *EM* 777.46, and Schulze, *Quaestiones Epicae* 266–7. Cf. A.R. 2.862–3 κατήμυσαν δ᾽ ἀχέεσσιν | θυμόν, Coluthus 338 ὑπημύουσι παρειαί (ὑπημύουσιν ὀπωπαί Tournier). For δεδάκρυνται cf. 16.7 (with comment).

This is a fine verse, with a chiastic structure, πάντα and παρειαί framing the two slow, melancholy verbs. It gives a very vivid picture of the humiliated and tear-stained child.

492 The verse is echoed at 499. ἄνεισι presumably means 'approaches' here.

493 Again notice the realistic visual detail: the child is trying desperately to attract the attention of these indifferent grown-ups, perhaps also asking for a suppliant's rights.

494-6 The tenses change here to a series of gnomic aorists.

494 κοτύλη elsewhere in the *Iliad* is used of the hip-joint (5.306, 307). Cf. however 23.34 κοτυλήρυτον; and *Od.* 15.317, 17.12 where κοτύλη is used of a beggar's cup. Various views about the word are given in Athenaeus 478D-9C, but it must be some kind of small cup. Cf. also G. Bruns, *Arch. Hom.* Q 44. τυτθόν is adverbial, 'for a little'.

495 The repeated verb gives a pathetic close to this gnomic verse.. ὑπερῴη ('palate') occurs only here in poetry; cf. Hippocrates, *Mochl.* 39, etc. This scene resembles Luke 16.21, where the beggar Lazarus is described as 'desiring to be fed with the crumbs which fell from the rich man's table'.

496-8 So too Hektor feared the shame of Andromakhe, when some Greek would point her out in her slavery as 'Hektor's wife' (6.459-63). For the vital importance of the feast as a vehicle for honour see on 12.311.

496 ἀμφιθαλής '(a boy) with both parents alive' again occurs only here in early epic or archaic poetry; in this sense cf. Pl. *Lg.* 927D (in a discussion about the protection of orphans against injury), Call. fr. 75.3; see also L. Robert, *HSCP* Supp. vol. 1 (1940) 509-19, Fraenkel on A. *Ag.* 1144-5 (where it is used metaphorically, as at A. *Ch.* 394). The form δαιτύς for δαίς is only found here. For ἐστυφέλιξε ('shoves him away') see on 21.380.

497 ὀνειδείοισιν: only here on its own, meaning 'reproaches'; cf. 1.519 (etc.) ὀνειδείοις ἐπέεσσιν.

498 ἔρρ' οὕτως has a coarse, colloquial ring to it (so T). Cf. 21.184 | κεῖσ' οὕτως. μεταδαίνυσθαι recurs at 23.207, *Od.* 18.48.

500-1 With the name Astuanax we return to the particular case which we left at 490. Cf. 6.474 where Hektor takes him in his arms. Still closer in tone is Phoinix' description of how he used to take the child Akhilleus on his knees and give him titbits of meat and wine to drink (9.485-91). For Homer's close observation of children's behaviour see also on 16.7-10, 16.259-65. μύελος recurs at 20.482, 2× *Od.*

502-4 νηπιαχεύειν occurs only once in later literature, in a verse epitaph (*RhM* (1879) 195); cf. νηπίαχος 3× *Il.* For ἐν ἀγκαλίδεσσι cf. 18.555 of boys harvesting; AbT take this as a diminutive form, suitable to the littleness of the children. We met the nurse at 6.399ff., 6.467ff. εὐνῇ ἐνὶ μαλακῇ occurs 3× *Il.*, 1× *Od.*, in this position. θαλέων ('good cheer') is only used here in Homer in this sense, later by Alcman and Callimachus; θάλεα is really the plural of θάλος, but closer in sense to θάλεια, θαλίη. The pathos is enhanced by the triple repetition of the prepositional phrases, ἐν . . . ἐν . . . ἐνὶ . . .; cf. the similar effect at 24.614–15.

505 For φίλου . . . ἁμαρτών cf. 6.411 σεῦ ἀφαμαρτούσῃ (Andromakhe to Hektor).

506–7 On the etymology of the name Astuanax cf. 6.402–3, which this recalls: τὸν ῥ' Ἕκτωρ καλέεσκε Σκαμάνδριον, αὐτὰρ οἱ ἄλλοι | Ἀστυάνακτ'· οἷος γὰρ ἐρύετο Ἴλιον Ἕκτωρ. This is echoed again by Priam at 24.499. The repetition of the name after 500 is rightly treated by the ancient commentators as a pathetic touch (bT 500): it has not pleased some modern critics. For ἐπίκλησιν see on 29, and for πύλας καὶ τείχεα μακρά | cf. 4.34. With the apostrophe in 507 we return to Hektor, the subject of Andromakhe's opening address (477–86).

508 νόσφι τοκήων: cf. 24.208, 24.211, and on this motif of dying (etc.) far from one's parents see again Griffin, *HLD* 106–12.

509 The sound patterns of this verse are remarkable. αἰόλαι εὐλαί ('wriggling worms'), entirely composed of vowels and liquids, is horribly appropriate, and the verse ends with a series of harsh *kappas*. The whole sentence culminates in the emphatic runover word γυμνόν.

510–14 Cf. bT 512–13: 'this is full of pathos and realistic: for together with the dead, people also destroy their finest possessions, as a precaution against their being used by others'. That is one possible reason for doing this. The usual explanation is that the possessions are intended for the dead man's use, as in the story of Periander's wife, whose ghost complained to him that she was cold and naked because the clothes he had given her had not been burnt (Hdt. 5.92η). On the practice among many peoples of burying or burning a dead person's property, and the explanations given for this, see E. Samter, *Volkskunde im altsprachlichen Unterricht* I Teil, *Homer* (Berlin 1923) 148–58; E. Rohde, *Psyche* (English version, London 1925) 17–18, 23; Kurtz and Boardman, *Burial Customs* 201–17.

Here, however, the point is not that Homer ignores the belief that a dead man could profit from such things. In addition to what is burnt by Akhilleus on Patroklos' pyre (23.166–77), he also promises him a share in the ransom for Hektor's body (24.592–5). The clothes are of no use because they cannot serve their purpose of wrapping his body for burial (cf. 16.680, 18.352–3, 24.580–1, 24.588, *Od.* 2.96–102 etc.). Instead, however, her act of burning them will be a kind of 'substitute' funeral rite in his honour. It is all that she can do, and it appropriately symbolizes both her devotion as a wife and her despair at his loss.

It is appropriate that her speech should close with the thought of Hektor's glory (κλέος), for this was the mainspring of all his actions during his lifetime, and this is what will now survive for those who are left behind.

510–11 For the thematic present form κέονται cf. *Od.* 11.341, 16.232, and Chantraine, *GH* 1 476. λεπτά τε καὶ χαρίεντα recurs at *Od.* 10.223, where the phrase is used of weaving again.

512–14 καταφλέγειν only occurs here in Homer; cf. Hes. *Aspis* 18 etc. οὐδὲν σοί γ᾽ ὄφελος is in apposition to the preceding verse. ἐγκεῖσθαι again occurs only here in Homer, but is common later. For ἀλλὰ ... Τρωϊάδων cf. 24.215 ἀλλὰ πρὸ Τρώων καὶ Τρωϊάδων βαθυκόλπων.

515 = 24.746; see on 429. The repetition in 23.1 of the theme of 515 shows that there is a strong break at this point (see on 6.311–12).

BOOK TWENTY-THREE

In the life of Schiller by Frau K. von Wolzogen it is recorded that 'Schiller once said in a melancholy mood: "If one had only lived in order to read the twenty-third book of the *Iliad*, then one could not complain about one's existence"' (*Schillers Leben*, Stuttgart and Tübingen 1845, 335). The gloomy splendour of Patroklos' funeral will have appealed especially to a Romantic of the *Sturm und Drang* period, but he must surely have also admired the funeral games whose tone is so different, and whose manifold variety won the praise of Goethe (cf. Lehrs, *De Aristarchi studiis* 428). In the first part of the Book all is πάθος, but in the second the interest is above all on ἦθος. Together they make a beautifully balanced whole, and also an excellent transition to the final scenes of the poem.

The Book is marked off not only by its unity of theme, but also by the way in which the opening themes of grief for Patroklos and the fate of Hektor's body (1–26) are resumed at the beginning of book 24. In this part of the poem the contrast between the treatment of the bodies of Patroklos and Hektor is all-important, and it is recalled again at 23.179–91 where, after setting light to the pyre, Akhilleus invokes Patroklos' spirit, saying that he will give Hektor's body to the dogs. The poet adds that Aphrodite and Apollo in fact protected it from harm. Against the dishonouring of Hektor the unique honours paid to Patroklos at his funeral, the main theme of book 23, stand out in powerful contrast.

The funeral ends in mid-verse at 257, with a typically rapid Homeric transition to the games. These occupy the remaining 640 verses, but more than half (262–652) are taken up by the chariot-race, which forms the central panel of the Book's structure. Seven other contests follow, of which the first three (boxing, wrestling and running) are clearly important and occupy 145 verses in all, whereas the last four (armed duel, weight-throwing, archery and javelin) are dealt with more briefly, in only 100 verses. There is thus a marked sense of *diminuendo*: first the great sequence of scenes of the funeral itself, followed by the chariot-race with all its excitement and the complexity of its subordinate episodes, and then a series of ever-shorter scenes, with a progressive relaxation of tension. This effect must be deliberate, and those scholars who have argued that most of the final hundred verses are a later addition seem to have missed this point. A function of the funeral games themselves, both as heroic institution and epic narrative, must be to defuse the intensity of passion accumulated in the struggles which have preceded, leaving us at the end with a strong sense of restoration of the normal, in terms of both emotion and conduct, in preparation for the resolution of book 24.

In the poem's overall architecture book 23 clearly balances book 2 (cf. Introduction, 'Structure'). Both fall into two main sections, in 2 the Achaean assembly and the Catalogues, in 23 the Funeral and Games, themselves also in catalogue-form. Book 2 paints a picture of a potentially demoralized and disorderly army, whose morale is restored with difficulty by the leaders, an ominous prelude to disasters to come, whereas in book 23 these disasters are mostly over, and order is restored and maintained in the games by the firm hand of Akhilleus. Both show the whole army gathered together, for war and for the contests which are 'the image of war without its guilt'. In 2 we hear the slow, majestic roll-call of the Achaean leaders and their followers, whereas in 23 we bid farewell to most of the major Greek heroes of the poem, who will not appear in its closing scenes. There are also many echoes of episodes in the intervening narrative, and several threads which can be traced forward beyond the story of the *Iliad* itself, which add to the Book's richness of texture.

In the funeral itself the aspect of excess in so much of the ritual is very striking, by comparison with other epic funeral scenes. The poet is depicting something on an exceptional scale, in keeping with the grandeur of the poem as a whole, but above all as a reflection of the immensity of Akhilleus' grief. The funeral procession, in which the whole army, charioteers in front, a vast throng of infantry behind, escort Patroklos' body and lay their offerings of hair upon the corpse, must remind us of the funeral scenes on the great *kraters* of the Homeric period. The catalogue of offerings placed on the pyre is unparalleled in scale elsewhere, and even the size of the pyre itself ('a hundred foot square') seems unusual, although it may be matched in reality by the great burial mound at Lefkandi in Euboea (see on 164). Unique too is the episode in which Iris summons the Winds to make the pyre burn: Akhilleus is the only mortal who could evoke such a divine response (see on 192–225).

After the intensity of the funeral, the games come as a welcome relief and the tone is remarkably different. Akhilleus is perfectly in control, the model ἀγωνοθέτης. There is great excitement and even laughter at times. In the chariot-race quarrels break out among spectators and contestants alike, and we are aware of the tensions still stored beneath the surface: but here, in contrast to the opening of the *Iliad*, they are resolved, and Akhilleus himself ensures that this is so. The Book closes with Akhilleus awarding Agamemnon the prize for the javelin, without allowing him to compete, because he is 'supreme in power' (891). This courteous gesture sets the final seal on their reconciliation, and Akhilleus' moderation and sense of propriety prepare us for his change of heart when he receives Priam's supplication.

The individual contests are full of vivid incident, but what stands out most is the way the poet uses them to bring out, once again, some of his heroes' strengths and weaknesses of character. It is in this sense that one can describe them as ethical, as the *Odyssey* was seen to be in antiquity. Both stand closer in some ways to later comedy than to tragedy (cf. F. Robert, *Mélanges Desrousseaux*, Paris 1937, 405–16). This is nowhere more evident than in the chariot-race. Running through its narrative can be discerned the contrast between passionate ambition, with its disastrous results, and reason, and also that between genuine good sense and skill misused. Nestor's lecture to Antilokhos before the race with its sermon on μῆτις (306–48) sets the tone, and the final quarrel between Menelaos and Antilokhos is very much concerned with these themes (566–613). After their reconciliation (a morally 'happy ending') Menelaos hands over the prize mare to Antilokhos' companion Noemon (612–13) (surely a significant name), and Akhilleus then awards the spare prize to wise old Nestor, whose speech of gratitude rounds off the episode (626–50). His speech is called an αἶνος (652), and it may contain a moral relevant to the chariot-race as a whole (see on 499–652).

If the whole poem until now has been largely concerned with the disastrous effects of strife, the games offer us a counterpart of a positive kind (like Hesiod's 'good strife'), marking a peaceful close to the internal dissensions of the Greeks.

1–34 When the Achaeans reach the ships, Akhilleus tells the Myrmidons to lament Patroklos, and they drive their chariots thrice round the corpse, while he leads their lament. He then gives them a funeral feast

This lament is more official or ritualized than those in books 18 (314–42) and 19 (282–302, 314–39), as is shown by the reference to it as a γέρας θανόντων (9), and also by the motif of processing three times round the corpse. This is echoed by Akhilleus when he drags Hektor's body three times round Patroklos' tomb (24.14–16), and the same motif occurs at the funeral of Akhilleus himself (*Od.* 24.68–70). This is primarily a way of paying tribute to the dead man, and perhaps also (as in other ceremonies where something is encircled in this way) of symbolizing one's attachment to him. This encirclement of the dead was also part of the mourning ritual of Germanic peoples and others in the past: cf. Jordanes, *Getica* ch. 49, *Beowulf* 3169–72, and M. Andronikos. *Arch. Hom.* w (Totenkult) 14–15.

The funeral feast of the Myrmidons here precedes the burial, an order which seems unusual. A feast follows the burial of Hektor (24.664–6,

24.801–4), and is mentioned also after the deaths of Klutaimestre and Aigisthos (*Od.* 3.309–10). In the classical period and later the περίδειπνον took place after the funeral, but in the past sacrifices preceded it according to [Plato], *Minos* 315c. Its placing here may be influenced by compositional considerations, since the poet goes on directly from the burial to the funeral games (contrast 257–8 with 24.801–2), and the feast would have interrupted this sequence. Cf. also *Od.* 24.72–92 (burial followed by games), and Andronikos, *op. cit.* 15–18. For parallels between the funeral of Patroklos and the Thracian rites in Herodotus 5.8 see A. Petropoulou, *AJP* 109 (1988) 492–3.

1–12 The lamentation for Hektor at Troy merges with the laments for Patroklos in the Achaean camp.

2–5 For 2 cf. 15.233, 18.150 φεύγοντες νῆάς τε καὶ Ἑλλήσποντον ἵκωνται/ἵκοντο. For ἐπεί see on 22.379. Verse 3 = 19.277. For 5 cf. 129 αὐτίκα Μυρμιδόνεσσι φιλοπτολέμοισι κέλευσε.

6 Μυρμίδονες ταχύπωλοι: Cf. Δαναῶν -οι ταχυπώλων -οι | 10× *Il.*

7 ὑπ' ὄχεσφι: elsewhere ὄχεσφι functions as a dative, here as an ablatival form. Cf. ὑπὸ ζυγόφιν (24.576), Chantraine, *GH* I 234–41.

9 ὃ γὰρ γέρας ἐστὶ θανόντων: the relative is used for metrical reasons instead of τό here, as at 12.344 = 357 ὃ γάρ κ' ὄχ' ἄριστον ἁπάντων, and *Od.* 24.190 ὃ γὰρ γέρας ἐστὶ θανόντων. Cf. τὸ γὰρ γέρας ἐστὶ θανόντων 2× *Il.*, 1× *Od.*

10 Cf. 98 ὀλοοῖο τεταρπώμεσθα γόοιο |, 24.513 | αὐτὰρ ἐπεί ῥα γόοιο τετάρπετο, *Od.* 11.212 κρυεροῖο τεταρπώμεσθα γόοιο |. bT quote Aeschylus (fr. 385 N.²): οἵ τοι στεναγμοὶ τῶν πόνων ἰάματα.

11 δορπήσομεν ἐνθάδε πάντες: at 19.206–14 and 303–8 Akhilleus refuses to eat until sunset. It looks as if he now intends to break his fast and share in the funeral feast, and perhaps he shares also in the meal with Agamemnon which follows (cf. 48).

13–16 At 19.211–13 Patroklos' body was in Akhilleus' hut, whereas here it is on the shore: it has obviously been moved in the meantime, but the poet does not need to account for such details.

13 ἐΰτριχας ... ἵππους: cf. 301, 351 ἐΰτριχας ὥπλισαθ' ἵππους |. The phrase occurs only in book 23; cf. καλλίτριχας -ες ἵππους -οι 11× *Il.*, 3× *Od.*

14 μετὰ δέ σφι Θέτις γόου ἵμερον ὦρσε: Thetis and the Nereids joined Akhilleus in lament at 18.35ff., and at Akhilleus' own funeral they all appear to mourn for him, and the Muses also lament (*Od.* 24.47–62). Here, however, Thetis is not actually said to appear in person to the Myrmidons. The mention of Thetis may be influenced by the epic tradition about Akhilleus' death: cf Kakridis, *Researches* 84; vol. v, p. 18.

15–16 The repetition of δεύοντο adds pathos, as do the runover word δάκρυσι and the wistful tone of τοῖον γὰρ πόθεον ... Virgil imitates these verses directly at *Aen*. 11.191 *spargitur et tellus lacrimis, sparguntur et arma*, in a passage influenced by this episode (*Aen*. 11.188–90 ~ 23.13–14, 11.197–9 ~ 23.30–3 and 166–7, 11.201–2 ~ 23.154–5). For μήστωρα φόβοιο see on 4.328.

17–18 These verses exactly repeat the description of Akhilleus' mourning for Patroklos in book 18 (316–17); see comment.

19–23 Akhilleus' speech recalls his promises at 18.333–7 and 22.354 (and cf. 21.27–32 where he took the twelve Trojan prisoners). It is echoed at 179–83.

19 καὶ εἰν Ἀΐδαο δόμοισι: '*even* in Hades'. Cf. the similar use of καὶ by Akhilleus in this context at 22.389–90 (εἰν Ἀΐδαο ... καὶ κεῖθι) and 23.103–4 (καὶ εἰν Ἀΐδαο δόμοισι).

20 τελέω is probably present, 'I am already accomplishing'; see on 179–83.

21 ὠμὰ δάσασθαι: cf. *Od*. 18.87 μήδεά τ' ἐξερύσας δώῃ κυσὶν ὠμὰ δάσασθαι (and similarly *Od*. 22.476). Here one can understand κρέα with ὠμά (cf. 22.347).

22–3 These verses repeat 18.336–7 (ἀποδειροτομήσω; see comment).

24 = 22.395 (see comment). Here it seems to refer primarily to the immediate action of leaving Hektor stretched out face downward in the dust (25–6), but presumably also to Akhilleus' continued maltreatment of the body later (24.14–18).

25–6 Cf. 24.17–18 τὸν δέ τ' ἔασκεν | ἐν κόνι ἐκτανύσας προπρηνέα. This is in itself an insult, as a body would normally be laid out on its back for burial. ἀφοπλίζεσθαι only occurs here in Homer, and rarely in later Greek.

27 χάλκεα μαρμαίροντα occurs 3× *Il*. For λύον δ' ὑψηχέας ἵππους see comment on 5.770–2 (*ad fin*.) ὑψηχέες ἵπποι. This epithet occurs only on these two occasions in Homer, and later once in Philostratus. Here there was a variant λύοντο δὲ μώνυχας ἵππους (?Did/A), and a few MSS read ὑψαυχένας which is a variant at 5.772 (in [Longinus] 9.5).

29 μύριοι recurs as an emphatic runover word of the whole Greek army at 134 and 2.468. For τάφον ... δαίνυ ('gave a funeral feast') cf. *Od*. 3.309 δαίνυ τάφον, and δαινύναι γάμον 19.299, *Od*. 4.3. τάφος always means 'funeral rites' in Homer, never 'tomb'.

30–4 An elaborate sentence with four parallel clauses describes the feast. Verses 30–3 consist of three clauses with emphatic repetition of initial πολλοί, runover in the first clause and an extended two-verse third clause: these refer to the slaughter of oxen, sheep and goats, and pigs (suggesting comparison with the later *suovetaurilia*, or sacrifice of pig, sheep and bull). Verse 34 rounds the sentence off with a vivid description of the blood flowing 'everywhere around the corpse'. The verses are similar to 9.464–9: ἣ μὲν πολλά ... λισσόμενοι κατερήτυον ... | πολλὰ δὲ ἴφια μῆλα καὶ εἰλίποδας ἕλικας βοῦς | ἔσφαζον, πολλοὶ δὲ σύες θαλέθοντες ἀλοιφῇ | εὑόμενοι τανύοντο διὰ φλογὸς Ἡφαίστοιο, | πολλὸν δ' ἐκ κεράμων μέθυ πίνετο τοῖο γέροντος. Cf. Thracian funeral rites (Hdt. 5.8): παντοῖα σφάξαντες ἰρήια εὐωχέονται, προκλαύσαντες πρῶτον.

30–1 These verses were athetized by some critics (T), on the ground that 'iron did not exist at that time'.

30 βόες ἀργοί: only here of oxen; cf. κύνες -ας (πόδας) ἀργοί -ούς 3× *Il.*, 3× *Od.*, where it is thought to mean 'swift', and ἀργὴν χῆνα (*Od.* 15.161), where it has its basic sense of 'shining'. bT objected that only black victims were sacrificed to the dead, but suggested as one answer that they are intended here as a feast for the living. Presumably this is correct, but the sense here may be 'sleek', 'glistening', rather than 'white'. Cf. Chantraine. *Dict. s.v.*

ὀρέχθεον: this occurs only here in Homer, once in Aristophanes (*Nub.* 1368), and frequently in Hellenistic and later verse. It was explained here as either 'bellowed' (cf. ῥοχθεῖν), or 'stretched themselves out', 'struggled' (cf. ὀρέγεσθαι), or 'were cut open' (cf. ἐρέχθειν = 'rend', 'break'). Modern philology has favoured the second view (Chantraine, *Dict.* s.v.). In Hellenistic poetry it seems to mean either 'throb', 'swell' or 'roar' (cf. Gow on Theocr. *Id.* 11.43). The ancient interpretation 'bellow' was based on the assumption that it was onomatopoeic (κατὰ μίμησιν ἤχου τραχέος πεποίηται τὸ ῥῆμα: bT etc.), and this deserves to be taken seriously, as in the case of ῥοχθεῖν (cf. schol. *Od.* 5.402).

32–3 Cf. 9.467–8 (quoted on 30–4). ἀργιόδοντες ὕες belongs to a formular group: cf. | ἀργιόδοντος ὑός 1× *Il.*, 3× *Od.*, σύες (ὣς) ἀργιόδοντες | 2× *Od.*, σῦν ἄγριον ἀργιόδοντα | 9.535, ὑῶν ἕνεκ' ἀργιοδόντων | *Od.* 14.416.

34 κοτυλήρυτον ... αἷμα: literally this means 'blood drawn off in cupfuls' (cf. ἀρύω). The epithet occurs only here and in Nicander (*Th.* 539), but the phrase is imitated by Callimachus (?) fr. 773 Pf. κυλικήρυτον αἷμα. Its uniqueness draws our attention to the scene. Aristarchus took it as meaning here 'abundantly enough to be taken up in cups' (Arn/A), which could well be right in this context. Leaf argued that the blood was actually caught in cups and then poured out as a gift for the dead man, and Mazon (*REA* 42 (1940) 255–6) independently takes the same view. Leaf compared the blood for the ghosts in the *Odyssey* (10.535ff. etc.), and (more appropriately) E. *Hec.* 534–8, where Akhilleus' ghost is offered Poluxena's blood. But one might expect the ritual to be more explicitly described, in this case. Cf. also Andronikos, *Arch. Hom.* w 16–17.

35–61 The leaders escort Akhilleus to Agamemnon and invite him to wash, but he refuses to do so until Patroklos is buried. He tells them to eat and to prepare for the funeral, and they take their supper and go to bed. Akhilleus then lies down to sleep at the edge of the sea

37 σπουδῇ means 'with difficulty', as at 2.99 etc.

38–41 For 38 cf. 11.617 οἱ δ' ὅτε δὴ κλισίην Νηληϊάδεω ἀφίκοντο, etc. Verse 39 = 2.442 (with κέλευσε). For 40–1 cf. 18.344–5 (with comment) ἀμφὶ πυρὶ στῆσαι τρίποδα μέγαν, ὄφρα τάχιστα | Πάτροκλον λούσειαν ἄπο βρότον αἱματόεντα. ἀμφὶ ... μέγαν also recurs at 22.443.

42 Cf. 19.304–8, where Akhilleus refuses food because of his grief, and *HyDem* 47–50 where Demeter in her grief at the loss of Persephone abstains from both food and washing (Richardson, *Hymn to Demeter* 165–8).

43 As Monro and Leaf pointed out, the use of ὅς τίς τε here after the antecedent Ζῆνα is unusual, since this combination of relative plus generalizing τε normally refers to an indefinite antecedent. This looks like an echo of the familiar religious formula exemplified by A. *Ag.* 160 Ζεὺς ὅστις ποτ' ἐστίν (cf. Fraenkel *ad loc.*, and E. Norden, *Agnostos Theos*, 4th edn. Darmstadt 1956, 144–7), whereby one makes allowance for uncertainty over the proper way to address a god. Leaf suggests 'Zeus, or by whatever name the highest of the gods is to be called'. θεῶν ὕπατος καὶ ἄριστος was used at 19.258 (= *Od.* 19.303), in an invocation of Zeus as witness to an oath. Here the whole verse adds a weighty religious sanction to Akhilleus' refusal.

44 οὐ θέμις: this phrase too probably implies a specifically divine sanction, as at 14.386 etc.: see Richardson on *HyDem* 207, where οὐ θεμιτόν is similarly used by Demeter in the context of her abstention from wine, and Parker, *Miasma* 68.

46 κείρασθαί τε κόμην recurs at *Od.* 4.198, and cf. *Od.* 24.46 κείραντό τε χαίτας. See on 127–53, where this is done for Patroklos.

47 Cf. ἄχος κραδίην καὶ θυμὸν ἱκάνει (4× *Il.*) etc., and 22.387–8 ὄφρ' ἂν ἔγωγε | ζωοῖσιν μετέω. The form μετείω for μετέω is due to metrical lengthening.

48 This resembles 8.502–3 = 9.65–6 (cf. *Od.* 12.291–2): ἀλλ' ἤτοι νῦν μὲν πειθώμεθα νυκτὶ μελαίνῃ | δόρπα τ' ἐφοπλισόμεσθα. Akhilleus implies that the whole idea of eating is still abhorrent and simply a matter of necessity: hence πειθώμεθα. Cf. *Od.* 7.216–21, where Odysseus describes his stomach as στυγερή, and explains how it compels him to eat despite his sorrow, and *Od.* 17.286–9, 18.53–4. The variant τερπώμεθα, mentioned by AT and found in one papyrus, is out of place, and presumably due to the idea that πειθώμεθα δαιτί is an odd expression.

49 ὄτρυνε was Bentley's reading for the MSS' ὄτρυνον (aorist imperative), to preserve the digamma of ἄναξ. This is an unnecessary change, and Allen reads ὄτρυνον in his edition of 1931.

50 ὄσσ᾽ ἐπιεικές: nearly all MSS read ὡς, as in 19.147 παρασχέμεν ὡς ἐπιεικές (etc.). This would require the omission of 51, which could in theory be an added verse. But it seems best to read ὄσσα and keep 51.

51 νέεσθαι ὑπὸ ζόφον ἠερόεντα: cf. 21.48, where νέεσθαι is used of going down to Hades.

52–3 ὄφρ᾽ ἤτοι ... ὀφθαλμῶν: a rather compressed way of saying 'so that the fire may burn him and he may be taken from our sight more quickly'.

54–8 For 55–6 cf. *Od.* 14.347 ἐσσυμένως παρὰ θῖνα θαλάσσης δόρπον ἕλοντο. Here the adverb picks up Akhilleus' note of urgency, and the poet describes the meal in a summary form (cf. bT). Verses 56–7 = 1.468–9 etc. For 58 cf. 1.606 (and 3× *Od.*) οἱ μὲν κακκείοντες ἔβαν οἶκόνδε ἕκαστος.

59–61 As elsewhere (1.348–50, 24.3–13) Akhilleus seeks relief from his sorrow on the edge of the sea: 'that Akhilleus lies down by the shore in the open is a manifestation of grief' (Eust. 1287.33); 'the overtones of θῖνα ... θαλάσσης and so on are often of tension or sadness' (Kirk on 1.34: see also on 1.350). Here, however, he is still surrounded by his companions, whereas in books 1 and 24 he seeks solitude, as Odysseus does too on Kalupso's island (*Od.* 5.81–4, 5.151–8).

61 ἐν καθαρῷ ὅθι: cf. 8.491 = 10.199. ἐν καθαρῷ means 'in a clear space'. The sound patterns of this verse, especially the insistent triple alliteration of *kappa* and the slow, spondaic ending, focus attention on this scene of Akhilleus lying in his misery on the seashore beside the resounding breakers.

62–108 Akhilleus sleeps, and Patroklos' ghost visits him in a dream and delivers instructions for his funeral. Akhilleus tries vainly to embrace him, but his spirit slips away and leaves him. He awakes and tells his companions of the vision

62 = *Od.* 20.56. Cf. *Od.* 23.342–3 ὅτε οἱ γλυκὺς ὕπνος | λυσιμελὴς ἐπόρουσε, λύων μελεδήματα θυμοῦ. For ὕπνος ἔμαρπτε cf. 24.679. μελέδημα only occurs here in *Il.*, 4× *Od.*

63 For νήδυμος ἀμφιχυθείς cf. 14.253. In neither case is it possible to treat νήδυμος as a false reading of -ν ἥδυμος, since it opens the verse, although that may be how the word came into being originally: see on 2.2.

64 Ἕκτορ᾽ ἐπαΐσσων: it seems best to take Ἕκτορ᾽ as accusative rather than dative here, 'harrying Hektor as far as Ilios': cf. 7.240, 12.308 μόθον/ τεῖχος ἐπαῖξαι.

65 ἦλθε δ᾽ ἐπὶ ψυχή: evidently a formula in such contexts, as at *Od.* 11.84, 11.90, 11.387, 11.467, of the successive appearances of new ghosts to Odysseus. Here and at *Od.* 11.387 the δέ is apodotic. This is the only occasion in the *Iliad* where a vision of a ghost is described, and the only other dream described at length occurs at 2.5–41 (see Introduction, 'Structure'). For Πατροκλῆος δειλοῖο cf. 17.670, 23.105, 23.221. δειλοῖο is used in the *Iliad* only in this phrase describing Patroklos (17.670–73n.). On dreams in Homer see also West on *Od.* 4.795ff., and E. Lévy, 'Le rêve homérique', *Ktèma* 7 (1982) 23–41.

66–7 'The detailed description of the appearance of the dream-vision is very effective: for Akhilleus still has his friend's voice ringing in his ears' (T). Verse 66 resembles the formular εἶδός τε μέγεθός τε φυήν τ' ἄγχιστα ἐῴκει (etc.) (2.58 etc.), and *Od.* 1.208 αἰνῶς μὲν κεφαλήν τε καὶ ὄμματα καλὰ ἔοικας. It is appropriate to single out Patroklos' 'lovely eyes' here. περὶ χροῒ εἵματα ἕστο occurs only here in *Il.*, 4× *Od.*

68 = 24.682 and 4× *Od.*; cf. 2.20, 2.59. The context is similar in all cases: an image of a god or a human appears to someone who is asleep or (*Od.* 20.32) unable to sleep. Cf. also 10.496–7, and see on 2.20–1. In later Greek literature a dream-figure is often said to 'stand over' (ἐπιστῆναι) the dreamer: cf. E. R. Dodds, *The Greeks and the Irrational* (Berkeley 1951) 105–6.

69–92 This is the longest speech by a dream-figure in Homer. Patroklos begins by rebuking Akhilleus for sleeping and forgetting him. This is typical of such scenes: cf. 2.23–4 εὕδεις ... | οὐ χρὴ παννύχιον εὕδειν ..., 24.683 ὢ γέρον, οὔ νύ τι σοί γε μέλει κακόν, οἷον ἔθ' εὕδεις ..., *Od.* 6.25 Ναυσικάα, τί νύ σ' ὧδε μεθήμονα γείνατο μήτηρ; also the reproach to a sleeper at 10.159, the opening εὕδεις at *Od.* 4.804, and Pindar, *O.* 13.67 εὕδεις, Αἰολίδα βασιλεῦ; A. *Eum.* 94 εὕδοιτ' ἄν, ὠή, καὶ καθευδουσῶν τί δεῖ; See also E. Lévy, *Ktèma* 7 (1982) 36–7.

He then instructs Akhilleus to bury him quickly, explaining why, and begs him to give him his hand for the last time, recalling their companionship in life. Reference to his own death leads him to foretell Akhilleus' impending doom, and this in turn to a further instruction that their bones should be buried together in a single coffin: once again this leads back to recollection of their closeness in life, as they grew up together in Peleus' house, when Patroklos was received there in exile for homicide. Verses 83–91 form a ring, 83–4 being answered by 89–91. Verse 92 is probably a later addition (see comment).

The structure of the speech deserves attention. It begins with a series of solemn, end-stopped sentences (69–74), containing the main message the ghost has to convey. Then the emotional level rises, as he refers to their companionship, and it is significant that we begin to get more complex sentences with some enjambment (75–81). The second instruction is expressed in three verses (82–4), followed by the more leisurely narrative development of 85–90, with the closing verse 91. It is typical of Homeric psychology that Patroklos' ghost gives an extra impulsion to what is already Akhilleus' own wish (cf. 52–3 and 71), as often with supernatural motivation.

69 λελασμένος ἔπλευ: cf. 13.269 λελασμένον ἔμμεναι.

70 ἀκήδεις: imperfect of ἀκηδέω; cf. 14.427 ἀκήδεσεν.

71–4 Patroklos states for the first time in Homer the common ancient view that it was cremation or burial which enabled the soul to enter Hades properly; hence the corollary that thereafter it would not revisit the world above (75–6). Arn/A on 73 notes that the (athetized) second Nekuia (*Od.* 24.1–204) contradicts this, as there the souls of the unburied suitors meet the other ghosts in Hades.

71 πύλας Ἀΐδαο περήσω: cf. 5.646 πύλας Ἀΐδαο περήσειν |. περήσω is probably subjunctive here ('let me pass' or 'that I may pass'): see on 22.418.

72 τῆλέ με εἴργουσι: elsewhere we find (F)έργω, ἐέργω, and here the reading perhaps represents an original μ' ἐέργουσι or με ἔργουσι (Chantraine, *GH* I 181). For ψυχαὶ εἴδωλα καμόντων cf. *Od.* 24.14, εἴδωλα καμόντων | *Od.* 11.476. καμόντας alone meaning 'the dead' occurs at 3.278.

73 ὑπὲρ ποταμοῖο: presumably this means the Styx (cf. 8.369). The oblique reference suggests that everyone would know what is meant.

74 ἀν' εὐρυπυλὲς Ἄϊδος δῶ: cf. *Od.* 11.571 κατ' εὐρυπυλὲς Ἄϊδος δῶ. The epithet occurs nowhere else, and like many descriptions of Hades suggests the multitude of the dead (see on *HyDem* 9, 379). There is an apparent contradiction between this statement and 71, but the topography of the Underworld is always vague.

75 καί μοι δὸς τὴν χεῖρ': this gesture is here presumably intended as an expression of both affection and farewell, as often in Greek art (cf. Neumann, *Gesten und Gebärden* 49–58), rather than simply as a confirmation of Akhilleus' pledge to bury Patroklos, as Mazon suggests (*REA* 42 (1940) 257). Cf. Odysseus' parting from Penelope before he went to Troy (*Od.* 18.257–8), where he clasps her right hand when giving her instructions about what to do after he has gone. Patroklos' own ignorance of how useless his request is adds to the pathos of the scene.

ὀλοφύρομαι: 'I beg you'. Leaf compares 2.290 ὀδύρονται οἴκόνδε νέεσθαι, but there the infinitive expression gives the content of ὀδύρονται.

76 Although elsewhere νίσομαι has a present sense, it seems to be used as a future here. It is related to νέομαι, νόστος. For ἐπήν με πυρὸς λελάχητε cf. 7.79–80, 22.342–3 ὄφρα πυρός με | ... λελάχωσι θανόντα, and see on 15.350.

77–91 These verses are quoted by Aeschines, *Contra Timarchum* 149, with a text which varies considerably from our vulgate, especially from 81 onwards.

77 οὐ μὲν γάρ: Aeschines and some of the city texts (Did/A) read οὐ γὰρ ἔτι.

78–9 ἀλλ' ἐμὲ μὲν κὴρ | ἀμφέχανε στυγερή: 'a hateful doom has gaped around me', a vivid expression. ἀμφιχάσκω occurs only here in early epic, and then in Attic tragedy and later poetry.

ἥ περ λάχε γεινόμενόν περ: one's day of death or doom is fixed at birth. Cf. 20.127–8 ἄσσα οἱ Αἶσα | γιγνομένῳ ἐπένησε λίνῳ, ὅτε μιν τέκε μήτηρ, 24.209–10, etc.

80–1 In the context of Akhilleus' death the formula θεοῖς ἐπιείκελ' Ἀχιλλεῦ is pathetic.

81 εὐηφενέων was the reading of Rhianus and Aristophanes (Did/A) for the vulgate εὐηγενέων. εὐηγενής occurs at 11.427, *HyAphr* 229, rarely in later poetry, and as a proper name at Eretria in the fifth century B.C. Εὐηφενής or Εὐαφενής occur as proper names several times (O. Masson, *Rev. Phil.* 39 (1965) 236–7; see also 239–40), and εὐηφενέοντα in epic verse at *P. Oxy.* 1794.13. But εὐηγενής is an abnormal formation for εὐγενής or ἠϋγενής, whereas εὐηφενής (cf. εὐ- + ἄφενος) is normal. Consequently modern scholars favour the latter, although it is not easy to see why this should have been replaced by an abnormal form, or why this should have proved so dominant in the tradition, whereas εὐηφενέων looks as if it might be a conjecture by Rhianus and Aristophanes. It is also not easy to see why the Trojans should be categorized as 'wealthy' here, in what is clearly not a formular expression, whereas 'noble' is the kind of general term one might expect. It seems better therefore to accept that the anomalous εὐηγενής may have already existed in the epic tradition at the time of the *Iliad*.

After this the Aeschines quotation adds an extra verse μαρνάμενον δηΐοις Ἑλένης ἕνεκ' ἠϋκόμοιο, which is composed of formular elements: cf. | μάρνασθαι δηΐοις(1) 4× *Il.*; Ἑλένης ἕνεκ' ἠϋκόμοιο 9.339, Ἑλένης πόσις ἠϋκόμοιο 6× *Il.*

82 This verse occurs only here instead of the formular ἄλλο δέ τοι ἐρέω, σὺ δ' ἐνὶ φρεσὶ βάλλεο σῇσιν (4× *Il.*, 7× *Od.*), which Aeschines' text reads. Cf. 21.293 αὐτάρ τοι πυκινῶς ὑποθησόμεθ', αἴ κε πιθήαι, and similarly *Od.* 1.279. This phrasing is obviously better suited to the pleading tone of Patroklos' ghost.

83 τιθήμεναι: this form of τιθέμεναι, lengthened *metri gratia*, recurs at 247; cf. 10.34 τιθήμενος.

83–4 After 83 Aeschines' text adds two verses:

ἀλλ' ἵνα πέρ σε καὶ αὐτὸν ὁμοίη γαῖα κεκεύθῃ (cf. 18.329)
χρυσέῳ ἐν ἀμφιφορεῖ τόν τοι πόρε πότνια μήτηρ
ὡς ὁμοῦ ἐτράφομέν περ ...

The second verse replaces 92, which this version omits.

84 ὡς τράφομέν περ: this (cf. Aeschines' ἐτράφομέν περ) was suggested by

Buttmann and La Roche, for the vulgate ὡς ἐτράφην περ (also in Lucian, *Paras.* 47), and the variant (in two papyri, several MSS, and mentioned by A) ἐτράφημεν. The short vowel before τρ (ἐτράφην) is rare in Homer, but it occurs where the word would not otherwise scan without distortion ('Αμφιτρύων, τετράκυκλον), which is the case here, and even where it could (φαρέτρης, ἀλλότριος, 'Οτρυντεύς): cf. Chantraine, *GH* ι 108. So it is not impossible, and there is more to be said for the singular ἐτράφην, since it is picked up by 85–90 (especially 89–90 ἔνθα με ... ἔτραφε ...); cf. van der Valk, *Researches* ιι 330–1.

85–90 Exile for homicide is a common motif in Homer: cf. 16.570–6, the story of another of Akhilleus' companions, Epeigeus, who was received by Peleus and Thetis after he had killed his cousin. Other examples are Tlepolemos (2.661–7), Medon (13.694–7), Lukophron (15.430–2 and 437–9), and in the *Odyssey* Odysseus in disguise (13.258–73), an Aetolian (14.379–81), and Theoklumenos (15.224ff., 272–6). Cf. the simile at 24.480–3, which suggests how common this may still have been in the poet's own times. For this motif see on 13.694–7, and Strasburger, *Kleinen Kämpfer* 29–31.

Peleus seems to be particularly associated with this theme of giving a new home to exiles: besides Patroklos and Epeigeus there was also Phoinix, who left home after a quarrel with his father over a concubine, and who in one version of the text had considered killing his father (9.447–84).

Another way of avoiding a blood-feud was by payment of a fine to the dead man's kinsmen (9.632–6, 18.497–508). In general see R. J. Bonner and G. Smith, *The Administration of Justice from Homer to Aristotle* ι (Chicago 1930) 15–21.

In the case of Patroklos, because he was only a boy his father took him to Peleus. Later, when Patroklos was about to join Agamemon's expedition, Menoitios is again said to have been present in Phthie (11.765–90), and Akhilleus speaks of having promised Menoitios that he would bring his son back safe to Opoeis (18.324–7).

87 παῖδα ... 'Αμφιδάμαντος: the name also occurs at 10.268–9, where it belongs to a man from Kuthera, and as that of the historical king at whose funeral games Hesiod won a prize, at Hes. *Erga* 654–6. But there seems no reason to suppose (as West does *ad loc.*) that Homer's choice of the name is influenced by Hesiod here.

88 νήπιος, οὐκ ἐθέλων: νήπιος suggests both folly and also childish irresponsibility here. οὐκ ἐθέλων makes it clear that the act was involuntary or accidental, an interesting point in view of the later historical importance attached to the distinction between different forms of homicide.

ἀμφ' ἀστραγάλοισι χολωθείς: the word ἀστράγαλος occurs as the name of a vertebra at 14.466, *Od.* 10.560, 11.65, but only here in Homer for the game of knuckle-bones, which were used as a form of dice in antiquity. Cf. Hdt. 1.94.3, where this is claimed by the Lydians as their invention, and Laser, *Arch. Hom.* τ 117–22. According to Did/AT the majority of early scholarly editions (αἱ πλείους τῶν κατ' ἄνδρα) here read ἀμφ' ἀστραγάλῃσιν ἐρίσσας, using an Ionic feminine form of the noun which was found in Anacreon (*PMG* fr. 53).

90 For ἔτραφε many MSS in fact read ἔτρεφε, and elsewhere ἔτραφον is intransitive (2.661 etc.), so we should probably prefer ἔτρεφε here. ἐνδυκέως recurs only 3× *Il.*, all in book 24, but 16× *Od.* 'With good will' would perhaps give the general sense. It is used particularly in contexts of caring for or feeding someone, and often the translation 'steadfastly' seems suitable, but the basic sense is not certain. Cf. Chantraine, *Dict.* s.v., Leumann, *HW* 311–12.

91 σορός: only here in early epic. Later it means a coffin, but it may have originally meant simply any container (Chantraine, *Dict. s.v.*). Patroklos' bones are actually put in a φιάλη after the cremation, and this is placed in Akhilleus' hut to wait until he too has died (243–4, 252–4). Hektor's bones are put in a λάρναξ (24.795), and the scholia assume that this is what is meant here, but it could be an urn. In actual practice, whereas inhumation burials in the late Bronze and early Iron Ages are sometimes laid in coffins, for cremation burials, especially in the early Iron Age and Geometric period, clay or metal urns are much more common: cf. Kurtz and Boardman, *Burial Customs* 21–67; Andronikos, *Arch. Hom.* w 71–6, 102–4; and especially the very fine bronze vessel containing the bones of the warrior of Lefkandi (M. Popham, E. Touloupa and L. H. Sackett, *Antiquity* 56 (1982) 169–74).

92 Cf. *Od.* 24.73–4 δῶκε δὲ μήτηρ | χρύσεον ἀμφιφορῆα, for Akhilleus' burial. It is there said to be a gift of Dionusos and the work of Hephaistos. Aristarchus saw that verse 92 had been added in order to make the passage agree with the account in *Odyssey* 24, and he athetized it (Arn/A, T). The verse is omitted by the Ptolemaic papyrus (pap. 12), and 'was not in all the MSS' used by Aristarchus. 'This is the only place where an ancient athetesis corresponds to an omission in a pre-Aristarchean papyrus' (West, *Ptolemaic Papyri* 171). Aeschines' text omits the verse, although the vessel is mentioned in the verses added after line 83. Cf. also R. Janko, vol. iv, p. 28.

Stesichorus later embroidered the story of this vessel, making it a reward to Thetis from Dionusos for her reception of him after his pursuit by Lukourgos (*PMG* fr. 57 *ap.* schol. ABD *Il.* 23.92; cf. 6.135–7). It may, then, be the vessel which Dionusos carries on the François Vase, as Rumpf suggested (*Gnomon* 25 (1953) 470). It is possible that the description of the amphora in *Odyssey* 24 was originally suggested by the mention at *Il.* 23.243 and 253 of the φιάλη in which Patroklos' bones are to be kept until Akhilleus' death. See also M. W. Haslam, *TAPA* 121 (1991) 35–45.

93 After this verse pap. 12 adds ἡδὺ μάλα κνώσσων ἐ]ν ὀνειρείῃσι πύλῃσιν, which is borrowed from *Od.* 4.809, where 810 resembles *Il.* 23.94.

94 Cf. *Od.* 4.810 τίπτε, κασιγνήτη, δεῦρ' ἤλυθες; and *Od.* 5.87 τίπτε μοι, Ἑρμεία χρυσόρραπι, εἰλήλουθας; For ἠθείη κεφάλη see on 22.229. According-ing to Arn/A it is an address used by a younger towards an older man, and Patroklos was in fact older than Akhilleus (11.787). Chamaeleon (fr. 19 Wehrli) read ὦ θείη κεφάλη here, which would be 'ridiculous when ad-dressed to a ghost' (Did, Arn/A). After 94 pap. 12 may have had another extra verse, and possibly two more again after 96: see West, *Ptolemaic Papyri* 172.

97–101 In the same way in *Od.* 11.204–22 Odysseus tries to embrace his mother's ghost, but she slips through his hands, and when he asks her why she explains that the soul is like a dream-image. Verses 97–8 resemble *Od.* 11.211–12 ὄφρα καὶ εἰν Ἀΐδαο φίλας περὶ χεῖρε βαλόντε | ἀμφοτέρω κρυεροῖο τεταρπώμεσθα γόοιο. Here ἀμφιβαλόντε probably governs ἀλλήλους, as τεταρπώμεσθα is usually intransitive (see on 23.10). The variant κρυεροῖο (A) in 98 may be derived from *Od.* 11.212. In 97, as often, μίνυνθα is pathetic; and 98 is a powerfully constructed four-word verse, with balance and assonance at the end of each hemistich.

99 ὠρέξατο χερσὶ φίλῃσιν: cf. *HyDem* 15 ὠρέξατο χερσὶν ἄμ' ἄμφω.

100–1 ψυχή ... τετριγυῖα: cf. *Od.* 24.5–9, where the souls of the suitors are like squeaking bats (24.9 τετριγυῖαι), and the fledgeling birds eaten by the snake at *Il.* 2.314, ἐλεεινὰ ... τετριγῶτας. The comparison to smoke is wonderfully effective. At *Od.* 11.207–8 the soul flies away σκίῃ εἴκελον ἢ καὶ ὀνείρῳ; cf. also *Il.* 18.110, where χόλος rises in men's breast ἠύτε καπνός.

101 ταφὼν δ' ἀνόρουσεν Ἀχιλλεύς recurs at 9.193, 11.777.

102 συμπλατάγησεν: a vivid onomatopoeic word, which occurs only here in early Greek literature, and rarely later, although πλαταγεῖν is commoner in Hellenistic and later poetry. Most of our MSS read συμπατ-άγησεν, presumably under the influence of the Homeric πάταγος.

ἔπος δ' ὀλοφυδνὸν ἔειπε: as at 5.683 (see comment), *Od.* 19.362. ὀλοφυδνός ('lamenting') is a Homeric gloss which recurs later in an epigram of Anyte (*AP* 7.486). According to Chantraine, *Dict.* s.v. ὀλοφύρομαι, it is a second-ary formation, like γοεδνός in relation to γοερός.

103–7 Akhilleus draws the natural conclusion from his dream that after all there *is* some kind of existence after death: the ψυχή and an image (εἴδωλον) of the person does survive. This suggests debate on this subject already in Homer's time; cf. the similar hesitancy of 24.592–3.

103–4 For τις some of our MSS read τι, i.e. 'the soul and image *are* something even in Hades' halls', or perhaps 'there *is* something . . . , a soul and image'. This may have been what Propertius read, as his *sunt aliquid manes* echoes it (4.7.1), and it seems preferable to τις, which goes rather awkwardly with ψυχή καὶ εἴδωλον. Cf. perhaps Pl. *Phaedo* 63c5 εὔελπίς εἰμι εἶναί τι τοῖς τετελευτηκόσι ('there is some existence for the dead').

The scholia (Did?, Arn/A) have a long discussion of 104, which is not easy to disentangle (cf. van der Valk, *Researches* I 540–2). The problem is that if one takes φρένες as meaning 'wits' it is odd to say of Patroklos' ghost, which has 'made a reasonable and intelligent speech', that it has no φρένες. They first suggest that 'the verse has been intruded (ἐνσέσεισται) from the *Odyssey*', i.e., presumably it reflects the view expressed at *Od.* 10.492–5, where Teiresias' ghost is said to differ from the others since his φρένες are ἔμπεδοι and he alone has intelligence. An alternative view is then offered (which seems to be that of Aristophanes), that φρένες has its physical sense here, referring to part of the body (i.e. the midriff), and so it means that the ψυχή has no physical existence. The scholia then quote what appears to be Aristarchus' opinion, that 'Homer assumes that the souls of the unburied dead still preserve their intelligence': i.e. after burial they have no sense, but Patroklos' unburied ghost still retains this faculty. Aristarchus probably quoted *Od.* 11.51–83, where Elpenor's unburied spirit converses with Odysseus without having drunk blood, whereas the other souls are unable to do this (cf. schol. *Od.* 11.51).

In addition, bT offer the explanation that Patroklos' ghost shows his lack of sense because he wrongly accuses Akhilleus of neglecting him (cf. also Leaf, *Iliad* II 621). bT have one other suggestion, that ἀτάρ . . . πάμπαν means that the ghosts have some intelligence, but it is not complete; i.e. οὐ πάμπαν means 'not altogether' rather than 'not at all'; and T quotes a variant πᾶσαι which would make this sense clearer.

As far as intelligence goes, 24.592–5 indicate that Akhilleus allows that even in Hades Patroklos may have some idea of what goes on in the world above, and may derive satisfaction from receiving a share in the ransom for Hektor's body. Perhaps the simplest answer is that of Aristophanes. Patroklos' ghost apparently displayed normal emotions, it could give Akhilleus instructions, and it looked just like him (105–7), but when Akhilleus tried to grasp it he realized that it had no *physical* substance.

105 παννυχίη: Akhilleus has the impression that his dream lasted 'all night'; dreams often do seem to last a considerable time, even when they are quite brief.

106 Cf. 6.373 πύργῳ ἐφεστήκει γοόωσά τε μυρομένη τε. For ἐφεστήκει see on 68.

107 θέσκελον: 'marvellously'; see on 3.130.

108 = *Od.* 4.183; cf. also *Il.* 23.153 τοῖσι δὲ πᾶσιν ὑφ᾽ ἵμερον ὧρσε γόοιο etc.

109–26 Dawn comes, and Agamemnon orders the Achaeans to fetch wood for the pyre of Patroklos. Meriones takes charge of this. They take mules to Mt Ida, cut down oak trees, and bring them back to the sea-shore, where they lay them ready for the pyre

After the intensely emotional scenes which have preceded we have an interlude of equally intense physical activity. The urgency and bustle is expressed in a passage where enjambment is noticeably frequent, and in 117–26 'periodic' or 'integral' enjambment occurs in seven out of ten verses. The extraordinary rhythm and sound-effects of 116 add to the impression of great numbers of men and animals moving ceaselessly in all directions over the hills.

109 Plutarch (*Mor.* 114E) quotes as Homeric μυρομένοισι δὲ τοῖσι μέλας ἐπὶ ἕσπερος ἦλθε. This is composed of the first hemistich of 109 and the second of *Od.* 1.423 = 18.306. It could well be due to faulty memory, or even deliberate adaptation, rather than being a genuine variant which would be quite out of place here. For μυρομένοισι δὲ τοῖσι cf. 19.340 | μυρομένους δ᾽ ἄρα τούς γε. – φάνη ῥοδοδάκτυλος ᾽Ηώς resembles the formular verse ἦμος δ᾽ ἠριγένεια φάνη ῥοδοδάκτυλος ᾽Ηώς (2× *Il.*, 20× *Od.*): see on 1.477. Macleod, *Iliad* XXIV 47–8, points out that in this poem the appearance of Dawn is several times linked with the theme of human sorrow or trouble: cf. 11.1–4 (Zeus sends Strife to the Greek ships); 19.1–6 (Thetis finds Akhilleus and the Myrmidons lamenting Patroklos' death); 23.226–8 (the flames of Patroklos' pyre die at dawn: see comment); 24.694–7 (Hermes leaves for Olumpos as Dawn comes and Priam brings Hektor's corpse into Troy with lamentation and groaning); 788–803 (the conclusion of Hektor's funeral at dawn). There is something similar at 7.421–9 (at sunrise the Greeks and Trojans prepare the dead for burial, with tears and grief), and 433–41 (just before dawn, in the early twilight, the Greeks gather round the pyre to build the mound and wall): the second of these suggests a particularly eerie and melancholy scene.

111 οὐρῆάς are 'mules'; cf. 1.50 | οὐρῆας. Many ancient copies omitted τε (Did/AT), which is an odd mistake. T compares the simile at 17.742–6, where Menelaos and Meriones carrying Patroklos' body out of the battle are like mules bringing down a tree-trunk from the mountain along a rocky path. It is interesting that in both these scenes Meriones is involved in the care for Patroklos' corpse: cf. also 16.632–7 (simile of woodcutters, after a reference to Meriones).

112 ἐπὶ δ᾽ ἀνὴρ ἐσθλὸς ὀρώρει: cf. *Od.* 3.471, 14.104 ἐπὶ δ᾽ ἀνέρες ἐσθλοὶ ὄροντο -ται. The poet must be using ἐπιορώρει here as a pluperfect of ἐπιόρομαι meaning 'watch over' (cf. ἐπίουρος 13.450). On these forms see Chantraine, *GH* I 311, 426.

113 In earlier books Meriones' whole-verse formula is Μηριόνης ἀτάλαντος Ἐννυαλίῳ ἀνδρειφόντῃ (4× *Il.*), which would presumably have too martial a flavour here. Having referred to him in this way here the poet repeats this alternative formula at 124 (see comment), and we have αὐτὰρ/ ἂν δ' ἄρα Μηριόνης θεράπων ἐΰς Ἰδομενῆος at 23.528, 23.860 and 888. There is no very obvious reason why the poet should select Meriones as commander here, except perhaps that he is a minor but efficient hero, and as a θεράπων he is suitable for a practical but not very heroic operation. It is worth noticing the thematic link with 17.742–6 (see on 111). For Meriones and his formulae see also on 13.246–8 and 249–50.

ἀγαπήνορος Ἰδομενῆος: the epithet is less common than one might expect. Cf. 15.392 ἀγαπήνορος Εὐρυπύλοιο |, 13.756, *Od.* 7.170 ἀγαπήνορα Πουλυδάμαντα/Λαοδάμαντα |, and the proper name Agapenor; see on 13.756.

114 ὑλοτόμους πελέκεας: ὑλοτόμος occurs only here and at 123 in Homer, in the second case as a noun; cf. Hes. *Erga* 807 etc. πελέκεας recurs in the same position in the verse at 851, 856 and 882, where ten axes are the first prize in the archery contest: by coincidence they are won by Meriones (882).

115 εὐπλέκτους: this epithet only recurs in Homer at 335 ἐϋπλέκτῳ ἐνὶ δίφρῳ, although we find ἐϋπλεκέες (2.449) and ἐϋπλεκέας (23.436).

116 'Many times uphill and downhill, alonghill and crossways they travelled.' ἄναντα and κάταντα occur only here in Homer, rarely later and usually together; πάραντα seems to occur nowhere else; cf. Homeric ἔσαντα, ἔναντα. δόχμιος occurs nowhere else in Homer, but cf. 12.148 δοχμώ. The verse is a particularly striking example of the poet's own skill in linguistic innovation. The use of a consistently dactylic rhythm and sequence of trochaic words is paralleled by for example *Od.* 11.598 αὖτις ἔπειτα πέδονδε κυλίνδετο λᾶας ἀναιδής (and see on 6.2, 21.406–11 and 23.263). The acoustic jingle adds to the effect, although in a rather obvious way. This verse has the highest number of *a*-sounds in the poem. See also Edwards, *HPI* 118.

117 For the phrase κνημούς ... πολυπίδακος Ἴδης see on 8.47–8, 21.449, 21.559, and for πολυπίδαξ cf. 14.157n. Timber-felling is still one of the main occupations of those who live around Mt Ida, and oak trees are abundant there (cf. 14.287–8n.).

118 δρῦς ὑψικόμους: cf. 14.398, *Od.* 9.186 δρυσὶν ὑψικόμοισιν |, δρυὸς ὑψικόμοιο 3× *Od.* ταναηκέϊ χαλκῷ is formular, 3× *Il.*, 1× *Od.* This verse is a rising threefolder.

119 ἐπειγόμενοι: pap. 12 reads ἀμειβόμενοι, but this has been corrected above the verse to ἐπειγόμενοι. At *Od.* 19.252 ἐπειγομένη is a false variant for ἀμειβομένη, and the papyrus variant has been preferred here by some scholars (cf. van der Valk, *Researches* II 562 n. 102). But there is no weight of authority in favour of it, and the MS reading is surely correct.

119–20 ταὶ δὲ ... πῖπτον: the spondaic runover word is effective, describing the slow fall of these great trees.

120 διαπλήσσοντες ('splitting'), Aristarchus' reading (Did/A) and that of nearly all our MSS, must surely be right. At *Od.* 8.507 he read διαπλῆξαι instead of διατμῆξαι. The compound recurs nowhere else.

121 ταὶ δὲ χθόνα ποσσὶ δατεῦντο: 'they divided the ground with their feet'. This appears to mean that their hooves cut furrows in the ground, in their eagerness to reach the plain. It is a unique phrase. At 20.394 δατέοντο is used of horses cutting up the body of a fallen man with the wheels of their chariots. There is a nice contrast with the smooth journey of Nausikaa's mules (*Od.* 6.318) αἱ δ' εὖ μὲν τρώχων, εὖ δὲ πλίσσοντο πόδεσσιν.

122 ἐλδόμεναι πεδίοιο: 'eager for the plain'; for ἔλδεσθαι with the genitive cf. *Od.* 5.210, 14.42. Pap. 12 seems to have read ἱέμεναι πεδίονδε (West, *Ptolemaic Papyri* 173).

διὰ ῥωπήϊα πυκνά: cf. 13.199, *Od.* 14.473 (with ἀνά and κατά respectively); also 21.559. The description suggests a picture of the mules eagerly forging a path through the thickets on the mountain.

123 ὑλοτόμοι: pap. 12 reads ὤμοισιν, which was preferred by Wilamowitz as more vivid (*IuH* 111 n. 1). ὑλοτόμοι could possibly be a gloss on πάντες, and one might object to the variation in use of the word from adjective to noun in 114 and 123. But these arguments do not seem strong enough to make one alter the traditional reading.

124 See on 113. Pap. 12 may have read ὀτρηρὸς θεράπων (cf. *Od.* 4.23, 217), and it is possible that the name has been inserted to clarify the text, as happens elsewhere (West, *Ptolemaic Papyri* 174). Either way, this verse repeats 113 in ring composition, rounding off the account of the expedition.

125–6 For ἐπισχερώ ('in a row', 'in order') cf. 11.668 etc. ἠρίον ('barrow', 'mound') only occurs here in Homer, instead of τύμβος, and in later prose and poetry from the sixth century onwards. It probably had an initial digamma. Cf. Chantraine, *Dict. s.v.*

127–53 Akhilleus tells the Myrmidons to arm and prepare their chariots. They do so and then escort the body of Patroklos in the funeral procession, after covering it with their hair. When they reach the pyre Akhilleus cuts off a lock of his own hair, and offers it to Patroklos

The first part of this passage describes the *ekphora* or funeral procession (cf. 24.786 ἐξέφερον θρασὺν Ἕκτορα). Here Patroklos' body is carried by his companions, probably on the bier (φέρτρον) mentioned at 18.236 (cf.

18.233 ἐν λεχέεσσι and 23.171 πρὸς λέχεα), with an escort consisting not only of the Myrmidons in their chariots but also of a vast number of soldiers on foot (133–4): so presumably the whole army joined this great procession. This scene inevitably invites comparison with the magnificent vases of the Geometric period which depict funerary scenes (cf. Andronikos, *Arch. Hom.* w 43–51): most of these are of the *prothesis* or lying-in-state, but a few do show the *ekphora*. Here the dead man is lying on a horse-drawn cart, with a procession led by men in armour and women following behind: cf. for example Kurtz and Boardman, *Burial Customs* pl. 5. This particular *krater* from the National Museum in Athens also shows a chariot procession in the register below the *ekphora* scene: cf. Andronikos, *op. cit.* 46, fig. 2. Similar chariot processions occur in association with some of the *prothesis* scenes. For an illustration of the bier being actually carried on the shoulders of a group of men we must look at the more simple scene on a later black-figure vase (Beazley, *ABV* 346 no. 7; cf. *Ath. Mitt.* 53 (1928) Beilage xv.2, Kurtz and Boardman pl. 35). There is a more detailed discussion of the Geometric examples, with ample illustration, by G. Ahlberg, *Prothesis and Ekphora in Greek Geometric Art* (Göteborg 1971). Whether or not they are directly related to or inspired by epic or Homeric accounts of funerals is an open question.

In the case of Patroklos the procession is associated with the offering of their hair by his companions, and it is followed by a separate scene in which Akhilleus offers a lock of his own hair, placing it in Patroklos' hands. In the account of Akhilleus' own funeral in *Odyssey* 24 the Greeks likewise cut off their hair (45–6), and this is mentioned as a regular mourning-ritual at *Od.* 4.197–8. In Aeschylus' *Choëphoroe* (6–7) Orestes offers a lock of hair at his father's grave, having first offered one to the river Inakhos in gratitude for his nurture. Aeschylus may have had this passage of the *Iliad* specifically in mind in associating these two offerings. In *Iliad* 23 the poet has (typically) taken a conventional ritual and given it new and deeper significance in the second scene of Akhilleus' offering: cf. vol. v, pp. 22–3.

Cutting one's hair in mourning was a common custom in ancient Greece at all times, as in many other societies. In the classical period it was most often, but not always, women who cut their hair, whereas men (whose hair was now usually shorter, in contrast to the fashion of the heroic age) would let their hair grow long in mourning. As Plutarch observed, mourning ritual involves the reversal of everyday customs (*Mor.* 267A–B). The actual offering of hair to the dead, or on a tomb, is less commonly attested in ancient Greece: it seems to occur particularly, if not exclusively, in mythical contexts and in the cults of heroes and heroines (Nilsson, *GgrR* 180). Offering one's hair to the local river, usually in thanksgiving for one's nurture, is again more commonly attested in mythology than by historical examples.

But like many other ancient customs it survived in Arcadia, where the boys of Phigaleia dedicated their hair to the river Neda (Pausanias 8.41.3). It is not clear whether the statue which Pausanias describes near the Kephisos in Attica of 'the son of Mnesimakhe cutting his hair for the Kephisos' (1.37.3) is of a mythical or historical figure: quite probably the latter, but it is significant that Pausanias calls this an 'ancient Greek custom' and invokes this passage of *Iliad* 23 to support this view. Hair-offerings to the nymphs, Artemis, Apollo, and other deities, on the other hand, are a regular practice in the historical period (Nilsson, *GgrR* 136–8).

On all of these rituals see Andronikos, *Arch. Hom.* w 18–20, and for hair-offerings W. H. D. Rouse, *Greek Votive Offerings* (Cambridge 1902) 240–5. For possible Minoan examples cf. E. N. Davis, *AJA* 90 (1986) 399–406, R. B. Koehl, *JHS* 106 (1986) 99–110, and C. Doumas in ΕΙΛΑΠΙΝΗ (Festschrift for N. Platon, Herakleion 1987) 151–9. E. Samter, *Familienfeste der Griechen und Römer* (Berlin 1901) 71–8 and *Geburt, Hochzeit und Tod* (Leipzig 1911) 179–83, and S. Eitrem, *Opferritus und Voropfer der Griechen und Römer* (Kristiania 1914) 344–72, are worth consulting for further details.

127 παρακάββαλον: this compound verb, the only Homeric instance of one with παρακατα-, occurs again at 683, and nowhere else in Homer. It presumably means that they put the wood down alongside the place for the pyre. The word is a good instance of a coinage which, once the poet has introduced it, recurs quite soon by a process of association. It is found later as a legal term, meaning 'deposit', 'make a deposition' in the Attic orators and inscriptions.

ἄσπετον ὕλην | recurs at 24.784 of the wood for Hektor's pyre, and 2.455 (see comment).

129–32 Pap. 12 diverges considerably here from our vulgate, but the text is very fragmentary. There was apparently at least one extra verse here. See West, *Ptolemaic Papyri* 147, 175–6.

129 For Μυρμιδόνεσσι φιλοπτολέμοισι in this position cf. 16.65.

130 χαλκὸν ζώννυσθαι: only here as an expression for arming, but cf. 11.15–16 ζώννυσθαι ἄνωγεν ... ἐν δ' αὐτὸς ἐδύσετο νώροπα χαλκόν. The verb recurs at *Od.* 24.89 in the context of Akhilleus' funeral and the games which accompany it.

131–2 ἐν τεύχεσσιν ἔδυνον, | ἂν δ' ἔβαν ἐν δίφροισι: cf. 10.254 ὅπλοισιν ἐνὶ δεινοῖσιν ἐδύτην, but *Od.* 22.201, 24.498 ἐς τεύχεα δύντε/ἔδυνον; *Il.* 23.352 ἂν δ' ἔβαν ἐς δίφρους (which is read here by schol. pap. XII (Erbse), but is metrically impossible). Cf. Chantraine, *GH* II 101–2 for other examples of ἐν with verbs of movement.

132 παραιβάται: this denotes the warrior riding alongside his charioteer. It occurs only here in Homer, later in Attic prose and poetry. At 11.104 Ἄντιφος αὖ παρέβασκε also refers to the fighting man in the chariot (there explicitly distinguished from the ἡνίοχος), whereas at 11.522 Ἕκτορι παρβεβαώς is used of the charioteer standing beside Hektor.

133 μετὰ δὲ νέφος εἵπετο πεζῶν: see on 4.274 ἅμα δὲ νέφος εἵπετο πεζῶν. There the metaphor is developed in the following simile, but here this would be out of place.

134 μύριοι: see on 29. There it referred to the Myrmidons, and it may do so again here. But at 156–62 it seems that the whole army must have joined the procession.

135–9 Leaf observes that we have a sequence of five dactylic lines here and at 166–70, but in both cases it looks as if this has occurred purely by chance.

135–7 As Mazon pointed out (*REA* 42 (1940) 257–8), we should envisage the Myrmidons as covering Patroklos' body with their hair as the procession advances. The series of imperfects indicates this, and the resulting scene is more impressive and solemn than if the cutting of hair had taken place all at once before the procession was under way. The two emphatic runover participles κειρόμενοι ... ἀχνύμενος express the leading themes of this scene.

135 καταείνυσαν: 'clothed', a vivid metaphor. The form (κατα)εινύω occurs only here in Homer (and later at Oppian, *H.* 2.673), although (κατα)ειμένος is closely related. Most of our MSS read καταείνυον, and καταείνυσαν is due to Aristarchus (Arn/AT): similar variants occur elsewhere (Chantraine, *GH* 1 473).

136 ὄπιθεν δὲ κάρη ἔχε δῖος Ἀχιλλεύς: Eustathius says that Akhilleus does this because the body is not being carried on a bier (1292.30), but it looks rather as if this is a customary expression of closeness to the dead man. At 24.710–12 Andromakhe and Hekabe touch Hektor's head as they express their grief, and at 724 Andromakhe holds his head in her hands while she sings her lament. Cf. 18.71, where Thetis holds Akhilleus' head as she comforts him, and Andronikos, *Arch. Hom* w 11–12.

In *prothesis* scenes on works of art the position at the head of the body is evidently one of some importance, and is usually occupied by a woman, on one occasion identified as the mother; cf. Zschietzsmann, *Ath. Mitt.* 53 (1928) 25–6, Boardman, *BSA* 50 (1955) 56–7. Occasionally the dead man's head is held in the hands of one of the mourners: a good example is on a vase by the Kleophrades painter (R. E. Arias and M. Hirmer, *A History of Greek Vase Painting*, London 1962, pl. 128). Cf. Arias and Hirmer pl. 129, Kurtz and Boardman, *Burial Customs* pl. 11, and other examples listed by Neumann, *Gesten und Gebärden* 89 n. 369. T says (oddly) that holding the head of the dead man was a Lindian custom.

After 136 pap. 12 has an extra verse, of which only the ending (δαΐζων) is preserved, but cf. 18.27 κεῖτο, φίλῃσι δὲ χερσὶ κόμην ᾔσχυνε δαΐζων.

137 ἕταρον γάρ ... Ἄϊδόσδε: the closing sentence of this passage is powerfully moving in its simplicity.

139 μενοεικέα: from its basic sense of 'satisfactory' this comes to mean here 'plentiful'.

140 ἔνθ' αὖτ' ἀλλ' ἐνόησε: only here and at 193 in *Il.*, but 5× *Od.* (with θεὰ γλαυκῶπις Ἀθήνη), and ἀλλ' ἐνόησε occurs 5× in other phrases in that poem.

141-53 For Akhilleus' offering of his hair see on 127-53.

142 Sperkheios is the main river of Akhilleus' homeland (see vol. 1, pp. 186, 228-9), and at 16.173-8 the river-god is also said to be the father of Menesthios by Peleus' daughter Poludore.

143-51 Akhilleus makes his speech facing westward towards his homeland. What he says almost amounts to a rebuke of the river-god for failing to answer Peleus' prayer.

144 ἄλλως: 'otherwise than has turned out to be the case', and so 'in vain', a sense which is common in Attic literature (cf. A); cf. *Od.* 14.124.

146-8 For sacrifices to a river or spring see on 21.131.

147 ἔνορχα: 'uncastrated', only here in Homer. This form of the epithet recurs in Hippocrates (*Vict.* 2.49); ἐνόρχης is the usual form. bT explain its use here as connected with the idea of water as a generative element.

148 ἐς πηγάς: Leaf takes πηγάς as meaning 'waters' here, because the sources of the river lie outside Phthie. But the springs seem the most suitable place for an altar and precinct. The sacrifice could have involved lowering the sheep into the water (cf. 21.132), or alternatively letting the blood flow into it: cf. for example Hor. *C.* 3.13.6-8.

ὅθι τοι τέμενος βωμός τε θυήεις: cf. 8.48 and on 8.47-8 *ad fin.*, *Od.* 8.363 ἔνθα δέ οἱ τέμενος βωμός τε θυήεις.

150 = 18.101. This use of νῦν δέ, to contrast reality with what might have been, is typical of Akhilleus: see on 18.88.

151 ὁπάσαιμι: 'I should like to give', an example of the optative expressing a wish.

152-3 Akhilleus places his lock of hair in the hands of Patroklos, a particularly touching gesture.

153-4 These verses resemble 108-9: lamentation is connected with the idea of dawn or sunset in each case.

154-91 Akhilleus tells Agamemnon to send the rest of the army away to eat, while the close associates of Patroklos prepare the pyre. The preparations are described: they include the slaughtering of sheep and cattle, the offering of honey and oil, and the sacrifice of four horses, two dogs, and twelve Trojan captives. Akhilleus lights the pyre, and bids Patroklos farewell, saying that he will give Hektor's body to be eaten by dogs. But the body of Hektor is preserved by Aphrodite and Apollo

154–5 Verse 154 = *Od.* 16.220, 21.226. This verse occurs only here in the *Iliad*, but for the sense of 154–5 cf. 24.713–15.

155–60 Pap. 12 differs considerably here from the standard text: for details see West, *Ptolemaic Papyri* 148, 176–9.

155 Ἀγαμέμνονι εἶπε παραστάς: Aristarchus (Arn/A) seems to have read Ἀγαμέμνονα, and pap. 12 appears to read Ἀγαμέμ]νονα ὡς προσέε[ιπεν.

156–60 Cf. the advice of Odysseus to Akhilleus that the Greeks should eat before fighting at 19.155–72, especially 171–2 ἀλλ᾽ ἄγε λαὸν μὲν σκέδασον καὶ δεῖπνον ἄνωχθι | ὅπλεσθαι, echoed here at 158–9.

157–8 γοοῖο μὲν ἔστι καὶ ἆσαι, | νῦν δ᾽ . . .: the construction with μέν and δέ suggests the meaning 'one can certainly (καί) have one's fill of mourning, if one likes: but for the moment . . .'

160 κήδεος: apparently an adjective meaning 'to be cared for', or in this context 'to be mourned'; cf. κῆδος, κήδιστος, κηδέμων. This form occurs nowhere else, but κήδειος is used at 19.294 (see comment). There seems to have been an alternative ancient view that the word was the genitive of κῆδος, meaning 'an object of care': cf. schol. A160a¹, and Erbse on 160d.

οἵ τ᾽ ἀγοί is the reading of most of our manuscripts and of Dionysius Thrax, but some read οἱ ταγοί with Aristarchus (Hrd/A). ταγός ('leader') occurs nowhere else in Homer, but it is used by the tragedians (always ταγός, except A. *Eu.* 296 ταγοῦχος), and survived in several dialects. C. M. Bowra (*JHS* 54 (1934) 56–7) and Ruijgh (τε *épique* §348) both argued that ταγοί is the correct reading here. The short *alpha* is morphologically correct, and it is understandable that the rare word should have been changed to the commoner epic one ἀγός, so they may well be right.

162 Pap. 12 adds the unnecessary verse κάπνισσάν τε κατὰ κλισίας καὶ δεῖπνον ἕλοντο (= 2.399), a typical 'concordance interpolation', as also after 165.

163 κηδέμονες: 'kinsmen', and more specifically here those who have the κῆδος of attending to the funeral. It occurs only here and at 674 in Homer. In later Greek it refers to anyone who takes care of someone or something, hence a protector or guardian.

164 ἑκατόμπεδον: only here in early epic; cf. Pindar (1. 6.22), etc. The pyre measured a hundred foot square, a vast size, equivalent to a πέλεθρον (cf. 21.407 with comment). But the building at Lefkandi in Euboea, of the tenth century B.C., which the excavators believe to be a *heroon* for the warrior buried at its centre, measures 45 by 10 metres, and the mound which covered it was even larger: cf. M. Popham, E. Touloupa and L. H. Sackett, *Antiquity* 56 (1982) 169–74; see also on 245–8.

165 Pap. 12 adds another extra verse after this one: μύρ[ι᾽ ὀνείατα χερσὶν ἀμησά[μενοι κατέθηκαν (with supplement by Blass).

166–76 The various objects added to the pyre are to some extent paralleled in the description of Akhilleus' own funeral at *Od.* 24.65–8. For the slaughter of many sheep and oxen (166–7) cf. *Od.* 24.65–6 πολλὰ δέ σ' ἀμφὶ | μῆλα κατεκτάνομεν μάλα πίονα καὶ ἕλικας βοῦς. For the amphorae of honey and oil (170–1) cf. *ibid.* 67–8 καῖεο δ' ἔν τ' ἐσθῆτι θεῶν καὶ ἀλείφατι πολλῷ | καὶ μέλιτι γλυκερῷ.

When Odysseus summons up the ghosts he slaughters sheep so that they may drink the blood, and he also vows to sacrifice an ox and a sheep to Teiresias on his return home (*Od.* 11.29–37). In the funeral scenes it is not made clear whether the animals are intended as offerings for the dead man, or in order to help the body to burn, or both. The fact that Patroklos' corpse is covered in the fat suggests that the second motive is relevant here, although this does not rule out the first (cf. AbT 168, bT 169). Sheep and oxen are quite often found in Greek burials of the Bronze and early Iron Ages (Andronikos, *Arch. Hom.* w 87–91).

Likewise the honey and oil could be partly intended to help the fire (cf. T 170–1), but these liquids are also used as offerings to the dead (cf. Burkert, *Religion* 71–2, Stengel, *Opferbräuche* 183–6). In addition Akhilleus pours out wine continually as he calls on the soul of Patroklos, while the pyre burns (218–21). Similarly Odysseus pours a drink-offering to the ghosts, consisting of honey and milk (μελίκρητον), wine and water (*Od.* 11.26–8). Such χοαί were sometimes called μειλικτήρια or μειλίγματα, i.e. propitiatory offerings. Again, they were often made at funerals in the Bronze and early Iron Ages, although the evidence is less easy to assess (Andronikos, *Arch. Hom.* w 91–7).

Akhilleus also sets on the pyre four horses and two dogs, and he adds the bodies of twelve Trojan captives, whom he first kills (171–6). The other funeral scenes in Homer offer no parallel for any of these. The horses and dogs are prize possessions and close companions of the Homeric hero, and they may be intended to accompany Patroklos' soul to Hades (for this idea cf. for example Lucian, *De luctu* 14). The captives have already been mentioned several times: after Patroklos' death Akhilleus vowed to kill twelve Trojans because of his anger (18.336–7; cf. 23.22–3), and when he took them prisoner it was so that they should be a ποινή for Patroklos' death, i.e. as a blood-payment (21.26–8). This makes it quite clear that his primary motive here is one of premeditated revenge.

The killing of horses and dogs, and probably also sometimes humans, did take place in the Bronze and early Iron Ages in Greece. The evidence for horses is now quite extensive, ranging from the early second millennium to the seventh century B.C. (cf. Andronikos, *Arch. Hom.* w 85–7). The most spectacular horse burials are those in the grandiose tombs of Salamis in Cyprus, of the eighth and seventh centuries, many of which contain one or more pairs of horses (or sometimes asses), usually together with a chariot or cart (cf. V. Karageorghis, *Excavations in the Necropolis of Salamis*, Nicosia 1967, I, and *Salamis in Cyprus*, London 1969, 23–150). The burials in the great tenth-century tumulus at Lefkandi also include four horses (*Antiquity* 56 (1982) 171), and another burial in this cemetery contains two horses (*Archaeological Reports for 1986–7*, p. 13). An interesting survival of this practice in the sixth century B.C. is mentioned by Herodotus (6.103): Cimon son of Stesagoras was buried together with the horses with which he had won three Olympic victories.

Dogs are occasionally found in burials of these periods, along with other animals (Andronikos, *Arch. Hom.* w 87–91). For an example of horses and dogs buried together in a cemetery, although separate from human tombs, at Prinias in Crete, cf. G. Rizza, in *Acts of the International Archaeological Symposium, 'The Relations between Cyprus and Crete'* (Nicosia 1978) 294–7.

The evidence for the actual killing of humans is more debatable, but many archaeologists believe that some cases cannot be explained away (cf. Andronikos, *Arch. Hom.* w 82–4). Again one can now add to Andronikos' discussion the possible case of the woman whose body was found in the Lefkandi tumulus, near to the urn containing the ashes of a warrior. Such double burials are found elsewhere in Cyprus, Crete and mainland Greece in this period (cf. also H. Catling, 'Heroes returned', in *Festschrift for Emily Vermeule*, forthcoming). It is significant that this warrior burial at Lefkandi shows a number of Homeric features together: cremation and the remains of a pyre, the horses, and the fact that as well as the warrior's bones the urn contained a decorated linen cloth (*Antiquity* 56 (1982) 172–3). Likewise at Salamis the dead are cremated, the bones are sometimes wrapped in a cloth and placed in a cauldron, and large amphorae are found which were thought to have held oil or honey: one of them had an inscription identifying its contents as olive oil (Karageorghis, *Salamis in Cyprus* 26–7, 71). In the *dromos* of another tomb were found human skeletons, which the excavators believed were probably killed at the time of the funeral (*ibid.* 30–1). Some scholars have thought that such Homeric features at Salamis and elsewhere in the eighth and seventh centuries could be explained as due to the influence of epic poetry (e.g. Coldstream, *Geometric Greece* 349–52). However, because of its earlier date the evidence of Lefkandi throws doubt on this theory. It seems more likely that the poet of the *Iliad* was aware that such practices existed in life, whether in the heroic past or (more probably) in recent times. See also D. D. Hughes, *Human Sacrifice in Ancient Greece*, London 1991.

Human sacrifice was a remarkably common theme of Greek mythology at all times (cf. A. Henrichs, *Entretiens Hardt* xxvII (Vandœuvres-Genève 1981) 195–235). But the most striking aspect of the funeral of Patroklos is that all these elements, the slaughter of horses, dogs and human captives, are unique in the Homeric poems. The poet, it seems, is trying to portray a funeral of a special kind, and the excesses of destruction in which Akhilleus indulges are above all a demonstration of his intense grief at Patroklos' loss.

166 = 9.466. See on 23.30–4.

167–9 Verse 167 resembles 24.622 σφάξ᾽· ἕταροι δ᾽ ἔδερόν τε καὶ ἄμφεπον, in the description of the preparations for a meal. Here the covering of Patroklos' corpse with fat also resembles the way in which the bones are wrapped in fat in a sacrifice to the gods. After the cremation this is what will happen to Patroklos' bones (243–4, 252–3). μεγάθυμος Ἀχιλλεύς in 168 is unusual for πόδας ὠκὺς Ἀ., to avoid repetition with ἐς πόδας (16.297–300n.).

169 For | ἐς πόδας ἐκ κεφαλῆς cf. 18.353, and 16.640n. δρατός for δαρτός (cf. Choerilus 4.5, etc.), meaning 'skinned', occurs only here. There was an ancient variant δρετά (Did, Arn/A).

170–1 Leaf observes that πρὸς λέχεα κλίνων suggests the type of pointed amphora which could be propped against something or stuck in the ground, and that the practice survived in the Attic funeral λήκυθοι which were placed round the bier of the dead. Pointed amphorae, however, belong to a later period than the eighth century B.C. (cf. Kurtz and Boardman, *Burial Customs* 102–5).

171 πίσυρας δ᾽ ἐριαύχενας ἵππους: the horse burials of the late Bronze and early Iron Ages are often pairs, or multiples of pairs, suitable for a chariot or cart. For actual four-horse chariots see 11.699 and perhaps 8.185.

173 τῷ γε ἄνακτι could in theory refer to either Patroklos or Akhilleus. Eustathius (1294.18) thought Akhilleus was the owner, as he is the subject throughout this passage, but it seems more appropriate that they should have belonged to Patroklos. For τραπεζῆες κύνες see on 22.69.

176 For χαλκῷ δηϊόων cf. 17.566, and for κακὰ δὲ φρεσὶ μήδετο ἔργα 21.19. There too it refers to great slaughter, although it is odd that here the phrase follows rather than precedes the act of destruction. Clearly attention is being drawn to the exceptional savagery of this action, even if we cannot necessarily take this as implying direct moral condemnation by the poet: cf. 7.478 where Zeus himself κακὰ μήδετο, and see on 22.395.

177 ἐν δὲ πυρὸς μένος ἧκε σιδήρεον: the epithet σιδήρεος suggests destructiveness and relentless force (cf. the metaphorical uses of this and σιδήρειος at 17.424, 22.357, 24.205, 24.521). Notice the juxtaposition of comparisons at 20.372 εἰ πυρὶ χεῖρας ἔοικε, μένος δ᾽ αἴθωνι σιδήρῳ. Eustathius (1294.29) observes that there is an exchange of images (ἀνταπόδοσις) at 177, since the metaphor of fire is often applied to fighting.

ὄφρα νέμοιτο: 'so that it might spread', but with the associated idea of feeding as in 182. See on 2.780 ὡς εἴ τε πυρὶ χθὼν πᾶσα νέμοιτο, and cf. Hdt. 5.101 τὸ πῦρ ἐπενέμετο τὸ ἄστυ πᾶν.

179–83 See on 19–23, which Akhilleus echoes here (179 = 19). At 180 most MSS read τελέω τὰ πάροιθεν as at 20, but pap. 12 and a minority of medieval texts have τετελεσμένα ὥσπερ, and this is mentioned as a variant by A. Some modern scholars prefer this reading (cf. Wilamowitz, *IuH* 73 n. 1, Leaf *ad loc.*). But part of Akhilleus' purpose is still unfulfilled (cf. 182–3 with 21), and there is no reason why one should not keep τελέω and treat it as either a future tense, or more probably a present. Cf. Mazon, *REA* 13 (1940) 258–9.

182–3 Pap. 12 reads:

τοὺς ἅμα σοι πάντας πῦρ ἀμφέπει, Ἕκτορα δ' οὐχί·
τόνδε γὰρ οὐ δώσω πυρὶ καέμεν, ἀλλὰ κύνεσσιν
ὠμησταῖς φαγέειν· τοσὰ γὰρ κάκ' ἐμήσατ' Ἀχαιούς.

This removes the powerful metaphor of πῦρ ἐσθίει, and 183 was probably also altered to remove the effective zeugma in the use of δαπτέμεν. The extra verse has a typically weak ending (cf. 22.392a).

Neither ἐσθίειν nor δάπτειν is used elsewhere in Homer in this metaphorical sense. Cf. Virgil, *Aen.* 2.758 *ignis edax*, 4.66 *est mollis flamma medullas*, with O. Lyne, *Words and the Poet* (Oxford 1989) 51–6.

184–91 Aphrodite keeps the dogs from harming Hektor's body, and anoints it with oil to protect it from mutilation, and Apollo covers it with a dark cloud so that the sun will not shrivel the flesh. The two main protecting deities of Troy intervene here, Aphrodite being given the task of anointing the body as one more suited to a female deity (cf. T 186). The passage is echoed at 24.18–21, where Apollo alone protects the corpse with the aegis (187 ∼ 24.21), and at 24.418–23. Cf. also 16.666–83 (Apollo's care for Sarpedon's body), 19.23–39 where Thetis protects Patroklos' corpse from flies and decay, pouring ambrosia and nectar into the nostrils, and 18.351 where the wounds are filled with ointment by Akhilleus' companions. These passages have been taken as evidence for Greek knowledge of the practice of embalming: see also on 7.85, 19.29–39.

This is the first clear sign that the gods are concerned about the fate of Hektor's body, and it foreshadows the events of book 24, with the allusion to the dragging of the corpse and the use of πρίν in 190, which implies that ultimately the body will be buried. The poet is reminding us that, as so often, Akhilleus' intentions will not be fulfilled, and he also keeps before us the contrast between the fates of Patroklos' and Hektor's bodies.

184 ἀμφεπένοντο: 'tended'; see on 21.203.

186 ἤματα καὶ νύκτας: a slightly unusual expression, as elsewhere (except at *Od.* 10.142 δύο τ' ἤματα καὶ δύο νύκτας) night comes first (5× *Il.*, 8× *Od.*). The order is presumably dictated here by metre, i.e. the position of the phrase at the beginning of the verse.

ῥοδόεντι ... ἐλαίῳ: 'oil of roses', later called ῥοδινόν (cf. Arn/AT 186). The epithet occurs only here in early epic (cf. Bacchylides 15.34, etc.), and ῥόδον first in *HyDem* 6, but compare the Homeric ῥοδοδάκτυλος. Pausanias (9.41.7) says that oil of roses was used as a medicine and also for preserving wooden statues.

187 ἀποδρύφοι: 'lacerate', apparently an aorist form of ἀποδρύπτω. The compound verb occurs only here and in the parallel verse 24.21 in *Il.*, but 3× *Od.* ἑλκυστάζειν occurs nowhere else except in these two verses.

188 κυάνεον νέφος: cf. 16.66 κυάνεον Τρώων νέφος as a metaphor.

188–91 The dark cloud with which Apollo covers the immediate area of the body is a rather unusual idea, perhaps similar to the cloud or mist which gods use to hide or rescue their favourites (cf. 3.380f. etc.).

191 'Should wither the flesh all around on the sinews and limbs.' σκήλει' is aorist optative of σκέλλω, a vivid verb which occurs only here in early epic; cf. A. *Pr.* 481 κατεσκέλλοντο (of men wasting away through lack of medicines), etc. It is related to σκελετός, σκληρός, etc.; cf. Chantraine, *Dict. s.v.* σκέλλομαι. The hiatus before ἶνες recurs at *Od.* 11.219, and it probably had an initial digamma; cf. Chantraine, *Dict. s.v.* ἴς 2.

192–225 When the pyre fails to burn Akhilleus prays to Boreas and Zephuros, and Iris goes to summon them. She finds the Winds feasting in the home of Zephuros and gives them Akhilleus' message. They cross the sea to Troy and fall upon the pyre, setting it ablaze. All night it burns, and Akhilleus continually pours wine on the ground, calling on the spirit of Patroklos with constant lamentation

This episode in which the Winds are summoned is a curious one. We have just heard of the care of Aphrodite and Apollo for the body of Hektor, which prevents Akhilleus' intention from being fulfilled. The failure of the pyre to burn is another check, and this in turn leads to further divine action. But the intervention of Iris of her own accord is unusual (cf. 3.121 where she comes unbidden to Helen), and it seems to be designed, like the episode as a whole, to give added importance to the whole narrative of the funeral. At the same time, Iris' visit to the Winds develops a momentum of its own, and forms an interlude in the action on earth, which is a relief after the intensity of what has preceded and a contrast with the picture of Akhilleus as he moves restlessly to and fro throughout the following night (cf. Wilamowitz, *IuH* 114). There seems to be no need here to invoke the theory of Kakridis (*Researches* 75–83), that the scene is modelled on one in a poem about Akhilleus' own funeral, where the Winds might be unwilling to come because of their grief at the death of Memnon their brother, and so they must be summoned.

The form of Iris' visit to the Winds (198–212) is also untypical, when compared with other scenes describing a messenger's journey or a visit. Normally she brings a message from a god to other gods or to mortals, whereas here she brings a request from a mortal to gods (cf. Arend, *Scenen* 58). This surely underlines the importance of Akhilleus: he is the only mortal who could evoke such a response. Iris' visit is most closely comparable with that of Patroklos to Nestor at 11.644ff. There too Patroklos refuses Nestor's offer of a seat (648 οὐχ ἕδος ἐστί ~ 23.205), because of the urgency of the situation; cf. also 6.360, where Hektor refuses Helen's offer of a seat.

Many readers have seen a touch of comedy in the portrayal of the Winds' party, and the eagerness of all of them to have Iris sitting beside them (202–3; cf. already T 203), although Kakridis protested that they are only showing proper epic courtesy (*Researches* 76–7, and cf. *Homer Revisited* (Lund 1971) 15). Iris' excuse, that she is going to join the other gods in the land of the Aithiopes, sounds very like a 'white lie' invented on the spur of the moment: this was already the view of some ancient scholars (bT 206a). L. Coventry, *JHS* 107 (1987) 178–80, suggests that it also contributes to the sense of the gods' detachment from the world of men (cf. bT 206b, Eust. 1296.25ff.).

Whatever the poet may have had in mind, the scene has an almost baroque quality to it. One thinks of Hellenistic poetry, Callimachus' *Lock of Berenice* for example, in which Zephuros also plays a part.

193 ἔνθ' αὖτ' ἀλλ' ἐνόησε: see on 140.

194 Cf. 1.35 πολλὰ δ' ἔπειτ' ἀπάνευθε κιὼν ἠρᾶθ' ὁ γεραιός, *Od.* 2.260–1 Τηλέμαχος δ' ἀπάνευθε κιὼν ... εὔχετ' Ἀθήνῃ, etc. See on 1.35–6.

195 For Βορέῃ καὶ Ζεφύρῳ cf. 9.5 (with comment) Βορέης καὶ Ζέφυρος, τώ τε Θρήκηθεν ἄητον. Here too these Winds seem to have their home in Thrace (229–30). The imperfect ὑπίσχετο goes better here with the imperfects in 194 and 196 than the variant ὑπέσχετο, which is read by pap. 12 and some medieval MSS.

After 195 and 209 pap. 12 adds the verse ἀρνῶν πρωτογόνων ῥέξειν κλειτὴν ἑκατόμβην, which occurs at 4.102, 4.120, and 23.864, 23.873, always in the context of prayers to Apollo by archers.

196 Pap. 12 reads πολλὰ δ' ἀποσπένδων ἠράσατο δῖος Ἀχιλλεύς, a very weak variant, with unnecessary repetition of the formula for Akhilleus after 193. Akhilleus' golden cup is paralleled at 219 by his golden *krater*. Cf. the very special libation vessel which he uses at 16.220–32.

197 φλεγεθοίατο νεκροί: most MSS read νεκρόν, which would make the verb middle instead of passive, and van der Valk supports this, since attention is focused on Patroklos rather than the dead Trojans (*Researches* II 581). It looks as if there was another ancient variant νεκρός, as Euphorion apparently used φλεγεθοίατο as a singular (T 197b with Erbse's comments).

198 ὕλη τε σεύαιτο was Aristarchus' reading (Did/A), against the variant ὕλην τε σεύαιντο (*sc.* ἄνεμοι), which probably went with the reading νεκρόν in 197. ὦκα δὲ Ἴρις was conjectured by Bentley for the vulgate reading ὠκέα δ' Ἴρις, and it is in fact read by pap. 12. The vulgate text probably arose from the common formula ὠκέα Ἴρις at the end of the line (18× *Il.*), and the papyrus reading, which respects the digamma of Ἴρις and gives the adverb ὦκα, is clearly better (*pace* Leaf).

199 Pap. 12 reads εὐχωλῆς instead of ἀράων. For μετάγγελος see on 15.143–5.

200–1 For the feasting of the Winds cf. Aiolos' family and their perpetual banqueting (*Od.* 10.8–11, 10.60–1).

200 Ζεφύροιο δυσαέος ... ἔνδον: i.e. in the house of Zephuros; cf. 20.13 Διὸς ἔνδον. Zephuros is normally a stormy wind in Homer: cf. *Od.* 5.295 Ζέφυρός τε δυσαής, 12.289 Ζεφύροιο δυσαέος. For δυσαής cf. also *Il.* 5.865.

201–2 ἐπέστη | βηλῷ ἐπὶ λιθέῳ: crossing or stepping on a threshold is often a way of expressing entry to a house in epic scenes of this type (e.g. *Od.* 1.680 etc.; see Richardson on *HyDem* 188); but usually the word for threshold is οὐδός rather than βηλός. The latter also occurs at 1.591 and 15.23, in both cases of the threshold of heaven from which gods were thrown by Zeus, and nowhere else in early epic. Later allegorists misinterpreted it as a word for heaven or part of the heavens (cf. AbT 1.591c, with Erbse's comments). Quintus of Smyrna has βηλὸν ἐς ἀστερόεντα (13.483) in a passage about winds stirring up the sea (NB: 482 δυσαέος).

202–3 The welcome of the Winds again follows a typical form for divine visits: cf. 1.533–4 (n.) θεοὶ δ' ἅμα πάντες ἀνέσταν | ἐξ ἑδέων σφοῦ πατρὸς ἐναντίον (of Zeus), 15.85–6 οἱ δὲ ἰδόντες | πάντας ἀνήϊξαν καὶ δεικανόωντο δέπασσιν (of Here), *HyAp* 3–4 καί ῥά τ' ἀναΐσσουσιν ἐπὶ σχεδὸν ἐρχομένοιο | πάντες ἀφ' ἑδράων. Here however κάλεόν τέ μιν εἰς ἓ ἕκαστος is a specific touch. Alcaeus made Zephuros the lover of Iris, and Eros their child (fr. 327 L–P): cf. Erbse on T 203. Later tradition saw Iris as ἐρωτική (bT 5.353, Eust. 555.30). T adds that the Winds are perhaps rather drunk (cf. T 15.86), which suits their boisterous behaviour!

204–5 Cf. 11.647–8 Πάτροκλος δ' ἑτέρωθεν ἀναίνετο, εἶπέ τε μῦθον· | οὐχ ἕδος ἐστί, γεραιὲ διοτρεφές, οὐδέ με πείσεις.

205–7 If this is supposed to be a subterfuge, as seems most likely, it is similar to the false pretexts offered by Here to Aphrodite and Zeus, when she says that she is going to visit Okeanos and Tethus (14.200–10, 301–11). For the visit to the Aithiopes cf. 1.423–4 and *Od.* 1.22–6 (with West's comments, *Od.* p. 75).

205–6 For ἐπ' Ὠκεανοῖο ῥέεθρα cf. 3.5 ἐπ' Ὠκεανοῖο ῥοάων, which a few MSS read here. Elsewhere we find ἀπ'/παρ' Ὠκεανοῖο ῥοάων, 19.1, *Od.* 22.197. For ἐς γαῖαν the city texts read ἐς δῆμον (Did/AT).

208–10 These verses recall the wording of 194–8. For Ζέφυρον κελαδεινόν ('resounding') cf. *Od.* 2.421 ἀκραῆ Ζέφυρον, κελάδοντ' ἐπὶ οἴνοπα πόντον, and their effect here at 212–18.

212–16 The Winds respond at once to Iris' request, and there is a vivid description of their turbulent journey and dramatic arrival. The poet does not give them the kind of brief speech of acceptance which would be usual after divine requests of this kind: their reaction is immediate.

212–13 Cf. 12.251–2, 13. 833–4 ὡς ἄρα φωνήσας ἡγήσατο· τοὶ δ' ἅμ' ἕποντο | ἠχῇ θεσπεσίῃ . . .

213 νέφεα κλονέοντε πάροιθεν: the winds 'drive' the clouds before them; cf. 11.305 ὡς ὁπότε Ζέφυρος νέφεα στυφελίξῃ, 12.157 ἅς τ' ἄνεμος ζαής, νέφεα σκιόεντα δονήσας, and 20.492 πάντη τε κλονέων ἄνεμος φλόγα εἰλυφάζει. Eustathius comments that the image is a military one here and at 217 φλόγ' ἔβαλλον (1296.32ff.).

214 πόντον ἵκανον ἀήμεναι: 'they reached the sea so as to blow on it'. Presumably the infinitive here is a development from phrases such as βῆ δ' ἰέναι etc., where the beginning of an action is described: cf. *Od.* 3.176 ὦρτο δ' ἐπὶ λιγὺς οὖρος ἀήμεναι.

215–16 For 215 cf. 13.590 πνοιῇ ὑπὸ λιγυρῇ, 18.67 Τροίην ἐρίβωλον ἵκοντο. θεσπιδαὲς πῦρ occurs 7× *Il.*, 1× *Od.* Here the fire is caused by a separate divine agency, but fire was in any case divine. There is an interesting parallel to this god-sent wind in the description of the tenth-century A.D. cremation of a Scandinavian chieftain on the Volga (C. Waddy and H. L. Lorimer, *Antiquity* 8 (1934) 62): when the pyre was lit, 'an awe-inspiring gale got up, so that the flames of the fire grew stronger and its blaze fiercer'. Then one of the spectators said 'out of love for him, his Lord has sent the wind to take him away this very hour'.

217–25 The repetition of παννύχιοι . . . πάννυχος gives added intensity to this scene: against the background of this howling tempest, and before the crackling flames of the pyre, we see Akhilleus slowly moving to and for throughout the whole night, constantly pouring wine upon the ground and calling on Patroklos' soul, his inconsolable grief being compared to that of a father who has lost his newly married son.

217 ἄμυδις φλόγ' ἔβαλλον: 'beat upon the flame together' ('as though the blasts were missiles', comments Monro).

218 λιγέως always occurs in this place in the verse, except at 3.214 (2× *Il.*, 4× *Od.*). It usually qualifies the verb κλαίειν, but cf. λιγέων ἀνέμων (3× *Il.*, 1× *Od.*) etc. ὠκὺς Ἀχιλλεύς is a good instance of a purely formular use of the epithet.

219–20 For | χρυσέου ἐκ κρητῆρος cf. *HyAphr* 206. ἑλὼν δέπας ἀμφικύπελλον | occurs at 9.656; cf. *Od.* 8.89 | καὶ δέπας ἀμφικύπελλον ἑλών. Here, however, most MSS and pap. 12 read ἔχων (also Did/A as a variant), which is clearly preferable, since Akhilleus' action is continuous. For the same reason the present ἀφυσσόμενος in 220 is better than the variant ἀφυσσάμενος. Cf. 3.295–6 οἶνον δ' ἐκ κρητῆρος ἀφυσσόμενοι δεπάεσσιν | ἔκχεον, where again ἀφυσσάμενοι is a variant (as at 10.579). For the rest of 220 cf. 7.480 οἶνον δ' ἐκ δεπάων χαμάδις χέον, and δεῦε δὲ γαῖαν | 13.655 = 21.119, *Od.* 9.290.

221 For ψυχὴν ... Πατροκλῆος δειλοῖο cf. 65, 105–6. Pap. 12 reads κικλήσκων ψυχὴν Πατρόκλου τεθνηῶτος, but the verse opens much more effectively with the single spondaic word ψυχήν, and the reading of the end of the verse in pap. 12 probably derives from 192. Arn/AT observe that 221 is wholly spondaic. It is a very solemn four-word verse, appropriate to the invocation which accompanies a libation (σπονδή). On such spondaic verses and their associations cf. Edwards, *HPI* 118–19, West, *Greek Metre* 55–6, L. P. Wilkinson, *Golden Latin Artistry* (Cambridge 1966) 60–1. Leaf objects that 'the original forms were certainly Πατροκλέϝεος and possibly δϝεελοῖο', and so it is wrong to see any special effect here: but we have no grounds for assuming that the words were still pronounced in this way at the time of composition of the *Iliad*. Other examples of wholly spondaic verses are 2.544, 11.130, *Od.* 15.334, 21.15, 22.175, 22.192. In general see D. W. Pye, *G&R* 11 (1964) 2–6. On the libation of wine to the dead cf. Stengel, *Opferbräuche* 183–6 and see on 166–76.

222–5 This is the last of a whole series of similes scattered throughout the poem in which the theme of parents and children is applied to Akhilleus or Patroklos, or as here to both together: cf. especially 16.7–11 (with comment) where they are like a mother and daughter, and 18.318–23 where Akhilleus' grief for Patroklos is like that of a lion which has lost its cubs, and see the analysis by Moulton, *Similes* 99–106. Moulton (106) comments that 'it is of course part of Achilles' sorrow that he has failed in his promise to Menoitios, and that he cannot restore the son to the father (cf. 18.324–7)'; and of the simile 'the vehicle fits no one more than the Priam of book 24, in whose grief for a married son there will be, paradoxically, a ground for a new understanding and humane respect on the part of the sorrowing hero'. This potential link with the theme of Priam's loss of so many sons, and the funeral of Hektor at the end of the *Iliad*, is surely significant. Cf. Griffin, *HLD* 123: 'the bereaved father is a dominant figure in the plot from Chryses to Priam, who appeals to Achilles in the name of another tragic father, Peleus; it seems natural to compare Achilles' grief for Patroclus (23.222) with that of a father mourning for his son'. See also on 22.44.

Here the pathos is increased by the fact that the son was νύμφιος, i.e. recently married but without a son of his own, as the father is thus deprived of two hopes at once (cf. bT 222–3, Eust, 1296.52).

The four verses are composed of two balanced couplets, in which 224 parallels 222 unusually closely: ὡς δὲ πατὴρ οὖ παιδὸς ὀδύρεται ὀστέα καίων | ... ὡς Ἀχιλεὺς ἑτάροιο ὀδύρετο ὀστέα καίων.

222 ὡς δὲ πατὴρ οὖ παιδός: cf. 9.481 ὡς εἴ τε πατὴρ ὃν παῖδα φιλήσῃ. But such a comparison is much commoner in the *Odyssey*: cf. 1.307–8, 2.47 (etc.), 16.17, 17.111, 17.397, and Moulton, *Similes* 141–5.

223 νυμφίου: only here in *Il.*; cf. *Od.* 7.64–6, where it refers to someone who had died without leaving a son, although he has produced a daughter (cf. AbT 223). After this verse pap. 12 adds χήρωσεν δὲ γυναῖκα μυχῷ θαλάμοιο νέοιο | ἀρητὸν δὲ τοκεῦσι γόον καὶ πένθος ἔθηκεν, which are adapted from 17.36–7. Plutarch (*Mor.* 117D) follows 223 with the second of these verses, and then adds μοῦνος τηλύγετος πολλοῖσιν ἐπὶ κτεάτεσσι, which is derived from 9.482 (where 481 ~ 23.222). It is natural that this simile should have suffered such expansion for emotional effect.

223–4 ὀδύρετο ... στεναχίζων: cf. *Od.* 13.219–21 ὁ δ' ὀδύρετο πατρίδα γαῖαν |'ἑρπύζων παρὰ θῖνα ... | πόλλ' ὀλοφυρόμενος. 'ἑρπύζων evidently expresses the weary movement of a broken-hearted man' (Leaf; cf. bT 225). It is only used here in *Il.*, and once elsewhere in *Od.*, of the aged Laertes (1.193); it recurs in Hellenistic and later verse. The present participles which frame the verse emphasize Akhilleus' continual sorrow and its physical expression.

226–61 At dawn the fire dies down, the Winds return home, and Akhilleus falls asleep exhausted. He is woken by the gathering of the leaders, and tells them to quench the pyre, collect Patroklos' bones, and build a mound: this will be enlarged after his own death, to cover both of them. They do as he orders, and he then makes the army sit down and brings out prizes for the contests

This scene, marking the end of the funeral and transition to the games, is paralleled by the conclusion of Hektor's funeral (24.788–803), where the people gather at dawn to quench the pyre with wine (791–2 ~ 23.250–1), and collect the bones, which are placed in a gold λάρναξ, wrapped in purple robes, and put into a grave, which is then covered by a layer of great stones and a mound (801 ~ 23.257). But it is striking how much variety there is in the language and ritual details of the two passages, and here our attention is focused especially on the rôle of Akhilleus. Cf. also 7.433–6 where the Achaeans gather at dawn to build a mound over their dead. At *Od.* 24.71–92 Akhilleus' own funeral concludes at dawn: his bones are collected, placed in wine and oil, and laid in a gold amphora together with those of Patroklos, and over them and Antilokhos' remains a great mound is built. Thetis then institutes funeral games in his honour.

226–8 The description of Dawn's arrival is unusually elaborate, with the mention of the morning-star as its harbinger (cf. *Od.* 13.93–4): see on 109 and 2.48–9, and cf. Wilamowitz, *IuH* 114: 'Dawn comes in its eternal beauty, unconcerned for the tears of the mortals, who have not been refreshed by the night.'

226 ἑωσφόρος, the Morning-star (i.e. the planet Venus), occurs only here in Homer: cf. Hes. *Th.* 381, where this star is the child of Dawn. There is no reason to suppose that the form of the word is Attic, as Wackernagel argued, since Ionic writers use ἑωθινός and similar forms (cf. West, *Theogony* p. 81). Here ἑωσφόρος must be scanned with synizesis (cf. Chantraine, *GH* I 69–72). For φόως ἐρέων cf. 2.49 φόως ἐρέουσα (Dawn).

227 Saffron-robed Dawn spreading over the sea (cf. 24.12–13) does not mean that the sun seems to *rise* from the sea, and cannot imply a poet who lives on an east coast as some have argued. As Leaf says, 'the dawn *spreads over* the sea to any observer on the shore, whether he looks N., E., S., or W.'; cf. Wilamowitz, *IuH* 508–9.

228 Cf. 9.212 αὐτὰρ ἐπεὶ κατὰ πῦρ ἐκάη καὶ φλὸξ ἐμαράνθη (in a description of cooking).

229–30 For the home of these Winds see on 195, and for οἴδματι θύων see on 21.234. Verse 229 is a rising threefolder.

231–5 Cf. 62–4 where Akhilleus falls asleep, exhausted after the pursuit of Hektor. To fall asleep at dawn is a reversal of normality, and Akhilleus' unquiet sleep is soon broken.

231–2 Verse 231 is again a rising threefolder. For ἐπὶ δὲ γλυκὺς ὕπνος ὄρουσεν cf. *Od.* 23.342–3 (and see on 62).

233 οἱ δ' ἀμφ' Ἀτρεΐωνα: i.e. 'Agamemnon and his companions'; see on 3.146–8.

234–5 Cf. 9.573 τῶν δὲ τάχ' ἀμφὶ πύλας ὅμαδος καὶ δοῦπος ὀρώρει, and *Od.* 10.556–7 κινυμένων δ' ἑτάρων ὅμαδον καὶ δοῦπον ἀκούσας | ἐξαπίνης ἀνόρουσε (of Elpenor's sudden awakening). For | ἕζετο δ' ὀρθωθείς cf. 2.42, with comment.

236 = 7.327, 7.385. Pap. 12 reads ἄλλοι ἐϋκνήμιδες Ἀχαιοί, as at 272 = 658.

237–8 It has been thought that quenching the pyre with wine may be archaeologically attested at Salamis in Cyprus and also on Ischia in the Geometric period: cf. Coldstream, *Geometric Greece* 349–50, P. Dikaios, *Archäologischer Anzeiger* (1963) 154–5, G. Buchner, *Expedition* 8 (1966) 5–6. The unburnt vessels found at such burials may, however, have been used to pour a libation to the dead man after the body had been burnt.

Virgil imitates this passage at *Aen.* 6.226–7, perhaps describing a similar Roman ritual. Wine was certainly poured on the pyre or over the bones (cf. Cic. *Leg.* 2.24.60, Pliny, *HN* 14.88, Petr. 65 etc.).

239 Akhilleus tells the others to quench the pyre, but will himself help to collect the bones (so T).

240 εὖ διαγιγνώσκοντες: cf. 470 | εὖ διαγιγνώσκω, and in the burial of the Greeks and Trojans at 7.424 ἔνθα διαγνῶναι χαλεπῶς ἦν ἄνδρα ἕκαστον, where the bodies are hard to recognize because covered in blood and wounds.

ἀριφραδέα: elsewhere in *Il.* only at 326 (5× *Od.*). Notice how the language of this verse is echoed in the following episodes, as though it is in the poet's mind. Pap. 12 reads ἀριφραδέως γὰρ ἔκειτο.

241-2 ἐπιμὶξ ἵπποι τε καὶ ἄνδρες: cf. 21.16, with comment. Pap. 12 reads αὐτοί τε καὶ ἵπποι (cf. 13.684, 17.644).

243-4 Cf. Patroklos' instructions to Akhilleus (80-91). Here the φιάλη is most probably a broad, shallow bowl (as in classical Greek), which is covered by fine linen (253) and kept in Akhilleus' hut until his death. Then their bones will be buried together in the σορός mentioned at 91 (see comment). Cf. Andronikos, *Arch. Hom.* w 30, and see on 270. φιάλη only occurs in Homer in this book (4×), but is common later.

243 δίπλακι δημῷ: a double layer of fat to protect the bones. Cf. δίπλαξ of a garment at 3.126 etc. At *Od.* 24.72-3 Akhilleus' bones are placed in 'unmixed wine and oil' before being buried in a golden amphora.

244 ἐγὼν Ἄϊδι κεύθωμαι: the variant ἰών for ἐγών is mentioned by A, and Arn/AT say that Aristarchus read κλεύθωμαι, whilst pap. 12 reads the aorist κλεύσωμαι. κλεύθωμαι, explained as a syncopated form of κελεύθωμαι meaning 'journey', 'travel', recurs only in the lexicographers. These variants may have been designed to avoid the use of Ἄϊδι in a local sense, unusual in Homer. The passive of κεύθω is also only found here in Homer, but the verb is used of burial at *Od.* 3.16 and later. Sophocles read κεύθωμαι, since he echoes the verse: *Aj.* 635 κρείσσων γὰρ Ἄϊδα κεύθων ὁ νοσῶν μάταν, and *Ant.* 911 μητρὸς δ' ἐν Ἀΐδου καὶ πατρὸς κεκευθότοιν (cf. also *OT* 968, A. *Pr.* 570 etc.). So we should keep the vulgate reading as in the OCT. For the idea cf. 22.482 Ἀΐδαο δόμους ὑπὸ κεύθεσι γαίης.

245-8 The tumulus will cover the pyre (255-6), which itself is a hundred feet square (164). It is to be a small one to begin with, and at first a cenotaph (cf. *Od.* 1.289-92, 4.584), but later when both heroes' remains are buried in it the Achaeans will make it broader and higher. Cf. *Od.* 24.80-4, where the final construction is described. There it is a great mound on a promontory looking over the Hellespont, and a landmark visible from far out at sea (cf. similarly 7.84-90). The tumulus built over the Achaean dead at 7.435-6 would have been a large one, and compare for example 2.811-14 where a high hill is called by the gods the 'tomb of Murine': see on 2.813-14, 7.86 for actual tumuli in the area, and for the ancient identification of barrows near the Sigeion headland as the tombs of Akhilleus, Patroklos and Antilokhos.

Andronikos (*Arch. Hom.* w 32–4) discusses these Homeric burial mounds, and (107–14) actual evidence for tumuli. Some of the most interesting examples from the Homeric point of view are found in northern Greece, at Halos and Vergina (*Arch. Hom.* w 112 and Lorimer, *HM* 108–10). At Halos a tumulus was erected in the eighth century B.C. over the site of sixteen pyres on which cremated human remains were found. 'Presumably they represent a family group over which the tumulus was raised when the direct line became extinct: no doubt each pyre was provisionally protected by a small mound' (Lorimer, *ibid.*, comparing 23.245–8). At Vergina we find many tumuli dating from the tenth to seventh or sixth centuries B.C. which have a circular enclosure of unworked stones as a base: some are as large as twenty metres in diameter (Andronikos, *Arch. Hom.* w 112). Near Larisa two very large tumuli of the archaic period contained multiple graves, with warrior cremation burials, some in bronze vessels (*AR* 1980–1, p. 25). Such tumuli continued in use in northern Greece into the Hellenistic period. Similar ones of the classical period in Thrace (cf. Hdt. 5.8) are discussed by A. Petropoulou (*AJP* 109 (1988) 493–5).

246 ἐπιεικέα τοῖον: 'just of moderate size'. ἐπιεικής is normally in Homer used in the phrase ὡς ἐπιεικές, or ἐπιεικές with an infinitive, and this qualifying use of τοῖον occurs only here in *Il.* but is common in *Od.* (1.209 etc.); it may be colloquial, as if accompanied by a gesture ('just *so* big').

247–8 ἐμεῖο | δεύτεροι: 'after me'. This use of δεύτερος with a genitive occurs only here in epic; cf. Hdt. 1.23 etc. Akhilleus' reference to his own death is very objective (cf. bT 248: 'in a noble way he does not lament his death').

251 βαθεῖα δὲ κάππεσε τέφρη: 'where the ash had fallen deep'.

252 ἑτάροιο ἐνηέος: almost exclusively of Patroklos in *Il.*; cf. 17.204, 21.96 ἑταῖρον ... ἐνηέα, 17.670 ἐνηείης Πατροκλῆος, and once of Nestor at 23.648, just after a reference to Patroklos (see comment).

252–3 ὀστέα λευκά | ἄλλεγον: cf. 24.793 ὀστέα λευκά λέγοντο, and 21.321 ἄλλεξαι (of collecting bones).

254 For ἐν κλισίῃσι δὲ θέντες cf. 19.280 ἐν κλισίῃσι θέσαν, etc. Leaf prefers the variant reading of some MSS ἐν κλισίῃ δ' ἐνθέντες, but the generalizing plural κλισίαι is quite common (2.226–7 etc.). For ἑανῷ λιτὶ κάλυψαν | cf. 18.352 ἐν λεχέεσσι δὲ θέντες ἑανῷ λιτὶ κάλυψαν, where Patroklos' body is covered in fine linen, and 24.796 πορφυρέοις πέπλοισι καλύψαντες μαλακοῖσιν of Hektor's bones. On ἑανός ('supple' or 'fine') see 5.734n. At Salamis in Cyprus cremated bones have been found together with or actually wrapped in fine cloth, and at Lefkandi the warrior burial has its funerary amphora wrapped in cloth: see on 166–76. For other examples of this practice cf. Coldstream, *Geometric Greece* 196–7, 350 (the burials at the West Gate of Eretria, *c.* 700 B.C.), and Kurtz and Boardman, *Burial Customs* 53, 98–9, describing Geometric and later burials in Attica in which the urns or cremated remains (or both) are wrapped in cloth. In the one illustrated there (pl. 23) the ashes 'were gathered from the pyre into a purple cloth, placed in a bronze cauldron, which was itself wrapped in cloth. The urn lay in a wooden chest inside a stone box, which was buried beneath a built tomb.' A celebrated example is that of the magnificent purple and gold cloth found in the antechamber of the late fourth-century B.C. 'Royal Tomb' in the great tumulus at Vergina: this was wrapped around the cremated bones, in a gold *larnax*, and the similar cremation in the gold *larnax* inside the main chamber was also probably wrapped in cloth. Cf. M. Andronikos, *Vergina: the Royal Tombs and the Ancient City* (Athens 1984) 73, 170, 191–2, pls. 156–7.

A. Petropoulou, *AJP* 109 (1988) 482–95, discusses further examples from Thrace, Macedonia and Rhodes of cinerary urns of the classical period of gold or silver, some of which are covered by cloth, and argues that the κλισίαι referred to here is not Akhilleus' hut (as is usually supposed) but the actual tomb itself (as suggested by Düntzer and Thielscher). κλισίαι does not have this sense elsewhere in Homer, but she quotes some examples from Hellenistic and later epitaphs. The strongest point in her favour is 24.16, where Hektor's corpse is dragged round Patroklos' tomb (σῆμα), which is odd if his bones are not there. But the lack of Homeric parallels makes it hard to take the word in this sense.

255–6 Finally they drew the circle (τορνώσαντο) of the mound, and set up around the circumference of the pyre a base of stones, which they then covered with earth. The verb τορνοῦσθαι occurs only here in *Il.*, at *Od.* 5.249, and occasionally in late epic, but τόρνος is the common Greek word for a type of compass for marking a circle. For θεμείλια cf. 12.28, *HyAp* 254. On the tomb's construction see Andronikos, *Arch. Hom.* w 32, 107ff.

256 χυτὴν ἐπὶ γαῖαν ἔχευαν: the word χυτός is used in Homer only to refer to a burial mound (cf. Arn/A): cf. *Od.* 3.258 χυτὴν ἐπὶ γαῖαν ἔχευαν |, *Il.* 6.464, 14.114 χυτὴ κατὰ γαῖα καλύπτοι/κάλυψε |.

257 This verse is similar to 24.801 χεύαντες δὲ τὸ σῆμα πάλιν κίον· αὐτὰρ ἔπειτα (followed by the funeral feast). It has been objected that κίον is an aorist form, and so there is an awkward transition here, as in fact the Greeks do *not* go away (cf. Leaf, Willcock). The poet may be using a regular phrase to describe the end of a burial.

258 ἵζανεν εὐρὺν ἀγῶνα: 'made the broad assembly sit down'; cf. 2.191 ἄλλους ἵδρυε λαούς (etc.), *Od.* 8.260 καλὸν δ' εὔρυναν ἀγῶνα. ἀγών means any gathering, and hence an assembly of spectators at a contest, or the place of the contest, and then the contest itself (cf. perhaps already *Od.* 8.259).

259–61 The general catalogue of prizes serves as the briefest introduction to the games, but by its richness of detail it marks the transition from the solemnity of the funeral rites to the more cheerful atmosphere of the following scenes.

Both Aristophanes and Aristarchus athetized these verses (Did/T). The scholia do not say why, although bT defend the use of νηῶν here to mean 'the place where the ships were', since the prizes were not kept in the ships themselves (cf. 564 οἰσεμέναι κλισίηθεν). Leaf suggests that they may have objected pedantically to the fact that horses, mules and oxen are mentioned, when only one of each is subsequently given as a prize, and to the application of ἔκφερε to such animals. We surely need an introductory passage at this point. Of the prizes actually mentioned later, some belong to Akhilleus (807–8, 826–9), others to Patroklos. Several have significant associations as spoils of the War. For their values see on 269, and in general cf. Laser, *Arch. Hom.* T 79–81.

259 For tripods as prizes cf. 11.700 (in Elis: cf. Olympia?), 22.164, Hes. *Erga* 657, with West's comment. The great series of tripods at Olympia and other sanctuaries, beginning in the ninth century, may have been dedications rather than prizes, although this is disputed: cf. M. Maass, *Die geometrischen Dreifüsse von Olympia* (Berlin 1978) 4, Fittschen, *Sagendarstellungen* 31. Fittschen lists depictions of contests for tripods in eighth- and seventh-century art (*Sagendarstellungen* 28–30). In addition to tripods we find shields and horses, possibly as prizes, in some Geometric scenes of contests (Andronikos, *Arch. Hom.* W 124).

260–1 The phrase ἵππους (θ') ἡμιόνους τε recurs 3× in book 24, but βοῶν ἴφθιμα κάρηνα is used only here in Homer: cf. *HyHerm* (4×); *Il.* 9.407 ἵππων ξανθὰ κάρηνα |. Verse 261 = 9.366 (see comment).

262–897 The games

The games in honour of Patroklos consist of eight contests. By far the longest episode is the first, the chariot-race (262–652). It is followed by boxing (652–99), wrestling (700–39), running (740–97), armed combat (798–825), weight-throwing (826–49), archery (850–83), and spear-throwing (884–97).

In Nestor's reminiscences a shorter list of five contests is mentioned, boxing, wrestling, running, spear-throwing, and the chariot-race (634–42), and Akhilleus mentions the first four of these in his speech to Nestor (621–3). In the Phaeacian games for Odysseus the five events are running, wrestling, jumping, discus-throwing, and boxing (*Od.* 8.120–30), but Odysseus boasts to the Phaeacians of his skill in archery and spear-throwing (8.214–29). Thus all the contests in the games for Patroklos recur elsewhere in Homer except the armed duel, although some modern scholars actually believe this to be the event from which funeral games developed (cf. L. Malten, *MDAI(R)* 38 (1923) 300–40, K. Meuli, *Die Antike* 17 (1941) 189–208, and *Der griechische Agon*, Cologne 1968, 15–67).

Nestor's games were at the funeral of Amarunkeus (630–1). In book 11 he mentions a four-horse chariot which his father had entered for a race in Elis, but does not specify whether this was at a funeral or not (698–702). Several other games in Homer are funerary: 23.678–80 (Oidipous), 22.162–4 (a simile), and *Od.* 24.85–92 (Akhilleus). It was believed later that all athletic festivals had originated as funeral games (cf. Pfeiffer on Call. fr. 384.30, Erbse on bT 22.164b), and this view is supported by Meuli. But not all games in Homer are of this type (cf. 4.385–90, *Od.* 8.100–3).

The motive for holding contests at a funeral is never explained in Homer, although 646 implies that they are designed to honour the dead man. In addition, when Akhilleus offers Nestor a prize he says that he should keep it as a memorial of Patroklos' funeral (618–19). The games are seen as a great commemorative occasion. The poet does not give us any hint of Patroklos' own spirit as taking pleasure in this, but the idea may well have been present in people's minds on such occasions. During the funeral itself Akhilleus continually called upon the ghost of his friend (218–21), but after the burning his spirit is in Hades (cf. 75–6). Whether he hears we are not told, but Akhilleus does address him again later, and promises him a share in Priam's gifts (24.591–5).

Structurally the games mark a transition to the last Book, preparing the way for Akhilleus' reception of Priam. They also show us the Greek heroes, for the last time, with many of their strengths and weaknesses of character displayed in speech and action. This Book forms a counterpart to book 2, which gave us our first picture of the Greek army as a whole: the marshalling of the Achaeans for war corresponds with their gathering for the games, war's peaceful counterpart. But the quarrels which break out among the leaders also recall book 1. There Akhilleus was the protagonist in the dispute, whereas here by contrast he is the mediator and restorer of concord (490–8, 555–62, 618–23). Honour is satisfied in the games and the risk of further conflict is avoided (see on 448–98).

Some of the episodes foreshadow events beyond the poem's scope, for example the wrestling match between Telamonian Aias and Odysseus, which brings to mind their later contest for Akhilleus' arms. The prominence of Antilokhos, and his close friendship with Akhilleus, suggests the rôle he is to play in the events described in the *Aithiopis*, where his death at Memnon's hands is avenged by Akhilleus: after Patroklos' death Antilokhos begins to replace him as Akhilleus' closest friend alive. We see heroes who play no part in the main events of the poem but may have been prominent elsewhere, such as Eumelos of Pherai (cf. 2.712–15, 2.763–7), and Epeios who later will make the Wooden Horse (cf. *Od.* 8.492–3, 11.523).

On the early history of funeral games cf. Andronikos, *Arch. Hom.* w 34–7, 121–6, and Laser, *Arch. Hom.* τ. For some literary aspects cf. M. M. Willcock, 'The funeral games of Patroclus', *BICS* 20 (1973) 1–11, and on the relationship of the games to book 1 see Macleod, *Iliad XXIV* 29–32, and M. W. Dickie, 'Fair and foul play in the Funeral Games in the *Iliad*', *Journal of Sport History* 11. 2 (1984) 8–17.

262–652 The chariot race

This falls into four main sections:

(a) Preparations for the race (262–361)
(b) The race itself (362–447)
(c) The argument between the spectators Idomeneus and the lesser Aias (448–98)
(d) The end of the race and the awarding of the prizes (499–652).

(a) *262–361 The preparations. Akhilleus offers prizes for the chariot race. The contestants are Eumelos, Diomedes, Menelaos, Antilokhos, and Meriones. Nestor advises Antilokhos on tactics. They draw lots for positions, and Akhilleus sets Phoinix as an umpire at the turning-point*

262–70 The list of prizes is varied: the postponement of τῷ πρώτῳ gives a neatly chiastic order to 265, and the placing and form of the verb is elegantly varied: | θῆκε ... ἔθηκεν | ... κατέθηκε ... θῆκε ... ἔθηκε |. The expression ἄεθλα θῆκε (etc.) is used for the first four contests of the Games (cf. 653, 700, 740), but for the later, more minor ones ἄεθλα is omitted and the prizes are listed as objects of the verb.

262 ἱππεῦσιν ... ποδώκεσιν: cf. 376 ποδώκεες ... ἵπποι, 17.614 ποδώκεας ... ἵππους. The adaptation of this expression has led to the transfer of the epithet from horses to riders. T mentions a variant ἵπποισιν, clearly designed to avoid the oddity of expression, and impossible with what follows.

263 Cf. 16.233 θῆκ' ἐπὶ νηὸς ἄγεσθαι, and 9.128 δώσω δ' ἕπτα γυναῖκας ἀμύμονα ἔργα ἰδυίας. The hiatus after γυναῖκα is inelegant, and may be due to the combination of the two types of phrase just quoted (cf. Chantraine, *GH* I 91). The succession of trochaic word breaks produces an uneven verse (cf. 116n.), although examples of this are not so uncommon: cf. Kirk, *YCS* 20 (1966) 95ff.

264 καὶ τρίποδ' ὠτώεντα: this phrase recurs at 513. The epithet ('with ears or handles') does not recur in Homer: cf. Hes. *Erga* 657 τρίποδ' ὠτώεντα, of the prize won by Hesiod in the funeral games for Amphidamas. The form οὐατόεις is most often used elsewhere (see West's comment). Tripod handles (οὔατα) are mentioned at 18.378–9.

δυωκαιεικοσίμετρον: 'holding twenty-two measures'; cf. the similar compound δυωκαιεικοσίπηχυ (15.678), with comment. These are the only cases in Homer of a single word filling the second half of the verse (Edwards, *HPI* 123), and both occur nowhere else. As this is five and a half times the quantity held by the cauldron in 267–8 it must have been a very large tripod bowl, but we do not know what the μέτρον here represents.

266 Cf. 655 ἐξέτε' ἀδμήτην, ἥ τ' ἀλγίστη δαμάσασθαι. ἀδμητος ought to mean 'untamed' (cf. 10.293). Delebecque (*Cheval* 160) considered it odd to use this of a six-year-old mare, and suggested that it should mean 'hard to master', but she could have been left wild up to then. βρέφος ἡμίονον κυέουσαν means 'pregnant with a baby mule'.

267–8 For ἄπυρον ('not yet exposed to fire') cf. 9.122 ἕπτ' ἀπύρους τρίποδας, and 23.270 ἀπύρωτον, 885 λέβητ' ἄπυρον. Here λευκὸν ἔτ' αὔτως (268) elaborates the point of ἄπυρον. For κεχανδότα ('containing') cf. *Od.* 4.96 and see on 24.192.

269 δύω χρύσοιο τάλαντα: cf. 614, 18.507. It is significant that two talents of gold are assigned only as the fourth prize. Ancient discussion concluded that the Homeric talent must have had a smaller value than in the classical period, and Aristotle (fr. 164 R.³) argued that its value cannot have been precisely fixed (cf. AbT 269 with Erbse's commentary, and F. Hultsch, *Griechische und römische Metrologie*, Berlin 1862, 128–9). The only weight terms used in Homer are the talent and half-talent, and these are only applied to gold, whereas other commodities are measured in different ways, especially in terms of oxen. Some scholars believe that the Homeric talent was equated in value with an ox. It has been argued that there was no attempt at standardization of weights before the introduction of coinage, but this is a debatable point: cf. C. H. Grayson, 'Weighing in ancient Greece' (Oxford D.Phil. thesis 1974) 285–6, 323, 326–30. In the Mycenaean period there appears to have been a more developed system of weights and measures: cf. Ventris and Chadwick, *Documents* 57–8 and Grayson, *op. cit.* 674–8. The Eretria gold hoard of *c.* 700 B.C. contains a number of what may be talents, as well as half pieces and fragments: P. G. Themelis, *Praktika* 1980, 89–91. For discussion of relative values of the prizes and other Homeric objects see A. L. Macrakis, *Studies Presented to Stirling Dow*, ed. K. J. Rigsby (Durham, North Carolina 1984) 211–15.

270 ἀμφίθετον φιάλην: according to Aristarchus (Arn/A) the Homeric φιάλη is a shallow bowl-shaped cauldron, and ἀμφίθετος means that it can stand either upright or upside down on its rim, but this seems unlikely. The sense of the epithet was uncertain, and Athenaeus (500F–501D) records many interpretations. The most likely seems to be 'with handles on both sides'. The word recurs at 616, and nowhere later. The φιάλη existed in Mycenaean Greek: cf. *pi-je-ra₃*, *pi-a₂-ra* in the Linear B tablets, which is depicted in the ideograms as 'a large shallow vessel, designed to expose a large area to the fire, and provided with high-swung handles for suspension' (Ventris and Chadwick, *Documents* 324–5). See also on 243–4, and F. Brommer, *Hermes* 77 (1942) 361, 368–9.

271 This verse is repeated before Akhilleus' introductory speeches to all the contests except the last two, at 456, 657 (272 = 658), 706, 752, 801, 830, and occurs nowhere else in Homer, a remarkable example of a formula confined to a single context (cf. Edwards, *HSCP* 74 (1970) 15, 27). Cf. in this Book 781 ὄνθον ἀποπτύων, μετὰ δ' Ἀργείοισιν ἔειπεν, 786 μειδιόων, καὶ μῦθον ἐν Ἀργείοισιν ἔειπεν, and 471 Αἰτωλὸς γενέην, μετὰ δ' Ἀργείοισιν ἀνάσσει. It looks as if the verse may have been invented by the poet for this episode. Alternatively, it could belong to the stock of epic accounts of games. Elsewhere we find 19.269 ἀνστὰς Ἀργείοισι φιλοπτολέμοισι μετηύδα, and 2.109, 9.16 ἔπε' Ἀργείοισι μετηύδα |.

272–86 Akhilleus' speech appropriately introduces the first and most important contest, by referring to the supremacy of his own horses (cf. 2.770), and to the loss of Patroklos, their driver. This reference is developed pathetically with the reminiscence of his gentle care for them and of their grief for him, a motif which recalls 17.426–56 and 19.400–24.

272 = 658 (with 657 = 271) at the beginning of the next episode. The same verse (with Ἀτρεΐδαι) occurred at 1.17. Here some MSS read ἀριστῆες Παναχαιῶν | as at 236.

273 'These prizes are set down in the assembly, awaiting the horsemen': δεδεγμένα (from δέχομαι) is applied here unusually to inanimate objects. Arn/A mention a variant ἱππεῦσι, and T says that some took δεδεγμένα as from δείκνυμι, meaning 'displayed for'.

274 ἐπὶ ἄλλῳ: the hiatus at the end of the second foot is rare, especially inside a phrase where the words cohere so closely.

276 περιβάλλετον: 'are outstanding'; only here and at *Od*. 15.17 in this sense.

277–8 At 16.866–7 and 17.443–4 we learnt that the gods gave Peleus immortal horses, presumably at his wedding to Thetis (cf. 18.84–5 and see on 16.140–4). Their parentage was described at 16.148–51; they were the offspring of Zephuros and the Harpy Podarge. Here we learn that they were a gift of Poseidon, presumably as the god of horses (so T). Leaf says that 'this is the only passage in Homer where Poseidon is brought into any special relation with the horse', but 584–5 is surely another instance, and perhaps 8.440–1, where Poseidon takes charge of the chariot and horses of Zeus.

277 αὐτούς: Leaf reads αὐτός, with the support of one or two MSS, but the anaphoric use of αὐτός appears occasionally in Homer: cf. Chantraine, *GH* II 157.

278 After this verse pap. 12 adds two more, ὡς τώ γ' ἀθάνατοι κ[... | θνητοὺς ἀθανάτοισι [..., whose sense probably was 'They are immortal, and mortals should (or do) not vie with immortals'; cf. *Od.* 5.212–13.

280 τοίου γὰρ κλέος ἐσθλόν: pap. 12 and some MSS read τοῖον ... σθένος. τοῖον must be a mistake, due to false assimilation with σθένος. κλέος ἐσθλόν occurs 3× elsewhere in *Il.* and 5× *Od.*, σθένος ἐσθλόν nowhere else. Either would be possible, but κλέος is more emotive and seems preferable (*pace* van der Valk, *Researches* II 110). The oblique reference to Patroklos without naming him is pathetic, as at 16 τοῖον γὰρ πόθεον μήστωρα φόβοιο.

281–2 Cf. Hektor's reference to Andromakhe's care of his horses (8.185–90). For the stress on Patroklos' gentleness see on 252. For ὅς σφωϊν pap. 12 and some MSS read ὅ σφωϊν, and this was Aristarchus' reading, with a comparison of 1.73 (AT). This is more euphonious. ὑγρὸν ἔλαιον ('liquid oil') occurs only here in *Il.*, but 3× *Od.*

283–4 These verses recall 17.426–40, where the horses mourn Patroklos' death, especially 434–40, where their stillness is like that of a funeral στήλη, they bow their heads to the ground (οὔδει ἐνισκίμψαντε καρήατα), and their manes are besmirched. Cf. also 19.405–6, where Xanthos bows his head in sorrow for Akhilleus and his mane reaches the ground. Here χαῖται (284) picks up the reference to the washing of their manes in 282, and the effect of contrast is rather like that of 22.401–4 and similar passages (cf. Griffin, *HLD* 135–6). The repetition in τώ γ' ἑσταότες πενθείετον ... τώ δ' ἕστατον ἀχνυμένω κῆρ dwells on this picture of the silent, sorrowing creatures: their continual stillness is abnormal and reveals their grief.

284 ἐρηρέδαται: 'rest on the ground'; cf. 7.145 etc. οὔδει ἐρείσθη. The form ἐρηρέδαται recurs at 329; cf. *Od.* 7.95 ἐρηρέδατο.

285–6 Nicanor preferred to take κατὰ στρατόν with the relative clause, rather than with what precedes, but the latter seems more natural. Some MSS read ἀλλ' ἄγε δή at the beginning of 285, and this is occasionally used with an address in the plural (1.62 etc.). For ἵπποισιν τε ... καὶ ἅρμασι κολλητοῖσιν see on 4.366 and 11.198.

287 Aristarchus took ταχέες as predicative, meaning 'quickly' (Arn/AbT), comparing 880 and 19.276, and this is probably correct (although cf. 262). He also preferred to read ἔγερθεν (Did/A), which is read by some of our MSS ('roused themselves'), in preference to ἄγερθεν ('gathered'). But ἐγείρεσθαι elsewhere in Homer always seems to be used of waking up.

288ff. For the form of this list cf. 7.162ff. ὦρτο πολὺ πρῶτος μὲν ἄναξ ἀνδρῶν Ἀγαμέμνων, | τῷ δ' ἐπὶ Τυδεΐδης ὦρτο κρατερὸς Διομήδης [=23.290], | τοῖσι δ' ἐπ' Αἴαντες (etc.), with Meriones in sixth place (cf.

23.351); also 23.708, 811–12, 836, 859. This listing seems to reflect the contestant's natural order of ability.

288–9 On Eumelos, his horses, and their connexion with Apollo, see 2.712–15, 2.763–7 with comments. His father Admetos was one of the contestants at the funeral games in honour of Pelias, a major event in early Greek poetry and art: cf. Paus. 5.17.9, *LIMC* I. I pp. 219–20 (B 7 and 10), L. Malten, *MDAI(R)* 38 (1923) 307–8.

290–2 The introduction here of the horses from the stock of Tros neatly links this episode with earlier parts of the poem, especially book 5: cf. their description at 5.222–3 and 260–73, their capture at 319–27, and Aineias' rescue by Apollo at 344–6 and 445–7; they are mentioned again at 8.105–8. In the ensuing race there are further important echoes of book 5, for here too Apollo attempts to thwart Diomedes' success, and Athene helps him, at the same time as she robs Eumelos' horses, which Apollo had looked after, of victory (382–400).

The ancient critics (T 291) were puzzled by Diomedes' ability to take part in the games (cf. 812–25 where he fights Aias in the duel), after he had been wounded in battle (11.376–8), a fact which had been recalled as recently as at 19.47–9. Given the frequency of cross-references in the games to earlier parts of the poem this may seem odd, but presumably the poet forgets Diomedes' wound for the purpose of these episodes. The same problem will apply to Odysseus' participation at 709ff., 755ff.

293–300 Menelaos competes with one of his own horses and one of his brother's, a neat way of bringing Agamemnon into the contest, since the poet could not easily have let him compete and lose, and a way of suggesting the unity of the two Atreidai (cf. bT 293, 295). The names of the horses, Fiery and Fleetfoot, are suitable (see on 8.185). They are dignified with a biographical sketch: Ekhepolos, a very rich inhabitant of Sikuon, avoided military service at Troy by giving Agamemnon the horse Aithe. Cf. the references to payment of a fine for this purpose by a Corinthian (13.669), and to conscription by lot (24.399–400). Both Corinth and Sikuon were in Agamemnon's own territory: see on 2.569–80.

Ekhepolos, son of Ankhises, has an appropriate name. Later mythographers (Acusilaus, Pherecydes) made him a descendant of Pelops (T 296), and it is interesting to find the name Ankhises in a Greek context. Plutarch (*Mor.* 32F) records the dry comment of Aristotle (fr. 165 R.³), that Agamemnon rightly preferred a warlike horse to an unwarlike man!

299 ἐν εὐρυχόρῳ Σικυῶνι: the epithet must originally have meant 'with broad dancing places', but it seems to have come to be used as if it were the same as εὐρύχωρος and meant 'spacious'. Hence it is applied, for example, to Hellas (9.478) and Elis (*Od.* 4.635: see West's comment), etc. Sikuon's position, by the rich plain on the north coast of the Peloponnese, would be suitable for a wealthy owner of horses.

300 ὅ γ': the variant τόθ' (a few MSS, and mentioned as a variant by A) was read by Leaf, but τὴν τόθ' is less attractive from the point of view of sound.

ἰσχανόωσαν: this verb normally means 'hold back' (5.89 etc.), but could theoretically mean 'cling to'. It is hard to see how it could mean 'desire' (*vel sim.*), and we should perhaps read the variant ἰχανόωσαν, which may be related to ἴχαρ ('desire', A. *Supp.* 850), and recurs as a variant at *Od.* 8.288. The verb survived in later Ionic (Herodas, Babrius), and ἰχαίνειν occurs in Callimachus fr. 178.22; cf. Wackernagel, *Kleine Schriften* 1 778, and see also on 17.570–3.

301–50 The list of contestants is interrupted at this point by Nestor's speech to Antilokhos, and will be concluded at 351. This gives us advance warning that Antilokhos will play a prominent part in the race. In earlier episodes he has appeared several times in association with Menelaos, who will be his rival in the race: at 5.561ff. he joined him in order to protect him from attack by Aineias, and at 15.568ff. he was encouraged by him to attack the Trojans (cf. bT 15.568 for the suggestion that their friendship stemmed from their being neighbours at home). At 17.651ff. Telamonian Aias asked Menelaos to find Antilokhos, so that he could bring Akhilleus the news of Patroklos' death. Thus the way is prepared for the touching conclusion to the ensuing quarrel of Menelaos and Antilokhos (566–613).

Nestor himself is ἱππότα by tradition (2.336 etc.) and he is descended from Poseidon, god of horses (T 301). Among his other speeches of tactical advice (see on 2.360–8) is one about the use of chariots in battle (4.297–309; see comments), and among his reminiscences are accounts of fighting with chariots (11.711–61) and of chariot-races (11.698–702, 23.638–42).

Here his two speeches before and after (cf. 626–50) frame the race, setting it in a context of traditional expertise. The first one has a typical ring-structure (cf. Lohmann, *Reden* 15–18):

306–8:   introduction
(a) 309–12: you are a good charioteer, but your horses are slower than the rest
(b) 313–18: you must make use of ingenuity (μῆτις)
(c) 319–25: contrasting descriptions of the bad and good driver
(d) 326–33: description of the turning-post
(c) 334–43: positive and negative advice on how to round it
(b) 343:   use your intelligence and take care!
(a) 344–8: if you turn the post well even the best horse in the world will not catch you

The structure of the speech neatly mirrors that of the race, 309–25 portraying the physical and psychological situation before the turn, 334–48 that after it, with the speech pivoting around 326–33, the central description of the turn. As such it forms a complement to the race, allowing the poet in the following narrative to dispense for example with any further description of the turning-post. As a general discourse on horsemanship it is a miniature forerunner of later works on the subject such as Xenophon's. It is also a sermon on the uses of μῆτις (practical intelligence): cf. M. Detienne and J.-P. Vernant, *Cunning Intelligence in Greek Culture and Society* (English translation, Harvester Press 1979) 11–26. On Nestor's speeches in general see Martin, *Language of Heroes* 101–13.

301 This formulation is repeated with Meriones at 351.

303–4 Πυλοιγενέες ... ὠκύποδες: see on 2.54 Πυλοιγενέος (of Nestor). The variant παλαιγενέες is due to 445, where they are said to be no longer young (bT). ὠκύποδες is a good example of a formular epithet, given the relative slowness of these horses (so Arn/A).

305 Nicanor judged it best to take εἰς ἀγαθά with μυθεῖτο (cf. 9.102 εἰπεῖν εἰς ἀγαθόν), and φρονέων νοέοντι καὶ αὐτῷ together, making an antithesis, but perhaps μυθεῖτ' εἰς ἀγαθὰ φρονέων all go together. The phrase is characteristic of Nestor: 9.102 is spoken by him, as is 11.789 ὁ δὲ πείσεται εἰς ἀγαθόν περ. Antilokhos' intelligence is often mentioned in what follows (440, 570, 586, 603–4), and Menelaos' distress is partly because it is out of character for him to be so reckless.

306–8 Aristarchus (Arn/A) and some MSS read ἐδίδαξεν in 307, referring only to Poseidon as god of horses, whereas Zenodotus preferred ἐδίδαξαν, which is surely right. Zeus may be included as author of divine gifts in general, but the emphasis can still be on Poseidon, who is especially suitable as the great-grandfather of Antilokhos. Cf. 13.554–5, where Poseidon protects him from the Trojan attack.

Nestor's introductory remarks are complimentary, and use the standard rhetorical device of saying that someone does not really need advice: cf. especially 787 εἰδόσιν ὔμμ' ἐρέω πᾶσιν, φίλοι ..., 1.577 μητρὶ δ' ἐγὼ παράφημι, καὶ αὐτῇ περ νοεούσῃ, Hes. *Erga* 202 νῦν δ' αἶνον βασιλεῦσ' ἐρέω, φρονέουσι καὶ αὐτοῖς (which resemble 305); and other examples in Macleod, *Iliad XXIV* 47.

309 περὶ τέρμαθ': in *Il.* always applied to the turning-post (22.162 and 6× in book 23). At 332 etc. this is called νύσσα.

310 βάρδιστοι: this superlative form of βραδύς occurs only here and at 530 in Homer; cf. Theocr. *Id.* 15.104. τῶ τ' οἴω λοίγι' ἔσεσθαι means 'therefore I think things will be troublesome for you'; cf. 21.533 νῦν οἴω λοίγι' ἔσεσθαι. Nestor's horses are said at 8.104 to be slow.

311 ἀφάρτεροι: 'swifter', a comparative from the adverb ἄφαρ, itself treated as an adjective at Theognis 716, τῶν ἄφαρ εἰσὶ πόδες. It recurs only in a fragment of Dionysius' *Bassarika* (frag. 5b2 Heitsch), and is noted as a *hapax* by Arn/A.

312–18 μητίσασθαι ... μῆτιν ... | μήτι ... | μήτι ... | μήτι: the rhetorical repetition develops into a threefold enumeration of instances of μῆτις, described by ancient commentators as an example of inductive reasoning (ἐπαγωγή); it could be regarded as a form of priamel (cf. Willcock), and suits the gnomic style of this part of the speech. See also vol. v, p. 44.

314 παρεκπροφύγῃσιν ('slip away past your grasp'): this splendidly elaborate compound, with its triple prefix, occurs only here.

315 δρυτόμος recurs in Homer only at 11.86; cf. ὑλοτόμος (114, 123).

317 ἐρεχθομένην ἀνέμοισι: the exact sense and etymology of ἐρεχθεῖν are uncertain. It occurs only here in *Il.*; cf. *Od.* 5.83 = 157 δάκρυσι καὶ στοναχῇσι καὶ ἄλγεσι θυμὸν ἐρέχθων, *HyAp* 358 ὀδύνῃσιν ἐρεχθομένη χαλεπῇσι, and perhaps Procl. *H.* 7.38 ἐρίχθομαι ... πρήξεσιν οὐχ ὁσίαις. It is usually taken as meaning something like 'trouble', 'distress'. AbT mention a variant ἐεργομένην, substituting a more common word, and there was a variant spelling ἐριχθομένην.

319–25 The ancient and medieval traditions are both divided over whether to read ἀλλ' ὅς or ἄλλος in 319, but ἄλλος μέν is surely right here (cf. e.g. 11.636–7). If we read ὅς μέν as a relative, either there is no apodosis or the apodosis is in 321, which is unsatisfactory as this is an expansion of 320. The variant πέποιθε in 319 is very weakly attested and probably a conjecture. Ptolemy of Ascalon took ὅς μέν as demonstrative, meaning 'one man', as in later examples of ὅς μέν ... ὅ δέ, etc. (Hrd/A 319), which is un-Homeric. Moreover the use of ἀλλά has no real point here (cf. Leaf).

320 'Thoughtlessly wheels wide to this side and that.' For ἀφραδέως cf. 426. At 309 and 466 ἑλίσσειν refers to taking the turn, and presumably the point is that one should not lose time by covering unnecessary ground at the turn (cf. 323).

321 πλανόωνται: only here in Homer, but common later.

322 κέρδεα: cf. 515 where Antilokhos is said to have defeated Menelaos κέρδεσιν, οὔ τι τάχει γε.

323–5 'Always keeping his eye on the turning-post wheels close to it, and he does not forget how from the start to keep (his horses) taut with the ox-hide reins, but he holds them steadily in hand, and fixes his gaze on the competitor in the lead.' Here, as elsewhere in this episode, one might suspect the use of the technical language of racing, for example in τανύσῃ: cf. 16.375 τανύοντο δὲ μώνυχες ἵπποι, 475 ἐν ῥυτῆρσι τάνυσθεν, 23.403 τιταίνετον (etc.).

326–33 The turning-post is described in great detail, suggesting that it will play an important part in the actual race. Here however the poet surprises us, since in the event all the attention will focus on the return lap (373ff.). In the context of Nestor's speech, however, the circumstantial details add credibility and focus attention on this crucial mark (326 σῆμα). Leaf fails to see the point: 'The whole passage is hopelessly obscure ... 328.

An irrelevant line and totally unlike Homer ... 331 ... no evidence whatever in antiquity for wooden posts having been used for sepulchral monuments ...' To object as he does that it is odd for Nestor to know about the race-course before Akhilleus has fixed it (358) is absurdly pedantic.

326 = *Od.* 11.126 (cf. *Od.* 23.273). Here the σῆμα is (*a*) the turning-post, marked out (358 σήμηνε) by Akhilleus, (*b*) a mark for Antilokhos to watch out for, and (*c*) coincidentally, it may also be a funerary σῆμα (331).

327 ὅσον τ' ὄργυι': the phrase ὅσον τ' ὄργυιαν recurs at *Od.* 9.325, 10.167, and ὄργυια is used only here in the *Iliad*.

328 τὸ μὲν οὐ καταπύθεται ὄμβρῳ: bT quote Theophrastus (*HP* 5.4.3) for the view that in some circumstances certain types of wood do not rot, in response to a difficulty raised by early critics as to why the post was not rotten, of which there are echoes in Aristotle (*Soph. El.* 166b1ff., *Poet.* 1461a21ff.). The most probable interpretation of what Aristotle says is that an earlier Homeric scholar, Hippias of Thasos (86 B 20 D–K), proposed the reading οὗ instead of οὐ in this line, giving the meaning 'part of this is rotted by rain' (cf. Wackernagel, *Kleine Schriften* 1077ff.). Leaf rightly describes this as marking 'the low water of Homeric criticism'. καταπύθειν occurs only here and at *HyAp* 371; cf. πύθειν *Il.* 4.174 etc.

329 The whiteness of the stones makes them a conspicuous mark: cf. 453–5 and on 22.294 λευκάσπιδα. ἐρηρέδαται means 'are fixed into the ground' (so *Etymologicum Magnum* s.v.), or alternatively 'are propped against it'; cf. 284.

330 ἐν ξυνοχῆσιν ὁδοῦ: 'at the place where the track narrows' or 'at the point where the two laps of the race meet' (cf. AT, Eust. 1304.17). In either case, it must refer to the turning-point. ξυνοχή occurs only here in Homer (cf. Aristotle, A.R., etc.).

λεῖος δ' ἱππόδρομος ἀμφίς: 'and there is smooth running for horses on either side (of the turning)'. ἱππόδρομος also occurs only here in early literature, and later means specifically a race-course for chariots (Pl. *Critias* 117c etc.). The point presumably is that this makes it easier to risk going really close to the turn.

331 Cf. 7.89 ἀνδρὸς μὲν τόδε σῆμα πάλαι κατατεθνηῶτος. The uncertainty as to whether it is a grave-marker or not is significant, suggesting that the landscape may have had many anonymous minor monuments of this kind (cf. 11.371–2 with comment). The objection by Heyne and Leaf that wooden posts were not used in this way is aptly answered by Eustathius' comparison (1304.20) with *Od.* 11.77 πῆξαί τ' ἐπὶ τύμβῳ ἐρετμόν.

332–3 Instead of both these verses Aristarchus apparently read ἠὲ σκῖρος ἔην, νῦν αὖ θέτο τέρματ' Ἀχιλλεύς, and according to T he took σκῖρος as meaning 'a root'. Why he preferred this text is quite unclear.

332 νύσσα is used only in this book of the *Iliad* (4×) and once in *Od.*

(8.121); it is rare later (Theocr. *Id.* 24.119, etc.). It is probably connected with νύσσω and means 'the thing which one touches' in turning, and so is a more concrete expression than τέρμα. For ἐπὶ προτέρων ἀνθρώπων cf. 5.637.

334–41 Nestor advises Antilokhos to steer as close as possible to the turn, leaning a little to the left and urging on the right-hand horse: the left-hand horse should just clear the turn, almost touching it with the nave of the wheel, but avoiding a crash. Cf. the chariot-race in Sophocles' *Electra* 720–2:

> κεῖνος δ' ὑπ' αὐτὴν ἐσχάτην στήλην ἔχων
> ἔχριμπτ' ἀεὶ σύριγγα, δεξιὸν δ' ἀνεὶς
> σειραῖον ἵππον εἶργε τὸν προσκείμενον

and Orestes' crash (743ff.).

335 ἐϋπλέκτῳ ἐνὶ δίφρῳ: cf. 436 δίφρους ... ἐϋπλεκέας, and similar expressions at Hes. *Aspis* 63, 306, 370. The epithet refers to the plaited leather thongs which were used for the breastwork of the chariot: see on 5.727–8, and Lorimer, *HM* 326, V. Karageorghis, *Salamis* v (Nicosia 1973) text p. 73, Crouwel, *Chariots* 59ff. Plato (*Ion* 537A) quotes κλινθῆναι δὲ καὶ αὐτὸς ἐϋξέστῳ ἐνὶ δίφρῳ, and Xenophon (*Symp.* 4.6) has ἐϋξέστου ἐπὶ δίφρου.

336 ἐπ' ἀρίστερα τοῖιν: 'to the left of the horses'.

337 κένσαι: only here in Homer; cf. Pindar, *P.* 1.28, etc., also 387, 430 κέντρον, and related words. The *Suda* quotes the proverb κεντεῖν τὸν πῶλον περὶ τὴν νύσσαν, of impetuous haste.

339–40 For πλήμνη ('hub') cf. 5.726 with comment, and for δοάσσεται see on 13.445–8. ἄκρον must refer to the edge or surface of the turning-post. The separation of κύκλου ποιητοῖο from πλήμνη is unusual.

342–3 This is a typically gnomic conclusion to the detailed advice in the previous verses. Verse 343 recalls the point of 313–14, and the alliteration of π and φ may be designed for emphasis. There were ancient variants ἀεικίη in 342 (Apollonius), and ἔσσεαι in 343 (T).

344 παρεξελάσηισθα: cf. 24.342 παρὲξ ... ἔλασσαν, 3× *Od.*

345 παρέλθηι: most MSS read παρέλθοι, which is unusual after the subjunctive ἔληισι, but surely not impossible (cf. Chantraine, *GH* II 248). The optative perhaps anticipates the mood of 346: 'there is no one who may catch you ... nor who could pass you, not even if he were driving ...'

346–7 Arion, Adrestos' divine horse, is a creature belonging primarily to the cycle of Theban legends. He was certainly referred to in the *Thebais* (fr. 4 Allen = Davies, *EGF* fr. 6A = Pausanias 8.25.8), although from what Pausanias says it looks as if his parentage was not specified there. According to the D-scholium on 346 he was the offspring of Poseidon (in the form of a horse) and Erinus, and this is said to derive from the Cyclic poets. As

Wilamowitz saw (*Der Glaube der Hellenen*, Berlin 1931, I 399), Homer quite possibly knew of a genealogy of this kind for Arion, but is characteristically vague in referring to such fantastic stories, which are common in the Cyclic poems. Cf. R. Janko, *CQ* 36 (1986) 51–5.

348 Laomedon inherited these horses, which were also divine, from Tros: see on 291, and especially 5.265–70. For οἳ ἐνθάδε γ᾽ ἔτραφεν ἐσθλοί cf. 21.279 ὃς ἐνθάδε γ᾽ ἔτραφ᾽ ἄριστος (with comment). Here too we might possibly read ἔτραφον (intransitive), with a few MSS.

350 ἑκάστου πείρατ᾽: 'the ways of achieving each thing'; cf. *Od.* 3.433 where a smith's tools are called πείρατα τέχνης, and Pindar, *P.* 4.220 πείρατ᾽ ἀέθλων δείκνυεν, etc., and see on 6.143.

351 Meriones rounds off the list of competitors. He will come last in the race itself, apart from Eumelos who crashes. bT suggest that the poet includes him because he has in mind the ensuing quarrel of his commander Idomeneus and Locrian Aias (450–98): see on 450–1, where Idomeneus is watching the race from a vantage-point.

352–8 The drawing of lots determines the placing of the contestants. Cf. 7.170–99, where lots are drawn to decide who is to fight Hektor. μεταστοιχί ('in a line') in 358 was taken by Aristarchus as meaning that they were drawn up in file (Arn/AT), but this seems very improbable. The point presumably is that the person who draws first takes the inmost place on the left, giving an advantage at the turn. We do not have much information about starting arrangements for later chariot-races, but at Olympia Pausanias describes a system designed to ensure that all the chariots started in line abreast (6.20.10–14); cf. Gardiner, *Sports* 453–5. The allotment here conveniently confuses the natural order of excellence, like a handicap, putting the best charioteer last, and Antilokhos before Eumelos.

358 = 757. μεταστοιχί occurs nowhere else.

358–61 As the turning-post is far away Phoinix is set to keep an eye on the race at this crucial point. Cf. the judge who sits by the turning-post in a foot-race, on a vase in Würzburg: Harris, *Athletes* pl. 4b and p. 161.

360 Phoinix is not given this description elsewhere, but this is the only time he is named in the accusative. He was last mentioned at 19.311.

361 μεμνέῳτο: an unusual form, presumably by metathesis of quantity from μεμνήοιτο (Chantraine, *GH* I 71, 465). At 24.745 the MSS have μεμνήμην, and later Attic has both μεμνῷτο and μεμνῇτο.

δρόμους was Aristarchus' reading (Did/AT), and it is that of a few of our MSS, against the vulgate δρόμου. The former would be better suited to a race with several laps and it is not clear why Aristarchus preferred it: δρόμου seems more appropriate here. ἀληθείην occurs only here and at 24.407 in *Il.*, but 7× *Od.*

(b) *362–447 The race. The start is described, and the race itself in general terms. On the return lap Eumelos takes the lead and Diomedes is just behind, until Apollo and Athene intervene. Athene makes Eumelos crash, and Diomedes takes the lead, with Menelaos behind. Antilokhos overtakes Menelaos where the track is narrow, and he has to give way to avoid a collision. Menelaos complains that Antilokhos is driving recklessly and begins to close the gap behind him*

As with the battle scenes, the detailed narrative of individual conflicts is preceded by a general description which very vividly gives a picture of the chariots bounding over the plain, and portrays the emotions of the competitors. This is followed by two 'duels', the contests between Eumelos and Diomedes and between Menelaos and Antilokhos (cf. A. Köhnken, *Hermes* 109 (1981) 144). In the first of these the gods intervene, just as in the battle scenes, Athene aiding Diomedes as previously and Eumelos being helped by Apollo, who had been the guardian of his horses at home in Pherai (cf. bT 383). In the second it is human guile that gives Antilokhos the advantage. For artistic representations (especially the François Vase) see Johansen, *Iliad in Early Greek Art* 86–92, *LIMC* I. 1, pp. 121–2.

362–72 The high frequency of periodic and integral enjambment adds to the dramatic effect. The opening motifs of the charioteers urging on their horses, and of the horses racing over the plain and raising clouds of dust (362–6) are repeated more briefly at the end (371–2), rounding off the passage. See also on 499–506.

362 ἅμα, i.e. all at the same moment, is much more effective than the variant ἄρα. Cf. S. *El.* 711–13 οἱ δ' ἅμα | ἵπποις ὁμοκλήσαντες ἡνίας χεροῖν | ἔσεισαν (where the whole passage imitates this part of the Homeric race). Virgil has this passage in mind at *G.* 3.103–12.

363 πέπληγόν θ' ἱμᾶσιν: this probably means that they shook the reins on the horses' necks, as understood by Sophocles, although Delebecque argues that ἵμαντες can mean 'whips' (*Cheval* 185), and LSJ gives this sense here; the word is used of a whip in some late Greek passages.

364–6 ἐσσυμένως ... ὦκα ... ταχέως: the recurrent adverbs stress the eagerness and speed. Verse 364 is similar to 2.785 = 3.14 ἐρχομένων· μάλα δ' ὦκα διέπρησσον πεδίοιο (and 3.13 refers to the dust storm raised by the two armies). For 365–6 cf. also 2.150–1 ποδῶν δ' ὑπένερθε κονίη | ἵστατ' ἀειρομένη, etc. νόσφι νεῶν (365) shows that the race began near the ships.

367 Cf. 1.529 χαῖται ἐπερρώσαντο, *Od.* 2.148 μετὰ πνοιῆς ἀνέμοιο.

368–9 These verses suggest the dangerous bumpiness of the course, as the light vehicles hurtle and bound over it.

370 πάτασσε δὲ θυμὸς ἑκάστου: cf. 7.216 θυμὸς ἐνὶ στήθεσσι πάτασσεν, 13.282.

372 This verse is echoed in 449. Cf. 13.820 κονίοντες πεδίοιο.

373-6 The turn is not described (see on 326–33). This must refer to the return lap, when the horses go flat out (375). ἂψ ἐφ' ἁλὸς πολιῆς must mean that they are going back from the plain towards the sea. This is Aristarchus' reading and that of most of our MSS, as against the ancient variant ἀφ' ἁλός. He apparently thought the race took place between the sea and the Achaean wall, so he presumably put the finish near the sea (cf. bT, Eust. on 365).

375-6 ἄφαρ δ' ἵπποισι τάθη δρόμος means 'at once (after the turn) the horses ran full stretch' (see on 323–5). αἱ Φηρητιάδαο are the mares of Eumelos, grandson of Pheres (2.763). Notice the distinction between Eumelos' mares and Diomedes' stallions. Cf. 407–9, where Antilokhos tells his stallions that it would be disgraceful to be beaten by Menelaos' mare Aithe.

375-81 These verses are echoed in the foot-race (758–66): 758–9 resemble 375–6; for ἐκφέρειν ('race ahead') cf. also Xen. *Eq.* 3.4 ('run away'). The vivid description of the closeness of the contestants (378–81) is echoed by 760–6; cf. especially 765 with 380–1. ἐπιβησομένοισιν (379) means 'being on the point of mounting', as at 5.46; cf. *Od.* 11.608 αἰεὶ βαλέοντι ἐοικώς. In 380–1 θέρμετο agrees with μετάφρενον as if the intervening phrase were a parenthesis (cf. Chantraine, *GH* II 19). For the formular phrase μετάφρενον εὖρέε τ' ὤμω cf. 16.791–2n. The rest of 381 means 'with their heads lying right on top of him they sped on'. Cf. 13.385 τὼ δὲ πνείοντε κατ' ὤμων, 17.502 ἐμπνείοντε μεταφρένῳ (both of horses); S. *El.* 718–19 ὁμοῦ γὰρ ἀμφὶ νῶτα καὶ τροχῶν βάσεις | ἤφριζον, εἰσέβαλλον ἱππικαὶ πνοαί; Virgil, *G.* 3.111 (the charioteers) *umescunt spumis flatuque sequentum*. Demetrius (*On Style* 210) praises the vividness of 379–81.

382-4 As in the battle scenes an event which was about to happen is dramatically averted by divine intervention (cf. Reinhardt, *IuD* 107ff.). Here one could rationalize 384 by saying that Diomedes dropped his whip, and this is attributed to the god's action. But at 388–90 the return of the whip by Athene must be a supernatural event, similar to her return of Akhilleus' spear at 22.276–7.

382 Cf. 527 τῶ κέν μιν παρέλασσ' οὐδ' ἀμφήριστον ἔθηκεν. ἀμφήριστος occurs only here in Homer, and then in Hellenistic and later literature. In later Greek a drawn contest is described as ἱερά, because the prize was consecrated to the god.

385 χωομένοιο: this verb often indicates frustrated distress more than anger; e.g. 22.291 etc.; cf. Arn/A, bT and A. W. H. Adkins, *JHS* 89 (1969) 13–14 and 17.

387 οἱ δέ οἱ was Aristarchus' reading, whereas Ptolemy of Ascalon preferred οἱ δὲ οἵ (=*sui*, 'his own'): cf. Hrd/A and Erbse, *Beiträge zur Überlieferung der Iliasscholien* (Munich 1960) 317 n. 1. The latter seems preferable for 'his own'. ἐβλάφθησαν ('were thwarted') is used, as often, with reference to a god; see on 22.15.

388–9 The interlaced word-order is unusual, and presumably designed to juxtapose the two gods' names in the same verse. ἐλεφηράμενος seems to mean something like βλάπτειν here, e.g. 'thwarting', or 'frustrating'. This rare epic word occurs only here in *Il.*; cf. *Od.* 19.565 where dreams which come through the gate of ivory (ἐλέφαντος) ἐλεφαίρονται, ἔπε' ἀκράαντα φέροντες (Privitera translates 'dannegiano', i.e. 'are harmful'); and Hes. *Th.* 330 where the Nemean lion ἐλεφαίρετο φῦλ' ἀνθρώπων, where it must mean 'damage'. Hesychius has ἐλεφῆραι· ἀπατῆσαι, and the verb is not otherwise attested.

391–2 κοτέουσα echoes 383. ἧξε ('broke') is aorist from ἄγνυμι, contracted from ἔαξε. Cf. *Od.* 19.539 κατ' αὐχένας ἧξε, and Chantraine, *GH* 1 34. bT observe that this verse (and perhaps the following ones; cf. bT 396) imitates with its roughness the sound of the breaking chariot.

392–4 Cf. 6.38–43, where Adrestos' horses break the end of their yoke-pole (ῥυμός) and run free, while he crashes (42 = 23.394); also 16.370–1, where many horses do this at the Achaean trench.

393 ἀμφὶς ὁδοῦ is 'off the track' (so bTD), and ἐλύσθη 'rolled' or 'slipped' to the ground (cf. Mazon, *REA* 42 (1940) 260–1).

394–6 Verse 394 = 6.42. All three verbs occur only in these verses in Homer, and θρυλίσσειν only once later in Lycophron. περιδρύφθη and θρυλίχθη are again harsh-sounding words (bT 396). The whole passage very vividly describes Eumelos' crash.

396–7 τὼ δέ οἱ ὄσσε ... φωνή = 17.695–6.

398–400 Diomedes skilfully avoids a collision and takes the lead, aided by Athene's inspiration of his horses.

401–57 We now come to the second contest, between Menelaos and Antilokhos, the most exciting incident in the games.

402 Cf. 19.399 σμερδαλέον δ' ἵπποισιν ἐκέκλετο πατρὸς ἑοῖο.

403–17 Antilokhos' speech of encouragement to his horses is similar to those addressed to a human audience, with its appeal to their sense of shame, its threat of reprisals if they fail, and its practical promise of support at the end.

403 'Get a move on, you two as well, go flat out!' ἐμβαίνειν is really an athletic term from other sports, like καταβαίνειν, meaning to enter the contest (cf. 'get in there and win!'): cf. E. *El.* 113, Ar. *Ran.* 377, *Ec.* 478, and Eustathius' comments here (1308.11ff.). For τιταίνετον see on 323–5.

405–6 Aristarchus (Arn/A) athetized these two verses, objecting that Antilokhos cannot know about Athene's aid, and also that it is not necessary to say they are Diomedes' horses as this is clear in any case. The first objection seems unreasonable, since it would be quite natural to infer divine aid for Diomedes from Athene here from previous occasions. The second point fits in with Aristarchus' general view of the way in which verses are added to fill out the sense. They *could* have been added for this reason, but in themselves there is nothing wrong with them. οἷσιν Ἀθήνη ... ἔθηκεν resembles 399–400.

408 ἐλεγχείην: cf. 342, and 22.100. In military speeches of exhortation the Achaeans are called ἐλέγχεα, ἐλεγχέες (4.242 etc.).

409 For Αἴθη θῆλυς ἐοῦσα cf. 19.97 Ἥρη θῆλυς ἐοῦσα (in the context of Zeus, the highest god, being deceived by 'Herē, a female'). τίη λείπεσθε, φέριστοι; is an urgent and cajoling appeal.

410 = *Od.* 16.440, and cf. *Il.* 1.212 etc. ὧδε γὰρ ἐξερέω, τὸ δὲ καὶ τετελεσμένον ἔσται. A verse of this kind is often used to introduce a threat.

411–14 Cf. 8.186–91 (with comment), where Hektor appeals to his horses to repay the provisions which Andromakhe gave them: νῦν μοι τὴν κομιδὴν ἀποτίνετον ... 191 ἀλλ' ἐφομαρτεῖτον καὶ σπεύδετον ... Schol. A mentions a variant βιοτή for κομιδή in 411, but the parallel with book 8 makes the case for κομιδή, and βιοτή only occurs in Homer at *Od.* 4.565 (cf. Wackernagel, *Kleine Schriften* II 1136).

412 This verse was condemned by Agar (*CR* 14 (1900) 4) as absurd, and as added to fill the sense of 411. He also disliked the contraction of -κτενέει to -κτενεῖ (but cf. 15.65, 15.68, 19.104). The first objection is literal-minded.

413 'If through your losing heart we win a worse prize.' The dual ἀποκηδήσαντε with φερώμεθα is odd. It is easy to say that the poet is no longer aware of the proper force of the dual, but it may mean 'you and I together', or else be influenced by the other duals in this passage: cf. Arn/A, Chantraine, *GH* II 27–8. ἀποκηδεῖν occurs only here in Homer, and once later in Sophron (78).

414 ἐφομαρτεῖτον: Did/AT mention a variant ἐφαμαρτεῖτον, which Aristarchus probably preferred. At 12.412 he read ἐφαμαρτεῖτε, and generally he wished to read ἁμαρτῇ, ἁμαρτεῖν etc., probably rightly, as the forms with *omicron* are likely to be due to Attic influence: cf. Wackernagel, *Sprachliche Untersuchungen* 70–1.

415–16 Antilokhos' skill and watchfulness echo Nestor's advice (cf. 312–18, 323, 326), although he uses a different ruse. For στεινωπῷ ἐν ὁδῷ cf. 7.143, and 419–21, 427 below. παραδύμεναι ('to slip past') is aorist of παραδύεσθαι, which occurs only here in Homer, but is common in classical Greek.

417–18 ὣς ἔφαθ' ... ἐπιδραμέτην: this is repeated at 446–7, after Menelaos' briefer speech of encouragement to his horses. Cf. Sarpedon's exhortation to his men at 12.408–12, followed at 413–14 by ὣς ἔφαθ', οἱ δὲ ἄνακτος ὑποδείσαντες ὁμοκλὴν | μᾶλλον ἐπέβρισαν ...

418–24 'And soon after warlike Antilokhos saw a narrowing of the hollow way. There was a gully in the ground, where pent-up torrent water had broken away part of the track, and hollowed out all the ground: along this

Menelaos drove, to avoid the wheels running side by side. But Antilokhos turned aside his horses and drove them outside the track, and diverting them a little he kept pressing on.'

The exact details of how Antilokhos succeeds in overtaking Menelaos are not immediately clear. It looks as if he is beginning to draw level at the point where they are reaching the narrow part of the track. Here Menelaos drives along what is left of the road, and Antilokhos begins to drive outside the track. At some stage he has to rejoin it: when he does so, it is too narrow for both of them and Menelaos gives way to avoid a collision (429–37). In any case, it is clear from the sequel that Antilokhos is engaging in dangerous and unfair tactics, even if he never quite admits that he was guilty (cf. 570–95).

The attempt by M. Gagarin (*CP* 78 (1983) 35–9) to prove that Antilokhos overtakes at the turn, and so is following Nestor's advice, fails to explain satisfactorily the point of 373–5, which explicitly states that they were on the return lap.

420 ῥωχμός: only here in Homer, and then in Hellenistic poetry and later prose. Herodian read ῥωγμός.

421–2 Aristophanes read ἔνερθεν instead of ἅπαντα (Did/T), and for τῇ Aristarchus read ᾗ. For ἔχειν meaning 'drive' see on 13.326–7. ἀματροχίη occurs only here in Homer, and then in Hellenistic poetry; cf. *Od.* 15.451 ἀματροχόων (or ἅμα τροχόων). It most probably refers to the two chariots running side by side, rather than to an actual collision of wheels. Porphyry (quoted by Erbse on 422) criticizes Callimachus (fr. 383.10) for using the word as if it meant the same as ἁρματροχίη, which occurs at line 505.

424 παρακλίνας presumably means that he followed a diversion, picking up the sense of 423. Schol. A mentions a variant παρακλινθείς, and a few MSS read παρεκκλίνας, which was probably Eustathius' reading (1309.12) and would be possible.

425–47 Menelaos' three speeches (426–8, 439–41, 443–5) are all only three verses long, reflecting both the urgency of the situation and also his own laconic character (cf. 3.213–15). In 426–8 the succession of abrupt, brief clauses is dramatically effective, and in 439–43 there is an unusual run of five verses without any enjambment. Cf. (for example) the staccato urgency of 16.126–30, and Higbie, *Measure and Music* 69–72.

426 ἱππάζεσθαι occurs only here in Homer, but is common in classical Greek.

427 εὐρυτέρη παρελάσσαι ('there will be more room to pass') seems to be the reading of T and one papyrus. εὐρυτέρη παρελάσσαις (optative), read by most MSS, is possible but less attractive.

428 ἅρματι κύρσας: either 'striking my chariot' or 'hitting me with your chariot'.

430 ὡς οὐκ ἀΐοντι ἐοικώς: 'as though like one who does not hear'. The double use of ὡς ... ἐοικώς stresses that Antilokhos is *pretending* not to hear.

431–3 ὅσσα δὲ ... τόσσον ἐπιδραμέτην: for such comparisons cf. 15.358–9 ὅσον τ' ἐπὶ δουρὸς ἐρωή | γίγνεται, ὁππότ' ἀνὴρ σθένεος πειρώμενος ᾗσι (with comment); 16.589–92 ὅσση δ' αἰγανέης ῥιπὴ τανᾶοῖο τέτυκται | ἥν ῥά τ' ἀνὴρ ἀφέη πειρώμενος ἢ ἐν ἀέθλῳ ... | τόσσον ἐχώρησαν Τρῶες ...; and similarly 10.351–4 ἀλλ' ὅτε δή ῥ' ἀπέην ὅσσον τ' ἐπὶ οὖρα πέλονται | ἡμιόνων ... | τὼ μὲν ἐπεδραμέτην ...

431 δίσκου οὖρα κατωμαδίοιο: 'the limits of a discus swung from the shoulder'; cf. also 523 ἐς δίσκουρα. κατωμάδιος occurs only here in Homer, and then in Hellenistic poetry; cf. κατωμαδόν 15.352, 23.500.

433 With αἱ δ' contrast 446 οἱ δέ of these horses; T reads τοὶ δέ here. One is female, one male (295). ἠρώησαν ὀπίσσω means that they slowed down and fell behind.

435–7 An elaborate tricolon to describe the potential crash and its results. Notice the parallel structure of the first hemistichs of 435 and 436, with their heavy spondaic scansion and two quadrisyllabic verbs, echoed more lightly by the verb in the same position in 437. The third, longer, clause forms the crescendo of the series, and effectively juxtaposes the contestants' eagerness for victory and their humiliating fall.

435 συγκυρεῖν (cf. 428 κύρσας) occurs nowhere else in Homer, but is common later. For δίφρους ... ἐϋπλεκέας cf. 335, with comment. ἀναστρέφειν occurs only here in *Il.*; cf. *Od.* 13.326 ἀναστρέφομαι.

439–41 Menelaos' first speech was more restrained. Now that he realizes Antilokhos' ploy is deliberate, he vents his feelings in an angry outburst.

439 Cf. 3.365 = *Od.* 20.201 Ζεῦ πάτερ, οὔ τις σεῖο θεῶν ὀλοώτερος ἄλλος; also *Il.* 15.569 (Menelaos) Ἀντίλοχ', οὔ τις σεῖο νεώτερος ἄλλος Ἀχαιῶν.

440 ἔρρ', ἐπεὶ οὔ σε ...: cf. 8.164 ἔρρε ... ἐπεὶ οὔκ ..., 22.498 ἔρρ' οὕτως· οὐ σός γε ..., *Od.* 10.75 ἔρρ', ἐπεὶ ..., etc. ἔρρε is a coarse expression, expressing strong emotion. For the rest of the verse see on 305. φάμεν is imperfect here.

441 Cf. 581–5, where Menelaos challenges Antilokhos to swear an oath that he has not deliberately used a trick to defeat him.

442–5 Verse 442 = 8.184. For ἔστατον ἀχνυμένω κῆρ (443) cf. 284. | φθήσονται τούτοισι ... | ἢ ὑμῖν are emphatic at the beginning of 444 and 445: '*their* feet and knees will tire first before *yours* do'. For this construction (φθάνειν ... ἢ ...) cf. *Od.* 11.58, Hdt. 6.108.

446–7 See on 417–18.

(c) *448–98 The quarrel between Idomeneus and the lesser Aias. Among the spectators Idomeneus says that Diomedes seems to be in the lead, but Aias abusively contradicts him, saying that Eumelos is. Akhilleus intervenes to prevent the quarrel from deteriorating*

This entertaining episode belongs to the type where the scene shifts from action to debate at a dramatic point, leaving the outcome in suspense.

The closest parallel is with 22.166–87, where after the simile comparing Akhilleus and Hektor to racehorses at funeral games the scene changes to the gods as spectators debating what is to happen (see comment). The poet shows us how violent are the emotions just below the surface: the quarrel flares up over nothing, in the most realistic way.

The quarrels arising from the chariot-race echo the main themes of the poem, Akhilleus' quarrel with Agamemnon and his fatal wrath. Now that this passion has finally spent itself, it is Akhilleus himself who controls the emotions of his companions, a remarkable reversal.

The scene also contrasts the characters of Idomeneus and Aias, the former polite, cautious and unassertive in his opening speech (cf. 4.266–71, with comment), the latter abusive and unreasonable, accusing Idomeneus of the very fault from which he himself suffers most (474 with AbT, 478–9 and 483–4). It is no coincidence that this foul-mouthed character will end the foot-race ignominiously by slipping in cow-dung and getting a mouthful of it, to the derision of the spectators (774–84 with AbT 777; cf. Thersites in book 2). The lesser Aias' inability to control his tongue will ultimately cause his destruction by the gods (cf. *Od.* 4.499–511, and see on 2.527).

448–9 The spectators of this race are well portrayed on the early-sixth-century Attic vase painting by Sophilos, which shows them on a stepped platform, some seated and others standing. Some of them are gesticulating excitedly as they look towards the four horses who approach, drawing a chariot. The nearest of the leading horses is white, outlined in purple (a reminiscence of 453–5?), two others have black faces and purple necks, and the fourth is black; cf. P. E. Arias, M. Hirmer and B. Shefton, *A History of Greek Vase Painting* (London 1962) pl. 39; and the description by Johansen, *Iliad in Early Greek Art* 91–2. In the scene of the funeral games of Pelias on the Chest of Cypselus the spectators were also portrayed (Pausanias 5.17.9). Cf. also Laser, *Arch. Hom.* T 83–5. Verse 449 resembles 372.

450–1 bT comment that Idomeneus was clearly anxious about his companion Meriones, and so went up to a vantage point to watch: not an unreasonable guess as to why the poet should choose to introduce him at this point. Cf. 681–2, where Diomedes supports his cousin Eurualos, and 24.697–702, where Kassandre is first to see Priam's return. For ἐν περιωπῇ (451) cf. 14.8, *Od.* 10.146 ἐς περιωπήν.

452–3 τοῖο ... ἔγνω: literally 'and hearing him while still afar urging on his horses he recognized him'. For ὁμοκλητῆρος ἀκούσας | cf. 12.273. The chiastic structure of 452–3 is neat, the two similar verbs being juxtaposed at the beginning of 453.

454 τόσον is 'so far', i.e. but for the mark on his brow; cf. 18.378–9, 22.322–5. φοῖνιξ ('chestnut') is used only here in Homer as an adjective.

455 περίτροχον ἠΰτε μήνη: 'circular, like the (full) moon'. περίτροχος is found only here in Homer, later in Hellenistic poetry, etc. μήνη recurs in Homer only at 19.374, σελήνη at 18.484.

456 = 271 etc. (see comment).

457–72 Idomeneus' speech has a ring-structure (cf. Lohmann, *Reden* 29–30):

(a) ⎰457–8   Do I alone see the horses, or do you too?
    ⎱459–60   The leading horses and driver seem different from before.
(b)   460–1   The others must have had an accident on the plain.
(c)   462–4   They were first round the turn, but I cannot see them now.
(b)   465–8   Perhaps the accident happened at the turn itself.
(a) ⎰469–70   You look as well, for I cannot see clearly.
    ⎱470–2   I think the leader is Diomedes.

Throughout the speech the suspense is built up, and at the end the postponement of the name Diomedes, and the increasing precision of his description in 470–2, are surely designed by the poet for deliberate effect. The frequency of integral enjambment (5× in 16 verses) reflects the excitement of the speaker.

457 = 2.79 etc.

458 αὐγάζομαι: 'discern', perhaps with the idea of seeing clearly (e.g. cf. A.R. 1.155 of Lunkeus); cf. West on Hes. *Erga* 478, 'I suppose the essential idea is "fix the gaze on" a particular object.' It occurs only here in Homer. The polite question at 457–8 resembles Nestor's in a similar situation at 10.533–4.

459–60 This is directly contradicted by Aias at 480–1, echoing Idomeneus' words. παροίτεροι ('in front') recurs at 459 and 480, and not again until Apollonius Rhodius (4.982); cf. Chantraine, *GH* I 258. For ἰνδάλλεται ('appears') cf. 17.214 and 2× *Od*.

460–1 αἱ δέ refers to Eumelos' mares, explained by αἳ ... ἦσαν. αὐτοῦ is 'out there', with ἐν πεδίῳ. κεῖσε means 'up to that point'; Zenodotus and Aristophanes read κεῖθι.

462–8 What Idomeneus presumably means is that he saw Eumelos' horses in front as they *reached* the turn, but could not see clearly what happened *after* that as they actually went round it, and he assumes that the accident happened there (so bT 462–3, although T adds that this actually *was* the place where Eumelos crashed). Several modern scholars have wished to delete 462–4, because they thought 462 was inconsistent with 465–6 (e.g. cf. Ameis–Hentze, Leaf). Von der Mühll suggested reading προτί instead of περί in 462, to remove the problem (*Ausgewählte Kleine Schriften*, Basel 1976, 10–11).

Another objection is that if Idomeneus could see the turn he should be able to see clearly who is in the lead on the home stretch. But Idomeneus may be modestly affecting uncertainty because he does not want to show off: this is what Eustathius quotes as the view of 'the ancient commentators' (1310.41 and 1311.12ff.), and it looks as if this was what bT said (on 458: one should probably read here, as in Eustathius, θρύπτονται γὰρ ὡς ⟨μὴ⟩ ἀκριβέστερον θεώμενοί τινες· ⟨οἱ δὲ⟩ καὶ ἐν ἤθει καταλαζονεύονται τῶν πολλῶν, i.e. among spectators of the games some are modest and unassertive, whereas others disdainfully show off their knowledge). That this is correct is suggested both by 450–5 and also by 485–7 where Idomeneus shows that in reality he is convinced that he is right.

462 τάς is 'those ones' (demonstrative). For περὶ τέρμα βαλούσας ('racing round the turn') cf. 639 πλήθει πρόσθε βαλόντες, and 11.722 εἰς ἅλα βάλλων. The intransitive use of βάλλειν is very rare (cf. Fraenkel on A. *Ag.* 1172, pp. 534–5), and Leaf may well be right to see its use here and at 639 as another instance of 'racing slang' (cf. also 572).

463 οὔ πη: there was an ancient variant οὔ πω, which some of our MSS read.

464 παπταίνετον: Aristarchus (Did/AT) read παπταίνεται.

465–6 This is presumably an alternative suggestion to 460–1. For οὐδὲ δυνάσθη cf. *Od.* 5.319; the usual Homeric form is δυνήσατο. Verse 466 means 'to keep good control at the post, and he failed to hold the turn'. For εὖ σχεθέειν cf. 325 etc.

467 σύν θ': A records a variant κατά θ', which some MSS have.

468 ἐξηρώησαν: 'swerved off the course'; the compound verb occurs only here in Homer, later only at Theocr. *Id.* 25.189 ἐξηρώησε κελεύθου.

469 ἀνασταδόν recurs at 9.671, and apparently nowhere else.

470–2 δοκέει ... Διομήδης: For the effect of climax see on 457–72. Aristarchus (Arn/A) athetized 471, as out of place in the mouth of Idomeneus, but ἀνήρ seems to require qualification, and the line adds to the climactic effect (cf. von der Mühll, *Ausgewählte Kleine Schriften* 9). Neither 471 nor 472 occurs elsewhere to describe Diomedes. For the phrasing cf. 19.122 ἤδη ἀνήρ γέγον' ἐσθλός, ὃς Ἀργείοισιν ἀνάξει (etc.), and 7.163 (etc.) Τυδείδης ... κρατερὸς Διομήδης |. Diomedes' father Tudeus was from Aetolia, but he himself was king in Argos (14.113–25).

473–81 Aias' reply is grossly insulting, for no apparent reason. bT (on 476) say that 'his abuse is boorish: but the poet is portraying the characteristic behaviour of spectators'. The most striking feature of the speech is the repetition of λαβρεύεαι ... λαβρεύεαι ... λαβραγόρην. λαβραγόρης seems to recur only once, in Adamantius Judaeus (fourth century A.D.), λαβρεύομαι nowhere else. λαβρός in Homer is always applied to the violent natural forces of wind and water, but later it is used metaphorically of rash or loud-mouthed people (Theognis 634, Simon. 177 Bergk, Pindar, *O.* 2.86, *P.* 2.87, S. *Aj.* 1147). These words aptly characterize Aias himself here (see on 448–98).

474 τί πάρος λαβρεύεαι; : 'why have you always had such a big mouth?' For πάρος in this sense cf. 4.264, *Od.* 8.36, etc.

475 | ἵπποι ἀερσίποδες: 3.327 is the only other Homeric instance of this phrase; cf. *HyAphr* 211 | ἵππους ἀρσίποδας. The phrase πολέος πεδίοιο δίενται implies that they still have plenty of ground to cover.

476 Cf. 13.361–2, where Idomeneus is said to be μεσαιπόλιος ('grizzled').

477 For the dual ὄσσε with singular verb see on 12.466.

479 Aristarchus (Arn/AT) unjustly athetized this verse, because he thought that it was added to fill up the sense of 478, and because he misunderstood the point of παρὰ ... ἄλλοι, which implies that Idomeneus should not show off in the presence of his betters.

480 αὐταί: 'the same ones'; cf. 12.225 etc. This is much better than the variant αὖτε.

481 εὔληρα ('reins') is a rare word, only here in Homer, and later only twice in Quintus of Smyrna (4.508, 9.156), but cf. Epich. 178 αὔληρα. Evidently Neoptolemus of Parium knew of other instances (cf. bT 481). It may be related to Latin *lora* (cf. Chantraine, *Dict.* s.v.).

483–4 Cf. 3.39 = 13.769 Δύσπαρι, εἶδος ἄριστε, γυναιμανές, 17.142 Ἕκτορ, εἶδος ἄριστε, μάχης ἄρα πολλὸν ἐδεύεο, and see on 24.261. Aristarchus (Did/AT) read νεῖκος, as do some MSS, against the vulgate νείκει. κακοφραδής occurs only here in Homer, later in Apollonius (3.936) and Euphorion (98.2). For ὅτι τοι νόος ἐστὶν ἀπηνής cf. 16.35, where it is used of Akhilleus.

485 The enclitic νυν occurs in Homer only here and at 10.105. περιδώμεθον means 'let us make a bet'. This form of the first person of the dual in -θον occurs elsewhere only at S. *El.* 950 and *Ph.* 1079, and twice in Athenaeus 98A (as examples of false archaism). The variant περιδώμεθα may be right, and περιδώμεθον due to Attic influence: cf. J. Wackernagel, *Vorlesungen über Syntax* I (Basel 1920) 81–2. περιδίδοσθαι recurs at *Od.* 23.78, and several times later in comedy, suggesting a colloquial flavour. It is amusing to find betting associated with horse-racing already in Homer.

486 ἵστορα: 'arbiter'; cf. 18.501.

487 Instead of the subjunctive γνώῃς nearly all MSS read the optative γνοίης, which may well be correct: cf. Chantraine, *GH* II 271. Idomeneus now shows just how sure he is that he is right.

488–98 This is a dangerous moment, as Aias springs to his feet in anger, but the quarrel is skilfully defused by Akhilleus. Verses 490–1 recall other moments of crisis, where disaster is averted by divine rather than human intervention. One also thinks of Nestor's unsuccessful attempt at mediation between Akhilleus and Agamemnon in the quarrel in book 1 (254–84), and that of Hephaistos in the divine scene at the end of that Book (573–83). Verse 488 = 754.

490 'And then the quarrel between both would have gone still further.'

491 'Akhilleus as director of the games (ἀγωνοθέτης) is also in charge of ensuring good discipline' (bT). This was an important function of the officials who presided over Greek games in the classical period: cf. Harris, *Athletes* 157–8, on measures to keep crowds of excited spectators under control. At Olympia an early inscription calls the judges διαιτατῆρες. For καὶ φάτο μῦθον A records the variant καὶ κατέρυκε, as in 734.

492–3 Verse 492 echoes 489. Verse 493 is a weak one, and κακοῖς seems intolerable after χαλεποῖσιν: T suggests ἄναξ, which is clearly a conjecture, and κακῶς (in two MSS) is little better. The scansion of Αἴαν as if it were a spondee (στίχος λαγαρός) is also very unusual: cf. Chantraine, *GH* I 103–4. The verse was rejected by Heyne, and could well be an addition.

494 Cf. *Od.* 6.286 καὶ δ' ἄλλῃ νεμεσῶ, ἥ τις τοιαῦτά γε ῥέζοι, and 1.47 ὡς ἀπόλοιτο καὶ ἄλλος ὅ τις τοιαῦτά γε ῥέζοι. For the optative cf. Chantraine, *GH* II 248. In view of Akhilleus' earlier conduct it is ironic that he should say this now.

495–8 Again the ancient commentators find this realistic in terms of their own experience. Cf. T (on 497): 'this is just how some older and steadier spectators behave nowadays at games, telling people not to anticipate the outcome before it occurs'.

(*d*) *499–652 The end of the race and the awarding of the prizes. Diomedes takes the first prize, followed by Antilokhos, Menelaos and Meriones, with Eumelos last. Akhilleus wishes to give Eumelos second prize, but is dissuaded by Antilokhos, and gives him an extra one instead. Menelaos accuses Antilokhos of cheating, but is appeased by Antilokhos' offer to give up his prize. The last prize is given to Nestor, who recalls his own athletic exploits in youth*

This remarkable scene is the dénouement of the chariot-race, in which the consequences of the earlier events are worked out and a resolution achieved. Akhilleus considers that the prizes should be awarded according to the true merits of the contestants, irrespective of the outcome. But this, as Antilokhos objects, disregards the divine patronage which tipped the scales in favour of Diomedes. The quarrel over the second prize also develops in a way which echoes the main theme of the poem: like both Agamemnon and Akhilleus in book 1, Antilokhos feels that he is being unjustly deprived of his due and refuses to accept this. Akhilleus' resolution of this issue sparks off the following protest of Menelaos: once again injured honour is at stake and he demands justice. But this quarrel takes a very different course from the quarrel of Akhilleus and Agamemnon, for first Antilokhos yields to the older man, and then Menelaos gives way to him in turn, recognizing the value of Antilokhos' past support and friendship. The touching quality of this reconciliation is beautifully expressed by the simile at 597–600.

Finally Akhilleus, who had ignored Nestor's mediating advice in book 1, now pays a special tribute to his venerable seniority. Nestor's speech, as well as complementing his earlier one to Antilokhos, may have a paradeigmatic function like his other reminiscences, for his defeat by the sons of Aktor echoes Antilokhos' defeat of Menelaos, in the suggestion that they had an unfair advantage which they used because of their jealous eagerness for victory (638–42; cf. 639 with 572). This final exchange between Akhilleus and Nestor also sets the games in a wider context: Nestor will keep the prize as a κειμήλιον in memory of Patroklos, whom they will see no more, and for Nestor himself the days of heroic exploits are long over (618–23). Characteristically the poet looks both to past and future here, and the whole episode closes quietly, on a nostalgic note not unlike what we find in parts of the *Odyssey*.

499–506 Diomedes' rapid arrival is described in a vivid passage which resembles the start of the race at 362–72. In both, the main motifs are the same: the charioteers whipping on their horses (362–4, 500), their speed (364–5, 500–1), the clouds of dust (365–6, 502), and the chariots skimming lightly over the plain (368–9, 503–6), and both are rounded off by a final reprise of the theme of the flying horses (372, 506).

500 Cf. 15.352 μάστιγι κατωμαδὸν ἤλασεν ἵππους (with comment). μάστι is an Ionic dative of μάστις, which recurs at *Od.* 15.182; cf. the verb μαστίω. Most of our MSS substitute the more familiar form μάστιγι, which would not scan here.

501 Cf. *Od.* 13.83 ὑψόσ' ἀειρόμενοι ῥίμφα πρήσσουσι κέλευθον. The idea is the same as at 475, ἵπποι ἀερσίποδες.

502 ῥαθάμιγγες ἔβαλλον |: cf. 11.536 = 20.501. There it is used of drops or sprinklings of blood (cf. probably ῥαίνω).

503–4 Cf. 2.777 ἅρματα δ' εὖ πεπυκασμένα (with comment on 777–8). There πεπυκασμένα refers to chariots being 'closely covered' or wrapped up when stored away, whereas here it must be used to describe a facing of metal plates which covers the chariot-body: cf. 4.226 (etc.) ἅρματα ποίκιλα χαλκῷ, 10.438 ἅρμα δέ οἱ χρυσῷ τε καὶ ἀργύρῳ εὖ ἤσκηται (of Rhesos' chariot), and 8.320 = 23.509 δίφροιο ... παμφανόωντος. Chariots plated with precious metals are attested in Egypt in the mid-second millennium B.C., and it is assumed that they were used also by the Greeks in the late Bronze Age: cf. Lorimer, *HM* 327, J. Wiesner, *Arch. Hom.* F 14 and 47. The Linear B tablets certainly attest the use of silver and bronze in connexion with the wheels of chariots: cf. Ventris and Chadwick, *Documents* 369–75, and Crouwel, *Chariots* 88–90. For tin as a precious metal cf. 11.25, 18.474, etc.

The poet draws attention to the chariots' ornamentation because the whole passage is graphic in character. T comment on 503–4: 'by emphasizing its costliness he makes us marvel at the scene. He has also given life to the chariot, as if it were speeding on of its own accord.' Plutarch (*Mor.* 747E) quotes 503–4 (ἅρματα ... ἐπέτρεχον) as an example of mimetic language, where the collocation and rhythm of the words imitate the sense. His other examples (E. fr. 985 N. and Pindar, *O.* 1.20–1) suggest that he has in mind the predominantly dactylic rhythm and the lightness of sound of ἅρματα ... πεπυκασμένα κασσιτέρῳ τε, and of ὠκυπόδεσσιν ἐπέτρεχον. The verb means that the chariot ran closely behind the horses, as if about to overtake them.

504–6 οὐδέ τι πολλή ... κονίη: T rightly comments that the hyperbole is moderated and made credible by the use of πολλή. Contrast 20.226–9, of semi-divine horses, and the imitation of 23.504–6 by Quintus of Smyrna (4.516–17) οὐδ' ἀρματροχίας ἰδέειν σθένον οὐδὲ ποδοῖιν | ἐν χθονὶ σήματα, τόσσον ὑπεξέφερον δρόμον ἵπποι. See also on 764. ἀρματροχίη (505) occurs only here in Homer, and then in Hellenistic and later literature.

507–13 After the flurry and excitement of Diomedes' arrival στῆ δὲ μέσῳ ἐν ἀγῶνι suggests the dramatically abrupt halt of the horses, as sweat pours from them. All is over in no time: Diomedes has dismounted and laid down his whip, and Sthenelos has already (without delay: οὐδὲ μάτησεν) claimed the woman and tripod as prizes, and handed them over to his companions, and is beginning to unyoke the horses, before Antilokhos and Menelaos arrive. In this way the poet not only gives us a sense of the brisk and lively scene at the winning-post, but also suggests that the others are some distance behind.

507–9 πολὺς δ' ἀνεκήκιεν ἱδρώς: cf. 13.705 πολὺς ἀνακηκίει ἱδρώς, and 8.543 = *Od.* 4.39 ἵππους ... ἱδρώοντας. Delebecque (*Cheval* 54) notes the accuracy of this description: a horse sweats especially from its neck and chest (cf. also 11.282). Verse 509 = 8.320 (see comment).

510–13 Sthenelos, Diomedes' close companion, is a lively and energetic character: cf. especially 4.403–10 (with comments), and perhaps also his name and epithet here, ἴφθιμος Σθένελος suggesting strength. For οὐδὲ μάτησεν | cf. 16.474, and for the prize 23.262–4. Here Aristarchus observed that ἄγειν and φέρειν are used in their proper and distinct senses (cf. Arn/AT 512–13, and Lehrs, *De Aristarchi studiis* 137). In 513 we should keep the imperfect ἔλυεν, as it implies that Sthenelos was just unyoking the horses when Antilokhos appeared. Leaf and others objected to the ῠ, but cf. *Od.* 7.74 λύει, and Chantraine, *GH* 1 372–3.

514 Νηλήϊος: as grandson of Neleus (cf. Αἰακίδης of Akhilleus, etc.). Elsewhere this is applied to Nestor.

516–27 Menelaos has caught up, as he said he would (444–5), but just fails to overtake in time. The comparison in 517–21 is unusual in being taken from the activity described, like expressions such as 'leading by a head'. In Bronze Age and Geometric representations the horses are usually shown as very close to the chariot, and sometimes their tails appear to touch the wheels: Cf. Wiesner, *Arch. Hom.* F 44 (Abb. 8), 47 (Abb. 10), Crouwel, *Chariots* pl. 77, P. A. L. Greenhalgh, *Early Greek Warfare* (Cambridge 1973) figs. 11, 14, etc. Within 517–27 there are five examples of progressive enjambment.

For 518 cf. 22.23 (with comment). Verses 19–21 are a typical expansion of the point of comparison. οὐδέ τι πολλή is repeated from 504, and πολέος πεδίοιο θέοντος (cf. 475, and 4.424 πολέος ... θέουσαι) echoes πεδίοιο τιταινόμενος in 518, rounding off the comparison.

523 ἐς δίσκουρα: 'as much as a discus-throw' (cf. 431 with comment). δίσκουρα is an absolute *hapax*.

525 Cf. 295 Αἴθην τὴν Ἀγαμεμνονέην. Here this mare is dignified with a whole-verse description.

526 εἰ δέ κ᾽ ... γένετο: cf. 490. This is the only instance in Homer of εἴ κε with the indicative (cf. an oracle in Hdt. 1.174), but κε with indicative is commoner in the apodosis of conditionals: cf. Chantraine, *GH* II 283.

527 See on 382. Zenodotus (Arn/A) read ἢ ἀμφήριστον ἔθηκεν here too, but the point is surely that Menelaos would have actually *defeated* Antilokhos.

528–9 Μηριόνης ... Ἰδομενῆος is repeated at 860 = 888, and cf. also 113 = 124. For δουρὸς ἐρωήν cf. 15.358, 21.251 ὅσον τ᾽ ἐπὶ δουρὸς ἐρωή |.

530–1 For βάρδιστοι see on 310. ἥκιστος ('weakest') occurs only here in Homer; cf. ἦκα, and Attic ἥκιστα. The epic forms have the normal Ionic psilosis (cf. Arn/AbT). These words are thought to be related to Latin *segnis* (cf. Chantraine. *Dict.* s.v. ἦκα); σιγά ('quietly') in modern Greek has also come to mean 'slowly'. Meriones' skills lie elsewhere, in archery and javelin-throwing (850–91).

532–3 Eumelos is indeed a pitiful figure, as he appears dragging his chariot behind him, and driving his horses in front, and he evokes Akhilleus' pity. As Eustathius says, the spectacle is also slightly comic (1314.61).

532 πανύστατος: only here and at 547 (of Eumelos again) in the *Iliad*; cf. *Od.* 9.452, where it refers to the ram of Poluphemos in the speech which its master makes to it. In all these cases there is an element of pathos, as often with these παν- compounds (see on 22.490).

533 For ἕλκων ἄρματα καλά cf. 10.505, where a chariot is light enough to be carried. Aristarchus (Arn/AbT) seems to have taken ἐλαύνων προσσόθεν ἵππους to mean that he was walking in front of the horses, leading them by the reins and whipping them on. More probably it means that he was driving them in front of him (cf. Eust. 1315.1). προσσόθεν occurs only here, and is related to πρόσω, πρόσθεν, πρόσωθεν; the scholiasts compare ἔξοθεν in Stesichorus and Ibycus (Erbse on 533). Zenodotus read ὠκέας instead, and a few MSS read μώνυχας.

534–5 Verse 534 = 16.5 (cf. also 11.814). For ποδάρκης ... ἀγόρευε cf. 22.376–7 ... ποδάρκης δῖος Ἀχιλλεύς, | στὰς ἐν Ἀχαιοῖσιν ἔπεα πτερόεντ᾽ ἀγόρευεν.

536–8 Akhilleus tactfully avoids depriving Diomedes of the first prize: T (538) detects signs of previous rivalry between them (cf. Arn/AT on 16.74, referring to Diomedes' contemptuous remarks about Akhilleus at 9.697–709), and suggests (T 536–7) that Eumelos' Thessalian origin makes Akhilleus favour him. But the point is surely more general: Eumelos is simply the best, and Akhilleus holds that he deserves recognition, on the principle that ἀρετή should not suffer because of τυχή (bT 536–7), a principle we might well expect Akhilleus to believe in.

536 λοῖσθος: only here in Homer; cf. Hes. *Th.* 921 etc. (but λοίσθιος is commoner in classical poetry), and 23.751 λοισθήϊα, 785 λοισθήϊον ... ἄεθλον.

537–8 ἄεθλον ... δεύτερ᾽: the plural δεύτερα in apposition to ἄεθλον is slightly odd but not impossible; cf. also λοισθήϊα meaning 'as last prize' in 751. After 537 some ancient texts added two verses: τὰ τρίτα δ᾽ Ἀντίλοχος, τέτρατα ξανθὸς Μενέλαος, | πεμπτὰ δὲ Μηριόνης θεράπων ἐὺς Ἰδομενῆος. These were justly condemned by Aristarchus (Arn/AT) as un-Homeric.

539–40 The emphasis on the approval of the Achaeans is a relevant point, since what Akhilleus proposes is not according to strict justice, as Antilokhos protests. For 539 cf. 7.344 = 9.710 ὣς ἔφαθ᾽· οἱ δ᾽ ἄρα πάντες ἐπήνησαν βασιλῆες.

541–2 For Ἀντίλοχος μεγαθύμου Νέστορος υἱός | cf. 5.565, 13.400. In 542 'with a formal appeal' may be the sense of δίκη, although later it means simply 'justly'.

543–54 Antilokhos' protest is direct and frank, as suits his youth and friendship with Akhilleus (cf. bT 543). But he has an argument in favour of his plea, which is that Eumelos failed to invoke divine aid. Verses 549–50 are effective with their rhetorical anaphora, suggesting how easy it would be for Akhilleus to solve the problem. Finally 553–4 close the speech with a very emphatic refusal to give up the prize, and a threat to anyone who dares to try to make him do so. Here the echoes of book 1 are particularly strong: cf. 1.29 τὴν δ᾽ ἐγὼ οὐ λύσω (Agamemnon refuses to give up Khruseis), and 298–303, where Akhilleus says that he will not fight over Briseis (298 χερσὶ μὲν οὔ τοι ἔγωγε μαχήσομαι ~ 23.554 χείρεσσι μάχεσθαι), but if anyone tries to take away any of his other possessions there will be bloodshed (302 εἰ δ᾽ ἄγε μὴν πείρησαι ... ~ 23.553 περὶ δ᾽ αὐτῆς πειρηθήτω ...). These parallels were already noted by Eustathius (1315.29ff., 53–4, 65ff.). He regards 553 as a parody of 1.29, and he says that 'Akhilleus knows by experience what it means to be robbed of one's prize', and that he recognizes in Antilokhos' echo of his own words at 1.298ff. a sign that they both share the same nobility of character: hence he smiles at his speech. Cf. also Martin, *Language of Heroes* 188–9.

544 ἀφαιρήσεσθαι ἄεθλον: cf. 1.161 (Akhilleus to Agamemnon) καὶ δή μοι γέρας αὐτὸς ἀφαιρήσεσθαι ἀπειλεῖς, and 182 (Agamemnon's reply) ὡς ἔμ' ἀφαιρεῖται Χρυσηΐδα Φοῖβος Ἀπόλλων.

545–6 ὅτι οἱ βλάβεν ἅρματα... | αὐτός τ' ἐσθλὸς ἐών: βλάπτειν is applied to horses at 6.39, 23.387 and 571; cf. 22.15 ἔβλαψάς μ', ἑκάεργε, with comment. αὐτός τ'... ἐών is an afterthought, 'and himself for all his skill'.

546–7 The principle stated here is illustrated later in the foot-race and archery contest (768–72, 863–5, 872–81).

547 τῶ κ' ('in that case') is Bentley's emendation. Most MSS read τό κεν, which would mean 'therefore', and some have τῶ κεν which is unmetrical. For πανύστατος see on 532.

548 Cf. 16.450 ἀλλ' εἴ τοι φίλος ἐστί, τεὸν δ' ὀλοφύρεται ἦτορ, and 14.337 ἀλλ' εἰ δή ῥ' ἐθέλεις καί τοι φίλον ἔπλετο θυμῷ. Here and at 16.450 (see comment) Aristarchus and some of our MSS read φίλος, against the vulgate's φίλον, but this may well be a learned 'improvement' in both cases.

549–51 Cf. 6.47–9 πολλὰ δ'... κειμήλια κεῖται, | χαλκός τε χρυσός τε... | τῶν κέν τοι χαρίσαιτο... (of ransom), and similarly 10.378–80, 11.132–4. It may be more relevant that Thersites' protest at 2.226–34 is similar. The casual order of the catalogue, together with the anaphora, are suited to Antilokhos' tone of protest (Eust. 1315.59ff.).

551–2 ἔπειτα... ἠὲ καὶ αὐτίκα νῦν: 'later... or even straight away now'; cf. *Od.* 20.63 αὐτίκα νῦν, ἢ ἔπειτα. For ἵνα... Ἀχαιοί cf. 539–40.

553–4 See on 543–54. For πειρηθήτω cf. also 21.225–6 Ἕκτορι πειρηθῆναι | ἀντιβίην.

555–6 Akhilleus smiles, for the first and only time in the whole poem, and is delighted by his friend's frankness. For the phrasing cf. 1.595 etc. ὡς φάτο, μείδησεν δέ, 1.121 etc. ποδάρκης δῖος Ἀχιλλεύς, 5.695 ὅς οἱ φίλος ἦεν ἑταῖρος.

558–62 Akhilleus' speech resembles that of the Phaeacian Euryalos at *Od.* 8.401–5, where in response to Alkinoos' suggestion of recompense for his insult he offers a valuable sword to the stranger (Odysseus): δώσω οἱ τόδ' ἄορ παγχάλκεον, ᾧ ἔπι κώπη | ἀργυρέη, κολεὸν δὲ νεοπρίστου ἐλέφαντος | ἀμφιδεδίνηται· πολέος δέ οἱ ἄξιον ἔσται. Cf. D. M. Jones, *Glotta* 37 (1958) 115–17, who argues that the *Odyssey* passage is influenced by this one.

558–9 Cf. 592–4 εἰ καί νύ κεν οἴκοθεν ἄλλο | ... ἐπαιτήσειας (etc.), and 7.364 = 391 πάντ' ἐθέλω δόμεναι καὶ ἔτ' οἴκοθεν ἄλλ' ἐπιθεῖναι. οἴκοθεν means 'from my store'.

560–2 This effectively recalls 21.182–3, where Akhilleus despoils Asteropaios. Cf. the use of Asteropaios' sword as a prize at 807–8, and the description of the mixing-bowl at 740–7, which recalls the story of Lukaon (21.34ff.). These were Akhilleus' last major victims before he killed Hektor, and the mention of these precious objects is a poignant reminder of his recent career of destruction.

The cuirass is of bronze, to which tin has been added as a decorative material. Either this means that the whole surface has been plated with tin (as D. H. F. Gray thought, in *JHS* 74 (1954) 2), or that the bronze is surrounded by a circle of tin overlay or inlay. The second (a surrounding circle) seems more probable. In any case, one can compare Agamemnon's cuirass with its bands of different precious metals (11.24–5).

561 χεῦμα: only here in Homer, later in Pindar (*N*. 9.39), tragedy, etc. περιχεύειν is used of silver or gold ornamentation (10.294 etc.). These words probably refer to a technique of overlay, rather than to actual pouring of metal: see Gray, *op. cit.* 4, for details of how this was done. For φαεινοῦ κασσιτέροιο | cf. 18.612 ἑανοῦ κασσιτέροιο |, 21.592 νεοτεύκτου κασσιτέροιο |.

562 ἀμφιδεδίνηται: this verb occurs only here in *Il.*, once in *Od.* at 8.405 (see on 558–62); cf. Bacchylides 17.105–7 ἀμφὶ χαίταις δὲ χρυσεόπλοκοι δίνηντο ταινίαι. It ought to mean 'is set round in a circle', but in *Od.* it is applied to an ivory scabbard enclosing a sword. δινωτός is used of objects decorated with precious materials, and again the precise sense is hard to determine: see on 3.391, and cf. the article by Jones mentioned on 558–62. The long compound word, occupying the first hemistich, is in itself an ornamental feature, adding dignity to the object described. The variant ἄξιον ('an object of value') is probably derived from *Od.* 8.405.

563 Automedon is a θεράπων of Akhilleus, and next in command after Patroklos: see on 9.209.

565 This verse is omitted by several MSS and a first-century B.C. papyrus. It is a slight variation of the formular verse 624 etc. (see on 1.446). Although not essential it does round off this episode more effectively than 564 would do without it.

566–85 We come now to the second round of the quarrel. Menelaos' protest is a far more solemn affair than that of Antilokhos. He is clearly furious (567), but controls his anger. He takes the sceptre, a sign that he is making a public speech, and appeals first to all the Achaean leaders for impartial justice, and then to Antilokhos' own conscience. One senses that their former friendship and Menelaos' admiration for Antilokhos' qualities (cf. 570 πρόσθεν πεπνυμένε, 581 διοτρεφές) make the situation even more distressing for him. As far as he is concerned Antilokhos has defeated him by deceit and treachery. The parallel with the resentment of Akhilleus at Agamemnon's conduct did not escape the notice of the ancient commentators: AT (565) quote 9.375 ἐκ γὰρ δή μ' ἀπάτησε καὶ ἤλιτεν (cf. also Eust. 1317.14).

Menelaos' speech throws light on the development of Greek justice (cf. R. J. Bonner and G. Smith, *The Administration of Justice from Homer to Aristotle*, Chicago 1930, 27–8). Two ways of settling the dispute are proposed, first by the arbitration of his fellow leaders, and second by an oath. The first has the disadvantage that the arbitrators may not be impartial, and so the judgement may be questioned later (cf. 574–8). The second is common to many societies at an early stage in the development of a legal system, and continued to be used in some circumstances in Greece in the classical period. It effectively makes the gods the witnesses, and so could be considered more secure, although Odysseus' grandfather Autolukos knew how to circumvent divine anger, since he surpassed all men in stealing and swearing on oath (*Od.* 19.395–6). Antilokhos subsequently offers Menelaos not only restitution but damages in addition, for fear of offending him and incurring divine displeasure (591–5).

567–9 ἐν δ᾽ ἄρα κῆρυξ ... ᾽Αργείους: cf. 2.278–81, where Odysseus holds the sceptre and Athene as herald orders silence, and *Od.* 2.37–8, where the herald Peisenor gives Telemakhos the sceptre before he speaks. The participation of the herald adds to the solemnity. For the association of the sceptre with oaths and judgements see on 1.234–9, 2.109, and cf. especially the trial scene at 18.505–6. Here, as at 1.234ff., it is held by someone who protests at an injustice he has suffered. In 568 χειρί is preferable to the variant χερσί, as at *Od.* 2.37, 18.103. For μετηύδα in this position in 569 cf. 24.32 (5 × *Od.*).

570–85 The speech has a simple ring-structure (cf. Lohmann, *Reden* 23):

A 570–2 Address to Antilokhos (᾽Αντίλοχε)
B 573–4 Appeal to Greeks for arbitration (ἀλλ᾽ ἄγετ᾽)
C 575–8 Imaginary speech against Menelaos
B 579–80 Alternative proposal of an oath (εἰ δ᾽ ἄγε)
A 581–5 Final address to Antilokhos (᾽Αντίλοχε).

570 πρόσθεν πεπνυμένε: see on 305.

571–2 ἤσχυνας μὲν ἐμὴν ἀρετήν means 'you have cast shame upon my valour'. It would be wrong to restrict the sense of ἀρετή here too closely, to mean for example 'skill' (so Leaf). For βλάψας see on 387, and for πρόσθε βαλών cf. 639 πρόσθε βαλόντες, and see on 462.

574 ἐς μέσον was taken by Aristarchus as meaning 'impartially' (Arn/ATD), probably correctly. μηδ᾽ ἐπ᾽ ἀρωγῇ means 'without favour to either side'; cf. 18.502 where the spectators at a trial are ἀμφὶς ἀρωγοί.

575–8 As often in Homer fear of what men say is a potent factor. For μή ποτέ τις εἴπῃσιν cf. 22.106. Verse 576 is a powerful four-word one, framed by the contrasting names. In 577–8 the two clauses introduced by ὅτι are in parataxis, although the first is really subordinate in sense: '*even if* his horses were worse he had the advantage in rank and power'. Verse 577 echoes the second half of 572, stressing the contrast. For αὐτὸς δὲ ... βίη τε cf. 9.498 τῶν περ καὶ μείζων ἀρετὴ τιμή τε βίη τε.

579–80 The suggestion of an oath arises naturally, as if it had just occurred to Menelaos as a better way of settling the issue, which is what δικάσω presumably means here. μ' probably represents the dative μοι with ἐπιπλήξειν, as at 12.211. For the idea of a 'straight judgement' cf. 18.508 δίκην ἰθύντατα εἴποι, 16.387 σκολιὰς κρίνωσι θέμιστας etc., and see Richardson on *HyDem* 152.

581 Ἀντίλοχ', εἰ δ' ἄγε δεῦρο, διοτρεφές echoes Menelaos' appeal to Akhilleus at 17.685, but here the repetition of εἰ δ' ἄγε after 579 suggests Menelaos' impatience. Aristarchus athetized this verse because he thought the honorific epithet διοτρεφές unsuitable (Arn/A). T compares the use of δῖον Ἀλέξανδρον at 3.352, where Menelaos is praying for vengeance against Paris, and other cases of this kind (6.377, 21.331), but Aristarchus athetized 3.352 and objected to 21.331. Although διοτρεφές is a formular epithet it can still be relevant here: it is as if Menelaos is appealing to Antilokhos' own sense of honour, and suggesting that it is not in his true character to act as he did.

For the formular ἣ θέμις ἐστί see on 2.73–5, 23.44. It indicates that the following procedure is laid down by convention or 'ritualized'.

582–5 The solemnity of the oath is indicated by the lengthy and complex prescription, with its various parenthetic and subordinate clauses. There is a similar lengthy build-up before Agamemnon's oath at 19.252–6. Antilokhos must take hold of his whip and of the horses themselves as he swears: cf. the oath by the sceptre which Akhilleus holds at 1.234 (and similarly 10.321), and 14.271–6 where Here is asked to take hold of earth and sea with each hand when swearing. The invocation of Poseidon may be due to his rôle as god of horses, in addition to his being Antilokhos' ancestor (see on 307).

583 For ἔχε a few MSS read ἔχων, and Eustathius quotes this, although his comments evidently assume the reading ἔχε. The whole of αὐτάρ ... ἔλαυνες is in parenthesis, giving variety to the construction. ῥαδινός occurs only here in Homer; cf. Hes. *Th.* 195, *HyDem* 183, etc. Its precise sense is not easy to pin down, but 'slender' or 'supple' seem possible.

584–5 For γαιήοχον ἐννοσίγαιον cf. γαιήοχος ἐννοσίγαιος 13.43 etc., -ῳ -ῳ 9.183 etc. The terms of the oath lay stress on the element of deliberate deceit, since Antilokhos could well have claimed that he did not actually intend to impede Menelaos. πεδῆσαι is a strong word, as Eustathius observes (1317.7). It is used by Pindar in Pelops' prayer to Poseidon for victory in the chariot-race at *O.* 1.76 πέδασον ἔγχος Οἰνομάου (etc.); cf. D. Gerber (*Pindar's Olympian One*, Toronto 1982, p. 120) on words denoting binding and impeding in magical *defixiones* concerned with chariot-races. Could the use of this verb here be another echo of the racing jargon? Cf. also Pind. *P.* 6.32 ἵππος ἄρμ' ἐπέδα (when Nestor is rescued by Antilokhos), and for δόλῳ πεδῆσαι cf. *N.* 5.26.

586 For the expression τὸν/τὴν δ' αὖ/αὖτ' ... πεπνυμένος ἀντίον ηὔδα (6× *Il.*, 43× *Od.*, but only of Telemakhos) cf. 3.203 etc. But here the epithet clearly echoes and answers 570: 'we are being told that Antilokhos is showing himself a sensible man after all' (Parry, *Language* 308). Cf. for example the use of this epithet of Pouludamas when he gives his vital warning to the Trojans at 18.249(n.)., and of Antenor at 7.347, when he advises the return of Helen.

587–95 Antilokhos' reply is a masterpiece of honourable conciliation, putting all the emphasis on the rashness of youth, paying respect to Menelaos' age, reminding him of their past friendship (594–5), and of his own accord offering extra recompense. He cleverly avoids having to take the oath, but at the same time does not actually admit that he cheated! Eustathius has a long and over-ingenious analysis of his speech, designed to show that its covert intention is to praise himself (1317.43ff.), but both he and bT (591–2) observe that Antilokhos still refers to the horse as his own prize, which is a good point.

587–91 Cf. the progression of thought at 19.216–20, where Odysseus says that Akhilleus is more powerful than him, but he is older and wiser, and goes on (220) τῷ τοι ἐπιτλήτω κραδίη μύθοισιν ἐμοῖσιν.

587–8 Unusually Antilokhos does not begin with a vocative formula, the name being postponed to 588, because the situation demands that he should immediately calm Menelaos' anger. ἄνσχεο νῦν sounds colloquial: 'Hold on, now!' For Antilokhos' youth cf. 15.568–71, where Menelaos appealed to him for help as the most agile of the younger Achaeans. These echoes of their previous closeness in battle (cf. above on 581 διοτρεφές) are by no means irrelevant here. For σὺ δὲ πρότερος καὶ ἀρείων cf. 2.707 ὁπλότερος γενεῇ· ὁ δ' ἄρα πρότερος καὶ ἀρείων.

589–90 Antilokhos seems to be echoing 3.106–8, where again it is Menelaos who fears that Priam's sons may not respect the oaths (107 ὑπερβασίη), and adds αἰεὶ δ' ὁπλοτέρων ἀνδρῶν φρένες ἠερέθονται. Menelaos 'is unusually conscious of himself as a middle-aged man' (Parry, *Language* 321). For similar gnomic statements about youthful folly cf. *Od.* 7.294, Theognis 629–30, and for the phrasing of 590 cf. 10.226 ἀλλά τε οἱ βράσσων τε νόος, λεπτὴ δέ τε μῆτις. λεπτή in these cases means 'slight', 'slender'. There is irony in the use of μῆτις here, given Nestor's remarks on the subject (313–18).

592–5 τὴν ἀρόμην means 'which I won' (aorist of ἄρνυμαι). From εἰ καί νύ κεν onwards the sentence structure becomes more complex, and we have three consecutive verses with integral enjambment, as Antilokhos makes his final, more emotional point. For 592–5 (εἰ καί ... βουλοίμην) see on 558–9, and for βουλοίμην ἤ cf. 1.117. In 594 διοτρεφές is a nice echo of Menelaos' use of this vocative at 581, undoubtedly being designed to soften him (cf. bT 594). σοί γε ... ἐκ θυμοῦ πεσέειν means 'to fall out of favour with you' (cf. 1.562–3), and δαίμοσιν εἶναι ἀλιτρός 'to be culpable in the eyes of the gods' (cf. 8.361 for ἀλιτρός). The last phrase presumably hints at the fact that in order to contradict Menelaos Antilokhos would have to commit perjury.

596–7 Antilokhos seals his reconciliation by actually handing over the horse himself (cf. T 596).

597–600 τοῖο δὲ θυμὸς | ἰάνθη ... θυμὸς ἰάνθη: 'and his spirit | was warmed, just like the dew upon the ears of corn | of a ripening crop, when the ploughlands are bristling: | even so, Menelaos, was the spirit in your heart warmed'.

'No poet ever wrote lines more adequate to the beauty of reconciliation than these' (F. M. Stawell, *Homer and the Iliad*, London 1909, 87). The simile has a ring-structure, being framed by the repetition of θυμὸς ἰάνθη, although in 597–8 the strong enjambment and prominence of ἰάνθη at the beginning of the verse make these words stand out as introduction.

From antiquity onwards too much ink has been spilt over the exact sense. ἰαίνω probably means 'warm', and from this it comes to mean 'soften', 'melt' (Chantraine, *Dict.* s.v.); it is used in a similar context at 24.119 (θυμὸν ἰήνῃ) and *Od.* 22.59. We should read ἐέρσῃ in 598 rather than ἑέρσῃ (as some modern editors have done). The early-morning dew on the ripening corn is warmed and evaporated by the increasing force of the sun. Apollonius Rhodius surely saw the point in his imitation, when he said of Medea, as she falls in love: ἰαίνετο δὲ φρένας εἴσω | τηκομένη οἷόν τε περὶ ῥοδέῃσιν ἐέρσῃ | τήκεται ἠώοισιν ἰαινομένη φαέεσσιν (3.1019–21). The echo of the Homeric simile by Aeschylus (*Ag.* 1391–2) suggests the general tone but is less close in detail: χαίρουσαν οὐδὲν ἧττον ἢ διοσδότῳ | γάνει σπορητὸς κάλυκος ἐν λοχεύμασιν. There is also a reminiscence of 598–9 by Virgil at *G.* 3.314–15: *spicea iam campis cum messis inhorruit, et cum | frumenta in viridi stipula lactentia turgent.* στάχυς is only here in Homer, later in Hes. *Erga* 473 etc. ἀλδήσκειν (599) occurs only here in early Greek literature; cf. Theocr. *Id.* 17.78 λήϊον ἀλδήσκουσιν.

600 For this use of apostrophe, or direct address by the poet to one of his characters, as an 'emphatic and pathetic device', see on 13.602–3, 17.674–5. Cf. also bT 4.127 ('the poet is sympathetic towards Menelaos'), and the sensitive discussion by Parry in *Language* 310–26. T (on 600) notes Menelaos' characteristic gentleness; cf. bT 6.51, 62 etc., *CQ* 30 (1980) 272. For the second half of 600 cf. 24.321 = *Od.* 15.165 γήθησαν, καὶ πᾶσιν ἐνὶ φρεσὶ θυμὸς ἰάνθη.

602–11 This moving speech is the last by Menelaos in the poem. He accepts Antilokhos' apology, although still with a sharp note of warning against making the same mistake again. Recalling all that Antilokhos, Nestor and Thrasumedes have suffered for his sake in the past he actually offers to give Antilokhos back the horse, as if moved by a deep impulse of sympathetic generosity. We may well be reminded here of Phoinix' sermon to Akhilleus on the virtues of yielding to entreaty when one is angry at injustice (9.496–605), and of Iris' warning to Poseidon not to go on cherishing resentment against his elder brother Zeus (15.200–4; at 202 Iris calls his speech ἀπηνέα, a word used by Menelaos at 611; and cf. 211 νεμεσσηθεὶς ὑποείξω with 602–3).

603 οὔ τι παρήορος οὐδ' ἀεσίφρων: 'in no way deranged or foolish'. παρήορος is applied to a trace-horse which runs beside the regular pair of horses at 16.471, 16.474 (cf. παρηορίαι meaning 'side-traces' at 8.18, 16.152). Here, however, it was taken in antiquity as meaning 'deranged', and this seems to be how Archilochus understood it: cf. fr. 130.5 West, νόου παρήορος, and 172.2 τίς σὰς παρήειρε φρένας; At 7.156 it is applied to a fallen warrior and the sense is again uncertain, perhaps 'sprawling' or something similar; see on 7.155–6 for further discussion. For οὐδ' ἀεσίφρων see comment on 20.183. The original form was probably ἀασίφρων; cf. Chantraine, *Dict.* s.v. ἀάω.

604 νῦν αὖτε νόον νίκησε νεοίη: the heavy alliteration is surely deliberate here, suggesting a proverbial expression. νεοίη is an absolute *hapax*, apparently meaning 'youth' or 'youthful folly', possibly formed from νέος, νεότης under the influence of ἀνοίη (which some scholars have wanted to read here: Leumann, *HW* 228 n. 23). Hesychius glosses νέοιαι as ἀφροσύναι; cf. Wackernagel, *Sprachliche Untersuchungen* 242–3. Antimachus apparently read νόημα (AT 604, fr. 138 W.), i.e. 'your plan (*or* ingenuity) got the better of your good sense'.

605–6 These two forbidding verses show that Menelaos' tolerance and gentleness have their limits. παρέπεισεν is used of Menelaos being dissuaded from action at 7.120 (and cf. 6.61 v.l.): 'Menelaus is always being persuaded' (Parry, *Language* 320).

607–8 For 607 cf. 9.492, where it is Phoinix who is speaking. Apart from the general exploits in battle of Nestor and his sons one thinks especially of 5.561–72, where Antilokhos comes to Menelaos' aid against Aineias, of 15.568–91, where they fight together, and of 17.651–99, where Menelaos asks him to bring Akhilleus the news of Patroklos' death.

610–11 Like Antilokhos, Menelaos continues to regard the horse as *his* prize. Generosity does not overrule the concern for honour in the older any more than in the younger man (cf. bT). Menelaos is concerned about what people will think of his character (cf. 575–8). ὑπερφίαλος καὶ ἀπηνής is applied to Zeus by Here at 15.94, but a more relevant parallel might be 16.35 (ὅτι τοι νόος ἐστὶν ἀπηνής), where Patroklos accuses Akhilleus of relentless inhumanity because he has refused to show pity for the Greeks.

612 Νοήμονι: after the emphasis on Antilokhos' μῆτις and intelligence throughout the course of the preceding scenes, one can hardly avoid think- ing that his companion's name has a point (as T notices). Cf. *Od.* 2.386–7, 4.630–7, where an Ithacan named Noemon, son of Phronios, sensibly lends his ship to Telemakhos (and is later said to own horses in Elis). Noemon recurs in a list of Lycian names at *Il.* 5.678.

612–23 For the prizes cf. 265–70. The last prize is left over because Eumelos has received an extra one, and with great courtesy Akhilleus gives it to Nestor, the old charioteer *par excellence*, whose exploits on Menelaos' behalf have just been recalled. We have travelled a long way since the moment in book 1 when Nestor's conciliatory advice to Akhilleus and Agamemnon was ignored, and in Akhilleus' respect for Nestor's great age there is a foreshadowing of his attitude to old Priam in book 24.

616–17 Like Antilokhos (596–7) Akhilleus honours the older man by personally handing him the gift.

618–23 Akhilleus' speech is dignified and sad. Patroklos is in his mind as at 280–4, but there is a noble restraint in the simplicity of 619–20: 'you will not see him again among the Greeks'. The speech is quite heavily enjambed, but develops in a natural way (cf. Higbie, *Measure and Music* 120).

The list of contests (621–3) is echoed by Nestor at 634–7, and with the chariot-race makes up a kind of early pentathlon. The same order is main- tained in the contests which follow the chariot-race, at 653–797 and 884– 97. Plutarch (*Mor.* 639A–40A) discusses whether or not this reflects the original order of these sports.

618–19 For τῇ νῦν ('here now') cf. 14.219 etc., and for κειμήλιον ... μνῆμ' ἔμμεναι see on 499–652. κειμήλιον ἔστω | recurs at *Od.* 4.600, and Xenophanes includes among honours for successful athletes δῶρον ὅ οἱ κειμήλιον εἴη (fr. 2.9 West).

621 The crucial word αὔτως ('just like that', i.e. without a contest) is emphatically placed, and then explained. For οὐ γὰρ ... παλαίσεις cf. *Od.* 8.103 πύξ τε παλαισμοσύνη τε, 246 οὐ γὰρ πυγμάχοι εἰμὲν ἀμύμονες οὐδὲ παλαισταί. The fact that these sports are mentioned first here, at 634–5 and *Od.* 8.206, was taken by Aristarchus as evidence in favour of the same author for both poems (Arn/A 621, 634–5).

622 ἀκοντιστύς occurs nowhere else; cf. ἀκοντιστής etc. ἐσδύσεαι means 'will enter for'; Aristarchus (Did/A) and most of our MSS read this, against the variant ἐνδύσεαι (Plut. *Mor.* 639C and some MSS). ἐσδύνω occurs only here in Homer (cf. Hdt. 1.193, etc.), and van der Valk argues for ἐνδύσεαι (*Researches* II 203), but ἐνδύνω with the accusative is normally used in Homer of putting on clothes, except at 19.366–7.

623 χαλεπὸν κατὰ γῆρας ἐπείγει: cf. *HyAphr* 233 χαλεπὸν κατὰ γῆρας ἔπειγεν. Most MSS have ἔπεισιν (as in 1.29), and this is mentioned by A as an ancient variant, together with ἱκάνει (cf. *Od.* 11.196 etc.) and ὀπάζει (cf. *Il.* 8.108, addressed to Nestor). ἐπείγει is more graphic.

624 = 797, 1.446 (see comment).

626–50 Nestor's speech resembles in style some of his earlier reminiscences: cf. 629–30 with 7.132–3, 157, 11.670–1, 643 with 11.762, etc. It has thematic links with these in the allusions to the Epeans and Bouprasion, and to the sons of Aktor (cf. 11.671ff., 11.756, 11.750–2); for Nestor's other legendary and monstrous opponents cf. the Centaurs at 1.267–8, and Ereuthalion at 7.136–56. Structurally it begins with the theme of his old age (626–8), which picks up the end of Akhilleus' speech. This leads to the account of his youthful successes and failure in the games (629–42). He then returns to his age and the contrast with the young men of today (643–5). The last verses answer the first part of Akhilleus' speech, with their reference to Patroklos' funeral and Nestor's gratitude for the gift (646–50). The central section contains a *paradeigma* which may be obliquely relevant to the contest which has just occurred (see on 499–652). See also on 11.670–762.

626 = *Od.* 18.170; cf. also *Il.* 1.286 etc. (with γέρον, φίλος instead of τέκος). It looks as if Aristarchus' text did not include this verse, since he comments on 627 as if it were the beginning of the speech (Arn/A: ὅτι ἀπὸ τοῦ γὰρ ἦρκται . . .). It is omitted by a papyrus and one MS, but bT discuss the verse.

627–8 Cf. 772 (etc.) γυῖα δ' ἔθηκεν ἐλαφρά, πόδας καὶ χεῖρας ὕπερθεν, 13.512 γυῖα ποδῶν, and Hes. *Th.* 150 τῶν ἑκατὸν μὲν χεῖρες ἀπ' ὤμων ἀΐσσοντ αι. The construction of 627 would be smoother without 628, which Nicanor may not have read, as he takes πόδες . . . χεῖρες as epexegetic to γυῖα. But bT seem to have read both verses, and 628 is very suitable to describe the action of a boxer or javelin-thrower: 'my arms do not dart out on each side from my shoulders nimbly'. The variant ἀπαΐσσονται is equally possible.

629–30 εἴθ' ὡς ἡβώοιμι . . . ὡς ὁπότε . . .: this is repeated from Nestor's words at 11.670–1, and cf. 7.132–3, 157. The verse recurs at *Od.* 14.468 (echoed at 503), in a reminiscence told by Odysseus to Eumaios, which is called an αἶνος (508) as at 652 here.

630–1 Amarunkeus is the father of Diores, one of the Epean leaders (2.622), who is killed at 4.517–26. Pausanias makes him an immigrant from Thessaly (5.1.8). For Bouprasion and the Epeans see on 2.615–24. παῖδες δὲ θέσαν βασιλῆος ἄεθλα means 'and his sons instituted games in honour of the king'. Cf. 22.163–4 ἄεθλον . . . ἀνδρὸς κατατεθνηῶτος, and Hes. *Erga* 654–6 ἄεθλα . . . Ἀμφιδάμαντος | . . . τὰ δὲ . . . ἄθλ' ἔθεσαν παῖδες μεγαλήτορος (with West's comments). The usual later expression was ἄθλα ἐπί τινι.

632–7 The inclusion of the Aetolians as well as the Pylians suggests an important event, which drew people to Elis from the neighbouring areas. Cf. 11.698–702, where Neleus sends a four-horse chariot to compete there. In 634–7 Nestor gives us the first athletic victory catalogue, as in later epinician poetry and inscriptions. The events are the same as at 621–3, with the addition of the chariot-race, which is postponed to the end because it is an exception to his successes. The name Klutomedes occurs only here in Homer, but Enops is more common (14.445, 16.401). The coincidence of Ankaios of Pleuron and Iphiklos must be related to their appearance in later versions of the legend of the Calydonian boar: in Bacchylides 5 (117–20, 127–9) they are respectively the brother and uncle of Meleager. Ankaios is the name of an Arcadian, father of Agapenor, at 2.609 (see comment), and the Ankaios of the Calydonian boar-hunt later has an Arcadian origin (Apollodorus 1.8.2, Pausanias 8.4.10, 8.45.2 and 7). Iphiklos too has a namesake, the Thessalian father of Podarkes (cf. 2.704–5, 13.698 with comment), who was later famous as a runner (Hes. fr. 62 M–W, Call. fr. 75.46), and who is mentioned in connexion with Neleus and Melampous at *Od.* 11.287–97. But to disentangle these various legendary coincidences here would take too long. Probably the name Ankaios has been chosen as suitable for a wrestler: cf. ἀγκάς (711), ἀγκάλη, etc. (bT 635). The association of the Thessalian Iphiklos with running may have influenced the poet's choice of this name. Phuleus is a son of Augeias, and according to 2.625–9 he had migrated to Doulikhion after a quarrel with his father: his son Meges commands the contingent from there at Troy (see on 2.627–30). Poludoros is otherwise unknown: the name is that of one of Priam's sons at 20.407 etc.

634 Ἤνοπος: some MSS read Οἴνοπος, as does Plutarch (*Mor.* 639c), and another ancient quotation has Φαίνοπος.

635 πάλη occurs only here in *Il.* Aristarchus preferred πάλην; *Od.* 8.206 has πάλη, but in later Greek the internal accusative πάλην is quite common (E. *Alc.* 1031 etc.). ὅς μοι ἀνέστη is 'who stood up as my opponent'. The verb is used thus of boxers and wrestlers etc. at 677, 709, *Od.* 18.334, S. *Tr.* 441.

637–42 The twin Aktorione were mentioned by Nestor as his opponents in battle at 11.709–10, 750–2 (see 750n.). There they are called Μολίονε, and are said to be sons of Poseidon, who rescued them from defeat by Nestor. At 2.620–1 the Epean leaders Amphimakhos and Thalpios are called υἷες ὁ μὲν Κτεάτου, ὁ δ' ἄρ' Εὐρύτου, Ἀκτορίωνε (see comment). So the Aktorione mentioned here are presumably called Kteatos and Eurutos, the fathers of Amphimakhos and Thalpios respectively. Their own supposed mortal father will have been called Aktor. In the Hesiodic *Catalogue* (frr. 17–18 M–W) and later authors (Ibycus fr. 285 *PMG* etc.) they are Siamese twins, and Aristarchus argued that this was already the case in the

Homeric version of their legends (Arn/A 638–42, Eust. 1321.20ff.). This would explain how they were allowed to compete as a pair against Nestor on his own, and it is possible that the poet has avoided a direct reference to their abnormal form, whilst hinting at it in the language of 639–42 (see comments, and cf. U. von Wilamowitz, *Pindaros*, Berlin 1922, 514, van der Valk, *Researches* II 255). The popularity of portrayals of apparent Siamese twins taking part in both battle and funeral scenes in Greek art of the eighth century B.C. shows that the poet could have known such a legend, even if these artistic representations are not of the Aktorione themselves. On the artistic evidence and the debate about these figures see R. Hampe in *LIMC* 1.1 472–6, and 1.2 364–5 for illustrations; cf. also J. Carter, *BSA* 67 (1972) 52–4, Coldstream, *Geometric Greece* 352–4.

639 πλήθει πρόσθε βαλόντες: 'forging ahead through their superior number'. This seems the simplest explanation of the phrase (cf. Eust. 1321.23ff.). Cf. 17.329–30 πεποιθότας ἠνορέη τε | πλήθεῖ τε σφετέρῳ, i.e. 'trusting in superiority of number' (etc.), the only other instance in Homer of the word πλῆθος (πληθύς being commoner). For πρόσθε βαλόντες cf. 572 τοὺς σοὺς πρόσθε βαλών, and see on 462. In antiquity other interpretations were offered (cf. Arn/A 638–42, Eust. 1321.20ff.). One was that the twins entered several chariots and so hindered their rivals, another that those in charge gave them an unfair advantage at the start. It looks as if Aristarchus took πλήθει as meaning 'through the support of the crowd', and explained that the spectators allowed them to compete as a pair (Arn/A; Eustathius' account of his views seems to be confused). But this would be an extremely compressed way of expressing this.

ἀγασσάμενοι περὶ νίκης: 'as they were jealously eager for victory', or 'as they begrudged (me) the victory'. There was an ancient variant ἀγασσαμένω (A). Cf. the quarrel of Menelaos and Antilokhos, who gets an unfair advantage because he begrudges victory to his rival.

640 'Because the greatest prizes were reserved for this contest.' This follows Aristarchus and our MSS in reading παρ' αὐτόφι, as an equivalent of παρ' αὐτοῖς (AbT), referring back to ἵπποισι in 638. Cf. παρ' αὐτόφι in 12.302, 20.140 (αὐτόφι is the vulgate reading there), and Chantraine, *GH* I 239–30. This is surely preferable to the variant παρ' αὐτόθι ('on this spot'). Cf. Hdt. 5.8 (Thracian funeral games) ἐν τῷ τὰ μέγιστα ἄεθλα τίθεται κατὰ λόγον μουνομαχίης.

641 δίδυμοι: only here in *Il.*; cf. *Od.* 19.227 αὐλοῖσιν διδύμοισιν. Aristarchus held that the word meant that they were joined together, whereas διδυμάονε (*Il.* 5.548 etc.) meant simply 'twins': cf. Erbse on schol. 641.

641–2 ὁ μὲν ... ἔμπεδον ἡνιόχευ': the third and last example of such anaphora of a hemistich in the *Iliad*; cf. 20.371–2, 22.127–8, with comments. Both ancient (bT) and modern commentators view the device as intended for emphasis. It suggests that there is something quite extraordinary about this pair's way of racing (cf. Eust. 1321.46ff.: 'a spontaneous way of expressing amazement'), as if the poet is hinting at their being Siamese twins. The *homoeoteleuton* of ἡνιόχευεν ... κέλευεν and the echo of this at the end of the first hemistich of 642 may also be a way of suggesting the close co-operation of the twins. For μάστιγι κέλευεν cf. 24.326.

643 ὡς ποτ' ἔον: cf. 11.762 ὡς ἔον, εἴ ποτ' ἔον γε, at the end of Nestor's earlier reminiscence of war with the Epeans. Here 643–5 round off the narrative section, returning to the theme of 626–8.

646 Leaf argued that καί here means 'also', i.e. as in the case of the men of old, because ἀλλ' ἴθι is usually followed by another imperative without a connexion, but as he says 24.336 and *Od.* 18.171 may be exceptions to this. ἀέθλοισι κτερέϊζε means 'give him funerary honours with contests (or prizes)'; cf. κτέρεα, κτερίζω. Verse 647, referring to Nestor's prize, might point to the second sense for ἀέθλοισι here.

648–9 'Because you are always mindful of me as a friend, and do not forget the honour with which it is proper that I should be esteemed among the Achaeans.' There are several oddities about these verses. ἀεί is rare, but cf. 12.211, *Od.* 15.379. μέμνησαι instead of μέμνηαι occurs only here in Homer. ἐνηέος presumably goes with μευ, meaning 'as being well-disposed to you', rather than with τιμῆς (as Nicanor suggested hesitantly, A 648–9). ἐνηής is elsewhere in *Il.* applied to Patroklos, in the formular phrases ἑταῖρον ἐνηέα, ἑτάροιο ἐνηέος (17.204 etc.; cf. 17.670 ἐνηείης Πατροκλῆος), and the reference to him in 646 may have suggested the word. τιμῆς may be a genitive dependent on λήθω, but ἧς is probably a genitive of value with τετιμῆσθαι (Chantraine, *GH* II 56 and 57–8).

650 The prayer for divine recompense is traditional in such contexts although not expressed in exactly these words elsewhere. Cf. 1.18–19, *Od.* 6.180–2, etc.

651–2 Akhilleus waits courteously until Nestor has finished, as Patroklos did at 11.655–803 (cf. T 652a). αἶνος (only here and 795 in *Il.*) means 'a tale', and usually one with a message for the hearer (cf. *Od.* 14.508), and hence is used later of fables, proverbs or riddles (Hes. *Erga* 202 etc.). From being a tale it acquires the sense of an account in praise of someone (cf. *Od.* 21.110). Here bT take the word as meaning 'a story with a hidden message', whereas Eustathius (1322.3ff.) refers it to Nestor's praise of Akhilleus. It could also presumably refer to Nestor's own praise of himself. Cf. Martin, *Language of Heroes* 106 on Nestor as 'a speaker whose rhetoric rests on eulogy'. At 795 the word is used again with a similar potential ambiguity: there 'eulogy' seems to fit well, but Antilokhos' speech is designed to illustrate the moral that the gods honour older men (an interesting link with the exchange between Nestor and Akhilleus). Here it is tempting to side with bT and see a reference to the paradeigmatic quality of the narrative (cf. Schadewaldt, *Iliasstudien* 83 and n. 2). In translation, however, one should probably leave it open and say 'the whole tale'.

653–99 Akhilleus offers prizes for boxing. Epeios issues a challenge, to which Eurualos alone responds. They fight, and Eurualos is knocked out

After the length and complexity of the chariot race the boxing match and the following events are narrated on a much smaller scale. Boxing was regarded as a major sport in ancient Greece, but some features of this scene do suggest a contrast with what has preceded. The prizes of a mule for the winner and a cup for the loser seem to be on a lower level; and although Eurualos is one of the Argive leaders (2.565–6), his opponent Epeios is not a heroic figure: as he says himself, he is not so good at fighting in battle (670), and he turns out later to be the carpenter who made the Wooden Horse (*Od.* 8.492–3, 11.523). In the weight-putting event he appears to have made a fool of himself with a bad throw (839–40). His challenge speech (667–75) is extremely boastful and grimly humorous, in a way typical of heavyweight boxers at all times, and some have seen him as a brutish and ridiculous figure in this scene. But he *is* described as a skilful boxer (665), and despite his dire threats he does behave generously towards his defeated opponent, setting him on his feet again, and he is aptly characterized at 695–6 as μεγάθυμος (cf. R. L. Howland, *PCPS* 183 (1954–5) 15–16). Unlike later literary accounts of boxing matches, such as those of Theocritus (*Id.* 22.27–134), Apollonius Rhodius (2.1–97) and Virgil (*Aen.* 5.362–484), this one plays down the brutality, and the fight itself is briefly described. The interest is primarily in the characters as in the preceding episodes. Cf. the somewhat comic match between the beggars Odysseus and Iros at *Od.* 18.1–107, where again the fight is over quite quickly, and attention focuses on the preliminaries. There are good accounts of the Homeric scenes, and of ancient boxing in general, in Gardiner, *Sports* 17–18, 402–34, and Harris, *Athletes* 97–101. See also Laser, *Arch. Hom.* T 43–9, and for Bronze Age boxers cf. E. Vermeule and V. Karageorghis, *Mycenaean Pictorial Vase Painting* (Harvard 1982) 43–4, 93.

653 πυγμαχίης ἀλεγεινῆς: cf. 701 παλαισμοσύνης ἀλεγεινῆς. Both sports were painful and dangerous and the epithet is well chosen.

654–6 ἡμίονον ταλαεργὸν ἄγων is repeated at 662. The noun–epithet formula recurs in the genitive at 666, 2× *Od.* and once in *HyHerm.* For 655 see on 266, and for δέπας ἀμφικύπελλον see on 1.584.

657–8 = 271–2. Verse 659 = 802.

660 ἀνασχομένω seems to be a technical word meaning 'putting up one's fists' in preparation for the fight. Cf. 686, and *Od.* 18.89 χεῖρας ἀνέσχον, 95 ἀνασχομένω.

660–1 The mythographical scholia (AD) say that Apollo was patron-god of boxing because he defeated the brigand Phorbas by this means, according to 'the cyclic poets'. Another legend made him defeat Ares in boxing at Olympia (Paus. 5.7.10), and the Delphians sacrificed to Apollo as πύκτης (Plut. *Mor.* 724c). The only athletic contest mentioned as pleasing Apollo on Delos at *HyAp* 149–50 is boxing. But he could be seen as a god of athletic achievement in general, as κουροτρόφος and patron of young men. Cf. Plut. *Mor.* 723B–C: 'this god is fond of athletics and of victory ... and is protector of contestants'.

661 δώη καμμονίην: see on 22.257. This is an endurance test. 'There were no rounds in Greek boxing. The opponents fought to a finish ... Usually the fight went on until one of the two was incapable of fighting any more, or acknowledged himself defeated ...' (Gardiner, *Sports* 415). Here γνώωσι ... Ἀχαιοί indicates that the victory needed to be confirmed by the spectators, whose part in deciding contests is suggested by their intervention at 822–3.

662 νεέσθω: ancient and medieval texts are divided between this and the variant φερέσθω. Aristarchus may have objected to this because he did not consider φέρειν suitable to use with an animate object (see on 259–61).

664 ὡς ἔφατ', ὄρνυτο δ' αὐτίκ': cf. 488 = 754. ἀνὴρ ἠΰς τε μέγας τε is applied to Agamemnon and the greater Aias at 3.167 (see comment) and 226, and both are said there to be exceptionally tall.

665 For Epeios see on 653–99. His father Panopeus is the eponym of the town in Phokis mentioned at 2.520 and 17.307. Stesichorus portrayed him as being made to carry water for the Achaean leaders, because of which Athene had pity on him (fr. 200 *PMG*), and later he became proverbial for cowardice, and a butt of comedy. He may be intended as a slightly ludicrous figure here already.

666–75 Epeios claims automatic possession of the first prize by taking hold of it, and he invites anyone who will to take the second, as he claims to be 'the greatest'. There is a touch of resentment in the rather pathetic reference to his being a poor fighter, and to boost his self-confidence still more he threatens to 'smash' his opponent. Verses 674–5 are grimly ironic: 'Let him have his family mourners ready to carry him off!' bT comment that the speech is 'full of character and very aggressive'.

667 Epeios ironically echoes Akhilleus' last words (663).

670–1 'To admit one's weaknesses adds credibility to one's claim for superiority' (AbT); cf. Plut. *Mor.* 543F, who adds that Epeios' confession seems rather ridiculous. For ἦ οὐχ ἅλις ὅττι cf. 5.349, 17.450, *Od.* 2.312, in speeches of protest. For μάχης ἐπιδεύομαι cf. 17.142 μάχης ... ἐδεύεο, 24.385 μάχης ἐπεδεύετ' Ἀχαιῶν, etc.

οὐδ' ἄρα πως ἦν ... δαήμονα φῶτα γενέσθαι: for οὐδ' ἄρα πως ἦν see 16.60–1n.; and for this gnomic reflection cf. 4.320, 13.729–34, and *Od.* 8.167–77, where Odysseus in the Phaeacian games replies to Eurualos' taunts, saying that one cannot be good at everything. The Phaeacian Eurualos, who occurs only in this episode of the *Odyssey*, has the same name as Epeios' opponent, and the phrase δαήμονα φῶτα has its only Homeric parallel at *Od.* 8.159 in Eurualos' speech to Odysseus. It is hard to avoid the suspicion that there is some reminiscence of the scene in the *Iliad*.

672 = 1.212 etc. For the variant καὶ μήν cf. 23.410.

673 ἀντικρύ: perhaps 'with a straight blow' here, rather than 'absolutely'. The threat is typical of prize-fighters in all ages. Cf. the threats of Odysseus and Iros before their fight (*Od.* 18.20–4, 18.26–33), and Amukos' challenge at A.R. 2.57–9.

674–5 For κηδεμόνες see on 163. There is an echo of 159–60, where those who have responsibility for Patroklos' burial are asked to remain (μενόντων), and ἐξοίσουσιν continues the word-play, as the verb suggests the ἐκφορά or funeral procession.

676 = 3.95 etc. Epeios' speech makes the desired impact on his audience.

677–82 Eurualos is mentioned in the Catalogue of Ships as the third Argive leader, after Diomedes and Sthenelos (2.563–6). Diomedes is his cousin both by blood and marriage, being the grandson through Deïpule of Adrastos, Mekisteus' brother, and husband of his aunt Aigialeia, Adrastos' daughter (5.410–15 and Τ 23.681–2). So he is indeed one of the κηδεμόνες mentioned by Epeios. His concern for Eurualos suggests anxiety about the outcome, and the way in which he prepares him for the fight reminds one of later trainers (cf. Τ 681–2 οἶδε καὶ τὰς παραινέσεις τῶν παιδοτριβῶν ὁ ποιητής).

677–8 Cf. 2.565 Εὐρύαλος ... ἰσόθεος φώς and 678 = 2.566 (see comment). The correct reading in 678, however, may be Μηκιστέος or Μηκιστέως: see on 15.339, 16.21.

679–80 This must refer to Mekisteus, rather than Eurualos or his grandfather Talaos. His exploit, in defeating all the Cadmeans at the funeral games of Oidipous, is similar to that of Diomedes' father Tudeus at 4.385–90, where he challenged them to contests and beat them all, during an embassy. It is clear that Oidipous died at Thebes in this version, and this agrees with *Od.* 11.275–80, where he remains at Thebes as king after his wife's suicide, and with the Hesiodic *Catalogue* (fr. 192 M–W). The story that he died at Athens seems to be an Athenian innovation, and the location at Colonus may be Sophocles' own invention. δεδουπότος might suggest that Oidipous fell in battle: cf. 13.426 where δουπῆσαι is used on its own in this sense. This was Aristarchus' view (Arn/A). Alternatively it may be used simply to mean that he had died: that is how it was taken by some Hellenistic poets (A.R. 1.1304, 4.557, Lyc. 492).

683 ζῶμα δέ οἱ πρῶτον παρακάββαλεν: the ζῶμα is the girdle or loin-cloth, later called διάζωμα or περίζωμα, which early Greek athletes wore; cf. *Od.* 18.30, 18.67–9, 18.76. Its abandonment in favour of nudity was probably a gradual process, adopted first for running races and only later for other contests. Cf. J. Jüthner, *Die athletischen Leibesübungen der Griechen* II.1 (Vienna 1968) 48–50, and bT 683 with Erbse's references. For παρακάββαλεν see on 127; it should mean that Diomedes puts the girdle down on the ground, rather than actually putting it on Eurualos, as he does this himself (685): cf. Mazon, *REA* 42 (1940) 262. It does not seem necessary to read περικάββαλε (suggested by Heyne).

684 ἱμάντας ἐϋτμήτους βοὸς ἀγραύλοιο: cf. 10.567, 21.30 ἐϋτμήτοισιν ἱμᾶσι. The boxers bind leather thongs round their hands for protection, a practice which continued into the classical period, when a harder type of glove called σφαῖραι began to supersede them. The thongs, being softer, were later known as μείλιχαι or ἱμάντες μαλακώτεροι (cf. Gardiner, *Sports* 402ff., Laser, *Arch. Hom.* τ 41ff.). By contrast in the fight between Odysseus and Iros bare fists seem to have been used (*Od.* 18.66–107).

685 This is repeated at 710, with slight variation.

686–7 Cf. 7.255–6 τὼ δ' ἐκσπασσαμένω δολίχ' ἔγχεα χερσὶν ἄμ' ἄμφω | σύν ῥ' ἔπεσον ... For ἀνασχομένω see on 660. ἄμφω is nominative here, as at 7.255. σὺν δέ σφι βαρεῖαι χεῖρες ἔμιχθεν is a vivid way of describing the way in which the boxers 'mingle' their heavy blows.

688 χρόμαδος: an absolute *hapax*, evidently onomatopoeic, to describe the grinding of their jaws or the crack of blows on their cheeks (AbT and Erbse *ad loc.*). Hesychius mentions the related forms χρόμη and χρόμος, with similar meanings. Cf. A.R. 2.82–4 ὡς τοῖσι παρήϊά τ' ἀμφοτέρωθεν | καὶ γένυες κτύπεον· βρυχὴ δ' ὑπετέλλετ' ὀδόντων | ἄσπετος ... and Virgil, *Aen.* 5.436 *duro crepitant sub volnere malae.*

689–94 Epeios knocks his opponent out with an upper cut on the jaw, at the moment when Eurualos is looking for an opening and evidently off guard. The blow lifts him off the ground, and his back arches as he falls like a leaping fish.

691 αὐτοῦ ... γυῖα: 'for his bright limbs failed him on the spot'. ὑπερείπω occurs only here in Homer, later in Plutarch, *Pomp.* 74.

692–4 The simile is brief but very effective in its details: the fish leaps out of the shallow water near the shore, as it is stirred by the north wind, and then disappears again into the dark ripples. Cf. 7.63–4 οἵη δὲ Ζεφύροιο ἐχεύατο πόντον ἔπι φρὶξ | ὀρνυμένοιο νέον, μελάνει δέ τε πόντος ὑπ' αὐτῆς, and see on 7.63–6 and 21.126. Here ἀναπάλλεται is used to mean 'leaps up', although it is from πάλλομαι, whereas ἀνέπαλτο in 694 is perhaps originally from ἀν-επ-ἄλλομαι (cf. Leumann, *HW* 60–4).

692 ὑπὸ φρικός: there was an ancient variant ὑπαὶ ῥιπῆς (T), substituting a slightly easier expression, as φρίξ should really refer strictly speaking to the water rather than the effect of the wind.

693 θίν᾽ ἐν φυκιόεντι: the epithet ('full of seaweed', 'weed-strown') occurs only here in Homer; cf. Theocr. *Id.* 11.14, 21.10, and *Il.* 9.7 φῦκος. – μέλαν δέ ἑ κῦμα κάλυψεν recurs at *Od.* 5.353.

694 Cf. 8.85 ἀλγήσας δ᾽ ἀνέπαλτο; 11.732, 11.744 ἀτάρ μεγάθυμοι ᾽Επειοί. Here too the variant ἀνέπαλτο· ἀτάρ ... should perhaps be preferred, since there seem to be no certain examples of αὐτάρ where the first syllable falls in the second half of the foot: see on 4.542, and cf. C. J. Ruijgh, *L'Elément achéen dans la langue épique* (Assen 1957) 45–6.

695-7 The aftermath is described with comic pathos. Cf. the end of Odysseus' fight with Iros, where Odysseus drags him by the foot outside the palace and leaves him propped against the courtyard wall (*Od.* 18.100– 7); also Virgil, *Aen.* 5.468–71 *ast illum fidi aequales genua aegra trahentem* | *iactantemque utroque caput crassumque cruorem* | *ore eiectantem mixtosque in sanguine dentes* | *ducunt ad navis.*

695 φίλοι δ᾽ ἀμφέσταν ἑταῖροι is repeated from 18.233.

697 αἷμα παχὺ πτύοντα: neither the phrase αἷμα παχύ nor the simple verb πτύω occur elsewhere in Homer; cf. 781 ὄνθον ἀποπτύων.

698 ἀλλοφρονέοντα: only here in *Il.*; cf. *Od.* 10.374 ἀλλ᾽ ἥμην ἀλλοφρονέων, where it means 'with other things in mind', whereas here it must mean 'dizzy' or 'groggy'; cf. Theocr. *Id.* 22.129 κεῖτ᾽ ἀλλοφρονέων (of Amukos, knocked out by Poludeukes). It may be connected with ἠλεός ('distraught', 'crazy'); cf. Chantraine, *Dict.* s.v.

699 δέπας ἀμφικύπελλον: cf. 656, 663, 667.

700–39 Akhilleus offers prizes for wrestling. Telamonian Aias and Odysseus fight. Eventually Akhilleus stops the contest, declaring it a draw

After the decisive outcome of the boxing, involving two minor heroes, comes the wrestling match between two leading figures, Odysseus and Telamonian Aias, which is inconclusive. Wrestling was one of the most popular sports in antiquity, and clearly a technique has been developed by the time of the *Iliad*. The fight, however, is briefly described, and some aspects are not explicit. Evidently it belongs to the type later known as 'upright wrestling', whose object was to throw the opponent to the ground, as opposed to 'ground wrestling' where the struggle continued on the ground until one contestant admitted defeat: this formed part of the *pankration* rather than wrestling proper. Later contests were decided only when an opponent had been thrown three times (cf. Soph. fr. 941.13 with Pearson's commentary). In the Homeric fight, however, it is not obvious how many throws were needed for victory. The fight has two main stages. In the first the two opponents stand locked together, each unable to throw the other. Then to break the deadlock they agree to lift each other off the ground. Aias lifts Odysseus, who uses one leg to kick Aias behind the knee, so that Aias falls backwards and Odysseus lands on top of him. Then Odysseus lifts Aias just a little off the ground, and at the same time uses his knee against him, probably applying pressure to one of Aias' legs to make him fall on his side; but again this results in their both falling together side by side. At this point Akhilleus stops the fight, telling them to divide the prizes equally: how they are to do this is left unexplained.

The main question is whether Odysseus has gained a technical advantage by causing Aias to fall twice, or whether the fact that he himself also falls means that these do not count as throws. It does look as though, morally speaking, Odysseus' greater skill (cf. 725) is prevailing over Aias' strength, or may do so in the long run. The fact that Akhilleus stops the fight is significant. His sympathy for Aias as a straightforward character, and his suspicion of Odysseus' indirectness, come out strongly in book 9 (cf. especially 308–13, 622–55). The implication may be that Akhilleus does not want to see Odysseus the victor by guile.

This contest has been seen by some modern scholars as related to the famous one for the armour of Akhilleus at his own funeral games, which led to Aias' suicide, an episode referred to by Odysseus himself in his meeting with Aias' ghost at *Od.* 11.543–64, and related in the *Aithiopis* and *Ilias Parva* (OCT vol. v, p. 106 lines 16–17, 20–3 = Davies, *EGF* p. 47. 29–30, 52.3–5, *Aithiopis* fr. 2 = fr. 1 Davies, *Ilias Parva* frr. 2–3 = frr. 2–3 Davies): cf. Kullmann, *Quellen* 81–2, 335. If this is right, Akhilleus' decision maintains a balance between the two opponents broken by the later contest. On the other hand Aias is said to be the best warrior after Akhilleus at 2.768–9, and Odysseus himself echoes this view at *Od.* 11.550–1, calling him second to Akhilleus in appearance and achievements (εἶδος and ἔργα). The wrestling match is a more specialized activity in which skill plays a large part, and one cannot use it as a test of ἀρετή in general.

For wrestling in early Greek art and literature cf. Laser, *Arch. Hom.* τ 49ff.

701 παλαισμοσύνης ἀλεγεινῆς: cf. 653 πυγμαχίης ἀλεγεινῆς. παλαισμοσύνη occurs only here in *Il.*; cf. *Od.* 8.103, 126. According to Eustathius (1387.40) Aristarchus read παλαιμοσύνη, as in a first-century B.C. papyrus and a few MSS; cf. Tyrt. 12.2 (West) παλαιμοσύνης (v.l. παλαισμοσύνης), Pindar, *P.* 2.61 παλαιμονεῖ. See Wackernagel, *Kleine Schriften* I 824.

702 ἐμπυριβήτην: this absolute *hapax*, meaning 'able to stand on the fire' (cf. 267 ἄπυρον, etc.), belongs to a rare type of compound epithet, the first part of which is composed of a prepositional phrase; cf. Hdt. 5.108 ἐγχειρίθετος. The type of vessel is discussed by Athenaeus (37Eff.).

703 'And this the Achaeans valued among themselves at twelve oxen.' At 6.235–6 Diomedes' bronze armour is worth nine oxen, Glaukos' golden armour a hundred, and at 23.885 a cauldron is valued at a single ox. The form τῖον with long iota is used interchangeably with the form τίον as at 705, according to metrical convenience.

704–5 The second prize is a skilled woman worth only four oxen. Contrast *Od.* 1.431, where Eurukleia was bought for twenty, evidently an unusually high price. Cf. also *Il.* 7.289–91, where a special gift of honour is either a tripod or two horses or a concubine. τεσσαράβοιος is an absolute *hapax*.

706 = 271 etc. For 707 cf. 753 = 831.

708–9 The two contestants are at once contrasted by their epithets, the huge Aias and the crafty Odysseus. Odysseus, like Diomedes, had been wounded in the fighting at 11.434–8, and was still affected by his wound at 19.48–9, but we should not stop to worry about this (as T 709 does). Odysseus' skill as a wrestler is mentioned again at *Od.* 4.341–5 = 17.132–6, where he defeats Philomeleides on Lesbos.

709 The repetition of the preposition (ἀν ... ἀνίστατο) is unusual (cf. *Od.* 5.260), and due to the influence of the usual formula without the verb, as at 3.268, 23.755 ἀν δ' 'Οδυσεὺς πολύμητις, where ὄρνυτο has occurred already. For κέρδεα εἰδώς cf. 322 ὅς δέ κε κέρδεα εἰδῇ, etc.

710–13 For 710 cf. 685. In 711–13 the two wrestlers take their stance, gripping each other with their heads down, so that they resemble the gable rafters of a house: cf. Gardiner, *Sports* 382–3 with figs. 3 (top left), 111, 113.

711 ἀγκάς normally means 'in one's arms' or 'with one's arms', and is used before a vowel (5.371 etc.). Consequently it has been taken as a dative form of ἀγκων (ἀγκάσι), whose origin has here been forgotten since it is found before a consonant (Chantraine, *Dict.* s.v.). Here it perhaps means that 'they grasped each other *by the arms* with their stout hands'. Cf. bT and Eust., who comment that this form of grip is 'ancient and unsophisticated' (παλαιὸς καὶ ἀγροικώδης), and that they take hold under their opponents' ribs with the right hand and grip the right elbow with the left hand.

712–13 This is the only explicit reference to a gabled roof in the Homeric poems, although it seems reasonable to assume that Akhilleus' hut had a pitched roof, as it is said to be thatched at 24.448–51. Cf. Lorimer, *HM* 418–19, Drerup, *Arch. Hom.* o 116–20. The passage is well illustrated by depictions of wrestlers in Geometric and later Greek art: cf. Laser, *Arch. Hom.* T 52–7, especially fig. 15.

712 ἀμείβοντες: '"interchangers", i.e. rafters that meet and cross each other' (LSJ). The word occurs only here in classical Greek literature, and rarely in late authors. The later technical word was συστάται (bT), which was used of athletes in close combat. At 12.456 ἐπημοιβοί is similarly used as an epithet of bars holding the double-door of the Greek wall.

713 = 16.213, where the verse again occurs in an architectural simile.

714–17 A detailed passage describes the effect of their effort on the wrestlers, as in the boxing match (688–9). Verses 714–15 mean 'and their backs creaked with the force of their strong arms as they were gripped firmly'. τρίζω is used of birds crying or bats squeaking in Homer (2.314, *Od.* 24.7), later of bones cracking, teeth grinding, etc. The formular phrase θρασειάων ἀπὸ χειρῶν (11.553 etc.) is slightly strained here.

715 κατὰ δὲ νότιος ῥέεν ἱδρώς is repeated from 11.811.

716–17 Cf. 2.267 σμῶδιξ δ' αἱματόεσσα μεταφρένου ἐξυπανέστη (of Thersites).

718 νίκης ἱέσθην: cf. 767, and also 371 etc.

719 σφῆλαι: the simple verb occurs only here in *Il.*; cf. *Od.* 17.464.

721 The variant ἐϋκνήμιδες Ἀχαιοί is possible, as the verb is used both transitively and intransitively in Homer, but Aristarchus preferred our text (Arn/A). Cf. *Od.* 4.460 ἀλλ' ὅτε δή ῥ' ἀνιάζ' ὁ γέρων.

724 bT explain that this is called λαβή, where each contestant in turn gives the other an opportunity of lifting him. Aias' speech is typically brief, and he leaves the issue to Zeus to decide. Cf. 17.575 τὰ δέ κεν Διὶ πάντα μελήσει.

725 δόλου δ' οὐ λήθετ' Ὀδυσσεύς: 'Odysseus forgot not his (habitual) cunning'.

726 κόψ' ὄπιθεν κώληπα τυχών: 'he caught and struck the back of his knee'. κώληψ (cf. κωλῆ etc.) seems to recur only at Nic. *Th.* 424. ὑπέλυσε δὲ γυῖα | recurs at 15.581.

727 ἔβαλ': Leaf prefers the variant ἔπεσ', weakly attested but read by A, on the grounds that the repetition of Ὀδυσσεύς in 727 implies a previous change of subject. This seems very reasonable.

728 = 881. The fact that the crowd are astonished suggests perhaps that they expected Aias to win!

729–31 Odysseus clearly has difficulty in lifting Aias at all, but he manages to hook his knee round Aias' leg, so that they fall sideways (cf. bT, Eust., and Gardiner, *Sports* 397). bT and Eust. give various technical names for this manoeuvre. ἐγγνάμπτω occurs only here.

732 μιάνθησαν δὲ κονίῃ: cf. 16.797.

733–6 This sequence resembles the way in which the duel between Hektor and Aias is cut short at 7.273–81: καί νύ κε δὴ ξιφέεσσ' αὐτοσχεδὸν οὐτάζοντο, | εἰ μὴ κήρυκες ... | ἦλθον ... | μέσσῳ δ' ἀμφοτέρων σκῆπτρα σχέθον, εἶπέ τε μῦθον | κῆρυξ Ἰδαῖος ... | "μηκέτι, παῖδε φίλω, πολεμίζετε μηδὲ μάχεσθον· | ἀμφοτέρω γὰρ σφῶϊ φιλεῖ νεφεληγερέτα Ζεύς, | ἄμφω δ' αἰχμητά ..." See on 7.273–81, and Kirk in Fenik, *Tradition* 38.

735 'Do not go on struggling, nor wear yourselves out with your efforts.' Cf. 12.457 etc. ἐρεισάμενος. The variant ἐρίζεσθον is less vivid.

736 ἀέθλια ἴσ' ἀνελόντες: cf. 823. Eustathius and the scholia are at a loss as to how the prizes could be equally divided. The poet presumably wishes to press on to the next contest, before his audience loses interest.

738 = 7.379 etc.

740–97 The foot race. Akhilleus offers a silver mixing-bowl as first prize, and others for second and third. The contestants are the lesser Aias, Odysseus and Antilokhos. Aias takes the lead, with Odysseus just behind, until Odysseus prays to Athene, who causes Aias to slip. Odysseus wins and Aias comes second. Antilokhos is last, and makes a diplomatic speech which leads Akhilleus to double the value of his prize

After the two close-combat sports the foot race comes as a relief. It is a very entertaining episode, which in several ways echoes the chariot race and forms a kind of coda to it (cf. A. Köhnken, *Hermes* 109 (1981) 129–48). After the combat between Odysseus and the greater Aias in the wrestling match we have the contrasting pair of Odysseus and the lesser Aias, who is (as his formular epithet indicates) one of the fastest runners among the Greeks (see on 14.521–2). Aias only just takes the lead over Odysseus, as in the chariot race Eumelos is only just ahead of Diomedes (375–81 ~ 758–66). Towards the end of the race (768 ~ 373) Athene's intervention in response to Odysseus' prayer resembles the intervention of Apollo and Athene in the chariot race, leading to Eumelos' crash and Diomedes' victory. Aias' ignominious defeat, which leaves him with a mouthful of dung, is appropriate for the man who had displayed such foulness of language in his dispute with Idomeneus (473–98). Odysseus' μῆτις triumphs because he prays to Athene at the crucial moment, and she responds to her favourite as usual (cf. 782–3). Athene's treatment of Aias foreshadows his later fate, after he had aroused her anger by his rape of Kassandre during the sack of Troy: cf. *Od.* 4.499–511, OCT vol. v, p. 108.2–6 (*Iliupersis*), 108.26–8 (*Nostoi*) = Davies, *EGF* pp. 62.23–7, 67.18–19 etc.

Antilokhos' rôle echoes his part in the chariot race. The emphasis there on his youthful folly in the race (587–90, 604) is picked up in his speech about how the gods favour older men (787–92), as if he is drawing the moral of the previous episode. There is also an echo of the exchange between Akhilleus and Nestor there (615–52). Moreover, there Antilokhos had offered to give up his prize to Menelaos, who had in turn allowed him to keep it. Here again his diplomacy gains him a dividend, for his tactful praise of Akhilleus leads to the doubling of his prize.

Thus as in the chariot race what gives the episode its life is the strong focus on the heroes' characters, and the interplay of this with divine intervention.

740–9 The first prize is described at greater length than any other in the games. It is very precious, both in the beauty of its workmanship and by association: it belonged to Patroklos, and its use to buy Lukaon reminds us of one of Akhilleus' most unfortunate victims. The breastplate of Asteropaios has already been given as a prize (560–2), and in the next contest Akhilleus will offer the armour of Sarpedon, which Patroklos stripped from him, and the sword of Asteropaios (797–808). Thus we are constantly reminded of the main threads of the narrative, and the purpose of the contests themselves. The poet does not *describe* these objects in detail but indicates their value by telling their histories, a point made in Lessing's *Laocoon* (translated by W. Ross, London 1836, 150ff.).

The Sidonians have been mentioned once before in the poem, as makers of the embroidered robes which Paris brought from Sidon on his journey to Troy with Helen: the finest of these was offered by Hekabe to Athene's statue (6.289–92). In the *Odyssey* Menelaos offers Telemakhos a silver mixing-bowl with gilded rim, given to him by king Phaidimos of Sidon when he stayed there on his travels; he says that this is the most beautiful and valuable of his treasures (4.613–19 = 15.113–19). Sidon is also referred to as πολύχαλκος at *Od.* 15.425.

In 743–4 the Sidonians are craftsmen, whereas Φοίνικες ἄνδρες are the merchants who bring the bowl to Lemnos. This is the only reference in the poem to the Φοίνικες, whereas they appear several times in *Odyssey* 13–15 (13.272 etc.), and the land Φοινίκη is mentioned twice (4.83, 14.291). At *Od.* 4.83–4 the Sidonians at first sight look as if they are a separate people, but Eumaios' Phoenician nurse is from Sidon (15.417, 15.425), and the Phoenician sailors go (home) to Σιδονίη at 13.272, 13.285. As a rule in Homer it seems that the name Sidonians is applied to the Phoenicians when at home, whereas abroad they are called Phoenicians. In some Old Testament texts referring to the Early Iron Age the term 'Sidonians' is applied to the Phoenicians at home, including the people of Tyre: for example I Kings 16.31, where Ethbaal, king of Tyre (*c.* 887–856 B.C.), is called 'king of the Sidonians'. This title 'king of the Sidonians' for the ruler of Tyre remained in use for over 170 years from Ethbaal's time onward, i.e. during the ninth and eighth centuries. The basic reason was that after its destruction by the Sea Peoples Tyre had been refounded as a Sidonian town, and it then came to dominate the area. Occasionally 'Sidon' is used in records of the period from *c.* 1100 B.C. onwards to denote this area, including Tyre: cf. W. F. Albright, *Cambridge Ancient History*, 3rd edn, II.2 (Cambridge 1975) 519–20, H. J. Katzenstein, *The History of Tyre* (Jerusalem 1973) 129ff. It is possible that references to Sidon rather than Tyre (never mentioned by Homer) could be due to the tradition that this was the more important city in the Late Bronze Age. But it is more likely that Sidon actually was the centre of production for works of art.

Decorated silver and bronze bowls, thought to be of Phoenician origin, have been found in various parts of the Near East and Mediterranean world, dating between the ninth and seventh centuries B.C.: cf. G. Markoe, *Phoenician Bronze and Silver Bowls from Cyprus and the Mediterranean* (Berkeley 1985), and *AR* 1984–85, p. 15 (two bronze bowls at Lefkandi, *c.* 900 B.C.). Significantly, however, silver (as opposed to bronze) bowls do not seem to appear in a Greek context before the eighth century.

It is unclear exactly how early the Phoenicians themselves began to trade in the Aegean area. Recent finds suggest that this may have been from at least 900 B.C. (cf. J. N. Coldstream, 'Greeks and Phoenicians in the Aegean', in *Phönizier im Westen*, ed. H. G. Niemeyer, Mainz 1982, 261–75). This has, however, been questioned (J. D. Muhly, 'Phoenicia and the Phoenicians', in *Biblical Archaeology Today*, Israel Exploration Society, Jerusalem 1985, 177–91), and some of the finds might only prove that the Greeks themselves were bringing these objects back from their travels, as Menelaos did (*Od.* 4.615–19). The objects from Lefkandi described by M. R. Popham, E. Touloupa and L. H. Sackett in *BSA* 77 (1982) 213–48, especially 242–5, 247–8, show trading connexions with the Near East already well established by *c.* 900 B.C., and at Kommos in Crete there seems to have been an actual Phoenician settlement from at least 800 B.C. or earlier (cf. J. W. Shaw, *AJA* 93 (1989) 165–83).

Greek tradition held that the Phoenicians settled in some Aegean islands (T. Braun, *CAH*, 2nd edn, III.3, Cambridge 1982, 6–7). Some historians view these traditions with scepticism, but they should not be dismissed. The case for Phoenicians in Thasos seems quite strong (A. J. Graham, *BSA* 73 (1978) 88–92), and they certainly settled in Rhodes at Ialysos, and perhaps also in Cos (Coldstream, *op. cit.* 268–9). Lemnos would fit into this pattern of Phoenician activity. The Lemnians themselves according to Homer traded with the coast of Asia Minor: at 7.467–75 Euneos' ships bring wine into the Greek camp at Troy and are paid in bronze, iron, hides, cattle and slaves. This agrees with 21.40–1 and 23.746–7, where Euneos buys Lukaon (as a slave) with this Phoenician bowl (see also on 14.230). In the *Odyssey* the Phoenicians trade in slaves (14.287–98, 15.415–84). One can easily imagine that, had Lukaon not been ransomed by Eetion of Imbros, he might have ended up in some distant slave-market, carried there by a Phoenician ship.

741 ἀργύρεον κρητῆρα τετυγμένον: cf. *Od.* 4.615–16 (=15.115–16) δώσω τοι κρητῆρα τετυγμένον· ἀργύρεος δὲ | ἔστιν ἅπας (see on 740–9). For τετυγμένον meaning 'of fine workmanship' cf. 14.9 etc.

742 κάλλει ἐνίκα: cf. 9.130, 9.272 αἳ (τότε) κάλλει ἐνίκων φῦλα γυναικῶν; for ἐνίκα meaning 'was first' cf. 18.252, *Od.* 3.121.

743 Σιδόνες πολυδαίδαλοι: one might have expected Σῑδόνες, since the

Semitic name was Saida, and the iota is long in related forms, e.g. *Od.* 15.425 Σῖδῶνος etc. The epithet πολυδαίδαλος is only applied to craftsmen here in Homer, elsewhere always to works of art (3.358 etc.).

744 ἐπ᾽ ἠεροειδέα πόντον: only here in *Il.*; cf. *Od.* 2.263 etc. (4×), and ἐν ἠεροειδέϊ πόντῳ *Od.* 3.294 etc. (6×). But ἠεροειδές alone is used at 5.770 in the context of someone looking out over the sea. The metrically equivalent ἐπ᾽ εὐρέα νῶτα θαλάσσης is used 3× *Il.*, 7× *Od.*

745 στῆσαν δ᾽ ἐν λιμένεσσι: cf. *Od.* 19.188–9 στῆσε δ᾽ ἐν Ἀμνισῷ ... | ἐν λιμέσιν χαλεποῖσι ..., *Od.* 12.305 στήσαμεν ἐν λιμένι γλαφυρῷ εὐεργέα νῆα. As in these cases the verb probably means 'they landed' (cf. bT), rather than 'they set it up' or 'weighed it'.

Θόαντι δὲ δῶρον ἔδωκαν: Thoas was king of Lemnos (14.230) and father of Hupsipule, who married Iason and produced Euneos (7.468–9). The gift could have been in return for the right to moor in the harbour (Eust. 1327.57), or to trade in Lemnos, but the poet does not explain.

746–7 Cf. 21.40–1 on Lukaon's purchase. At 21.79 Lukaon says that he was sold for a hundred oxen. This was the value of the golden armour of Glaukos (6.234–6); see also on 23.703. Was the cup alone worth this much?

748–9 These verses return to the point of 740 with greater elaboration. With ὅς τις we must understand the antecedent 'for that man'.

751 λοισθήϊα: 'as last prize'; cf. 785 λοισθήϊον ... ἄεθλον. These appear to be the only instances of λοισθήϊος in surviving literature; cf. 23.536 λοῖσθος, and later λοίσθιος. For the plural form cf. 275 τὰ πρῶτα, 538 δεύτερα. The variant λοισθῆϊ (as if dative of λοισθεύς) is rejected by T.

752–3 =830–1 (cf. 271 etc., 706–7). The false variant πειρήσεσθον here (Zenodotus and a few texts) is derived from 707.

754 =488, perhaps a reminder of Aias' quarrel with Idomeneus. At 14.520–2 Aias is said to be the fastest of the Achaeans in pursuit of the enemy.

755 ἂν δ᾽ Ὀδυσεὺς πολύμητις: cf. 709, 3.268. Here too as at 709ff. Odysseus' intelligence will be shown in what ensues, and the epithet is functional.

756 At 15.569–71 Menelaos had said that Antilokhos was the fastest runner of the younger generation (cf. also *Od.* 3.112, 4.202). For ποσὶ πάντας ἐνίκα cf. 20.410 πόδεσσι δὲ πάντας ἐνίκα.

757–67 This section resembles the opening part of the chariot race.

757 =358. Aristarchus thought this verse an addition, because of his theory that μεταστοιχί meant 'in file', which is probably wrong (see on 352–8).

The chariot race itself started with a general description (362–72), of which there is only one verbal echo (370–2 ∼ 766–7), with significant variation. This was followed by a description of the return stretch, where the horses went at full gallop, with Eumelos in the lead and Diomedes only just behind (373–81). This is echoed by 758–66, although there is a displacement of the order, in that 373 (ἀλλ' ὅτε δὴ πύματον τέλεον δρόμον) is postponed to 768, where it introduces the last and decisive stage of the foot race.

758–9 These verses resemble 375–6: ... ἄφαρ δ' ἵπποισι τάθη δρόμος· ὦκα δ' ἔπειτα | ... ἔκφερον ἵπποι ~ τοῖσι δ' ἀπὸ νύσσης τέτατο δρόμος· ὦκα δ' ἔπειτα | ἔκφερ' 'Οϊλιάδης ... The description of Diomedes' horses, so close to Eumelos that they warmed his back with their breath (377–81) is echoed at 759–66, where the motif of Odysseus' breath on Aias' head is preceded by an elaborate simile stressing how close he was, and the further point that his feet landed in Aias' tracks before the dust had settled. The emphasis on the nearness of the contestants suggests that it would take very little to reverse the order, and whereas at 370–2 it is the contestants who urge on their horses in their zeal for victory, here it is the spectators who urge on Odysseus as he strives to win (766–7), as if they think that he deserves to come first, and that Aias ought to lose.

758 = *Od.* 8.121. At 332 and 338 νύσσα referred to the turning-post, whereas here it seems to be the start, and the phrase means 'right from the start they ran at full stretch'. bT reasonably assume that the race was a single lap, but Köhnken takes it as a δίαυλος as in the chariot race (*Hermes* 109 (1981) 133–4), and the phrase could mean that it was after the turning-post that they began to go flat out (cf. R. D. Williams on Virgil, *Aen.* 5.317–18).

759 ἔκφερ' 'Οϊλιάδης: cf. 376–7 (with comment). Zenodotus read ἔκθορ' ὁ 'Ιλιάδης (Did/A), as in other cases where Aias' patronymic occurs (see on 13.203).

759–64 This simile emphasizes the closeness of the two runners: cf. 760 ἄγχι μάλα, 762 ἀγχόθι ... στήθεος, 763 ἐγγύθεν. The weaver stands right up to the vertical loom, and draws the horizontal shed rod (or one of two such rods) towards her breast, in order to separate the alternate threads of the warp (μίτος). Through the opening thus created between the two sets of threads the spool (πηνίον) which carries the weft thread is passed, and this is probably attached to the shuttle (κερκίς: cf. 22.448). Cf. H. B. Blümner, *Technologie und Terminologie der Gewerbe und Künste bei Griechen und Römern*, 2nd edn, i (Leipzig 1912) 148–54, and G. M. Crowfoot, *BSA* 37 (1936–7) 36–47.

κανών occurs only here in Homer in this sense (later in Aristophanes etc.), but cf. 8.193, 13.407 where it refers to the rods supporting the framework of a shield. πηνίον and μίτος occur nowhere else in Homer: πηνίον recurs in Theophrastus (*HP* 6.4) and rarely later, μίτος in classical and later Greek. As so often the language of the simile is precise and technical.

Fränkel (*Gleichnisse* 78–9) suggests that the choice of simile was due to the resemblance between the movement to and fro of the κανών on the loom and that of the runners' feet, so close to each other and yet never meeting. This has the advantage of drawing 763–4 within the field of the comparison.

760 γυναικὸς ἐϋζώνοιο: word-break after the fourth trochee is rare in Homer ('Hermann's Bridge'): cf. West, *Greek Metre* 37–8. It is found a number of times before a five-syllable word, as here: cf. 10.317, *Od.* 1.241, 4.684, 18.140. For other comparisons drawn from women's work cf. 4.141–5 (ivory-staining), and 12.433–5 (spinning).

760–3 In ὡς ὅτε ... κανών we must understand ἄγχι again with στήθεος. For παρὲκ μίτον ('out past the warp') cf. 24.349 etc. The repetition of στήθεος at the beginning of 761 and 763 draws attention to the main point of the simile.

764 The vividness of this verse is praised by Macrobius (*Sat.* 5.13.4–5): the dust settles so soon that we sense the extraordinary closeness of the runners' feet. Virgil's *calcemque terit iam calce Diores* (*Aen.* 5.324), although it has the virtue of compression, fails to match the Homeric expression, as Macrobius admits. The poet often refers to the dust in these episodes (cf. 315–16, 372, 437, 449, 502, 504–6, 732, 739), as in the battle-scenes.

765 This verse is a variation on 380–1. Odysseus is taller than Aias, and so breathes down on his head (bT). ἀϋτμήν occurs only here in *Il.* and at *Od.* 3.289 for the usual ἀϋτμή. Here it avoids the heavy spondaic fourth foot followed by word-break, which is relatively uncommon (cf. West, *Greek Metre* 37).

767 Cf. 371–2 νίκης ἱεμένων, κέκλοντο δὲ οἷσιν ἕκαστος | ἵπποις ... Some papyri and MSS read ἱέμενοι, and Eustathius seems to have known a variant ἱεμένων (as at 371). For μάλα δὲ σπεύδοντι κέλευον Eustathius compares the proverbial σπεύδοντα ἐποτρύνεις (1328.40f.).

768–79 The last and decisive stage of the race is described in two sections of five verses each, both introduced by ἀλλ' ὅτε δή ... (768–72, 773–7), followed by the result in two concluding verses (778–9). In the first Odysseus prays silently to Athene, who responds by giving him an extra burst of speed, the spurt of the runner at the end of a race. In the second Athene causes Aias to slip in the cow-dung at the very last moment. Odysseus then takes up the bowl, which evidently stood right at the finish so that the winner was the first to seize it, and Aias takes hold of the ox as second prize.

Aristarchus (Arn/A) wanted to reject 772, in which Athene gives Odysseus a spurt: 771–2 are repeated from 5.121–2, and Aristarchus argued that as the runners were so close Odysseus should have won anyway as a result of this help, and there was no need for Aias' slip as well. However, Köhnken has argued in reply (*Hermes* 109 (1981) 135ff.) that 772 is the answer to

Odysseus' prayer to help his own running, and that 772 and 774–7 are really simultaneous events, which the poet describes consecutively in his usual manner. The double character of Athene's intervention is similar to 388ff., where Athene assists Diomedes positively by returning his whip and causes Eumelos to crash.

Whether or not the two events are really simultaneous in the foot race perhaps does not matter, as the other points made by Köhnken seem convincing, and it is appropriate that Athene's response should be both positive and negative. Köhnken points out that Odysseus' victory is not *simply* the result of divine intervention, since it is his prayer at the crucial moment which prompts this. As usual human and divine motivation work together but Odysseus initiates the process, true to his character as πολύμητις (755), the attribute which makes him Athene's favourite (cf. 782–3). From a spectator's viewpoint Athene *represents* Odysseus' μῆτις, which enables him to know when to put on the spurt, and this action distracts Aias, who slips and falls (cf. Köhnken, *op. cit.* 141). But the poet sees things differently, and he is at pains to point the moral for us twice (782–3 and 787–92).

768 ἀλλ' ὅτε ... δρόμον echoes 373, but here it refers to the last part of the race, there to the second lap. Cf. Virgil, *Aen.* 5.327–8 *iamque fere spatio extremo fessique sub ipsam | finem adventabant* ... (when Nisus slips).

769 εὔχετο ... ὃν κατὰ θυμόν: cf. *Od.* 5.444 εὔξατο ὃν κατὰ θυμόν, of Odysseus praying to the river-god when he reaches Phaeacia. The scholia there suggest that a silent prayer is appropriate for the exhausted swimmer, and this could apply here too (so Eust. 1329.19–20), but equally Odysseus may not wish his rivals to hear. Silent prayer was unusual: cf. 7.194–6 (with comment on 195), where Telamonian Aias asks the Greeks to pray for his success in the duel with Hektor 'silently, lest the Trojans hear, or even openly, since after all we are afraid of no man'. Later one prayed silently especially when wishing someone harm, or when one did not want to disclose one's wishes for other reasons; cf. H. S. Versnel, in *Faith, Hope and Worship* (ed. Versnel, Leiden 1981) 25ff.

770 For ἐπίρροθος see on 4.390, where it is used of Athene, and cf. ἐπιτάρροθος of her at 5.808 etc. Odysseus' prayer is suitably brief (bT).

771–2 See on 768–79. Verse 772 = 5.122, 13.61. T comments: 'they say that the hands of fast runners are like wings'. Early Greek vases show sprinters using their outstretched arms and hands: cf. Laser, *Arch. Hom.* T 34–6.

773 ἔμελλον ἐπαΐξασθαι ἄεθλον: 'they were likely to dart upon the prize' seems less satisfactory than the variant ἐπαΐξεσθαι, which would give the sense 'they were on the point of ...' (cf. Leaf).

774 For ὀλισθάνω cf. 20.470 (nowhere else in Homer). The μέν is answered by αὖτε at 778. βλάπτειν here means 'disable': cf. 782, 7.271 etc., and for its use of a divine action see on 22.15.

775–81 The cow-dung from the sacrifice at Patroklos' funeral (166–9) is another reminder, ludicrous though it may be, of the occasion of the games. Virgil is reluctant to be so explicit in naming the dung in his imitation at *Aen.* 5.328–33 (cf. 328 *levi ... sanguine ...*, and 332–3 *in ipso | ... immundo fimo sacroque cruore*), and he omits the picture of the loser with his mouth full of dung, spitting it out. It is hardly surprising that the word ὄνθος occurs only here in *Il.* or *Od.*: a comic episode introduces cruder language, as at 2.212ff., and the poet repeats ὄνθος three times, to emphasize the effect. The usual word for dung was κόπρος (*Od.* 9.329 etc.). ὄνθος recurs (for example) in Aeschylus' *Psychagogoi* fr. 275.2 N.² and Radt, a burlesque version of Teiresias' prophecy about Odysseus' death.

777 'He who called the older man λαβραγόραν (479) receives his punishment in the mouth' (AbT).

779–81 It cannot be coincidental that Aias receives an ox as prize, and the picture of him holding the ox by the horn as he spits out the ox-dung is ludicrous. In 779 Aias is called φαίδιμος, an epithet elsewhere reserved for his more illustrious namesake (cf. 11.496n.): this sounds ironic here.

781 ἀποπτύων: elsewhere in Homer only at 4.426; see on 697 (πτύοντα), in another comic scene.

782–3 Aias recognizes that Athene is the cause. In *Il.* she assists or protects Odysseus at 2.169ff., 5.676ff., 11.434ff., and especially in book 10, where cf. 245 φιλεῖ δέ ἑ Πάλλας Ἀθήνη, and Odysseus' prayer to her at 278–82: κλῦθί μευ, αἰγιόχοιο Διὸς τέκος, ἥ τέ μοι αἰεὶ | ἐν πάντεσσι πόνοισι παρίστασαι, οὐδέ σε λήθω | κινύμενος ... Athene's 'special relationship' with Odysseus in the *Odyssey* is anticipated here; cf. Stanford, *Ulysses Theme* 25–42.

782 ἦ μ' ἔβλαψε θεὰ πόδας: probably μ' represents με, with double accusative as at *Od.* 14.178, although cf. also 571 βλάψας δέ μοι ἵππους.

783 μήτηρ ὥς: cf. the more extended simile at 4.127–33, where Athene deflects the arrow of Pandaros to save Menelaos, like a mother keeping a fly away from a sleeping child.

784 = *Od.* 20.358, 21.376. Cf. 2.270 (when Thersites has been punished by Odysseus) οἱ δὲ καὶ ἀχνύμενοί περ ἐπ' αὐτῷ ἡδὺ γέλασσαν, and see comment there. That episode also involved Athene's assistance to Odysseus (2.169ff.) and Odysseus' triumph over an opponent who is a braggart, to the amusement of the spectators. Odysseus' comic defeat of the braggart Iros (*Od.* 18.1–117) suggests a narrative pattern here, and may foreshadow Odysseus' later rôle in comedy (on which see E. D. Phillips, 'The comic Odysseus', *G&R* 6 (1959) 58–67).

785–97 Antilokhos was mentioned at the beginning as the third runner

(756), but his part in the race was not described, as with Meriones in the chariot race (351, 528–31). The main point is the speech which he makes and its consequences. In tune with the laughter over Aias he smiles as he takes the last prize, and his speech is light-hearted but pointed. He echoes Aias' inference that the gods are behind the outcome, but draws a moral which picks up the theme of respect for age from the chariot race. His characterization of Odysseus as belonging to a past generation may be a humorous exaggeration, and whatever the exact sense of ὠμογέροντα, this word seems to have a colloquial and slightly mocking ring to it (although Eustathius says that it is not abusive, 1330.12). A further irony is that Antilokhos must know that Odysseus' victory was due more to his wit than his speed: it exemplifies the kind of μῆτις which Antilokhos tried to display in the chariot race, and Antilokhos himself shows ingenuity in turning his present defeat to advantage and winning the approval of Akhilleus.

785 λοισθήϊον: see on 751.

787 εἰδόσιν ὕμμ' ἐρέω πᾶσιν, φίλοι: for this tactful form of opening see on 306–8.

787–8 ὡς ἔτι καὶ νῦν . . . : i.e. perhaps the traditional view on this subject still holds good. Leaf says 'as they honoured them when they were young, so they continue to honour them when they are old', but this surely misses the point. For the view expressed here cf. 15.204 etc.

790–1 It is unnecessary to speculate how old Odysseus ought to be (cf. Stanford, *Ulysses Theme* 256, additional note). In the *Odyssey* Telemakhos is a baby when Odysseus leaves for Troy (11.447–9), but such cross-references run into difficulties. It may be fair to say that 'Antilochus was a very young man and to such even the moderately middle-aged often seem old' (Stanford, *loc. cit.*).

791 ὠμογέροντα: only here in Homer; cf. Call. fr. 24.5, etc. Aristophanes of Byzantium explained it (probably rightly) as meaning 'advanced in years', i.e. on the verge of old age, ὠμός meaning 'not yet ripe', 'early': cf. W. J. Slater, *Aristophanis Byzantii Fragmenta* (Berlin 1986) 34–5. This may be the sense in Callimachus, and probably in Arrian, *Ind.* 9.7; cf. also *AP* 7.363.9, Galen 6.379. The alternative explanation ('prematurely aged') came perhaps from interpretation of *Od.* 15.357 ἐν ὠμῷ γήραϊ θῆκεν. Virgil's *iam senior, sed cruda deo viridisque senectus* (*Aen.* 6.304) glosses the Homeric word in the former sense; cf. Tac. *Agric.* 29.4 *quibus cruda et viridis senectus.*

791–2 ἀργαλέον δὲ . . . Ἀχιλλεῖ: 'and it is hard for any of the Achaeans to compete in running (with him), apart from Akhilleus'. Antilokhos cleverly ends his speech with a compliment to Akhilleus, which wins his immediate favour.

792 ἐρῑδήσασθαι appears to be aorist infinitive based on ἐριδαίνω. The long iota is puzzling, since ἐρῐδῆσᾰσθαῑ could fit into the verse, and one would expect ἐριδήνασθαι. The ancient variant ἐριζήσασθαι (T) would be an odd formation from ἐρίζω, for which ἐρίσσασθαι would be normal (cf. 3.223 ἐρίσειε, *Od.* 4.80 ἐρίσσεται). Ἀχιλλεῖ with contracted -εῖ in the dative may be unique in Homer, since Πορθεῖ at 14.115 could be scanned Πορθέϊ (cf. also 24.61 Πηλέϊ). But we do find other contracted forms of nouns in -εύς, e.g. 4.384 Τυδῆ, 15.339 Μηκιστῆ, *Od.* 24.398 Ὀδυσεῦς (cf. Chantraine; *GH* I 224). It looks as if T may have wanted to read either εἰ μὴ Ἀχιλλῆ (so Heyne) or εἰ μὴ Ἀχιλῆϊ with synizesis (cf. A. Ludwich, *Aristarchs homerische Textkritik* I, Leipzig 1884, 492.30ff.). But as Ludwich observes (*op. cit.* II 258 n. 218), 'hundreds of contracted forms of all kinds are unshakeably embedded in the Homeric poems: therefore it is absurd to explain a select number of contractions as "impossible", merely because they can be removed more or less easily'.

793 ποδώκεα Πηλεΐωνα: after 791–2 this is an excellent example of a name-formula directly relevant to its context.

794 The formular τὸν δ' ἀπαμειβόμενος προσέφη πόδας ὠκὺς Ἀχιλλεύς is avoided here, after 793. For the alternative expression see on 3.437.

795 'Antilokhos, your eulogy shall not be spoken in vain'; for the meaning of αἶνος see on 651–2.

796 ἡμιτάλαντον: only here in Homer, later in Hdt. 1.50, 51, etc.; see on 269. Akhilleus' gesture is a typically spontaneous response revealing again his fondness for Antilokhos (cf. 555–6).

797 = 624, 1.446; see on 1.446. The formular verse is used effectively to close the episode.

798–897 The last four contests

The last hundred lines of this Book describe the armed combat (798–825), weight-throwing (826–49), archery (850–83), and javelin (884–97). Javelin-throwing is mentioned in Akhilleus' speech to Nestor (621–3), in Nestor's reminiscences (637), and in Odysseus' boast to the Phaeacians (*Od.* 8.229). Most modern scholars have accepted this contest as part of the original narrative, whereas many have suspected the intervening episodes (798–883) as a later addition: cf. Lehrs, *De Aristarchi studiis* 429–30; K. F. Ameis and C. Hentze, *Anhang zu Homers Ilias* VIII (Leipzig 1886) 57–61; Leaf, Introduction to book 23, p. 469 ('a long addition absolutely devoid of poetical merit, and standing in the harshest contrast with its surroundings ...'); more recently Kirk, *Songs* 223 ('a lamentable decline'); Chantraine and Goube, pp. 15–17 (who are hesitant); and Willcock on 798–883 ('we may well suspect that these three were added to the Games by a rhapsode (or perhaps by Homer himself) after the time of the first composition'). On the other hand, P. Mazon (*Introduction à l'Iliade* (Paris 1942) 225) detects links with the earlier contests in the way in which Meriones, so unsuccessful in the chariot race, wins the archery, and Epeios, victor in the boxing, is laughed at for his failure in the weight-throwing (840). Moreover, discus-throwing and archery are mentioned as contests in the Phaeacian games (*Od.* 8.129, 215–28), and discus, javelin and archery are the pastimes of the Myrmidons at 2.773–5. The only sport not referred to elsewhere in Homer is the armed duel. Yet this is probably a very archaic element in Greek games, and one which survived into the historical period in Greece (cf. the works by Malten and Meuli in the comment on 262–897 and Laser, *Arch. Hom.* T 186). Hence for all its strangeness it may have been something which the poet felt ought to be included.

798–825 Akhilleus offers as prizes for the armed duel the armour of Sarpedon and the sword of Asteropaios. Telamonian Aias and Diomedes fight, and when Diomedes apparently gains the advantage the Achaeans stop the contest

There are uncertainties about the course of this event. In Akhilleus' speech proposing the contest (802–10) 805 refers to the first person who succeeds in 'reaching fair skin', i.e. presumably touching or striking his opponent's body, but 806 adds 'and who touches his innards (*or* interior) through armour and black blood'. This peculiar verse was athetized by Aristarchus. Without it we should not have to assume that one opponent actually had to wound the other, which would be extraordinary. If the verse is genuine it must be part of an older formular introduction to such duels. In the fight itself Aias fails to touch Diomedes' body, whereas Diomedes 'always kept on threatening to strike (κῦρε) his neck with the bright spear's point' (821). At this point the spectators call a halt, fearing for Aias' life, and order the contestants to share the prizes equally. In 824–5, however, Akhilleus awards Asteropaios' sword to Diomedes, thereby proclaiming him as victor. Again these verses were athetized by both Aristophanes and Aristarchus, among other reasons because they seem to conflict with the indecisive character of the fight. They could have been added by someone who thought that the sword should be mentioned separately, since it was the first prize and could not be divided between both fighters (cf. 736n.), or else because it looked as if Diomedes really ought to have won. If the verses are genuine then Akhilleus really does consider Diomedes morally the victor, and since there is a clear contrast between 818–19 and 820–1 this seems likely to be the right answer.

798–800 The armour of Sarpedon, won by Patroklos (16.663–5), again reminds us of the hero in whose honour the games are being held, and of recent battles, just as Asteropaios' sword (807–8) recalls Akhilleus' exploits (see on 560–2, 740–9). The prizes are appropriate to the contest, as in the case of the weight-throwing (bT 826), archery (AT 850–1), and javelin-throwing (894).

798 = 884; first half of 799 = 886. ἀσπίδα καὶ τρυφάλειαν | recurs at 18.458.

801–4 Verse 801 = 271 etc., 802 = 659, where it is followed by an infinitive in 660. Here, however, one first-century B.C. papyrus and several MSS omit 804, where the corresponding infinitive occurs, and Nicanor's comments on 802–7 strongly suggest that he did not read this verse either. It looks as if Aristarchus must have omitted it, whether because he followed an earlier text which did not have it, or because he deliberately cut it out, as van der Valk supposes (*Researches* II 495–6). It is not easy, however, to see why he should have wished to remove it. Nicanor argues that κελεύειν can be used absolutely, comparing 24.90 τίπτε με κεῖνος ἄνωγε μέγας θεός; ·and *Od.* 21.175 ὡς φάτο, καί ῥ' ἐκέλευσε Μελάνθιον, but these are different, and we cannot really do without the infinitive, especially as περὶ τῶνδε cannot easily stand on its own. Verse 804 is a suitably solemn four-word verse with spondaic ending. Verse 803 is nicely balanced. For ταμεσίχροα χαλκόν cf. 4.511 χαλκὸν... ταμεσίχροα, 13.339–40 ἐγχείῃσι | ... ἃς εἶχον ταμεσίχροας (see on 13.339–44). The epithet is appropriate, suggesting the danger of the duel (cf. χρόα in 805, 819).

805–6 At 16.314 and 322 ἔφθη ὀρεξάμενος with an object is used to denote that someone actually succeeds in wounding his opponent by a spear-thrust. Here too it presumably means at least that the body is touched or struck (as in fencing): so AbT and Eust. The word ἔνδινα occurs nowhere else in literature, and there was debate as to whether it meant 'innards' (so Aristarchus) or 'that which is within the armour', i.e. any part of the body. The former seems more likely: cf. the similar formation *intestinus* (Chantraine, *Dict.* s.v. ἔνδον). The second hemistich of 806 recurs at 10.298 and 10.469, where it fits the context better. Aristophanes read for 805–6 ὁππότερός κε πρόσθεν ἐπιγράψας χρόα καλόν | φθήῃ ἐπευξάμενος διά τ' ἔντεα καὶ φόνον ἀνδρῶν. This must be a conjecture to avoid the danger implied, as Eustathius says (1331.6). Aristarchus' rejection of 806 is attractive, but it is possible that the verse is a formula inherited from contests where blood was actually spilt.

807–8 φάσγανον ἀργυρόηλον (cf. 14.405 in the genitive) is a variant formula for the more usual ξίφος ἀργυρόηλον (see on 2.45). A great Thracian sword is mentioned at 13.576–7 (see comment). The Thracians were not far from Asteropaios' home by the river Axios (cf. 2.844–50 with comments). Verse 808 resembles 560.

809 ξυνήϊα occurs only here and at 1.124, and nowhere else later; cf. ξυνός, also ξυνήων (Hesiod etc.). Although equal division of a set of armour might seem difficult, this is what Hektor proposed in the case of Patroklos' spoils (17.229–32).

810 Aristarchus athetized this verse because it seemed odd for Akhilleus to offer a feast only to this pair of contestants. But there is a precedent at 7.313–22, where Aias was offered a banquet after his duel with Hektor, and it is reasonable that a feast should be given to those sharing such risks (as T suggests). A subtler explanation is offered in Plutarch's *Moralia* (736D), that 'Akhilleus wished that through sharing a banquet and table together the contestants should lay aside and relinquish any anger or ill-feeling which might have arisen during their duel.' Banquets in honour of victorious athletes were common later, as well as the privilege of regular meals at public expense (σίτησις ἐν πρυτανείῳ): cf. Xenophanes fr. 2.8–9 West, and C. M. Bowra, *Problems in Greek Poetry* (Oxford 1953) 31–4.

παραθήσομεν: the (vulgate) reading παραθήσομαι seems preferable, as it should be Akhilleus who offers the feast; cf. *Od.* 15.506 ὁδοιπόριον παραθείμην (of a meal), and van der Valk, *Researches* II 625.

811–25 The fight itself and its conclusion are largely made up of recurrent elements. Verse 811 = 708, 812 = 290. Verses 813–15 resemble the opening of the duel between Menelaos and Paris: 813 = 3.340, 814–15 ~ 3.341–2; and 814 is almost identical with 6.120 and 20.159. Verse 816 = 3.15, 6.121, 20.176 etc. The end of 817 resembles 13.559 σχεδὸν ὁρμηθῆναι. For 818 cf. 3.347 etc. In 819 νύξ(εν) is common in this position (13× *Il.*), and with 818–19 cf. 7.260 (Aias and Hektor), 12.404 Αἴας δ' ἀσπίδα νύξεν ἐπάλμενος, ἡ δὲ διαπρὸ / οὐδὲ διαπρὸ, and 11.352 οὐδ' ἵκετο χρόα καλόν, 15.529 πυκινὸς δέ οἱ ἤρκεσε θώρηξ. Verses 820–1 are less formular, which suggests that the description is designed for this scene (821 ~ 11.253 φαεινοῦ δουρὸς ἀκωκή, etc.). Verse 822 ~ 11.508 τῷ ῥα περίδεισαν ... Ἀχαιοί, 823 ~ 15.176 παυσάμενόν σ' ἐκέλευσε μάχης ... (etc.), 23.736 ἄεθλια δ' Ἴσ' ἀνελόντες. The gift of the sword at 824–5 is similar to that by Hektor to Aias after their duel, at 7.303–4 ὡς ἄρα φωνήσας δῶκε ξίφος ἀργυρόηλον, | σὺν κολεῷ τε φέρων καὶ ἐϋτμήτῳ τελαμῶνι. The relationship of the formal duels in books 3 and 7 to this passage is discussed by Kirk in Fenik, *Tradition* 18–40 (especially 35ff.).

811–12 It is natural that the contestants should be Telamonian Aias, the great master of the standing fight (cf 7.206ff.) and Diomedes, who takes Akhilleus' place in books 5–6 especially. Cf. 7.179–80, where the Achaeans pray that Aias, Diomedes or Agamemnon may be allotted the task of facing Hektor in the duel. One might have expected Aias to gain the advantage, but it looks as if Diomedes is more skilled (820–1), as Odysseus appeared to be in the wrestling match.

814 The variant ἀμφοτέρων derives from 6.120 = 20.159, where it refers to the two armies.

815 This may be simply an echo of 3.342 (n.), or a traditional feature of other duels of this type. θάμβος is a strong word, and the powerful reaction is appropriate before such an event. The variant εἰσορόωντας derives from 3.342.

817 Leaf considers this 'devoid of sense', since it is impossible to tell what is the difference between the meaning of the two phrases. Willcock more reasonably says that 'this describes two formal movements, the advance into action and the attack at close quarters', comparing the formalism of karate or bayonet drill. Presumably each contestant advances and closes with his opponent three times, and either during or after these manoeuvres Aias hits Diomedes' shield and pierces it, while Diomedes constantly threatens Aias' neck. For τρὶς ... τρὶς see on 16.702–6.

818–21 The ancient commentators (bT and Eust.) observe that Aias' technique is more straightforward, whereas that of Diomedes is more cunning and effective. κύρειν is normally used of touching or hitting something, but the imperfect probably means that he was *trying* to do so (cf. H. Ebeling, *Lexicon Homericum*, Leipzig 1885–7, s.v.). The variant ἀκωκήν produces a construction with κύρειν for which there is no evidence elsewhere.

824–5 For the athetesis of these verses see on 798–825. The second verse = 7.304, in the exchange of gifts after the duel between Hektor and Aias.

826–49 Akhilleus next offers a very valuable lump of iron as a prize for the man who can throw it furthest. Polupoites, Leonteus, Telamonian Aias and Epeios compete, and Polupoites wins, with Aias second

There is only one prize for this contest (unlike all the others), the weight itself which is to be thrown (bT 826). This is a massive lump of iron, which Akhilleus says will be big enough to keep a farmer supplied for five years (832–5). Elsewhere we hear of discus-throwing (2.774 etc.), and in the Phaeacian games this is the contest in which Odysseus shows his strength (*Od.* 8.186–93), with a stone discus (190). Weight-lifting and throwing are occasionally referred to later, but as an exceptional feat rather than a regular event, especially in the sixth century B.C. Cf. 5.302–8, 12.445–62, *Od.* 9.481, 9.537, 10.121, where heroes and giants lift or throw massive rocks. Two sixth-century inscriptions record the lifting or throwing of rocks weighing 143 and 480 kilos. Cf. E. N. Gardiner, *JHS* 27 (1907) 1ff., and on weight and discus throwing see also Gardiner, *Sports* 22–4, 313–37, J. Jüthner, *Die athletischen Leibesübungen der Griechen* II.1 (Vienna 1968) 225–303, Laser, *Arch. Hom.* T 58–63.

The interest lies first in the history of the prize, which Akhilleus had taken from Andromakhe's father Eetion; second in the information about its value, which throws light on the relationship of country and town in the Homeric period; and finally in the contestants (see on 836–8). There is an interesting blend here of motifs suited to the 'heroic age' and the realism of the poet's own (or recent) times (see on 826, 832–5).

826 σόλον αὐτοχόωνον: σόλος occurs only here and in 839, 844 in Homer; cf. Eumelos fr. 9 K. (= A.R. 3.1372), and Hellenistic and later epic poetry. The meaning is uncertain, but clearly it refers to a lump of metal of some kind. The word σολοίτυπος is explained by Hesychius as meaning μυδροκτύπος (μύδρος is a mass of molten metal), or 'a type of bronze in Cyprus'. σόλος is probably a loan word, whose derivation is uncertain (Chantraine, *Dict.* s.v.). The place-name Soloi in Cilicia and Cyprus may well be connected with it.

αὐτοχόωνος means 'self-moulded' or 'self-cast' (cf. χόανος 18.470, with comment on 468–73), and recurs only in Nonnus (*D.* 37.667). The form is presumably due to metrical lengthening of αὐτο-χῶνος, and may represent an original αὐτο-χόανος with artificially lengthened α (cf. Chantraine, *GH* I 82, 104), or simply be an example of 'false diektasis' (Leaf *ad loc.*, W. F. Wyatt, Jr, *Metrical Lengthening in Homer*, Rome 1969, 225–6).

There was debate in antiquity over the sense of both words: cf. AbT 826, Erbse *ad loc.*, and J. Jüthner, *Antike Turngeräthe* (Vienna 1896) 18ff. Modern scholarship has been divided between explaining the phrase as referring to a meteorite, or a mass of iron as it comes from the smelting furnace. However, a meteorite cannot easily be forged, and the second explanation must surely be right: cf. R. J. Forbes, *Arch. Hom.* κ 31, and D. H. F. Gray, *JHS* 74 (1954) 13. A parallel would be the mass of iron (μύδρος σιδήρεος) which the Phocaeans threw into the sea before leaving home in Hdt. 1.165.

This valuable commodity was the property of Eetion of Thebe in the Troad: this might suggest that iron was more readily available here than in Greece itself. On the other hand what Akhilleus says about its use by a farmer to make his own implements indicates that knowledge of its working was already common in Greece, and this reflects the conditions of the early Iron Age: cf. Gray, *op. cit.* 1–15 (esp. 13ff.).

827–9 Eetion, Andromakhe's father, himself used to employ the σόλος for the same purpose as in the games: with all his wealth he could afford to treat it so lightly. Again we have an echo of Akhilleus' past exploits; on Akhilleus' killing of Eetion see especially 6.414–28. From the spoils of Thebe Akhilleus had won his lyre (9.186–8) and the horse Pedasos (16.152–4), and Agamemnon had received Khruseis (1.366–9), the ἀρχή κακῶν of the poem's story. In 829 σὺν ἄλλοισι κτεάτεσσι echoes 6.426(n.), in the account of Andromakhe's family.

827 ῥίπτασκε: for this form see on 15.23–5.
830 = 271 etc. Verse 831 = 753 (cf. 707).

832–5 'Even if the victor's fertile fields are very remote indeed, he will have it to supply his needs for five full years; for it will certainly not be through want of iron that any shepherd or ploughman of his will have to go to the town, but it will supply them.' This shows that a period is envisaged in which the πόλις is a centre for trade in such precious commodities as iron, but a local landowner could forge it into tools on his own estates, whether by using a skilled member of his own work-force or by employing an itinerant smith. On these two alternatives cf. M. I. Finley, *The World of Odysseus* (2nd edn, London 1977) 55–6, and see also H. Strasburger, *Gymnasium* 60 (1953) 99, who compares Hes. *Erga* 432 where the farmer makes his own ploughs at home.

This glimpse of settled life at home naturally introduces some Odyssean phrases: cf. *Od.* 4.757 ἀπόπροθι πίονας ἀγρούς, περιπλομένων ἐνιαυτῶν (-ου -ου) *Od.* 1.16 (11.248); *Il.* 8.404 etc. περιτελλομένους ἐνιαυτούς (etc.). The present tense χρεώμενος occurs only here in Homer; elsewhere the perfect is used; on the synizesis see Chantraine, *GH* 1 70. For ἀτέμβεσθαι with genitive see on 445. The ploughman (ἀροτήρ) recurs in Homer (significantly) only at 18.542, on the Shield of Akhilleus.

836–8 Polupoites and Leonteus are the giant leaders of the Lapiths (2.738–47n.), whom we last saw defending the gates of the Achaean wall (12.127–94), their only scene together in the fighting. μενεπτόλεμος Πολυποίτης | is used of this hero at 844, 2.740 and 6.29; cf. 848 Πολυποίταο κρατεροῖο, with 12.129, 12.182 κρατερὸν -ὸς Πολυποίτην -ης. For Leonteus' description cf. 16.189 Ἐχεκλῆος κρατερὸν μένος Ἀκτορίδαο, and for Λεοντεύς, ὄζος Ἄρηος (841) cf. 2.745, 12.188.

The greater Aias is a natural contestant here, as in the wrestling and duel. Epeios was the heavyweight winner of the boxing match, but does less well here. For Τελαμωνιάδης cf. 9.622–3n.

840 Epeios 'whirled the weight round and let it fly'. Cf. *Od.* 8.189 τόν ῥα περιστρέψας ἧκε στιβαρῆς ἀπὸ χειρός (Odysseus' discus-throw), and *Il.* 13.204 (of a severed head) ἧκε δέ μιν σφαιρηδὸν ἑλιξάμενος δι' ὁμίλου (see comment). At 431 a discus is described as 'thrown from the shoulder' (κατωμαδίοιο). The normal method of throwing a discus in antiquity was by a circular or semi-circular movement of the body, pivoting on the right foot: cf. Gardiner, *Sports* 318–37, Harris, *Athletes* 86–92. It has been suggested, however, that the σόλος would have been much too heavy to whirl in this way, and consequently that the Achaeans laughed at Epeios' throw because he had no idea how to 'put the weight', i.e. he had the strength but not the skill (R. L. Howland, *PCPS* 183 (1954–5) 16).

843 Cf. *Od.* 8.189 (see 840n.), and 192 ὁ δ' ὑπέρπτατο σήματα πάντων. The 'marks' are the points reached by the other throws, which are registered by the umpire (cf. *Od.* 8.193 where Athene does this). Aristarchus athetized this verse because πάντων is used with reference to two throws (Arn/A).

845–7 For this type of measure of distance cf. 431–3 ὅσσα δὲ δίσκου οὖρα ... | ὅν τ' αἰζηὸς ἀφῆκεν ἀνήρ ... | τοσσὸν ἐπιδραμέτην, and the parallels quoted there (also 517–23). The word καλαύροψ occurs only here in early literature; cf. Antimachus fr. 91 W. πάντες δ' ἐν χείρεσσι καλαύροπας οὐατοέσσας, and A. R. 2.33, etc. It refers to a throwing-stick, which according to the commentators was equipped with a string for holding it, and a weight at the other end: Antimachus' epithet οὐατοέσσας must refer to the string which formed a 'handle' (bT 845 and references in Erbse *ad loc.*). It has been compared to the *bolas*, 'a weapon consisting of a string with one or more stones attached to it, which is used in Spanish America for throwing at and catching cattle' (J. L. Myres in E. N. Gardiner, *JHS* 27 (1907) 5). Schol. b say that the καλαύροψ was used for separating cattle from a herd (cf. Eust. 1332.47). Cf. the λαγώβολον, discussed by Gow on Theocr. *Id.* 4.49. Whatever the weight of the σόλος, clearly this is meant to be an exceptional throw.

847 παντὸς ἀγῶνος: either the whole area in which the spectators were (cf. *Od.* 8.190–2), or more probably the whole of the area marked out for the contest.

850–83 For the archery contest Akhilleus offers two prizes, for the man who hits a dove tied to a mast and the one who hits the string. Meriones and Teukros compete. Teukros fails to make a vow to Apollo, misses the bird, but hits the string and cuts it. The bird flies up into the clouds, but Meriones quickly seizes the bow, makes a vow to Apollo, and shoots. He hits the bird, which falls on to the mast-head, and then on to the ground. Meriones and Teukros take first and second prize respectively

The last contest which actually takes place involves dramatic elements of divinely inspired luck similar to those of the chariot race and foot race. It is a rapid and exciting piece of narrative. Nevertheless, it has always aroused critical objections. The most serious of these is the point already made by Aristarchus (Arn/AT 857), that the poet should not have made Akhilleus foresee what was about to happen by accident, the cutting of the string which tied the bird to the mast. It is hardly surprising that Virgil avoids this apparent oddity in his imitation (*Aen.* 5.485–518). Other minor objections (cf. Leaf) are that the sudden change from narrative to direct speech at 855, without a formal speech-introduction, is unusual, and that this transition occurs only here in mid-verse; that 871 is oddly expressed; and that the description of the bird being shot and dying (875–81) is very confused, as the mast is far away (853) and yet the arrow falls in front of Meriones' foot, whilst the bird lands on the mast before falling to the ground.

A possible answer may be that the poet is deliberately introducing a more fantastic episode as part of his 'coda'. As so often Virgil is Homer's best commentator, for he catches this tone of 'the marvellous' and the divinely inspired outcome in the close of his own archery contest, when Acestes' arrow spontaneously bursts into flames and shoots through the sky like a comet, as a portent of things to come (*Aen.* 5.519–40). Here too the spectators react with wonder (529 *attonitis haesere animis*), and this shows that Virgil is developing the Homeric ending to this scene (881). Even Akhilleus' foresight could be assigned to divine inspiration, since (as has often been said) nothing in Homer occurs purely by chance (cf. 22.329n.). If this argument is dismissed as special pleading, one might ask whether a version in which this scene did not exist at all is likely or preferable: for most of the problems are integral to the passage and rejection of individual verses cannot solve them.

850 τοξευτῆσι: only here in early literature; cf. Call. fr. 70.2 Pf., etc. The normal classical word is τοξότης (11.385, etc.). For archery as a sport cf. 2.774, etc., *Od.* 8.229.

ἰόεντα σιδηρόν: the epithet occurs only here in Homer; cf. the (early epic) *Phoronis* fr. 2.6 K. = Davies, *EGF* fr. 2.6, where it refers to iron in general, and Nicander (*Alex.* 171), Quintus of Smyrna (6.48). Aristarchus (Arn/A) took it as meaning 'suitable for arrows', pointing out that this made the prize an appropriate one. The alternative explanation was 'dark', as in ἰοειδέα πόντον (11.298 etc.), where it should mean 'dark blue', 'violet'. Elsewhere iron is called αἴθων (4.485 etc.) or πόλιος (9.366 etc.). Despite this variation in colour-terminology, the second explanation for ἰόεις seems more likely, and fits its use in the *Phoronis* passage.

851 The prizes are 'ten (double) axes and ten single ones'. ἡμιπέλεκκον recurs nowhere outside this passage (cf. 858, 883). Aristarchus (Arn/A) saw a connexion with the archery contest in the *Odyssey*, where the contestants must shoot through twelve axes (19.572–81, 21.73–6, 21.120–430); cf. also Laser, *Arch. Hom.* τ 24 n. 109. These axes were themselves prizes won by Odysseus (21.61–2, and cf. 117), and there too the axe-heads are of iron. Some authorities record that πέλεκυς and ἡμιπέλεκκον were used as measures of weight, for example in Boeotia and at Paphos in Cyprus (TD and Eust., Hesychius, quoted in Erbse). C. H. Grayson ('Weighing in ancient Greece', Oxford D. Phil. Thesis 1974, 1 286) compares the Bronze Age double-axe bronze ingots which may have been used as units of value or weight. It is unclear whether in fact these prizes were axe-shaped ingots of iron which could be used for arrows or other tools (like the σόλος), or whether they were actual axes or axe-heads. For their use in battle, however, cf. 13.611–13, 15.709 with comments, and see also H. W. Catling, in *Lefkandi* 1 256. The one-bladed adze-axe occurs in some warrior burials of the Early Iron Age and could be what is meant by ἡμιπέλεκκον. For a hoard of 21 bronze axes with a bronze tripod in an undated burial at Mycenae cf. *AR* 1985–6, p. 27.

852 Cf. 878, *Od.* 14.311 ἱστόν ... νηὸς κυανοπρῴροιο, and νεὸς κυανοπρῴροιο 15.693, 8× *Od.*

853 τρήρωνα πέλειαν: cf. 855, 874, 22.140 (and 5.778n.).

854 μήρινθος occurs only in this passage in Homer (858 etc.); cf. Ar. *Th.* 928, etc. The scholia record the variants πόδα for ποδός and ὡς γὰρ ἀνώγει. bT (855) point out that the dove would be harder to hit if tied by the foot, as it could flutter about.

855–6 The direct speech is introduced simply by ἀνώγει, as at 4.301–9 (see comment). This is unusual (and noted by AbT), but there is a wide range of different examples of 'anomalous speech introductions' in Homer: see M. W. Edwards, *HSCP* 74 (1970) 1–36, especially 20ff. What is unparalleled is the transition to speech within a verse, which leads Edwards to call this 'the oddest speech introduction in Homer' (27). All the other contests so far have been introduced by the same formal introduction στῆ δ᾽ ὀρθὸς καὶ μῦθον ἐν Ἀργείοισιν ἔειπεν (271 etc.). But the abbreviated style continues a stage further at 884–6, since there is no introductory speech by Akhilleus there. For parallels to the shift from indirect to direct speech see on 15.346–7.

855 τοξεύειν: only here in Homer for τοξάζεσθαι (*Od.* 8.220 etc.), but the normal verb in classical prose and poetry.

856 οἴκόνδε: the variant κλισίηνδε is equally possible.

857–8 For the oddity of this see on 850–83. ἥσσων γὰρ δὴ κεῖνος is a parenthesis and the δέ in 858 is apodotic. The point may be that if one hits the string one has failed to hit the target itself, but the shot is still remarkable and deserves a prize.

859–60 Teukros, Telamonian Aias' half-brother, regularly uses a bow in the battle-scenes (8.266–334 etc.), and is called the best Greek archer at 13.313–14. Meriones usually fights with a spear (and enters for the javelin contest at 888), but he uses a bow at 13.650–2 (see comment), and this suits his Cretan origins. These are the only two Greek heroes who actually fight with a bow in the *Iliad* itself, though Odysseus boasts later that he was surpassed as an archer at Troy only by Philoktetes (*Od.* 8.219–22). Meriones' success may reflect his energetic, practical character (cf. 113n.), whereas Teukros tends to have bad luck: cf. 8.324–9 where he is hit by a stone which breaks his bow-string, and drops his bow, and 15.461–70 where his new bow-string again breaks thanks to divine influence. For βίη Τευκροῖο ἄνακτος cf. 13.770 (etc.) βίη δ᾽ Ἑλένοιο ἄνακτος (etc.). Verse 860 = 888.

861–2 The contestants draw lots as at 352–8. The first to shoot might have an advantage as he could hit the bird and win outright. Verse 861 = 3.316 (cf. *Od.* 10.206). For κλήρῳ λάχεν cf. 24.400.

863–4 The underlying sense of ἀπειλεῖν seems to be 'to make a declaration', and from this come the senses 'to boast', 'to threaten', 'to promise' or as here 'to make a vow' (cf. Chantraine, *Dict.* s.v., A. W. H. Adkins, *JHS* 89 (1969) 10–12, 18–20). A first-century B.C. papyrus and a few MSS (including T) omit 864 (=873, 4.102, 4.120). This could have been added to supply the infinitive phrase with ἠπείλησεν; Aristarchus (Arn/AT) glosses the verb as ηὔξατο, which could be used without an infinitive, and no comment by him on 864 is recorded. πρωτόγονος occurs only here in Homer; cf. Hes. *Erga* 543, etc. The sacrifice is the same as that vowed by Pandaros before his successful bow-shot (4.102ff.). As Leaf observes, a hecatomb of first-born lambs 'seems to be regarded as Apollo's fixed price for a successful shot'. It would certainly have been a major offering.

865 'This is an incentive to piety' (bT). For μέγηρε referring to a god 'begrudging' someone success cf. 15.473 συνέχευε θεὸς Δαναοῖσι μεγήρας, which refers to the breaking of Teukros' bow-string by Zeus's power, and *Od.* 3.55–6 κλῦθι Ποσείδαον γαιήοχε, μηδὲ μεγήρῃς | ἡμῖν εὐχομένοισι τελευτῆσαι τάδε ἔργα.

868 παρείθη: 'fell down', aorist passive of παρίημι, only here in Homer; cf. Chantraine, *GH* I 402, 406, where the spread of aorists in -θην is described as a relatively late development in Homeric grammar.

869 The spectators applaud (cf. 847), clearly regarding this as an achievement.

870–1 'And then in haste Meriones snatched from his hand the bow; but the arrow he had long been holding, while Teukros was making his shot' (cf. bT). As with the weight-throwing and javelin the same weapon is used by both competitors (so Aristarchus, Did/A). Leaf objects that 'the idea seems absurd, the change of subject in ἴθυνεν is very harsh, and ὡς does not mean *while*'. The first point seems unfair, but the second and third carry some weight. The conjecture of Voss (on *HyDem* 273) ὡς ἰθύνοι ('so that he might shoot') would remove these objections, but has no authority. If ὡς can mean 'when' in Homer its use here does not seem impossible, and the change of subject, if abrupt, is intelligible. The passage was found difficult in antiquity, and seems to have given rise to several conjectures. Antimachus of Colophon's reading is recorded in two different ways by A and T (cf. fr. 139 Wyss):

(A) σπερχόμενος δ' ἄρα Μηριόνης ἐξείλετο τόξον | χερσίν,
(T) σπερχόμενὸς δ' ἄρα Μηριόνης ἐξείρυσε Τεύκρου | τόξον· χερσὶ δ' ὀϊστὸν ἔχεν πάλαι, ὡς ἴθυνεν.

It seems likely that T's version records what Antimachus actually read: cf. Wyss on Antim. fr. 139, van der Valk, *Researches* I 428–9. The Massaliote text read σπερχόμενος δ' ἄρα Μηριόνης ἐπεθήκατ' ὀϊστὸν | τόξῳ· ἐν γὰρ χερσὶν ἔχεν πάλαι, ὡς ἴθυνεν (AT). This removes part of Leaf's objections, since it gives Meriones his own bow, but the reading looks like a conjecture.

872–3 Cf. 863–4, with comment.

874 ὕψι δ' ὑπὸ νεφέων: cf. 16.374–5 ὕψι δ' ... | ... ὑπὸ νεφέων. In both cases most MSS rightly read ὑπαί as at 15.625 (see on 16.372–6).

875–9 'ὑπὸ πτέρυγος seems to imply a side shot, in which case it can only have been by a miracle that the arrow fell at Meriones' feet; if the bird was directly overhead it is equally miraculous that she should have been able to fly to the mast "far away" (853, 880) after letting the arrow through' (Leaf). These objections have some force.

875 τῇ: '(up) there'; the variant τήν is equally possible, but is less likely to have been changed to τῇ than vice versa.

877 ἡ ὄρνις: the article here perhaps marks the opposition with what preceded, i.e. 'but she, the bird' (cf. Chantraine, *GH* II 161). But there are several uses of it in books 23 and 24 in a relatively weak sense: cf. 75, 257, 465, 24.388, 24.801, Chantraine and Goube 23, Chantraine, *GH* II 164.

878–9 The bird resting on the mast, with its neck hanging down and drooping feathers, is a vivid and pathetic picture. Verse 878 (cf. 852) is a four-word one. In 879 Aristarchus seems to have read λίασσεν, from the active λιάζω, which occurs once in Lycophron, meaning 'loosen'. λίασθεν (or the variant λιάσθη) means 'dropped' or 'drooped'; cf. 15.543 etc. of a fallen warrior.

880 ὠκύς is emphatic here, meaning 'swiftly' (cf. Arn/AT). Elsewhere in the *Iliad* the nominative singular only occurs in the formula ὠκὺς Ἀχιλλεύς, except 11.478 ὠκὺς ὀϊστός. Cf. 13.671–2 = 16.606–7 ὦκα δὲ θυμὸς | ᾤχετ' ἀπὸ μελέων.

880–1 τῆλε δ' ἀπ' αὐτοῦ | κάππεσε: probably 'and it (the bird) fell far from the mast' (Mazon, Willcock), rather than 'far from him' (Leaf). Cf. 16.117 τῆλε δ' ἀπ' αὐτοῦ | , 18.395 τῆλε πεσόντα. Verse 881 = 728.

884–97 Finally Akhilleus offers as prizes for spear-throwing the spear itself and a cauldron. Agamemnon and Meriones rise to compete, but Akhilleus says that Agamemnon is the best and gives him the cauldron and Meriones the spear, without a contest

The final scene is the briefest, bringing the marked *diminuendo* to a close. Javelin-throwing was mentioned in the lists of contests at 621–3 and 634–8, and cf. 2.774 etc., *Od.* 8.229, and Laser, *Arch. Hom.* T 53–6. It becomes clear that the spear will be the second prize, the valuable cauldron the first. Akhilleus diplomatically does not allow Agamemnon to compete, but when he says (890–1) 'we know how far you surpass all others, and how much you were always the best in power and in casting the spear', one cannot fail to catch the relevance of these words to the quarrel between the two leaders in the earlier part of the *Iliad*. Contrast especially 1.161–8, 225–30, where Akhilleus accused Agamemnon of taking the best of the prizes of war without having the courage to fight for them. This brief speech seals the reconciliation achieved in book 19.

884–6 Verse 884 = 798, first half of 886 = 799. For λέβητ' ἄπυρον cf. 267 ἄπυρον κατέθηκε λέβητα (with comment). For ἀνθεμόεντα cf. *Od.* 3.440 ἐν ἀνθεμόεντι λέβητι, 24.375 κρητῆρα πανάργυρον ἀνθεμόεντα. The scholia (AbT) explain it as meaning either 'dedicatory' (ἀναθεματιαῖον) or 'decorated with (embossed) flowers, which are called ἄνθεμα', and they compare Pind. *O.* 2.72 ἄνθεμα δὲ χρυσοῦ, which are used to make necklaces and garlands. The second explanation (or something like it) must be correct. Cf. also *HyHom* 6.9, where ἄνθεμα of orichalc and gold are used as ear-rings, *IG* I² 286.60 ὅρμος ἀνθέμων, IX 2.164 B 25 ἄνθεμα κοτταβείων (i.e. rosettes decorating basins), and Leumann, *HW* 249. Such decorative flowers or rosettes on vases occur occasionally in the Mycenaean period, the best example being from the Shaft Graves at Mycenae (cf. Helbig, *Homerische Epos* 386). F. Canciani (*Arch. Hom.* N 39–40 and fig. 10) suggests an alternative connexion with a late Geometric or early Orientalizing-period type of cauldron with lotos flowers on the handles, but this seems less likely.

886 ἤμονες: 'javelin-throwers', an absolute *hapax*, as is ἧμα (891) meaning 'a throw'; cf. ἵημι etc. (*Od.* 8.198 ὑπερήσει of a javelin-throw). Both words could well be technical terms belonging to this sport. The ancient variant ῥήμονες (Arn/A, bT, Plut. *Mor.* 675A), meaning 'orators' and implying a reading ῥήμασιν in 891, would introduce a contest in speaking which would be quite out of place here. Eustathius (1334.49ff.) notices the absence of an introductory speech by Akhilleus and discusses reasons for this. Abbreviation of narrative is presumably one factor (cf. 855–6n.), together with the point that his speech to Agamemnon follows so soon.

887–8 For 887 cf. 1.102 etc. Verse 888 = 860.

889 This combination of formulae (cf. 2.336 etc., 1.121 etc.) occurs only here.

890 Cf. 6.125 πολὺ προβέβηκας ἁπάντων |; 16.54 ὅ τε κρατεῖ προβεβήκῃ. In the second case Akhilleus was referring to Agamemnon's claim to superiority in connexion with his removal of Briseis.

891 δυνάμει τε καὶ ἥμασιν: an odd combination of nouns, δύναμις being chosen by the poet perhaps because it could refer not merely to individual physical strength but to Agamemnon's 'power' in general, although this sense does not seem to occur elsewhere in Homer. For ἧμα see on 886.

892 ἀλλά: the implication is presumably 'but do not feel the need to display your supremacy'.

894 ἐθέλοις: the optative makes the suggestion slightly more hypothetical than the variant ἐθέλεις (which would be more usual after πόρωμεν), and fits Akhilleus' courteous tone better. Cf. 17.488–9 εἰ σύ γε θυμῷ | σῷ ἐθέλεις (v.l. ἐθέλοις). In κέλομαι γὰρ ἔγωγε (cf. 18.254) the point may be 'for it is *I* who am urging you to do this'.

895–7 Verse 895 = 2.441. Agamemnon himself gives the spear to Meriones, and then hands the first prize to his herald Talthubios, whom we first saw when he was ordered by the king to go and take Akhilleus' prize, Briseis (1.318–25). Here, by contrast, Akhilleus gives a prize to the king of his own free will, in friendship. On this quiet and dignified note the games for Patroklos are concluded.

BOOK TWENTY-FOUR

The last book of the *Iliad* is remarkable for its clearly-defined theme and structure. In this respect it resembles its counterpart, the opening Book, whose theme was Akhilleus' anger and its consequences (see Introduction, 'Structure and themes'). Book 24 is wholly concerned with the fate of Hektor's body, and its keynote is pity, on both the divine and human planes. As the poem began with Akhilleus (1.1), so it ends with Hektor (24.804): these two are the pillars which buttress the whole work.

It is not the most obvious ending, given the tone of the rest of the poem. This could have come after Hektor's death, or (more quietly) after Patroklos' funeral. Alternatively, given the continuity of epic tradition, the story could have progressed further, for example as far as the death of Akhilleus himself. An ancient variant of the final verse in fact exists, linking the poem to the *Aithiopis* (see on 804). What we have is quite different. At the beginning of the Book we seem to revert to the tone of book 22, with Akhilleus' repeated mutilation of Hektor's body. But then the gods are moved to pity, and with Apollo's speech the train of events is begun which leads to the ransoming and funeral.

As Macleod says, the plot 'may be divided into three parts: (*a*) the gods show pity, (*b*) a man accepts supplication, (*c*) a lament and burial are achieved' (*Iliad XXIV* 14). If we look more closely, we can see that the major action, Priam's visit to Akhilleus, together with his journey to and from the Greek camp (322–718), is preceded by two main movements, the complex sequence of divine preparations (1–187) and those on the human level (188–321). Both involve debates, between Apollo, Here and Zeus, and between Priam and Hekabe. This elaborate and leisurely build-up creates great suspense, and the tension is increased throughout Priam's journey, up to the momentous point of his appearance in Akhilleus' hut (see on 469–84). Relief comes with Akhilleus' response to Priam's plea, in the scene where both men share their grief (507–12), followed by Akhilleus' great speech of consolation (518–51), although even then there is an ever-present sense of Priam's danger (cf. 559–72, 582–6, 591–5, 649–55, 671–2, 683–9). Finally the lamentations of Andromakhe, Hekabe and Helen and the brief, restrained account of the burial close the poem on a note of quiet dignity, not unlike the ending of some Greek tragedies.

The rôle of Apollo, as initiator of the poem's action, and as the agent of its resolution, has been discussed in the Introduction ('Structure'). In book

272

24 he is above all a god concerned with the ethical themes of pity and respect, whose opening speech of protest against Akhilleus (33–54) sets the moral tone of the Book, which, like much else, brings it closer to the *Odyssey* than the rest of the *Iliad* (see Introduction, 'The end of the *Iliad* in relation to the *Odyssey*'). This is underlined by the emphasis on Priam's piety and extraordinary faith in the gods. In this context the lengthy scene of the meeting between Hermes and Priam is important (see on 349–442). Equally remarkable are Akhilleus' prompt response to Zeus's command (139–40), his self-restraint, and his sympathy and admiration for Priam.

In the end, then, the gods do show their concern for men and their sufferings. Although Akhilleus describes them as 'free of care' (ἀκηδέες) in his speech to Priam (526), this is by contrast with mortals, for whom some degree of trouble and sorrow is unavoidable. From the human viewpoint the sufferings which the gods send may seem inexplicable, and they themselves may appear indifferent to men's pleas for justice. But the poet shows that this is not the whole story, through the action of book 24 itself. Of course, as with all endings of great narrative and dramatic works, the resolution which this brings, satisfying and moving though it is, leaves much that is unresolved: the implacable hostility of Here, Poseidon and Athene to Troy (cf. 25–30), the imminent death of Akhilleus, the city's fall and all the horrors which this will bring, and beyond this, yet more troubles in store for the returning Achaeans. In this respect again, the *Iliad*'s structure resembles that of many later tragedies, especially those of Sophocles.

On book 24 see especially Beck, *Stellung*, Deichgräber, *Letzte Gesang*, and Macleod, *Iliad XXIV*, Introduction.

1–21 The Achaeans disperse, eat their supper, and go to bed. But Akhilleus is unable to sleep. At dawn he yokes his chariot, drags Hektor three times round Patroklos' tomb, and leaves him stretched out face downward in the dust. But Apollo protects his corpse from harm, covering it with his aegis

After the ending of the games, in which Akhilleus' normality and composure were emphasized, there is a clear break, marking off this Book from what precedes, since the opening passage reverts to the earlier motifs of Akhilleus' grief, the mistreatment of Hektor's body, and Apollo's protection of it; cf. especially 23.1–26, 23.178–91. The contrast between the dispersal of the army and Akhilleus' sorrow recalls both the opening of book 23 and 23.57–61, where the army sleeps but Akhilleus lies grieving on the shore until sleep overtakes him. The motif of a single individual's sleeplessness also occurred at the beginning of books 2 and 10, and is repeated at 677–81. On this theme and its use here cf. E. Minchin, *Parola del Passato* 40 (1985) 269–75.

1 The long *upsilon* of λῦτο (= ἔλυτο) is due to epic lengthening. For ἀγών meaning 'gathering' see on 23.258, where the assembly for the games begins.

2-3 μέδοντο ... ταρπήμεναι: 'they took thought of ... so as to have pleasure in them'.

3-4 bT comment on how the poet uses the respite of the games to suggest the abatement of Akhilleus' sorrow, and then dramatically returns to this leading theme, when Akhilleus is again left on his own. Notice the contrast between the meal taken by the army and Akhilleus' implied abstention: this recurs at 122-5.

4-5 οὐδέ μιν ὕπνος ᾕρει πανδαμάτωρ: the epithet occurs first here; cf. *Od.* 9.372-3 κὰδ δέ μιν ὕπνος ᾕρει πανδαμάτωρ. It is paradoxical and virtually concessive, as if to suggest that Akhilleus' grief was so intense as to overcome even all-mastering sleep.

5-11 Akhilleus' restlessness is most vividly expressed by 5 + 10-11, and 6-9 form a parenthesis, expanding the point of φίλου ἑτάρου μεμνημένος. These four verses were athetized by Aristophanes and Aristarchus for various reasons, the main one being that they weaken the dramatic effect. Aristarchus also objected to the use of ἀνδροτῆτα here, apparently because he took the sense as 'courage', which he considered un-Homeric, and then went on to argue that the word was tautologous with μένος. To these points Leaf adds that verse 8 is Odyssean (8.183, 13.91, 13.264), and so is the verb τολυπεύειν (but cf. *Il.* 14.86), that the rare synizesis of ἄλγεα suggests direct borrowing from *Od.* 13.263, and finally that 'the allusion to the hardships of the sea evidently belongs to the *Od.* rather than the *Il.*'

The resemblances to the *Odyssey* are not an argument against originality, in view of the frequency of Odyssean language and motifs in this Book (cf. Introduction), and the theme of endurance will be important later (see on 49 etc.). But it is true that without these verses the sense would run on smoothly from 5 to 10, and they are too general to add much to the portrayal of Akhilleus' grief.

6 ἀνδροτῆτα: the word recurs in Homer only at 16.857 = 22.363, at the deaths of Patroklos and Hektor; see on 16.855-8 (also for the scansion). It must mean 'manhood', i.e. one's nature as a man, virtually one's living self and strength, rather than 'courage'. This was the view of Aristarchus (and bT on 16.857), although here he seems to have failed to realize that the sense 'manhood' is possible, and that the combination with μένος is similar to the phrase ἀνδροτῆτα καὶ ἥβην in 16.857.

6-8 Akhilleus longs for Patroklos, and remembers with longing all that they had endured together, a slight but natural zeugma in the use of ποθέων. The addition of verse 8 creates a second zeugma, as πόλεμον -ους τολυπεύειν is a common phrase, especially in the *Odyssey* (14.86, 4× *Od.*), but πείρων governs both 'wars' and 'waves', although it goes better with the second noun. It looks as if there is some association here between the senses of πειράω ('try', 'experience') and πείρω ('pierce', 'cut through'). In 7 the scansion ὁπόσα is paralleled by *Od.* 12.396 ὀπταλέα τε καὶ ὠμά, and the synizesis ἄλγεα occurs only here. In the *Odyssey* verse 8 always occurs in the context of Odysseus' wanderings and sufferings, being preceded by the phrases μάλα πολλὰ πάθ' ἄλγεα and ἐγὼ πάθον ἄλγεα θυμῷ at 13.90–1, 263–4.

10–21 Up to verse 11 the description seems to refer to a single night, but the frequentative verbs in 12–17 evidently describe Akhilleus' actions over several nights: cf. especially λήθεσκεν of Dawn (13), and the fact that the next stage (Apollo's protest to the gods) only occurs on the twelfth day (31).

12–13 This solitary and restless activity of Akhilleus, pacing up and down on the sea shore, is typical of his unquiet spirit: see on 23.59–61, and cf. the sequence at 23.218–28, where Akhilleus moves restlessly to and fro all night long beside Patroklos' pyre, until Dawn comes, spreading her light across the sea.

Plato's adaptation of verse 12 (*Rep.* 388A), πλωΐζοντ' ἀλύοντ' ἐπὶ θῖν' ἁλὸς ἀτρυγέτοιο, suggests an odd variation πλωΐζεσκ' ἀλύων, but may be due to misquotation from memory.

14–18 The threefold dragging of Hektor's body round Patroklos' tomb repeats the initial treatment of the corpse at 22.395–404, and is a kind of tribute to Patroklos (although the tomb is empty; see on 23.243–4, 254), like the threefold procession of the Myrmidons around his body at 23.12–13. Aristotle observed the parallel with a later Thessalian custom of dragging a murderer round his victim's tomb (see on 22.401–4). The optative ζεύξειεν indicates a repeated action ('whenever he had yoked'), and δέ in 15 is apodotic, marking the main clause. In 17 we should perhaps follow Herodian and most MSS in reading τόνδε δ' ἔασκεν.

18 ἐν κόνι ... προπρηνέα: cf. 23.25–6 (with comment) πρηνέα ... τανύσσας | ἐν κονίῃς; προπρηνές 3.218.

18–21 At 23.184–91 Aphrodite and Apollo protect Hektor's corpse, one with immortal oil, the other with a dark cloud. The golden aegis is a variation of the latter, and 21 echoes 23.187. At 15.307ff. Apollo has an aegis, and is also clothed in cloud, and at 18.203–6 Athene puts the aegis round Akhilleus' shoulders and a golden cloud round his head. Aristarchus (Arn/A) athetized 20–1, and the scholia offer various objections: (*a*) the verses are unnecessary; (*b*) the divine aegis should not be polluted by death; (*c*) it belongs to Zeus, not Apollo; (*d*) the verses disagree with the account in book 23. These are poor arguments.

19 ἀεικείη occurs only here in *Il.*; cf. *Od.* 20.308. ἄπεχε χροΐ means 'kept away from his flesh'; cf. *Od.* 20.263 κερτομίας τοι ἀφέξω.

20–1 Aristarchus preferred αἰγίδα ... χρυσείην, as in 18.343 τοῖόν τοι ἐγὼ νέφος ἀμφικαλύψω (and similarly 21.321), and Leaf reasonably assumes that this requires the change to παντί (cf. also R. R. Dyer, *Glotta* 42 (1964) 356). For the aegis see on 2.446–51.

22–76 The gods pity Hektor and urge Hermes to steal his body, but Here, Poseidon and Athene object. On the twelfth day Apollo protests at the gods' neglect of Hektor's corpse and support for Akhilleus. Here answers that Akhilleus deserves more honour, but Zeus supports Apollo. He orders Thetis to be summoned so that she can tell Akhilleus to accept Priam's ransom

The theme of the gods' pity for Hektor introduces a crucial new development, preparing the way for Apollo's protest, and the debate gives us a last vivid picture of the clash between pro-Greek and pro-Trojan deities, with Zeus as arbitrator. Apollo stands out as a god concerned with fundamental Greek ethical principles, whereas Here's objections are more personal and vindictive. Zeus's decision strikes a proper balance: the respect due to Hektor will not detract from Akhilleus' honour. On the overall structure of the three speeches see Lohmann, *Reden* 152–4. Cf. also Reinhardt, *IuD* 471–4, who points to the structural similarity between this scene with its sequel and the divine assembly at the beginning of the *Odyssey*, leading to Telemakhos' mission and Odysseus' rescue. In fact the parallels are even more striking than Reinhardt observes (see Introduction, 'The end of the *Iliad* in relation to the *Odyssey*').

23–30 bT record that these eight verses were athetized (by whom they do not say). They then defend 23 but reject 24–30, and ascribe this athetesis to Aristarchus. But Aristonicus (A 25–30) records the athetesis of 25–30 only, and it looks as if this was really Aristarchus' opinion. He does not seem to have rejected 24, since he is not said to have objected to the parallel verse 109 (although he did regard 71–3 as an interpolation). bT argue against 24 that the idea of Hermes' stealing the body is unsuitable for the gods (θεοῖς οὐ πρέπον), and that it does not make sense to give this as the suggestion of all the gods and then to add Apollo's speech accusing them. The idea of Hermes' stealing the corpse is odd but not impossible, and the point about the contradiction with Apollo's speech could equally be applied to 23, which is presumably intended to prepare the ground for what follows (22–76n.).

The objections of Aristarchus to 25–30 are more serious: (*a*) it is absurd to speak of all the gods agreeing, and then exclude three of the most powerful deities; (*b*) the judgement of Paris is nowhere else mentioned by Homer, whereas it ought to have been referred to more often as an explanation of the goddesses' hostility; (*c*) νείκεσσε (29) is misused, since it cannot mean 'judged'; (*d*) μαχλοσύνη (30) means γυναικομανία, whereas what Aphrodite gave to Paris was not this but Helen, the most beautiful woman of the time; and the word is in any case Hesiodic (cf. Hes. fr. 132 M–W).

To these points bT add: (*e*) that gods should not show the same kind of resentment as Akhilleus; (*f*) that Poseidon's support of the Greeks is not explained by the story of the judgement; (*g*) that according to Homer Paris was brought up and educated in the city (cf. 3.54–5), whereas 29 indicates that he was a rustic; (*h*) that μαχλοσύνη is not used elsewhere of men, but only of women; (*i*) that it is out of place for Athene and Here to engage in a beauty-contest with Aphrodite, the goddess of love, especially as Here elsewhere treats her as her child (14.190) and knows that she possesses all the arts of persuasion (14.198–9). Finally bT give a list of passages where they think that the judgement could or should have been mentioned, of which the most striking is 4.31–2, where Zeus asks Here why she hates Troy so much, and no explanation is offered. It should be noted that nearly all of these objections could be avoided by the omission simply of 29–30, leaving 25–8 unaltered.

Most analytical scholars accepted this condemnation of the passage as conclusive, but a spirited defence was made by F. G. Welcker in *Der epische Cyclus* (Bonn 1865) 113–20 (cf. also J. A. Scott, *CJ* 14 (1919) 326–30, and other references in Griffin, *HLD* 195 n. 49). Following Welcker's lead Reinhardt (in 1938) argued that the whole poem presupposes the story of the judgement, but the poet keeps it in the background because it does not suit him to attribute the gods' hostility explicitly to such a petty motivation ('Das Parisurteil', reprinted in *Tradition und Geist*, Göttingen 1960, 16–36).

Reinhardt's article has been proclaimed 'a landmark in Homeric studies' (Griffin, *loc. cit.*), but it has rightly been pointed out (M. Davies, *JHS* 101 (1981) 56–62) that he does not actually offer an explanation of why the poet should choose to mention the story *at all* at this point in the work, nor does he answer some of the ancient objections, especially concerning the awkward way in which Poseidon is sandwiched between the two goddesses, when his hostility should be due to other reasons, and the reference to Aphrodite's reward to Paris as μαχλοσύνη. Davies suggests that the story's position near the end of the poem emphasizes that the anger of the gods hostile to Troy still persists even then, in contrast to Akhilleus' appeasement.

The lateness of the reference in the poem had already struck Eustathius (1337.29–30). In his words, 'the poet has held in reserve to the end the event which was most responsible for the Trojan war, thereby keeping the hearer in great suspense'. Likewise E. Drerup compared the way in which authors delay the solution to a puzzle until the end of a long work (*Das Homerproblem in der Gegenwart*, Würzburg 1921, 360 n. 1).

The most significant passages where Reinhardt detected the influence of the judgement story are 4.5ff., where Zeus contrasts Aphrodite's constant protection of Paris with the apparent indifference to the Greeks of Here and Athene, provoking their anger and Here's outburst against Troy, and 5.418–25 and 21.418–34, in which the two goddesses triumph over Aphrodite and mock her as the cause of Helen's abduction (see on 21.418–34). Moreover at 5.130ff. Athene deliberately and explicitly incites Diomedes to wound Aphrodite and no other deity (cf. Scott, *CJ* 14 (1919) 328). Kullmann (*Quellen* 230–44) gives a list of other allusions in the poem to the enmity of Here and Athene against Troy. But the poet could presuppose the legend without mentioning it explicitly, and the introduction of it at the end still requires explanation. The passage as a whole prepares the way for Here's protest at 56–63, and it helps to explain the reference at 107–8 to a nine-day dispute in heaven, although this would still be the case even without verses 29–30. The allusion to the judgement, however, is in the abbreviated, elliptical style typical of such epic summaries, especially where the poet seems unwilling to be too explicit about the details. In conclusion it is probably fair to say that the passage as a whole should be regarded as part of the original poem, despite some doubts over 29–30.

The story was definitely told in the *Cypria* (Homer, OCT vol. v, p. 102.14–19, Davies, *EGF* p. 31.7–11), and it appears in art from the second half of the seventh century B.C. onwards. On the development of the myth see T. C. W. Stinton, *Collected Papers on Greek Tragedy* (Oxford 1990) 17–75, and I. Raab, *Zu den Darstellungen des Parisurteils in der griechischen Kunst* (Bern 1972).

24 This verse is echoed at 109. Hermes is the god of theft, as at *Od.* 19.394–8 and in *HyHerm.* The formula ἐΰσκοπος Ἀργειφόντης (etc.) occurs only here and at 109 in *Il.*, 2× *Od.*, and 3× in the Homeric Hymns. ἐΰσκοπος means something like 'keen-sighted', 'watchful'. For Ἀργειφόντης see on 2.103.

25 ἐήνδανεν: this anomalous form, which recurs at *Od.* 3.143, probably represents ἐ(ϝ)άνδανεν, the *eta* being due to the influence of the later form ἥνδανεν; cf. Chantraine, *GH* 1 480.

25–6 οὐδέ ποθ' Ἥρῃ ... κούρη: cf. 1.399–400, where these three deities plot to bind Zeus. A personal reason for Poseidon's enmity is given at 21.441–60, when he recalls Laomedon's treachery to himself and Apollo. For the elision of Ποσειδάων (1) cf. Chantraine, *GH* 1 86. γλαυκώπιδι κούρη occurs only here in *Il.*; cf. *Od.* 2.433 (with Διός), 24.518 (κούρη γλαυκώπιδι καὶ Διὶ πατρί). It is unusual to find the phrase without a reference to Zeus as father; 8.373, where Zeus calls Athene φίλην γλαυκώπιδα, is different.

27 ἀλλ' ἔχον ὥς: 'but they persisted (in their hostility), as ...'; cf. 12.433 ἀλλ' ἔχον ὥς τε ...

27–8 Ἴλιος ἱρή | καὶ Πρίαμος καὶ λαός: these words echo 4.45–6 and 4.164–5 = 6.448–9. In the first case Zeus proclaims his exceptional favour towards Troy because of its people's piety, in his dispute with Here over its fate. In the second passage Agamemnon prophesies its doom because of the Trojans' treachery, and these two verses are echoed by Hektor in book 6. Here, the expression λαὸς ἐϋμμελίω Πριάμοιο (as in the other passages) is cut short to allow the powerfully contrasting hemistich Ἀλεξάνδρου ἕνεκ' ἄτης, which suggests the moral theme that a whole city suffers for one man's error.

28 Ἀλεξάνδρου ἕνεκ' ἄτης: some MSS read ἀρχῆς; for this variation see on 3.100, 6.356 where the same phrase occurs. Here ἄτης is certainly more appropriate. See also Stinton, *Collected Papers* 71, who quotes parallels from tragedy (S. *Aj.* 643, 909, E. *El.* 1307, *HF* 917) for ἄτη with a personal genitive. It is worth noticing that without 29–30 one would take this phrase as referring to Paris' rape of Helen, as at 6.356 and 3.100 (if ἄτης is right there).

29 ὃς νείκεσσε θεάς: with a direct personal object the verb elsewhere means 'reproach' (1.521 etc.), but from this to 'find fault with' and hence to 'insult' is not a difficult transition. It is contrasted here with ᾔνησε (30). Cf. A. W. H. Adkins, *JHS* 89 (1969) 20: 'When Paris gave his judgment that Aphrodite had won, the other two goddesses naturally felt his words to be hostile, and indeed would feel ἐλεγχείη at their defeat.' ὅτε οἱ μέσσαυλον ἵκοντο recurs at *Od.* 10.435. Paris is a herdsman, like other sons of Priam at 11.104–6, 15.545–8, or Aineias at 20.188–90; cf. Stinton, *op. cit.* 47–9, 58–60.

30 ἥ οἱ πόρε μαχλοσύνην ἀλεγεινήν: the noun (meaning 'madness for sex') occurs only here in Homer, as Aristarchus observed (Arn/A 25), citing Hes. fr. 132 M–W on the daughters of Proitos, εἵνεκα μαχλοσύνης στυγερῆς τέρεν ὤλεσεν ἄνθος. μάχλος is used again of women at Hes. *Erga* 586 etc., but once of men (Lucian, *Alex.* 11 μάχλος καὶ γυναικομανής), and it fits the description of Paris at 3.39–55 (39 γυναιμανές etc.). μαχλοσύνη or its equivalent is more usually something sent by Aphrodite as a punishment than as a reward (cf. Davies, *JHS* 1981, 57–8), but the point may be that what appeared to be a gift really turned out to be disastrous (cf. ἀλεγεινήν) for Paris and for Troy. The easier variant ἥ οἱ κεχαρισμένα δῶρ' ὀνόμηνε, read by Aristophanes and some city texts (Did/A), may have been due either to the difficulty of the phrase or to prudishness.

31 = 1.493, where it refers to the time between Thetis' meeting with Akhilleus and her visit to Zeus. Here (as bT observe and as 413–14 confirm) it must mean the whole time since Hektor's death, including the three days of Patroklos' funeral and the nine days' quarrel of the gods (107–8). On the parallel with book 1 see Introduction, 'Structure'.

32 Cf. *HyAp* 130 αὐτίκα δ᾽ ἀθανάτησι μετηύδα Φοῖβος Ἀπόλλων, and see on 23.569.

33–54 Apollo's speech opens with a dramatic and passionate protest: σχέτλιοι, δηλήμονες are strong words. He goes on to contrast the gods' unfair treatment of Hektor's body and their support for Akhilleus, and then speaks at length of the extreme inhumanity of Akhilleus, his lack of normal pity and respect, returning at the end to Hektor's fate. There are similarities to Aias' protest at Akhilleus' rejection of their embassy, at 9.624–42: cf. especially 9.628–38 and 24.49. At the beginning of the poem too, Apollo showed his concern for αἰδώς and ἔλεος (1.8–52).

33 σχέτλιοί ἐστε, θεοί, δηλήμονες: cf. *Od.* 5.118 σχέτλιοί ἐστε, θεοί, ζηλήμονες ἔξοχον ἄλλων. There Kalupso is complaining to Hermes about the jealousy of the gods for mortals who are loved by goddesses. σχέτλιοι could be translated 'relentless' here. δηλήμων ('destroyer') occurs only here in *Il.*, 3× *Od.*, always in the phrase Ἔχετον βασιλῆα βροτῶν δηλήμονα πάντων (18.85 etc.); it recurs in Herodotus and late prose. It is possible that ζηλήμων in *Od.* 5.118 is modelled on this word, and the *Odyssey* passage may echo this one; cf. Usener, *Verhältnis der Odyssee zur Ilias* 148–55.

33–4 Cf. *Od.* 1.60–1 (Athene to Zeus) οὔ νύ τ᾽ Ὀδυσσεὺς | Ἀργείων παρὰ νηυσὶ χαρίζετο ἱερὰ ῥέζων; This protest at the beginning of the *Odyssey* is parallel to Apollo's (see on 22–76). The point is echoed and stressed by Zeus at 66–70; see also on 20.297–9, 22.170–2. αἰγῶν τε τελείων occurs only here and at 1.66.

35 οὐκ ἔτλητε: 'you could not bring yourselves to'.

36–7 ἥ τ᾽ ἀλόχῳ ... λαοῖσί τε: the enumeration of all those concerned with Hektor's loss is very emphatic.

38 κήαιεν ... κτερίσαιεν: the optative ending -αιεν occurs only here in Homer, apart from a possible variant reading τίσαιεν at 1.42, and κτερίσειαν is attested as a variant by Didymus and in some MSS. A first-century B.C. papyrus reads κτερέουσιν. Macleod suggests that κήαιεν may have been preferred for phonetic reasons, and κτερίσαιεν naturally attracted to this form. But optative aorist in -αιμι, -αις, -αι, etc. occurs a number of times elsewhere in Homer: cf. Chantraine, *GH* I 464–5. κτέρεα κτερίσαιεν is 'give funerary honours to him'; κτέρας means 'offering', 'gift' (10.216, 24.235), but in the plural it is used exclusively of honours paid to the dead at a funeral. In this sense it occurs only here in *Il.*, but 7× *Od.*, in all but one case with κτερίζειν or κτερεΐζειν.

39 ὀλοῷ Ἀχιλῆϊ occurs only here and expresses the strength of Apollo's feelings. The repeated vocative θεοί (cf. 33) stresses that all the gods share responsibility here.

40–1 Cf. *Od.* 18.220 οὐκέτι τοι φρένες εἰσὶν ἐναίσιμοι οὐδὲ νόημα. The moral tone naturally leads to the use of Odyssean language. For νόημα γναμπτὸν cf. Phoinix' appeal to Akhilleus not to be relentless: at 9.497

even the gods are στρεπτοί, at 514 honour paid to Prayers ἐπιγνάμπτει νόον ἐσθλῶν. The epithet is used metaphorically only here.

41–3 Akhilleus' inhuman savagery is compared to that of a marauding lion. Cf. Moulton, *Similes* 105–6, 112–14, for a discussion of Akhilleus' lion-similes; also 16.33–5 where his lack of pity leads Patroklos to say that his parents must be the sea and the rocks. In 42–3 the words ὅς τ' ἐπεί are both followed by a single verb, a type of anacoluthon similar to that found at 8.230, 17.658–64 (see comment). It is as if the ἐπεί had lost its function of introducing a clause. AT (Nicanor) propose εἴξῃ or εἴξῃσ' in 43 to avoid this, but this is unnecessary. Moulton (114) observes that 42–3 suggest 'that the lion may be conceived as having better instincts, which could sometimes restrain him'; cf. 15.586 θηρὶ κακὸν ῥέξαντι ἐοικώς, with comment on 586–8.

In 43 βροτῶν seems at first sight unnecessary, but it is a god who is speaking. Aristarchus is thought to have held that δαίς was properly used in Homer only of a human meal (see on 1.5, and cf. Pfeiffer, *History of Classical Scholarship* 111–13), but there is no evidence that he wanted to athetize 24.42–3. Possibly he took βροτῶν δαῖτα together here, as Lehrs suggested (*De Aristarchi studiis* 87).

44–5 Pity and respect (ἔλεος and αἰδώς) are keynotes of the whole of this Book: cf. 207–8, 503, and see on 21.74, 22.82. On the varying senses of αἰδώς ('awe', 'respect', 'shame') see J. T. Hooker, *G&R* 24 (1987) 121–5. ἀπώλεσεν is a dramatic word, whether it means 'destroyed' or simply 'lost'. Verse 45 is evidently a proverbial one, which recurs at Hes. *Erga* 318 (αἰδώς ἥ τ' etc.), on which see West's comments. Aristarchus rejected it (Arn/AT), on the grounds that it was inappropriate to speak of αἰδώς as harmful here, and the verse had been added to supply a verb with the end of 44, a common type of interpolation (cf. 558, etc.). This could well be right, as the sense here must be 'respect', whereas in Hesiod it is rather 'shame'. It is true that in such 'polar' expressions one often finds that in a particular context only one of the two alternatives is relevant (cf. 10.249 μήτ' ἄρ με μάλ' αἴνεε μήτε τι νείκει, etc.), but here the extra verse rather weakens the rhetorical effect.

46 μέλλει μέν πού τις ... ὀλέσσαι: 'I presume that a man is likely to have lost even someone closer to him in the past'. The ironic though serious expression resembles 18.362 (in a protest by Here), καὶ μὲν δή πού τις μέλλει βροτὸς ἀνδρὶ τελέσσαι.

47 ὁμογάστριον: i.e. of the same mother as well as the same father. The word occurs once elsewhere in Homer at 21.95 (see comment).

48 μεθέηκε: 'he relented', i .e. after a period of grief; cf. 23.434 μεθέηκεν ἐλαύνειν.

49 τλητός occurs only here in Homer (cf. ἄτλητος, etc.), and nowhere else in the active sense 'enduring', but such verbal adjectives can be either active or passive: cf. 1.415 ἀδάκρυτος, 'without tears' etc., and

J. Wackernagel, *Vorlesungen über Syntax* I (Basel 1926) 288. Μοῖραι also occurs in the plural only here in Homer, but at *Od.* 7.197–8 we meet the Κλῶθες, who spin the thread of a person's destiny (see Hainsworth on *Od.* 7.196–8). The Moirai as a group are firmly established in Hesiod's *Theogony* (217, 904–6). As Apollo is protesting at the gods' failure to intervene it would have been less appropriate for him to ascribe endurance to the gods' favour. This idea of the value of endurance (τληµοσύνη) is unusual in the *Iliad*, and much commoner as a motif in the *Odyssey* and later poetry (see Richardson on *HyDem* 147–8). But it is another essential leitmotif of this Book (see especially on 518–51).

The solemnity of this gnomic verse is increased by its spondaic rhythm, and the emphasis falls heavily on the opening τλητόν. It is echoed by Archilochus fr. 13.5–7:

> ... ἀλλὰ θεοὶ γὰρ ἀνηκέστοισι κακοῖσιν
> ὦ φίλ' ἐπὶ κρατερὴν τληµοσύνην ἔθεσαν
> φάρµακον.

50–4 Apollo returns at the end of his speech to the fate of Hektor with which he began. ἕλκει is heavily emphatic at the beginning of 52, and followed by the strong expression of moral condemnation and a final warning of retribution.

52 οὐ ... ἄµεινον: the ominous understatement is typical of such solemn warnings: cf. 7.352–3 τῶ οὔ νύ τι κέρδιον ἡµῖν | ἔλποµαι ἐκτελέεσθαι, ἵνα µὴ ῥέξοµεν ὧδε, *Od.* 7.159, Hes. *Erga* 750 οὐ γὰρ ἄµεινον, 759, and similar positive assertions at 570 etc.; also Hdt. 1.187.2, etc. Apollo will in fact cause Akhilleus' death: cf. the warning of the dying Hektor at 22.358–60.

53 bT record that this verse was athetized on the grounds that Apollo could not describe Akhilleus as ἀγαθός after he had called him ὀλοός, and they then give the alternative explanation that the word means 'brave' here. There is no reference, however, to the athetesis by A, and Aristarchus is said to have read νεµεσσηθέωµεν here instead of our manuscripts' νεµεσσηθῶµεν. ἀγαθός is used in its sense of 'noble' or 'outstanding', as at 1.131, etc. (see on 1.275–6); cf. A. A. Long, *JHS* 90 (1970) 128. For parallels to νεµεσσηθέωµεν or νεµεσσηθῶµεν (from -θήοµεν) see Chantraine, *GH* I 64, 459. The word-order, with οἵ postponed, is unusual, and the neglect of digamma in οἵ is also relatively rare in Homer (Chantraine, *GH* I 147–8). This displacement is presumably due to the desire to put the emphasis on ἀγαθῶ περ ἐόντι.

54 κωφὴν ... γαῖαν means 'mute earth'. For this idea of the body's 'earthly clay' cf. 7.99 ἀλλ' ὑµεῖς µὲν πάντες ὕδωρ καὶ γαῖα γένοισθε, Soph. *El.* 244 ὁ µὲν θανὼν γᾶ τε καὶ οὐδὲν ὢν | κείσεται τάλας, etc. Verses 53–4 are echoed by Aeschylus in his *Phrygians* or *Ransoming of Hektor*, fr. 266 N.² and Radt.

55–63 Herē's reply is bitterly scornful, in a way typical of her speeches, and as bT remark she fails to answer the main point of Apollo's charge. The opening is sarcastic: 'Certainly even what you say, Apollo, could well be true, if all of you are really going to ascribe the same status to both Akhilleus and Hektor', an idea which, she goes on to point out, would be absurd, given the contrast in their origins and upbringing. The climax comes with her allusion to the wedding of Peleus and Thetis at which all the gods were present, including Apollo himself, whom she ends by accusing of treachery because of his support for Hektor and the Trojans.

56 For this form of expression cf. *Od.* 15.435 εἴη κεν καὶ τοῦτ', εἴ μοι ἐθέλοιτέ γε, ναῦται (etc.).

57 The dramatic switch to an apostrophe to all the gods is similar to that at 2.235, *Od.* 4.681–9, etc.; cf. [Longinus] 27.3–4 for a discussion of this device in Homer and later literature.

58 γυναῖκα ... μαζόν: a double accusative, as at 170 etc. This is the emphatic point, since it will be contrasted with Herē's own upbringing of Thetis. The verb θῆσαι occurs only here in *Il.*; cf. *Od.* 4.89, *HyAp* 123, *HyDem* 236.

59–60 In the *Cypria* (OCT vol. v, fr. 2 Allen = Davies, *EGF* fr. 2) Thetis is said to have refused marriage with Zeus as a favour to Here, and the story of Here's upbringing of Thetis is mentioned in A.R. 4.790–8 and Apollod. 3.13.5. B. K. Braswell (*CQ* 21 (1971) 23–4) notes the contrast with Here's suspicion of Thetis in book 1, and suggests that this motif may have been invented by Homer for this occasion, to supply a reason why Here should show special favour to Thetis and her son. Verse 60 is an effective 'tricolon crescendo', although the first two verbs go closely together.

62–3 For the wedding of Peleus and Thetis and the gods' gifts see on 16.140–4 and 18.429–56. ἀντιάω is used only here in Homer in the middle, later in Apollonius Rhodius. Herē ends by rounding on Apollo again. For ἔχων φόρμιγγα cf. 1.603 where Apollo's lyre accompanies the gods' feast. κακῶν ἕταρε sounds colloquial (cf. Hes. *Erga* 716 κακῶν ἕταρον), and the last two phrases are powerfully compact. Apollo's treachery in 'betraying' Akhilleus perhaps foreshadows the part he will play in causing his death (cf. 21.277–8, 22.359–60). These verses inspired the famous speech of Thetis in Aeschylus (fr. 350 N.[2] and Radt), where she recalls how Apollo sang of her future happiness at her wedding, and declares that he has now betrayed her by killing her son (7–9):

> ὁ δ' αὐτὸς ὑμνῶν, αὐτὸς ἐν θοίνῃ παρών,
> αὐτὸς τάδ' εἰπών, αὐτός ἐστιν ὁ κτανών
> τὸν παῖδα τὸν ἐμόν.

64–76 Zeus diplomatically resolves the quarrel, quietly but firmly reassuring Here and at the same time supporting Apollo's plea.

64 There was an ancient variant τὴν δὲ μέγ' ὀχθήσας (T), as again at 138.

65 ἀποσκύδμαινε: cf. 592 σκυδμαινέμεν. The verb occurs nowhere else, but is a variant form of σκύζομαι meaning 'be angry' (see on 113).

66–7 Zeus implies that Akhilleus will have special honour, perhaps referring to Priam's gifts (cf. 110), but he is unspecific about this. Verse 67 resembles and contrasts with 61.

68–70 Zeus amplifies Apollo's insistence on Hektor's piety (see on 33–4). We should read ὣς ('so') at the beginning of 68 (as in Allen's *editio maior*, 1931). Verses 69–70 = 4.48–9, where Zeus speaks of his special love for Priam and his people.

71–3 These verses were athetized by Aristarchus, on the grounds that Thetis was not really present with her son all the time: but the exaggeration is quite natural. The verses refer back to 24 (see on 23–30). ἐάσομεν is a short-vowel subjunctive, and κλέψαι is treated as if it were the object: 'but as for stealing, let us forget about it'. Antimachus read ἀμήχανον instead of ἐάσομεν, evidently finding the phrase difficult. In 72 νέκυν Ἕκτορος was an ancient variant (T), presumably because θρασύν was thought inappropriate when Hektor was dead: cf. however 786. For αἰεὶ ... παρμέμβλωκε cf. 4.11 αἰεὶ παρμέμβλωκε, again said by Zeus to Here, of Aphrodite protecting Paris (see comment). For ὁμῶς νύκτας τε καὶ ἦμαρ cf. *Od.* 24.63.

74 ἀλλ' εἴ τις καλέσειε: for this form of wish or polite request cf. 10.111 ἀλλ' εἴ τις καὶ τούσδε μετοιχόμενος καλέσειεν, etc. Tactfully Zeus leaves open which god should undertake this errand.

75–6 Zeus finally and briefly reveals the plan, which will dominate the rest of the poem.

77–119 Iris visits Thetis in the sea, and summons her to Olumpos. They arrive and Thetis is welcomed. Zeus then asks her to instruct her son to receive Priam and accept the ransom for Hektor

Iris' summoning of Thetis is the first stage of a double action, the second being her visit to Priam (143–87). Cf. 15.49–280, where Zeus sends Here to summon Iris and Apollo, and then despatches Iris to tell Poseidon to withdraw from the battle, and Apollo to rouse Hektor (see on 15.151–280). Similarly, on a larger scale, the action of the *Odyssey* opens with the sending of Athene to Ithaca and this is complemented in book 5 by Hermes' mission to Kalupso's island. On the typical form of such divine messenger scenes see Arend, *Scenen* 54–61. Iris' journey, however, is described in an individual way, and by means of a vivid and unusual simile.

77 = 8.409, 24.159. Iris responds at once.

78 Cf. 13.33 (Poseidon's cave) μεσσηγὺς Τενέδοιο καὶ Ἴμβρου παιπαλοέσσης (see comment), and 24.75 ἐς Σάμον ἔς τ' Ἴμβρον. Samos is Samothrace in these passages (see on 13.10–12).

79 Iris plunges into the sea with a great impact. The artificially lengthened form μείλανι (*metri gratia*) occurs only here in Greek, but cf. Μειλανίων. ἐπεστενάχησε is the reading of the majority of MSS, with the variants ἐπεστονάχησε, ἐπεστενάχιζε, ἐπεστονάχιζε, ἐπεστενάχισ(σ)ε. This compound occurs only here in Homer; cf. Hes. *Th.* 843 ἐπεστονάχιζε (with variants). For λίμνη meaning 'sea' cf. 13.21 etc., and for sea or earth 'groaning' see on 16.389–92.

80–2 She then plummets straight to the bottom like a lead weight attached to a piece of ox-horn on a fishing-line. Cf. *Od.* 12.251–3:

> ὡς δ' ὅτ' ἐπὶ προβόλῳ ἁλιεὺς περιμήκεϊ ῥάβδῳ
> ἰχθύσι τοῖς ὀλίγοισι δόλον κατὰ εἴδατα βάλλων
> ἐς πόντον προΐησι βοὸς κέρας ἀγραύλοιο,

and *Il.* 16.406–8 for another fishing simile (see comment). A divine journey is often illustrated by a simile; cf. 4.74–8, 15.78–83, 15.168–72, 15.236–8, and especially *Od.* 5.51–4, where Hermes is compared to a sea-bird hunting for fish, etc. (cf. Introduction, pp. 22–3).

μολύβδαινα occurs only here in Homer (cf. Hippocrates, *Mul.* 2.188, etc.), and so does βυσσός (Hdt. 2.28, 96, etc.); cf. βυσσοδομεύειν in the *Odyssey*. The piece of horn was explained by Aristarchus (Arn/A; cf. Plutarch, *Mor.* 977A, where this is ascribed to Aristotle, perhaps wrongly) as being fastened to the line above the hook, to prevent the fish from biting through the line. An alternative modern theory is that the piece of horn was used as an artificial bait: cf. C. E. Haskins, *Journal of Philology* 19 (1891) 238–40. Other views are mentioned by AbT. On early Greek fishing in general see H.-G. Buchholz, *Arch. Hom.* J 169ff.

Plato (*Ion* 538D) has ἐμμεμαυῖα in 81, and in 82 ὠμησταῖσι μετ' ἰχθύσι πῆμα, which correspond closely with variants mentioned by A (πῆμα being the reading of some city texts). ἐμμεμαυῖα would be possible, but πῆμα is said by A to be due to misgivings about applying the word κῆρα to fish. Cf. van der Valk, *Researches* II 323–4.

83–6 On arrival it is typical for a visitor to 'find' (εὗρε) someone engaged in a particular activity, and often surrounded by companions. Here Iris finds Thetis among her nymphs, lamenting her son's coming death, whereas immediately afterwards, when she and Thetis go to Olumpos, they find the gods drinking, and Thetis is welcomed with a cup. The parallel language of 83–4 and 98–9 points up the contrast. Likewise, when Thetis visits Akhilleus she finds him among his companions, lamenting (122–4), and again Iris comes upon Priam surrounded by his sons and with all his family, in deep mourning for Hektor (160–8). Cf. also L. Coventry, *JHS* 107 (1987) 179–80.

For the scene of Thetis lamenting among the nymphs cf. 18.35–64, *Od.* 24.47–59. Once again the poet looks forward beyond his work to Akhilleus' death, and bT comment that 'it is full of pathos to lament for one who is still living.' Cf. the laments for Hektor at 6.500–2 and Priam at 24.327–8, and *CQ* 30 (1980) 269. For death 'far from home' see on 16.458–61, 538–40, and Griffin, *HLD* 106ff.

83 ἐνὶ σπῆϊ γλαφυρῷ: cf. 18.402 ἐν σπῆϊ γλαφυρῷ (and 3× *Od.*).

85–6 Aristarchus (Arn/A) athetized 86 (cf. 16.461), as added to supply the sense of ὅς οἱ ἔμελλε, which he took as standing on its own, and meaning '(the doom) which was destined for him'. This seems virtually impossible. Rhianus read ὃς τάχ' ἔμελλεν.

87 = 2.790 etc.

88 This one-verse speech is urgent in its brevity (see on 20.428–9). Ζεὺς ἄφθιτα μήδεα εἰδώς occurs only here in Homer; cf. Hes. *Th.* 545, 550, 561 (all in the context of Zeus's superiority over Prometheus), *HyAphr* 43, and *HyDem* 321 Δήμητερ, καλέει σε πατὴρ Ζεὺς ἄφθιτα εἰδώς. This expression may be used here (instead of καλέει σε πατὴρ ἀνδρῶν τε θεῶν τε or Κρόνου πάϊς ἀγκυλομήτεω) to give more weight to Iris' request. At any rate Thetis, despite her reluctance, recognizes the urgency of the situation.

89 Cf. 18.127, 19.28.

90–2 μέγας θεός picks up the solemn tone of 88. Thetis' unease at mingling with the gods is caused by her grief and entanglement in mortal affairs. ἔχω δ' ἄχε' ἄκριτα θυμῷ is characteristic of Thetis in its tone of self-pity (cf. 18.429–31, etc.). Verse 92, however, is resolute (μέν adversative, and adding stress: 'I *will* go, all the same'), and in her recognition of Zeus's authority she echoes his famous promise to her in book 1 (524–7). Cf. 224 (Priam resolved to go to Akhilleus), and *Od.* 2.318 εἶμι μέν, οὐδ' ἁλίη ὁδὸς ἔσσεται ἣν ἀγορεύω (Telemakhos to the suitors). Thetis' words are similar to the ending of Helen's speech at 3.399–412, where she *refuses* to obey Aphrodite and visit Paris: cf. 410 κεῖσε δ' ἐγὼν οὐκ εἶμι … 412 ἔχω δ' ἄχε' ἄκριτα θυμῷ (see on 399–412, 410–12).

93–7 Cf. the journey of Thetis and the Nereids at 18.60–8:

> ὣς ἄρα φωνήσασα λίπε σπέος· αἱ δὲ σὺν αὐτῇ
> δακρυόεσσαι ἴσαν, περὶ δέ σφισι κῦμα θαλάσσης
> ῥήγνυτο· ταὶ δ' ὅτε δὴ Τροίην ἐρίβωλον ἵκοντο,
> ἀκτὴν εἰσανέβαινον ἐπισχερώ …

For the sea dividing before the deities cf. also 13.29 (Poseidon's journey).

93–4 κάλυμμα occurs only here in Homer, for καλύπτρη (22.406 etc.). Cf. *HyDem* 42 κυάνεον δὲ κάλυμμα κατ' ἀμφοτέρων βάλετ' ὤμων (with

comment). This is also the only place in Homer where the use of black in
mourning is mentioned: bT comment that 'black is suitable to a goddess
of the sea, and one who is in mourning'. ἔσθος occurs only here in Homer,
later in Aristophanes (*Av.* 943, lyric; *Lys.* 1096, Laconian); cf. ἐσθής in the
Odyssey.

97 ἀκτὴν δ' ἐξαναβᾶσαι: this is Aristarchus' reading, and is said to be
that of 'most texts' by Did/A. Our MSS have εἰσαναβᾶσαι as in the parallel
passage at 18.68, and Leaf prefers this on the grounds that ἐξαναβαίνειν with
accusative rather than genitive is unusual . But cf. ἀτραπὸν ἐξανάβα (*Epigr.
Gr.* 782), and ἐξικέσθαι with accusative (8.439, 9.479).

98–102 For this scene of arrival and welcome in heaven cf. 15.84–8,
where Here arrives and finds the gods in assembly; they rise and greet her
with their cups, and she receives the cup offered by Themis. In 99 the
formula μάκαρες θεοὶ αἰὲν ἐόντες is Odyssean (4×), and occurs only here in
the *Iliad*. It may be chosen to stress the contrast between Thetis' mourning
and the blessed life of the immortals. Thetis' reception is portrayed as
courtly and decorous: Athene, who sits in the place of honour at Zeus's side,
gives up her seat to her. T quotes Pindar (fr. 146 Snell) of Athene: πῦρ
πνέοντος ἅ τε κεραυνοῦ | ἄγχιστα δεξιὰν κατὰ χεῖρα πατρὸς | ἵζεαι. Herē's
greeting accords with her favour to Thetis at 59–61. There could hardly be
a more marked contrast with the balancing scene in book 1, where Thetis
visits Zeus privately, he tells her to leave before Here sees her, and Here at
once attacks him for receiving her (493–569).

102 ὤρεξε πιοῦσα: 'handed it back when she had drunk'.

103–19 Zeus's speech is sympathetic (105), and he reassures Thetis that
he will continue to maintain the honour due to Akhilleus and herself. At the
same time he makes it plain that she must tell her son that he and the other
gods are severely displeased over the treatment of Hektor's corpse, and
announces his plan for Priam's visit to Akhilleus. Structurally the speech is
quite simple, with little enjambment, except in the final part (113–19).

104 ἤλυθες: for this form of greeting (usually friendly) to a visitor cf.
3.428 (scornful), *Od.* 16.23, 16.461, 17.41, and in later literature Alcaeus fr.
350.1 L–P, Theognis 511, Ar. *Av.* 680, Theocr. *Id.* 12.1–2, and other
examples quoted by Gow *ad loc.*

105 For ἄλαστος see on 22.261. οἶδα καὶ αὐτός is a touching expression
of sympathy, at the same time forestalling yet another of Thetis' outbursts
of self-pity (cf. 91n.). Cf. *Od.* 10.457 οἶδα καὶ αὐτή, where Kirke is expressing sympathy for Odysseus' sufferings, and *Od.* 5.215 οἶδα καὶ αὐτός
(Odysseus consoling Kalupso), etc.

107–9 These verses echo 23–4 and 31. In 108 Ἕκτορος νέκυι meaning
'the corpse of Hektor' may be paralleled by 17.240 νέκυος Πατρόκλοιο; such
expressions occur later (e.g. Hdt. 1.140.1, 3.16); for disyllabic νέκυι cf.

16.521–6n. In 109 the vulgate reading is ὀτρύνεσκον as at 24, whereas the Massaliote and Chian texts read ὀτρύνουσιν. Either seems possible; the former could derive from 24, but the latter could equally well be an unnecessarily fussy correction (van der Valk, *Researches* II 167, and Macleod's comment).

110 κῦδος must refer at least primarily to the honour which Akhilleus will receive from Priam's ransom (cf. 119). The expression κῦδος προσάπτειν is found only here in Homer; cf. Pindar, *N.* 8.36–7 κλέος ... προσάψω, etc., and the Homeric ἐπὶ κῦδος ἔθηκεν (23.400). Zenodotus and Aristarchus (in his *Against Comanus*) and some of our MSS read προϊάπτω, with the sense of προϊάλλω, but this verb seems inappropriate here. On the present tense for immediate future see 16.849–50n.; it is especially appropriate to an announcement by Zeus.

111 'With the intention of preserving your respect and friendship in future': this could mean either Zeus's respect for her or vice versa, but more probably the former. Cf. 18.386, where Thetis is described by Hephaistos as αἰδοίη τε φίλη τε, and similarly 14.210, 10.114.

113 σκύζεσθαι in *Il.* is used particularly of the gods (4.23, 8.460, 8.483), once of Akhilleus (9.198). Cf. 65 ἀποσκύδμαινε (Here), 592 (Patroklos).

115 Hektor himself had asked Akhilleus to ransom his body if he killed him (22.258–9).

116 αἴ κεν πως is unexpectedly courteous after 112–15, in harmony with Zeus's tactful handling of Thetis. Cf. Athene to Akhilleus at 1.207, αἴ κε πίθηαι (see comment). But there is still an ominous note of warning in ἐμέ ... δείσῃ.

117–19 This is the second prong of the double action: see 77–119n. Before λύσασθαι (etc.) we must understand 'to tell him to'. Verses 118–19 are repeated at 146–7, 195–6, and with variation at 175–6. This fourfold repetition is surely not just a formular device, but is designed to bring out the importance of this central theme.

119 Cf. the gifts of Agamemnon to Akhilleus at 19.172–4: τὰ δὲ δῶρα ... οἰσέτω ... ἵνα ... σὺ δὲ φρεσὶ σῇσιν ἰανθῇς. This serves to remind us that it is the second time in the poem that Akhilleus will receive gifts. ἰαίνειν seems to be used in the *Iliad* particularly of appeasement: cf. 15.103, 23.598, 23.600.

120–42 Thetis comes to Akhilleus and delivers her message. Akhilleus at once consents

120–7 Thetis' journey and arrival are described in largely formular terms, combining features of 'messenger' and 'arrival' scenes: cf. Arend, *Scenen* 28ff. (especially 29 n. 1). For 122–5 see on 83–6. Akhilleus' abstention from food is emphasized by Thetis in her address to him (129).

124 ἐντύνοντ' ἄριστον: the reading ἐντύνοντο must be wrong, as the alpha of ἄριστον is long. This is due to the tendency to write words in full without elision in ancient texts. This word for the early-morning meal occurs only here in *Il.*, once in *Od.* (16.2), as Arn/A and T note.

125 This brief description of a sacrifice is untypical. ὄϊς λάσιος is used only here (λάσιος 4× *Il.*, 1× *Od.*), and the form ἱέρευτο is odd: it is presumably pluperfect, but one would expect a form with long *iota*. The short vowel may be *metri gratia* (cf. Leaf, Chantraine, *GH* I 422).

126–42 Thetis' dialogue with her son recalls some of the language and themes of her first visit in the balancing scene at 1.357–430. Verses 126–7 echo 1.360–1, and Thetis again begins by asking why Akhilleus is lamenting (128–30, 1.362–3), although here she is advising him not to go on doing so to no purpose. Her reference to his coming death (131–2) echoes 1.417–18, as well as her other predictions of his fate (18.95–6 etc.). Her instructions to him from Zeus (133–7) contrast with 1.393–412, where Akhilleus charges her with his request to Zeus for honour: here (although she does not say so) Zeus has promised him honour (110), but only if he accepts Priam's ransom. Moreover, in book 1 Akhilleus expressed his own anger and grievance at the dishonour done to him, whereas here it is the gods who are angry with him, on account of the dishonouring of Hektor's corpse. It is in this context that Thetis speaks of the need for Akhilleus not only to eat but also to sleep with a woman (130–1), and although the woman is not named, when Akhilleus finally sleeps it is with Briseis at his side (675–6). The poet must surely be looking back to the theme of book 1, the quarrel over Briseis and Agamemnon's removal of her, which Akhilleus described there in his speech to his mother (365–92).

128 μέχρις is used only here in Homer, and μέχρι once at 13.143, instead of the commoner ἄχρι(ς), in order to avoid hiatus. For ὀδυρόμενος καὶ ἀχεύων | cf. 9.612.

129 σὴν ἔδεαι κραδίην: cf. 6.202 ὃν θυμὸν κατέδων, θυμὸν ἔδοντες (etc.) *Od.* 9.75 = 10.143, and 10.379 where (as here) this is combined with fasting because of unhappiness. See also on 617.

130–2 These verses were athetized by Aristarchus (Arn/A, T), as improper for a mother to say to her son and also as unsuitable advice before fighting. In 130 περ must be taken as emphasizing the whole phrase γυναικί ... μίσγεσθαι (cf. Denniston, *Particles* 482). For γυναικί περ (in this position) cf. *Od.* 11.441. For 131–2 cf. 16.852–3 (the dying Patroklos to Hektor), οὐ θην οὐδ' αὐτὸς δηρὸν βέῃ, etc. (see comment).

133 Cf. 2.26 = 63 (νῦν δ' ἐμέθεν, etc.), said by the Dream to Agamemnon.

134–7 The first three verses repeat the message of 113–15, and 137 summarizes the point of 117–19, without however mentioning who it is who will bring the ransom. For ἕέ in 134, replacing ἐμέ in 113, cf. 20.171; Chantraine, *GH* I 264.

139–40 Akhilleus' reply is brief and to the point. He accepts at once without showing any sign of hesitation, but his tone might seem almost dismissive, as if he does not want to think further about the whole issue. The OCT punctuates τῆδ' εἴη· ὅς ..., and so does Leaf. This means 'let it be so: may he who brings the ransom take away the corpse'. τῆδε for οὕτως or ὧδε is, however, unusual in Homer, and in cases such as 14.107, 17.640 εἴη ὅς ... means 'let there be someone who would ...' If we take τῆδε in its usual sense of 'here' and delete the colon we could translate 'let the man be here who would bring the ransom and take the corpse'. This is still rather awkward, and a third alternative, given by bT, was to treat εἴη as an anomalous form of εἶμι (*ibo*), instead of ἴοι or ἰείη (19.209). This occurs nowhere else (Chantraine, *GH* 1 285), but it is possible that the poet took it as such in this form of expression (see Macleod, comparing *Od.* 14.407–8 τάχιστά μοι ἔνδον ἑταῖροι | εἶεν). For πρόφρονι θυμῷ meaning 'wholeheartedly' cf. 8.23 πρόφρων (of Zeus), and similarly 8.39–40 = 22.183–4. For Akhilleus' immediate assent to a divine request T aptly compares 1.216–18.

141–2 This variation on the formular ὡς οἱ μὲν τοιαῦτα πρὸς ἀλλήλους ἀγόρευον suggests with delicate pathos that mother and son remain talking for a long time, aware of how little time Akhilleus has left to live. To leave them thus together is a most unusual way of closing the scene, as normally the divine visitor would return to heaven. Another remarkable case of unreported speech occurs in the scene between Priam and Akhilleus (632). ἐν νηῶν ἀγύρει is a variant of νεῶν (νηῶν) ἐν ἀγῶνι (15.428 etc.); cf. 16.661 ἐν νεκύων ἀγύρει.

143–87 Zeus instructs Iris to visit Priam, and to tell him to go to Akhilleus with gifts of ransom, promising that Hermes will be his escort. Iris comes to Priam, and finds him and his family in deepest grief. She delivers her message

144–58 This is the second stage of Zeus's plan (see on 77–119). This speech is again measured in tone, especially the last part (152–8), which contains hardly any enjambment.

144 βάσκ' ἴθι, Ἶρι ταχεῖα: cf. 8.399 etc.

145 This is a rather compressed way of saying 'Go to Troy and tell Priam ...'; cf. 143, and *Od.* 4.775 μή πού τις ἐπαγγείλησι καὶ εἴσω.

146–7 = 118–19. Verse 148 is an important addition, with the emphatic οἷον and the following explanatory phrase to stress it. The ancient variant οἷος (also in 177) probably arose because of the shift to direct speech in this verse. The accusative follows on after ἰόντ(α) in 146, and this goes closely with the infinitive λύσασθαι.

149–51 These verses are then a kind of qualification of 148: 'let no Trojan man go with him: but a *herald* should accompany him, an older man, to drive …' The herald's office and age would help to ensure safe-conduct (cf. bT). This version differs significantly from the usual one in later art and literature. In artistic representations of Priam and Akhilleus from the sixth century onward, Priam was normally accompanied by a retinue of attendants (sometimes including women): cf. Johansen, *Iliad in Early Greek Art* 127–38 (but cf. 49–51 for a sixth-century bronze relief on which Priam is accompanied only by Hermes). Likewise in Aeschylus' *Phrygians* or *The Ransoming of Hektor* the chorus was composed of Priam's attendants: *Tragicorum Graecorum Fragmenta* III (ed. Radt) p. 364. Cf. also *LIMC* vol. I.1, pp. 147–61, I.2, pp. 121–9. Priam's visit to Akhilleus was the most popular scene to be represented in Greek and Roman art of all the episodes in the *Iliad* (*LIMC* I.1, p. 161).

150 ἡμιόνους καὶ ἄμαξαν ἐΰτροχον: cf. 189, 266, 711 ἄμαξαν ἐΰτροχον (ἡμιονείην), *Od.* 6.37 | ἡμιόνους καὶ ἄμαξαν.

152 Cf. 10.383 θάρσει, μηδέ τί τοι θάνατος καταθύμιος ἔστω. θάνατος and τάρβος are virtually a hendiadys for 'fear of death'. τάρβος occurs only here and in the repeated line 181 in Homer, but is common in Attic tragedy; cf. ταρβεῖν.

153–4 This kind of reassurance of divine aid is clearly traditional. Cf. 21.288(n.), and especially 15.254–7:

> θάρσει νῦν· τοῖόν τοι ἀοσσητῆρα Κρονίων
> ἐξ Ἴδης προέηκε παρεστάμεναι καὶ ἀμύνειν,
> Φοῖβον Ἀπόλλωνα (etc.)

and *Od.* 4.825–8:

> θάρσει, μηδέ τι πάγχυ μετὰ φρεσὶ δείδιθι λίην·
> τοίη γάρ οἱ πομπὸς ἅμ᾽ ἔρχεται …
> Παλλὰς Ἀθηναίη …

Here, however, πομπός is especially suitable for Hermes and is used again of him at 182, 437, 439, and 461.

154–5 ὅς ἄξει … ἄγων … ἀγάγησιν: emphatic repetition. In ὅς ἄξει the first syllable is treated as long, as in 22.236 (etc.), but it seems unnecessary to read (for example) ὅς ϝ᾽ ἄξει (conjectured by Brandreth; cf. Leaf). ἔσω occurs only here (= 184) in *Il.*, 4× *Od.*, instead of εἴσω. In the later artistic representations (see on 149–51) Hermes is often portrayed as actually present in Akhilleus' hut. Cf. 460–9, where he leaves Priam at the entrance.

157–8 bT comment that the three epithets ἄφρων, ἄσκοπος and ἀλιτήμων refer concisely to the three sources of wrong-doing, folly, carelessness and deliberate malice, and that Zeus is defending Akhilleus against Apollo's charge at 40–5. For the emphatic triple negative prefixes ('privative tricolon'), common in moral and religious contexts, cf. 9.63 ἀφρήτωρ ἀθέμιστος ἀνέστιος, and later examples in Fraenkel, *Aeschylus, Agamemnon* II 217. ἄσκοπος ('heedless') and ἀλιτήμων are found only here and at 186 in early epic; ἄσκοπος recurs in Parmenides (1.35) and tragedy, ἀλιτήμων in Hellenistic poetry. For ἐνδυκέως ('with kindness') see on 23.90. Akhilleus' respect for suppliants and the defeated was shown in the past, before the main action of the poem began: cf. 1.84–91 (Kalkhas), 6.414–19 (Eetion), etc.

159 = 77 etc. Here, however, the poet omits any description of Iris' journey, in contrast to 78–82.

160–70 For Iris' arrival and the scene of mourning which she finds see on 83–6, 120–7. But in this case the manifestations of grief are much more extreme; cf. their immediate reactions to Hektor's death at 22.405–28.

160 ἐνοπή is associated specifically with the Trojans at 3.2, 10.13, 16.782, 17.714; cf. E. *Ba.* 159 ἐν Φρυγίαισι βοαῖς ἐνοπαῖσί τε.

162 δάκρυσιν εἵματ' ἔφυρον: cf. *Od.* 17.103 etc. αἰεὶ δάκρυσ' ἐμοῖσι πεφυρμένη. The verb occurs only here in *Il.*, 5× *Od.*

163 ἐντυπὰς ἐν χλαίνῃ κεκαλυμμένος literally must mean 'covered in his cloak in such a way as to show the impression of his body' (so Arn/A, bT). ἐντυπάς occurs only here and then in Apollonius Rhodius (1.264, 2.861) and Quintus of Smyrna (5.530); cf. ἐντυπόω ('mould', 'impress') in Aristotle etc. It could well have been coined by the poet for this occasion, as a graphic and concise way of indicating Priam's despair. Cf. Odysseus' covering of his head so that the Phaeacians should not see his tears at *Od.* 8.84–6. Aeschylus is said to have portrayed the grieving Akhilleus and Niobe seated in silence, with their faces similarly covered (Ar. *Ran.* 911–13 with *Trag. Graec. Frag.* III ed. Radt, pp. 239–40, 265ff., 365–6). Eustathius (1343.6off.) links this scene in the *Iliad* with the Aeschylean ones. Cf. vase-paintings of the mourning Akhilleus (Johansen, *Iliad in Early Greek Art* 123–4, 156ff., etc.), and O. Taplin, *HSCP* 76 (1972) 58–76. In Euripides' *Hercules Furens* (1159–1234) the mourning Herakles covers his head, partly from shame and partly lest he pollute Theseus. In art the painter Semanthes of Sicyon was thought to have been inspired by Homer in his portrayal of Agamemnon with his head covered at the sacrifice of Iphigeneia (Eust. *loc. cit.*).

163–5 Priam's rolling in and covering himself with dung echoes 22.414 (see comment). καταμάειν (165) occurs only here in Homer; cf. *Od.* 9.247 ἀμησάμενος, *Od.* 5.482 ἐπαμήσατο.

166–8 Priam's daughters and daughters-in-law lament for all those warriors who have been killed, not only Hektor; cf. 6.242–50 for the 'extended family' structure of Priam's palace (with 22.59–65), *Od.* 3.451 θυγατέρες τε νυοί τε. The spondaic ending ὠδύροντο of 166 is appropriate: cf. Theocr. *Id.* 1.71, 75.

170 Iris speaks quietly, possibly lest she be heard by Priam's family, but most probably to avoid alarming him (so bT); yet he is still terrified at the divine epiphany (see Richardson on *HyDem* 188–90, pp. 208 and 210–11). τυτθόν means 'softly', 'in a low voice'; cf. the later μέγα, μικρὸν λέγειν. A god appears to one person alone at 1.198, 15.243–62.

171–4 Iris begins by reassuring Priam, a common response by gods to the fear of those who are visited by them: see on 153–4, and cf. *HyAphr* 193 θάρσει, μηδέ τι σῇσι μετὰ φρεσὶ δείδιθι λίην, *Hy.* 7.55–7, etc.

172 For κακὸν ὀσσομένη cf. 1.105 κάκ' ὀσσόμενος. τόδ' ἱκάνω probably means 'I have come to this (place)'; see on 14.298–9.

173–4 Cf. 2.26–7 (174 = 27), with comment. ἄνευθεν ἐών implies that despite the physical remoteness of Zeus he is still concerned with human affairs.

175–87 These verses are closely modelled on Zeus's instructions at 146–58. It is striking that Priam does not repeat Iris' promise of a divine escort when he relates her message to Hekabe (194–6), and even when he meets Hermes he does not realize who he is. Throughout all the following episodes Priam's journey is seen as a great and perilous enterprise. This is dramatically effective and psychologically realistic. Priam's experience of divine reassurance in no way detracts from his sense of risk and anxiety.

188–227 Priam orders his sons to prepare the waggon, and tells Hekabe of Iris' visit. She tries to dissuade him, but he insists on going

188 = 8.425 etc.

189–90 ἄμαξαν ... ἠνώγει: cf. 150 etc., *Od.* 6.37 ἡμιόνους καὶ ἄμαξαν ἐφοπλίσαι. The order for the preparation of the waggon is left unfulfilled, until it is repeated at 263–4 with more urgency, thus framing the intervening scenes: cf. Edwards, *HPI* 306.

190 πείρινς occurs only in this episode (cf. 267) in *Il.*; cf. *Od.* 15.131. It was explained in antiquity as a wicker-work basket tied on to the top of the vehicle to hold baggage (AbT etc.), and this fits the *Odyssey* passage, where it is attached to a chariot. Cf. J. Wiesner, *Arch. Hom.* F 5–6.

191–2 Cf. 6.288 αὐτὴ δ' ἐς θάλαμον κατεβήσετο κηώεντα (this contained a store of fine garments), and for similar basement store-chambers cf. *Od.* 2.337–47, 15.99–108 (15.99 = *Il.* 24.191). It is dignified by the epithets κέδρινον ὑψόροφον. The first occurs only here in Homer; cf. *Od.* 5.60 κέδρου, said to be the prickly cedar, *Juniperus oxycedrus* (cf. Hainsworth *ad loc.*). For ὑψόροφος cf. 3.423 ὑψόροφον θάλαμον, and 24.317. γλήνεα, from γλῆνος, is a Homeric *hapax*. According to bT it survived in Elean dialect as a word for 'possessions', and it recurs in Hellenistic poetry; cf. γλήνη (8.164 etc.), τρίγληνος (14.183 etc.). The best sense here would be 'treasures', 'precious things', and it may be linked etymologically with γαλήνη, γέλως, etc., with the basic sense of 'shining' (Chantraine, *Dict.* s.v.). For κεχάνδει cf. 23.268, *Od.* 4.96. One papyrus reads κεχόνδει, and there was another variant κεκεύθει in the Massaliote text (cf. Did/A, T). Analogy with λέλογχα etc. suggests that κέχονδα may well be the original form (cf. Chantraine, *GH* I 427, Wackernagel, *Kleine Schriften* I 825).

193. This verse is an untypical speech-introduction (cf. 3.161 Πρίαμος δ' Ἑλένην ἐκαλέσσατο φωνῇ). Priam calls Hekabe to join him in the store-chamber, and then addresses her. For the scansion -ον Ἑκάβην cf. 16.716–20n.

194–9 Priam's account of his vision is extremely brief, repeating only the crucial message (195–6 = 118–19; see on 117–19, 175–87). He asks his wife for her opinion, but when she gives it he refuses to listen: a good piece of psychological observation. bT observe that he has already made up his mind, but behaves in a typically human way in asking for his wife's support. His speech contains what may be some reflections of colloquial style, such as δαιμονίη, a familiar form of address (like 'my dear') which sometimes suggests remonstrance but here probably just affection (cf. E. Brunius-Nilsson, ΔAIMONIE, Uppsala 1955, 12ff., and see on 1.561). In 197 τί τοι φρεσὶν εἴδεται εἶναι; may be a colloquial way of saying 'how does the situation look from *your* point of view?', and in 198 αἰνῶς (like English 'terribly') is probably drawn from everyday speech: it occurs 19× in *Il.*, of which 15 are in speeches, and 13× *Od.*, always in speeches (see also on 3.158). For the form Διόθεν (194, 561, 15.489) see on 15.489.

198–9 Priam's assertion that his desire to go to Akhilleus coincides with the divine command is an example of the familiar pattern of 'double motivation'; cf. 8.218–19, 9.702–3, 11.714–17, etc.

200–16 Hekabe reacts to Priam's proposal with horror and incredulity, as well she might, for it sounds a lunatic scheme. Her speech is in the strongest language, directly reflecting her deepest feelings: 'have you gone crazy?' (201–2), 'your heart is made of iron' (205), 'a ravenous, faithless man he is' (207), 'if only I could fasten my teeth into the middle of his liver and eat it' (212–13). Much of this could reflect colloquial idioms. There is frequent enjambment throughout, expressing her agitation, and in the long sentence from 209 to 216 the sense develops and changes direction with Hekabe's train of thought, reflecting her mixture of reasoning, pity and bitter hatred (cf. bT 209–16, Eust. 1345.23). The protest of Eurukleia at the news of Telemakhos' intended journey in *Od.* 2.361–70 may echo this speech (24.200 ∼ *Od.* 2.361, 203 ∼ 364–5, 208–9 ∼ 369–70). Cf. Beck, *Stellung* 107–9.

200 For κώκυσεν see on 22.407–9. For the pattern of this verse cf. 424 ὣς φάτο, γήθησεν δὲ γέρων, καὶ ἀμείβετο μύθῳ (and 571 = 1.33). ἀμείβετο μύθῳ occurs only here in *Il.*, 3× *Od.* (and ἠμείβετο μύθῳ 5×); cf. 3.171 μύθοισιν ἀμείβετο (with comments on 3.161, 437), and M. W. Edwards, *HSCP* 74 (1970) 9–10. Aristarchus read ἀνήρετο here (Did/A, T).

201–2 Cf. 5.472 Ἕκτορ, πῇ δή τοι μένος οἴχεται ὃ πρὶν ἔχεσκες; οἴχεσθαι is similarly used at 13.219–20. ἔκλε᾽ for ἐκλέεο is unusual; cf. Chantraine, *GH* I 73. This verb occurs only here in *Il.*, 3× *Od.*

203–5 These verses are echoed by Akhilleus at 519–21 (πῶς ἔτλης etc.). οἷος is emphatic. Hekabe has not been told this, but assumes it quite naturally. For ἀνδρὸς ἐς ὀφθάλμους cf. 462–3, and for the oblique reference to Akhilleus see on 22.38. For σιδήρειον ... ἦτορ cf. 22.357 ἦ γάρ σοί γε σιδήρεος ἐν φρεσὶ θυμός, 20.372, etc.

After 205 there was an extra verse in some ancient texts:

ἀθάνατοι ποίησαν Ὀλύμπια δώματ᾽ ἔχοντες (Arn/A)
ἀθάνατοι ποίησαν οἳ οὐρανὸν εὐρὺν ἔχουσιν (T)

This was clearly added to supply a verb after 205.

206–8 Verse 206 is a natural form of *hysteron proteron* (cf. bT). ὠμηστής in 207 is only used here of a person in Homer; it is justified by 22.346–7, and echoed by Hekabe's own wish at 212–13. ὠμηστής ... ὅ γε are a parenthesis. For Akhilleus' lack of ἔλεος and αἰδώς see on 44–5.

208–9 ἄνευθεν probably means 'away from Hektor', as in 211, emphasizing the contrast with normal rites of mourning and burial; see on 22.508 (νόσφι τοκήων). ἥμενοι implies their helpless inactivity, as at 540–2 etc.

209–10 For this expression and the idea of Destiny as the spinner of one's fate at birth cf. 20.127–8 (with comment), *Od.* 7.197–8. If we take ὥς as 'thus' here (cf. Leaf) the sentence is complete, whereas if it means 'as' there must be an anacoluthon at 213. The first seems slightly preferable, but given Hekabe's state of mind the second is possible.

211 ἀργίπους occurs only here in Homer, and once in Sophocles (*Ajax* 237); cf. κύνες (πόδας) ἀργοί (etc.) 3× *Il.*, 3× *Od.* The unusual epithet adds vividness to what is already a painfully realistic expression.

212–13 Hekabe's wish that she might fasten on and devour Akhilleus' liver is, in its precision of language, even more awful than the similar but vaguer allusions to eating someone raw at 4.34–6 and 22.346–7. προσφῦναι (only here in *Il.*) is used once in the *Odyssey* (12.433) of Odysseus clinging to a tree 'like a bat', to escape Skulla and Kharubdis. It perhaps suggests a leech here.

213 τότ᾽ ἂν τιτὰ ἔργα γένοιτο: ancient opinion was divided between ἂν τιτά and ἄντιτα, but in view of *Od.* 17.51 (=60) αἴ κέ ποθι Ζεὺς ἄντιτα ἔργα τελέσσῃ, we should probably read the latter here too. The word seems to be from ἀντί-τιτος by haplography (cf. *LfgrE* s.v.); cf. παλίντιτα ἔργα 2× *Od.*

214–16 Hekabe naturally remembers only Hektor's courage in facing

Akhilleus, and not his flight. κακίζεσθαι ('play the coward') occurs only here in Homer; cf. E. *Med.* 1246, etc. For 215 cf. the end of Andromakhe's speech at 22.514 (hence probably the variant πρός here). In 216 φόβου means 'flight', as often in Homer, and ἀλεωρῆς 'shelter' (cf. 15.533n.).

217 This name–epithet formula for Priam is used only in book 24, always in speech-introductions (7×), except for 483 (accusative). In the context of Priam's journey and meeting with Akhilleus it emphasizes his piety and godlike character.

218–27 Priam's reply is unexpectedly resolute, putting Hekabe firmly in her place. Notice the emphatic placing of initial words in 222–6: ψεῦδος ... νῦν δ' ... εἶμι ... τεθνάμεναι ... βούλομαι.

218–19 μηδὲ ... πέλευ: κατερυκάνω for κατερύκω occurs only here. The 'evil omen' is Hekabe's own speech with its foreboding of death. Cf. 12.243 εἷς οἰωνὸς ἄριστος ἀμύνεσθαι περὶ πάτρης. A 'bird of omen' within one's own house would be paradoxical and even worse in its implications than something outside one's home. Cf. Hesiod's ominous crow perching on one's roof, *Erga* 747 (with West's comment). For the scansion ὄρνῖς see on 12.218. οὐδέ με πείσεις (6× *Il.*, 1× *Od.*) is extremely decisive here: cf. 18.126, in a similar context.

220–4 Scepticism about or suspicion of prophecies and religious phenomena or characters runs through Greek literature: in the *Iliad* cf. 1.106–8, 12.237–43. Here the language echoes Nestor's when he was expressing his opinion about Agamemnon's dream at 2.80–2 (and 222 = 2.81); see on 2.80–1. In 221 μάντιες ... θυοσκόοι should probably be taken together: θυοσκόος means 'one who examines a sacrifice' (cf. *haruspex*), and recurs in the *Odyssey* (3×). Cf. the probable distinction at 1.62–3 between μάντις, ἱερεύς and ὀνειροπόλος.

223 The insistence on the *personal* experience, by hearing and direct vision, of a divine epiphany, is characteristic of such assertions of faith: cf. (e.g.) *Od.* 3.420 (ἐναργής), and in the New Testament, St John's First Epistle 1.1–3, etc.

224 εἶμι ... ἔσσεται: cf. 92 (Thetis).

226–7 βούλομαι is an emphatic runover word: 'I am ready'. Priam ends by expressing his willingness to die, if only he might first clasp his son in his arms and relieve his longing for lamentation. For this form of extreme wish ('may I die if only ...') cf. *Od.* 7.224–5 ἰδόντα με καὶ λίποι αἰὼν | κτῆσιν ἐμὴν (etc.), *HyAphr* 153–4 βουλοίμην κεν ἔπειτα ... | σῆς εὐνῆς ἐπιβὰς δῦναι δόμον Ἄϊδος εἴσω. It is quite common later (cf. Garvie on A. *Cho.* 438, etc.). Priam really means it here (cf. 244–6).

228–80 Priam selects the precious possessions which he will take as ransom. He then drives the Trojans out of his palace with an angry speech, and bitterly reproaches his

remaining sons, telling them once again to prepare and load the waggon. They obey,
and these preparations are described

The precision with which the preparations for Priam's journey are described adds to its significance: 265–74 give an account of the equipment of a waggon unparalleled in Homer. At the same time the tension and misery of the old man can only find relief in the outbursts of anger with which he drives away the Trojans and expresses his contempt for his living sons. This is in marked contrast with the portrayal of him elsewhere as moderate and kind (T 248 compares 3.103, 24.770), and the poet observes with fine insight the state of mind of someone in this almost unbearable situation. Cf. Reinhardt, *IuD* 475: 'Nowhere else in the *Iliad* or in the *Odyssey* is the character of old age portrayed thus.' In later Greek literature one could think of parallels: above all old Oidipous in Sophocles' last play.

228 φωριαμοί, meaning 'chests', recurs in Homer only at *Od.* 15.104, where again they contain fine πέπλοι, and the scene is one of preparations for the departure of Telemakhos from Sparta (see on 281–321). Later it was used only by Apollonius Rhodius (3.802) and Nonnus, but there was a place-name Φωριαμοί in Elis (Stephanus Byzantius). The etymology is uncertain: perhaps connected with φέρω, φώρ, etc. (Chantraine, *Dict.* s.v.).

ἐπίθημα is a Homeric *hapax*; cf. Hipponax 56, etc.

229–37 The list of gifts resembles that at *Od.* 24.274–9, where 276–7 ~ *Il.* 24.230–1, and seven talents of gold and a silver mixing-bowl are included. Verse 232, however, is repeated from 19.247 (with ἔφερεν for Ὀδυσεύς), in the list of gifts of Agamemnon to Akhilleus. Here it may be an interpolation (see comment). The ransom would then consist of fine clothing, blankets or rugs, and precious vessels.

229 πέπλοι are usually women's garments, but at 796 are used to cover Hektor's corpse at his burial, and at 5.194 to cover chariots.

230 ἁπλοΐς is found only here and in the repeated verse at *Od.* 24.276, and later once in the *Greek Anthology* (Agathias, *AP* 5.293) as a noun meaning 'single garment' (like ἁπληγίς); cf. δίπλαξ (3.126 etc.), χλαῖνα διπλῆ (10.133–4), and the later διπλοΐς ('double cloak'). τάπητες are rugs or blankets used to cover furniture or beds (see on 9.200).

231 The vulgate reading is καλά as in *Od.* 24.277, but the variant λευκά is more likely to be right, in view of περικαλλέας at 229 and περικαλλές at 234. Whereas a χλαῖνα was woollen, the φᾶρος was almost certainly made of linen, hence the colour; cf. 18.353 φάρεϊ λευκῷ. On these garments see Lorimer, *HM* 370–5, S. Marinatos, *Arch. Hom.* A 6–11.

232 = 19.247. Here the verse breaks the run of the passage (ἔξελε ... ἐκ δὲ ... ἐκ δὲ ...), and ἔφερεν is unsuitable as Priam is taking things from the chests. Also the idea of weighing has been thought unnecessary here, as no exact amount has been specified, but that is a minor objection. Leaf argued on these grounds for interpolation, and he could well be right (so also Macleod). The reference to gold at 22.351–2 and in the later tradition of the ransoming (see comment there) could have led to the insertion.

233 Cf. 9.122–3 (etc.) ἕπτ' ἀπύρους τρίποδας ... | αἴθωνας δὲ λέβητας ἐείκοσι ...

234–7 The most valuable object is the cup given to Priam when he went on an embassy by the Thracians. Cf. 11.632 πὰρ δὲ δέπας περικαλλές, ὃ οἴκοθεν ἦγ' ὁ γεραιός (Nestor's cup). The Thracians were suitable donors, as heavy drinkers (T), as well as near neighbours of the Trojans. ἐξεσίη ('a mission') recurs at *Od.* 21.20 (ἐξεσίην ... ἦλθεν), and later in Callimachus (fr. 82.4 Pf.). For ἐξεσίην (acc. of respect, 'on a mission') cf. 4.384 etc. κτέρας means 'a present' here; see on 38. ὁ γέρων in 236 perhaps has a touch of pathos, as at (e.g.) 1.33, 8.87 (so bT on both these verses), and the whole of 235–7 (οὐδέ ... υἱόν) are added to stress the great worth of this possession, περὶ δ' ... being explanatory ('for he longed intensely ...'). The poet gives us an insight into the old man's mind.

239 ἔρρε(τε) is always a violent word (cf. 8.164 etc. and see on 22.498), and λωβητήρ is abusive (2.275, 11.385). For ἐλεγχέες see on 4.242, and cf. the abusive κάκ' ἐλέγχεα at 2.235 etc.

239–40 οὗ νυ καὶ ὑμῖν ... κηδήσοντες: 'Haven't you enough of your own to weep for at home, that you have come to tend my grief?' κηδήσοντες seems to be a word-play, for κήδειν means 'to *cause* distress', but κῆδος etc. is used of mourning (cf. κηδεύειν of attending to a corpse, i.e. burial-rites). So here by their grief the mourners only give Priam worse distress (cf. T).

241 ἦ ὀνόσασθ': this was Aristarchus' reading (Did/A), from ὄνομαι, meaning 'have you made light of it, that ...?' It looks like a conjecture for the vulgate reading οὔνεσθε, which can be explained as the second person plural indicative of ὄνομαι, with epic lengthening, or as a misspelling of the imperfect ὤνεσθε. In both cases the sense will be virtually the same as that of Aristarchus' reading, and the closest parallel is *Od.* 17.378 (Antinoos abusing Eumaios) ἦ ὄνοσαι ὅτι τοι βίοτον κατέδουσιν ἄνακτος (etc.). For Κρονίδης Ζεὺς ἄλγε' ἔδωκε cf. 2.375; 18.431.

242 παῖδ' ὀλέσαι τὸν ἄριστον is 'to lose the best of sons', in apposition to ἄλγεα, and ἀτὰρ γνώσεσθε καὶ ὕμμες 'but you yourselves shall learn', i.e. by bitter experience, what this means; cf. 8.406 etc.

243–4 Cf. 18.258 ῥηΐτεροι πολεμίζειν, etc. Here the comparative is reduplicated by μᾶλλον: cf. 334, LSJ s.v. μάλα ΙΙ 2.

244–6 αὐτὰρ ἔγωγε ... εἴσω: for this type of 'death-wish' cf. especially 6.464–5 (at the end of Hektor's speech to Andromakhe, envisaging her capture), and 4.182, 8.150. The reduplication of the long participles in 245 adds greater force.

247 ἦ, καὶ σκηπανίῳ δίεπ' ἀνέρας: cf. 13.59 ἦ, καὶ σκηπανίῳ, and 2.207

ὡς ὅ γε κοιρανέων δίεπε στρατόν, where Odysseus is restoring order in the army, using the sceptre to do so. δίεπε means 'he controlled them', i.e. drove them out of the palace.

248–51 This list of Priam's sons contains some well-known names (Helenos, Paris, Polites, Deiphobos), and others which occur only here and may be invented by the poet for the occasion. The names Agathon, Pammon, Antiphonos and Dios do not recur in the poem, and in the case of Δῖον ἀγαυόν there was debate as to which word was the proper name, Pherecydes being quoted in favour of Dios (Arn/A, T). Hippothoos recurs as a leader of the Pelasgians (2.840), killed at 17.298–303. The shadowy character of some of them emphasizes Priam's point that his favourite sons are dead.

253–64 Priam's bitter invective, now directed at his own sons, begins in a way structurally similar to the previous speech (239 ~ 253), and then returns to the cause of his grief, with its emphatic repetition of Hektor's name at the beginning of 254 and 258. The opening is picked up in the magnificently contemptuous description of the remaining sons at 261–2 as parasitic layabouts. It emerges at the end of the speech that they have failed to react to his earlier order to prepare the waggon (189–90), and with this renewed order the main thread of the narrative is resumed. For criticism of Priam's sons and sons-in-law as cowards cf. also 5.472–6.

253 κατηφόνες: 'downcasts', i.e. people who suffer from κατηφείη ('dejection'), who are κατηφέες (*Od.* 24.432): see on 22.293. The word recurs in Philo of Alexandria and the scholia to Hermogenes. Such nouns in -ων can often be derogatory, e.g. ἀλαζών, δηλήμων, κέντρων ('rogue'), τρίβων, etc.; cf. C. D. Buck and W. Petersen, *A Reverse Index of Greek Nouns and Adjectives* (Chicago 1945) 247. Aristarchus thought that the word had a feminine connotation here, whereas Crates read κατηφέες (Did/A).

255–6 These verses are echoed by Priam at 493–4, where he expands this theme in his plea to Akhilleus; see also on 22.44–5. The highly rhetorical compound πανάποτμος occurs nowhere else, and could well be a coinage of the poet (for ἄποτμος see 388): cf. M. Pope, *CQ* 35 (1985) 5, J. Griffin, *JHS* 106 (1986) 41.

256 Τροίη ἐν εὐρείη: the only Iliadic parallel (apart from 494) for this phrase is at 774, ἐνὶ Τροίη εὐρείη |. The first formula occurs 3× *Od.*, the second 2×.

257 Oddly enough, neither Mestor nor Troilos is mentioned elsewhere in Homer. Apollodorus (*Epit.* 3.32) mentions Mestor in connexion with Akhilleus' raid on Aineias' cattle, and he crops up in some other late versions of the Trojan War (Dio Chrys. *Or.* 11.77, Dictys 6.9). The killing of Troilos by Akhilleus was related in the *Cypria* (OCT vol. v, p. 105.12 = Davies, *EGF* p. 32.81–2), and was clearly a popular story, as it is often shown in art from the early archaic period onwards: cf. Johansen, *Iliad in Early Greek Art* 45, 53, 83, K. Schefold, *Myth and Legend in Early Greek Art* (London 1966) figs. 28, 34, 35, pls. 48a, 73a, F. Brommer, *Vasenlisten* (3rd edn, Marburg 1973) 357–66. The epithet ἱππιοχάρμην (only here in *Il.*, 1× *Od.*) is given point by later versions of the story: on the François Vase Akhilleus on foot pursues Troilos on horseback (Schefold, *op. cit.* pl. 48a), and this was the version of οἱ νεώτεροι according to Arn/A, whilst T tells us that in Sophocles' *Troilos* he was exercising his horses when ambushed (cf. *Trag. Graec. Frag.* IV, p. 453 ed. Radt). In Virgil he has a chariot, whose horses bolt (*Aen.* 1.474–8).

258–9 Hektor's godlike status is twice emphasized by Priam (cf. 22.394, 22.434–5, and Griffin, *HLD* 81ff.). As often the contrast between ἀνδρός and θεοῖο frames 259. The most godlike of Priam's sons is dead, and those who are left seem mere nobodies to him by contrast.

260–2 The invective style evokes highly individual language: ψευστής occurs only here in Homer (cf. Pindar, *N.* 5.29, etc.); ὀρχηστής recurs at 16.617 (ὀρχηστήρ 18.494); χοροιτυπίη is only here in early literature (cf. χοροιτύπος *HyHerm* 31, etc.); ἐπιδήμιος at 9.64 and 2× *Od.*; ἁρπακτήρ only here and in late literature (Oppian, Nonnus, Julian); finally the phrase ἀρνῶν ἠδ' ἐρίφων is Odyssean (3×). The structure of the verses is also effective: 260 is a balanced contrast of μέν and δέ clauses with dactylic rhythm, 261 a 'tricolon crescendo' with emphatic spondaic opening and the long abstract formation χοροιτυπίῃσιν giving weight to the ending, and 262 again has a climactic effect, emphasized by its spondaic ending:

τοὺς μὲν ἀπώλεσ' Ἄρης, ‖ τὰ δ' ἐλέγχεα πάντα λέλειπται,
ψεῦσταί τ' ‖ ὀρχησταί τε, ‖ χοροιτυπίῃσιν ἄριστοι,
ἀρνῶν ‖ ἠδ' ἐρίφων ‖ ἐπιδήμιοι ‖ ἁρπακτῆρες.

The accusations remind one particularly of the *Odyssey*: e.g. Alkinoos' description of liars (11.363–6), the young men of Phaeacia, unwarlike and brilliant at dancing, and the suitors of Penelope who devour Odysseus' animals. Such derogatory descriptions are neatly echoed by Hor. *Ep.* 1.2.27–31. But cf. also *Il.* 3.39 = 13.769 Δύσπαρι, εἶδος ἄριστε, γυναιμανές, ἠπεροπευτά, 1.231 δημοβόρος βασιλεύς, ἐπεὶ οὐτιδανοῖσιν ἀνάσσεις, and 3.106, where Priam's sons are described as ὑπερφίαλοι καὶ ἄπιστοι. ἄριστοι in 261 picks up and bitterly echoes υἷας ἀρίστους in 255; for the word's sarcastic use cf. 17.142, 23.483, Hdt. 3.80.4, Thuc. 3.38.5. Dancing and fighting are contrasted at 3.393–4, 15.508 (see comment). In 262 each word has its point: lambs and kids would be particular delicacies, and ἐπιδήμιοι is paradoxical ('robbers in your own land'); bT compare Ar. *Pax* 1189–90 οἴκοι μὲν λέοντες, ἐν μάχῃ δ' ἀλώπεκες. Robbing livestock outside one's community was no disgrace in heroic society, as Thucydides observed (1.5.1); cf. Caes. *BG* 6.23.6 *latrocinia nullam habent infamiam quae extra fines cuiusque civitatis fiunt* (among the Germans, and especially in training young warriors). For modern Greek parallels cf. J. Th. Kakridis, *Gymnasium* 78 (1971) 513–15.

263 Cf. *Od.* 6.57 (Nausikaa to Alkinoos) πάππα φίλ', οὐκ ἄν δή μοι ἐφοπλίσσειας ἀπήνην ... As Leaf observes, 'The very different tone expressed here by the same construction shews how rash it is to put down certain formulae as "polite" or "hesitating" requests; such a connotation belongs to the context rather than the words.' For this construction (οὐκ ἄν δή with optative), expressing a command or suggestion, gentle or contemptuous, cf. 3.52, 5.456. On the relation of this episode to the scene in *Odyssey* 6 cf. Reinhardt, *IuD* 474–7, Usener, *Verhältnis der Odyssee zur Ilias* 180–1.

264 ταῦτα refers to all the objects which Priam has brought out for the ransom (229–35), although they are as yet still in the store-room, and so presumably not visible (cf. 275). ἵνα πρήσσωμεν ὁδοῖο means 'so that we can get going on our way', with the verb having the root sense of 'pass over', 'traverse' (cf. περάω etc.) and ὁδοῖο used of the space in which this occurs. Once again the phrase as a whole is Odyssean, cf.:

3.476 ζεύξαθ' ὑφ' ἅρματ' ἄγοντες, ἵνα πρήσσησιν ὁδοῖο
15.47 ζεῦξον ὑφ' ἅρματ' ἄγων, ὄφρα πρήσσωμεν ὁδοῖο
15.219 αὐτοί τ' ἀμβαίνωμεν, ἵνα πρήσσωμεν ὁδοῖο.

265–74 After the dramatic scene of Priam's anger and impatience the technical account of how the waggon is prepared and harnessed makes a complete contrast: as often in Homer, an emotional scene is followed by one of practical action (cf. for example 23.109–26 with comment). The style is similar to that of other technical descriptions, such as the construction of Odysseus' raft (*Od.* 5.233–57) or Hesiod's instructions for making a waggon or plough (*Erga* 423–36), but it is not altogether matter-of-fact: as bT (266) say, 'the poet has dignified an everyday and commonplace action by the variety (ποικιλία) of his poetic expressions'. The interpretation of some of the details remains uncertain, despite more than a century of modern discussion. Here is a provisional translation of 268–74: 'And they took down from the hook the yoke for the mules, made of box-wood, with a knob on it, well-fitted with rein-guides. Then they brought out the nine-cubit-long yoke-binding, along with the yoke. And the yoke they fitted properly on to the well-polished pole, at its front end, and put the ring over the peg, and tied it (the binding) three times on each side of the knob, and then bound it fast in a succession of turns and tucked it in under the hook.'

Much of the language is individual: for πρωτοπαγής, meaning 'joined together for the first time', see on 5.194; it recurs in Hellenistic and late

Greek. The following are Homeric *hapaxes*: πύξινος (fifth-century and later literature); οἴηξ, which later always means 'a ship's tiller'; ζυγόδεσμον (Plutarch, etc.); πέζα (Hippocrates, etc.; said to be used in Arcadian and Doric, but cf. τράπεζα, and the epic compounds ἀργυρό- and κυανό-πεζα); κρίκος (Hdt. etc.); ἕστωρ (otherwise only in Aristobulus' account of the Gordian knot, *FGH* 139.7, quoted by Plutarch and Arrian); and γλωχίν or γλωχίς (cf. Sophocles etc., and the Homeric compounds τανυ- τρι- χαλκο-γλώχις, 5.393 etc.).

This waggon is four-wheeled (324). ἄμαξα may have its basic sense here, referring to the wheeled framework or *chassis*, πείρινς being the superstructure and ἀπήνη denoting the whole vehicle (cf. N. J. Richardson and S. Piggott, *JHS* 102 (1982) 226 on Hesiod's waggon). It is usually thought that the οἴηκες were hooks or rings attached to the yoke through which the reins were passed. The length of the yoke-binding, nine cubits or about four metres, is puzzling, and it has been suggested that as well as being lashed around the yoke and pole this was used to form 'yoke braces', which ran forward from the pole diagonally to either yoke-arm and helped to keep the pole level. Such braces were certainly used in Near Eastern chariots of the Late Bronze Age, and they appear on later Assyrian reliefs: cf. M. A. Littauer and J. Crouwel, *JHS* 108 (1988) 194–6. However, given the precision of the Homeric verses, it is odd that there is nothing in the text referring to them. The κρίκος was probably a ring attached to the yoke, which was passed over a peg (ἕστωρ) fastened through the pole: it was by removing this peg, according to Aristobulus, that Alexander undid the Gordian knot. The ὀμφαλός was a boss on the yoke itself, around which the binding was passed three times, before being bound fast in a succession of turns (ἐξείης κατέδησαν) around the pole. The end was then possibly tucked under a hook on the pole, if that is what γλωχίς means: ὑπὸ γλωχῖνα probably go together (rather than ὑπὸ ... ἔκαμψαν), because of the position of δέ, and γλωχίς normally means 'a barb'. There are discussions and diagrams in Leaf's Commentary, vol. II, pp. 623–7, J. Wiesner, *Arch. Hom.* F 6–9, 16–18, F. H. Stubbings in Wace and Stubbings, *Companion* 539–41; see also Willcock's comments on 268–74.

265–7 For 265 cf. 12.413 etc. ὡς ἔφαθ'· οἱ δὲ ἄνακτος ὑποδείσαντες ὁμοκλήν, and for 266–7 cf. 189–90. The fact that the waggon is 'newly-constructed' adds to its importance.

268–70 For κὰδ δ' ἀπὸ πασσαλόφι cf. *Od.* 8.67, 105 | κὰδ δ' ἐκ πασσαλόφι. For some reason Zenodotus omitted 269 (Did/AT). For the οἴηκες ('terrets', 'rein-guides') see on 16.470–5. ἐννεάπηχυς recurs at *Od.* 11.311, *HyAp* 104.

271–2 Cf. 6.40, 16.371 ἐν πρώτῳ ῥυμῷ, and 5.729–30 where the yoke is bound to the front end of the chariot-pole (see comment).

274 Most MSS read the unmetrical ἔγναμψαν, a minority ἔκαμψαν.

275-6 The word ἀπήνη is first mentioned here in the poem and recurs several times in book 24. Verses 275–6 are echoed at 578–9.

277-8 For 277 cf. *Od.* 6.253 ζεῦξεν δ' ἡμιόνους κρατερώνυχας. This epithet is usually applied to horses. ἐντεσιεργός is an absolute *hapax*, meaning 'working in harness'; cf. Pind. *O.* 13.20, A. *Pers.* 194 for this sense of ἔντεα. The noble epic diction dignifies these homely beasts: cf. the story of Simonides' reluctance to write an ode for a mule-race victor until paid well, after which he wrote χαῖρετ' ἀελλοπόδων θύγατρες ἵππων (Arist. *Rhet.* 1405b23–8), and Pindar's elaborate praise of Hagesias as victor in the mule-car race, *O.* 6.22–8. Verse 278 gives them a homeland and special association, as in the case of the Thracian cup at 234–5. T points out that the Mysians were neighbours of the Enetoi, ὅθεν ἡμιόνων γένος ἀγροτεράων (2.852; see comment), and quotes Anacreon (377 *PMG*): ἱπποθόρων δὲ Μυσοὶ | εὗρον μίξιν ὄνων. The mules are masculine here, feminine at 325.

279-80 Priam drives his own chariot (322), while Idaios drives the waggon. The variant Τρῳούς in a few MSS for Πριάμῳ in 279 would avoid the repetition of Πριάμῳ in 278–9 and would make the horses belong to the famous breed of Tros (5.222–3 etc.), but it is very weakly attested and probably an echo of 23.291. For 280 cf. 5.271 τοὺς μὲν τέσσαρας αὐτὸς ἔχων ἀτίταλλ' ἐπὶ φάτνῃ. εὔξεστος occurs three times in this passage (cf. 271, 275), perhaps by a simple process of association.

281–321 While preparations are being made Hekabe brings a cup of wine, and tells Priam to make a libation, pray for a safe return, and ask for a good omen from Zeus. Priam does so and Zeus sends a great eagle in response

Libation and prayer before a journey were a normal Greek practice (cf. Burkert, *Religion* 71). In the *Iliad* the other chief occasion for this was at the departure for battle of Patroklos (16.220–52), where Akhilleus prayed to Zeus for his safe return (16.231–2 ~ 24.306–7), but there in vain. In the *Odyssey* the Phaeacians send Odysseus on his homeward voyage with a libation (13.36–62), but the departure of Telemakhos and Peisistratos from Sparta is closer to this scene (15.147–81). Verses 284–6 are echoed closely by *Od.* 15.148–50, and there is a similar favourable omen of an eagle, with similar reactions. In both the Odyssean scenes the departure is accompanied by guest-gifts, which makes a further indirect resemblance to the preparation of the ransom-gifts in book 24 (see on 228). See also Arend, *Scenen* 77–8.

281-2 The middle ζευγνύσθην means that they supervised the yoking of the mules and horses (cf. AbT). Verse 282 = 674. For πυκινὰ ... ἔχοντες cf. *Od.* 19.353 πυκινὰ φρεσὶ μήδε' ἔχουσα. Priam and the herald have much to think about, both here and still more at 673–4.

283–6 For 283 cf. 4.529, 16.820 ἀγχίμολον δέ (ῥά) οἱ ἦλθε, and ἀγχίμολον δέ σφ' ἦλθε 5× *Od.* Verse 284 = *Od.* 15.148 (ἔχων), 285 = 15.149 (with variant ἐν δέπαϊ χρυσέῳ), 286 ~ 15.150.

287–98 Hekabe naturally seeks for comfort and reassurance both in prayer and in an omen from Zeus. Only with divine confirmation will she acquiesce in Priam's plan.

287–9 For τῇ cf. 14.219, 23.618. In 288–9 σέ γε ... ἐμεῖο μέν ... are strongly contrasted, μέν with the subordinate clause having a virtually concessive force. For other examples of a subordinate μέν clause cf. Denniston, *Particles* 378–9.

290–1 εὔχεο is in synizesis: cf. 17.142 ἐδεύεο, etc. ἔπειτα may mean 'in addition' (i.e. to praying for safe return), rather than 'after all that has been said', as Leaf proposed. In 291 the specification of Zeus as god of Ida (cf. 16.603–7n.), and as watching over Troy, gives a reason why he should respond: in Akhilleus' prayer at 16.233–48 Zeus is god of Dodona and the Pelasgians, i.e. of northern Greece and Akhilleus' homeland. Here κατά ... ὁρᾶται implies protection, as in the case of ἐφορᾶν (etc.) later, of the gods (cf. Griffin, *HLD* 181). For καθορᾶν -ᾶσθαι of Zeus cf. 11.337 (from Ida), 13.4, and (of Artemis) Anacreon, *PMG* 348.6 (ἐσκατορᾷς), etc.

292–8 This is the only time in the *Iliad* where an omen is actually prayed for: again an Odyssean motif. In 292 there was a variant ἐόν for ταχύν (Did/AT and a papyrus), mentioned again as a variant at 310 by A: cf. 296 where ἐὸν ἄγγελον is the correct reading. In 292 and 310 it would be possible, ἑός meaning 'his own' here and 'your own' in 310 (cf. Chantraine, *GH* I 273–4). But it is less likely to be correct here, in view of ὅς τέ οἱ αὐτῷ etc. which follows, and ταχύν should stand in both verses. In 293 καί εὐ κράτος ἐστὶ μέγιστον conforms to a formular pattern: τοῦ γὰρ (ὅ τε/ ὅου/ οὗ τε/ καί εὐ) κράτος ἐστὶ μέγιστον 6× *Il.*, 2× *Od.* The eagle's power is greatest, just as in the case of Zeus, its lord. For the superlatives in such a context cf. 15.237–8 (n.), etc., and for ὅς τε ... καί εὐ, with change from relative clause to main clause 1.78–9 etc. Zenodotus' reading οὗ is unnecessary, but originally it may have been καί ἑō κράτος.

δεξιόν in 294 is emphatic, and means that the bird flies 'towards the right' from the point of view of the observer: cf. 12.239 ἐπὶ δεξιά, 13.821 (etc.) δεξιὸς ὄρνις. In 295 there was a variant χαίρων ἐνὶ θυμῷ| (A), but this would hardly suit Priam's mood. The use of οὐ after εἰ (296) is not uncommon in Homer: cf. Chantraine, *GH* II 333.

299–301 Priam's answer is very brief. For the speech-introduction 299 see on 217. His pious comment (301) is similar to that at 425–8, and helps to characterize him. αἴ κ' ἐλεήσῃ -ης occurs 5× *Il.* (357 etc.), 1× *Od.*

302–7 Before prayer and libation washing of hands and purification of the cup was normal: 6.266–8, 16.228–30, *Od.* 2.261, 12.336. For 302 cf. *Od.* 16.152 ἀμφίπολον ταμίην ὀτρυνέμεν ὅττι τάχιστα. ἀκήρατος ('pure') recurs at 15.498, *Od.* 17.532, meaning 'untouched'; it is used of pure water at Soph. *OC* 471, 690; cf. *Od.* 9.205 οἶνος ἀκηράσιος, and see on 15.498. Verse 304 resembles the Odyssean verse χέρνιβα δ' ἀμφίπολος προχόῳ ἐπέχευε φέρουσα (6×), which always occurs in the formular passage describing preparations for a meal. χέρνιβον is found only here in early literature, in a fourth-century B.C. inscription, and in Gregory of Nyssa, but was used in Hellenistic Greek: this is attested by Arn/A, who reports Aristarchus' athetesis of the verse because he thought the word post-Homeric, in place of λέβης. χέρνιψ means 'water for washing the hands', and χέρνιβον (or χερνιβεῖον in classical Greek) the basin containing this. Aristarchus may have disliked the idea of *two* vessels being mentioned, and bT argue, in fact, that χέρνιβον means the water itself (cf. Pollux 2.149). πρόχοος occurs only here in *Il.* (προχοαί 17.263). T mentions a reading of the Massaliote text which is uncertain but seems to have ended ταμίη μετὰ χερσὶν ἔχουσα, thus cutting out the πρόχοος (cf. Erbse on schol. 304b). For 305 cf. 1.596 μειδήσασα δὲ παιδὸς ἐδέξατο χειρὶ κύπελλον. The two verbs seem to be in a *hysteron-proteron* relationship. Verses 306–7 = 16.231–2 (see comment).

308–13 Priam's prayer is again brief and to the point. Verse 308 = 3.276. Verse 309 is paralleled in Odysseus' prayer to Athene at *Od.* 6.327 δός μ' ἐς Φαίηκας φίλον ἐλθεῖν ἠδ' ἐλεεινόν, but it is significant that instead of praying for a safe return (287–8), Priam asks to receive friendship and pity when he comes to Akhilleus' hut, again stressing the vital theme of pity (cf. 301 etc.), and reminding us that until now Akhilleus was his worst enemy. Verses 310–13 on the other hand are a close repetition of 292–5.

314–16 Verse 314 = 16.249 (at the end of Akhilleus' prayer before Patroklos' departure); 315 = 8.247 (see comment). Arn/A observes that τελειότατον does not mean 'physically perfect' but 'most capable of bring-ing fulfilment'; cf. Zeus τέλειος (A. *Supp.* 525–6, A. *Ag.* 973, Fraenkel *ad loc.*). The epithet could well mean both, 'most perfect' symbolizing 'most capable of fulfilment'. In 316 μόρφνος and περκνός occur only here in Homer. μόρφνος reappears at Hes. *Aspis* 134, apparently again as an epithet of an eagle, and in Aristotle (*HA* 9.32) the eagle mentioned here is said to be called πλάγγος and 'duck-killer', as well as μορφνός (so accented), and to haunt valleys, glens and lakes. Lycophron (838) treats it as a noun, and so does the *Suda*. περκνός means 'dusky', 'dark-coloured', and recurs in Hellenistic and later literature; cf. ὑποπερκάζουσιν of ripening grapes at *Od.* 7.126. Aristarchus seems to have treated περκνος as the substantive here (Hrd/A). The original sense may have been 'dappled', 'with dark patches': cf. Chantraine, *Dict.* s.v. The eagle in question might be the same as the one described in the simile at 21.252–3 (see comment), although it looks as if they may be distinguished in Aristotle (*loc. cit.*). Given the size of its wing-span (317–19), the golden eagle would be a good candidate, as its span can reach seven feet and it is dusky in colour. Whatever type of bird it may be, the effect of the elaborate description is to make it more awe-inspiring, and this is increased by the simile which follows.

317–19 For this kind of measure of size compare the description of Poluphemos' club as like the mast of a twenty-oared ship (*Od.* 9.322–4). For the language cf. 3.423 ὑψόροφον θάλαμον (*Od.* 2.337), *Od.* 4.121 θαλάμοιο ... ὑψορόφοιο; *Il.* 24.482 ἀνδρὸς ἐς ἀφνειοῦ. The singular θύρη occurs only here and at 453 in *Il.*, 7× *Od.*

In 318 Aristarchus read ἐϋκλήϊς as one word, meaning 'well-closed' (the word would be an absolute *hapax*; cf. εὔκλειστος), and all MSS have this reading, whereas Tryphon preferred ἐὺ κληῖσ'. Aristarchus objected to the elision of the dative plural -ῖσι, which seems possible given other elided datives in *iota*. Against the compound word is the fact that ἀρηρώς (etc.) is usually joined to an adverb or a dative elsewhere, but cf. 4.134, 19.396, where it probably stands on its own. Elsewhere doors seem to have a single κληΐς, whether lock or bolt (cf. 12.456, 14.168, 24.455), but this may not be a relevant objection to the plural. On the whole it seems better to treat ἐὺ κληῖσ' ἀραρυῖα as a single phrase, rather than dividing it into two separate epithets.

319–21 'And it appeared to them darting towards the right through (or over) the city.' Most MSS have ὑπὲρ ἄστεος, διά being a variant in A and a few others. The initial digamma of ἄστυ is usually observed, but ὑπέρ seems better of an eagle. Verses 320–1 are echoed closely at *Od.* 15.164–5, of the portent at Telemakhos' departure from Sparta. Cf. also *Od.* 2.154 (two eagles) δεξιὼ ἤϊξαν διά τ' οἰκία καὶ πόλιν αὐτῶν. For θυμὸς ἰάνθη cf. 23.597–8, 23.600.

322–48 Priam and the herald Idaios set off, escorted by Priam's family until they leave the city. Zeus then instructs Hermes to conduct Priam to Akhilleus unseen by the rest of the Greeks, and Hermes comes down to Troy disguised as a young man

At last the perilous journey begins. After the departure the whole focus in the next 140 verses or so is on the meeting of Hermes with Priam, which virtually replaces any description of the journey itself.

322 Most MSS read ὁ γέρων ξεστοῦ (cf. Leaf), A and a few others ὁ γεραιὸς ἑοῦ, which the OCT prefers. Cf. 8.44 = 13.26 ἑοῦ δ' ἐπεβήσετο δίφρου, ἐϋξέστου ἐπὶ δίφρου 2× *Od.* There would be a point in ἑοῦ, since Priam and Idaios have different vehicles (so Macleod).

323 This verse belongs to the type-scene of departures by chariot from a palace (Arend, *Scenen* 88–9), and recurs 3× in *Od.* of Telemakhos (3.493, 15.146, 15.191). The αἴθουσα is the portico around the outer courtyard (cf.

9.472); see Lorimer, *HM* 415. It is ἐρίδουπος (as a generic epithet) in the *Odyssey* even in cases where no noisy activity is being described (3.399 etc.), presumably because of its echoing capacity. T compares κατὰ δώματα ἠχήεντα (*Od.* 4.72). ἐρίδουπος, however, occurs only here in the *Iliad*, and may well have its point, the thundering of the horses' hooves: cf. 11.152 ἐρίγδουποι πόδες ἵππων, and Reinhardt, *IuD* 492–3. Usener, *Verhältnis der Odyssee zur Ilias* 156–64, argues that the phrase is specifically designed for *Iliad* 24, and only becomes a formula through its use in the *Odyssey*.

324 For τετράκυκλος cf. *Od.* 9.241–2 (ἄμαξαι). This would be in contrast to chariots, which were two-wheeled, although some early Greek ἄμαξαι do appear to have been two-wheelers (cf. Richardson and Piggott, *JHS* 102 (1982) 225–9). The scansion τετράκυκλον is *metri gratia*: at *Od.* 9.242 τετράκυκλοι involves another metrical expedient, the lengthened *alpha*.

325 Idaios the Trojan herald appeared at 3.248, 7.276 etc.

326 For μάστιγι κέλευε cf. 23.642.

327–8 Despite the recent portent and Priam's vision, his family still lament at his departure as if he were going to his death (cf. Deichgräber, *Letzte Gesang* 58–9). Cf. the lament of the women when Hektor returns to battle at 6.500–2, and see on 24.83–6. θανατόνδε is used elsewhere in the poem only of the summons to death by the gods of Patroklos and Hektor (16.693, 22.297).

329–32 For 329 cf. *Od.* 24.205 οἱ δ' ἐπεὶ ἐκ πόλιος κατέβαν, τάχα δ' ἄγρον ἵκοντο, and for 330 cf. *Il.* 3.313 (τὼ μὲν ...). On εὐρύοπα Ζῆν cf. 8.206, 14.265 (with comment). Zeus's pity in 332 answers Priam's hopes (301) and echoes 174 (etc.).

333–48 Hermes has not been active in the poem up to now, and even in the Theomachy he declined to fight against Leto (21.497–501). Here he is employed by Zeus in his rôle as an escort (334–5) and helper of travellers (e.g. *Od.* 10.277–306), and more particularly because he has the power to lull men to sleep with his magic wand (343–5), and so is able to conduct Priam through the Greek camp unnoticed (337–8, 445–7). His power to act by stealth has already been shown at 24, where the gods urged him to steal Hektor's corpse (cf. 5.388–91, etc.). For Hermes πομπαῖος cf. A. *Eu.* 90–2, S. *Ph.* 133, [Theocr.] *Id.* 25.4–6 (etc.), and for his rôle as helper of mankind in general *Od.* 8.335 etc. (δῶτορ ἐάων), Ar. *Pax* 392–4 ὦ φιλανθρωπότατε καὶ μεγαλοδωρότατε δαιμόνων, etc.

Zeus's sending of Hermes is paralleled in the *Odyssey*, where Hermes is treated as a messenger when he is sent to Kalupso's island to release Odysseus, replacing Iris, who does not appear in this poem. For 333–5 cf. *Od.* 5.28–9:

Ἦ ῥα, καὶ Ἑρμείαν, υἱὸν φίλον, ἀντίον ηὔδα·
"'Ἑρμεία, σὺ γὰρ αὖτε τά τ' ἄλλα περ ἄγγελός ἐσσι ...'"

Verses 339–45 = *Od.* 5.43–9 (and 340–2 ~ *Od.* 1.96–8, 343–4 = *Od.* 24.3–4); moreover 347–8 are similar to *Od.* 10.278–9, where Hermes appears to Odysseus to help him before he meets Kirke. In *Odyssey* 5, however, Hermes' wand has no function and is merely an attribute (as T observes; schol. *Od.* 5.47); and here Hermes' disguise as a young man leads to the delightful scene between him and the aged Priam, where the contrast of youth and age creates a moving relationship of sympathy, whereas the same disguise in *Odyssey* 10 has no particular significance (cf. Reinhardt, *IuD* 479–82). For other similarities with *Od.* 10.277–306 see on 360–3, 375–7. Usener, *Verhältnis der Odyssee zur Ilias* 165–79, argues that the whole episode of Hermes' meeting with Priam has influenced several parts of the *Odyssey*.

335 For ἑταιρίσσαι ('act as companion to') cf. 13.456 ἑταρίσσαιτο (with accusative), *HyAphr* 95–6 (Χάριτες) αἵ τε θεοῖσι | πᾶσιν ἑταιρίζουσι. καί τ' ἔκλυες ᾧ κ' ἐθέλησθα is 'and you listen to whomever you like'; for the dative with κλύειν or ἀκούειν of a god hearing a mortal request cf. 5.115 (etc.) κλῦθί μοι, 16.575, etc.

336 βάσκ' ἴθι: elsewhere this always comes at the beginning of a speech by Zeus, with a vocative (2.8n., 5× *Il.*). Here it is displaced by the explanatory clause in 334–5: Zeus treats Hermes with more elaborate courtesy than either the Dream or Iris, and in any case, a reason for the choice of Hermes is necessary here.

338 For this contrast between the other Greeks and Akhilleus cf. 2.674 = 17.280 τῶν ἄλλων Δαναῶν, μετ' ἀμύμονα Πηλεΐωνα. This is the only case in Homer where -δε is added to a personal name, as if it meant 'to the house of Akhilleus': cf. however Ἀϊδόσδε ('to the house of Hades'). This extension of the usage seems natural, and is imitated by Apollonius Rhodius (Ἀλκινοόνδε, αὐτοκασιγνητήνδε). T compares 7.312 (etc.) εἰς Ἀγαμέμνονα.

339–45 See on 333–48 for the Odyssean parallels.

339 For διάκτορος see on 2.103. If it was thought to mean 'conductor' it would be especially appropriate here (cf. 378 etc.).

340–2 Hermes' divine sandals, which carry him over sea and land, were portrayed as winged in archaic and later art: T criticizes Aristotle (or perhaps Aristophanes, according to Rose) for regarding them as such here, but why should he not be right? Cf. J. Chittenden, *Hesperia* 16 (1947) 101; L. Deroy, *Athenaeum* 30 (1952) 59–84.

343–5 Hermes' wand has 'magical' powers: cf. *Od.* 10.302–6, where he gives Odysseus the magic plant μῶλυ. The description of the wand sets the tone for the whole of what is to follow, with its atmosphere of the wonderful and supernatural. In *Od.* 24.1–10 he uses his wand to shepherd the ghosts of the suitors down to Hades, and in the *Odyssey* (3×) and *Hymns* (3×) Hermes is χρυσόρραπις. The wand is described at *HyHerm* 528–32 where it is called τριπέτηλον, suggesting the more elaborate form of the κηρύκειον or *caduceus* with which he is later portrayed (cf. Allen, Halliday and Sikes *ad loc.*, and Càssola, *Inni Omerici* 162–3, 540–1). Hermes' ῥάβδος seems to have combined the functions of a shepherd's staff, a herald's sceptre and a magic wand. Here not only does Hermes put the Greek guards to sleep (445–7), but he also wakes Priam secretly at 679–89. For ἐθέλει (Aristarchus' reading) the variant ἐθέλῃ (Did/A) is possible in such a generic relative clause, and it is preferred by Hainsworth at *Od.* 5.48. In ὑπνώοντας the *omega* is presumably *metri gratia*, on the analogy of verbs such as ἱδρώω etc.: cf. Chantraine, *GH* i 365–6.

347–8 The form αἰσυμνητήρ is found only here for αἰσυμνήτης, which means an umpire in the Phaeacian games at *Od.* 8.258, and later was used of a ruler or magistrate in various Greek states. αἰσυμνητῆρι is Aristarchus' reading here, with some of our MSS, the majority having αἰσυητῆρι whose meaning was variously explained (bT, Eust., and Erbse on 347). Presumably αἰσυητήρ is a variant spelling of αἰσυμνητήρ, which is probably a loan-word (*LfgrE*, Chantraine, *Dict.* s.v.). Cf. the name Αἰσυήτης (2.793, and 13.427 with comment). Here the most likely sense would be 'royal', 'princely'. At 397–9 Hermes says that he is a squire of Akhilleus and son of a wealthy Myrmidon. Cf. *Od.* 13.221–3 where Athene is disguised as a young man, 'soft-skinned, like the sons of kings'.

Verse 348 = *Od.* 10.279, again of Hermes in disguise as a young man. ὑπηνήτης occurs only in these verses in Homer. In later Greek ὑπήνη ('moustache') is common, ὑπηνήτης very rare, and sometimes directly from Homer (Pl. *Prt.* 309B, Lucian, *Sacr.* 11). Hermes' youth is part of his disguise; in early Greek art he is nearly always fully bearded: cf. L. R. Farnell, *Cults of the Greek States* v (Oxford 1909) 44–61.

349–442 At dusk they stop to water the horses in the river. Hermes approaches and converses with Priam. He tells him that Hektor's body is intact. Priam offers him a cup, which he refuses, but he promises to escort him safely, and takes charge of his chariot

This episode is unusually extended, and the dialogue is more elaborate than on other occasions in the *Iliad* where god and man meet. In its grace and irony it reminds one of similar scenes in the *Odyssey* and Homeric Hymns, especially the meeting between Odysseus and Athene disguised as a young prince, at *Od.* 13.321–440; cf. the rôle of Athene in *Odyssey* 3, and still closer, the escort and assistance of Athene in disguise to Odysseus at 7.14–81 before his supplication of Arete and Alkinoos; and see Richardson on *HyDem* 98ff., pp. 179–80. It is one of the most delightful scenes in the poem, and yet it is surely not here simply for its own sake. One of its functions is to prepare for the encounter of Priam and Akhilleus, for in the young Myrmidon prince Priam finds someone who treats him as a father (362, 371), and whose kindness and sympathy establish a bond of trust. Hermes' admiration for Hektor, and his account of how the gods have miraculously protected his body, confirm Priam's own trust in divine protection and justice, and (as at 301) his piety is shown by his comments at 374–7 and 425–8. The irony of these remarks, when Priam is speaking to a god, and of his attempt to give Hermes a gift at 429 in accompaniment to his prayer for protection, is typical of such scenes. The whole episode illustrates the Odyssean precept that the gods frequent the society of men in disguise, ἀνθρώπων ὕβριν τε καὶ εὐνομίην ἐφορῶντες (17.487).

349 The tomb of Ilos (cf. 20.230–6) was mentioned as a landmark at 10.415, 11.166, 11.372.

350–1 στῆσαν ... ἐν ποταμῷ probably go together: cf. *Od.* 14.258 στῆσα δ' ἐν Αἰγύπτῳ ποταμῷ νέας, and for the river as watering-place cf. *Il.* 18.521. They presumably stopped at the ford (cf. 692–3), and δὴ γάρ ... γαῖαν explains that this was a safe time to stop as it was already dark.

352–7 This is a dramatic moment, as Idaios suddenly catches sight of an unknown man through the gathering darkness. It is brought about by an unusual change from the poet's normal technique, for in other scenes of divine visitation the god's journey is usually followed by the description of his approach to the person concerned, whom he 'finds' engaged in some activity (as at 83, 98, 122–3 etc.). Here the focus has switched from Hermes to the travellers, and it is they whose reactions are described (cf. Edwards, *HPI* 307). In 353–4 the high frequency of π- and φ-words may be deliberate; φάτο φώνησέν τε recurs only at *Od.* 4.370. In 354–5 Idaios' anxiety is expressed by his rapid sentences with asyndeton; cf. (for example) 16.126–9, and [Longinus] 19 with Russell's comments. Verse 354 means 'Beware, offspring of Dardanus: there is need for a wary mind.' The repetition of φράζεο ... φραδέος is emphatic (cf. also 352 ἐφράσσατο), as well as being characteristic of such explanatory maxims: cf. 7.282, 11.793, 13.115, 15.203, Hes. *Erga* 352, 369. In several cases this leads to the use of an unusual epithet or noun, as here: 11.793 παραίφασις, 13.115 ἀκεσταί, 15.203 στρεπταί, Hes. *Erga* 369 φειδώ; hence φραδέος, an absolute *hapax* (although Hesychius has φραδῶς), analogous to ἀρι-/ἀ-φραδής etc. For ἔργον (ἔστι) with genitive meaning 'it is a matter for', and hence 'there is a need for' cf. LSJ s.v. ἔργον IV 1, and the similar development of *opus est* in Latin.

355 τάχα ... ὀΐω: cf. *Od.* 1.251 τάχα δή με διαρραίσουσι καὶ αὐτόν, and *Il.* 17.727 διαρραῖσαι. bT take it as future passive, but the middle (with ἄνδρα) is possible.

356 ἐφ' ἵππων means 'on the chariot', leaving the waggon to its fate (bT). ἔπειτα means 'as the next best alternative': cf. perhaps 13.743, and *Od.* 20.63.

357 Cf. 21.65 γούνων ἅψασθαι, 10.455 ἁψάμενος λίσσεσθαι etc., and for αἵ κ' ἐλεήσῃ see on 301.

358–60 Priam's reaction is very violent: the hair on his limbs stands up ('goose-flesh'), and he is paralysed with terror. bT say that the 'hyperbaton', i.e. tmesis and word-order of σὺν δὲ γέροντι νόος χύτο, imitates his distress (cf. Eust. 1001.42, in a general discussion of tmesis). The motif of 'goose-flesh' occurs only here in Homer: cf. Andromakhe's physical manifestations of panic at 22.448, 22.451–3, etc. Hesiod (*Erga* 539–40) has ἵνα τοι τρίχες ἀτρεμέωσιν | μηδ' ὀρθαὶ φρίσσωσιν ἀειρόμεναι κατὰ σῶμα, in a different context (winter cold). ἐνὶ γναμπτοῖσι μέλεσσι occurs at 11.669 (in a speech by old Nestor) and 4× *Od.*, 1× *Hymns*. In all these cases there is a contrast between the supple limbs of youth and those of old age. Originally the sense may have been simply 'jointed (or flexible) limbs', but here the poet may have intended the 'bent limbs' of old age. See on 11.669, and cf. B. Snell, *Gesammelte Schriften* (Göttingen 1966) 62–4. For στῆ δὲ ταφών cf. 11.545, 16.806.

360–3 Hermes takes Priam's hand to greet and reassure him, and asks what he is doing in such a dangerous situation. Cf. his similar meeting with the lonely Odysseus at *Od.* 10.280–2 (278–9 ~ *Il.* 24.347–8): ἔν τ' ἄρα μοι φῦ χειρὶ ἔπος τ' ἔφατ' ἔκ τ' ὀνόμαζε· | "πῇ δὴ αὖτ', ὦ δύστηνε, δι' ἄκριας ἔρχεαι οἶος, | χώρου ἀΐδρις ἐών;" For the gesture of reassurance cf. also Poseidon in disguise at 14.137, Akhilleus at 24.671–2, etc. For ἐριούνιος see on 20.34. It is usually an epithet but stands on its own also at 440.

362–71 Hermes addresses Priam as πάτερ at the beginning, and at the end of his speech (with ring composition) he says that he reminds him of his own father: this is why he will protect him. The emphasis is on the age of Priam and his herald, and the extraordinary risks he is running. Priam responds by calling Hermes φίλον τέκος (373; cf. 425 ὦ τέκος), and Hermes later compares his own aged father to Priam (398). In this exchange with the young squire of Akhilleus we have a preview of the relationship between Akhilleus and Priam, who is explicitly compared to Akhilleus' own father. Priam himself has lost all the best of his sons and above all Hektor, and in Hermes he finds the sympathy and reassurance which a son should have given him.

363 Cf. 10.83 = 386 νύκτα δι' ὀρφναίην, ὅτε θ' εὕδουσι βροτοὶ ἄλλοι; νύκτα δι' ἀμβροσίην 10.41, 10.142 (the night expedition there prompts similar expressions).

365 ἀνάρσιος occurs only here in *Il.*, 5× *Od.*; δυσμενέες καὶ ἀνάρσιοι *Od.* 14.85.

366–7 Verse 366 = 653; for θοήν ... μέλαιναν cf. 10.394, 10.698. ὀνείατα in the plural elsewhere always refers to food (3× *Il.*, 13× *Od.*), but ὄνειαρ is used of anything beneficial. For τίς ... εἴη cf. Virgil, *Aen.* 4.408 *quis tibi tum, Dido, cernenti talia sensus ...?*'

368–9 The variation in the two hemistichs of 368 is elegant. Cf. *Od.* 16.71–2 αὐτὸς μὲν νέος εἰμὶ καὶ οὔ πω χερσὶ πέποιθα | ἄνδρ' ἀπαμύνασθαι, ὅτε τις πρότερος χαλεπήνῃ, and *Od.* 21.132–3; *Il.* 19.183 ἄνδρ' ἀπαρέσσασθαι, ὅτε τις πρότερος χαλεπήνῃ. Here the infinitive is epexegetic with γέρων, i.e. 'he is too old for self-defence', as at 662–3, etc.

370–1 Failure to understand that οὐδέν means 'not at all' or 'in no way' has led to the variant οὐδ' ἄν σε, and to κακόν in most MSS, with a few reading ἠδέ or εἰ δέ after it. The compound ἀπαλέξειν occurs only here in *Il.*: cf. *Od.* 17.364.

372–7 Priam's reply is full of unconscious irony, since the young man is indeed a divine protector, and μακάρων has a double sense in 377 as it can be applied to the gods (see also on 397–8). Despite Iris' promise that Hermes will escort him (181–3) Priam apparently fails to realize directly who he is, and yet as often in such cases it is as if he is half-aware of his identity, and when Hermes reveals himself (at 460–1) he shows none of the usual reactions of surprise etc.

373 οὕτω πη τάδε γ' ἐστί ... ὡς ἀγορεύεις sounds like a variation of more colloquial answers such as οὕτως, οὕτω γε πως, ἔστι ταῦτα (Pl. *Theaet.* 160A, 165C, *Soph.* 244D); cf. LSJ s.v. οὕτως I.

374 Did/A seems to have read εἴ τις, with some of our MSS, but it is hard to see how this can be right. ἔτι ... καὶ ἐμεῖο stresses Priam's surprise that the gods should indeed show concern for him, after all his sufferings. For ὑπερέχειν χεῖρα(ς) of divine protection cf. 5.433 etc.

375–7 ὁδοιπόρος occurs only here in Homer, but cf. ὁδοιπόριον *Od.* 15.506; ὁδοιπορίη *HyHerm* 85. αἴσιος is also a Homeric *hapax* (cf. Pindar, *N.* 9.18, etc., and Homeric ἐναίσιμος, ἐξαίσιος, παραίσιος). It surely refers to the fact that 'chance' meetings could be ominous or lucky, and Hermes himself is a god of lucky chances (ἑρμαῖα), as well as of ways and travellers. Cf. his meeting with Odysseus when he is travelling on his own on Kirke's island (*Od.* 10.277–306; note 277 ἀντεβόλησεν). In 376–7 bT ingeniously find the three 'goods' of the later philosophical schools: physique, intelligence and good birth. The last, praise of parents as 'blessed' (a form of 'makarismos'), is paralleled at *Od.* 6.154–5 (cf. T), E. *Ion* 308, etc. For the second hemistich of 377 cf. 387 etc.

378 = 389, 410, 432.

379–85 The opening verse is traditional but especially apt here, since Priam's words are more true than he realizes. Hermes then suggests two possible reasons for Priam's journey. The first, to take Troy's treasures abroad for safe-keeping, becomes the opening motif of Euripides' *Hecuba*, where Priam sends his son Poludoros with the gold of Troy to Polumestor of Thrace before the city's fall (*Hec.* 1–12; cf. bT). For the second, total desertion of Troy, cf. 22.382–3 where Akhilleus sees this as a possibility after Hektor's death. Here too this leads Hermes on to mention Hektor's fall, with a note of admiration and sympathy. With sensitive tact he thus introduces the most important theme of this dialogue.

379 = 1.286, 8.146, and cf. similar answer-formulae elsewhere.

380 = 10.384 etc. The verse occurs twice in book 10 and twice in book 24 (cf. 656), but 13 × *Od.*; see on 10.384.

381–2 Cf. 9.330 κειμήλια πολλά καὶ ἐσθλά |; ἄνδρας ἐς ἀλλοδαπούς, 2× *Od.*; *Od.* 13.364 ἵνα περ τάδε τοι σόα μίμνῃ.

383–5 Cf. 22.383 ἢ καταλείψουσιν πόλιν ἄκρην τοῦδε πεσόντος. For δειδιότες in runover position followed by an explanatory clause cf. 6.137, 15.628. 21.24. Verses 384–5 delicately introduce Hektor indirectly, 'such a man, the best, has fallen – your son', with σὸς πάϊς in emphatic position. Cf. 16.521 ἀνὴρ δ' ὤριστος ὄλωλε |. οὐ ... Ἀχαιῶν probably means 'for he never failed in battle with the Achaeans'. For μάχης ἐπιδεύεσθαι cf. 13.310, 17.142, 23.670, and for the genitive Ἀχαιῶν with μάχη cf. 11.542. This seems better than 'he did not fall short of the Achaeans in battle' (cf. 23.483).

386–8 Priam's surprise and curiosity prevent him from answering Hermes' questions. For 387 cf. 6.123, 15.247 τίς δὲ σύ ἐσσι, φέριστε, and 377 μακάρων δ' ἒξ ἐσσι τοκήων. In 388 the vulgate reading is ὅς, which would be explanatory here (as at 434 etc.), but the exclamatory ὡς seems more effective. For ἀπότμου cf. 255 = 493 πανάποτμος, again spoken by Priam. ἄποτμος -ότατος occur 2× *Od.*

389–404 Hermes' answer is again subtle and courteous. He says that he understands what is really uppermost in Priam's mind, the desire to know what has happened to Hektor's body. This leads him to speak of the Greeks' admiration for his prowess, and thence to answer Priam's actual question about his identity. Finally he explains what he is doing, by reference to the Greeks' preparations for battle: the motive is left a little vague, but the real point is presumably the reminder that the present inactivity is only a temporary lull in the conflict.

390 The first hemistich is repeated at 433. For πειρᾷ see on 14.198–9, 21.459. The assonance in this verse is notable: πειρᾷ ἐμεῖο, γεραιέ, καὶ εἴρεαι ... For εἴρεαι with accusative meaning 'you are asking about' cf. 6.239 etc.

391–3 For 391–2 cf. 6.124 οὐ μὲν γάρ ποτ' ὄπωπα μάχῃ ἐνὶ κυδιανείρῃ, where 123 resembles 387. The second part of 393 is a variant of the formular δεδαϊγμένος -ον ὀξέϊ χαλκῷ.

394 ἡμεῖς ... θαυμάζομεν is repeated from 2.320, ἑσταότες implying 'standing idle' here.

396 νηῦς εὐεργής occurs only here in *Il.*, 2× *Od.*, 2× *Hymns*; cf. εὐεργέος ... δίφρου 2× *Il.*

397–8 Hermes gives his origin and his father's name, this being sufficient to identify one: see on 21.153, and for this formulation cf. *Od.* 15.267 ἐξ Ἰθάκης γένος εἰμί, πατὴρ δέ μοί ἐστιν Ὀδυσσεύς, where again Telemakhos does not name himself. The name Poluktor recurs in the *Odyssey* (17.207, 18.299, 22.243), and is suitable for a rich man, -κτωρ being probably related to κτέρας etc.; cf. von Kamptz, *Personennamen* §21. As at 377 there may be irony, as Hermes himself is the 'giver of good things' (*Od.* 8.335 etc.). In 398 γέρων ... ὧδε stresses the bond of sympathy between this young man and Priam. ὧδε probably picks up ὡς σύ περ, 'even so, just as you are'.

399–400 For 'six ... the seventh' cf. 7.247–8. In 400 Aristarchus took τῶν μέτα together. Leaf objected that μετά meaning 'with' rarely takes the genitive in Homer, but it certainly sometimes does (see on 21.458). Hermes implies selective conscription by lot, one brother from each family (T), but this need not have been supposed to be general.

401–4 Presumably Hermes pretends to have come on a reconnoitring expedition (cf. bT), as in book 10, with which this scene has some points of contact. The impatience of the Achaean army in 403–4 is similar to that of the Myrmidons earlier in the poem (16.156–66, 16.200–9), and Hermes seems to suggest that the leaders would like to prolong the spell of quiet but cannot do so. In 403 Leaf follows a handful of MSS in reading οἵ γε, on the grounds that οἵδε 'is merely anaphoric and can have no deictic force', an objection which seems pedantic and hard to understand. For ἐσσυμένους πολέμου cf. 13.315 ἐσσύμενον πολέμοιο, etc.

405–9 Priam now comes to the crucial point, asking Hermes to tell him 'the whole truth' about his son's body, however awful it may be. In 407 the runover word εἷς is regarded by Leaf as 'intolerably weak for so emphatic a position', but with εἰ μὲν δή it carries weight: 'if in truth you really *are*'; cf. Denniston, *Particles* 392, and for other examples of forms of εἶναι in this position cf. 6.225, 16.515, *Od.*4.95, 17.159. πᾶσαν ἀληθείην κατάλεξον belongs to the Odyssean formular group (πᾶσαν ἀληθείην καταλέξω/ κατέλεξα (6× *Od.*, 1× *HyHerm*). In 409 μελεϊστὶ ταμών is Odyssean: cf. *Od.* 9.291 μελεϊστὶ ταμών, 18.339 διὰ μελεϊστὶ τάμῃσιν. Priam's fear that Akhilleus has chopped the body in pieces before giving it to the dogs goes even further than Akhilleus' own threats.

410–23 Hermes' reply amplifies the theme of the miraculous preservation of the corpse, leading up to the emphatic statement that the gods have taken care of Hektor after his death.

411 Cf. 22.335–6 σὲ μὲν κύνες ἠδ' οἰωνοὶ | ἑλκήσουσ' ... (etc.).

412–13 κεῖνος is probably deictic: 'there he lies', as in 3.391 etc. κεῖται is picked up by the runover κειμένῳ in 414, and κεῖται in 419. αὖτως means 'just as he was'.

413–14 δυωδεκάτη ... κειμένῳ 'this is the twelfth day that he has been lying there'; see on 31. ἠώς is the vulgate reading, with the variants ἥδε in a few MSS and ἤδη in one or two. As it is now night Leaf and van Leeuwen object to ἠώς, arguing that it has come in through the influence of 1.493 or 21.80. If one reads ἥδε or ἤδη the use of δυωδεκάτη as a substantive can be supported by, for example, 1.425, *Od.* 2.374. But equally these readings could be due to scholarly qualms in antiquity over ἠώς, and it may well be used simply to mean 'day': cf. (e.g.) 13.794 etc.

414–15 These verses are paralleled by the description of decay at 19.25–7, and 19.31 which is almost identical with 415.

416–17 Cf. 12–16, where the neutral Μενοιτιάδαο θανόντος is used instead of the more emotive ἑοῦ ἑτάροιο φίλοιο; and for the first part of 417 cf. 22.465 ἕλκον ἀκηδέστως (see comment). Here, however, the lack of due κῆδος is contrasted with the gods' care for the body (422 κήδονται).

418–23 The divine protection by Aphrodite and Apollo was described at 23.184–91 and 24.18–21. Here it is something to excite wonder (θηοῖο): the body's freshness (ἑερσήεις) would accord with the dark cloud spread over it by Apollo to keep off the sun's rays (23.188–91), the 'washing of blood' and closure of wounds with Aphrodite's anointing (23.186–7). The motif of wonder here, together with the recollection at 421 of the many wounds given by the Greeks, echoes the description at 22.369–71 of how the Achaeans wondered (θηήσαντο) at Hektor's body as they all ran up and stabbed him (cf. T on 24.418 and 421). Cf. the reference at 24.394 to their admiration for him.

418 θηοῖο, a contracted form of the second person singular present optative of θηέομαι (cf. θεάομαι), is the spelling of Aristarchus (Did/T) and some MSS. The majority have θείοιο, which presumably comes from confusion with forms such as θείομεν etc. (cf. Monro, *HG* Appendix c, pp. 384–6). αὐτὸς ἐπελθών | is Odyssean (5×); cf. ἄλλος/οἷος ἐπελθών | etc. in *Il.*, usually in a hostile context.

419 ἑερσήεις: cf. 757 ἑρσήεις, again of Hektor's body. The epithet is applied to λωτός at 14.348, just before the description of the divine cloud from which drip shining dewdrops (350–1). In περὶ δ' αἷμα νένιπται the noun is probably an internal accusative ('he is washed of blood'); cf. 16.667, 18.345 etc.

420 μιαρός occurs nowhere else in Homer, and seems to keep its original connexion with μιαίνω here, meaning 'stained' (with blood etc.). It reappears in Heraclitus (61) and later. (συμ)μύω is also new, and recurs only at 637 (μύσαν); cf. fifth-century tragedy and later poetry and prose. T describes this statement as miraculous (παράδοξον), since wounds made after

315

death would not normally close, and there seems to have been debate over this point going back at least to Aristotle (fr. 167 R.), whom T quotes.

422–3 This forms the climax of Hermes' speech: divine responsibility is after all vindicated. In this context κήδονται presumably has a double sense, as at 21.123, 22.465, 24.417. For the form ἑῆος ('your') see on 15.138. T records that 423 was athetized as unnecessary, and because the use of the pronoun σφι here was un-Homeric. The criticisms seem to go back to Aristophanes. The second is untrue, and, as to the first, the verse does in fact add something important: even if the gods could not save Hektor from his fated death, they are still concerned for him as one who was dear to them (cf. 33–8, 66–70, etc.). Priam's answer echoes this and draws the general moral (425–8). Moreover, 422–3 are again echoed by Hekabe in her lament at 749–50, just as 754–9 echo 416–21.

424 ὣς φάτο, γήθησεν δέ: cf. 6.212, 17.567, 5× *Od.*, and for the whole verse cf. 200.

425–8 These verses pick up the theme of Zeus's speech at 66–70: again Priam's piety is revealed (see 301n.). Cf. *Od.* 24.351–2, where old Laertes exclaims that after all the gods do exist on Olumpos, if the suitors have truly paid for their insolence. Both statements are thematically significant, occurring as they do at the end of each poem. ἐναίσιμα δῶρα recurs in this position in the verse at *HyDem* 369, of offerings to the gods. διδοῦναι is a unique form, presumably lengthened *metri gratia*, for διδόναι, the nearest parallel being ζευγνῦμεν (16.145); cf. Chantraine, *GH* I, 104, 486. It appears to have troubled Aristophanes (Erbse *ad loc.*), and shocked Eustathius (1357.19ff.). In 426 εἴ ποτ' ἔην γε ('if ever in fact he was') is a formular phrase expressing 'nostalgia and regret at how things have changed' (Kirk on 3.180). Eustathius says that it is 'spoken in a very pathetic and characteristic way, as if such a great man as Hektor never really existed' (περιπαθῶς λεχθὲν καὶ συνήθως, ὡς εἰ μὴ γέγονέ ποτε ὁ τοσοῦτος Ἕκτωρ).

In 428 τῷ ('therefore') is the vulgate reading, but some MSS have τῶν (also, in T as variant), with which one would have to understand the antecedent 'his offerings'; this, however, is rather remote. For ἀπεμνήσαντο in this context cf. Hes. *Th.* 503 οἳ οἱ ἀπεμνήσαντο χάριν εὐεργεσιάων, Thuc. 1.137.2 αὐτῷ χάριν ἀπομνήσεσθαι ἀξίαν, E. *Alc.* 299 σύ νύν μοι τῶνδ' ἀπόμνησαι χάριν. The compound verb occurs only here in Homer. Many MSS read ἐπεμνήσαντο, and forms of this compound occur at 15.662, 17.103, but it is less appropriate here (so Eustathius). The phrase καὶ ἐν θανάτοιό περ αἴσῃ recurs at 750, in the similar comment of Hekabe.

429–31 After Priam's pious observation he unconsciously exemplifies what he has said, by offering a drinking-cup to Hermes, and asking in return for protection and safe escort with the favour of the gods, using language typical of prayers. The ἄλεισον is a two-handled drinking-cup: cf.

11.774, and 6× *Od.*; for καλὸν ἄλεισον cf. *Od.* 4.591, 22.9. It is sometimes a synonym for δέπας (ἀμφικύπελλον); cf. *LfgrE* s.v., F. Brommer, *Hermes* 77 (1942) 356–7, 363–4, G. Bruns, *Arch. Hom.* Q 43. T (on 433–4) assumes that this is the Thracian cup described at 234–5 as the most precious vessel in the ransom (cf. Eust. 1357.31ff.). For (430) πέμψον ... σύν γε θεοῖσιν cf. 9.49 σὺν γὰρ θεῷ εἰλήλουθμεν, etc.

432–9 Hermes ironically again suggests that Priam is 'testing' him, since he cannot accept a gift without Akhilleus' orders. But he promises with great warmth to escort him wherever he wishes to go.

433 This verse echoes 390, again with assonance, and γεραιὲ νεωτέρου are artfully juxtaposed. For οὐδέ με πείσεις | cf. 219 etc. (6× *Il.*, 1× *Od.*).

434 κέλεαι (with synizesis) is a modern editorial spelling (Wolf), for the manuscripts' κέλη (with contraction). Elsewhere in *Il.* we find κέλεαῑ (cf. | ὅς κέλεαι at 12.235, 14.96, objecting to a suggestion), whereas in the *Odyssey* we have | καί με κέλεαι (4.812), | ἤ με κέλεαι (5.174), πῶς γάρ με κέλεαι (10.337). It hardly matters which spelling we choose here, but for -ῃ see 13.818 with comment, Chantraine, *GH* I 57. παρὲξ Ἀχιλῆα means 'behind Akhilleus' back', παρέκ having an implication of deception or disregard; cf. 10.391 παρὲκ νόον ἤγαγε, etc.

435–6 For this mixture of reverence and fear of one's superior cf. 1.331, 3.172, etc. (with Richardson on *HyDem* 190), and especially *Od.* 17.188–9, where Eumaios says of his master Telemakhos ἀλλὰ τὸν αἰδέομαι καὶ δείδια, μή μοι ὀπίσσω | νεικείῃ· χαλεπαὶ δὲ ἀνάκτων εἰσὶν ὁμοκλαί. For the form συλεύειν (instead of the normal συλᾶν) cf. 5.48.

437–9 For ἄν ... κε cf. 11.187 etc., Chantraine, *GH* II 345. One papyrus offers σοὶ μέν here, which Chantraine thinks could be original, but no change seems necessary. The repetition of πομπός ... πομπόν in 437 and 439 is suitable in allusion to Hermes' rôle as divine escort (cf. πομπαῖος, ψυχοπομπός), as at 153, 182, and again at 461. The phrase κλυτὸν Ἄργος occurs only here, and presumably implies 'all the way to my home in Greece', i.e. Pelasgian Argos in Thessaly (cf. 2.681). For ἐνδυκέως in 438 see on 23.90, and for the combination of 'by ship ... on foot (πεζός)' cf. 9.328–9, *Od.* 1.171–3 (etc.), 11.58, 11.159, Pind. *P.* 10.29. Here the phrase acts as a hyperbole: 'or even (if you ask) on foot' (T). Verse 439 means '(if I did so) no one would (dare to) fight with you, thinking lightly of me as your escort'. Cf. 9.55 | οὔ τίς τοι τὸν μῦθον ὀνόσσεται.

440–2 Suiting action to words Hermes at once leaps aboard the chariot, seizes the reins, and inspires the horses and mules with strength. That is all that we hear of the rest of the journey, which is accomplished (one assumes) with the briskness of divine inspiration. Hermes' swiftness is again stressed at 446 (ἄφαρ), although there it is more remarkable. | ἦ καὶ ἀναΐξας is repeated at 621, of Akhilleus; cf. 1.584 ὣς ἄρ᾽ ἔφη· καὶ ἀναΐξας. For 440–1 cf. 17.481–2 Ἀλκιμέδων δὲ βοηθόον ἄρμ' ἐπορούσας | καρπαλίμως μάστιγα καὶ ἡνία λάζετο χερσίν; and for 442 cf. 17.456 ἵπποισιν ἐνέπνευσεν μένος ἠΰ |.

443–69 When they reach the Achaean wall Hermes puts the guards to sleep and opens the gates. They arrive at Akhilleus' hut, whose structure is described. Hermes opens the great doors, and they enter. He then reveals his true identity, tells Priam to entreat Akhilleus, and departs

443–7 The main clause after ἀλλ' ὅτε ... comes probably at 445. The guards were described as being in the space between wall and trench at 9.66–7, 9.87, etc. πύργους νεῶν means 'the fortifications of the ships'. For the association of δόρπα with φυλακτῆρες cf. 9.66 δόρπα τ' ἐφοπλισόμεσθα· φυλακτῆρες δὲ ἕκαστοι | λεξάσθων ... In 445 τοῖσι δ' ἐφ' ὕπνον ἔχευε belongs to an Odyssean group of phrases: ὕπνον ἔχευεν with dative, and variations, occurs 7× *Od.*, 1× *HyAphr.* For Hermes' soporific power cf. 343–4. ἄφαρ in 446 stresses again the divine ease with which he accomplishes what Akhilleus says no mortal could easily do (565–7). Cf. for example the infant Hermes' miraculous speed of action at *HyHerm* 15–23, 43–6, etc. For 446 cf. 21.537 οἱ δ' ἄνεσάν τε πύλας καὶ ἀπῶσαν ὀχῆας.

448–56 Akhilleus' κλισίη (perhaps we should say 'quarters' rather than 'hut'; the German *Lager* would be a good equivalent for κλισίη, which is related to κλίνω etc.) was never described in detail earlier in the poem. Here it has become a full-scale dwelling, with thatched roof, a great courtyard, and a heavily bolted door. Later its αἴθουσα (644), μέγαρον (647), and πρόδομος (673) are mentioned, as in the palaces of the *Odyssey*, although its thatched roof and fence of stakes suggest its rustic quality (see on 452–3). Such a description of a dwelling-place is common at this stage of an 'arrival scene' (6.240–50, 6.313–17, *Od.* 5.55–75, 7.81–133, 14.5–22; cf. Arend, *Scenen* 31–2, 37–8, 42–3, etc.), but it has its own special functions here, the most obvious being to build up the impression of Akhilleus' greatness, as if we saw the scene through the apprehensive eyes of Priam and Idaios (as at 352–60, etc.; cf. the onlooker's reaction of wonder at *Od.* 5.75, 7.82–3, 7.133). Like other forms of αὔξησις, it prepares for the momentous meeting which is to follow. Akhilleus' own physical strength is shown by the detail of 454–6, as well as Hermes' miraculous aid. Moreover, the scale of Akhilleus' quarters will later enable Hektor's body to be washed and anointed without Priam's seeing it, an important precaution as the poet explains (582–6), and will allow Priam and Idaios to sleep apart from Akhilleus and Briseis, like guests in the *Odyssey* (673–6).

Thus the aggrandizement of the κλισίη (so disturbing to Leaf and the analysts) is a natural consequence of the poet's narrative techniques, although again he comes much closer here to Odyssean patterns than in the rest of the poem.

448 This verse belongs to a formular pattern: 11.618 οἱ δ' ὅτε δὴ κλισίην Νηληϊάδεω ἀφίκοντο, etc.; cf. also 431.

449 The phrasing resembles 20.146–7 (τεῖχος) ὑψηλόν, τό ῥά οἱ ... | ... ποίεον ...

450–1 A gabled roof is described in the simile at 23.712–13 (see comment) and is presumably meant here, since it is thatched. ἔρεψα | is used of roofing at 1.39 (temple); cf. *Od.* 23.193 (Odysseus' bedroom) εὖ καθύπερθεν ἔρεψα. Verse 451 means '(they roofed it) with shaggy thatch, reaped from the meadows'. It is a particularly euphonious four-word verse, with strong assonance of liquids and nasals, and a spondaic ending. The ancient commentators claim that ὄροφος signifies a type of straw, a view supported by either Aristotle or Theophrastus (Pollux 10.170 = Arist. fr. 268 R.). As Leaf pointed out, the English 'thatch' actually means 'roof' (cf. German 'Dach'), and so the interchange of sense would be natural. Apart from this Homeric use and the Aristotelian fragment, the form ὄροφος occurs nowhere else, and this might support a specialized sense. ὀροφή, a later word for 'roof', is used at *Od.* 22.298. Theocritus imitates λειμωνόθεν (*Id.* 7.80), Apollonius ἀμήσαντες (1.688); cf. Call. *Hy.* 3.164 ἐκ λειμῶνος ἀμησάμεναι.

452–3 The courtyard is surrounded by a close fence of stakes: cf. Eumaios' farmstead at *Od.* 14.11–12 σταυροὺς δ' ἐκτὸς ἔλασσε διαμπερὲς ἔνθα καὶ ἔνθα, | πυκνοὺς καὶ θαμέας. σταυρός occurs nowhere else in Homer (cf. Hdt. 5.16, etc.), the usual word being σκόλοψ.

453–6 The door is held by a single great beam, called ἐπιβλής (cf. ἐπιβάλλειν), and at 455 μεγάλην κληΐδα. ἐπιβλής, a Homeric *hapax*, occurs rarely later (Lysias, inscriptions, epigrams). ἐπιρρήσσειν recurs only at 456 (cf. 18.571 ῥήσσοντες) and is the Ionic form of ἐπιρράσσειν (S. *OT* 1244 πύλας ... ἐπιρράξασ' ἔσω, etc.), meaning 'slam shut' here. The contrast between Akhilleus' strength and that of others is a motif which occurred at 16.140–2, 17.76–8, 19.387–9 (his spear), and cf. 5.302–4, 11.636–7 (with comment), for similar comparisons.

457–9 The innovative contracted form ᾦξε occurs only here in Homer: cf. 446 ὤϊξε, etc. Verse 458 is a variant form of 447, and 459 resembles 3.265, 8.492 ἐξ ἵππων (δ') ἀποβάντες ἐπὶ χθόνα.

460–7 Hermes reveals his identity just before his departure, and instructs Priam how to approach Akhilleus. As Aristarchus observed (Arn/A 2.791), the moment of a god's departure was one of the most usual occasions for self-revelation: cf. 13.71–2, 21.7–13, *Od.* 1.319–20, 3.371–9, and see Richardson on *HyDem* 188–90 (p. 208), 275ff. (p. 252). For the typical language of this revelation see on *HyDem* 256–74, 268, and cf. especially here *Od.* 19.548–9 (the eagle in Penelope's dream) ἐγὼ δέ τοι αἰετὸς ὄρνις | ἦα πάρος, νῦν αὖτε τεὸς πόσις εἰλήλουθα. In such cases 'I have come' often implies 'to your aid'. The runover word Ἑρμείας in 461 is emphatic here. The rest of 461 recalls Zeus's promise (153, 182).

462–70 For εἴσομαι ('I shall hasten') see on 21.334–5. εἴσειμι occurs only here in *Il.*, 4× *Od.* In verses 463–4 νεμεσσητὸν ... ἄντην is usually taken to mean 'it would be offensive for mortals to entertain an immortal god in this way face to face'. Apart from 16.192 ἀμφαγαπαζόμενος, ἀγαπάζειν is Odyssean (5×, once in active, otherwise middle), meaning 'to greet', 'to show affection to'. It would also be possible to take it as 'for an immortal god thus to greet mortals face to face'. In the *Iliad*, only the remote Ethiopians have the privilege of giving hospitality to the gods in their true form, but in the *Odyssey* the Phaeacians can also do so (7.201–6). In the past, however, the gods came in person to the wedding-feast of Peleus and Thetis (*Il.* 24.62–3).

465–7 Hermes ends by advising Priam on how to supplicate Akhilleus. The form is traditional: for clasping the knees, and invoking the family of the supplicated person, see on 22.338. Akhilleus' only son Neoptolemos was mentioned by him together with his father Peleus at 19.326–37 (see comments); cf. *Od.* 11.492–540. In fact Priam will not only clasp his knees but also kiss his hands, a gesture which adds a new dimension to this act of suppliancy (478–9, 505–6), and he will invoke only his father Peleus, in such a way as to link his own fate to that of Akhilleus' father (486–506).

468–9 ὣς ... ἀπέβη is a traditional formula for departure (cf. 6.116 etc.), and the whole sentence is echoed at 694. The usual account of human reactions to a divine self-revelation or epiphany (see on *HyDem* 188–90, 275ff.) is here omitted, because it would detract from the main focus on Priam's approach to Akhilleus. In any case, Priam had already been told by Iris that Hermes would help him.

469–691 Priam's visit to Akhilleus

In general structure the whole of this episode corresponds to the schema of 'Visit' scenes, as described by Arend (*Scenen* 34–53, and on 322–691 see pp. 37–9). Normally in the *Iliad* the visitor enters and finds the host and his companions engaged in some activity. He is seen, and the reaction of those inside is sometimes described. He is then welcomed, offered a seat, and usually invited to share in a meal. After these preliminaries conversation at last begins. Finally, a bed is sometimes prepared for the guest for the night.

Many of the main motifs of this typical structure are present here, but the nature of the situation gives rise to a series of significant variations, and the extensive dialogue sections create a different narrative technique from that of other visit scenes in the *Iliad* (cf. Arend, *Scenen* 38–9). Thus Priam is unseen until he reaches Akhilleus. It is he who speaks first, in supplication. The offer of a seat (522) comes in Akhilleus' reply, but this leads to his long consolatory reflection on human misfortunes. Priam's refusal of this offer, because of his anxiety to complete his task (552–8), stirs Akhilleus' dormant anger and nearly destroys the precarious balance of sympathy just created between them (559–70). Priam then obeys (571). The traditional schema is interrupted by the series of actions through which the actual ransoming is effected (572–95), including the washing of Hektor's body, itself a feature of a Visit scene (see on 587–90). There follows Akhilleus' invitation to Priam to share in a meal, extended by the paradeigmatic story of Niobe (596–620). The meal is prepared and they eat together (621–7), but afterwards no further dialogue is reported. Instead, they simply gaze in wonder at each other (628–32), although in 632 καὶ μῦθον ἀκούων suggests that Priam speaks. Finally Priam requests that he may be allowed to go to bed, and preparations are made for this, but with special precautions in case his presence is detected by the other Greek leaders, and there is further discussion of the truce for Hektor's funeral (633–72). They sleep: but Priam is soon woken by Hermes, who escorts him out of the Greek camp (673–91).

Within the *Iliad* the visit of the ambassadors to Akhilleus in book 9 (182–668) is the nearest parallel, and its differences are interesting. They find him playing the lyre and singing κλέα ἀνδρῶν, accompanied only by Patroklos, who sits in silence. They enter, and Akhilleus leaps up in astonishment (193 ταφών). They are welcomed and seated, and food and drink is served. There follows the dialogue (222–655), after which they leave, except Phoinix who stays and sleeps in Akhilleus' quarters (656–68).

Still closer, however, is the description in the *Odyssey* of Odysseus' arrival at the palace of Alkinoos, and his reception there as a suppliant (*Od.* 7.14ff.; cf. Arend *Scenen* 42–4). Odysseus is escorted by the disguised Athene as far as the palace, and advised by her to supplicate Arete. Athene has cast over him a cloud of invisibility as he goes on his way. At his approach to the palace he stops and wonders at it, and it is described at length. Then he enters and finds the Phaeacians pouring their last libation of the day. He is still invisible until he reaches Arete. He clasps her knees, and the cloud disperses. All in the palace are silent in amazement. He makes his supplication, which is followed by a stunned silence, and sits down at the hearth. At length the process of receiving him begins to get under way. Alkinoos takes him by the hand, raises him and seats him on a chair, and from then on the normal courtesies reassert themselves to a large extent. The general tone of the Odyssean scenes is quite different, but the points of comparison are striking.

469–84 Priam enters the house, leaving Idaios outside, and finds Akhilleus who has just finished eating. Unnoticed by him or his companions he approaches, clasps his knees and kisses his hands. Akhilleus and the companions are struck with amazement

469–76 The narrative is rapid here with a very unusual run of six sentences with enjambment and sentence breaks in mid-verse, a type defined as 'skewed sentences' by Higbie, *Measure and Music* 77, 112–20.

469–72 For 469 cf. 5.111 etc. ἀφ'/ἐξ ἵππων ἆλτο χαμᾶζε |.

472–6 Akhilleus sits alone, with his companions a little apart (at a distance which respects his state of mind), except his two squires Automedon and Alkimos, who are busy attending him. He has just finished eating and the table is still beside him. In book 9 it was Patroklos who sat with him while he sang, and it used to be he who served his meals (9.186–91, 201–20, 19.315–18), and at 572–5 we shall be reminded that they have taken the place of Patroklos after his death as Akhilleus' comrades. Akhilleus has broken his fast as Thetis urged him to do (128–30), and as we shall soon hear that Priam has not eaten since Hektor's death (641–2), and both share a meal together (621–7), the poet's mention of this particular detail must be significant. It suggests that Akhilleus' mood is quieter and more normal (cf. Deichgräber, *Letzte Gesang* 64, Macleod on 472–6, Nagler, *Spontaneity* 186–7). It may also add to the sense of Akhilleus as the lordly figure (Διΐ φίλος in 472 perhaps suggests his majesty) who is in control of the situation, as he dines among his retainers, like Alkinoos and the Phaeacians who have just dined when Odysseus arrives (*Od.* 7.136–8, 188), or Menelaos who is giving a wedding-feast when Telemakhos comes to Sparta (4.1–19): cf. Edwards, *HPI* 308–9.

474 For Automedon see 9.209 etc., and for Alkimos (the short form of Alkimedon, to avoid the verbal jingle with the first name) cf. 16.197 etc. The two recur together at 574, 19.392.

475–6 Cf. *Od.* 5.196–7 τίθει πάρα πᾶσαν ἐδωδήν, | ἔσθειν καί πίνειν, and | ἔσθων καί πίνων 2× *Od.* Verse 476 was athetized (T) on the trivial ground that in Homer tables were not removed directly after eating: cf. Arn/A on 4.262, and schol. *Od.* 7.174. The problem is discussed in Athenaeus (12A–B), where the right answer is given, that as Akhilleus is in mourning one would not expect the table to remain throughout the following scene (so also schol. D and T).

477–9 Πρίαμος μέγας occurs only here. At this momentous point it is appropriate to speak of 'mighty Priam' entering unseen, and it helps to prepare for the shock of surprise when he is suddenly seen, present in all his greatness.

At 8.371 Athene says that Thetis 'kissed Zeus' knees and took hold of his chin with her hand' (which is more than she is actually said to do at 1.500–2 and 1.512–13, where she just clasps his knees); cf. *Od.* 14.279, where Odysseus in a false tale supplicates the king of Egypt by kissing his knees. Only here in Homer does a suppliant kiss the hands, a gesture which is a sign of affection and welcome at *Od.* 21.225, 22.499–500, and especially 24.398. The next verse spells out the awful significance of this action. Verse 479 is a 'tricolon crescendo'. with heavy opening spondaic word (δεινάς), followed by the more explicit ἀνδροφόνους, which in turn is 'glossed' by the still more precise relative clause αἵ οἱ πολέας κτάνον υἶας (cf. 16.261n. for such glosses on compound words). χεῖρας ... ἀνδροφόνους was used at 18.317, 23.18 of Akhilleus placing his hands on the breast of the dead Patroklos. Otherwise the epithet is nearly always (e.g. 509) applied in the genitive to Hektor (11×; 2× with Lukourgos and Ares). Here, in the context of the death of Priam's sons, this creates a strange reverberation, perhaps similar to the reversal of rôles in the following simile. These verses are echoed by Priam himself at 505–6, underlining still further the significance of his action. Supplication by touching or clasping someone's hands seems to be rare in later literature; cf. E. *Hec.* 273–6, 342–5. In the case of Priam, his action in kissing the hands of Akhilleus, the killer of his sons, perhaps 'defuses' their power to harm. The scene is portrayed on a fine silver bowl of the Augustan period, found in Denmark: *LIMC* I. 1, p. 154, no. 687.

480–4 This must be the most dramatic moment in the whole of the *Iliad*, and its character is marked by a simile which is extremely individual. The effect of 477–9, followed by the elaboration of 480–4, is rather like that of a flash of lightning from a sky heavy with black clouds, followed by the long rumble of thunder. The simile concerns a homicide who goes into exile and seeks refuge in the house of a rich man, in the hope presumably of becoming his retainer: for this theme see on 23.85–90. The ἄτη which has seized him could refer both to the circumstances which led him to kill and to the disastrous consequences of the act: he has become a man 'under a cloud' of disaster. It is this which (partly at least) causes the shock of surprise to those into whose house he enters when he appears in the doorway. As J. Gould remarks (*JHS* 93 (1973), 96 n. 111), this may not be so far from the later idea of pollution for bloodshed. It cannot, surely, be simply the unexpected suddenness of a stranger's appearance which is the point of comparison with Priam's entry and actions (cf. bT, although they also thought that the homicide was seeking purification; Macleod on 480–4: 'the bystanders are amazed simply at the unexpectedness of the arrival'; Parker, *Miasma* 135 n. 124: 'no more than surprise and curiosity'). But the way in which the simile is introduced suggests that there is more to it than that.

The aspect of the comparison which has most impressed modern readers is the reversal of rôles (already noted by Eustathius). In the narrative it is the supplicated man who is the killer, and the suppliant who is the rich man. Moreover, Priam is in his own homeland, whereas Akhilleus is a hostile invader. But the emotional charge involved in both situations is similar, and the poet has chosen an event, doubtless common in his own time, which would suggest to his audience more directly the intensity of the moment in the narrative. Cf. also Moulton, *Similes* 114–16.

480 ἄτη πυκινή implies that ἄτη has got a tight grip on the man.

482 The view that the homicide seeks purification led T to say that 'this may be an anachronism', i.e. something reflecting the poet's own times which occurs in a simile but not in the narrative, and on 11.690 T notes that purification for homicide does not occur in Homeric society.

482–4 This is a variation on the common reaction of surprise at an unexpected visitor in such scenes: cf. 9.193, 11.777 ταφὼν δ' ἀνόρουσεν Ἀχιλλεύς; *Od.* 7.144–5 (silent amazement of the Phaeacians in the parallel suppliant scene), 10.63 οἱ δ' ἀνὰ θυμὸν ἐθάμβεον (Aiolos and family at Odysseus' second visit), 16.12–14 ταφὼν δ' ἀνόρουσε συβώτης (who drops the vessels he is holding). θάμβος denotes a strong reaction (cf. 23.815n.), and this is emphasized by the repetition θάμβος ... θάμβησεν ... θάμβησαν, rounded off by ἐς ἀλλήλους δὲ ἴδοντο. Cf. Keats:

> Or like stout Cortez when with eagle eyes
> He stared at the Pacific – and all his men
> Look'd at each other with a wild surmise...

In 483 Πρίαμον θεοειδέα is more than just formular, and is in fact the only case of this phrase in the accusative (with synizesis; cf. Ἀλέξανδρον θεοειδέα). It is not just Priam's presence, but his godlike character, that impresses Akhilleus. See on 217, and on 472 (Διῒ φίλος), 477 (Πρίαμος μέγας).

485–512 *Priam supplicates Akhilleus. They both weep*

486–506 *Nam epilogus quidem quis unquam poterit illis Priami rogantis Achillem precibus aequari?* (Quintilian 10.1.50; he may really be thinking here of the whole of the last Book, as the poem's epilogue; see also on 776). ˙

Priam's entreaty is based on the comparison of himself to Akhilleus' father, establishing a bond of sympathy between them. He begins and ends with this theme (486–9, 503–4), and in both cases this leads to the reflection that Priam is even more deserving of pity than Peleus (490–4, 504–6). In the first part Priam's exceptional misfortune is developed by the theme of the loss of so many of his children, by contrast to the survival of Peleus' only one, and this culminates in the reference to the death of the 'only' child who defended Troy, Hektor (493–501). After this emotional climax comes the reason for his journey, mentioned as briefly as possible (501–2). On the overall ring-structure see Lohmann, *Reden* 121–2, and on this theme of father–son relationships elsewhere in the poem see vol. v, p. 10.

486 The opening is very abrupt and direct, with no preamble. The vulgate reading σεῖο was supported by Zenodotus, σοῖο being that of Aristarchus and a group of MSS. The possessive adjective σοῖο is what is wanted. As with θεοειδέα in 483, θεοῖς ἐπιείκελε surely has point: 'in calling him dear to the gods and godlike he averts the risk of dishonouring a suppliant', say bT, comparing *Od.* 5.447–8 on divine respect for ξεῖνοι.

487 τήλικος occurs only here in *Il.*, 1× *Od.* The phrase ἐπὶ γήραος οὐδῷ was used once before in the poem, again by Priam of himself in an appeal for pity: see on 22.60, and cf. 515–16n.

488–9 περιναιέτης occurs only here and then in A.R. 4.470; cf. περιναιετάειν (4× *Od.*) and περικτίονες. ἀμφὶς ἐόντες perhaps glosses the epithet, as in 479; cf. *Od.* 2.65–6 περικτίονας ἀνθρώπους | οἳ περιναιετάουσι. ἀμφίς seems here to mean 'around', whereas elsewhere in Homer it means 'on either side'. Priam assumes that Peleus is harassed by those around him, just as he himself is harassed by the Greeks (e.g. cf. 6.255–6 τείρουσι of the Achaeans attacking the Trojans). Akhilleus is already anxious for his father at 19.334–7. In *Od.* 11.494–505 Akhilleus' ghost is eager to hear whether Peleus has lost his kingdom, but Odysseus cannot tell him. Later legends filled in the story with accounts of how he was dispossessed by Akastos or his sons: cf. E. *Tro.* 1126–8 with scholia, Sophocles' *Peleus*, *TGF* IV, ed. Radt, pp. 390–2, Soph. *Fragments* ed. Pearson, II, pp. 140–3, Apollodorus, *Epit.* 6.13, etc.

490–2 Peleus' one consolation is the news that his son is alive and hope for his return, although there is an underlying irony here, for we have been told so often that they will not meet again. For ἐπί τ' ἔλπεται ... | ὄψεσθαι cf. *HyDem* 35–6 ἔτι δ' ἤλπετο μητέρα κεδνὴν | ὄψεσθαι. The form Τροίηθεν occurs only here in *Il.*, 6× *Od.*; 3× (ἀπὸ) Τροίηθεν ἰόντα (etc.). It is natural that it should occur more often in the *Odyssey*. Some MSS and one papyrus read ἀπὸ Τροίηθε(ν) μολόντα, but -θεν is regular in such case-forms.

493–4 = 255–6 (with ὤ μοι ἐγώ...). There, however, Priam was contrasting the sons who survived with those who were lost, but here he thinks only of the dead, and goes on to elaborate in more detail their number and parentage.

495–7 For Priam's fifty sons cf. 6.242–6. 'It is the custom for foreign kings to have children from several women', say bT, and it is fairly clear that Homer is depicting Priam as a polygamous ruler, in contrast to Greek custom (cf. Hall, *Barbarian* 42–3). bT list as known wives, besides Hekabe (mother of nineteen according to 496), Arisbe daughter of Merops, Alexiroe daughter of Antandros, and Altes' daughter Laothoe. The first two do not occur in Homer, but the last was mentioned at 21.84–5, 22.46–8, as mother of Lukaon and Poludoros. At 8.302–5 we also hear of Kastianeira, mother of Gorguthion. Of Priam's fifty sons, twenty-two are mentioned in the *Iliad*. Two (Mestor and Troilos) died earlier in the war (257), eleven are killed in the course of the poem, and the remaining nine are named at 249–51. If we exclude the three children said to be from other wives (Lukaon, Poludoros and Gorguthion) we are left with nineteen, and so it is possible that all the nineteen sons of Hekabe are mentioned by the poet in the course of his narrative, although only five are explicitly said to be hers (Hektor, Paris, Antiphos, Deiphobos, Polites). For more complete lists cf. Apollod. 3.12.5; M. C. van der Kolf, *RE* s.v. Priamos, xxii, 1845–7. See also her article in *Mnemosyne* 7 (1954) 9–11 for reflections on the political background to Priam's marriages.

498–501 Priam contrasts the many whom furious Ares has destroyed with the 'only' son whom Akhilleus has just killed, Hektor. The name is postponed and stressed by its position, as at 742, 22.426, etc. On 498 the b scholia comment that 'in fear he does not say "you (killed)", in order not to anger him' (cf. 520–1, 22.423), and it is true that elsewhere the subject of γούνατ᾽ ἔλυσεν is always a specific hero. But the rhetorical effect of climax is an important factor here. Leaf objected to 498 that it was a weak and unnecessary line, and that the rhythm was 'unusually bad and un-Epic'. But the rhythm of the first part of 498 actually recurs at 500:

$$-- \mid -- \mid -\cup \parallel$$

Really, however, τῶν μὲν πολλῶν should be treated as a single metrical unit:

$$\overset{1}{---- \mid} \overset{2}{-\cup\cup- \mid} \overset{3}{\cup\cup-\cup\cup-} \times$$

This is unusual, but not impossible.

Of 499 bT say that it is a form of hendiadys, meaning 'he who was the only one to protect the city', which may be right (cf. 6.403 οἶος γὰρ ἐρύετο Ἴλιον Ἕκτωρ, and 22.507). But οἶος does have the implication of 'the only son who really counted at all'. ἄστυ καὶ αὐτούς means 'the city and its inhabitants'; cf. 14.47 νῆας ... καὶ αὐτούς, *Od.* 9.40 πόλιν ἔπραθον, ὤλεσα δ᾽ αὐτούς. This is the vulgate reading. The variant καὶ αὐτός would mean 'by himself', but after οἶος this would hardly be necessary. In 500 πρώην means 'lately' as at 5.832; cf. 2.303 (n.). ἀμυνόμενον περὶ πάτρης appropriately recalls Hektor's own exhortations at 12.243, 15.496.

501–2 'He does not go into detail about the gifts: for this would have destroyed the pathos' (T on 504). Verse 502 resembles 1.13 = 372 λυσόμενός τε θύγατρα φέρων τ᾽ ἀπερείσι᾽ ἄποινα, of Khruses' supplication of the Greeks and Agamemnon, a significant echo in view of the analogies between the opening and close of the poem: cf. Reinhardt, *IuD* 63–8, Macleod, *Iliad XXIV* 33–4, and see Introduction, 'Structure'.

503–6 The conclusion echoes the opening (486–94; cf. bT 504), but with new developments, the appeal to reverence the gods and show pity to Priam, and the culminating reference to his unique act of kissing the hands of his son's killer. For 503 cf. 21.74 σὺ δέ μ' αἴδεο, καί μ' ἐλέησον, 22.82 (with comments), and *Od.* 9.269 ἀλλ' αἰδεῖο, φέριστε, θεούς (mentioned by A as a variant reading). In view of 478–9, 506 ought to mean 'to stretch the hands (χεῖρε) of my son's killer towards my mouth'. This is an unusual sense of ὀρέγεσθαι, which elsewhere means 'to reach out (one's own hands) for something', but the middle can surely also mean 'to reach to myself' as here. The alternative, favoured by Leaf, is to translate 'to reach with my hand (χειρί) to the mouth (etc.)', i.e. to touch his mouth or chin as a suppliant, the gesture described at 1.501–2 etc. This is what Priam does on a sixth-century B.C. relief inspired by this scene (Johansen, *Iliad in Early Greek Art* 49–51; cf. *LIMC* 1.1, p. 148, no. 642). Eustathius (1360.56ff.) seems to have read χεῖρας ὀρέξαι, and to have taken this as referring to Priam stretching out his hands to Akhilleus' chin. This version would give a less complex word-order, with ἀνδρὸς παιδοφόνοιο ποτὶ στόμα going together, whereas with the first version there is an interlacing effect, but this can be explained by the need to give prominence to ἀνδρὸς παιδοφόνοιο. The epithet occurs only here in early literature (cf. Hdt. 7.190, Euripides, etc.), and echoes 479.

507 = *Od.* 4.113 (Telemakhos weeps when Menelaos speaks of his father). On the difference in tone of the two scenes cf. Reinhardt, *IuD* 493–4 (echoed by Griffin, *HLD* 67–9).

508 Akhilleus takes Priam by the hand, a gesture of acceptance, but instead of raising him at once from his suppliant position and seating him (cf. 515, 522), he gently pushes him away, overcome by emotion, and the storm of grief breaks. For the normal sequence denoting acceptance of the suppliant cf. *Od.* 7.159–71, Thuc. 1.137.1. The emotional tension or conflict is shown by Akhilleus' gesture of pushing Priam away, which would normally imply rejection (cf. 6.62–3 ὁ δ' ἀπὸ ἕθεν ὤσατο χειρὶ | ἥρω' Ἄδρηστον), but here is qualified by ἦκα ('gently'). The sequence is wonderfully natural and powerfully effective. Cf. J. Gould, *JHS* 93 (1973) 78–80.

509–12 τὼ δὲ μνησαμένω picks up μνησάμενος in 504 (cf. 486), but Priam's speech has recalled to both their causes for grief, and in Akhilleus' case not just his father but also Patroklos. Cf. the effects of the laments for Patroklos in book 19 (301–2, 338–9): in the second of these it is the mention of Akhilleus' family left at home which stirs memories in his audience. Likewise in the *Odyssey* (4.183–202) Menelaos' regret for Odysseus' absence leads all who are present to weep, as they remember those whom they have lost. The sentence-structure τὼ δὲ ... ὁ μὲν ... αὐτὰρ Ἀχιλλεύς resembles 7.306–7, 12.400–4, *Od.* 8.360–2. In 510 Priam's self-abasement is clearly described: he is 'crouched' or 'curled up' (ἐλυσθείς) before Akhilleus' feet. This may be a further aspect of his suppliancy (cf. 22.220–1, and Gould,

JHS 93 (1973) 94–5), but it surely also depicts his abject sense of grief, as at 162–5, 22.414.

513–51 Akhilleus then raises Priam to his feet and addresses him. He asks him to sit down, and offers him consolation, reflecting on the nature of human misfortune, and comparing Priam's fate with that of Peleus

513–14 For 513 cf. 23.10 αὐτὰρ ἐπεί κ' ὀλοοῖο τεταρπώμεσθα γόοιο, 23.98. Chrysippus (quoted by Galen, *De plac. Hipp.* 4.7.26 ed. P. de Lacy) read the alternative verse ἀλλ' ὅτε δὴ κλαίων τε κυλινδόμενός τε κορέσθη which is derived from *Od.* 4.541, 10.499. For 514 cf. *Od.* 6.140 θάρσος ἐνὶ φρεσὶ θῆκε καὶ ἐκ δέος εἵλετο γυίων. The verse was athetized (Arn/A) as unnecessary, and because of Aristarchus' view that γυῖα referred only to the hands and feet, not to all the limbs, and so was out of place here; see on 23.627, but contrast bT on 3.34, who disagree. Passages such as *Od.* 10.361–3, 18.236–42 suggest that γυῖα can have a wider sense (cf. *LfgrE* s.v.), and in Homer it is quite natural for the desire for tears to be seen as something physical, which affects the body as a whole: cf. Eust. 1362.12ff., and R. B. Onians, *The Origins of European Thought* (2nd edn., Cambridge 1954) 79.

515–16 Cf. *Od.* 7.168–9 (Alkinoos) χειρὸς ἑλὼν Ὀδυσῆα ... | ὦρσεν ... καὶ ἐπὶ θρόνου εἷσε φαεινοῦ. Verse 516 echoes 22.74, in Priam's appeal to Hektor (cf. 487n.), and at last fulfils the hope of 22.418–20.

518–51 Akhilleus' speech answers and to some extent mirrors the structure of Priam's (cf. Lohmann, *Reden* 121–4). He begins by echoing and sympathizing with Priam's description of his misfortunes (518–21, 493–501). The ring-form is signalled by the repetition of ἄνσχεο σὸν κατὰ θυμόν (518) in ἄνσχεο ... σὸν κατὰ θυμόν at the end (549), although the verb is aorist indicative in the first place, imperative in the second; and the theme of 522–4 is picked up at 550–1 ('there is no use in grieving'). Verses 525–33 are a general gnomic section (the jars of Zeus), illustrating the moral that all men have a certain share of miseries, and some are even worse off because they have unmixed troubles, rather than a mixture of good and ill. This is illustrated by the cases of Peleus and Priam (534–48), which are compared as in Priam's speech. But whereas Priam had seen his own fate as worst of all (493 πανάποτμος), Akhilleus shows how both old men have had a mixture of blessings and sorrows, and Priam's reference to Akhilleus as the son who can still give Peleus joy (490–2) is answered by the description of himself as παναώριον (540), a unique coinage which echoes and contrasts with Priam's πανάποτμος. Verses 538–40 pick up and answer 493–501: Priam's lost sons, and his 'only' son Hektor, are echoed by Peleus' failure to have sons who will succeed, and the doom of his only son Akhilleus. The structure of this whole section (534–48) resembles that of 488–502, since both speakers begin with Peleus, then move on to Akhilleus, and then make the comparison with Priam. But Akhilleus' reply is more general and reflective. In its use of *gnomai*, allegory and *paradeigmata* it resembles that of his tutor Phoinix (9.434–605; cf. Deichgräber, *Letzte Gesang* 69).

The speech is consolatory and foreshadows the themes of later *consolationes*, which express sympathy but correct the tendency to excessive grief, by pointing out that weeping has no practical use, suffering is common to all, others have endured worse, or that the person consoled has himself had worse to suffer before. Cf. R. Kassel, *Untersuchungen zur griechischen und römischen Konsolationsliteratur* (Munich 1958) 49–103, and Nisbet and Hubbard on Hor. *Odes* 1.24. The *Consolatio ad Apollonium* quotes 522–33 as an example of Homer's particular skill in this genre (Plutarch, *Mor.* 105 C–D). The emphasis on endurance, as man's response to the divine gift of troubles, is standard in later literature: see on 49 and *HyDem* 147–8. In the *Iliad* it occurs in Dione's consolation of Aphrodite at 5.382–402, where by a paradoxical reversal it is applied to *divine* endurance of troubles inflicted by giants or mortals.

518 ἆ δειλ' is often used at the opening of a speech of pity; cf. 17.201, 17.443 etc., and especially *Od.* 11.618 (Herakles' ghost to Odysseus) ἆ δειλ', ἦ τινὰ καὶ σὺ κακῶν μόρον ἡγηλάζεις.

519–21 These lines echo Hekabe's at 203–5 (πῶς ἐθέλεις), where see comment. Verses 520–1 also pick up Priam's reference to his sons (493–501), but Akhilleus is more explicit in taking responsibility for their deaths.

522–3 The formal invitation to the suppliant visitor to sit down, postponed to this late point, is here joined to the justification that they must lay their sorrow aside. Likewise Peisistratos is embarrassed at his tears, and Menelaos says ἡμεῖς δὲ κλαυθμὸν μὲν ἐάσομεν (*Od.* 4.193–5, 4.212). For ἄλγεα ... ἐάσομεν cf. 18.112 = 19.65 (Akhilleus) ἀλλὰ τὰ μὲν προτετύχθαι ἐάσομεν ἀχνύμενοί περ. ἐν θυμῷ κατακεῖσθαι means 'to lie undisturbed in our hearts'; cf. 527, of the jars 'stored' in Zeus's floor.

524 Both the word πρῆξις and this form of the sentiment are Odyssean: πρῆξις 6×; cf. *Od.* 10.202 = 568 ἀλλ' οὐ γάρ τις πρῆξις ἐγίγνετο μυρομένοισιν. Here cf. also 550, echoing 524, and 1.562 πρήξαι δ' ἔμπης οὔ τι δυνήσεαι. Herakles' words imitate Akhilleus in his reply to Meleager's ghost at Bacchyl. 5.162–4 ἀλλ' οὐ γάρ τίς ἐστιν | πρᾶξις τάδε μυρομένοις, | χρὴ κεῖνο λέγειν ὅτι καὶ μέλλει τελεῖν (cf. Maehler's comments on the relationship of this to the *Iliad* scene, and on the other parallels). A and T have οὐ γάρ τίς τ' ἄνυσις as a variant. κρυεροῖο γόοιο recurs at *Od.* 4.103, 11.212; cf. *Il.* 13.48 κρυεροῖο φόβοιο |. *Od.* 4.100–4 possibly echo *Il.* 24.522–4: cf. Reinhardt, *IuD* 494–5. For the theme as a later commonplace cf. Nisbet and Hubbard on Hor. *Odes* 1.24.13.

525–6 If we read ὡς the construction is suspended during the long passage on the jars of Zeus (527–33), and the apodosis comes with the example of Peleus at 534. It seems better, however, to follow Leaf and read ὥς in 525, with 526 explaining the previous verse: 'for in such a way have the gods spun (destiny) for wretched mortals, that they should live in sorrow; but they themselves are free of care'. The verb ἐπικλώθειν occurs only here in *Il.*, but 7× *Od.*, and always of a god or gods allotting destiny. For this idea, however, of the spun thread of fate see on 209–10, and cf. *Od.* 7.197 where the Fates are called Κλῶθες. In 526 ἀχνυμένοις is the vulgate reading, but ἀχνυμένους is well-attested, and as this is a normal Homeric construction it is probably correct; cf. 145–8, 6.207–8, etc. ἀκηδέες is contrasted with ἀχνυμένους. The epithet usually means 'uncared for', but 'uncaring' at 21.123, *Od.* 17.319, and 'without care' covers both. On the theme of these verses cf. Griffin, *HLD* 189–91.

T reasonably comments that 'he means τὸ φύσει θεῖον (i.e. true divinity), since he portrays the gods of poetry as experiencing sorrow', and compares the Epicurean view of divinity. The point is rather that the gods' troubles do not strike deep, as those of mortals do. Nevertheless, the 'carefree' gods seem to be a step closer to the less involved deities of the *Odyssey*: cf. *Od.* 6.41–6, where 'Olumpos' is a remote place of permanent radiance and calm, in which the gods take their pleasure for all time.

527–33 The jars of Zeus can be regarded as a moral allegory, like the descriptions of Prayers and Ruin in the speeches at 9.502–12, 19.91–136; but this account of the nature of evil is more down-to-earth, less abstract than those ('not so much an allegory as a survival in popular fancy of what may once have been regarded as a real explanation', in Leaf's view). The popular character of the theme is suggested by its recurrence in Hesiod's story of Pandora's πίθος (*Erga* 90–104; bT and schol. *Erga* 94 think the Hesiodic story was inspired by the Homeric passage). The πίθος is a large storage jar, sunk into the floor of a store-room, as in the Mycenaean and Minoan palaces of the Late Bronze Age. In antiquity there was doubt as to whether Akhilleus speaks of two jars (one of evil and one of good) or three (two of evil and one of good). Pindar (*P.* 3.80–1) apparently took the second view:

μανθάνων οἶσθα προτέρων·
ἓν παρ' ἐσλὸν πήματα σύνδυο δαίονται βροτοῖς
ἀθάνατοι.

Plato, however (*Rep.* 379D), took the first, although he gives a different text for 528, κηρῶν ἔμπλειοι ὁ μὲν ἐσθλῶν αὐτὰρ ὁ δειλῶν. Aristarchus evidently thought there were only two (Arn/A 527–8; cf. Arn, Nic/A 528), and this is surely right. ἕτερος most naturally refers to one of two, and for the ellipse of ἕτερος μέν before κακῶν cf. 22.157 φεύγων, ὁ δ' ὄπισθε διώκων, 7.240, etc.

The language of the whole passage is untypical. The word πίθος occurs first here; cf. *Od.* 2.340, 23.305. ἐν Διὸς οὔδει is an unusual phrase, but cf. 5.734, 8.385 πατρὸς ἐπ' οὔδει, again with reference to Zeus's palace. In 528 the form ἑάων occurs first here, and then at *Od.* 8.325, 335 and 2× in the *Hymns*, in the phrases δωτῆρες/δῶτορ ἑάων; also 4× in the *Theogony*. It must be a genitive plural of ἐΰς, meaning 'of good things'; for theories about the formation cf. Hainsworth on *Od.* 8.325. It should properly be written with psilosis, ἑάων. The hiatus before it is unusual, and the Derveni papyrus (fourth century B.C.) quotes the line with ἕτερος δέ τ' ἑάων, which Bentley had conjectured: cf. the text in *ZPE* 47 (1982), p. 12, col. xxii, line 7. But there is no obvious reason why the τε should have been lost in all other texts, and it is more likely to be due to a conjecture. If δῶτορ ἑάων is connected with Sanskrit *dātā vásūnām* an initial digamma has been thought to explain the hiatus, but there is absolutely no other trace of this; cf. Chantraine, *Dict.* s.v. ἐΰς.

In 529 the compound ἀνα-μείγνυμι occurs first here (2× *Od.*); καμμίξας is given in most manuscripts, but it is better to keep the κε here. κύρεται (530) is the only instance of the middle of κύρειν in surviving Greek literature; for the sense cf. Hes. *Erga* 691 πήματι κύρσας. In 531 λωβητός ('degraded') occurs first here; cf. Hes. *Aspis* 366, etc. βούβρωστις (532) is a highly individual word, which recurs in Callimachus (*Hy.* 6.102 κακὰ βούβρωστις) and other Hellenistic and later poetry. It was interpreted in anitquity as meaning originally 'great hunger', 'famine', and hence (as here) 'great distress' (AbT, etc.). T mentions that at Smyrna there was a cult of Βούβρωστις, and that this was a deity invoked against one's enemies (cf. Plutarch, *Mor.* 694A–B). The sense 'ravening hunger' seems quite possible, in view of the connexions (as in the *Odyssey*) between this and the poverty of the outcast wanderer and lack of respect for him (despite pleas that beggars are under special divine protection). On the intensifying sense of βου- in such compounds cf. Chantraine, *Dict.* s.v., and see on 13.824. The comparison with the ultimate fate of Bellerophon (made by bT) is not inappropriate:

> ἀλλ' ὅτε δὴ καί κεῖνος ἀπήχθετο πᾶσι θεοῖσιν,
> ἤτοι ὁ κὰπ πεδίον τὸ Ἀλήϊον οἶος ἀλᾶτο,
> ὃν θυμὸν κατέδων, πάτον ἀνθρώπων ἀλεείνων· (6.200–2)

Here too the victim of Zeus's displeasure becomes an outcast and vagrant, wholly ἄτιμος (533).

bT (527–8) suggest that Zeus's defence of the gods as not to blame for men's troubles, at *Od.* 1.36–43, is designed to answer Akhilleus' words (cf. Introduction, 'The end of the *Iliad* in relation to the *Odyssey*', and E. R. Dodds, *The Greeks and the Irrational*, Berkeley 1951, 32). Notice however that in the *Odyssey* Zeus does not deny that the gods are responsible for *some* troubles. What he says is that men add to their proper share of these, by their own follies (33–4). There is no direct contradiction with Akhilleus' speech.

529–30 Cf. *Od.* 4.236–7 (in a consolatory speech by Helen) ἀτὰρ θεὸς ἄλλοτε ἄλλῳ | Ζεὺς ἀγαθόν τε κακόν τε διδοῖ, 6.188–90 (... σὲ δὲ χρὴ τετλάμεν ἔμπης), etc.

534–42 These verses apply the reflections of 525–33 to Peleus, and especially the point of 529–30, for Peleus is an example of mixed good and evil fortune, as is Priam (543–8).

534–7 The exceptional favour of the gods to Peleus was shown above all by his marriage to a goddess, and the other gifts associated with this (16.380–1, 17.194–6, 18.84–5, 24.59–63, etc.). Cf. Hes. fr. 211 M–W, where at his wedding the song is τρὶς μάκαρ Αἰακίδη καὶ τετράκις ὄλβιε Πηλεῦ (etc.), and Pindar, *P.* 3.86–96 (in a passage echoing Akhilleus' speech), etc. But Peleus is also seen here as a rich and powerful ruler, in such a way as to stress the comparison with Priam (543–6). Verse 534 echoes the wording of 16.381 etc., 536 that of 16.596 (ὄλβος only here in *Il.*, 8× *Od.*).

538–40 Akhilleus has in mind here Priam's words about his own lost sons, and the death of his 'only' son Hektor (cf. 518–51n.). Verses 538–9 mean that Peleus has no sons destined to succeed as rulers (κρειόντων). γονή occurs only here in *Il.*, 1× *Od.*, 2× *HyAp*.

In 540 πανάωριος is a Homeric *hapax*, which recurs only in some late epigrams. ἄωρος in classical Greek means 'untimely', and can be used of death or of those who have died before their natural time. πανάωριος was usually interpreted as meaning 'altogether untimely', although an alternative view took it as 'altogether despised' (Hdn/A, Eust.). Modern scholars have usually translated it as 'doomed to die young'. M. Pope (*CQ* 35 (1985) 1–8) suggests that it means 'untimely in all things', but this is contested by A. W. James (*CQ* 36 (1986) 527–9). Akhilleus' failure to return home and care for Peleus may well be associated with the idea of early death, as in the passage about his choice of fates at 9.410–16 and elsewhere in the poem (4.477–9, 17.301–3). It is, however, possible that πανάωριον has a similar general sense to the corresponding πανάποτμος of 493, meaning 'unlucky in all ways'; cf. Leumann, *HW* 105, who translates both words by '(ganz) unglücklich'.

540–2 In Greek society failure to care for one's parents in old age has always been regarded as one of the worst faults. Here it is even worse for Akhilleus, since he is not only unable to look after Peleus, but is forced to waste his life at Troy, giving trouble to Priam and his children. The emphatic ἧμαι in 542 has the sense of 'I just sit around' as often (cf. 18.104 of Akhilleus, 1.134, 2.137, 2.255, etc.), and κήδων is bitterly ambiguous, 'troubling' or 'caring for', Akhilleus' lack of care for Peleus being contrasted with his 'concern' for the Trojans.

543–6 ἀκούομεν means 'we have heard tell'; cf. 14.125, etc. ὄλβιος occurs only here in *Il.*, 14× Od. (cf. ὄλβος 536, ὀλβιοδαίμων 3.182).

Verses 544–5 define the whole area within which Priam's kingdom lies, surrounded by Lesbos to the south, Phrygia to the east, and the Hellespont to the north. For the whole sentence cf. *HyAp* 30–45 ὅσσους Κρήτη τ' ἐντὸς ἔχει ... (37) Λέσβος τ' ἠγαθέη Μάκαρος ἕδος Αἰολίωνος | ... τόσσον ἐπ' ... ἵκετο Λητώ, and 2.845 ὅσσους Ἑλλήσποντος ἀγάρροος ἐντὸς ἐέργει (see on 844–5). ἄνω occurs only here in the poem (cf. *Od.* 11.596) and appears to mean 'out there' or 'out to sea' (cf. ἀνάγειν); and καθύπερθε seems to mean 'inland' here. Makar was a legendary colonist of Lesbos, which was called Makaria after him. Cf. AbT and references in Erbse ad loc.; *RE* s.v. Makar(eus). Two quotations in Plutarch and Dio Chrysostom, one second-century A.D. papyrus and a few MSS read μακάρων, which could well be due to an ancient conjecture (cf. van der Valk, *Researches* II 597–8). The epithet ἀπείρων in 545, applied only here to the Hellespont, is at first sight puzzling, and has been explained as referring to the whole sea off Troy and Thrace, not just the modern channel. It is called 'broad' at 7.86, 17.432. But the phrase could be influenced by memory of πόντος ἀπείρων (Hes. *Th.* 678); cf. πόντον ἀπείρονα (Aristarchus' reading in 1.350, and *Od.* 4.510).

Verse 546 echoes 535–6, only adding 'sons' here to 'wealth'. Cf. *Od.* 14.206 ὄλβῳ τε πλούτῳ τε καὶ υἱάσι. For the depletion of Priam's wealth cf. 18.288–92. Lesbos had been sacked by Akhilleus himself (9.129 etc.). τῶν in 546 presumably means 'among the inhabitants of these places', and uncertainty about its reference perhaps led to the variant τῷ.

547–8 Verse 547 balances 538. For 548 cf. 7.237 μάχας τ' ἀνδροκτασίας τε, and *Od.* 11.612.

549–51 ἄνσχεο ... σὸν κατὰ θυμόν echoes the opening theme (518), here with strong imperatives, and 550 recalls 524. For ἀλίαστον ('incessantly') of lamentation cf. 760. Verse 551 is a typically emphatic way of saying 'you will not be able to bring him back to life, *whatever you do*', i.e. 'even if you suffer more yourself for his sake, it will not do any good': Arn/A takes it this way, and compares 1.29 τὴν δ' ἐγὼ οὐ λύσω· πρίν μιν καὶ γῆρας ἔπεισιν ... It would be clearer if we place a colon after ἀνστήσεις. The theme is common in later consolations: cf. Soph. *El.* 137–8, fr. 513 N. (=557 Radt), Hor. *C.* 1.24.11–18.

552–95 Priam refuses the offer of a seat, and asks Akhilleus to release Hektor's body as soon as possible. Akhilleus, however, warns him not to anger him and Priam gives way. The ransom is removed from the waggon, and the body is washed, dressed and put on a bier, which is placed on the waggon. Akhilleus asks Patroklos not to be angry because he has released the body of his enemy, and promises him a share in the ransom

That a visitor should refuse the offer of a seat owing to the urgency of the situation is a motif which has occurred already at 6.360–2 (Hektor with Helen), 11.648 (Patroklos' visit to Nestor) and 23.205 (Iris and the Winds). But here, by a touch of the poet's wand of genius, this theme suddenly takes on great importance, since it threatens to precipitate a crisis, and shows how in spite of the detached and gnomic speech which he has just made Akhilleus is still in a precarious state of tension which could easily be broken. Yet he *does* control himself, and in the preparation of Hektor's body he personally supervises what is done, and takes special care to avoid any further risk of provocation (583–6). A final sign of the conflict of his feelings is his brief speech to Patroklos' spirit, in which we see the embers of the urge for vengeance momentarily flicker into flame, and then die away for the last time. bT (569) aptly quote the view of Aristotle (fr. 168 R.), that his character is 'uneven' or 'inconsistent' (ἀνώμαλον); cf. Arist. *Poet.* 1454 a26–8, b8–15 and Eust. 1365.62–1366.2. An alternative view (bT 559, 569) was that Akhilleus shows anger in order to prevent Priam from upsetting him by his grief: this is based on 583–6. Plutarch (*Mor.* 31A–C) quotes Akhilleus' ability to master his anger as an example of self-control and self-knowledge. Cf. Deichgräber, *Letzte Gesang* 71: 'Man kann (mit Schadewaldt) fragen: Wo kennt sonst jemand sich selbst wie Achill hier?'

There are echoes of the opening scene of the poem (cf. Introduction, 'Structure'). Priam's request to Akhilleus and his accompanying prayer for his safe return home (554–7) are parallel to the prayer and request of Khruses (1.17–21), Akhilleus' warning to Priam not to anger him is paralleled by Agamemnon's response (560, 569–70 ∼ 1.26–8, 32). Both Agamemnon and Akhilleus refer to the divine support the suppliant receives, the first with contempt, the second with respect. Priam's fear and acquiescence are expressed in the same words as those applied to Khruses (571 = 1.33). But in book 1 the request for ransom is refused, whereas here it will be fulfilled. Cf. also E. Minchin, *Greece and Rome* 33 (1986) 11–19, on Akhilleus' speech and the parallels with book 1.

553–5 For the subjunctive form κεῖται cf. 19.32, Chantraine, *GH* I 457. ἀκηδής has the specific sense here of 'without the proper care due to a dead body'; cf. *Od.* 24.187. The situation is echoed at *Od.* 10.383–7, where Odysseus explains to Kirke that he cannot bear to eat until his companions have been restored to their normal form: cf. especially 386–7 ἀλλ' ... | λῦσον, ἵν' ὀφθαλμοῖσιν ἴδω ἐρίηρας ἑταίρους. For 555 cf. 137.

556–8 Aristarchus athetized 556–7 'because such prayers are unsuitable in the mouth of Priam, and the insincerity would be obvious' (Arn/A). The prayer of Khruses that the Greeks will take Troy and return home safely aroused similar debate (schol. Ab 1.18–19). But the parallelism of the two passages supports the second one. Leaf objected to the lengthening of με in the second half of the fourth foot before πρῶτον, as a breach of 'Wernicke's Law', but there are a number of other exceptions to this, and με πρῶτον presumably would go closely together. Cf. his Appendix N, vol. II, especially pp. 636–7, and West, *Greek Metre* 37. πρῶτον must mean 'from the very first' here.

Verse 558 is omitted by several MSS, and is ignored by the scholia and Eustathius. In fact Herodian and Didymus discuss various explanations of ἔασας which assume that it stood on its own, and Sidonius read ἐπεί με πρῶτ' ἐλέησας in 557. Probably it is a late interpolation designed to complete the construction of ἔασας, which stands on its own at 569, 684, and elsewhere. For a similar case of probable interpolation with ἐᾶν cf. 20.312 with comment. Van der Valk (*Researches* II 218–21; see also *GRBS* 23 (1982) 301–3) argues that 20.312 and 24.558 were removed from the text by Aristarchus, but his case is not convincing. ζώειν/ζώει καὶ ὁρᾶν/ὁρᾷ φάος ἠελίοιο occurs elsewhere 2× *Il.*, 5× *Od.*, and so its appearance at *Od.* 10.498, in a scene probably influenced by *Iliad* 24, does not automatically prove that 24.558 is genuine (as suggested by G. Beck, *Philologus* 109 (1965) 11). Cf. also *Od.* 13.359–60 αἵ κεν ἐᾷ πρόφρων με ... | αὐτόν τε ζώειν, and *Od.* 16.388.

559 = 1.148 etc.

560–70 Akhilleus' speech is framed by the warnings to Priam not to upset him further (560, 568–70), between which are two balanced statements of the divine motivation behind the scenes, first Thetis' visit to her son (120–42), and second Akhilleus' realization that a god must have escorted Priam. The point he is making is that given this motivation any failure to respect Priam as a suppliant would be a direct offence against the orders of Zeus (570). Note also the 'ring' motif of 561 Διόθεν ... ἄγγελος, 570 Διὸς ... ἐφετμάς.

560–2 Verse 560 echoes 1.32 μή μ' ἐρέθιζε, in Agamemnon's warning to Khruses (see on 552–95). For 561 cf. 194–5. The first hemistich of 562 resembles 1.352; for the second cf. 1.538, 1.556.

565–7 Cf. *Od.* 23.187–8 (Odysseus' bed) ἀνδρῶν δ' οὔ κέν τις ζωὸς βροτός, οὐδὲ μάλ' ἡβῶν, | ῥεῖα μετοχλίσσειεν. There is more point to οὐδὲ μάλ' ἡβῶν here, in relation to Priam, than in the *Odyssey* passage (cf. Reinhardt, *IuD* 483–4). In 566 the form φυλακός, for φύλαξ, occurs only here in Homer, except as a proper name (6.35, *Od.* 15.231), and seems to be Ionic (cf. a sixth-century inscription from Thasos, Herodotus, etc.); φύλακας is a minority variant. ὀχῆα is the reading of Aristarchus and a few MSS, the majority having ὀχῆας. The plural is perfectly possible, in spite of the singular bolt of 453–5. The bolt(s) of the Achaean Wall are similarly referred to as either singular or plural (12.121 etc., 12.455–62; see on 13.124–5). The compound μετοχλίζειν ('shift by force') occurs only here and in the *Odyssey* passage above, and then occasionally in Hellenistic and later authors. But cf. 12.447–8 (in the context of breaking open the Achaean gates with a great rock) τὸν δ' οὔ κε δύ' ἀνέρε δήμου ἀρίστω | ῥηϊδίως ... ἀπ' οὔδεος ὀχλίσσειαν, and the similar passage at *Od.* 9.241–2.

568–70 For ἐν ἄλγεσι A gives the commoner ἐνὶ φρεσί as a variant (cf. *Od.* 15.486). But cf. *Od.* 21.88 κεῖται ἐν ἄλγεσι θυμός. Verses 568–70 echo 1.26–8 (Agamemnon to Khruses) μή σε, γέρον ... κιχείω ... | μή νύ τοι οὐ χραίσμῃ σκῆπτρον καὶ στέμμα θεοῖο. Khruses had also invoked divine sanction (1.21), but in vain. οὐδ' αὐτόν here is emphatic, 'not even yourself' (for μή ... οὐ cf. also 584, and Chantraine, *GH* II 336–7). Verse 569 picks up 557 ἐπεί με πρῶτον ἔασας. Verse 570 is echoed by 586. Διὸς ἐφετμάς refers specifically to Zeus's message to Akhilleus via Thetis, as well as more generally to Zeus as god of suppliants (*Od.* 13.213 etc.).

571 = 1.33, making quite clear the parallelism of the two scenes.

572–5 Akhilleus' sudden and rapid exit 'like a lion' dramatically indicates his state of mind: cf. bT 'the simile refers both to his ease of movement and his fierce appearance, in order that he may alarm Priam'; Moulton, *Similes* 114 'the short simile flashes by with a reminder of the strength and danger that are deep in Achilles' nature, even at the moment when he performs an act of respect and reconciliation'. Akhilleus was compared to a lion by Apollo at 41–3 because of his savage lack of respect and pity, but the simile recalls earlier passages where Akhilleus and other heroes were compared to a lion when attacking in battle: cf. 20.164–74 (Πηλείδης δ' ἑτέρωθεν ἐναντίον ὦρτο λέων ὥς, etc.), 11.129, etc. Verse 573 belongs to the formular pattern 'not only, with him/her (followed two attendants, etc.)', for which see on 2.822–3, 3.143. Verse 574 recalls 474, but here the poet adds that the two squires were Akhilleus' most honoured companions after Patroklos' death. This echoes the description of Automedon at 16.145–6, and at *Od.* 24.78–9 Antilokhos replaces Patroklos in this place of honour. Patroklos will be in our minds, as in Akhilleus', during the following scene (582–90n., 591–5).

576–8 Normally in a Visit scene the horses (and mules) would be unyoked on arrival (e.g. *Od.* 4.35–42, and similarly *Il.* 8.433–5), but here this has been displaced by the unusual nature of the scene. καλήτωρ ('crier', 'summoner') occurs as a proper name at 13.541, 15.419, and nowhere else in literature; but it is surely a common noun rather than proper name here (*pace* 15.419–21n.). Cf. Arn/A, D, and 701 κήρυκά τε ἀστυβοώτην. With due courtesy he too is seated, although on the simpler δίφρος (cf. T). Verses 578–79 recall 275–76, where the ransom was loaded on to the waggon. The ancient variant ἐϋσσώτρου (Did/A, T, one papyrus, a few MSS) would mean 'with good wheels' (cf. σῶτρον, 'felloe', in Pollux; Homer's ἐπίσσωτρον, 'tire'), and it occurs once elsewhere, at Hes. *Aspis* 273 (ἐϋσσώτρου ἐπ' ἀπήνης). Van der Valk (*Researches* II 578) thinks this is the right reading here, and it was adopted by Leaf. The argument (cf. Macleod) that it would be un-Homeric to vary the epithet (from 275) is not necessarily conclusive, and the commoner ἐϋξέστου could well have replaced the unusual word.

580–1 From the ransom itself three garments are set aside to dress and cover the body, a χίτων to be placed round it, and two larger robes to put under and over it. Hektor will thus be wrapped in Trojan clothing, rather than Greek (cf. the fine garments referred to by Andromakhe in her lament at 22.410–14). Cf. 18.352–3, where Patroklos' corpse is covered 'with fine linen ... and above with a white robe'. Solon was said to have limited the number of garments used for burial to three (Plutarch, *Sol.* 21.5); cf. the fifth-century funerary law from Iulis in Ceos (*IG* 12.5.593.1–4): κατὰ τά]δε θά[πτ]εν τὸν θανόντα· ἐν ἐμ[α]τίο[ις τρι]σὶ λευκοῖς, στρώματι καὶ ἐνδύματι [καὶ ἐ]πιβλέματι· ἐξῆναι δὲ καὶ ἐν ἐλάσ[σ]οσ[ι]. On this and similar regulations see I. von Prott and L. Ziehen, *Leges Graecorum Sacrae* (Leipzig 1896) 219, 263. For the second half of 580 cf. 18.596 χιτῶνας ... ἐϋννήτους, *Od.* 7.97 πέπλοι ... ἐΰννητοι.

582–90 Akhilleus himself supervises the washing, anointing and clothing of the body, and it is he who places it on the bier (589). The same rituals were performed for the body of Patroklos when it was brought back from the battle, at 18.343–53 (washing and anointing, placing on the bier and covering). These preparations would normally be performed by members of the dead man's own family, and it is highly significant that they should be undertaken by Akhilleus. The washing and anointing were strictly speaking unnecessary since the gods had kept the body fresh and clean, and Aphrodite herself had anointed it with ambrosial oil (413–23, 23.185–7). The poet's careful detailing of this ritual must be designed to stress the propriety with which Akhilleus now treats the body of his former enemy, just as again his concern to avoid distressing Priam and causing a breach of their understanding is emphasized. For a similar concern with funerary ritual shown by an enemy or a stranger in tragedy cf. S. *Aj.* 1378–95 (Odysseus and Aias), E. *Supp.* 765–8, *Tro.* 1150–5.

582–6 ἐκκαλεῖν occurs first here, 2× *Od*. The maids are ordered to wash the body in a place where Priam cannot see it, lest he should become distressed and so risk being killed through Akhilleus' anger. The sentence develops with an elaborate series of dependent clauses, unfolding the potential consequences. In 584 there were ancient variants κότον or γόον for χόλον, and κατερύκοι for ἐρύσαιτο (cf. οὐ κατερύξει in some MSS). Herodian objected to χόλον and preferred γόον, which could well be a conjecture, but κατερύκοι is possible. For ἐρύσαιτο meaning 'keep hidden' cf. *Od*. 16.459. Verse 585 echoes 568 and 586 recalls 570, but καί ἑ κατακτείνειε is much more explicit. Leaf regards 586 as 'no doubt an interpolation', because 'the subj. ἀλίτηται after the historic tense is indefensible', and it is more effective if the consequences of Akhilleus' anger are left undefined, as at 569–70. This is reasonable, but the variation between optative and subjunctive is not so unusual (cf. 686–8, 14.162–5 with comment, etc.), and despite the length of the periodic structure (582–6) the explicit statement of 586, with all its shocking implications, should probably stand.

587–90 Verse 587 resembles 18.350 (the washing of Patroklos' body). But 587–8 also belong to the normal scene of washing someone in Visit scenes in the *Odyssey*: see on 18.343–55, and cf. *Od*. 3.467–8, 23.154–5, and similarly 4.49–50, 8.454–5, 17.88–9, with Arend, *Scenen* 124 n. 1. That is why only one φᾶρος is mentioned, instead of two. The washing of the dead body follows the same sequence as in the normal life of the living; the poet is adapting a motif typical of a Visit scene for a new purpose here. Placing the body on the bier (cf. 720, 18.352) was envisaged as the mother's task by Akhilleus in his speeches to Lukaon and Hektor at 21.123–4, 22.352–3. αὐτὸς τόν γ' Ἀχιλεύς emphasizes Akhilleus' own participation, leading up to his outburst in the following verses.

591–5 Akhilleus still fears the resentment of Patroklos' ghost, and promises him a share in the ransom gifts. This is one of the very few points in the Homeric poems where we glimpse the idea that the living could fear the continuing anger of the dead (cf. Parker, *Miasma* 133–4), or that the dead might require any form of offerings after the actual burial was completed (cf. *Od*. 11.29–33).

Verses 594–5 were athetized (apparently by Aristarchus: Arn/A) on the grounds that it was incorrect for Akhilleus to speak of the gifts as a reason for releasing Hektor's body, when he was really obeying Zeus's command. But clearly the two motives go together, and Zeus himself had decreed that the ransom should be paid (119, 137). bT discuss how Akhilleus could make gifts to the dead man, which shows awareness that in Homer this is an unusual procedure. They add that it was customary to purge a murder by material compensation (quoting 9.632–4). The supposed 'materialism' of

Akhilleus attracted the criticism of Plato (*Rep.* 390E): 'we shall not allow that Akhilleus could be so materialistic ... as to release a dead body only in exchange for payment, and otherwise to be unwilling to do so'. This could be the ultimate source of the later athetesis.

In 591 φίλον δ' ὀνόμηνεν ἑταῖρον perhaps reminds us of the fact that Akhilleus has up to now avoided mentioning Patroklos' name. In 592 the form σκυδμαινέμεν is paralleled only by ἀποσκύδμαινε at 65 (see comment). αἴ κε πύθηαι | εἰν Ἀϊδός περ ἐών implies some doubt as to whether Patroklos really can hear or not. Such expressions of uncertainty were common later: cf. K. J. Dover, *Greek Popular Morality* (Oxford 1974) 243–6.

596–632 Akhilleus returns inside, sits down opposite Priam, and invites him to share a meal, telling the story of Niobe as a precedent. The meal is prepared, they eat and drink, and then gaze at each other in wonder

The ransoming is completed (599), and the procedure of hospitality can be resumed even in these extraordinary circumstances. Normally a meal would have been offered to the guests on arrival, but here this was out of the question. Its occurrence now symbolizes and cements the bond of sympathy between Priam and Akhilleus (cf. Griffin, *HLD* 16: 'eating with old Priam resolves the passionate separateness of the hero'). At the same time it signifies the need for practical action in spite of grief, as was the case in book 19, where Akhilleus had to be persuaded to allow the army to eat before returning to battle (154–237). By contrast, however, it is here Akhilleus himself who urges Priam to break his twelve-day fast (cf. 641–2), and the function of the story of Niobe is to stress that this is justified even in the case of extremest sorrow.

596–8 Akhilleus' seat, called a θρόνος at 515, is here a κλισμός. Sometimes the two are distinguished, but they can be used as synonyms, e.g. 11.623, 11.645, and cf. West on *Od.* 1.130. Akhilleus sits 'by the opposite wall' to Priam, a phrase used of Akhilleus sitting facing Odysseus in the Embassy (9.218–19), and also applied to Penelope opposite Odysseus in the Recognition scene at *Od.* 23.89–90. It presumably suggests some distance or formality.

599–620 Akhilleus' speech is a clear example of ring-composition centred on a paradeigmatic story (cf. R. Oehler, *Mythologische Exempla in der älteren griechischen Dichtung*, Aarau 1925, 7, and Lohmann, *Reden* 13):

A 599–601 Your son is free: you will see him tomorrow.
B 601 Now let us think of eating,
C 602 For even Niobe did so.
D 603–12 Niobe's story.

C 613   She ate, when she had tired of weeping,

614–17 And now she still nurses her grief, even when turned to stone (cf. 619–20?).

B 618–19 But come, let us also think of eating.

A 619–20 After that you can mourn your son, when you have brought him back to Troy. He will cost you many tears.

Verses 614–17 were athetized by Aristophanes and Aristarchus (see comment), and the fact that they apparently interrupt the ring-structure has been taken as confirmation of this view. But they provide a parallel with the conclusion of Akhilleus' speech, for just as Niobe continues to mourn her children, so will Priam lament his son on his return to Troy (cf. von der Mühll, *Hypomnema* 385, Leaf on 614–17, Macleod on 596–620).

The version which Akhilleus gives of the myth of Niobe contains some puzzling features, which do not recur in later versions, except where these are clearly dependent on Homer. After her children are killed they lie unburied for nine days, because Zeus has 'turned the people to stone', and on the tenth day the gods themselves bury them (610–12). It is commonly believed that the story has been adapted to suit Priam's situation: the motif of Niobe breaking her fast is then an innovation. The period of her mourning for her unburied children parallels the time when Hektor has lain in Akhilleus' hut, or else the nine-day mourning which will take place at Troy (664–5, 784–7; cf. Eust. 1367.41ff.); and the gods' personal care for the burial echoes the gods' concern for Hektor's body. The motif of the people turned to stone derives from Niobe's petrifaction, and is introduced to explain why the Niobids lie unburied. Cf. Oehler, *op. cit.* 5–7, Kakridis, *Researches* 96–105, M. M. Willcock, *CQ* 14 (1964) 141–2, Macleod on 569–620; doubts about the above views are expressed by Lesky, *RE* xvii 646 s.v. Niobe; and see also W. Pötscher, *Grazer Beiträge* 12/13 (1985/6) 21–35 for a quite different view.

Whatever the truth about these details the chief point of the example is its function as an argument *a fortiori*. Priam has lost many sons killed by Akhilleus, but Niobe's were all killed together by Apollo and Artemis, and she is (by implication) a more famous figure of the past, especially if we accept 614–17 as genuine. Her story was later the subject of tragedies by Aeschylus and Sophocles (*TGF* ed. Radt, iii, pp. 265–80, iv, pp. 363–73), and was always popular as an *exemplum* (e.g. S. *Ant.* 824–31, *El.* 150–2).

601 Akhilleus' suggestion that they share a meal is all the more significant since he has in fact recently eaten (475–6), as bT note (618–19).

602–9 The details of Niobe's parentage and origins varied in later versions (AbT 602, 604, with Erbse). Her father was either Tantalos (mentioned at Od. 11.582–92) or Pelops, and her home either Thebes or Lydia.

The number of her children also varied. The narrative is told with elegant economy. Verse 603 is picked up at the end of this section by 609 (ὄλοντο ... ὄλεσσαν), and the balanced structure of 604 is developed in chiastic order in 605–6 (θυγατέρες ... υἱέες ... τούς μέν ... τάς δ᾽ ...). Likewise the repetition in 608–9 stresses the bitter recompense for Niobe's boast. Verses 603–4 are echoed by *Od.* 10.5–6 (Aiolos) τοῦ καί δώδεκα παῖδες ἐνὶ μεγάροις γεγάασιν, | ἓξ μέν θυγατέρες, ἓξ δ᾽ υἱέες ἡβώοντες. For ἀργυρέοιο βιοῖο | in 605 cf. 1.49 (Apollo as plague-god), and 8.279 τόξου ἀπό κρατεροῦ ... ὀλέκοντα. In 607 the frequentative form ἰσάσκετο is unique; cf. 12.435 ἰσάζουσα. Verse 608 means 'she boasted that Leto had borne only two, whereas she herself had borne many'. According to Sappho (fr. 142 L–P), Leto and Niobe were close friends, just as Tantalos was the gods' companion in later legends.

610–12 For the nine-day period see on 660–7. Turning people into stone is a common motif in folk-tales, but there may be influence from the similarity of λαός and λᾶας (stone), as in the story of Deukalion (noted by Eust. 1367.47ff.; cf. Hes. fr. 234 M–W, Pindar, *O.* 9.41–6). Cf. also 2.319 λᾶαν γάρ μιν ἔθηκε Κρόνου πάϊς ἀγκυλομήτεω of the snake at Aulis, *Od.* 13.163 ὅς μιν λᾶαν θῆκε of the Phaeacian ship turned to stone by Poseidon. bT assume that the people are petrified as an extension of Niobe's punishment (cf. Hes. *Erga* 240–3), but we are not given a reason.

614–17 These verses were rejected for several reasons (Arn, Did/A, bT):

(i)   If Niobe was turned to stone, how could she eat?

(ii)   It is an absurd consolation to say 'eat, for Niobe ate and was petrified'.

(iii)   The style is Hesiodic, especially ἀμφ᾽ Ἀχελώϊον ἐρρώσαντο (616).

(iv)   ἐν is repeated thrice.

(v)   How can Niobe nurse her sorrows when turned to stone?

bT add

(vi)   Akheloos is in Aetolia, not near Sipulos.

These objections are groundless. The origin of the story was clearly a rock-image on Mt Sipulos, identified as the sorrowing Niobe, the water flowing down its face being her tears, as Eustathius observed (1368.10ff.): compare the simile at 16.3–4 (see comment). This explains 617, which is echoed by Priam at 639 (κήδεα μύρια πέσσω). The image is described by Pausanias (1.21.3). The other objections are answered by Leaf: the triple use of ἐν is paralleled at 22.503–4 (see comment): ἐρρώσαντο of dancing is Hesiodic (*Th.* 8), but a natural extension of the Homeric sense 'move nimbly' (see on 1.529–30); an unknown Akheloos in Lydia is not strange, since the name is applied to many rivers; finally, Niobe was turned to stone not as punishment but because of her grief, which continues like Priam's.

These are, in fact, memorable and evocative verses, whose style is not out of place in Akhilleus' mouth. Cf. J. Griffin, *JHS* 106 (1986) 53: 'A last feature of Achilles' speech . . . is his tendency to invoke distant places and resounding names, lines which . . . open out into a spacious rhythm which goes with a vision of places far removed from the battle-ground of Troy or the crowded assembly of the Achaeans' (cf. also 56). This is especially true of these verses, which lift Akhilleus' consolation on to a different plane, as we rest our eyes on this great, solitary and distant figure, frozen in the image of perpetual grief.

Eustathius (1367.16ff.) praises the verbal echoes of the dative plural forms in 614 and the genitive plurals in 615–16, as well as the repetition of the preposition in 614–15, as adding to the beauty of the verses. For ἐν οὔρεσιν οἰοπόλοισιν | cf. *Od.* 11.574. Mt Sipolos is north-east of Smyrna, and was regarded as the home of Tantalos (e.g. Pind *O.* 1.38). Verse 615 resembles 2.783 (again referring to a legendary place in Asia Minor) εἰν Ἀρίμοις, ὅθι φασὶ Τυφωέος ἔμμεναι εὐνάς; T compares Pindar (*N.* 1.3) Ὀρτυγία δέμνιον Ἀρτέμιδος. The nymphs have their dwellings on Sipolos, and dance around the local river, like Hesiod's Muses who haunt Mt Helikon and dance round a spring on the mountain (*Th.* 1–8); cf. *Th.* 8 ἐπερρώσαντο δὲ ποσσίν. bT however offer other mythological explanations of θεάων εὐνάς, especially one which associated Sipolos with Rhea and her daughters. Instead of Ἀχελώϊον in 616 'some' read Ἀχελήσιον, said to be a river in Lydia, after which Herakles named a son by Omphale according to T (cf. Panyassis fr. 17 K. νύμφαι Ἀχελήτιδες). A offers the variant Ἀχελήϊον. For Ἀχελῷος as a generic name for rivers or water in general, see on 21.194. In 617 θεῶν ἐκ could go either with κήδεα or πέσσει ('by the grace of the gods'), but the former seems more likely. For the metaphorical use of πέσσει ('digests' and so 'broods on', 'nurses') see on 4.512–13. Similar metaphors connected with food are used in the context of eating at 128–9 and *Od.* 10.378–9; cf. Pindar, *O.* 1.55–6 καταπέψαι μέγαν ὄλβον in a sympotic context, with Gerber's comment.

618–20 These verses resume the themes of 599–601, with σίτου in emphatic position. πολυδάκρυτος recurs 3× *Od.*; cf. πολυδάκρυος at *Il.* 17.192, πολύδακρυς 6× *Il.*, and for the phrase *Od.* 19.404, *HyDem* 220 πολυάρητος δέ τοι (μοι) ἐστίν.

621–32 The description of the meal follows conventional patterns: cf. Arend, *Scenen* 64–70 and Schema 8. Thus 623–4 = 7.317–18 (cf. *Od.* 19.422–3; 624 4× *Il.*, 1× *Od.*); 625–6 = 9.216–17 (Automedon here replaces Patroklos); 627–8 = 9.91–2, 9.221–2, etc. A meal is often followed by conversation (cf. 632, and 634ff.), but here this is varied by 629–32, a wonderful innovation: cf. T 630 ταῦτα δὲ πρὸς ἔκπληξιν τῶν ἀκροατῶν.

621-2 For the first hemistich of ᾗ21 cf. 440. ὄϊν ἄργυφον occurs only here; cf. *Od.* 10.85 ἄργυφα μῆλα, and ἀργύφεος. For ἔδερόν τε καὶ ἄμφεπον cf. 23.167.

629-32 The mutual admiration of the two heroes is expressed in two balanced couplets, 631 echoing 629 with interchange of cases (*diptoton*) and repetition of the full patronymic formula for Priam, 630 and 632 giving the reasons for wonder, Akhilleus' godlike physique, Priam's noble appearance and words. For ὅσσος ἔην οἷός τε of Akhilleus cf. 21.108 οὐχ ὁράᾳς οἷος καὶ ἐγὼ καλός τε μέγας τε; The phrase θεοῖσι γὰρ ἄντα ἐῴκει('for he was like the gods to look upon') is echoed at *HyDem* 241. In 632 the balanced and chiastic order, with framing participles, is also effective. For Priam as wise counsellor bT compare 7.366 Δαρδανίδης Πρίαμος, θεόφιν μήστωρ ἀτάλαντος. H. J. Mette, *Glotta* 39 (1961) 52, calls this 'one of the finest scenes in Homeric epic'; cf. Deichgräber, *Letzte Gesang* 73-5.

633-76 Priam asks to be allowed to go to sleep, and Akhilleus orders beds to be prepared under the portico. A truce of eleven days is agreed for Hektor's burial. Idaios and Priam go to sleep outside, while Akhilleus sleeps in the hut with Briseis beside him

After the meal for the guests comes sleep, again a typical motif: cf. Arend, *Scenen* 101-5, with Schema 12. A similar but much briefer version of the theme occurred at the end of the Embassy, when Phoinix slept in Akhilleus' hut (9.658-68), but the closest parallels come in *Odyssey* 4.294-305 and 7.335-47. Verses 643-4 echo 9.658-9, where it was Patroklos who gave the order to the attendants, and 675 = 9.663. At 9.664-8, however, Akhilleus slept with a captive from Lesbos, Diomede, and Patroklos with one from Skuros, Iphis, whereas here Briseis is mentioned for the last time, reunited with Akhilleus (another echo of the opening of the poem), but Patroklos is gone. In *Odyssey* 4 Telemakhos takes the initiative in asking to go to bed as Priam does here (635-6 ~ *Od.* 4.294-5), and *Od.* 4.296-305 closely resemble *Il.* 24.643-8 and 673-6, with several identical verses (644-7 = *Od.* 4.297-300, 673 = 4.302). *Od.* 7.335-47 repeat the pattern closely, and 648 resembles *Od.* 7.340.

In the *Odyssey* it is normal for guests to sleep under the portico, rather than within the palace (cf. *Od.* 3.397-403, 20.1, 20.143), and even at *Il.* 9.662-6 Phoinix seems to be apart from Akhilleus and Patroklos, although he is not outside. Here, however, Akhilleus gives a special justification for Priam's sleeping outside, which is oddly introduced by ἐπικερτομέων (649-58). Eustathius rightly observes that this speech is really a poetic device to enable Priam to leave in secret on Hermes' orders (1370.11-2). Thus another normal motif of epic hospitality is used for a special purpose (cf. C. Rothe, *Die Ilias als Dichtung*, Paderborn 1910, 331). Given Priam's age and status it could have seemed discourteous to make him sleep outside, and that may be the point of ἐπικερτομέων, which suggests some apparent lack of respect (see on 649).

635–6 For λέξον ('put me to bed') cf. 14.252 ἔλεξα. ὄφρα καὶ ἤδη ... κοιμηθέντες recur at *Od.* 4.294–5 and 23.254–5. Aristarchus and some MSS read παυσώμεθα for ταρπώμεθα (Did/AT), probably a conjecture since the reason for preferring this is said to be that 'taking pleasure' in sleep would be unsuitable (ἀπρεπές, ἄκαιρον) in this context. The same variant occurs at *Od.* 23.255.

637–42 Priam's grief has manifested itself in the same way as that of Akhilleus, in sleeplessness (3–12), self-defilement (18.22–7; cf. 22.414, 24.162–5), and fasting (19.205–14, 19.303–8). For μύσαν cf. 420 (μέμυκεν). In 637–8 there is a chiastic antithesis, the two prepositional phrases with ὑπό being juxtaposed and framed by their accompanying verbal clauses. κήδεα ... πέσσω (639) echoes Niobe in 617, and for 640 cf. 11.774 and 22.414. For λαυκανίης (642) cf. 22.325, with comment.

643–8 See on 633–76, 9.658–61. The epic word ῥῆγος ('blanket') occurred at 9.661 and is common in *Od.*; it is related to ῥέζειν ('to dye') etc. (cf. Chantraine, *Dict.* s.v. ῥέζω), hence here πορφύρεα. Cf. Ibycus 316 *PMG* ποικίλα ῥέγματα, Anacreon 447 *PMG* ἀλιπόρφυρον ῥέγος. For τάπητες see on 230. Even in what appears to be the mundanely typical material of these verses the language and colometry are elegantly varied, the opening infinitive phrase (644) being developed with an effective tricolon, the first clause in enjambment (644–45), the second (645) in chiasmus with the first, and the third longer and more elaborate (646). Thus the poet adds dignity to such simple, everyday actions. Likewise the description in 647–8 of how the orders are carried out falls into two balanced whole-verse clauses (almost entirely dactylic) with *homoeoteleuton*, whether or not this feature was intentional. Both δάος (for δαΐς) and ἐγκονέειν occur only here in *Il.*, and then in similar scenes in *Od.* (4.300, 7.339–40, 22.497, 23.291, 23.294).

649 For τὸν δ' ἐπικερτομέων προσέφη cf. 16.744, *Od.* 22.194. The verb occurs only in this form in Homer. It ought to mean 'speaking provocatively' or something like this: cf. J. T. Hooker, *CQ* 36 (1986) 32–7. The scholia do not comment on the word, but Eustathius discusses it (1369.54ff.). He explains it as meaning μετρίως χλευάζων ('with gentle mockery'), and adds that 'it introduces a false fear, so that the aged king should not be upset at being forced outside,' and that this fear is strengthened by Hermes' warning to Priam (683–9). Leaf suggests that the word either refers to Akhilleus' tone in speaking of Agamemnon (in which case he means what he is saying), or else means 'bantering,' which he thinks is a possible sense at *Od.* 24.240, κερτομίοις ἐπέεσσιν; unfortunately that passage is almost as puzzling. Willcock adopts the same translation, 'in a bantering tone', and adds 'what seems to be the case is that Achilles does not mean what he is saying', i.e. his speech is just a pretext designed by Akhilleus to enable Priam to escape. Cf. Macleod who translates 'teasing', 'mystifying', and says that it is used here of deception, not mockery. Hooker objects that κερτομεῖν does not have any *inherent* connotation of deception, even if it may acquire this in some contexts. But teasing provocation often *is* insincere, and this could be the point here, as if Akhilleus were to say 'I'm afraid, old man, that you will have to sleep outside. I can't risk having you in here, you know', in a gently provocative or mocking tone. Cf. 4.6 where Zeus speaks with ulterior motivation and παραβλήδην ἀγορεύων probably stresses the insincerity (see comment); *Od.* 13.325–7 (where Odysseus thinks Athene is not telling the truth, but just teasing him); Hes. *Erga* 788–9 where κέρτομα βάζειν goes with words for deception etc.; S. *Ph.* 1235; E. *Hel.* 619, *IA* 849; Theocr. *Id.* 1.62. κερτομεῖς often later has the sense of 'you're joking, surely!'. A further interpretation is offered by P. V. Jones, in *CQ* 39 (1989) 247–50, who translates 'cutting him to the quick', and argues that the real or popular etymology of κερτομεῖν (from κῆρ + τέμνειν) supports this. But there is no sign that Akhilleus' speech has this direct effect on Priam.

650–2 γέρον φίλε is an advance on Akhilleus' earlier γέρον (560, 599), and it fits his semi-serious tone here. The actual chances of one of the other leaders turning up suddenly during the night are surely slender, and 651–52 is hardly true of the recent past. In fact, it looks as if ἣ θέμις ἐστί is slipped in here to add a specious justification, as in the case of the testing of the troops, at 2.73; see on 2.73–5, where Kirk says 'It can also serve, vague as it is, to justify a kind of behaviour which a character – or the poet himself – does not wish to spend time in elaborating further.'

653–5 Verse 653 = 366. This warning, together with Hermes' similar words at 686–8, are the last we hear of Agamemnon, and they remind us of his brutality in the early parts of the poem. ἀνάβλησις λύσιος is a euphemistically abstract expression, with two nouns in -σις, for which 686–8 are more explicit. λύσις occurs only here in *Il.*, 1× *Od.* Cf. 2.380 ἀνάβλησις κακοῦ. For the shift from optative to subjunctive in 653–5 see on 582–6. A papyrus and some MSS have the easier γένοιτο, but the subjunctive suggests that the hypothetical case is likely to occur, and (*pace* Leaf) seems preferable here (cf. also 686–8).

656–8 This essential piece of 'business', the discussion of the truce, is neatly slipped in here at the end of the scene, so that it does not interfere with the impact of the rest, and acts as a transition to the final scenes of the poem. For the Odyssean verse 656 see on 380. ποσσῆμαρ is an absolute *hapax*, formed in an unusual way by analogy with αὐτῆμαρ, ἐννῆμαρ, etc. On these compounds with -ημαρ see Leumann, *HW* 98–101. κτερεΐζέμεν here refers to the whole process of burial, including the preparations.

660–7 Priam begins his speech with a courteous introduction: 'if you are really willing . . . then if you were to act as follows you would do me a kindness'. Cf. the use of χαρίζεσθαι meaning 'to oblige someone' (11.23 etc.). The reason given for a long truce is the practical difficulty of collecting wood for the pyre. In the case of Patroklos' funeral this only took part of a day (110–26), but Priam adds that the Trojans are under siege and afraid to leave the city. This motif is echoed at 778–81 and again at 799–800, and this emphasis right at the end of the poem reminds us of how fragile is the truce, and looks forward to the renewal of conflict soon to come. Aristarchus seems to have explained the nine-day period as due to ancient custom (Arn/A 665–6). On the other hand, at *Od.* 24.63–5 Akhilleus is mourned for seventeen days and burned on the eighteenth. According to Plutarch (*Lyc.* 27.2) Lycurgus prescribed a limit of eleven days for mourning, and at Athens in the classical period there was a ceremony on the ninth day *after* the burial (τὰ ἔνατα), but here it is a question of nine days *before* the funeral. However, ἐννῆμαρ μὲν . . . τῇ δεκάτῃ δὲ . . . is a conventional period of time which recurs elsewhere in epic (see on 1.53–4, and Richardson on *HyDem* 47, p. 166). Above all it corresponds to the duration of the plague at 1.53–4, and thus forms the outermost element in the series of structural correspondences at the beginning and end of the poem (cf. Introduction, 'Structure'). One of the opening scenes is that of the plague and the pyres on which the Greek dead are burned, and the work ends with the pyre of Hektor and his burial.

For the funeral feast (665) see on 23.1–34, 29–34. To hold the feast directly after the burning and before the burial mound is built would be normal. In fact, the order is changed at 788–803 (see on 801–3). δαινῦτο is optative like ἐκδῦμεν (16.99), δαινύατο (*Od.* 18.248), etc.: cf. Chantraine, *GH* I 51. Verses 664–7 have a wearisomely repetitive character, each verse beginning with one of the series of time-references, and 667 concludes the speech on a note of sad resignation: 'on the twelfth day then let us fight, if we really must'.

669–70 Akhilleus' reply is brief and equally courteous. Verse 669 resembles 21.223. For examples of ἔσται ταῦτα and similar expressions of assent in classical Greek cf. E. Fraenkel, *Beobachtungen zu Aristophanes* (Rome 1962) 77–89. These are the last words Akhilleus speaks in the poem. They set the seal on his reconciliation with Priam, and leave us with an impression of him as a commanding figure, in full control of the situation.

671–2 Akhilleus' gesture is described as one of reassurance (cf. 360–3 with comment). Grasping the hand ἐπὶ καρπῷ recurs at *Od.* 18.258, where Odysseus is saying goodbye to Penelope before leaving for Troy. There it may be a gesture of farewell, and perhaps a pledge of their love (cf. Fittschen, *Sagendarstellungen* 55). See also on 14.136–7.

673–6 See on 633–76, and for the πρόδομος cf. Lorimer, *HM* 415–17. προδόμῳ δόμου is a common type of 'pleonastic' expression, as in αἰπόλος αἰγῶν (*Od.* 17.247) etc. Verse 674 = 282. In 675–6 Akhilleus follows his mother's advice (128–32), again a sign of the restoration of a more normal pattern of life. But the mention of Briseis sleeping with him, at the moment when we leave Akhilleus for the last time, has great poignancy, and if we recall book 9, where Patroklos too was mentioned at this point in the parallel scene (666–8), this adds a further tinge of sadness (cf. O. Taplin, in *Chios* 17–18).

677–718 Hermes comes to Priam and urges him to leave, and he and Idaios do so, under his escort. At the ford of the Skamandros Hermes leaves them. At dawn they reach the city. Kassandre sees them and announces the news to the Trojans, who come out to meet them with Hekabe and Andromakhe, amid general lamentation

The transition from the scene in Akhilleus' hut to Troy is rapidly narrated. The return mirrors the outward journey (a type of ring-structure), but here the description is brief. Attention is focused on the arrival at Troy and the intense emotional reactions which this arouses. This sets the scene for the three great final laments of the poem (723–76).

677–86 This passage resembles the opening of book 2, where Zeus lies awake debating what to do (677–8 ~ 2.1–2), and then sends the Dream which reproaches Agamemnon for sleeping and urges him to action (2.5–34). Cf. 10.1–4 (10.2 = 24.678) where Agamemnon lies awake pondering what to do, and see on these passages. The pattern is discussed in connexion with dream-sequences by Arend, *Scenen* 61–2. E. Lévy (*Ktema* 7 (1982) 23–41) argues that Hermes actually comes to Priam in a dream, but this is surely not the case here.

681 For ἱερούς πυλαωρούς cf. 10.56 φυλάκων ἱερὸν τέλος. The epithet indicates the solemnity of their commission: cf. P. Wülfing von Martitz, *Glotta* 38 (1960) 300–1.

682 = 23.68 (see comment), etc.

683–8 Hermes rebukes Priam for sleeping at a time of such danger. For such rebukes by figures in visions and dreams see on 23.69–92. One could, if one wished, see this speech as an allegory, Hermes representing Priam's own good sense which suddenly reasserts itself, prompted by Akhilleus' warning. But Hermes' aid goes beyond more suggestion, here as elsewhere. In waking Priam he performs the rôle which is attributed to him at 24.344.

685–8 The ransoming itself is made the theme of Hermes' warning. παῖδες τοι ... λελειμμένοι means 'your sons, the ones who are left behind at home'. παῖδές τοι ... would be possible for 'the sons left behind by you'. In 686–8 we have a shift from optative to subjunctive similar to those at 582–6, 653–5, etc. The repetition of the verb in 688 adds to the urgency.

689–91 Verse 689 resembles 1.33, 24.571 etc. Hermes himself yokes the horses and mules and takes charge of them for greater speed, and the dactylic rhythm of 691 (with ῥίμφα) is typical of such brief descriptions of journeys: cf. 6.511, 13.29–30, 20.497, and Richardson on *HyDem* 89, 171. The end of 691 echoes and contrasts with 688.

692–7 Verses 692–3 = 14.433–4, 21.1–2. Verse 693 is omitted in two papyri and some MSS, and is probably an addition (cf. 351 where the river's name is not given). Verse 694 = *Od.* 10.307, and 695 = *Il.* 8.1 (μέν). Hermes departs at the same point where he met them on the outward journey, the boundary perhaps of Trojan territory, and just as he appeared at nightfall, so he leaves at dawn. They reach Troy 'with lamentation and groaning' soon after dawn. 'The god leaves for the home of the gods; dawn illumines the earth where there is suffering and sorrow' (Macleod, *Iliad XXIV* 48). For the imperfect ἕλων cf. *Od.* 4.2, Chantraine, *GH* 1 354.

697–9 Verses 697–8 pick up 691 ('no one saw them ... except ...'); for οὐδέ τις ἄλλος | ἔγνω (etc.) ... ἀλλά ... cf. 18.404–5, and for 698 cf. 7.139 ἄνδρες ... καλλίζωνοί τε γυναῖκες, *Od.* 23.147 ἀνδρῶν ... καλλιζώνων τε γυναικῶν, and *HyAp* 154.

699–702 Kassandre makes a brief but memorable appearance here. The only other mention of her in the *Iliad* was at 13.365–7 where Othruoneus was said to have tried to marry her, and she was called the fairest of Priam's daughters (see comment). The comparison of her to Aphrodite fits this description. In *Od.* 11.421–3 her later death at Klutaimestre's hands is recounted by Agamemnon's ghost. bT comment that she is watching because she is deeply anxious about her brother and father, and not because the poet has any knowledge of the tradition which made her inspired. They compare Nestor at 10.532; one could add Idomeneus at 23.450–1 (see comment). We cannot tell whether the poet really does have in mind her prophetic gifts, or whether her rôle as announcer of sad news may have helped to foster the later tradition of her as prophetess of doom. As often, however, one is inclined to think that the poet knows more than he tells us, and to read the scene in the light of what we ourselves know from later tradition.

For ἰκέλη χρυσέη Ἀφροδίτη cf. 19.282 (Briseis) where the situation is similar: Briseis sees the body of Patroklos and laments him. Kassandre has gone up to the highest point in the city to watch: cf. Idomeneus at 23.451. The scene resembles the τειχοσκοπία in book 3, where Helen watches from the walls (161–244), and cf. Andromakhe at 6.381–403. At 701 ἀστυβοώτης ('city-crier') is an absolute *hapax*, with -βοώτης by diectasis from -βώτης, a contracted form of -βοήτης. Cf. 577 καλήτορα. These two unique words for the same idea are good evidence, if such were needed, of the great range of vocabulary which the poet had at his command. In 700–2 the sequence 'her father ... the herald ... and *him* ...' is dramatic. Hektor is not named, but he is above all the one she is hoping to see.

703–6 For | κώκυσέν τ' ἄρ' ἔπειτα cf. 18.37. ὄψεσθε is most probably aorist imperative, as at *Od.* 8.313; cf. ἄξετε (778 etc.), Chantraine, *GH* I 418. Kassandre dwells on the past joy of Hektor's safe return from battle (χαίρετε ... χάρμα), in contrast to the present grief. Cf. 17.207 and 22.444, where again μάχης ἐκ νοστήσαντι was applied to Hektor in the context of his death. Here there is a bitter, almost ironic edge to Kassandre's words, as if Homer has in mind her rôle as the unwelcome harbinger of grief.

707–18 Kassandre's cry is the signal for a scene of great dramatic power (cf. bT 707–8), which recalls the scene of despair in Troy at Hektor's death (22.405ff.). In both cases this is the prelude for the more formal laments which follow. The technique resembles that of the battle-scenes, where individual episodes are preceded by more general descriptions of fighting. The impatience of Priam to make a way through the crowd is similar to the manner in which he angrily disperses the crowd and rebukes his sons at 237–64 (cf. Deichgräber, *Letzte Gesang* 79). Cf. also 6.238–41, where the women crowd round Hektor when he enters Troy.

708 For ἀάσχετον see on 5.892.

710–12 Andromakhe and Hekabe tear their hair in mourning for Hektor: τόν γε is accusative with τιλλέσθην, as if this meant 'they mourned him'. This is common with verbs of mourning ritual, e.g. Hdt. 2.61 τὸν δὲ τύπτονται, E. *Tro.* 623 κἀπεκοψάμην νεκρόν, etc. For the action see on 22.77–8. They also throw themselves upon the waggon, and touch the dead man's head: cf. 724 where Andromakhe holds his head during her lament, and see on 23.136.

713–15 πρόπαν ἦμαρ ἐς ἠέλιον καταδύντα is formular (3× *Il.*, 6× *Od.*), but for the whole sentence cf. 23.154–5 καί νύ κ' ὀδυρομένοισιν ἔδυ φάος ἠελίοιο, | εἰ μή ... εἶπε ..., with comment.

716–17 Priam's words are peremptory, almost harsh: 'Let me pass through with the mules! Later you can have your fill of weeping...' ἄσεσθε is a 'permissive' future, as in 6.70–1 ἔπειτα ... συλήσετε, etc. κλαυθμός occurs only here in *Il.*, 6× *Od.*

718–76 Hektor is brought home and laid on a bed. By it they set singers, who lead in singing a dirge, and the women join in keening. Andromakhe begins their lament, followed by Hekabe and Helen. All join in lamentation

Of all the scenes of lamentation in the last third of the poem this is the most formal. Only here is the mourning led by professional singers, who sing θρῆνοι, formal laments, and the women set up an accompaniment of cries. Against this accompaniment are set the individual spoken laments of the women of the family, Hektor's wife, mother, and sister-in-law. These in turn are supported by more general lamentation. The speeches of Andromakhe and Hekabe echo and complement those in book 22 (431–6, 477–514), where again there were three speeches after Hektor's death, Priam's being the first (416–28). There, however, the poet kept Hektor's wife to the end, whereas here it is natural that she should lead the laments. That Helen should be the last to speak is, however, less expected, and it is surely significant that she, who was the cause of the war, should speak thus so near the poem's end.

To some extent the three laments are similar in structure. Each one is introduced and followed by parallel verses with variations (723, 747, 762; 746, 760, 776). Each begins by addressing the dead man, as husband, son, brother-in-law. The opening themes, Andromakhe's sense of loss of a husband, Hekabe's pride that her son was and is dear to the gods, Helen's loss of her only friend at Troy, are resumed at the end of each speech. The central part is a narrative section, Andromakhe's vision of Troy's fate, Hekabe's recollection of the deaths of her sons, Helen's memory of Hektor's kindness. There is closer parallelism between the shorter speeches of Hekabe and Helen. The openings (748–69, 762–63) are very similar to each other, and both speeches are concerned with Hektor's φιλία, his nearness to the gods and to Helen. Both contain a contrast between Hektor and others (the rest of Hekabe's sons, Paris and the rest of Helen's relations by her marriage). On their structure see Lohmann, *Reden* 108–12, Alexiou, *Ritual Lament* 132–3.

There is also a clear association with Hektor's homecoming in book 6. There he was greeted by Hekabe, Helen and Andromakhe (254–62, 344–58, 407–39), and there are many links with these scenes, for example in Hekabe's concern there with Hektor's piety, Helen's self-reproach and sympathy for Hektor, Andromakhe's preoccupation with her own fate and that of her child. Each of the women speaks in character, in a way consistent with the speeches which they make elsewhere. On Andromakhe's lament and its connexions with books 6 and 22 see Lohmann, *Andromache-Szenen* 70–4.

Finally these laments are 'praise poems', encomia, like later funeral speeches. They praise Hektor's prowess in war, his piety, and his kindness. Cf. Reiner, *Die rituelle Totenklage* 62–7, 116–20, who comments on the close association between such praise poems and the development of epic poetry, κλέα ἀνδρῶν. It is appropriate that these speeches should come at the *end* of the *Iliad*. So too, *Beowulf* ends in mourning and praise for the hero (3169–82, translated by M. Alexander):

Then the warriors rode around the barrow,
twelve of them in all, athelings'.sons.
They recited a dirge to declare their grief,
spoke of the man, mourned their King.
They praised his manhood and the prowess of his hands,
they raised his name; it is right a man
should be lavish in honouring his lord and friend,
should love him in his heart when the leading-forth
from the house of flesh befalls him at last.
This was the manner of the mourning of the men of the Geats,
sharers in the feast, at the fall of their lord:
they said that he was of all the world's kings
the gentlest of men, and the most gracious,
the kindest to his people, the keenest for fame.

For a sensitive treatment of the whole theme of ritual lament see P. Levi,
The Lamentation of the Dead (Anvil Press Poetry 1984).

719–22 The body is laid on a bed within the house. This is the beginning
of the *prothesis*, which later would normally take place inside the house, and
which was the chief occasion for the ritual lament; cf. 19.210–13, and
Reiner, *Die rituelle Totenklage* 35ff. For τρητοῖς ἐν λεχέεσσι cf. 3.448 ἐν
τρητοῖσι ... λεχέεσσι (with comment), and similar phrases 4× *Od.* The
epithet probably refers to the holes bored in the frame for leather thongs
or fibres to be passed through to support the bedding: cf. Laser, *Arch.
Hom.* P 30–2.

Verses 720–2 mean 'and by the bed they set singers, leaders of the
dirges, who in the mournful song themselves led the dirge, while the women
wailed in accompaniment'. The form of the sentence is broken after ἀοιδήν,
and instead of the simple verb ἐθρήνεον, the sentence is divided into μέν
and δέ clauses. ἀοιδός, θρῆνος, θρηνεῖν, and ἔξαρχος occur only here in
the poem; cf. ἀοιδός frequently in *Od.*, ἀοιδή etc. in *Il.*, θρηνεῖν *Od.* 24.61,
ἐξάρχειν common in *Il.* ἔξαρχος is rare later, and particularly used in
connexion with the cults of Dionusos and Sabazios in the classical period
(E. *Ba.* 141, Dem. 18.260). The vulgate reading is θρηνούς, which would
presumably be taken as an epithet (cf. θρηνῳδούς AT), and most MSS
have ἐξάρχουσ(ι) as a verb with the relative clause οἵ τε ... ἀοιδήν. But
there is no evidence for this sense of θρῆνος, and the word order is un-
Homeric. ἔξαρχος and ἐξάρχειν are virtually technical terms for leading
a group of singers or dancers: cf. (ἐξ)ῆρχε γόοιο 18.316, 24.723, 24.747,
24.761, and 18.605–6 etc. In the laments for Patroklos the captive Trojan
women take up the refrain (18.28–31, 18.339–42, 19.301–2), and at
Akhilleus' funeral the Nereids (presumably led by Thetis) lament and the

Muses sing a dirge antiphonally (*Od.* 24.55–61). Later, hired mourners were not uncommon: cf. A. *Cho.* 733, Pl. *Laws* 800E, Plut. *Solon* 21.4 (probably), and Alexiou, *Ritual Lament* 10–14. θρῆνοι themselves developed into a particular type of lyric composition, like those of Simonides, Pindar and others (Reiner, *Die rituelle Totenklage* 71–100). It is possible that even in Homer there is a distinction between the more or less spontaneous γόος of relatives or friends, and the θρῆνοι sung by outsiders or professionals (cf. 720–1, *Od.* 24.60–1, Reiner, *Die rituelle Totenklage* 9 etc., Alexiou, *Ritual Lament* 11–14).

In antiquity the practice of singing dirges was believed to be originally non-Greek or oriental (Reiner, *Die rituelle Totenklage* 59–61, 66), and ancient scholars noted that θρῆνοι are mentioned only here in a Trojan context, and not in connexion with Patroklos (cf. T, Eust., *Suda* s.v. θρηνούς). T adds that this is a reason for athetizing *Od.* 24.60–1. They may well be right to detect in this another feature differentiating the Trojans from the Greeks (cf. von der Mühll, *Hypomnema* 387; Hall, *Barbarian* 44, is sceptical). In the laments of Andromakhe and Hekabe, however, there is nothing obviously foreign, and their restraint is one of their remarkable features. In many societies such laments are primarily, or exclusively, the affair of women; E. Samter, *Volkskunde im altsprachlichen Unterricht*, 1 *Homer* (Berlin 1923) 124–30, collects many examples.

723–4 Andromakhe holds Hektor's head in her hands as she utters her lament (see on 23.136). The poet could have used the phrase ἁδινοῦ ἐξῆρχε γόοιο in 723, as at 747 and 761. Instead he prefers the epithet λευκώλενος for Andromakhe, which he had used of her in book 6 (371, 377), but otherwise reserved almost exclusively for Here (24×; once of Helen). This could be a further sign that he has in mind the meeting of Hektor and Andromakhe in book 6. Mark Edwards sees this as a visual touch: 'it is hard not to think that the change of the adjective is intended to evoke more vividly the picture of her bare arms around the corpse' (*HPI* 314). Instead of the majority reading ἀνδροφόνοιο two papyri and some MSS have ἱπποδάμοιο. But ἀνδροφόνοιο is surely better, in view of what she will say of Hektor's prowess at 736–9. For the two formulae see on 16.717–18.

725–45 She begins with the themes of Hektor's early death, her widowhood, and the fate of her child, with a clear echo of her lament in book 22 (725–7 ~ 22.482–5; cf. also 6.407–9). The one protector of Troy is gone (728–30 ~ 22.507, 6.402–3), and she foresees the slavery in store for herself and the other Trojan women (731–2 ~ 6.410–13, 6.450–63). Astuanax will either follow them into slavery, or else he will be killed, thrown from the wall by an Achaean in revenge for Hektor's killing of a kinsman (732–8). This goes beyond any earlier prediction about his fate

(6.476–81, 22.487–506). It leads to the subject of Hektor's fierceness in war (739), which will be counterbalanced by what Helen will say of his kindness, and this brings Andromakhe back to the sense of loss felt by the people, Hektor's family, and herself above all (740–2). She closes with a very personal touch: in dying, he could not stretch out his hands to her from his bed, or speak a last word which she could keep in her memory to console her grief (743–5). Just so at the end of her lament in book 22, she spoke of the clothes which should have been used for his funeral, but which were now no use to him. In both cases the underlying theme is the same, the denial of the normal consolations and rites associated with death. The speech moves naturally from one theme to the next, with a high frequency of enjambment, so that the thematic transitions often occur in mid-verse or mid-sentence, and many of the emphatic words (especially verbs) occur at the beginning of verses. This flowing style is similar to that of her speeches in books 6 and 22.

Andromakhe's vision of impending disaster is paralleled by one of the laments at the end of *Beowulf* (3150–5):

> A woman of the Geats in grief sang out
> the lament for his death. Loudly she sang,
> her hair bound up, the burden of her fear
> that evil days were destined her
> — troops cut down, terror of armies,
> bondage, humiliation. Heaven swallowed the smoke.

725–6 She does not name him as Hekabe and Helen do, but simply calls him 'husband'. ἀπ' αἰῶνος νέος ὤλεο is an unusual expression, which seems to mean 'you have been robbed of your (proper) span of life while still young' (cf. Eust. 1373.23). For ὄλλυσθαι with ἀπό or ἐκ cf. 18.107, *Od.* 15.91, and for χήρην see on 22.484. The sound-patterns of 725 are striking:

> ἄνερ, ἀπ' αἰῶνος νέος ὤλεο, κὰδ δέ με χήρην.

For the complaint of desertion in 725ff. see on 22.484–6.

726–8 In 726–7, παῖς δ' ... δυσάμμοροι = 22.484–5. In a natural way at 727–8 Andromakhe speaks of her son dying when Troy is sacked, whereas at 732–5 she envisages that he may survive, and then again that he may be killed.

728–30 For κατ' ἄκρης in connexion with Troy's sack cf. 13.772–3, 15.557–8, 22.411. ἐπίσκοπος ('guardian') is glossed by the relative clause; see on 22.255. The frequentative imperfect ῥύσκευ (cf. ῥύομαι) occurs only here. ἔχες alludes to the etymology of Hektor's name (cf. T, and Pl. *Crat.* 393A–B), as with Astuanax (6.402–3, 22.506–7); cf. 5.473–4, where Sarpedon reproaches Hektor for thinking that he can 'hold the city alone', unaided by his allies. The chiastic order of the relative clause, with the two verbs juxtaposed at the beginning of 730, emphasizes the main idea. For 730 cf. 4.238 (with comment), etc.

731–2 Macleod suggests that 'ὀχήσονται seems to continue the word-play, this time with a pathetic contrast: before, Hector "kept" them, now they "will be carried (off)"'. For ὀχεῖσθαι in connexion with the sea cf. *Od.* 5.54; it is commonly used later of being on a ship. In the Cyclic epics and later tradition Andromakhe becomes the slave and concubine of Neoptolemos; cf. *Iliupersis*, OCT vol. v, p. 108.9 (= Davies, *EGF* p. 62.31), *Ilias Parva* fr. 19 (= Davies, *EGF* fr. 20), etc.

732–40 Here Andromakhe addresses Astuanax instead of Hektor. Whether he is actually present or not we are not told, but the pathos of the apostrophe is the same. Cf. 741–2, where she again addresses Hektor in mid-sentence (and bT on 732, 739). In 732–3 (ἢ ἐμοὶ αὐτῇ ... ἐργάζοιο) the frequency of vowel-sounds and hiatus is noticeable, especially in ἔργα ἀεικέα ἐργάζοιο which mirrors the ugliness of what she has in mind. Again in 734 ἀθλεύων πρὸ ἄνακτος ἀμειλίχου has strong assonance. ἀμείλιχος is used of Hades and Erinus at 9.158, 9.568, the only other occurrences in the poem, and it is echoed by 739. πρό means 'in the face of' and so virtually 'on behalf of' (cf. 8.57).

734–9 That a child should be thrown from the walls in vengeance would, one imagines, not be so uncommon in a sack (cf. bT 735, Eust. 1373.43), and need not reflect a precisely formed tradition. In fact, Aristarchus (Arn/A, T) thought that this passage was the origin of the later legends. In the *Iliupersis* Astuanax is killed by Odysseus, apparently by being thrown from the wall: OCT vol. v, p. 108.8 and *Iliupersis* fr. 2 (= Davies, *EGF* p. 62.30, fr. 3). In the *Ilias Parva* (fr. 19.3–5 = Davies, *EGF* fr. 20.3–5) Neoptolemos seizes him by the foot and hurls him to his death:

παῖδα δ' ἑλὼν ἐκ κόλπου ἐϋπλοκάμοιο τιθήνης
ῥῖψε ποδὸς τεταγὼν ἀπὸ πύργου, τὸν δὲ πεσόντα
ἔλλαβε πορφύρεος θάνατος καὶ μοῖρα κραταιή

(cf. Paus. 10.25.9). The language of this version echoes or parallels that of the *Iliad*, and it looks as if the poet is trying to outdo the Homeric version, by substituting ποδὸς τεταγών for χειρὸς ἑλών, as in *Il.* 1.591 (Hephaistos' fall from heaven). In Euripides' *Troades* Odysseus persuades the Greeks that Astuanax must die, and he is thrown from the wall (721–5, 1134–5). The death of Astuanax was often portrayed in archaic and later art (*LIMC* II.1 s.v. Astyanax I), but it is uncertain whether he is the subject of two early representations, one on a late Geometric vase, the other on the Myconos pithos of the early seventh century (*LIMC* II.1 s.v. Astyanax I nos. 26 and 27), although in the second case many scholars have assumed that he is.

Andromakhe speculates that the agent of her son's death may be someone angry over a kinsman's death at Hektor's hand. This is not precisely mirrored in the later versions, but that does not tell us what tradition already existed. For vagueness over a similar future event, certainly already fixed by legend, cf. for example Akhilleus' uncertainty about his predicted death at 21.111–13, with comment. On the relationship of this passage to later versions see also Beck, *Stellung* 157–68. E. *Tro.* 742–4 look like an echo of this passage: (Andromakhe to Astuanax) ἢ τοῦ πατρὸς δέ σ᾽ εὐγένει᾽ ἀποκτενεῖ, | ἢ τοῖσιν ἄλλοις γίγνεται σωτηρία, | τὸ δ᾽ ἐσθλὸν οὐκ ἐς καιρὸν ἦλθέ σοι πατρός.

The grimness of 734–5 is justified by the equally grim assertions of 736–9, and λυγρὸν ὄλεθρον (735) is echoed by ἐν δαῒ λυγρῇ (739), ἄλγεα λυγρά (742), as 739 also picks up 734. ἄναξ meaning 'master' of a slave occurs only here in *Il.*, frequently in *Od.* For 738 cf. 7.105, for 737–8 cf. 19.61 τῷ κ᾽ οὐ τόσσοι Ἀχαιοὶ ὀδὰξ ἕλον ἄσπετον οὖδας.

740–2 These verses form a tricolon crescendo: 'the people ... his parents ... myself above all', with effective variation in the phrasing of each clause. The subject changes in each case, as does the tense of the verb (present, past, future), and the change to apostrophe in mid-sentence is particularly vivid, with Ἕκτορ in emphatic runover position, followed at once by ἐμοὶ δέ. For this juxtaposition and contrast of dead man and mourners cf. 725–6 (etc.), and Alexiou, *Ritual Lament* 171–7. Later, classical laments and epitaphs often emphasize the sorrow which the dead man has left to those who survive: S. *Aj.* 972–3 Αἴας γὰρ αὐτοῖς οὐκέτ᾽ ἐστίν, ἀλλ᾽ ἐμοὶ | λιπὼν ἀνίας καὶ γόους διοίχεται, and (e.g.) W. Peek, *Griechische Versinschriften* I (Heidelberg 1955) 697.5–6, 2002.7–8; R. Lattimore, *Themes in Greek and Latin Epitaphs* (Illinois 1962) 179–82.

Verse 741 = 17.37, and we should probably read ἄρρητον in both cases (see comment there). Cf. also 5.155–8.

743–5 bT (on 744) say 'this is true to life: for in one's sorrows the last words of those dear to one are a sweet thing for consolation'. Cf. Plut. *Mor.* 117B: 'if the dying man spoke to them, they always keep this in their mind as a kindling for grief'. At the end of the *Agricola* (45.5) Tacitus regrets that he and Agricola's daughter were not present at his death: *excepissemus certe mandata vocesque, quas penitus animo figeremus.* Cf. Alexiou, *Ritual Lament* 183–4 for modern Greek examples. πυκινὸν ἔπος (75, etc.) has particular force here: 'a word full of meaning', something enduring and substantial; cf. Martin, *Language of Heroes* 35–6. For the optative μεμνήμην see on 23.361, and Chantraine, *GH* I 465.

746 = 22.515. The poet varies the verse describing this refrain after each lament (cf. 760, 776, and see on 22.429). Here it is the women, echoing 722, at 760 the γόος is more general, and at 776 it is the whole of the δῆμος ἀπείρων.

747 This verse echoes 723 and is picked up again at 761; cf. 22.430 (Hekabe), etc.

748–59 Hekabe's lament at 22.431–6 was passionate and despairing (cf. 22.82–9, 24.201–16), but here she is unusually controlled. It is above all her fierce pride in the greatest of her sons which stands out, and this fits her character (cf. 22.432–6, 24.215–16). There may be an implicit sense of triumph, that after all Akhilleus failed in his attempt to disfigure Hektor's corpse, and all that he did was of no use to Patroklos after his death. By contrast the theme of Hektor's piety and the special divine protection of his body appears for the last time, and forms the chief encomiastic element in her lament. For this theme cf. especially 416–23, closely recalled here by her words. The speech falls into four sections of three verses each (noted by von Leutsch: see Leaf on 723). This gives it a steadily measured quality.

748–50 Verses 748–49 are echoed by Helen's opening words (762–3). For the comparison between life and death in 749–50 cf. Hekabe's first lament at 22.435–6 (with comment on 430–6). The repetition of περ ... περ ... stresses the antithesis: 'certainly in *life* you were dear to the gods: and after all (ἄρα), even in *death* ...' Verse 750 resembles Priam's pious reflection at 425–8.

751–6 Hekabe speaks as if Akhilleus had spared the lives of several of her sons, in contrast to his savagery against Hektor. Cf. Isos and Antiphos (11.104–6) whom he ransomed, and Lukaon (21.34ff.) who was sold by him to Euneos of Lemnos. Akhilleus himself spoke of the many Trojans he had spared before Patroklos' death (21.99–102). In 753 Samos is Samothrace, as at 78 etc. ἀμιχθαλόεις occurs only here in Homer, and again at *HyAp* 36 Ἴμβρος τ' εὐκτιμένη καὶ Λῆμνος ἀμιχθαλόεσσα; Antimachus (fr. 141 W.) apparently read μιχθαλόεσσαν. Callimachus (fr. 18.8 Pf.) has ἀμιχθαλόεσσαν ἤερα of a dark sea-mist; cf. Colluthus 208 ἀμιχθαλόεντος ἀπ' ἠέρος ὄμβρον ἱεῖσα. The word was said to have survived in Cypriote with the sense εὐδαίμων, but van der Valk doubts this (*Researches* I 488). There is a discussion of it in a papyrus commentary on Callimachus (A. Henrichs, *ZPE* 4 (1969) 23–30, with Erbse v 509). The chief ancient suggestions were: prosperous, rocky and steep, hard to approach or inhospitable (ἄμικτος), misty and hard to catch sight of. The cloud of uncertainty around this foggy gloss has not been lifted by modern scholarship (Chantraine, *Dict.* and *LfgrE* s.v., Leumann, *HW* 214, etc.), unless I have myself failed to catch sight of a solution. The translation 'misty' would fit here.

ἐξέλετο ψυχήν is not a formular expression for killing someone (cf. 22.257 σὴν δὲ ψυχὴν ἀφέλωμαι). For ταναηκέϊ χαλκῷ see on 23.118. The frequentative form ῥυστάζω occurs only here in *Il.*, 2× *Od.* (16.109 = 20.319); cf.

Od. 18.224 ῥυστακτύς. Both words denote rough or brutal handling. Verse 755 resembles 51–2, 416–17. The conclusion of 756 is bitter: cf. Akhilleus' words to Priam about Hektor at 551, οὐδέ μιν ἀνστήσεις.

757–9 For ἐρσήεις see on 419. πρόσφατος (only here in Homer; common in later Greek) means 'fresh'; the original sense was probably 'newly killed' (cf. Chantraine, *Dict.* s.v. θείνω). Verses 758–59 resemble several Odyssean passages referring to a sudden, painless death, sent by Apollo or Artemis or both: 3.279–80, 5.123–4, 11.172–3, 11.198–9, 15.410–11. A quotes the variant οἷς ἀγανοῖσι βέλεσσιν … καταπέφνῃ, which a papyrus has (and καταπέφνῃ in some MSS), and the 'generalizing' subjunctive seems better here than the aorist. Apollo's protection of the body (18–21, 23.188–91) makes this comparison particularly suitable (cf. Reinhardt, *IuD* 484), and these verses make a lovely, quiet close to this lament. Contrast the opening scene of book 1 (8–52): Apollo the destroyer becomes Apollo the preserver, who even in death keeps Hektor's body intact (see Introduction, 'Structure', pp. 5–6).

760 See on 746, and cf. 20.31 πόλεμον δ' ἀλίαστον ἔγειρε.

762–75 Helen's speech is a masterpiece of characterization and pathos, which should be compared with her speeches to Priam in book 3 (172–80), and to Hektor in book 6 (344–58). There and elsewhere (e.g. 3.242, 3.404, 3.410–12) remorse and bitterness about her marriage with Paris and contempt for him (cf. 3.428–36) were prominent. But her respect for Priam, who treated her so gently (3.162–5), and her sympathy for Hektor, who bore the chief burden of the fighting for her sake, also came out strongly (3.172, 6.354–8). Here too she stresses Hektor's kindness, and Priam's (770), in contrast by implication to her husband Paris and the other Trojans. Self-reproach comes out in her wish to have died before coming to Troy (764, if that is the right reading), and self-pity in 773–5, again characteristic of Helen (e.g. 3.411–12, 6.357–8). There is also a note of longing for home in 765–6, where she speaks of having been away for twenty years: cf. 3.174–6, 3.232–42 (Idomeneus, her brothers), and *Od.* 4.259–64. Throughout all Helen's speeches there runs a preoccupation with her complex family relationships, at home in Greece and here in Troy: that is why kinship words (δαήρ, ἑκυρός, ἑκυρή, πόσις, υἱός, παῖς, αὐτοκασιγνήτω, γνωτοί, γαλόῳ, εἰνάτερες) recur so often (see on 3.180). Verses 762–63 echo 748–49. Helen uses δαήρ of Hektor at 6.344, 6.355, and of Agamemnon at 3.180; cf. 24.769. It must be scanned δαέρων at 769, and either thus or δᾱέρων here.

763–7 The train of thought is 'truly Paris is my husband, and I had no right to expect such kindness from Hektor as I did from him: and yet …'

764 The vulgate reading is ὡς πρὶν ὤφελλ' ἀπολέσθαι (as at 7.390), but Aristarchus (Did/T) and some MSS read ὡς πρὶν ὤφελλον ὀλέσθαι. At

3.428–9 Helen wishes that Paris had been killed in his duel with Menelaos, but that was in an outburst of contempt against him just after that event. On the other hand her wish to have died herself echoes what she said both to Priam at 3.173–5 and to Hektor, even more passionately, at 6.345–8. Such a wish is common in laments: cf. Hekabe at 22.431–2, and Andromakhe at 22.481 (ὡς μὴ ὤφελλε τεκέσθαι), with comment there.

765–7 Helen's point is that it is a very long time since she left home, and yet Hektor was never unkind to her. Twenty is a standard figure in Homer (e.g. 13.260, 16.847, *Od.* 4.360, 5.34, and Reinhardt, *IuD* 488–9). The *Iliad* takes place in the tenth year of the war, and for a longer period twenty is the next major figure: cf. 9.379, 22.349, 11.33–4, etc. AbT and Eustathius explained this as due to the time taken to gather the expedition (cf. 4.27–8, 11.765–70, *Od.* 24.115–19). One could add the wanderings of Paris on the way to Troy (6.289–92), or later traditions of an abortive first expedition which landed in Mysia, of Akhilleus' stay in Skuros (schol. 19.326), and of the delay at Aulis before sailing for Troy, all of which were related in the Cyclic epics (cf. Kullmann, *Quellen* 189–200). But this is all unnecessary, and the poet may well have invented this detail *ad hoc* for Helen's speech (cf. J. T. Kakridis, *Gnomon* 32 (1960) 407). In the *Odyssey* Odysseus returns home in the twentieth year since he left, but this does not need to be reconciled with what Helen says. Her words at 765–6 are paralleled by *Od.* 19.222–3 (with reference to Odysseus); for discussion of the two passages and their possible relationship cf. Reinhardt, *IuD* 485–90, J. T. Hooker, *La Parola del Passato* 127 (1986) 111–13.

For the pattern of 765–7 cf. 2.798–9 ἦ μὲν δὴ μάλα πολλὰ μάχας εἰσήλυθον ἀνδρῶν, | ἀλλ' οὔ πω τοιόνδε τοσόνδε τε λαὸν ὄπωπα, and 10.548–50, *Od.* 4.267–70. In 767 ἀσύφηλον is a rare word, which recurs at 9.647 and very occasionally later (Quintus of Smyrna 9.521 and late prose). It must mean something like 'rude' or 'harmful' here; see Chantraine, *Dict.* and *LfgrE* s.v. Cf. *Od.* 4.690 (Odysseus) οὔτε τινὰ ῥέξας ἐξαίσιον οὔτε τι εἰπών.

768–72 This is the only case in Homer of a conditional clause with 'iterative' optative, but it is a natural corollary to temporal and relative clauses of this kind, and is common later (cf. Chantraine, *GH* II, 224–5). Most MSS read ἐνίσποι, which perhaps reflects A's variant ἐνίσσοι, itself a possible reading. But ἐνίπτειν is commoner and occurs on its own, without ἐπέεσσιν etc. For γαλόῳ and εἰνάτερες see on 22.473. The contrast in 770 suggests what the rough edge of Hekabe's tongue could do, and Priam's fatherly gentleness recalls 3.162–5 (cf. Priam's φίλον τέκος in 3.162). The picture of Hektor's kindness to her in 771–2 is enhanced by the repetitions and sentence-structure, with σὺ ... σῇ ... σοῖς ... stressing his exceptional behaviour, ἐπέεσσι ... ἐπέσσι framing the whole, and ἀγανοφροσύνῃ ...

ἀγανοῖς ἐπέεσσι dwelling on his gentleness. There is similar pathos in the speech of Odysseus' mother at *Od.* 11.202-3:

ἀλλά με σός τε πόθος, σά τε μήδεα, φαίδιμ' Ὀδυσσεῦ,
σῇ τ' ἀγανοφροσύνῃ μελιηδέα θυμὸν ἀπηύρα.

The contrast there with οἷς ἀγανοῖς βελέεσσιν at 199, and the fact that 199 repeats *Il.* 24.759, suggests that the *Iliad* scene is in the poet's mind here, especially since ἀγανοφροσύνη occurs nowhere else in Homer (cf. 20.467 ἀγανόφρων) or later.

773-5 Helen returns to the present, her grief at the loss of Hektor, her self-pity and desolation. Like Andromakhe she links grief for Hektor with sorrow for herself, and καὶ ἔμ' ἄμμορον recalls Andromakhe at 6.408 (cf. 24.727). The ending leaves a very bitter taste, with πεφρίκασιν ('shudder at') as the final word: cf. 19.325 ῥιγεδανῆς Ἑλένης.

776 'Not only the women lament here; for she aroused greater grief. With the greatest pathos (ἔλεος) the poet concludes the *Iliad*', comment bT, comparing later perorations. Leaf says that 'δῆμος is nowhere else used in the sense of *multitude*', but it presumably means the whole people of Troy; cf. 3.50 πόληΐ τε παντί τε δήμῳ, etc. ἀπείρων elsewhere in Homer is applied to sea or land, except for *Od.* 8.340 δεσμοὶ ἀπείρονες; but cf. *HyAphr* 120 ὅμιλος ἀπείριτος, Hes. *Aspis* 472 λαὸς ἀπείρων, *HyDem* 296 πολυπείρονα λαόν.

777-804 Priam orders the Trojans to collect wood for the pyre, and for nine days they do so. On the tenth day Hektor's body is burnt. Next day the pyre is quenched, the body is buried, and the people hold the funeral feast in Priam's palace

By contrast with the funeral of Patroklos, and with the leisurely pace of the narrative in this Book, the final description of Hektor's funeral rites is economical (cf. Eust. 1375.30ff.), although at 788-801 the actual burial is described in detail as at 23.250-7. The train of events resembles that for Patroklos, although not always in the same order. There (unusually) the funeral feast came before the burial (see on 23.1-34), and after the gathering of wood (110-26) the *ekphora* took place (128-37), followed by the building of the pyre (163-4), the burning (177-225), and burial. There is no mention here of funeral games, which would be quite out of place; they would not suit the state of siege and shortness of the truce. Moreover the poet wants as quiet and simple a close as possible, with all the emphasis falling on the burial itself. On the order of ceremonies see M. W. Edwards, 'The conventions of a Homeric funeral', in *Studies in Honour of T. B. L. Webster* (edd. J. H. Betts, J. T. Hooker and J. R. Green), 1 (Bristol 1986) 84-92.

778–81 Priam's speech contains the briefest of instructions (778), with a reassurance against ambush (cf. Akhilleus' promise at 669–72), echoed at 799–800. ἐπέτελλε means that Akhilleus gave orders to this effect as a guarantee of security.

782–7 ἀγινεῖν recurs at 18.493, 4× *Od.*, 5× *HyAp*. For ἄσπετον ὕλην in this context cf. 23.127. The building of the pyre is taken for granted. Verse 785 = 6.175 (with ῥοδοδάκτυλος, which is a variant here too). φαεσίμβροτος occurs first here; cf. *Od.* 10.138, Hes. *Th.* 958 φαεσιμβρότου Ἠελίοιο. It is perhaps used because of ῥοδοδάκτυλος in 788. ἐξέφερον is the technical word for the funeral procession; cf. Hdt. 7.117, etc., and see on 23.127–53. Verse 787 echoes 23.165 (ἀχνύμενοι κῆρ).

788–801 The burial takes place after dawn, as at 226–57. Cf. *Od.* 24.72, and *Il.* 7.433–6 (twilight before dawn), where 434 closely resembles 789; in both cases we should read ἤγρετο ('gathered'), with a few MSS here, for the vulgate ἔγρετο ('woke up'). Verse 788 = 1.477. For this Odyssean verse see comment there; but (*pace* Kirk) the echo of book 1 may be significant. Likewise the Odyssean 790 recalls 1.57 (see comment). Both assemblies follow immediately after the reference to 'nine days... on the tenth' (1.53–4, 24.784–5), even if in book 24 the gathering is actually on the *eleventh* day, not the tenth (but see on 801–3). Verse 790 is omitted by one papyrus and several groups of MSS including A, and it is dispensable, but the repetition in 789–90 is paralleled by *Od.* 2.8–9.

Verses 791–801 should be compared with 23.250–7, with comments. Verse 791 = 23.250, and the first half of 801 = 23.257. But the language of the rest is significantly varied, although the basic series of actions is similar. In both cases, after the pyre has been quenched with wine, the bones are gathered and covered with cloth, and a mound is built. There the tomb was to be a cenotaph (see on 254) until Akhilleus' own death. At 23.253 Patroklos' bones were put in a golden φιάλη for the time being, whereas here the bones can be placed directly in a coffin (λάρναξ), the equivalent of the σορός which will ultimately hold the remains of both Patroklos and his friend (see on 23.91). For the word λάρναξ cf. 18.413, the only other occurrence in Homer. The grave is mentioned only here. κοίλην κάπετον of a grave recurs twice in Sophocles' *Ajax* (1165, 1403). Verses 797–8 seem to indicate a layer of stones over the grave, whereas the verb χέω (799, 801) suggests that these are then covered by a mound of earth: see on 255–6. The simple κλαίοντες of 23.252 is here developed into the full verse 794, with emphatic runover μυρόμενοι. Verse 796 is a lovely, euphonious four-word verse to describe the purple clothing with which the bones are covered: see on 23.254, both for this practice and for the colour described. Verse 798 is again a majestic four-word verse of similar type and almost identical rhythm, with three long dative forms framing the verb, which occurs only here in *Il.*, 2× *Od.* In 799–800 ῥίμφα is significant: there is no time to delay, and the mention of the scouts and danger of attack are vivid touches, reminding the audience for the last time that this is only a brief pause in the larger action of the war. For σκοποὶ ἥατο cf. 18.523.

The effect of the great burial-mounds of the Troad such as Hektor's is nowhere better described than by Hektor himself, before his duel with Aias, where he speaks of how his opponent's will become a landmark for passing sailors, who will pronounce his epitaph and so commemorate Hektor's own fame for ever (7.86–91).

801–3 At 665 Priam speaks of holding the feast directly after the funeral on the tenth day, before the building of the tumulus, whereas it actually occurs on the eleventh as the final ceremony, thus giving the quiet but celebratory ending. Mark Edwards comments: 'Perhaps this implies again the Trojans' fear of a Greek attack, but more probably it is to enable the poet to concentrate his ending not only upon the dead Hector but also upon the living and doomed Trojans and their city' (*HPI* 315). In 802 εὖ means 'in due fashion', like Latin *rite*; cf. 2.382–4, etc. (δαίνυντ') ἐρικυδέα δαῖτα is Odyssean (4×). For Πριάμοιο διοτρεφέος βασιλῆος cf. 5.464. That the feast should take place within the palace, rather than near the pyre, could again be due to the focus on Troy itself, but it may simply be the natural place for it to be held, since Priam would be the giver of the feast. Whatever the truth, these lines have a stately dignity appropriate to the conclusion.

804 Some ancient texts (T, one first-century A.D. papyrus) offered an alternative ending, which linked the *Iliad* to the *Aithiopis*:

ὣς οἵ γ' ἀμφίεπον τάφον Ἕκτορος· ἦλθε δ' Ἀμάζων,

followed by

Ἄρηος θυγάτηρ μεγαλήτορος ἀνδροφόνοιο (T)

or

Ὀτρήρ[η]⟨ς⟩ θυγάτηρ εὐειδὴς Πενθεσίλ⟨ε⟩ια (pap. 104)

Cf. the summary of the *Aithiopis* (OCT vol. v, p. 105.22–3 = Davies, *EGF* p. 47.4): Ἀμάζων Πενθεσίλεια παραγίνεται Τρωσὶ συμμαχήσουσα, etc.

This simple but noble verse closes the poem, which began with the wrath of Akhilleus, and ends with the burial of Hektor, tamer of horses.

General index

INDEX OF GREEK WORDS FOR ALL VOLUMES

Bold roman numerals refer to the volume of the commentary in which the immediately following Homeric book- and line-numbers occur. Italic figures refer to page-numbers in the introduction to the volume in question, or in introductory material later in the volume.

369

Index of Greek words

371

διιπετής **IV**: 16.173–5; **V**: 17.263–6
διΐφιλος (Διΐ φίλος) **III**: 11.419; **IV**: 13.674–8
δίκη **IV**: 16.386–8
δινωτός **I**: 3.391; **IV**: 13.406–7; **VI**: 23.562
Διόθεν **IV**: 15.489
δῖος **III**: 9.538; 12.21; **IV**: 14.75–7
διοτρεφής **VI**: 23.581
δίσκουρα **VI**: 23.523
δίφρος **II**: 5.608–9, 5.727–8, 5.729–31; 6.354; **III**: 9.200
Διώρης **I**: 4.517; **V**: 17.471–4
δμήτειρα **IV**: 14.256–61
δοάσσετο **IV**: 13.445–8
δοκέω **IV**: 15.728–30
Δόλων **III**: 10.314
δόρυ **IV**: 13.246–8, 13.561; 16.141–4, 16.812–17
δούλη **III**: 9.336
δουπέω **II**: 5.58; **IV**: 13.424–6; 15.419–21; 16.593–9; **VI**: 23.679
δραίνω **III**: 10.96
δρατός **VI**: 23.169
δριμύς **IV**: 15.696–8
δρυτόμος **IV**: 16.633–4; **VI**: 23.315
δύναμις **VI**: 23.891
δυσαριστοτόκεια **V**: 18.54
δυσκλέα **III**: 9.22; **IV**: *34*
δύσμορος **VI**: 22.60, 22.481
δυσπέμφελος **IV**: 16.747–8
δυωκαιεικοσίμετρος **VI**: 23.264
δῶ **IV**: 14.173

ἑ, ἕ **IV**: *13*; 13.163–4, 13.492–5, 13.561, 13.802–5; 14.162–3; 15.165–7; 16.207–9, 16.735–6; **V**: 17.547–52; 20.170–1
ἔαγη **III**: 11.559
ἐαδότα **III**: 9.173
ἑανός **IV**: 14.172–4, 14.175–7, 14.180
ἔασουσι **IV**: 13.315–16
ἑάφθη **IV**: 13.541–4
ἐάω **IV**: 15.472–5; 16.95–6
ἐγγυαλίζω **IV**: 15.490–3
ἔγρετο **IV**: *35*
ἐγρήγορθαι **III**: 10.67, 10.419
ἐγρηγορτί **III**: 10.180–2
ἔγχελυς **VI**: 21.203
ἔγχος **I**: *34*; 3.330–8, 3.346–7, 3.355–60, 3.379–80; **II**: 5.568–9, 5.623–4, 5.625–6; 6.29–36, 6.124–7, 6.305–6; **IV**: 13.292–4, 13.518–20, 13.597; 16.313–15
ἐδανός **IV**: 14.172–4
ἔδνον **III**: 9.146–8; **IV**: 13.365–7
ἐεδνωτής **IV**: 13.378–82
ἐείκοσι **IV**: *17*; 13.260–1
ἐεισάμην **IV**: 15.414–15, 15.539–45
ἕζομαι **IV**: 14.436–7

ἔῆος **IV**: 15.138; **V**: 19.342–3
ἐθείρω **VI**: 21.347
ἔθων **III**: 9.540
εἰ **III**: 9.49; **IV**: 15.372–6, 15.568–71; 16.556–62
εἴασεν **III**: 10.299
εἴατο **IV**: 15.10–13
εἰδέω **IV**: 14.235–6
εἴδομαι **I**: 2.791–5; **II**: 7.59–60; **IV**: 13.191; 16.710–11, 16.716–20
εἰδυῖα **V**: 17.3–6
εἰκαιότεραι **IV**: *22*
εἴκοσι **IV**: *17*; 13.260–1
εἰκοσινήριτος **VI**: 22.349
Εἰλείθυια **III**: 11.270
εἰλήλουθμεν **III**: 9.48–9
εἷλκον **IV**: 16.402–6
εἰλυφάζω **V**: 20.490–2
εἰλύω **VI**: 21.319
εἰμι **III**: 11.808; **IV**: *16, 17*; 13.317–18; 14.271–4, 14.331–3; 15.10–13, 15.80–3; 16.514–16
εἰνατέρες **VI**: 22.473
εἰνί **IV**: 15.150
εἷος **V**: 20.41–3
εἶπε **V**: 17.237–9
εἶραι **I**: 18.530–2
εἴσατο, καταείσατο **III**: 11.358; 12.118–19
εἴση **III**: 11.61
εἶσθα **III**: 10.450
ἔϊσκω **III**: 11.799; **IV**: 13.446–7; 15.539–45
εἰσωπός **V**: 15.653–4
εἵως **IV**: *18*; 13.141–2, 13.143–4; **V**: 17.730
ἐκ **IV**: 13.492–5; 15.78–9; 16.364–5
Ἑκάβη **IV**: 16.716–20
ἑκάεργος **I**: 1.474; **II**: 5.439; 7.23; **IV**: *12*; 15.252–3; **VI**: 21.599–601
ἔκαθεν **IV**: 13.107–10; 16.633–4
ἕκαστος **III**: 9.88; **IV**: 15.286–93, 15.502–6; 16.168–72
ἑκατηβόλος **IV**: 15.231–2
ἑκατόμβη **I**: 1.65; **II**: 6.234–6
ἑκατόμπεδος **VI**: 23.164
ἐκγίνομαι **IV**: 14.115–20
ἐκδῦμεν **IV**: 16.97–100
ἐκεῖνος **III**: 9.63; 11.653; **IV**: 15.45–6
ἐκηβόλος **IV**: 15.231–2; 16.716–20
ἔκηλος **III**: 11.75–6
ἔκπαγλος **I**: 1.145–6; 3.357–9, 3.415; **IV**: 13.413–16; **VI**: 21.452
ἐκτάδιος **III**: 10.134
Ἑκτόρεος **III**: 10.46; **IV**: *16*
ἐκφέρω **VI**: 23.376
ἐκφεύγω **IV**: 14.402–8
ἐλαύνω **IV**: 13.315–16; 16.467–9
ἐλελίζω **VI**: 22.448

Index of Greek words

κήλεος **IV**: 15.742–6
κήρ **I**: 4.46; **II**: 5.811–13; 7.99–100; 8.73–4;
  III: 9.411; 12.326–7; **IV**: 5; 16.684–7
κῆρ **IV**: 16.481
κῆτος **IV**: 13.27–31
κινυρός **V**: 17.3–6
κιχείς **IV**: 16.342–4
κλέα **III**: 9.189; **IV**: 34
κλέος **II**: 5.2–3, 5.172–3; 6.357–8; 7.91; **III**:
  9.413; **IV**: 10
κλήδην **III**: 9.11–12
κληῒς **II**: 6.86–98; **IV**: 14.166–9; 16.168–72
κλῆρος **IV**: 15.494–9
κλισίη **IV**: 13.260–1; **VI**: 24.448
κλισμός **III**: 9.200; 11.623
κλιτύς **IV**: 16.389–92
κλοτοπεύω **V**: 19.149–50
Κλυταιμήστρη **I**: 1.113
κλύω **I**: 3.86–7; **II**: 8.5–6; **IV**: 16.514–26
κνήμη **IV**: 13.70–2
κνημῖδες **I**: 34; 3.330–1
κνίση **I**: 1.315–17, 1.447–68; 4.48–9; **II**: 12
κόϊλος, κοῖλος **III**: 10.525; **IV**: 13.107–10,
  13.358
κοιναί **IV**: 22
κόλος **IV**: 16.114–18
κομιδή **II**: 8.186–90; **VI**: 23.411
κομίζω **IV**: 14.454–7; **VI**: 22.286
κομόωντες **I**: 2.536, 2.542; 3.43
κοναβέω, κοναβίζω **IV**: 13.496–501
κονίω **IV**: 14.143–6
κορυθάϊξ **VI**: 22.132
κορυθαίολος **III**: 11.315; **V**: 20.38–40
κόρυμβος **III**: 9.241–2
κόρυς **I**: 2.816; 3.371–2; 4.274, 4.424–6; **II**:
  7.206; **IV**: 13.130–1, 13.712–18
κορύσσω **I**: 2.272–7; 4.274, 4.424–6,
  4.440–1; **II**: 7.206; **IV**: 13.795–9; **VI**:
  21.306
κότος **IV**: 13.516–17
κοτύλη **VI**: 22.494
κοτυλήρυτον **VI**: 23.34
κούρητες **III**: 9.529; **V**: 19.192–3
κοῦρος **IV**: 13.95–6; 15.281–5
κραταιός **III**: 11.118–19; **IV**: 13.345–60
κρατερῶνυξ **IV**: 16.722–5
κράτεσφι **III**: 10.156
κράτος **III**: 9.39
κρείουσα **VI**: 22.48
κρείσσων **IV**: 24, 34; 16.688–90
κρήγυον **I**: 1.106
κρήδεμνον **IV**: 14.184; 16.97–100; **VI**:
  22.470
κρίκος **VI**: 24.272
Κρονίων **IV**: 14.244–8
κρόσσαι **III**: 12.258–60

κρυόεις **III**: 9.2, 9.64; **IV**: 15
κτεατίζω **IV**: 16.56–9
κτέρας **VI**: 24.38
κτιδέη **III**: 10.334–5
κτίλος **IV**: 13.492–5
κυάνεος **VI**: 22.402
κύανος **III**: 11.24; **IV**: 13.562–3
κυανοχαίτης **IV**: 13.562–3; 15.100–3
κυβιστάω **IV**: 15.535–6; 16.745–50
κυδάνω **IV**: 14.71–3
κυκεών **III**: 11.638–41
κυλλοποδίων **V**: 18.369–71; **VI**: 21.331
κῦμα **I**: 1.469; **II**: 4.422–3; 6.348
κύμβαχος **II**: 5.586; **IV**: 15.535–6
κύμινδις **IV**: 14.290–1
κυνάμυια **VI**: 21.394
κυνέη **I**: 34; 3.330–8, 3.336, 3.371–2; **III**:
  10.258; 11.41; **IV**: 13.712–18
κυνῶπα **I**: 1.225; **II**: 6.344
Κύπρις **II**: 5.327–30
κύρομαι **VI**: 24.530
κύρω **VI**: 23.821
κύων **I**: 3.180; **II**: 6.344; 8.423–4; **III**:
  10.360–4; **VI**: 22.345
κωκυτός **VI**: 22.409
κωκύω **VI**: 22.407
κώληψ **VI**: 23.726
κωφός **IV**: 14.16–19

λαβραγόρης **VI**: 23.479
λαβρεύομαι **VI**: 23.474, 23.478
λαβρός **VI**: 23.473–81
λαθικηδής **VI**: 22.83
λάϊνεος **VI**: 22.154
λαισήϊα **III**: 12.425–6
λαιψηρός **IV**: 14.16–19; 15.269–70
Λαμπετίδης **IV**: 15.526
λαμπετόωντι **IV**: 15.526
λανθάνω **IV**: 13.269–71, 13.720–2;
  15.58–61
λαός **IV**: 17, 18
λαοσσόος **IV**: 13.126–8; **V**: 20.38–40
λάρναξ **VI**: 24.795
λαυκανίη **VI**: 22.325
λέγω **I**: 2.435; 3.188; **IV**: 13.275–8
λειριόεις **IV**: 13.830–2
Λειόκριτος **V**: 17.343–4
λέλαχον **IV**: 15.348–51
λεληκώς **VI**: 22.141–2
λελιμένοι **III**: 12.106
λεξάσθων, λέξεο **III**: 9.66–7, 9.617
λευγαλέος **IV**: 13.97–8
λευκάσπις **VI**: 22.294
λευκός **IV**: 13.837; 14.185–6; 15.313–17
λευκώλενος **IV**: 15.92
λέων **IV**: 15.592–5; **V**: 17.133–6